# THE RISING COST OF STATE GOVERNMENT

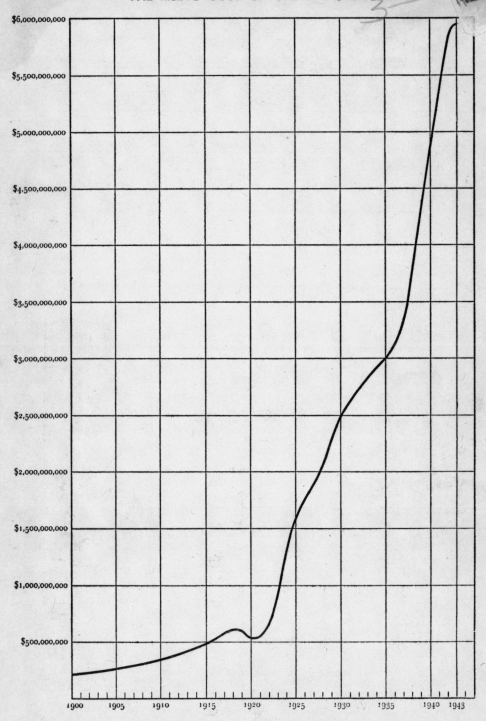

# AMERICAN STATE GOVERNMENT
# AND ADMINISTRATION

# CROWELL'S SOCIAL SCIENCE SERIES

*Edited by* SEBA ELDRIDGE *University of Kansas*

LABOR PROBLEMS. *By* Gordon S. Watkins and Paul A. Dodd

MAN AND CULTURE. *By* Clark Wissler

SOCIAL PATHOLOGY. *By* Stuart A. Queen and Jennette R. Gruener

THE AMERICAN RACE PROBLEM. *By* Edward Byron Reuter

ELEMENTS OF RURAL SOCIOLOGY. *By* Newell Le Roy Sims

INTRODUCTION TO AGRICULTURAL ECONOMICS. *By* Fred Roy Yoder

AMERICAN CITY GOVERNMENT AND ADMINISTRATION. *By* Austin F. Macdonald

SOCIAL CONTROL OF THE MENTALLY DEFICIENT. *By* Stanley P. Davies

URBAN SOCIETY. *By* Noel P. Gist and L. A. Halbert

AMERICAN STATE GOVERNMENT AND ADMINISTRATION. *By* Austin F. Macdonald

SOCIAL ORGANIZATION AND DISORGANIZATION. *By* Stuart A. Queen, Walter B. Bodenhafer, and Ernest B. Harper

GOVERNMENT FINANCE. *By* Jens P. Jensen

THE PROBLEM OF SOCIAL CHANGE. *By* Newell Le Roy Sims

AN INTRODUCTION TO SOCIOLOGY. *By* L. L. Bernard

THE FAMILY. *By* Ruth Shonle Cavan

ORIGINS OF AMERICAN SOCIOLOGY. *By* L. L. Bernard and Jessie Bernard

SOCIAL-ECONOMIC MOVEMENTS. *By* Harry W. Laidler

# AMERICAN STATE GOVERNMENT AND ADMINISTRATION

*Third Edition*

AUSTIN F. MACDONALD
*Professor of Political Science*
*University of California*

THOMAS Y. CROWELL COMPANY, *New York*

*To* JAMES T. YOUNG

# PREFACE

THIRTEEN years ago, when the first pages of the first edition of this volume were written, the states were grappling desperately with the problems of a severe industrial depression. The "New Deal" was still a campaign slogan, and social security was merely the expression of a pious hope. War was far from the minds of peace-loving Americans. But many things have changed since that time. Systems of unemployment compensation and old-age insurance have been established; proposals for minimum wages and maximum hours in industry have been enacted into law and upheld by the courts; and, more recently, the United States has been transformed into the world's greatest military power, with its armed forces fighting on foreign soil and its factories geared to the requirements of total warfare.

These changes have necessitated a re-examination and rearrangement of the traditional line of demarcation between federal and state authority. The federal government has been obliged to assume control of many matters that were once thought to be within the exclusive competence of the states. Yet state government continues to function with unabated vigor. The states are now spending more money, employing more persons, and performing more functions than ever before. In co-operation with the federal government and with one another they have found their new role in our developing federal system. That role is traced in the pages of this new edition.

There are new chapters on indebtedness and on direct legislation and the recall. Substantial modifications have been made in many sections—for example, those dealing with absent voting, federal aid for highways, conservation of oil and gas, water power, utility regulation, hours of labor, wages, and the right to strike. Despite these changes and additions, however, the spirit of this volume, like the spirit of American state government, remains unchanged.

AUSTIN F. MACDONALD

Berkeley, California
*May 1, 1945*

# CONTENTS

*Part One*

## STATE GOVERNMENT

*Part Two*

# STATE ADMINISTRATION

*Part One*

# STATE GOVERNMENT

Part One

STATE GOVERNMENT

# Chapter One ✦✦ HISTORY OF AMERICAN STATE GOVERNMENT

THE English colonies established in North America were not governed according to a uniform plan during the first part of the seventeenth century. There were, in fact, substantial differences in the provisions of their charters and also in the methods of enforcement. At the very beginning some of the colonies did not even possess charters, so their leading citizens prepared and adopted constitutions. The laws of England were supreme, of course, throughout colonial America, and colonial legislation was supposed to be in harmony with the acts of the English Parliament. But this restriction had little significance because the laws enacted by the colonists were not submitted for English approval until the latter part of the colonial period.

Not only did the colonies differ widely from one another in their early forms of government, but also in other ways. It is not difficult to understand why these differences arose. Some colonies were created for purposes of trade; others were established to escape religious persecution. Some were in the hands of wealthy, cultured men; others were dominated by persons who lacked both wealth and culture. Then, too, the founding of the thirteen colonies extended over a century and a quarter, and during that period English policies underwent a transformation.

## ESTABLISHMENT OF UNIFORM COLONIAL GOVERNMENTS

The first suggestions for a uniform type of government in the colonies were made at a rather early date. We know that Charles II received such proposals from his advisers in 1661, though he made no attempt to put them into effect. But soon afterward disquieting reports arrived from America—reports that seemed to indicate the need for greater uniformity in colonial affairs and for closer supervision by England. The colonies were quarreling with the royal collectors of customs and with one another. The royal revenues were seriously menaced by widespread illegal trading. At last the English government was obliged to take action. The early policy of *laissez-faire* was

3

abandoned, and in its place was established a carefully devised plan of imperial control. A number of the colonies lost their original charters and in their stead received documents that were far less liberal; the right of the crown to disallow provincial laws was generally accepted, though not without a struggle; [1] and cases were frequently appealed from the colonial courts to the Privy Council in England.

Before the middle of the eighteenth century, therefore, a fairly uniform plan of government had been established. Eight colonies had become "royal provinces," a term that indicated a rather high degree of dependence on the crown; and the governments of the remaining five did not differ from them radically in organization or powers. In every colony the leading figure was the governor, who was appointed by the king or by the colony's proprietor,[2] and charged with the responsibility of keeping the colonists obedient. The legislative body usually consisted of two houses—a popularly chosen assembly or house of representatives, and a somewhat smaller council whose members were generally selected by the authorities in England upon the governor's recommendation. The councillors also performed a number of administrative and judicial duties. Individually they acted as colonial secretaries and treasurers; and sitting as a body, with the governor, they comprised a court of appeals in civil cases.

As a rule the governor could rely upon the support of the council, whether he was engaged in furthering his own schemes or in executing orders received from England. The councillors understood quite well that the authority that had put them into office could sweep them out again with equal ease, and they showed no desire to dispute the governor's leadership. There were some few exceptions, of course, as in Massachusetts, where the lower house had a voice in the selection of councillors, and in Virginia, where the local aristocracy was frequently at odds with the representative of royal authority; but in general it can be said that the governor and the council worked harmoniously together. All the executive and judicial powers of the colonial governments were in their hands, and they exercised a large measure of control over legislation. In most colonies, laws passed by the assembly had to receive the approval of the council and the governor's veto power was absolute.

---

[1] Connecticut, Rhode Island, and Maryland differed from their neighbors, however, in that the laws enacted by their assemblies were not subject to the royal veto.

[2] Except in Rhode Island and Connecticut, where the governor was elected by the people.

### THE STRUGGLE BETWEEN THE GOVERNORS AND THE COLONIAL ASSEMBLIES

Although the governor found it comparatively easy to dominate the council, he soon learned that the popularly chosen assembly could not so readily be swayed. In fact, the central theme of the entire colonial period is the struggle between the governor and the assembly for control of provincial policies.

The governor was the personal representative of the crown or of the proprietor; in either case he was the symbol of external control. He was charged with the duty of enforcing regulations that were frequently unpopular with the colonists, and that often worked hardships on rich and poor alike. Whenever the interests of the colonies and of England were in conflict, he was certain to champion the mother country's cause. His personal views had nothing to do with the matter; orders came to him from across the sea, and he carried them into effect.

The assembly, on the other hand, represented the people. It was the one popular element in the whole scheme of colonial government, and its members accepted with due seriousness their obligation to resist the encroachments of the crown and, subsequently, of Parliament. In a number of colonies they enacted bills of rights fashioned after the English model, though in all cases these laws were disallowed when they reached the central authorities in England. Every assembly session marked the beginning of fresh disputes and new attempts to limit the governor's authority. Sometimes the members of the assembly were shortsighted and selfish, disregarding the broader aspects of imperial policy. Sometimes they exercised their authority in ways that reflected little credit on their judgment. Fundamentally, however, they were right, for they stood for the vital principle of local self-government that Englishmen on both sides of the Atlantic had come to regard as essential.

In a struggle between the governor and the assembly, it would seem that the odds should have been overwhelmingly in favor of the governor. He controlled the administration and the courts; he could block any legislation that failed to please his fancy. There were, however, a number of factors that operated to the advantage of the people's representatives.

For one thing, the source of the governor's authority was in England, and England was many miles and many months away. Before a decision on any vital matter could be obtained from the Privy Council or the Board of Trade, the facts of the case might change so materially as to make necessary still further instructions. The colonists, of course, had no such handicap: in a few hours their spokesmen could always be brought together, ready to make the most of any circumstance that might seem to suggest a change of policy. The assembly met only at infrequent intervals, and then at the call of the governor; [3] but the assembly's leaders, as individuals, might meet when and where they pleased.

Still more important, the assembly gradually established its right, in colony after colony, to grant or withhold appropriations, including the appropriation for the governor's salary. The home government, however, did not recognize this right without a struggle. It issued instructions to the governors, directing them to insist upon permanent settlements; but every attempt to obey these instructions resulted in a deadlock between governor and assembly. William Burnet, who assumed the governorship of Massachusetts in 1728, argued strongly for a permanent civil list as necessary to his freedom of action. He was strongly supported by the Privy Council, and even the House of Commons passed a resolution decrying the attitude of the colonists as tending "to shake off the dependency of said Colony upon their kingdom"; but the Massachusetts assembly remained obdurate and eventually it had its way. Burnet's successors still argued for fixed salaries, but they accepted whatever the assembly was willing to appropriate. In New York the salary list was long granted for five-year periods, but finally the assembly voted to appropriate revenue for one year only, and after several years of bitter controversy the governor was instructed not to press the matter. Everywhere the outcome was the same.

And so the colonial governor found himself unable to exercise many of the powers that he nominally possessed. His most cherished projects were crippled by lack of funds. His right of veto had to be exercised with care, lest the assembly take offense and refuse to vote the annual appropriation for his salary. On the other hand, he could not yield too readily to the demands of the colonists, for fear of incurring royal displeasure and receiving orders terminating his appointment. His lot was not a happy one. As a contemporary writer

[3] In most of the colonies, laws were passed providing for biennial or triennial assembly meetings, regardless of the wishes of the governor. Several of these acts were disallowed, however, when they reached England.

observed: "Every . . . Governor has two Masters: one who gives him his Commission and one who gives him his Pay." [4]

Although the laws that colonial assemblies frequently forced upon unwilling governors had to receive the approval of the home government, there were various ways of evading this requirement. "Temporary" legislation remained in force for surprisingly long periods. In Massachusetts, where the charter specifically stated that statutes must be disallowed by the crown within three years or else remain in effect until repealed by the provincial assembly, reasons were found for not sending questionable laws to England until the three-year limit had almost expired. But these evasions did not escape the attention of the central authorities. Governors were given more specific instructions concerning legislation. They were directed to withhold their assent from every law dealing with certain specified subjects unless it contained a suspending clause—that is, a clause suspending operation until the crown should take final action.

For many years the royal veto was used unsparingly. A single order of the queen's ministers disallowed fifty Pennsylvania laws in 1706, and the legislation of many other colonies received similar treatment. The reasons for disallowance varied widely. Some statutes were vetoed because they conflicted with acts of Parliament or with the common law; others met with disfavor because they seemed inimical to British economic interests or to the jealously guarded prerogatives of the crown. Sometimes the whim of a single official seems to have been the deciding factor.

During the latter part of the colonial period the provincial assemblies began to realize the futility of enacting laws that could not possibly hope to win approval; and so they displayed in public a much greater degree of respect for British policies, while striving secretly to find new ways of evading imperial control. The use of the royal veto therefore became less frequent. But the demands of the colonists for self-government were no less vehement; on the contrary, they grew in intensity and bitterness until the course of events fanned the spark of colonial dissent into a flame of revolution.

### SUFFRAGE IN THE COLONIES

In one matter, at least, colonial governments were given considerable leeway by the mother country: they were permitted to grant or

---

[4] *Historical Review of the Constitution and Government of Pennsylvania,* quoted in Evarts B. Greene's *Provincial America,* p. 198.

withhold the suffrage practically as they saw fit. And in every colony the leading colonists saw fit to restrict the privilege of voting within very narrow limits. They regarded democracy as a dangerous experiment, "unfit for church or commonwealth," as John Cotton once declared. Property qualifications were universal. No man could vote in Georgia unless he possessed a "freehold" of at least fifty acres of land. Virginia offered an alternative: fifty acres *or* twenty-five acres and a house twelve feet square. Several colonies permitted personal property to be substituted for real estate—a concession to the townspeople that caused country squires to shake their heads disapprovingly. But there was no abandonment of the generally accepted principle that voting should be the privilege of the wealthier classes. The masses of the people, it was said and believed by those who controlled colonial affairs, "had little interest in the country, making tumults at the elections and disturbing his majesty's peace." [5]

Religious and racial discriminations were also quite common. In New England, especially, men were disqualified from voting because they lacked church membership or because they would not subscribe to sectarian dogmas. "Grosly scandalouse" conduct, such as lying, drinking, or blasphemy, was quite commonly regarded as a sufficient reason for disfranchisement. Under one pretext or another Roman Catholics and Jews were kept from voting in most of the colonies, and the discrimination sometimes extended to Quakers and Baptists. Negroes were generally excluded from political rights. These restrictions served to disfranchise the overwhelming majority of the people in every colony. Only sixteen per cent of the total population of Massachusetts was included in the voters' lists just prior to the Revolution, and even that percentage was considered exceptionally high. In Philadelphia not more than one person in fifty was entitled to vote. And this state of affairs was vehemently defended by the little group of patricians who controlled American politics during most of the colonial period. Emphatically they were *not* democrats.

### DISSENSION AMONG THE COLONIES

In 1776, when complete separation from England was finally agreed upon, the men who framed the Declaration of Independence labeled themselves the representatives of the "United States of America." If the newly formed states were really united, it was only through their

---

[5] Andrews, Chas. McLean, *Colonial Self-Government*, pp. 208–209.

common hatred of England.    Every attempt to unite them as colonies
had proved a dismal failure.

In 1643 four of the New England colonies had entered into "a firm
and perpetual league of friendship and amity," but this "perpetual"
league lasted only about twenty years as an actively functioning organization, though it was not formally dissolved for another two decades.
Petty jealousies and unseemly bickerings marked every stage of its
existence.    When the home government tried the plan of appointing
one governor for two or more colonies, as it did on several occasions,
serious friction invariably developed.    The smaller and weaker
colony usually complained that its interests were being sacrificed and
its rights ignored.    Boundary disputes were common.    Massachusetts
had controversies of this nature with at least four of its neighbors, and
nearly all the other colonies were similarly involved with one another.
They were seldom able to reach an amicable agreement; usually the
Lord Chancellor in England had to take a hand.    Then, too, there
were trade disputes, characterized by sharp practices and consequent
ill will.    Feeling at times ran high.    Each colony spoke of its neighbors in slurring terms.    Typical was the action of the South Carolina
agents in London, who pictured North Carolina as "the receptacle of
all the vagabouns and runaways of the main land of America, for
which reason and for their entertaining Pirates they are justly con-
temned by their neighbors." [6]

It is no surprise, therefore, that the six years of the Revolution were
marked by still further quarrels among the states.    At first there
seems to have been little thought of creating a permanent union.
Each state was free, sovereign, and independent, and intended to remain so.    Joint action with the other states was admittedly necessary
for the successful prosecution of the war, but joint action meant nothing more than free co-operation among equals, who might at any time
decide to go their separate ways.    "Where are your landmarks, your
boundaries?" asked Patrick Henry, in a burst of eloquence.    "The
distinctions between Virginians, Pennsylvanians, New Yorkers and
New Englanders are no more." [7]    That was mere rhetoric, however,
as everyone well knew.    Henry's listeners hastened to remind him
that the separate identity of their respective commonwealths was a
precious thing.    They did not propose to be swallowed up.

[6] *North Carolina Colonial Records*, Vol. II, pp. 394–396, quoted by Evarts B. Greene,
*op. cit.*, p. 194.
[7] Van Tyne, Claude H., *The American Revolution*, p. 178.

Although the Continental Congress was composed of representatives from the several states, it possessed virtually no authority. At the time it seems to have been regarded as little better than an interstate advisory committee, and many leaders spoke of it with ill-concealed contempt. Most of its important decisions were reached after consultation with state officials, and the delegates of each state had specific instructions that they dared not ignore. When such vital matters as independence and the establishment of new state governments came up for consideration, Congress merely made recommendations or else marked time until its members received instructions from their respective states. Every state acted as befitted a sovereign nation. Virginia, for example, ratified the treaty of 1777 with France and sent its own agents abroad to contract a loan. The United States of America, like Napoleon's Italy, was little more than a geographical expression.

### CONFEDERATION AND UNION

To produce even a semblance of unity among thirteen independent nations, each jealous of its newly gained prerogatives, was a task for statesmen. It taxed to the utmost the ingenuity of Congress, though that body included in its membership some of the ablest men in America.

**The Articles of Confederation.** As early as July of 1776 a plan of union was presented by a committee of which John Dickinson was chairman. This scheme definitely recognized the supremacy of the states. Almost its first words were: "Each State retains its sovereignty, freedom, and independence, and every power, jurisdiction, and right, which is not by this confederation expressly delegated to the United States, in Congress assembled." [8] Congress was given no power to levy taxes, to regulate commerce, or to bring its authority directly to bear upon individuals.

With the central authority thus restricted, the proposed scheme of government was little more than a league of friendship. Yet it aroused a veritable storm of opposition among those members who feared that in some mysterious manner the rights of the sovereign states might be menaced. "If the Plan now proposed should be adopted," declared Rutledge, "nothing less than Ruin to some Colonies will be the consequence of it. . . . I am resolved to vest the Congress with no more Power than is absolutely necessary, and, to use

[8] Articles of Confederation, Art. II.

a familiar expression, to keep the Staff in our own hands; for I am confident, if surrendered into the Hands of others, a most pernicious use will be made of it." [9]   Other members expressed fears similar to those voiced by Rutledge, but eventually the obvious need for greater unity of action produced a majority favorable to the plan, and after numerous amendments and protracted discussion it was finally adopted by Congress in the fall of 1777.   Not until nearly four years later, however, was ratification by the legislatures of all the states completed.

INEFFECTIVENESS OF CONGRESS.   The "Articles of Confederation and perpetual Union," as the new scheme of government was officially styled, soon demonstrated the folly of the extreme proponents of separatism.   Congress did not become a dangerous "supergovernment," dictating state policies and menacing the liberties of the people, as had been so freely predicted.   On the contrary, it manifested a helplessness that was at once ludicrous and pathetic.   Its powers were narrowly restricted, and it was totally without authority to enforce its decisions, even with regard to those few matters that had been placed under its jurisdiction.   It had no federal courts to execute its decrees.   Still more serious, it had no money and no effective way of getting any.   It could borrow, of course; but American credit was at a low ebb, and apparently destined to go still lower.   It could make requisitions upon the states, but if the states failed to respond there was no way of coercing them.   As a matter of fact, only two or three states ever responded fully to the repeated appeals of Congress for adequate revenue.   The others doled out occasional pittances, or else sent nothing.   The inevitable result was that the interest on the public debt fell into arrears, and even the most pressing national business had to be curtailed for lack of funds.

Equally serious was the inability of Congress to regulate commerce. American trade was languishing because of British restrictions upon importations from the United States, though American merchants were still buying in British markets much as they had done before the war.   Congress twice requested authority to enact retaliatory measures, but the necessary permission was never given.   In the meantime, the states plunged into a petty commercial warfare with one another that threatened to split the Union into fragments.   New York discriminated against New Jersey and Connecticut.   Pennsylvania laid heavy burdens on the trade of New Jersey and Delaware, and these

[9] Quoted by Van Tyne, Claude H., *op. cit.*, p. 184.

states promptly struck back with restrictions of their own.  Maryland several times used unfair tactics in an effort to steal Virginia's commerce, while the ethics of Virginia were not above reproach.  When the ports of some states were closed to British shipping, the ports of neighboring commonwealths were immediately thrown wide open. Generally speaking, the people of the Northern states would have been glad to give Congress control over commerce, and thus end the petty bickering.  But the Southern planters, fearful that the power might in some way be used to injure them, withheld their assent.

During the eight years that the Articles of Confederation remained in effect, they were violated by nearly every state.  Some entered into alliances with the Indian tribes or with one another without troubling to inform Congress, though the approval of that body was expressly required.  Others passed laws without regard for Congressional treaties which were supposed to be binding upon all the states alike. Congress could remonstrate, and it frequently did; but nothing ever came of its protests.  For since it lacked coercive power, it was treated by the state governments with an indifference that at times bordered on contempt.

**Adoption of the Constitution.**  In view of the disregard in which the confederation was held, it obviously could not continue for any great length of time.  Some men thought that a central government possessing very much broader powers should be created.  Others, at the opposite extreme, proposed the dissolution of all the political ties that bound the states.  The possibility of monarchy was freely discussed, "without horror."  Proposals to amend the Articles of Confederation were made as early as 1782, and finally, in the spring of 1787, a convention met in Philadelphia for this purpose.  The delegates to the convention understood quite clearly that their instructions did not permit them to go beyond a revision of the Articles, but they knew also that a mere revision would not suffice.  Early in their deliberations, therefore, they adopted a momentous resolution: "that a national Government ought to be established consisting of a supreme Legislative, Executive, and Judiciary."  This decision irrevocably fixed the form of the new government.  The powers of the central authority were to be materially increased—at the expense of the states, of course.  The complete independence of action that the thirteen commonwealths had enjoyed since the Revolution was to be seriously restricted.  A *national* government, *supreme* in its own sphere, was to take the place of an impotent confederation.

But there were many matters still to be decided—matters so vital and so controversial that they threatened to wreck the convention on more than one occasion. What should be the basis of representation in the new national legislative body? Should every state have an equal voice, or should voting power be proportioned to population? If population were accepted as the proper basis, should slaves be included in the enumeration? What control over commerce should the national government be given?

Agreement was finally reached on all these points, and many others in addition; but the compromises thus effected were generally received without enthusiasm. Like most compromises, they failed to satisfy anyone completely. A number of the delegates were so disappointed that they refused to sign the finished document. And when it was made public it encountered a veritable storm of abuse, especially from the rural sections and from the poor people in all parts of the country. Taxes, it was freely predicted, would mount so rapidly that the country would speedily become bankrupt. So much centralization of authority would destroy the liberties of the people and speedily lead to the establishment of monarchy. The power of Congress to regulate commerce would be used to destroy agriculture. Arguments of every sort were advanced against the ratification of the new Constitution, only to be met by the closely reasoned arguments of Hamilton and Madison, the merciless logic of James Wilson, and the impassioned eloquence of Gouverneur Morris. Opinion seemed to be rather evenly divided throughout the states, and for a time the fate of the plan hung in the balance. Ratification by nine states was necessary for adoption. Five acted promptly, but the others delayed. In Massachusetts Elbridge Gerry led a bitter opposition, and such influential men as John Hancock and Samuel Adams were long in doubt. New York gave its approval by the narrow margin of three votes, and then only after the nine necessary ratifications had already taken place. Rhode Island did not agree to enter the Union until May, 1790, thirteen months after Washington had been inaugurated as the first president.

## STATES' RIGHTS

With the adoption of a national constitution, which was by its own terms the supreme law of the land,[10] and the establishment of a national government to serve the people of all the states, it would be

[10] Constitution, Art. VI.

natural to suppose that the question of state sovereignty was settled for all time. Actually, however, it proved to be one of the most troublesome issues facing the new government. The spirit of localism was far from dead. Many a man placed his state before the nation, and gave to it his first allegiance.

In 1793, when the Supreme Court of the United States in the now famous case of Chisholm *v.* Georgia [11] ruled that any state might be haled into federal court by a citizen of another state, the popular disapproval was so general and so spontaneous that both parties speedily united to amend the Constitution.[12] Later, during the early days of the nineteenth century, the conflicting interests of the different sections of the country led to bitter denunciation of the broad-construction policies of Congress and the Supreme Court, and there was frequent talk of secession. "I have even gone so far," wrote Pickering in 1814, "as to say that the separation of the Northern section of the States would be ultimately advantageous." [13] The same year a group of delegates representing most of the New England states met at Hartford, chiefly to register a protest against recent federal policies and to devise means of preventing what they considered federal usurpation of power. The resolutions adopted by this convention hinted at rebellion, without openly advocating it; and though they had no immediate political effect, they served to show the attitude of the day.

Still later, as bitter disagreement between North and South developed over the tariff and slavery, the states' rights school acquired a more definite philosophy and a still larger following. Its adherents during this period came chiefly from the South instead of New England. In 1828 appeared a paper prepared for the use of the South Carolina legislature by John C. Calhoun, who had long been an ardent nationalist but had found it necessary to change his views in order to retain the confidence of his political allies. This document, later known as the South Carolina Exposition, set forth the doctrine that every state had the right to decide for itself whether federal laws should be enforced within its boundaries. The states, it was argued, were sovereign, and the federal government was simply their agent.

[11] 2 Dallas 419 (1793).

[12] Amendment XI, which provides that "The judicial power of the United States shall not be construed to extend to any suit in law or equity, commenced or prosecuted against one of the United States by citizens of another State, or by citizens or subjects of any foreign State," is the result.

[13] Quoted by Babcock, Kendric C., *The Rise of American Nationality*, p. 161.

From this premise it followed naturally that if any sovereign state should become dissatisfied with the acts of its agent—in other words, if it should regard any law of Congress as unconstitutional or oppressive—it could refuse to consider itself bound. The necessary state action, according to Calhoun, was to call a convention, which would declare the objectionable statute inoperative within the state. Thus, any state might set at naught the authority of the federal government, and its decision to nullify a federal law could be overruled only by action of three fourths of the states assembled in national convention.

The theory of nullification was not new. It had been asserted, in a milder form, as early as 1798,[14] but Calhoun vitalized it and made it a convenient tool for the Southern statesmen who were trying to protect the interests of their section against the policies of the dominant North. In the United States Senate it was warmly defended by Robert Hayne, and denounced with equal vigor by Daniel Webster. Then, in 1832, came an opportunity to put the theory into practice. The legislature of South Carolina, incensed by the tariff acts of 1828 and 1832, called a convention which met and declared these laws null and void, and at the same time prohibited the payment of duties at South Carolina ports. Faced with this crisis, President Jackson acted promptly and decisively. He issued a proclamation setting forth his intention of enforcing the laws of the Union, and prepared to collect the customs by a resort to arms if necessary. Meanwhile South Carolina tooks steps to make its resistance effective. Civil war was in prospect. It was averted, however, by the action of Congress, which hastily agreed upon a compromise tariff. The South Carolina nullification ordinance was thereupon repealed, though the *right* of nullification was still asserted with vigor. Each side claimed victory, but actually the incident was inconclusive. It took four years of bloody civil war to establish permanently the supremacy of the national government.

The quarter of a century following the South Carolina episode was a period of increasing sectionalism, with Northern supremacy becoming more certain every year, and Southern dissatisfaction more acute. The breach created by the divergent views of the two sections concerning slavery was growing wider rapidly. Clay's "Great Compromise" of 1850 had no lasting effect; only a few years later "bleeding Kansas"

[14] See the famous Virginia and Kentucky Resolutions. The text of these resolutions may be found conveniently in *American History Leaflet* No. 11.

was the center of a bitter struggle between the friends and foes of human slavery. Eventually, therefore, the statesmen of the South became convinced that the protection of their economic system necessitated withdrawal from the Union. The election of Lincoln as president brought matters to a head, and even before he was inaugurated eight states had severed their relations with the Union.

To Lincoln, and probably to most Northerners, secession was an act of rebellion, not sanctioned by the Constitution and contrary to the fundamental principles of American government.[15] "The Union of these States is perpetual," he declared in his inaugural address. "No State upon its mere notion can lawfully get out of the Union." But the spokesmen of the cotton states were equally insistent that secession was their constitutional right. "It is the right of the people to alter or abolish governments," said Jefferson Davis, "whenever they become destructive of the ends for which they were established. The declared purpose of the compact of the Union was 'to establish justice, insure domestic tranquillity, provide for the common defense, promote the general welfare, and secure the blessings of liberty to ourselves and our posterity'; and when, in the judgment of the sovereign States now composing this Confederacy, it had been perverted from the purposes for which it was ordained, a peaceful appeal to the ballot box declared that, so far as they were concerned, the Government created by that compact should cease to exist. In this they merely asserted a right which the Declaration of Independence of 1776 had defined to be inalienable; of the time and occasion for its exercise they, as sovereigns, were the final judges, each for itself. . . . Thus the sovereign States here represented proceeded to form this Confederacy, and it is by abuse of language that their act has been denominated a revolution."

Between these two conflicting views there was no possible middle ground, no room for compromise. Either the Union was indestructible, fusing all the states into a single nation; or else it was a treaty of friendship among sovereign nations, and could be abrogated at any time. The force of Northern arms drove home the contention that the union of the states was perpetual, and the issue passed into history.

[15] Some of the opponents of slavery took a different view, however. Horace Greeley declared editorially: "We hold, with Jefferson, to the inalienable right of communities to alter or abolish forms of government that have become oppressive or injurious; and, if the cotton states shall decide that they can do better out of the Union than in it, we shall insist on letting them go in peace." For a concise statement of the conflicting views of this period, see Raymond G. Gettell's *History of American Political Thought*, Chap. XI.

THE FIRST STATE GOVERNMENTS

**State constitutions.** Although the fundamental basis of federal-state relationships remained a matter of dispute until the close of the Civil War, the forms of state government were molded very much earlier. Before the end of the Revolution nearly every state had adopted a new constitution,[16] though these documents did not differ radically from the colonial charters. In nearly all cases they were the handiwork of the legislatures; the people were afforded little opportunity to express their approval or dissent.[17] Most of the powers of government were given to the legislature, which was made bicameral for a number of reasons, but chiefly because Americans were accustomed to legislative bodies of two houses.[18] The members of both houses were popularly chosen, of course,[19] and for very short terms. Annual elections were the rule for members of the lower house; [20] in the upper house or senate the terms were somewhat longer. The structure of the courts remained much the same under the new regimes as under the old. Judges were chosen by a variety of plans— appointment by the governor, selection by the legislature, selection by a committee of senators. A little later, popular election became the commonly accepted method of choosing judges, but at the outset it was regarded with disfavor.

RESTRICTIONS OF GUBERNATORIAL POWER. The men who framed the first state constitutions had stronger aversions than preferences. They were by no means agreed as to the form of government they desired, but there were certain features of their old charters that they knew did *not* want for their new constitutions. One of these objectionable features was a strong executive. For more than a century they had suffered under the tyranny of royal governors; now that the government was in their own hands, they were determined to write into the fundamental law provisions that would prevent the

[16] Connecticut and Rhode Island were the only exceptions, and they speedily adapted their old charters to changed circumstances.

[17] In Massachusetts, where the people were allowed to vote upon their new constitution, they rejected the draft first submitted by the legislature.

[18] Georgia and Pennsylvania, which had single-chambered legislatures in colonial days, retained the unicameral form for nearly a decade and a half after they became states. When Vermont entered the Union in 1791 it had a unicameral legislature, which it kept until 1836.

[19] In Maryland, however, the members of the state senate were chosen indirectly through the medium of an electoral college.

[20] South Carolina was the only exception. The members of its lower house were chosen biennially.

chief executive from ever becoming a tyrant. This they did very effectively, and as a result the governors of the new states were pitiable figures—"ciphers," as Madison picturesquely described them. In eight states they were chosen by the legislatures, and thus subjected to legislative domination. One-year terms were the rule; their power of veto was commonly withheld; and their appointing power was restricted within narrow limits. Provision was carefully made for impeaching them if necessary, and councils of state or similar bodies were created for the purpose of "giving advice"—which meant, in practice, preventing any unreasonable exercise of gubernatorial authority. Virginia, still mindful of unhappy colonial experiences, denied to the governor the right to adjourn the legislature, and its example was generally followed.

Thus did the passions of men obscure their judgment, and blind them to the need of effective leadership. Failing to distinguish between the agents of a distant monarch and the executives of their own choosing, they imposed upon their state governors a series of limitations that would have been more appropriate had they still been dealing with the representatives of the British crown. They reasoned, illogically enough, that because royal governors had been despotic, all governors must be despotic. Therefore all governors must be restrained. Their viewpoint was narrow, but under the circumstances it was quite natural. As Jay said, "It takes time to make sovereigns out of subjects." [21]

GUARANTEES AND RESTRAINTS. Not only did the fathers look with suspicion upon their governors; they distrusted all government. To them government was at best a necessary evil, and must be carefully restrained lest it degenerate into tyranny. "That government is best which governs least," declared Jefferson, and he expressed a generally accepted dogma. Men were fearful that their own popularly chosen representatives, once possessed of power, would use that power for evil instead of good. The liberties of the people, wrested by force of arms from a jealous king, might be trampled underfoot by unscrupulous demagogs. So every precaution was taken to prevent public officials from abusing their authority. Terms of office were short. In many states the governor was declared ineligible to succeed himself—at least until another term had intervened. Bills of rights, based in large measure on Magna Carta and the Declaration of Independence, were written into the constitutions of seven states, and every one of the

[21] Van Tyne, Claude H., *op. cit.*, p. 144.

other state constitutions contained some specific guarantees of individual liberty. Freedom of speech and of the press were assured. Freedom of religious worship was guaranteed, and also the right of trial by jury. General search warrants could not be issued, as in colonial days; instead, every warrant must describe specifically the place to be searched and the person or thing to be seized. Cruel and unusual punishments were prohibited, as were excessive bail and unreasonably heavy fines. Taxes might not be levied without the consent of the people or their representatives.

OTHER CHECKS ON POWER. Thus the framers of the first state constitutions aimed to preclude a recurrence of despotism. But they were not satisfied with formal guarantees. They believed that the most effective way to prevent the abuse of power was to divide it into so many parts, and scatter it among so many officials, that no one man could possibly obtain enough authority to make himself master. This doctrine of the separation of powers had received widespread publicity through the writings of the Frenchman Montesquieu, and in the early days of American independence it was quite generally accepted. "It will not be denied," wrote Madison, "that power is of an encroaching nature, and that it ought to be effectually restrained from passing the limits assigned to it. After discriminating, therefore, in theory, the several classes of power, as they may in their nature be legislative, executive, or judiciary, the next and most difficult task is to provide some practical security for each against the invasion of the others." [22] How could this "practical security" best be obtained? By setting every branch of government to watch every other, and act as a check upon its activities. With power thus nicely apportioned, any tendency toward usurpation of authority would speedily be restrained.

And so the fathers put their theory into practice, though with some reservations. They established the governor as a somewhat feeble check upon the legislature, and the council of state as a very effective check upon the governor. The judiciary was designed to restrain all the other branches of government. Every official was supposed to curb every other official, so that a proper balance might be maintained. Had this creed been carried to its logical extreme, the immediate result would probably have been a complete deadlock. The restrictions intended to prevent evil action would almost inevitably have led to complete inaction. As Theodore Roosevelt said more than a century later: "You cannot tie a man's hands for evil, and leave them free for

[22] *The Federalist*, No. 48.

good." In actual practice, however, the statesmen of that earlier day were not entirely consistent. They subscribed to the doctrine of an equal division of powers among the three main departments of government, but they adopted constitutions that definitely subordinated the executive to the legislature. Denying the desirability of legislative supremacy, they yet accepted it in part. There were checks upon legislative action, of course, such as the bills of rights and the power of the courts to declare state laws unconstitutional—a power still open to question at that time. But these limitations were as nothing compared with the restrictions placed upon the governor. Americans had not yet learned that a popularly elected assembly could be quite as tyrannous as a representative of royal authority.

SUFFRAGE RESTRICTIONS. The restricted suffrage of the colonial era was carried over into the first period of independence. Not one of the thirteen states, in framing its original constitution, provided for universal manhood suffrage. Property qualifications were imposed, both for voting and office-holding, though in general the requisite amount of property was made considerably smaller than before the Revolution. In Pennsylvania, Delaware, North Carolina, and Georgia, any taxpayer might vote. Religious restrictions still existed in some states, but they were far less common. Racial discriminations continued until the Civil War, and even that great conflict with its resultant constitutional amendments did not put an end to them in the South.[23] During the early years of the nineteenth century the aggressive democracy of the frontier was destined to sweep triumphantly into power, and brush aside contemptuously most of the voting restrictions based on the ownership of property; but the closing days of the eighteenth century saw the forces of aristocracy still in the ascendant.

## STATE GOVERNMENT IN 1850

The period from 1800 to 1850 witnessed substantial modifications in the form and substance of state government. By the middle of the century eighteen new commonwealths had joined the original thirteen, and had adopted constitutions that reflected the changing spirit of the new era. Every one of the original states, save Massachusetts and South Carolina, had completely revised its constitution one or more times, and Massachusetts had adopted thirteen amendments.

[23] See pp. 104–105.

The state constitutions of 1850, therefore, were substantially different documents from those of 1800.

**Limitations on the legislature.** The state constitutions differed most markedly, perhaps, with respect to the powers of the legislature. At the beginning of the century the state assemblies were still regarded as the guardians of the liberties of the people. They were treated with wholesome respect, as befitted the lineal descendants of colonial legislative bodies that had stood firmly against the encroachments of the British crown. They were given the balance of power in the newly formed states, despite the widespread belief that the authority of every department of government must be narrowly restricted. But the results of several decades of legislative supremacy were bitterly disappointing. Members of the state assemblies showed a greater concern for the affairs of their local communities than for the welfare of the commonwealth. They habitually decided broad questions of policy on the basis of local or even personal interest, and spent most of their time quarreling with one another over matters of little or no importance. Not unnaturally, therefore, numerous limitations on legislative authority began to appear in the constitutions of the early nineteenth century, and these restrictions became more numerous and more specific as the legislatures continued to demonstrate their incompetence. By 1850 legislative supremacy had disappeared in fact, if not in theory.

The constitution that Michigan adopted in 1850 illustrates the tendency of the period to limit the legislature's freedom of action. This document specified not only the purposes for which debt might be contracted, but also the minimum size of the sinking fund and its minimum rate of increase. The exact manner of assessing property and levying taxes was explicitly stated. The legislature was forbidden to charter private corporations under special laws, or for more than thirty years. It was denied the right to authorize lotteries, to grant divorces, to allow private claims, to establish a state newspaper. Its control over education was limited by sundry clauses specifying the exact nature of the public school system. Nearly every grant of power was coupled with a detailed statement of the manner in which it was to be exercised. And Michigan's 1850 constitution was by no means the handiwork of a group of extremists; it simply reflected the growing belief of the people in every state that the legislature could not be trusted.

**Increase of governor's powers.** While the legislature was losing its hold on public confidence, the governor was gaining in importance. By 1850 he had become an elective official in every state, with authority to veto the acts of the legislature. His right to pardon criminals was recognized by nearly all the newer constitutions. Only by courtesy, however, could he be called the head of the state government. His appointing power was limited to a few offices, and was still further restricted by the requirement of senatorial confirmation. Most of the administrative officials with whom he shared the obligation of conducting the day-to-day business of the state were also popularly elected, or else chosen by the legislature; in either case he had no means of controlling their conduct. Restrictions on his right to succeed himself were still common.

**Tenure of office.** During the first half of the nineteenth century there was a distinct trend toward longer terms of office for public officials. John Adams' dictum that "Where annual elections end, there slavery begins," no longer received widespread acceptance. In the constitutions of the new states of the West especially, two-year terms for governors and legislators were the rule. Even terms of four years were not unknown. However, the tenure of office of state judges was commonly shortened. Originally they had been selected for life or for very long terms; but by the middle of the century six- or seven-year terms had become the rule. And almost everywhere they were popularly chosen.

**Amendment and revision of constitutions.** In many of the earliest state constitutions no provision was made for amendment or revision. It was assumed that the legislature, in its unquestioned wisdom and sovereign might, would make such alterations from time to time as might be required for the welfare of the people. Several constitutions specifically authorized the legislature to make necessary changes.[24] In time, however, as the distinction between ordinary legislation and the fundamental law of the constitution was more clearly drawn, a widespread belief developed that constitutional amendments should not be put into effect without the approval of the people, and that extensive revisions should be the work of conventions —popularly elected bodies especially chosen for that purpose. During the year 1850 seven new state constitutions were drafted, and every one of them was prepared by a convention.

[24] Safeguards against undue haste were sometimes provided, however. A two-thirds vote, or affirmative action by two successive assemblies, might be required.

**The spoils system.**   By the middle of the century the spoils system had become an accepted feature of public life in the United States. Federal, state, and local governments alike were blighted by this warped philosophy.   When William Marcy, during the course of a Senate address in 1832, declared: "We can see nothing wrong in the doctrine that to the victor belong the spoils of the enemy," he merely condoned a practice already widely adopted.   But his epigram furnished the spoilsmen with a ready means of justifying their activities. If politics was really a modified form of warfare, with every election a sublimated battle, then surely the spoils of victory should go to those veterans who had been in the heart of the fight and borne the brunt of the attack.   Public office need not be regarded as a public trust. On the contrary, it should be considered the property of the party in power, to be bestowed as a reward for partisan service.   Men should be appointed to office because of party loyalty and not because of any technical qualifications that they might possess.   And if their faction should suffer defeat at the polls, they must expect to make way for the opposition.

This theory was rigorously applied in every state.   Each new election was made the excuse for a clean sweep of state offices.   Even minor employees were not exempt.   "Deserving" but wholly incompetent Democrats replaced equally "deserving" but equally incompetent Whigs, only to give way at the next election to other Whigs as the popular fancy changed once more—over and over in a vicious circle of pitiful ineptitude.   Public officials showed but scant regard for the duties of public office, for they understood quite well that their tenure depended solely on the success of their party at the polls.   The inevitable result of the spoils system was to destroy all possibility of efficient government.

### STATE GOVERNMENT AFTER THE CIVIL WAR

The Civil War temporarily diverted men's minds from the problems of state government, and focused attention upon national issues. Then followed a period of reconstruction, during which the Southern states were treated like so many conquered provinces.   The period of formal reorganization ended in 1870, when the last of the seceded states was finally restored to its full place in the Union; but actually another decade was required to erase all traces of Negro supremacy and "carpetbagger" rule.

**Increase in corruption.** Meanwhile, in every part of the country, state government was becoming increasingly corrupt and inefficient. The concept of "spoils" had acquired a new and more sinister significance. Not only did it include the appointment and election of persons to public office, but also the granting of franchises and special privileges to those who would meet the legislature's price. For a time the railways were under the necessity of seeking favors from the state, and they had their lobbyists at every state capitol. Bribery, direct and indirect, was the order of the day. So successful were the railway lobbyists that they managed to secure virtually complete control over many legislatures. Not without reason did this period of legislative history become known as the railroad era. A little later, when the railways had secured all the franchises, privileges, and exemptions they desired, they permitted other special interests—for a substantial consideration, of course—to use the highly efficient staffs of lobbyists that they had organized with such infinite care. After the railroad era came the public utility period of legislative corruption. The "trolley crowd" and the "gas combine" were potent factors in state affairs.[25]

**Reaction to corruption.** Then followed the inevitable reaction. Serious efforts were made to put an end to corruption in state government. A considerable number of states imposed heavy penalties for improper attempts to influence legislation. Public-spirited citizens devoted their time, energy, and wealth to the task of purging state politics, with some degree of success. They experienced more defeats than victories, of course, for they were matching their unorganized forces against the highly trained and rigidly disciplined cohorts of the professional politicians. But they won some notable victories none the less, and paved the way for significant changes in the form and spirit of state government. During the last two decades of the nineteenth century such men as Grover Cleveland and Theodore Roosevelt of New York, Hazen Pingree of Michigan, and Robert Pattison of Pennsylvania were elevated to the governorship, and their unceasing advocacy of the cause of reform stimulated the popular demand for honest and efficient administration. In 1883 the work of the newly formed National Civil Service Reform League bore important fruit when the merit system of selecting public employees was established in New York. Massachusetts followed the next year, but for two

25 See the excellent history of this period in Paul S. Reinsch's *American Legislatures and Legislative Methods*, pp. 328–393.

decades thereafter no other state saw fit to abandon its time-honored spoils system.

**Changes in power of the governor and the legislature.**  The closing years of the nineteenth century witnessed a further increase in the power and prestige of the governor.   His appointing power was made somewhat broader, and for certain appointments the requirement of senatorial approval was waived.   His term of office was lengthened, becoming four years in many states, though the two-year term predominated.   His salary was quite generally increased.   He became a very important figure in the popular imagination.   And yet he still lacked much of the substance of power.   He had no way of controlling the popularly elected chief administrative officials, such as the secretary of state, the treasurer, and the attorney-general, though compelled to rely on them for the enforcement of state policies.   And so he was placed in the unenviable position of assuming the responsibility for efficient administration, while denied sufficient authority to insure satisfactory results.

During this period the influence of the legislature suffered a still further decline.   Legislators had added venality to their original sin of ignorance, and as a result the public saw fit to restrict their power for good or evil by adding still further constitutional limitations. Thus state constitutions grew longer and longer.   The Virginia constitution of 1776 contained only about three thousand words, but when this document was discarded in 1830 a constitution nearly twice as long was adopted in its stead.   Then came the document of 1870, swollen to nearly six times original proportions; and in 1902 Virginia adopted a constitution of about thirty-five thousand words.   Texas doubled the length of its constitution in a little over three decades, and many other states did approximately the same.   The newer provisions dealt with a great variety of subjects—the regulation of corporations and other businesses, with special attention to public utilities, banks and insurance companies; the structure and control of local government; educational organization and methods; the protection of labor; taxation and finance.   These matters might well have been left in the hands of the legislature, to deal with as it saw fit.   But most people felt that the legislature had forfeited its right to be trusted.

## RECENT TRENDS IN STATE GOVERNMENT

During the present century some of the older tendencies in state government have continued, while others have virtually disappeared.

Long terms for public officials are increasing in favor; the governor is now elected for four years in more than half of the states; and four-year terms predominate for members of the state Senate. Most governors are still hampered by a multiplicity of elective officials, though the process of administrative reorganization in a number of progressive commonwealths has tended to correct this evil.[26] State constitutions continue to grow in length, if not in quality.

On the other hand, the nineteenth century's dogmatic insistence upon universal manhood suffrage has produced a mild reaction against such promiscuous distribution of the franchise. The actual number of voters has been materially increased by the adoption of the Nineteenth Amendment to the federal Constitution, which confers upon women the privilege of voting; [27] but this privilege has been denied to illiterates in a number of states. When the Southern states adopted literacy tests for voting, shortly after the Civil War, their obvious purpose was to exclude the Negro vote; and they have since found the device reasonably effective.[28] Twelve other states, however, scattered throughout the North and West, make use of literacy requirements simply to secure a more intelligent expression of public opinion. The line they draw is not a color line, but a line of defense against the forces of ignorance.[29]

**Growth of public welfare activities.** Probably the most important development of the present century in the field of government is the multiplication of public services, a growth that is characteristic of all present-day governments—federal, state, local. In part it is a result of man's increasing knowledge and increasing ability to satisfy his desires. In part it is a recognition of the obvious fact that some of the forces released by science are too powerful for any one individual or group, and require social control. In part it is a consequence of changing concepts concerning the proper sphere of government. No single reason offers a complete explanation of increasing governmental activity; it is the inevitable outgrowth of modern civilization.

The first state governments were chiefly agencies of repression. Their function was to establish and enforce the fundamental rules of

---

26 See pp. 323–328.

27 "The right of citizens of the United States to vote shall not be denied or abridged by the United States or by any State on account of sex."

28 See pp. 105–106.

29 It must not be assumed, however, that the literacy requirements of the Northern states are entirely a product of the present century. The first literacy test for voting in the United States was adopted by Connecticut in 1855.

conduct.   Beyond that they did not venture.   Today, however, state governments are highly complex organizations.   In addition to enforcing fundamental rules, they regulate innumerable intimate aspects of individual and corporate affairs.   There are public utility commissions, banking commissions, insurance commissions; boards to maintain proper professional standards for accountants, lawyers, physicians, dentists, oculists, pharmacists, barbers, embalmers.   But repression is no longer the primary function of state governments. They have become service agencies, busily engaged in promoting the public welfare.   Their time and funds are devoted largely to such matters as the conservation of natural resources, the protection of health, the promotion of education and recreation, the improvement of living and working conditions, the development of means of communication.   Government has ceased to be a necessary evil, and has become a necessary good.

Additional services and higher standards have, however, inevitably led to larger expenditures.   Even when reduced to a per capita basis, the cost of running the state governments has risen ninefold in less than three decades.   Neither depression nor war has reversed this trend. Nearly all candidates for public office emphasize the necessity of reducing public expenditures, and some of them solemnly promise to curtail the "spending orgy."   But such pledges seldom have any noticeable effect upon the tax rate.[30]

Since 1900—and especially since 1930—the sphere of state authority has been materially restricted.   By means of formal amendments, executive orders, judicial decisions, and informal "bribes" or subsidies, power has been transferred from the states to the nation.   Just as the failure of the Articles of Confederation emphasized the need for a more perfect union, just as the secession of the Southern states ultimately resulted in a stronger national government, so the onward sweep of modern civilization has almost destroyed the economic significance of state boundaries, and has correspondingly enhanced the importance of the nation.   During the depression years of the 1930s and the war years of the 1940s the urgent need for increased governmental activity has accelerated the movement.   This rising tide of nationalism is regarded by some statesmen and publicists as a positive evil; few consider it an unmixed blessing; but it is the product of

[30] For a more detailed consideration of the rising cost of state government, see p. 345.

economic forces that neither statesmen nor publicists have power to control.[31]

## SELECTED REFERENCES

Anderson, Dewey, *California State Government*, Palo Alto, 1942.

Andrews, Chas. McLean, *Colonial Self-Government, 1652–1689*, 1904.

——, *The Colonial Background of the American Revolution*, New Haven, 1931.

Cochran, Thomas C., *New York in the Confederation*, 1932.

Cottman, George S., *Indiana: Its History, Constitution, and Present Government*, Indianapolis, 1925.

Dealey, J. Q., *Growth of American State Constitutions*, Chaps. I and III, 1915.

Dodd, Walter F., and Dodd, Sue H., *Government in Illinois*, 1923.

Folwell, William Watts, *A History of Minnesota*, 4 vols., St. Paul, 1921–1930.

Garst, Doris S., *The Story of Wyoming and Its Constitution and Government*, Douglas, 1938.

Gray, Robert A., and Tryon, Florence R., *The Government of Florida*, 1941.

Green, F. M., *Constitutional Development in the South Atlantic States, 1776–1860: A Study in the Evolution of Democracy*, Chapel Hill, N.C., 1930.

Greene, E. B., *The Provincial Governor in the English Colonies of North America*, 1898.

Holloway, W. W., and Smith, C. W., Jr., *Government and Politics in Alabama*, University, Ala., 1941.

Irwin, Leonard B., *New Jersey; the State and Its Government*, 1942.

Johnson, Samuel A., *Missouri; the State and Its Government*, 1943.

Kalijarvi, Thorsten V., and Chamberlin, William C., *The Government of New Hampshire*, Durham, 1940.

Martin, Roscoe C., *The Growth of State Administration in Alabama*, University, Ala., 1942.

McNutt, W. S., and Others, *A History of Arkansas*, Little Rock, 1932.

Morrison, Leonard S., *The Government of New Hampshire*, Concord, 1943.

Nevins, Allan, *The American States During and After the Revolution, 1775–1789*, 1924.

Odum, Howard W., and Others, *Alabama, Past and Future*, 1942.

Patterson, C. P., and Others, *State and Local Government in Texas*, 1940.

Pollard, Lancaster, *History of the State of Washington*, 4 vols., 1938.

Selsam, J. Paul, *The Pennsylvania Constitution of 1776*, 1936.

Sikes, Pressly, *Indiana State and Local Government*, Bloomington, 1940.

——, *The State Government of Indiana*, Bloomington, 1937.

Stewart, Frank M., and Clark, Joseph L., *The Constitution and Government of Texas*, 1930.

Tanger, Jacob, and Alderfer, H. F., *Pennsylvania Government, State and Local*, rev. ed., Harrisburg, 1939.

Turner, F. J., *The Frontier in American History*, 1920.

Vaughan, John H., *History and Government of New Mexico*, Albuquerque, 1927.

[31] The growth of national power is discussed at length in the next chapter. See pp. 31–42.

## Chapter Two  ⁊ FEDERAL-STATE RELATIONS

THE government of the United States is federal in form—that is, the powers of government are divided between the nation and the states, and neither the nation nor the states may disturb the balance that has thus been established. This does not mean that the original apportionment of authority is perpetual, and may never be altered to meet changing conditions. It means, instead, that every reallocation of power must be the result of agreement between the nation, as represented by Congress, and the states, as represented by their legislatures or by conventions chosen for that purpose. In order to set up a government of the federal type it is necessary to establish, by means of a written constitution, the line of demarcation between federal and state powers. Otherwise there would be no basis for settling the disputes that might arise between the states and the nation as to the exact scope of their authority. Experience has shown that such controversies are frequent.

Outside of the United States the federal type of government has not proved very popular. It is used by a few other nations,[1] but most countries prefer the unitary form. Under the unitary plan of government, all power is vested in the national authorities. Some of this power they may delegate to local agencies of government; in a large country they usually find it necessary to do so. Thus the central government in England permits the county and municipal boroughs to handle many important matters; and even in France, the classic land of centralization, the communes are given a certain measure of local self-government. But this distribution of authority in England or in France does not indicate a trend toward federalism, for the essence of power still remains in the hands of the national government. It may reapportion authority at any time, and in any way it sees fit. It may even abolish all the agencies of local government—counties, municipal boroughs, or communes—at a single stroke. For under the

[1] Five Latin American republics: Argentina, Brazil, Venezuela, Colombia and Mexico; two British dominions: Canada and Australia; and one European nation: Switzerland. The Soviet Union is also included by some writers, but its government is not truly federal. Argentina and Brazil seem to have abandoned their federalism, at least temporarily.

unitary plan the local governments are merely creatures of the nation, and possess only such measure of authority as the nation may care to bestow. The federal form, on the other hand, makes provision for a national government and for state governments as well, each independent of the other within its own sphere of action.

## POWERS OF THE FEDERAL GOVERNMENT

After a federal scheme of government has been decided upon, there are two practicable methods of preparing a dividing line between state and national authority. One plan is to make a careful list of state powers, and then specify that the remainder of governmental authority shall vest in the nation. That was the procedure followed in establishing the present Dominion government of Canada in 1867. But it did not appeal to the men who met in Philadelphia in the spring of 1787 "for the sole and express purpose of revising the Articles of Confederation"—a task so impossible of satisfactory attainment that they ended their deliberations by approving a new constitution. Most of the delegates to the Convention had taken a more or less prominent part in the Revolution, and had long been accustomed to regard local self-government as the corner stone of liberty. Their experience under the Articles of Confederation had prepared them for a stronger and "more perfect union," but they still agreed that the rights of the states must be carefully protected. Not unnaturally, therefore, they enumerated the powers of the federal government, and assumed that all authority not delegated to the nation would continue to reside in the states. In 1791 this arrangement was made emphatically clear by the adoption of the Tenth Amendment to the federal Constitution. The amendment did not in any way alter the original plan; it simply recorded an existing fact. Its exact form follows:

The powers not delegated to the United States by the Constitution, nor prohibited by it to the States, are reserved to the States respectively, or to the people.

**Delegated powers.** The federal government, therefore, is a government of *delegated* powers. It may exercise those powers that are conferred upon it by the Constitution, and no others. It has no authority to legislate for the general welfare of the people, and the mere fact that a matter requiring urgent attention—public health, for example—is neglected by the states does not constitute a sufficient reason for the federal government to interfere. The test of federal authority over any activity of government is not the importance of the activity, nor the extent or manner of its control by state officials, but whether it has been included among the federal powers listed in the Constitution.

**Implied powers.** The federal government, however, is not limited to those powers *expressly* conferred upon it. The Constitution authorizes Congress "to make all laws which shall be necessary and proper for carrying into execution" [2] the powers expressly granted, and this clause has been interpreted quite liberally. Thus, under the power "to establish post-offices and post roads," [3] Congress has arranged for the transportation of mail by railroad, boat, and airplane; it has placed armed guards in railway mail cars as a protection against robbery; it has prohibited interference with the United States mails, and has prescribed suitable penalties; it has provided for federal supervision of the construction of a great national highway system, and has even authorized road building directly by the federal government; [4] it has excluded seditious, salacious, and fradulent matter from the mails; and in 1912 it established a federal express business under the name of parcel post. The power "to lay and collect taxes, duties, imposts, and excises" had also proved capable of broad interpretation. It has been the basis of Congressional action, not only in imposing taxes for the purpose of raising revenue, but also in building up a system of protective tariffs, regulating the distribution of narcotics, establishing a comprehensive scheme of unemployment insurance, and controlling the sale of certain foodstuffs. The implied powers of the federal government, therefore, are quite as important as those granted to it in express terms.

**Transfer of power to national government.** Ever since the adoption of the Constitution there has been a tendency to increase the authority of the federal government at the expense of the states. National prestige and influence have grown steadily, while the importance of the states has declined. This transition has been especially noticeable during two periods in American history. Immediately after the Civil War there was a great wave of nationalism—a reaction against the extreme states' rights view of the South; and the powers of the federal government were materially increased. And now, during the twentieth century, a similar expansion of national authority is

2 Art. I, Sec. 8, Cl. 18.
3 Constitution, Art. I, Sec. 8, Cl. 7.
4 The Cumberland Road, which played an important part in the early development of the Middle West, was built by the federal government. For many years it was under federal control, and was known as the Great National Pike.

taking place.   A striking example of this trend is the National Labor Relations Act of 1935, designed to insure labor's right of collective bargaining.   This statute directs the National Labor Relations Board to ascertain the workers' choice of labor union representatives and to compel employers to deal with those representatives in all labor disputes.   Orders of the Board may be enforced in the Courts.   Although the declared purpose of the act is "to eliminate the causes of certain substantial obstructions to the free flow of commerce," its provisions have been applied not only to persons engaged in commerce, but also to those in manufacturing—a local occupation, and therefore traditionally regarded as free from federal control.   But several court decisions [5] have made clear that manufacturers, also, come within the scope of federal regulation if they obtain their raw materials from sources outside the state or sell their finished products across state boundaries.   Other recent laws have increased the scope of federal activity in various other ways.   Thus many powers formerly vested in the states have already been or are being transferred to the federal government; the balance of power is shifting gradually to the nation.

In December, 1941, came the Japanese treachery at Pearl Harbor, and the immediate aftermath of this attack was a veritable deluge of statutes, decrees, and orders designed to strengthen the position of the federal authorities, in order to subordinate every aspect of American life to the war effort.   There was general agreement that nothing must be permitted to interfere with complete victory at the earliest possible moment.   Therefore the national government assumed control of rents, prices, wages, profits, and hours of labor, with virtually no regard for the traditional limits of its authority.   It rationed gasoline, tires, shoes, and even food.   It established priorities for innumerable categories of goods regarded as necessary to the conduct of the war.   It ordered the removal from the Pacific Coast of thousands of persons of Japanese ancestry, many of whom were American citizens.   But these drastic steps did not represent an attempt by the federal government to secure permanent control of local affairs. State officials recognized this fact, and co-operated heartily with the national authorities in carrying out the vast war program.   State laws were amended to conform to federal specifications.   Most of the actual work of rationing gasoline and other articles was performed by

---

[5] National Labor Relations Board *v.* Jones & Laughlin Steel Corp., 301 U.S. 1 (1937); National Labor Relations Board *v.* Freuhauf Trailer Co., 301 U.S. 49 (1937); and National Labor Relations Board *v.* Friedman-Harry Marks Clothing Co., 301 U.S. 58 (1937).

local boards. The care of evacuated Japanese-Americans became the joint responsibility of the nation, the states, and the counties.

**Increase in power through constitutional amendments.** It must be recognized, however, that the expansion of federal power is not merely a by-product of war. It is a trend that continues decade after decade, in war and in peace. The transfer of authority from the states to the nation has been accomplished in part by means of formal amendments to the Constitution. Thus the Sixteenth Amendment, proclaimed in 1913, made possible an effective system of federal income taxation. When the Eighteenth Amendment, which placed in the hands of Congress concurrent jurisdiction over the manufacture, transportation, and sale of intoxicants, was proclaimed six years later, an important legal controversy arose. It was urged that the original distribution of authority between the nation and the states could not be disturbed by amending the Constitution in the customary manner —despite the very obvious fact that it had already been so disturbed in a number of instances; and that any amendment purporting to transfer power from the states to the nation was unconstitutional unless ratified by state conventions instead of the state legislatures. This argument was palpably weak. Its main theme—that a duly adopted part of the Constitution might be unconstitutional—seemed to be a contradiction in terms, and was so regarded by the Supreme Court of the United States. When asked to set aside the Eighteenth Amendment, the Court, said in part: "That Amendment, by lawful proposal and ratification, has become a part of the Constitution, and must be supported and given effect the same as other provisions of that instrument." [6]

If changes in federal-state relations could be made only by means of formal amendments to the Constitution, however, the transfer of powers from the states to the nation would be a difficult and tedious operation. In nearly a century and a half the Constitution has been amended but twenty-one times, and ten of those twenty-one amendments were virtually a part of the original document. So cumbersome is the amending process that only proposals of the greatest importance have even a slight chance of adoption, and the opposition of substantial minority is sufficient to prevent favorable action. First, a proposed amendment must be approved by a two-thirds vote in each

[6] National Prohibition Cases, 253 U.S. 350 (1920). Substantially the same argument was advanced in U.S. *v.* Sprague, 282 U.S. 716 (1931), and was answered by the Supreme Court in the same manner.

house of Congress.   Almost invariably this means that it must be acceptable to both major parties, for neither Republicans nor Democrats can hope to control two thirds of the Senate and the House of Representatives, except at rare intervals.   Then it must be ratified by three fourths of the states.[7]   Small wonder that few amendments are adopted!

**Broadening power through judicial interpretation.**   But there are other ways of broadening the sphere of federal authority.   One of these is commonly known as judicial interpretation.   Every year the courts are called upon to determine the exact significance of some word or phrase of the Constitution, and their decisions have a profound effect upon the scope of the nation's powers.   Take, for example, the control of the federal government over interstate commerce.   "Congress," declares the Constitution, "shall have power to regulate commerce . . . among the several States." [8]   It would seem that nothing could be clearer than this simple statement, or less likely to cause disagreement as to its meaning, yet it has produced an astounding amount of litigation.   As early as 1824 the Supreme Court was asked to define commerce.   The contention had been advanced that commerce comprised only "traffic—buying and selling, or the interchange of commodities," and did not include navigation.   Had this narrow view prevailed, the authority of Congress would have been seriously restricted.   But the Court refused to accept any such interpretation.   Speaking through Chief Justice Marshall, it said: "All America understands, and has uniformly understood, the word 'commerce' to comprehend navigation. . . . The word used in the Constitution, then, comprehends, and has been always understood to comprehend, navigation within its meaning; and a power to regulate navigation, is as expressly granted, as if that term had been added to the word 'commerce.' " [9]

---

[7] The first twenty amendments to the federal Constitution were proposed by Congress and ratified by the state legislatures.   This is not the only possible method of amendment, however.   Article V of the Constitution states: "The Congress, whenever two thirds of both houses shall deem it necessary, shall propose amendments to this Constitution, or, on the application of the legislatures of two thirds of the several States, shall call a convention for proposing amendments, which in either case shall be valid to all intents and purposes as parts of this Constitution, when ratified by the legislatures of three fourths of the several states, or by conventions in three fourths thereof, as the one or the other mode of ratification may be proposed by the Congress."   But conventions for proposing amendments to the federal Constitution have never been called, and conventions for ratifying a federal amendment were first used in connection with the Twenty-first Amendment.

[8] Art. I, Sec. 8, Cl. 3.

[9] Gibbons *v.* Ogden, 9 Wheaton 1 (1824).

Half a century later another issue was raised that threatened to restrict the sphere of national power. The Pensacola Telegraph Company, denying the right of Congress to interfere with its affairs, argued that the framers of the Constitution could not possibly have intended to include telegraphy within the meaning of *commerce,* since telegraphy was not known until many years afterward. Had this contention been upheld, it would subsequently have prevented the federal government from regulating the interstate movements of automobiles and airplanes, in fact, all the newer agencies of communication. But the Supreme Court took a broad, statesmanlike view. "The powers thus granted . . . are not confined to the instrumentalities of commerce, or the postal system known or in use when the Constitution was adopted," declared Chief Justice Waite, speaking for the Court, "but they keep pace with the progress of the country, and adapt themselves to the new developments of time and circumstances. They extend from the horse with its rider to the stagecoach, from the sailing vessel to the steamboat, from the coach and the steamboat to the railroad, and from the railroad to the telegraph, as these new agencies are successively brought into use to meet the demands of increasing population and wealth. They were intended for the government of the business to which they relate, at all times and under all circumstances." [10]

In 1837 the Supreme Court of the United States stated that persons were not the "subject of commerce," and therefore could not be controlled under the interstate commerce clause of the Constitution.[11] Subsequently, however, it ruled otherwise in a number of far-reaching decisions, thus broadening materially the scope of national authority. Upholding an act of Congress that prohibited the transportation of women from state to state for immoral purposes, the Court said in part: "Commerce among the States . . . consists of intercourse and traffic between their citizens, and includes the transportation of persons and property. There may be, therefore, a movement of persons as well as of property; that is, a person may move or be moved in interstate commerce." [12]

These liberal decisions have been a vital factor in the growth of federal prestige and the expansion of federal power. They have per-

---

[10] Pensacola Telegraph Co. *v.* Western Union Telegraph Co., 96 U.S. 1 (1877).

[11] New York *v.* Miln, 11 Peters 102 (1837).

[12] Hoke *v.* U.S., 227 U.S. 308, 320 (1913). See also Gloucester Ferry Co. *v.* Pennsylvania, 114 U.S. 196, 203 (1885).

mitted national authority to keep pace with national problems, at least in part. They have obviated the necessity of amending many essential features of the Constitution. They have encouraged orderly evolution, and thus made revolution unnecessary. Of course, the courts have not invariably looked with approval upon the acts of Congress. In a number of instances they have set aside important legislation on the ground that it exceeded federal authority. But the general effect of court decisions, from Marshall to Stone, has been to uphold or increase the power of the nation.

**Expansion of power through federal aid.** The growth of federal influence has not been solely the product of constitutional amendment and judicial interpretation, however. In recent years Congress has discovered a very effective means of securing a measure of control over matters not mentioned in the Constitution, and therefore presumably reserved to the states. The plan has worked so well that it is now an established part of federal administration. Its essential features are quite simple. Congress offers a sum of money to the states for agricultural extension work, forest fire prevention, or some other activity, *provided they will match the federal grant dollar for dollar, or in some other ratio, and agree to accept federal supervision of their work.* This offer is in no sense a club. It is an inducement, and the states are free to accept or reject it as they see fit. But the inducement is so powerful that acceptance follows almost as a matter of course. Every state, almost without exception, receives practically every subsidy offered by Congress and agrees to the conditions of the federal grant.

CONDITIONS GOVERNING GRANTS. Under the terms of a typical subsidy law the actual details of administration remain in the hands of state officials. They formulate policies, prepare plans, choose subordinates, spend the combined federal-state money. They carry on the day-to-day work for which the money was appropriated. The federal government merely acts in an advisory and supervisory capacity. But state budgets, policies, plans, and even personnel must receive federal approval. They must at least measure up to minimum federal standards, though the states are freed to exceed the minimum in any way they desire.

When a state legislature accepts the provisions of a federal grant, it is required to establish a state agency to co-operate with federal officials, or else designate an existing state agency for that purpose. The state agency—extension director, vocational education board, forester, highway commission, or whatever it may be—prepares a detailed plan showing exactly how the money is to be spent. Although this plan must conform to certain specifications of the federal government, state officials are given considerable leeway. No attempt is made to impose exactly the same conditions on all states, without regard to local conditions. The state plan is supposed to reflect local needs, even though it must measure up to the prescribed minimum. Thus the Federal Highway Act, authorizing the payment of federal funds to the states for the construction of state road systems, specifies that "only such durable types of surfaces and kinds of material shall be adopted for the construction and reconstruction of any highway . . . as will adequately meet the existing and probable future traffic needs and conditions thereon." [13] But the United States Public Roads Administration, which administers this subsidy law for the federal government, understands quite well that "durable" may mean many different things—varying with climatic and soil conditions, and the amount and nature of traffic. It insists upon durable roads whenever a state plan is offered for its approval, but *durable* does not have the same significance in the sparsely settled ranch lands of Montana as in the thickly populated valleys of New York.

Federal suggestions frequently cause a modification of state plans, though only minor details are involved in most instances. Once federal approval has been given, a state is free to proceed with its program. It can be absolutely certain of receiving its allotment of federal funds—provided, of course, that it respects its part of the agreement. But when a state fails to carry out a plan that its own officials have prepared, the result is likely to be a withdrawal of federal aid. A number of states have acted in bad faith from time to time, and have been forced back into the straight and narrow path by the threatened or actual cutting off of federal funds. Incidents of this sort are now infrequent; most state officials have learned that in order to continue to get the cash they must keep the faith.

A federal bureau administering a subsidy law usually has a staff of inspectors who visit the states from time to time, audit state accounts, and report on the development of state programs. Sometimes these inspectors serve also as instructors, keeping state officials in touch with recent improvements and current practices in other states. Unsatisfactory conditions are reported promptly to Washington and in most cases are remedied without the necessity of resorting to threats. The

[13] 42 Stat. L. 212.

large majority of co-operating state officials value federal advice highly
and follow it as a matter of course.

RESULTS OF FEDERAL AID.   Federal funds are granted to the states
in support of a wide variety of different activities—construction of
highways, vocational education, re-education of physically handicapped persons, financial assistance to the blind and the aged, and to
dependent children, promotion of maternal and child welfare, maintenance of public employment offices, administration of unemployment compensation, extension work in agriculture, forest fire prevention, upkeep of state agricultural colleges and experiment stations.
Even this long list is not complete.   But some of the laws offering
grants to the state deviate from the standard pattern by requiring little
or no effective federal supervision of state activities.   The earliest
subsidy laws omitted all reference to federal approval of state plans,
and some of the more recent statutes—especially those relating to the
federal government's social security program—leave matters almost
exclusively in state hands.

Every year since 1922 the total of annual federal appropriations to
the states has been in excess of one hundred million dollars.   Every
year since 1936 it has exceeded five hundred million dollars, and in
1943 it was considerably more than three-quarters of a billion.
Nearly seventy-five per cent of this huge sum is for old age assistance
and other aspects of social security; another eighteen per cent is for
highways.[14]

This system of federal aid to the states has materially stimulated
state activity.   It has produced results; in fact, it has bought results;
and in nearly every instance the federal government has secured its
money's worth.   Agricultural extension work was unknown until it
was introduced as an experiment by the United States Department of
Agriculture.   Within a year after Congress first offered a subsidy for
the re-education of disabled persons, the number of states engaged in
this activity had tripled.   Most of the other federal grants have been
equally effective.   Not only has more state money been spent, however; it has been spent more efficiently.   State standards have greatly
improved as a result of federal supervision.   The federal influence is
traceable in better equipment for vocational schools, more training
and higher salaries for teachers of vocational subjects, better methods
of forest fire prevention and highway construction, better farms, and

[14] The most recent figures may be obtained conveniently in the Census Bureau's
annual publication, *State Finances*.

better rural homes. A few of the more progressive states have not been affected to any considerable extent by federal supervision, because their standards have always been higher than the federal minimum. But they are rare exceptions.

OPPOSITION TO FEDERAL AID. Despite the results accomplished by the federal subsidy system, it aroused a great deal of opposition during the first years of its expansion. Men high in public life charged it with stifling local initiative, ignoring local conditions, and forcing all local activities into a uniform mold. "There is scarce a domain in the field of government properly belonging to the municipality or the state," declared Frank Lowden, then governor of Illinois, "which the federal government is not seeking to invade by the use of the specious phrase 'federal aid.' . . . This rapid extension of federal administration not only means greatly increased expense because of duplication of efforts, but it means the gradual breaking down of local self-government in America." [15] Since 1930 most of the critics of federal aid have been silenced by the obvious need of the states for additional revenue. Grants for new services have been made, and grants for established services have been increased.[16]

The question of the subsidy system's constitutionality was presented to the Supreme Court of the United States in 1923. A taxpayer's suit to prevent the enforcement of the Federal Child Hygiene Act had been brought by a resident of Massachusetts, and when the suit reached the Supreme Court it was joined to a separate action of the State of Massachusetts, also contesting the constitutionality of the child hygiene law. The Court dismissed the two cases for want of jurisdiction, pointing out that no justiciable issue was presented; but in handing down its decision it took occasion to brush aside the constitutional objections to federal aid. The chief argument against the system, that it was "an effective means of inducing the states to yield a portion of their sovereign rights," the Court answered by saying: "Probably it would be sufficient to point out that the powers of the States are not invaded, since the statute imposes no obligation, but simply extends an option which the State is free to accept or reject. But we do not rest here. . . . What burden is imposed upon the States, unequally or otherwise? Certainly there is none, unless it be the burden of taxation, and that falls upon their inhabitants, who are

[15] Convocation Address, University of Chicago, June, 1921.
[16] For a more complete discussion of the American subsidy system, see *The Administration of Federal Grants to States*, by V. O. Key. See also A. F. Macdonald's *Federal Aid*.

within the taxing power of Congress as well as that of the State where they reside. Nor does the statute require the States to do or yield anything. If Congress enacted it with the ulterior purpose of tempting them to yield, that purpose may be effectively frustrated by the simple expedient of not yielding." [17]

**Reasons for the expansion of federal power.** And so the scope of federal power has gradually broadened—by formal amendments to the Constitution, by judicial interpretation, by grants from the federal treasury to the states. Since the Civil War the centralizing process has continued virtually without interruption; the centripetal forces of government have been in the ascendant. It is worth while, therefore, to make inquiry concerning the causes of this expansion of national authority. In part, at least, the greater efficiency of the federal government as compared with that of state governments has been responsible. Though the methods of administering national affairs have at times been open to serious criticism, they have usually been far ahead of current state practices. Some persons contend that this greater efficiency has been due to the relatively narrow scope of national activities—that the federal government has been more efficient because it has had less to do. And it must be admitted that the record of the war years has added force to this argument. The marked expansion of federal activities, expenditures, and personnel seems to have caused a deterioration of federal standards—at least, in certain fields. But federal efficiency still contrasts favorably with the relative inefficiency of many states. As long as this situation continues, many men will doubtless favor federal assumption of every task that has proved difficult for the state governments.

Nor must it be forgotten that those who are interested in improving social and economic conditions turn naturally to the federal government. They welcome federal control over matters that seem to need correction, for they know that the task of influencing Congress, difficult though it may be, is as nothing compared with the burden of bringing sufficient pressure to bear upon forty-eight state legislatures. Professional reformers, therefore, are usually proponents of a strong national government—unless their special hobby happens to be the preservation of the rights of the states.

But the chief reason for the expansion of national power has been the broadening scope of modern civilization. Present-day industry pays scant attention to state boundaries. Present-day commerce

[17] Massachusetts *v.* Mellon and Frothingham *v.* Mellon, 262 U.S. 447 (1923).

crosses them at will. The United States is bound together by a network of railways, highways, and airways. Giant corporations and
super-corporations extend their activities to the nation's boundaries
and beyond. Labor unions operate on a national scale. Time and
distance have lost much of their former significance. Small wonder,
therefore, that national power has been increased to meet this rapidly
changing situation! State officials have struggled to control nation-
wide or world-wide forces, and have failed dismally in the attempt.
The public has witnessed this partial collapse of state administration
and has tired of the uninspiring spectacle. It has begun to realize
that governmental authority must be as broad as the problems with
which it has to deal. And so it has accepted as natural, and almost
inevitable, the flow of power from the states to the nation.

**Arguments against excessive centralization of power.** To a
certain extent this expansion of federal authority *is* natural and almost inevitable. But it should not be permitted to continue indefinitely, lest it prove a menace to popular government. Excessive
centralization is quite as dangerous as excessive decentralization, and
quite as likely to become an inefficient method of control. This principle is fundamentally sound, regardless of the nation or the century to
which it may be applied; but it has an especial significance for present-
day America. The United States has a population of more than one
hundred and thirty million and an area equal to three fourths of all
Europe; it has great metropolitan centers, rich farm lands, vast
stretches of trackless desert, mountain peaks where the snow never
melts, and valleys where the snow never falls. Among the people of
the nation there are differences of color, custom, and creed. The
forty-eight states are too diverse to be fitted into an absolutely uniform
mold. No central government, however efficient, can solve all their
problems. While it can scarcely be disputed that the nation should
have authority over national affairs, this principle should not be distorted to justify federal control over matters of purely local concern.

It must be remembered, also, that an overburdened national government may become topheavy and unresponsive to the wishes of the
people. Federal bureau chiefs, seated at their desks in Washington,
may be entirely out of touch with local conditions and entirely ignorant of local needs. However proficient they may be in their chosen
professions, they may lack the personal touch that is so essential to
successful administration. Overwhelmed by the complexity of their
task, they may take refuge behind a set of rules poorly suited to meet

every possible contingency. Thus government may cease to be a personal matter and may become instead an arbitrary routine.

There is still another reason why excessive centralization is undesirable: it prevents local experiments in government. The states are sometimes characterized as "experiment stations." They afford an opportunity to try new plans, new theories, new dogmas, without involving the entire nation. If a state is convinced of the advisability of adopting any new reform, from the short ballot to the single tax, it may do so without hindrance. Its experience may induce other states to follow its lead, or instead may save them from costly error. In either case the experiment has been worth while. But if all authority were centered in the national government, the opportunity to try new schemes on a small scale would disappear.

One of the most perplexing problems of American government, therefore, is to strike a proper balance between the powers of the states and the nation. It is easy to say that the federal government should confine its attention to national matters, whereas the states should limit their activities to state affairs. Virtually everyone assents to this statement of principle. But when it becomes necessary to apply the principle in specific cases—in other words, to classify the functions of government according to their local or national character —the difficulties are at once apparent. Men may agree in principle, but with regard to specific functions they almost invariably differ.

The delegation of certain powers to the federal government is not necessarily a denial of those powers to the states. In some cases both the states and the nation may have jurisdiction over the same matter —that is, they may exercise *concurrent* authority. The concurrent powers of the states are not very numerous, however. They may borrow on their own credit, while the federal government may borrow on the credit of the nation. They may impose taxes on commodities, incomes, and the like, even though those commodities and incomes have already been taxed by the federal government. From 1919 until 1933 they had concurrent power to enforce the prohibition against the manufacture and sale of intoxicants, by virtue of a specific provision of the federal Constitution.[18] Control over the state militia is divided between the nation and the states.[19]

In addition, the states may even invade the sphere of national au-

[18] Eighteenth Amendment, Sec. 2. "The Congress and the several states shall have concurrent power to enforce this article by appropriate legislation."
[19] Constitution, Art. I, Sec. 8, Cls. 15 and 16.

thority to some extent for the purpose of protecting the welfare of their inhabitants, provided Congress has not acted in the matter. Thus reasonable state laws concerning safety appliances on interstate railroads will be upheld in the absence of Congressional legislation, despite the fact that Congress is vested with control over commerce among the states.[20]  Reasonable anchorage and pilotage rules will also receive judicial approval, even when applied to vessels from other states and other nations,[21] unless Congress sees fit to supplant state regulations with regulations of its own.  When Congress acts, however, its decisions are final within the sphere of national authority. Any conflicting state legislation becomes inoperative at once.[22]  For long periods in American history there was no federal legislation on the subject of bankruptcy, though this matter was specifically placed under the control of Congress.[23]  Each state, therefore, controlled bankruptcy in such a manner as it saw fit, and these state laws remained in force until the passage of a national bankruptcy law.[24]  It must be understood, however, that a state may not under any circumstances exercise control over a matter prohibited to it by the Constitution.  For example, it may not enter into treaties with foreign nations.[25]  Nor may it regulate matters of an exclusively national character, such as naturalization, even in the absence of an express constitutional prohibition.

### POWERS OF THE STATES

It has already been pointed out that the federal government is a government of delegated powers.[26]  The state governments, on the other hand, are governments of *reserved* or *residual* powers.  To them is reserved, generally speaking, all the authority not specifically or impliedly given to the nation.  They possess the residue of power. Therefore it is not necessary to search the federal Constitution for specific grants of power in order to determine the scope of state authority.

**Due process of law versus police power.**  Unless clearly prohibited

[20] New York, New Haven and Hartford Railroad *v.* New York, 165 U.S. 628 (1897).
[21] Cooley *v.* Port Wardens of Philadelphia, 12 Howard 299 (1851).
[22] Pennsylvania Railroad *v.* Pennsylvania, 250 U.S. 566 (1919).
[23] Constitution, Art. I, Sec. 8, Cl. 4.
[24] Congress enacted a bankruptcy law as early as 1800, but repealed it three years later. Subsequently it passed and repealed two other bankruptcy statutes, and did not permanently occupy the field until 1898.
[25] Constitution, Art. I, Sec. 10, Cl. 1.
[26] See p. 30.

from doing so, a state may make any reasonable regulations to promote the health, safety, morals, convenience, or comfort of its people. This right to take reasonable action for the general welfare is known as the police power of the state. It is the legal justification for a vast quantity of social legislation that has been enacted by the states during the last few decades. Such laws have not always been upheld by the courts, however; in many instances they have been declared void as contrary to the Fourteenth Amendment to the federal Constitution. That Amendment declares that no state shall "deprive any person of life, liberty, or property, without due process of law." [27] This phraseology should be noted carefully. A state is not prohibited from depriving a person of his life, liberty, or property, but only from doing so *without due process of law*. If due process of law is observed, nothing more can be demanded. It becomes necessary, therefore, to know the exact meaning of the phrase *due process of law*. According to the courts, *due process* includes the idea of *reasonableness*. The powers of the state must be exercised "within the limits of those fundamental principles of liberty and justice which lie at the base of all our civil and political institutions." [28] Thus the due process clause of the Fourteenth Amendment and the police power of the state are always in potential conflict.

A single illustration may suffice to show how readily this conflict arises. A state may limit the hours of work in mines to five a day. By so doing it deprives men of their liberty—that is, their liberty to work more than five hours daily if they feel so disposed, for *liberty* includes more than mere freedom from imprisonment. In includes "the right of a citizen to be free in the engagement of all his faculties; to be free to use them in all lawful ways; to live and work where he will; to earn his livelihood by any lawful calling; to pursue any livelihood or avocation; and for that purpose to enter into all contracts which may be proper, necessary, and essential to his carrying out to a successful conclusion the purposes above mentioned." [29] But is the limitation imposed by this statute reasonable, and likely to improve the welfare of the people of the state? If so, it is constitutional, as falling within the state's police power. If it is simply an arbitrary enactment, however, it is contrary to the due process clause of the Fourteenth Amendment, and void for that reason. Some person or group of persons must

27 Sec. 1.
28 Hurtado *v.* California, 110 U.S. 515, 535 (1884).
29 Allgeyer *v.* Louisiana, 165 U.S. 578 (1897).

decide, therefore, whether the statute is reasonable or arbitrary. Since this is a question of policy, and not of law, it would be natural to assume that final judgment would rest with the legislature. The legislature's primary function is to determine policy, and the mere fact of enacting a law is sufficient evidence that it considers the law reasonable. But the courts refuse to accept this viewpoint, and so they declare unconstitutional any such statute that seems to them unreasonable. Thus the Fourteenth Amendment, as judicially interpreted, may operate as a serious limitation upon the police power of the states.

**Constitutional limitations.** Although the federal Constitution reserves to the states a large measure of authority, it specifically limits state power in a number of ways. Some of these restrictions are virtually self-explanatory, and need little or no comment:

No State shall enter into any treaty, alliance, or confederation; grant letters of marque and reprisal; [30] coin money; emit bills of credit; make anything but gold and silver coin a tender in payment of debts; pass any bill of attainder,[31] *ex post facto* law,[32] or law impairing the obligation of contracts, or grant any title of nobility.[33]

No State shall, without the consent of Congress, lay any imposts or duties on imports or exports, except what may be absolutely necessary for executing its inspection laws; and the net produce of all duties and imposts, laid by any State on imports or exports, shall be for the use of the Treasury of the United States; and all such laws shall be subject to the revision and control of the Congress.[34]

No State shall, without the consent of Congress, lay any duty of tonnage, keep troops or ships of war in time of peace, enter into any agreement or compact with another State [35] or with a foreign power, or engage in war, unless actually invaded or in such imminent danger as will not admit of delay.[36]

[30] Letters of marque were commissions issued by a belligerent state to vessels owned and manned by private persons, either its own citizens or neutrals, authorizing them to carry on hostilities at sea against the enemy. Such commissions are no longer issued by civilized nations.

[31] In English law a bill of attainder was a bill introduced into Parliament convicting a person, without trial in an ordinary court of justice, of a high crime, and prescribing the penalty of death and the forfeiture of the estates of the person accused. For two centuries, at least, this was the usual English method of dealing with influential political offenders.

[32] A retroactive criminal law is known as an *ex post facto* law. Under this heading would come legislation which provided a penalty for an act that was not a crime at the time it was committed, or which increased the penalty for an offense already committed.

[33] Constitution, Art. I, Sec. 10, Cl. 1.

[34] *Ibid.*, Cl. 2.

[35] There are many examples of interstate agreements made with the approval of Congress. See p. 54.

[36] Constitution, Art. I, Sec. 10, Cl. 3.

The right of citizens of the United States to vote shall not be denied or abridged . . . by any State on account of race, color, or previous condition of servitude.[37]

The right of citizens of the United States to vote shall not be denied or abridged . . . by any State on account of sex.[38]

**Privileges and immunities.** Then there are a number of other constitutional limitations upon the power of the states that require at least a few words of explanation. Article IV specifies that "The citizens of each State shall be entitled to all privileges and immunities of citizens in the several States," [39] and the Fourteenth Amendment extends this guarantee:

No state shall make or enforce any law which shall abridge the privileges or immunities of citizens of the United States; nor shall any State deprive any person of life, liberty, or property without due process of law; nor deny to any person within its jurisdiction the equal protection of the laws.[40]

The "privileges and immunities" clauses just quoted might seem to be a guarantee that privileges granted by one state could be carried into every other state. If the citizens of each state are "entitled to all privileges and immunities of citizens in the several States," what is to prevent a man from securing the privilege of practicing medicine, or driving a motor car, in some state where such privileges are easily secured, and insisting upon his constitutional right to do likewise in every other commonwealth? The barrier that effectually prevents such action, with its resultant destruction of state standards, is the attitude of the United States Supreme Court. Interpreting the "privileges and immunities" clauses, it has said that "special privileges enjoyed by citizens in their own States are not secured in other States by this provision. It was not intended . . . to give to the laws of one State any operation in other States." [41] Therefore special privileges granted by one state—exemption from certain taxes, permission to practice law, medicine, or any other profession, and the like—are not recognized in other states unless as a matter of comity. No obligation to recognize them exists.

What, then, are the "privileges and immunities" guaranteed by the Constitution? The Supreme Court has refused to make a complete

37 Fifteenth Amendment.
38 Nineteenth Amendment.
39 Sec. 2.
40 Sec. 1.
41 Paul *v.* Virginia, 8 Wallace 168, 178 (1868).

enumeration,[42] but it has said that they include the right "to pass into any other State of the Union, for the purpose of engaging in lawful commerce, trade, or business, without molestation, to acquire personal property, to take and hold real estate, to maintain actions in the courts of the States, and to be exempt from any higher taxes or excises than are imposed upon the state by its own citizens." [43]  To this list the Court added, in 1935, the right to make a lawful loan of money in any state other than that in which the citizen resides.[44]  It should be noted, however, that a corporation is not a citizen [45] and that its creation by one state does not give it the right to enter other states for the purpose of doing business.  Other states may exclude it, or may admit it on such terms as they choose.[46]

EQUAL PROTECTION OF THE LAWS.  As already indicated, no state may deny to any person within its borders the equal protection of the laws.[47]  Even aliens are entitled to this protection; so are corporations, which are artificial persons.[48]  This clause does not mean that all persons must be treated alike, however.  Distinctions may be made by the state, which has a wide scope of discretion in this regard. It is necessary only that the distinctions have a reasonable basis. Thus taxes may be imposed upon certain trades, and not on others; special assessments may be levied against specially benefited property, while other property is permitted to escape this burden.  But the classification of persons or property for the purpose of according them different treatment must be reasonable—in other words, it must bear some relation to the purpose to be accomplished.  As the Supreme Court said in a leading case: "Class legislation, discriminating against some and favoring others, is prohibited, but legislation which, in carrying out a public purpose, is limited in its application, if within the sphere of its operations it affects alike all persons similarly situated, is not within the amendment." [49]

FULL FAITH AND CREDIT.  The Constitution specifies that "Full

---

[42] Conner v. Elliott, 18 Howard 591, 593 (1856).
[43] Ward v. Maryland, 12 Wallace 418, 430 (1871).
[44] Colgate v. Harvey, 296 U.S. 404 (1935).
[45] Paul v. Virginia, 8 Wallace 168, 178 (1868).
[46] Pembina Mining Co. v. Pennsylvania, 125 U.S. 181, 189 (1888).  A corporation may not be excluded, however, if it wishes to enter for purposes of interstate commerce (because control over interstate commerce is given to Congress by the Constitution); or if it desires to enter for the performance of some "governmental or quasi-governmental" functions of the federal government. Hooper v. California, 155 U.S. 648, 652 (1895).
[47] Fourteenth Amendment, Sec. 1.
[48] Santa Clara County v. Southern Pacific Railway Co., 118 U.S. 394, 396 (1886).
[49] Barbier v. Connolly, 113 U.S. 27, 31 (1885).

faith and credit shall be given in each State to the public acts, records, and judicial proceedings of every other State." [50] Included under this heading are records of deeds, mortgages, marriages, and the like, kept in public offices. But this does not mean that the acts of one state are necessarily binding upon other commonwealths. It does not, for example, indicate that a divorce issued in one state must be honored by every other state of the Union.[51] The only effect of the "full faith and credit" clause is to establish a binding rule of evidence, so that the facts properly determined in one state need not be judicially re-determined in another commonwealth.[52]

ARREST AND DELIVERY OF FUGITIVES. "A person charged in any State with treason, felony, or other crime," states the Constitution, "who shall flee from justice, and be found in another State, shall, on demand of the executive authority of the State from which he fled, be delivered up, to be removed to the State having jurisdiction of the crime." [53] The meaning of this clause is unmistakable. It has been supplemented by Congressional legislation which imposes upon the state governor the duty of arresting and delivering fugitives on demand. The question may well be raised, however: What means is provided for enforcing this command? If the governor of a state refuses to give up fugitives when properly requested to do so, is there any way of coercing him? When this question was presented to the Supreme Court of the United States, it answered that the governor's obligation was merely moral, and not legal. Said the Court: "The performance of the duty, however, is left to depend on the fidelity of the State Executive to the compact entered into with the other States when it adopted the Constitution of the United States, and became a member of the Union. It was so left by the Constitution. . . ." [54]

---

50 Art. IV, Sec. 1.

51 In the important case of Williams *v.* North Carolina, decided May 21, 1945, the Supreme Court of the United States specifically upheld the right of every state to challenge the validity of a domicile acquired in another state solely for purposes of divorce. The defendants left their respective spouses in their home state of North Carolina and went to Nevada, where they received divorces after residing for six weeks in an auto court. Then they were married, and returned to North Carolina as husband and wife. Later a North Carolina court convicted them of bigamous cohabitation, on the ground that their six weeks' stay in Nevada did not constitute a bona fide domicile necessary for divorce, and the United States Supreme Court sustained this conviction. Mr. Justice Black, in a vigorous dissent, declared that the Court's opinion "will cast a cloud over the lives of countless numbers of . . . divorced persons," and he is doubtless right; but that is one of the inconveniences of our federal system of government.

52 Virginia *v.* Tennessee, 148 U.S. 503 (1893).

53 Art. IV, Sec. 2, Cl. 2.

54 Kentucky *v.* Dennison, 24 Howard 66 (1861).

Despite this decision state governors have generally recognized their "moral duty," and only occasionally is a request for the return of a fugitive refused.

REPUBLICAN FORM OF GOVERNMENT. The Constitution also specifies that "The United States shall guarantee to every State in the Union a republican form of government." [55] Since *republican government* is guaranteed to the states, it necessarily follows that every other form of government is prohibited. But the Constitution provides no means for enforcing this clause. It establishes no test by which a republican form may be clearly distinguished from all others. Nor will the Supreme Court undertake to define the meaning of the term. It has said that the determination of whether a state has a republican form of government is a political rather than a judicial matter, and therefore within the control of Congress.[56] Actually, Congress has never attempted to pass upon the question. It could do so, no doubt, by refusing to admit Senators and Representatives to its membership on the ground that their state government was not republican in form; and it might even use the armed forces of the United States to eject an unrepublican government.

DENIAL OR ABRIDGMENT OF VOTING RIGHTS. The Fourteenth Amendment provides, among other things, that any state denying or abridging the right to vote to "any of the male inhabitants of such State, being twenty-one years of age and citizens of the United States, . . . except for participation in rebellion, or other crime, . . ." shall suffer a proportionate reduction in the number of its Congressmen. But this section of the Constitution has never been enforced, for reasons that are considered in a subsequent chapter.[57]

STATE TAXATION OF NATIONAL GOVERNMENT. Another limitation on state power, not found in the exact words of the Constitution but long regarded by the Supreme Court as an inherent part of the American federal system, is the rule that no state may tax the federal government or its agencies. This rule originated in the fear that the states might otherwise impose such heavy taxes on the national government as to impair its functions or even drive it out of existence. "The power to tax," declared Chief Justice Marshall in 1819, speaking for a united court in the famous case of McCulloch *v.* Maryland,[58] "involves

---

[55] Art. IV, Sec. 4.

[56] Pacific States Telephone Co. *v.* Oregon, 223 U.S. 118 (1912); Mountain Timber Co. *v.* Washington, 243 U.S. 219, 234 (1917).

[57] See pp. 103–104.

[58] 4 Wheaton 316 (1819).

the power to destroy." Half a century later the converse of this principle—that the national government might not tax the state or its agencies—was also affirmed by the Supreme Court of the United States, in Collector *v.* Day.[59] In the spring of 1939, however, the Court specifically reversed its earlier stand, and permitted state taxation of the salaries of federal employees.[60] It is now assumed that non-discriminatory federal taxation of state salaries is permissible, also, and such taxation has been accepted by the states without further protest. At last the Supreme Court has rejected Marshall's "power to destroy" dictum in favor of the words of Holmes: "The power to tax is not the power to destroy while this court sits." [61]

**Change in relationship between nation and states.** It has already been pointed out that the relationship of the nation to the states has undergone a mighty transformation since the adoption of the Constitution. In a century and a half the federal government has largely discarded the part of an agent and has assumed instead the role of master. The letter of the Constitution is much the same, but its spirit is very different. In 1789 the Union was composed of thirteen states, whose independence preceded the formation of the national government by a number of years. These states were, in a very real sense, the creators of the nation. Today, however, the nation stands as the creator of the states. Thirty of the forty-eight commonwealths that now comprise the United States were carved out of the national domain and admitted into the Union by act of Congress. The fact that they were once territories under Congressional control has no legal bearing on their present status, but unquestionably it has been an element in the development of national prestige.

## ADMISSION OF NEW STATES

The Constitution empowers Congress to admit new states into the Union.[62] The first step is usually a petition from the people of a territory to Congress, requesting admission as a state. If Congress approves this petition it passes a so-called *enabling act,* authorizing the people of the territory to frame a constitution and specifying the exact

---

[59] 11 Wallace 113 (1870).
[60] Graves *v.* New York, 306 U.S. 466 (1939).
[61] Dissenting opinion in the case of Panhandle Oil Co. *v.* Knox, 277 U.S. 218 (1927).
[62] Art. IV, Sec. 3, Cl. 1. This clause continues: "but no new states shall be formed or erected within the jurisdiction of any other States; nor any State be formed by the junction of two or more States or parts of States, without the consent of the legislatures of the States concerned as well as of Congress."

manner in which this is to be done. After the constitution has been framed and has been ratified by the people, it must receive the approval of Congress before the territory is admitted to statehood. In some instances the people of a territory have framed their constitution before receiving the sanction of Congress, but subsequent Congressional approval has remedied this irregularity.

Since the federal government has absolute power to determine whether a territorial petition for admission to the Union shall be granted or denied, it is able to impose any conditions that it may see fit, and to insist upon those conditions as a *sine qua non* of statehood. In a number of instances federal restrictions have actually been inserted in enabling acts. Utah, for example, was admitted in 1896 on condition that polygamy be prohibited. Because of the insistence of President Taft, Arizona and New Mexico were not permitted to enter the Union until clauses providing for the recall of judges had been deleted from their new constitutions. Oklahoma, admitted in 1907, was required to agree that its capital would not be removed from the City of Guthrie prior to 1913. In 1910, however, the Oklahoma legislature violated this pledge by moving the state capital to Oklahoma City, and thereby created a serious legal problem. Granted that the federal government may impose conditions when admitting a territory into the Union, does it have any means of enforcing those conditions after statehood has been acquired? Or is the new state's duty to respect its agreement merely a moral obligation, unenforceable by any federal agency? The Supreme Court decided the matter in the case of Coyle *v.* Smith [63] and ruled that the federal government possessed no authority to rob the states of a portion of their control over local affairs by forcing burdensome restrictions upon them. As territories they might agree to the terms of Congress, but as states they could not be compelled to keep their promises. Otherwise Congress might impose all sorts of unreasonable conditions, and establish different classes of states with varying degrees of power. Such an arrangement, said the Court, would clearly be contrary to the Constitution, for the Union "was and is a union of States, equal in power, dignity, and authority, each competent to exert that residuum of sovereignty not delegated to the United States by the Constitution itself."

It must be clearly understood, however, that by admitting a territory to statehood Congress does not in any way surrender its control over

[63] 221 U.S. 559 (1911).

national affairs, even within the boundaries of the new state. Therefore it may include in the enabling act a provision concerning interstate commerce, bankruptcy, or some other matter within the scope of national authority, and such a provision is enforceable even after the territory has become a state. This principle was made clear in the case of Ervien *v.* United States.[64] The enabling act for the admission of New Mexico had granted national lands to the state government and had specified how the proceeds from their sale were to be used. In defiance of federal requirements the New Mexico legislature subsequently authorized the expenditure of some of this money for the purpose of advertising the natural resources of the state, but the federal Supreme Court unanimously ruled that the conditions imposed by Congress must be respected. "The United States, being the grantor of the lands, can impose conditions upon their use, and has the right to exact performance of the conditions," it declared.

While it is true, generally speaking, that the states are "equal in power, dignity, and authority"—to use the exact words of the Supreme Court—there are two respects in which the states are quite unequal in power, dignity, and authority. State representation in the federal House of Representatives is on the basis of population, so that the states with large numbers of inhabitants have proportionately greater voting power than the less populous commonwealths.[65] And state voting power is roughly equivalent to state population in selecting the president of the United States.[66] In the United States Senate, on the other hand, the legal equality of the states is recognized by giving equal representation to every state.[67]

## SELECTED REFERENCES

Ball, Carleton R., *Federal, State and Local Administrative Relationships in Agriculture,* 2 vols., Berkeley, Cal., 1938.

Benson, G. C. S., *The New Centralization; A Study of Intergovernmental Relationships in the United States,* 1941.

Bittermann, Henry J., *State and Federal Grants-in-Aid,* 1938.

Blough, Roy, and Others, *Tax Relations among Governmental Units,* 1938.

Burdine, John A., *National-State Cooperation with Special Reference to Texas,* Dallas, 1935.

[64] 251 U.S. 41 (1919).

[65] Constitution, Art. I, Sec. 3, Cl. 3, and the Fourteenth Amendment, Sec. 2.

[66] The Constitution specifies that "Each State shall appoint . . . a number of electors, equal to the whole number of senators and representatives to which the State may be entitled in the Congress." Art. II, Sec. 1, Cl. 2.

[67] "The Senate of the United States shall be composed of two senators from each State. . . ." Constitution, Art. I, Sec. 3, Cl. 1.

Clark, Jane P., *Rise of a New Federalism,* 1938.

Council of State Governments, *Handbook of Interstate Crime Control,* 1942.

Green, Thomas S., Jr., *Liquor Trade Barriers,* 1940.

Heinberg, John G., *Manual on Federal-State Relations for the Missouri Constitutional Convention of 1943,* Columbia, 1943.

Howell, R., *The Privileges and Immunities of State Citizenship,* Johns Hopkins University Studies in History and Political Science, Series XXXVI, No. 3, 1918.

Hughes, Charles E., *The Supreme Court of the United States,* 1928.

Johnsen, Julia E., comp., *Interstate Trade Barriers,* 1940.

Kallenbach, Joseph E., *Federal Cooperation with the States under the Commerce Clause,* Ann Arbor, Mich., 1942.

Key, V. O., Jr., *Administration of Federal Grants to States,* 1937.

Macdonald, Austin F., *Federal Aid,* 1928.

Mort, Paul R., and Others, *Principles and Methods of Distributing Federal Aid for Education,* Washington, D.C., 1939.

Reed, Thomas H., *Federal-State-Local Fiscal Relations,* 1942.

Ribble, Frederick D. G., *State and National Power over Commerce,* 1937.

Studenski, Paul, and Mort, Paul R., *Centralized versus Decentralized Government in Relation to Democracy,* 1942.

Tax Institute, *Tax Barriers to Trade,* Philadelphia, 1941.

Williams, Mrs. Juanita K., *Grants-in-Aid under the Public Works Administration; A Study in Federal-State-Local Relations,* 1939.

Vol. 207 of the *Annals of the American Academy of Political and Social Science,* January, 1940, is entitled "Intergovernmental Relations in the United States."

THE Constitution of the United States sets forth in great detail the relationships of the states to the nation and carefully draws a dividing line between state and national powers. It is not greatly concerned, however, as to the dealings of the states with one another. Not only does it make no attempt to establish interstate co-operation, but, instead, it forbids the states to make mutual agreements except with the approval of Congress. As a result, interstate co-operation has developed slowly. Disagreements have been more numerous than agreements, every state tending to regard its neighbors with suspicion, instead of working with them for the common good.

But there are a number of examples of interstate co-operation under formal compacts that have received federal approval. New York and New Jersey have established a joint commission, known as the New York Port Authority, for the purpose of developing New York harbor. Agreements involving a number of states have been made concerning the waters of the Colorado, Columbia, and Delaware Rivers. Twelve states have signed a formal compact designed to prevent waste in the production of petroleum, and nearly three fourths of the states have entered into an agreement concerning penal jurisdiction.

Still more common are instances of informal co-operation, which do not necessitate action by Congress. The Supreme Court has said that the constitutional requirement of Congressional approval does not apply to all understandings among the states, but only to agreements "tending to increase the political power of the States, which may encroach upon or interfere with the just supremacy of the United States." [1]

## DIVERSITY OF STATE LEGISLATION

For many years the wide diversity of state legislation on matters requiring uniform treatment has produced very unfortunate results. Some states have tried to discourage divorce by making it a difficult

[1] Virginia *v.* Tennessee, 148 U.S. 503 (1893).

proceeding; others have made a strong bid for the divorce business of the nation by reducing the necessary residence period to six weeks and at the same time legalizing gambling in order to provide for the recreation of those awaiting divorce decrees. An act regarded as a felony in one commonwealth may be treated simply as a misdemeanor in another; in still another state it may not even be illegal. Murder, robbery, burglary, and larceny are words whose meanings vary greatly from state to state. Tax laws, labor laws, statutes regulating trade and industry, laws concerning the ownership and operation of motor vehicles [2]—these are just a few examples of diverse state legislation in fields where uniformity is urgently required. Although it is understood that local conditions should be given due recognition in the enactment of state laws, this elementary principle should not be made the justification for differences that represent only the idiosyncrasies of individual lawmakers.

An unfortunate development of recent years, growing out of the industrial depression of the thirties, has been the enactment of numerous state laws designed to protect local manufacturers, merchants, and farmers against competition from other states. Trade barriers have been erected by the states against the products of their neighbors, and the result has been a large crop of retaliatory legislation. Today, therefore, we find many of the states engaged in bitter "trade wars" with one another, apparently oblivious to the obvious fact that no commonwealth can hope to sell its commodities to other states unless it accepts their products in exchange.

The situation is vaguely reminiscent of the chaotic condition that existed under the Articles of Confederation [3]—a condition presumably corrected by the adoption of the federal Constitution. Congress was given control of interstate commerce, and it has never relinquished that authority. But the state governments have found numerous ways to evade the letter of the fundamental law. Sometimes they impose special taxes and license fees on "foreign" corporations (that is, corporations from other states); sometimes they tax "foreign" trucks and buses at excessive rates; sometimes they impose heavy tax burdens on local products manufactured from out-of-state

---

[2] Following the entry of the United States into the Second World War, the states forgot their rivalries long enough to adopt uniform size and weight requirements applying to trucks. These requirements had already been approved by the War Department, and their adoption eliminated many of the legal difficulties encountered by heavy trucks or interstate journeys.

[3] See pp. 11–12.

raw materials. In many instances discriminations against the goods of other states are accomplished by means of quarantine and inspection measures allegedly enacted for the protection of the public health or safety. A maximum grade for "fresh" eggs may be set so high that it can only be met by domestic hens. Some of the competing agricultural products of other commonwealths may be excluded, or made to pay exorbitant inspection fees—and such legislation may be justified as a health measure.

Not every such law is upheld by the courts. A few years ago the Supreme Court of the United States was asked to pass upon the validity of a 1937 Florida statute requiring inspection of all imported cement and imposing an inspection charge of fifteen cents per hundred pounds.[4] This measure was alleged to protect the public from some of the dangers of faulty construction; its preamble declared that "it is of paramount importance to the public safety that only cement measuring up to a minimum standard should be offered for sale, sold, or used in the State of Florida." The highest court of the state upheld the law,[5] but the Supreme Court of the United States, intent upon safeguarding interstate commerce, refused to follow suit. "The scheme for inspection and for the inspection fee," declared Mr. Justice Frankfurter, speaking for the Court, "applies only to cement imported or brought into the State of Florida from any foreign country. . . . The statute thus renders the seventy per cent domestic cement immune from its requirements of inspection and its attendant fee. . . . So far as public safety demands certain standards in the quality of cement, such safety is dependent on assurance of that quality by appropriate inspection no less of the seventy per cent domestic cement than of the thirty per cent obtained from abroad. That no Florida cement needs any inspection while all foreign cement requires inspection at a cost of fifteen cents per hundred weight is too violent an assumption to justify the discrimination here disclosed. . . . No reasonable conjecture can here overcome the calculated discrimination against foreign commerce. . . . It would not be easy to imagine a statute more clearly designed than the present to circumvent what the commerce clause forbids."[6]

The Twenty-first Amendment to the federal Constitution, which repeals the prohibition amendment, specifically authorizes the states

[4] A. B. Hale *et al. v.* Binco Trading Co., Inc., 306 U.S. 466 (1939).
[5] State *v.* Hale, 129 Fla. 588 (1937).
[6] A. B. Hale *et al. v.* Binco Trading Co., Inc., 306 U.S. 466 (1939).

to impose such restrictions as they may see fit upon liquor imported from other commonwealths. "The transportation or importation into any state, territory, or possession of the United States for delivery or use therein of intoxicating liquors, in violation of the laws thereof, is hereby prohibited." This clause was obviously designed to protect "dry" states from the activities of their "wet" neighbors, but it has served equally well to protect liquor-producing commonwealths from unwelcome competition. In 1935 the State of Minnesota prohibited the importation for sale of non-registered liquors, and applied this rule to unregistered intoxicants brought into the state by an Illinois corporation before the enactment of the law. The corporation, alleging denial of the equal protection of the laws, turned to the Supreme Court of the United States for relief. But the Court held the "equal protection" clause of the Fourteenth Amendment inoperative in this case, because of the words of the Twenty-first Amendment conferring upon the states plenary power to regulate the liquor traffic.[7]

### INTERSTATE CO-OPERATION

**Efforts to promote uniformity in legislation.** Serious efforts have been made to bring some measure of order out of the wilderness of state legislation. Some of these efforts were begun nearly half a century ago. The National Conference of Commissioners on Uniform State Laws, for example, was established in 1892. It is composed of representatives of the several states and territories—usually three commissioners from each state and territory, appointed by the governor. They are united in a permanent organization and come together for four or five days every year to consider the work of their standing committees. The commissioners are prominent members of the legal profession—judges, practicing attorneys, and law school professors. They serve without compensation and usually pay their own expenses. They have at various times drafted and recommended to the states nearly one hundred "model" acts, in addition to approving a few standard statutes drafted by other organizations. But the states have been discouragingly slow to adopt the statutes thus prepared. Only a handful of recommended laws have received anything like unanimous state approval.[8]

Every year the governors of the several states hold a conference, nor-

---

[7] Mahoney *v.* Joseph Triner Corp., 304 U.S. 401 (1938).

[8] An interesting volume, *The Handbook of the National Conference of Commissioners on Uniform State Laws,* is published annually by the Conference.

mally of three days' duration, for "an exchange of views and experiences on subjects of general importance . . . the promotion of uniformity in state legislation and the attainment of greater efficiency in state administration." [9]   The first conference of governors was called by President Theodore Roosevelt in 1908, with such satisfactory results that it was decided to hold annual meetings.   But subsequent sessions have fallen short of their early promise.   Many governors of important states are habitually absent, and the speakers deal chiefly in platitudes.[10]

Occasionally the chief executives of a number of states sharing some common problem, such as the regulation of the oil industry or the control of flood conditions in a river basin, meet less formally to discuss possible solutions.   These conferences have no regular meeting dates; instead, they are called when actual crises arise.   They have proved much more effective than the formal annual conferences of all the governors—largely because of the more limited scope of the agenda, the greater need for immediate action, and the increased likelihood of representation from all the interested states.

THE AMERICAN LEGISLATORS' ASSOCIATION.   In 1925 the American Legislators' Association was formed.   The idea of such an association was conceived by Henry W. Toll, a Colorado state senator, who sent letters to seventy-five hundred state legislators inviting them to participate in the task of organization.   Many accepted the invitation, and shortly afterward legislators from ten states met in the senate chamber at Denver.   The Association was formally established, and a program of activity approved.   But interest in the movement soon lagged, and lack of funds proved a serious handicap.   When, therefore, Mr. Toll called a second meeting in 1927, only five persons appeared at the appointed time and place.   Four of them were newspaper reporters; the fifth was a lobbyist.   It seemed that the American Legislators' Association had ceased to be more than a name.

But new interest arose in 1929.   A number of state legislators contributed substantial sums, and shortly afterward a private foundation made a large grant for the expansion of existing activities and the establishment of new projects.   The Association then began publication of an official monthly magazine, *State Government*, which replaced a small leaflet that had previously been circulated.   Association headquarters were moved from Denver to Chicago, and member-

[9] *Articles of Organization of the Governors' Conference*, Art. III.
[10] See the annual volume of *Proceedings* published by the Governors' Conference.

ship increased rapidly. More recent developments have swept away all doubt as to the success of the movement. The Association has now received the formal endorsement of the legislatures of all forty-eight states.

Impressed with the need for a united attack by state legislatures upon common problems, the American Legislators' Association organized a convention of state legislators in 1933. Approximately one hundred legislators from thirty-two states met in the national capital in February of that year and devoted a number of busy days to questions of overlapping and conflicting taxation, and the like. This gathering was known officially as the First Interstate Legislative Assembly. Other conventions have since been held at two-year intervals; they now include administrators as well as legislators.

The legislators attending the First Interstate Assembly were handicapped in their study of tax conflicts by lack of information concerning existing conditions. Few members were familiar with the proposals already made by various groups for improving the nation's tax structure. It was obvious, therefore, that conventions of legislators must be supplemented by permanent research staffs and that legislators' resolutions must be based on expert fact-finding and analysis. So the members of the convention directed the presiding officer to appoint an Interstate Commission on Conflicting Taxation—a permanent body consisting of ten representatives and seven senators. This commission promptly appointed an expert research staff, which presented a scholarly report on tax conflicts to the Second Interstate Assembly (1935). By this time it was generally understood that the tax difficulties of the states involved not only interstate complexities, but also conflicts of authority between the states and the nation; therefore a Tax Revision Council was set up, with members representing the federal government as well as the states and the local communities.

INTERSTATE COMMISSIONS. Interstate commissions on a number of other subjects have been established from time to time. One such commission, dealing with the problem of crime—and especially the problem of plugging the loopholes in interstate criminal law enforcement—arose directly from a conference called by the State of New Jersey in 1935. The commission now has one or more members from each of the states and an executive committee of eight members. Its research staff has prepared a number of model statutes dealing with such matters as extradition and parole supervision, and some of these statutes have been widely adopted. An Interstate Commission on

Social Security, similarly organized, has already completed a number of important studies.

When a public problem affects only a small group of states similarly situated or possessing similar resources, there is no reason why all forty-eight commonwealths should be asked to find a solution. Better results can usually be obtained by enlisting the co-operation of the states directly concerned. This principle underlies the previously mentioned regional governors' conferences.[11] It has also been made the basis for establishing a number of interstate commissions of limited geographic scope, such as the Interstate Commission on the Delaware River Basin, which is typical of this group. The Commission represents the states of New York, New Jersey, Pennsylvania, and Delaware. Each state designates four members—two legislators, an administrator, and a member or the executive of the state planning board. Problems of water pollution and water supply and the conservation of forest resources and wild life are studied by the Commission's technical staff, which is jointly financed by the four states.

THE COUNCIL OF STATE GOVERNMENTS. Here, then, are a number of agencies concerned with various aspects of the problem of interstate co-operation. Most of these agencies have recently been united as branches or affiliates of a sort of "holding company" of interstate co-operation—the Council of State Governments. The plan for such a council was first broached at a meeting of the planning board of the American Legislators' Association early in 1935. Administrators as well as legislators were to be included in the council's membership, and authority was to be derived from forty-eight commissions on interstate co-operation—one in each of the states.

New Jersey was the first state to establish such a commission. On March 12, 1935, the governor signed the necessary legislation, and appointed five administrative officers—the attorney-general and the tax commissioner, among others—to serve as the commission's administrative members. Five members from the state senate were appointed by its president, and five members from the lower house were chosen by its presiding officer. Colorado followed New Jersey's example a few weeks later. Before the end of the year commissions on interstate co-operation had been established in nine states. Others promptly fell into line, bringing the total number to thirty-seven in 1937. Today [12] there are only four states that have failed to act.

11 See p. 58.
12 1945.

Most of the state commissions on interstate co-operation follow the original New Jersey pattern—five members from each house of the legislature, and five administrators. One of the administrators commonly serves as chairman. Some commissions are fully organized, and have been equipped with offices and permanent secretaries. Other commissions, however, maintain no regular staffs for clerical work and meet infrequently. The more progressive commissions frequently invite their neighbors to conferences on common problems, ranging from banking practices to highway safety; and take the lead in promoting uniform legislation and uniform administrative practices.

The Council of State Governments is the central agency of the state commissions on interstate co-operation. Each commission contributing to the Council's work is entitled to one representative on its board of managers, which meets semiannually to review past activities and formulate future policies. The central secretariat of the Council, located in Chicago, maintains separate divisions for publications, research, organization, and public relations. During the last few years the work has been facilitated by the establishment of an office in the national capital, as well as regional offices in New York and San Francisco. The Council maintains closest relations with other agencies that are working for interstate co-operation. It operates clearing house services for the Governors' Conference, the American Legislators' Association, the National Association of Attorney-Generals, and the National Association of Secretaries of State. The executive director of the Council serves also as director of the American Legislators' Association and as secretary-treasurer of the Governors' Conference. These affiliated organizations are all represented on the Council's board of managers. Numerous other organizations, such as the American Society of Planning Officials, the American Public Welfare Association, the Civil Service Assembly, and the Governmental Research Association, maintain offices in the same building as the Council of State Governments and share some of its research facilities.

It should, perhaps, be emphasized that the Council of State Governments and its affiliated organizations are concerned primarily with research. They have no authority to shape the policies of any agency of state government. Instead, they make studies of state and interstate problems and publish their findings in various bulletins and periodicals and in an official reference work, the biennial *Book of the States;* they maintain consultant services for scores of state agencies and for private citizens; they sponsor regional and national conferences on dozens of important public questions. But no administrative officer is required to heed their advice; no legislature is bound to accept their recommendations. Their influence arises solely from the fact that they are expert, impartial agencies, completely unconcerned with the ebb and flow of politics. And it must be confessed that even yet the machinery created for interstate co-operation is more impressive than the results achieved. But the movement is still young and represents one of the first intelligent, large-scale attempts to co-ordinate the activities of the forty-eight states.[13]

### SUITS AGAINST A STATE

The framers of the federal Constitution realized that disputes involving the state governments would inevitably arise, and they made provision for the settlement of such disagreements. "The judicial power of the United States," declares Article III,[14] "shall extend . . . to controversies between two or more States; between a State and citizens of another State. . . . In all cases . . . in which a State shall be a party, the Supreme Court shall have original jurisdiction." It was generally assumed, when the Constitution was adopted, that these clauses did not confer upon any private citizen the right to sue a state. The British king was not suable,[15] and this immunity was thought to inhere in the states of the American Union. In 1793, however, as previously pointed out,[16] the Supreme Court of the United States took a contrary view and upheld a private action against the State of Georgia.[17] So firmly entrenched was the doctrine of states rights in those days that the Eleventh Amendment to the Constitution was promptly adopted, depriving the federal courts of jurisdiction over such disputes. Therefore a state cannot be sued without its consent by a citizen of another state, by one of its own citizens,[18] or by a citizen of any foreign nation. But it can be sued by another state of the Union, and such suits are not infrequent. The nation cannot be sued without its consent, and this limitation applies even to actions brought by a state.[19]

---

[13] This description of the Council of State Governments and its affiliated organizations is drawn largely from the several volumes of the *Book of the States.*

[14] Sec. 2.

[15] This legal fiction has become a mere technicality in England, however.

[16] See p. 14.

[17] Chisholm *v.* Georgia, 2 Dallas 419 (1793).

[18] Hans *v.* Louisiana, 134 U.S. 1 (1890).

[19] Kansas *v.* United States, 204 U.S. 331 (1907). The non-suability of the United States is not expressly stated in the federal Constitution, but is declared by the Supreme Court to be a fundamental principle of government.

## SELECTED REFERENCES

Buell, Raymond L., *Death by Tariff; Protectionism in State and Federal Legislation,* 1939.

Governors' Conferences, *Proceedings,* 1909—(published annually).

Graves, William B., *Uniform State Action,* Chapel Hill, N.C., 1934.

Green, Thomas S., Jr., *Liquor Trade Barriers,* 1940.

Interstate Commission on Conflicting Taxation, Research Staff of the *Conflicting Taxation,* Chicago, 1935.

Johnsen, Julia E., comp., *Interstate Trade Barriers,* 1940.

Melder, Frederick E., *State and Local Barriers to Interstate Commerce in the United States,* Orono, Me., 1937.

National Conference of Commissioners on Uniform State Laws, *Handbook,* Washington, D.C., 1892—(published annually).

Scott, James Brown, *Judicial Settlement of Controversies between States of the American Unions,* 2 vols., 1918.

Tax Institute, *Tax Barriers to Trade,* Philadelphia, 1941.

---

Bolles, Blair, "Balkanizing America; Trade Wars among the States," *Current History,* L, 16–19, July, 1939.

Rogers, James H., "From States' Rights to State Anarchy; Tariff Barriers between the States," *Harper's Magazine,* CLXXVII, 646–650, November, 1938.

Rose, Marcus A., "States Get Together," *Current History,* XLVIII, 25–27, May, 1938.

Schnader, William A., "Progress toward Uniform State Laws," *State Government,* XIII, No. 11, 219–220, November, 1940.

Toll, Henry W., "To Form a More Perfect Union," *Nation's Business,* XXVII, 42–45, March, 1939.

Tylor, W. Russell, "Regionalism in Practice," *American Journal of Sociology,* XLIV, 379–390, November, 1938.

Williams, Pierce, "State Walls and Economic Areas," *Survey Graphic,* XXVI, 192–196, April, 1937.

---

*The Book of the States,* published biennially by the Council of State Governments, contains a wealth of information concerning interstate relations.

# Chapter Four ∘∘∘ STATE CONSTITUTIONS

EVERY state of the American Union has a constitution—a written document setting forth the fundamental principles by which it is governed.   Trivial, inconsequential details and matters of a temporary nature may be included also, but always the fundamentals are there. For the constitution of a state is its supreme law, just as the federal Constitution is the supreme law of the entire nation.   Any state legislative act or administrative decree in conflict with the state constitution is therefore void and unenforceable, and the courts will set it aside when properly called upon to do so.   Like the federal Constitution, which is above the power of Congress to change, the constitution of a state is beyond the reach of the legislature.   It may be altered only by some special procedure, such as the action of an extraordinary majority in the legislature plus popular ratification at the polls.[1]

While the state constitution is supreme within its own sphere, it is necessarily subordinate to the Constitution of the United States within the realm of national authority.   It must conform to the federal Constitution, and also to properly enacted federal laws and treaties.   The restrictions imposed upon state power by the federal Constitution [2] cannot be swept lightly aside.   But the limits of national jurisdiction are still rather narrow, despite the expansion of recent years, so that a broad field of activity is retained by the state.   Most problems of government do not affect the nation, but fall instead within the purview of the state or its local subdivisions.

## ORGANIZATION AND SUBJECT MATTER OF STATE CONSTITUTIONS

**Lack of originality.**   Among forty-eight state constitutions, designed for as many states whose local conditions and internal problems are widely different, one would naturally expect to find great variations in organization and subject matter.   But even a cursory examination is sufficient to show that state constitutions closely resemble one another.   The fundamentals are the same in every case; only the details give any indication of originality.   When the framers of a new

[1] See pp. 73–77.
[2] See pp. 45–50.

state constitution begin their task, it seldom occurs to them to question the underlying principles with which they are already familiar. The popularly elected executive, the legislature of two houses, the independent judiciary, the nicely adjusted system of checks and balances—these things are commonly accepted as a matter of course.

As Judge Cooley once declared: "The vital things; the most important things—the great landmarks are decided instantly—settled before the convention meets. . . ." [3] Some experiments are made, of course; all the state constitutions are not merely "proof impressions of a single original," as they are sometimes described. But the publicity that every innovation receives is sufficient evidence that American constitution-makers usually follow the beaten path. Even the newer states of the West, which are commonly regarded as a fertile field for liberal ideas, prove quite conservative when new constitutions are proposed. "These new commonwealths of ours, pioneered though they have been by hardy and daring men, free as they are from the fetters of custom, and impatient of leading strings as of nothing else, are yet as hesitant as the oldest when they come to the serious business of setting up the foundations of a system of self-government," declared an observer of the convention that drafted North Dakota's first constitution.

Not only do the states borrow ideas from one another; often they copy the exact phraseology of constitutional provisions. Sometimes they do so for the purpose of securing clauses that have already been judicially interpreted, and are therefore comparatively free from the danger of troublesome litigation. In other instances they borrow simply because borrowing is easier than creating new terms. When they copy blindly, the result is almost invariably bad. Constitutional provisions that have proved unworkable in one state and are about to be discarded, sometimes become the model for similar clauses in other state constitutions. Fortunately, however, such blind copying is becoming increasingly unfashionable. The delegates to nearly all recent constitutional conventions in the more progressive states have been supplied with up-to-the-minute, authentic information concerning the constitutions and governments of other commonwealths, and therefore have been in a position to know the probable effect of any clauses that they might see fit to borrow. [4]

[3] Quoted in John D. Hicks' *The Constitutions of the Northwest States*, pp. 32–33. This monograph is published in Vol. XXIII of the University of Nebraska studies.
[4] See p. 78.

Of course, it must not be assumed that similarity in fundamentals, and even in style, indicates complete uniformity in all details—far from it. Some of the superficial differences among state constitutions are so great that the underlying resemblances are nearly hidden. The governor may have virtually an absolute veto over certain types of legislation, or no veto power whatever. The legislature may meet annually or biennially. The means provided for amending the constitution may be very simple or very complex. The clauses dealing with labor, public utilities, and other matters may vary widely. But these differences do not affect the broad outlines of any state constitution. The fundamentals are accepted by nearly everyone as a matter of course.

It may well be asked, therefore, why the constitution-makers of forty-eight states have displayed so little originality in creating the framework of their governments. In part, at least, their conservatism is explained by the homogeneity of the American people. Possessing substantially the same background, the same culture, the same traditions of government, they have learned to regard the underlying principles as axiomatic. Knowing only one general plan of governmental organization, they have not thought to question it. Nor is this at all surprising. The people of every state read the same magazines, drive the same motor cars, smoke the same cigarettes, wear the same styles of clothing. Why should they experiment with new fashions in government when the very foundations are involved?

**The preamble.** Nearly every state constitution [5] begins with a preamble—a statement of reasons for drafting the document and objects to be attained. This is almost invariably combined with the enacting clause.[6] The preamble serves no real purpose, save that it sometimes furnishes the members of the constitutional convention with an opportunity to express their political philosophy. Thus the Massachusetts preamble, which is several hundred words in length, states the reasons for maintaining the institution of government, the nature of the body politic, and the duty of the people to the state. It also recognizes expressly the right of revolution,[7] though the men who now control the state's government might refuse to accept any such interpretation. Contrasted with this wordy introduction is the brief preamble of Arizona: "We, the people of the State of Arizona, grateful

[5] There are three exceptions—New Hampshire, Vermont, and West Virginia.

[6] Delaware's constitution is the only exception.

[7] "Whenever these great objects are not obtained the people have a right to alter the government, and to take measures necessary for their safety, prosperity, and happiness."

to Almighty God for our liberties, do ordain this Constitution." It is interesting to note that most state constitutions, unlike the Constitution of the United States, contain some reference to the Deity.[8] This reference is commonly an expression of gratitude for benefits received; sometimes it is also a request for continued blessings and for guidance. In either case it is placed in the preamble.

**The bill of rights.** After the preamble comes the declaration or bill of rights, setting forth the fundamental guarantees designed to protect life, liberty, and the pursuit of happiness. Every state constitution has its bill of rights, the length varying from fifteen to forty-five provisions. Usually this part of the constitution is a curious mélange of old theories and new ideals. Some of the statements most commonly found are lineal descendants of the Declaration of Independence and Magna Carta; others are a product of the modern era of gigantic corporations and quasi-monopolistic public utilities. Some guarantees are phrased in such general terms that they have little or no significance; some are positively detrimental to the social development of present-day commonwealths; while still others deal with matters that cannot by any stretch of the imagination be classed as fundamental rights.

USELESS OR UNWISE CLAUSES. The clauses in state bills of rights that serve chiefly to consume additional space are surprisingly numerous. "All government, of right, originates with the people, is founded on their will alone, and is instituted solely for the good of the whole. Its only legitimate end is to secure justice to all, preserve peace, and promote the interest and happiness of the people," declares the Constitution of Louisiana.[9] The large majority of state constitutions assert, in but slightly varying language, that all men are created equal and that they have certain inalienable natural rights, including the enjoyment of life and liberty and the opportunity to pursue happiness. The people of Arkansas believe that property ownership should be included among these natural rights;[10] the people of Washington, on the other hand, deny the right of property ownership to aliens ineligible to citizenship.[11] Kentucky sees fit to include a lengthy statement of political theory, vintage of 1776, in its bill of rights. "Absolute and arbitrary power over the lives, liberty, and property of

8 Such a reference is found in the constitutions of forty-three states.

9 Art. I.

10 Constitution of Arkansas, Art. II, Sec. 2.

11 Constitution of Washington, Art. II, Sec. 33. Most state constitutions, however, reflect the Arkansas view on this point.

freemen exists nowhere in a republic, not even in the largest majority. All men, when they form a social compact, are equal. . . . All power is inherent in the people, and all free governments are founded on their authority and instituted for their peace, safety, happiness, and the protection of property. For the advancement of these ends, they have an inalienable and indefeasible right to alter, reform, or abolish their government in such manner as they may deem proper." [12] Some of these statements are certainly false; most of them are debatable; and all are so vague that they add nothing to the more specific clauses of the bills of rights. It may well be suggested, therefore, that their omission from future constitutions would be desirable.

FREEDOM OF RELIGION. Among the specific guarantees, freedom of religion has a very important place. It is mentioned in every state constitution, though in language that varies considerably from state to state. Thus Michigan specifies that "Every person shall be at liberty to worship God according to the dictates of his own conscience. No person shall be compelled to attend, or, against his consent, to contribute to the erection or support of any place of religious worship, or to pay tithes, taxes, or other rates for the support of any minister of the gospel or teacher of religion." [13] Oklahoma expresses the same thought in fewer words: "Perfect toleration of religious sentiment shall be secured, and no inhabitant of the state shall ever be molested in person or property on account of his or her mode of religious worship." [14]

Clauses such as these are frequently coupled with other provisions designed to insure even more fully the complete separation of church and state. Civil and political rights may not be denied on account of religious beliefs; no religious test may be required as a qualification for public office; jurors and witnesses may not be disqualified because of their religious views. Two states [15] even make ministers of the gospel ineligible to membership in the legislature. Grants and donations to sectarian institutions are prohibited by the constitutions of twenty-four states. Religious instruction in the public schools is quite commonly forbidden.

There still remain, however, some curious examples of religious intolerance. Although the preambles to the constitutions of Arkansas and Mississippi, for example, specify that no religious test shall be re-

12 Constitution, Secs. 2, 3 and 4.
13 Constitution, Art. II, Sec. 3.
14 Constitution, Art. I, Sec. 2.
15 Maryland and Tennessee.

quired as a qualification for public office, they declare in subsequent clauses that "No person who denies the existence of a God shall hold any office in the civil departments of this state." [16]    Six other states [17] also require every officeholder to declare his belief in God, and two of these [18] demand in addition an expression of belief in a future state of rewards and punishments.    Maryland, under its somewhat time-worn constitution of 1867, specifies that jurors and witnesses must believe "in the existence of God, and that under His dispensation [every] person will be held morally accountable for his acts, and be rewarded or punished therefor in this world or the world to come" [19]—presumably on the theory that fear of future punishment is the only effective safeguard against lying.    Eventually such clauses will doubtless be stricken from all state constitutions, but at present they still serve as a reminder of the days when religious intolerance was everywhere accepted as a matter of course.

PROTECTION OF LIFE AND LIBERTY.    The bills of rights of state constitutions contain a large variety of provisions designed to prevent governmental interference with life and liberty.    Every person accused of crime shall be entitled to a speedy public trial; he shall have opportunity to confront witnesses against him and to summon witnesses in his own behalf.    He shall be permitted to obtain his release on bail unless a capital offense is charged, and if convicted he shall not be subjected to cruel or unusual punishment.    He shall not twice be put in jeopardy of life or limb for the same offense.    *Ex post facto* laws [20] are commonly prohibited; so, too, are bills of attainder. [21]    The privilege of the writ of habeas corpus [22] may not be suspended. [23]    Protection against unreasonable searches and seizures, a guarantee that had no practical significance for a long period of years, subsequently acquired considerable importance during the most active period of prohibition enforcement.    Many state constitutions declare the right

16 This is the exact wording of the Arkansas constitution, Art. XIX, Sec. 1.   Mississippi's constitution provides, Art. XIV, Sec. 265, that "No person who denies the existence of a Supreme Being shall hold any office in this State."

17 Maryland, North Carolina, Pennsylvania, South Carolina, Tennessee, Texas.

18 Pennsylvania and Tennessee.

19 Declaration of Rights, Art. 36.

20 For a definition of an *ex post facto* law, see footnote 32 on p. 45.

21 Bill of attainder is defined in footnote 31 on p. 45.

22 A writ of habeas corpus is a writ, issued by a court of competent jurisdiction, directing that a prisoner be brought before it, in order that it may determine whether he is lawfully detained.   This writ is a safeguard against arbitrary imprisonment.

23 Some of the more recent state constitutions make this prohibition absolute; the older constitutions generally follow the federal Constitution by adding "unless when in cases of invasion or rebellion the public safety may require it."

of jury trial to be inviolate and then violate the declaration by specifying in other clauses that jury trial may be dispensed with under certain
circumstances.[24]

*Criticism of provisions guaranteeing protection.* The constitutional provisions that afford protection to persons accused of crime
have been subjected to a great deal of adverse criticism in recent years.
It is frequently pointed out that they seriously handicap the state in
its fight against professional criminals. Broad guarantees designed to
shelter the innocent from the arbitrary acts of capricious officials have
become the means of escape for thousands of wrongdoers. Murderers,
thieves, bribe takers, racketeers have learned how to make effective use
of constitutional and legal technicalities. Judicial interpretation has
given to some constitutional guarantees meanings that were probably
never intended by the men who framed them. In a Michigan case,
for example, the supreme court of the state ruled that a sentence of
a five-year probationary period, conditioned upon leaving the state
within thirty days, was a "cruel and unusual" punishment and therefore prohibited by the constitution.[25] It seems clear that bills of
rights should be so amended as to eliminate all unnecessary technicalities, while continuing to furnish the substance of necessary protection to persons wrongfully accused of crime.

PROPERTY RIGHTS. State bills of rights also contain provisions
intended to safeguard the ownership of property. Private property
may not be taken or damaged for public use without just compensation; private property may not be taken without due process of law.
These guarantees have been strictly enforced by the courts. Sometimes it is said that the judiciary is more interested in upholding
property rights than in preserving human liberty. At any rate,
private property has received its full measure of protection under the
terms of both federal and state constitutions.

THE RIGHTS OF FREE SPEECH AND A FREE PRESS. The clauses
guaranteeing freedom of speech and of the press have been treated
rather lightly by state legislatures, and the courts have regarded this
attitude with approval. Such guarantees are found in all state constitutions and are upheld, of course; but everyone now understands
that they are conditional and not absolute. Free speech and a free
press do not carry with them the right to slander at will, nor do they

---

[24] For a discussion of recent modifications of the original rule of jury trial, see pp.
246–247.
[25] People *v.* Baum, 231 N.W. 95 (1930).

assure freedom from libel suits. They do not imply the right to inflame others against the government when war is imminent and the undivided loyalty of all classes is urgently required. A considerable number of court decisions have made clear that the right of free speech and the right of a free press are both conditioned upon their proper use.

In war time, especially, they may be restricted almost to the vanishing point. The viewpoint of the courts in this matter is well illustrated by the case of Gompers *v.* Bucks Stove and Range Company,[26] which was carried to the Supreme Court of the United States. "The most stringent protection of free speech," declared the Court, "would not protect a man in falsely shouting fire in a theatre, causing a panic. We admit that in many places and in ordinary times the defendants, in saying all that was said in the circular, would have been within their constitutional rights. But the character of every act depends upon the circumstances in which it is done. . . . When a nation is at war many things that might be said in time of peace are such a hindrance to its effort that their utterance will not be endured so long as men fight, and that no court could regard them as protected by any constitutional right." This and similar decisions have fostered the belief that freedom of speech and of the press are merely peace-time rights, having no significance after the outbreak of war, but the courts have carefully pointed out that such is not the case. All the guarantees of individual liberty remain in force in time of war as in time of peace; their exact meaning may undergo a transformation, however, when war is declared.

IRRELEVANT PROVISIONS. The newer state constitutions include in their bills of rights many provisions that have no place in any recital of fundamental principles. There are clauses concerning lotteries, lobbying, dueling, pensions, slavery, contempt of court, tenure of office. Maryland sees fit to include in its declaration of rights a statement that Annapolis shall be the meetingplace of the legislature,[27] and also affirms that "monopolies are odious, contrary to the spirit of a free government and the principles of commerce, and ought not to be suffered." [28] Montana attempts to assure the use of modern penal methods by specifying that "laws for the punishment of crime shall be founded on the principles of reformation and prevention" [29]—ap-

---

[26] 221 U.S. 418 (1911).
[27] Art. 11.
[28] Art. 41.
[29] Art. III, Sec. 24.

parently without pausing to consider that these two principles may often be in hopeless conflict. The folly of including such provisions in a list of basic rights is obvious.

**The structure of government.** Following the bill of rights are found the clauses dealing with the structure of government. One article is commonly devoted to the legislature, one to the executive department, and one to the judiciary. In these sections are specified the officials of the state, how they are to be selected and how they may be removed, their terms of office, qualifications, powers, and duties. Some constitutions even fix the salaries of state officials, instead of leaving that matter to the legislature. Legislative procedure is commonly prescribed in considerable detail. The doctrine of the separation of powers, inherited from a political theory long since discredited, is solemnly enunciated as a matter of course, the phraseology varying but little from state to state. The constitution of Florida is typical in this respect: "The powers of the government . . . shall be divided into three departments—Legislative, Executive and Judicial; and no person properly belonging to one of the departments shall exercise any powers appertaining to either of the others, except in cases expressly provided by the Constitution." [30]

SEPARATION OF POWERS. In the closing quarter of the eighteenth century, when the first state constitutions were framed, men actually believed that the public business could best be administered by putting every branch of the government into a separate, power-tight compartment, so that power could not possibly flow from one to the other. With every public official thus forced to adopt a policy of magnificent inaction, the danger of wrongdoing would be reduced to a minimum. It has already been pointed out [31] that this theory proved unsound and unworkable when put into practice. During the last century and a half Americans have gradually been learning that they must concentrate authority in order to prevent the diffusion of responsibility. They have rejected many of the implications of the doctrine of the separation of powers, especially in the more progressive states. But the doctrine, in very explicit language, still has a prominent place in most state constitutions, even though, as one commentator observes, it "is rapidly falling into a condition of harmless senility." [32]

[30] Art. II.
[31] See pp. 19–20.
[32] Dealey, James Q., *Growth of American State Constitutions*, p. 264.

OTHER PROVISIONS. After the structure of government has been covered in sufficient detail, the state constitution commonly devotes itself to a variety of other matters. As a rule there are articles dealing with finance, education, labor, corporations, local government. Under these various titles are included economic, social, and cultural provisions of every description. Boards and commissions are established and their powers defined—boards of health, boards of education, parole boards, public service commissions, tax commissions, industrial commissions. The list could be expanded almost indefinitely. There must also be a portion of the constitution devoted to suffrage requirements; frequently the suffrage article is placed directly after the bill of rights.

Since the structural, administrative and franchise provisions of state constitutions are to be considered at length in subsequent chapters, we may pass on to those clauses dealing with constitutional amendment and revision. Amendment, in this connection, is used to indicate the making of specific changes without altering the general purport of the document; revision is the process of general overhauling. Amendments may be required at rather frequent intervals; revision should only occasionally be necessary.

**Amendment.** The men who framed the first state constitutions did not distinguish clearly between amendment and revision. They specified that all changes should be made by the legislature, as in Delaware, Maryland, and South Carolina; [33] or by constitutional conventions specially chosen for the purpose, as in Georgia, Massachusetts, and Pennsylvania; or else they failed to provide any method of altering the fundamental law, as in nearly half of the thirteen original states. At the outset there seemed to be no good reason to indicate more than one way of changing the constitution.[34]

TWO METHODS OF ALTERATION. After several decades, however, it became obvious that one method would not suffice. A constitutional convention could best accomplish the task of complete revision; but

[33] The process of legislative amendment differed from ordinary law-making, however. Delaware required an extraordinary majority; so did Maryland; and South Carolina specified that "no part of this constitution shall be altered . . . without the consent of a majority of the members of the senate and house of representatives"—as distinguished from a mere majority of those present.

[34] A state employing the convention method of making amendments might, however, provide two ways of calling the convention. Thus the Pennsylvania constitution specified that a convention might be called by the legislature or by the council of censors—a body of men chosen every seven years for the primary purpose of determining "whether the constitution has been preserved inviolate in every part."

one or two specific changes, however urgent, would scarcely justify the calling of a special convention. As early as 1790 South Carolina recognized two methods of altering its constitution—convention and legislative action. Though Delaware did likewise two years later, no other state followed South Carolina's example for nearly half a century. Then, about 1835, it became common practice to authorize both methods of constitutional change. More than half of the state constitutions adopted between the years 1835 and 1885 provided for amendment by legislative action and also by constitutional convention—the legislative mode to be used in most cases, and the convention reserved for those rare occasions when a few specific amendments would not suffice.

REVISION METHODS IN VARIOUS STATES. Today thirty-five states authorize both types of change, and most of the others use both methods on occasion, though not explicitly empowered to do so. In fact, there is now only one state—New Hampshire—that has no discretion as to the method of altering its constitution. By express provision of its fundamental law it must rely on constitutional conventions; the legislature is given no authority to propose changes. Rhode Island is one of twelve states whose constitutions make no reference to the calling of a constitutional convention. In the other states of this group, however, conventions have been called from time to time without express constitutional sanction, and the absence of constitutional provisions on the subject has been regarded as immaterial, especially in view of the fact that the work of conventions must usually be submitted to the people for their approval. But the Rhode Island supreme court ruled, in 1883, that a convention might not be held for the purpose of amending the state's constitution, so that Rhode Island was obliged to rely solely on legislative action until 1935, when the highest tribunal reversed its earlier stand.[35]

Frequent reference to amendment by action of the legislature must not lead to the assumption that the legislature has a final voice in the matter. In some of the earlier constitutions, it is true, the legislature was given complete power to frame and adopt amendments, though by some extraordinary procedure that would serve to emphasize the important distinction between constitutional provisions and ordinary legislation. Thus the Maryland constitution of 1776 specified that no change should be made "unless a bill so to alter, change, or abolish

[35] Following the court's change of front, the state legislature, in January, 1936, ordered a referendum on a call for a convention, but the proposal was defeated at the polls.

the same shall pass the general assembly, and be published at least three months before a new election, and shall be confirmed by the general assembly, after a new election of delegates, in the first session after such new election." *General assembly* was, and still is, the official designation of the Maryland legislature. The requirement of action by two successive legislatures was thought to be a satisfactory means of securing popular control. The intervening election would afford the voters an opportunity to elect senators and representatives who adequately expressed their views, so that the action of the new legislature might be considered the direct result of a popular mandate.

*Popular ratification.* This plan, or some modification of it, was adopted by a number of states; Delaware still uses it.[36] South Carolina and Mississippi give the people an opportunity to vote directly on amendments proposed by the legislature, but amendments approved at the polls do not go into effect without further legislative action.[37] The legislature, therefore, makes the final decision. But these commonwealths are exceptional. In forty-five states the vote of the people is conclusive.

As early as 1818 Connecticut introduced the plan of popular ratification of amendments. Every amendment, before adoption, must be passed at two successive sessions of the legislature and then approved at the polls. The next year Maine simplified this procedure by requiring the action of but one legislative session, followed by a popular vote. The Maine plan was not immediately popular, however. As the states in increasing numbers provided for popular ratification of amendments, most of them followed Connecticut's lead by requiring action at two sessions of the legislature prior to submission to the people. Nor is this at all surprising, for the trend of the times was in the direction of a more difficult amending process. Until the latter part of the nineteenth century it was assumed, almost as a matter of course, that the sanctity of the fundamental law ought to be preserved

[36] The Delaware constitution of 1897, Art. XVI, Sec. 1, specifies: "Any amendment or amendments to the Constitution may be proposed in the Senate or House of Representatives; and if the same shall be agreed to by two-thirds of all the members elected to each House, such proposed amendment or amendments shall be entered on their journals, with the yeas and nays taken thereon, and the Secretary of State shall cause such proposed amendment or amendments to be published three months before the next general election in at least three newspapers in each county, in which such newspapers shall be published; and if in the General Assembly next after the said election such proposed amendment or amendments shall upon a yea and nay vote be agreed to by two-thirds of all the members elected to each House, the same shall thereupon become part of the Constitution."

[37] Constitution of South Carolina, Art. XVI, Sec. 1, and Constitution of Mississippi, Art. XV.

by placing obstacles in the way of change.   Clauses were adopted requiring the concurrence of three fifths or two thirds of the legislature, or specifying that an extraordinary majority of the voters must approve, or limiting the number of proposals that might be made at any one legislative session.   State constitutions were the basis of the whole scheme of state government, and the statesmen of the mid-nineteenth century were determined that they should not lightly be altered.

*Simplification of amendment procedure.*   Toward the end of the century, however, the increasing length and complexity of state constitutions made necessary easier methods of amendment.   The so-called "fundamental laws" were rapidly degenerating into detailed manuals of legislative and administrative procedure—a movement that is still under way; [38] and all the details placed in the newer constitutions of that day could not well be left unchanged for long periods of years.   So the amending process was simplified in many states.   Typical of this group is North Carolina, whose constitution of 1876 provides: "No part of the Constitution of this State shall be altered unless a bill to alter the same has been agreed to by three-fifths of each House of the General Assembly.   And the amendment or amendments so agreed to shall be submitted at the next general election to the qualified voters of the whole State, in such manner as may be prescribed by law.   And in the event of their adoption by a majority of the votes cast, such amendment or amendments shall become a part of the Constitution of the State." [39]

The present trend is distinctly in the direction of an easy amending process.   Thirteen states, led by Oregon in 1902, permit proposal of amendments by a certain percentage of the voters; such proposals then become part of the constitution when duly ratified at the polls, without the necessity of receiving the legislature's approval.   This device is known as the *initiative*.   Though its exact form varies somewhat from state to state, the underlying principle is everywhere the same. The first step in initiating a constitutional amendment is to prepare a petition, together with the exact text of the proposal.   The petition must then be signed by a portion of the electorate—either a specified number of voters, as in North Dakota, where ten thousand signatures are required; or a certain percentage of the total vote cast for the governor or some other state officer at the preceding election, as in Nebraska, where the percentage is fixed at fifteen.   California and Oregon re-

[38] See pp. 81–83.
[39] Art. XIII, Sec. 2,

quire but eight per cent.[40]   After the proper number of signatures
has been obtained, the petition is presented to the appropriate state
official—usually the secretary of state—who places the proposed
amendment upon the ballot at the next election.   A simple majority
of those voting on the proposal is sufficient for adoption in most states
that use the initiative for amending their constitutions.[41]   The merits
and defects of the initiative as a method of changing state constitutions
need not be discussed at this point, since the entire problem of direct
legislation is considered at some length in a subsequent chapter.[42]

*Retention of cumbersome methods in some states.*   Although the
tendency of the times is to simplify the procedure of constitutional
amendment, there are still many states that cling to the old, cumbersome forms.   About one fourth of all the states require action by two
successive legislatures before an amendment may be submitted to the
people.   About one fourth specify that the approving popular vote
must be more than a bare majority of those voting on the amendment.
Some of these states, and some others also, limit the number, frequency, or character of proposals that may be submitted for popular consideration.   Kansas, for example, prohibits the submission of
more than three propositions to amend at any single election.[43]
Tennessee forbids the legislature to propose amendments to the constitution oftener than once in six years.[44]   New Mexico declares that
certain sections of its constitution dealing with education and suffrage
may not be amended except by a very large majority, both in the legislature and at the polls.[45]   Limitations such as these are found in the
constitutions of eleven states.   Most of them were adopted a number
of years ago and will probably be amended or repealed when it is more
generally realized that they serve only to hamper the work of the state.

## CONSTITUTIONAL CONVENTIONS

State constitutions deal with many matters of transitory importance.
They include numberless details that have no place in the funda-

---

[40] Massachusetts restricts the use of the initiative in a number of ways.   See the Massachusetts constitution, Art. XLVIII of the amendments.

[41] There are some exceptions, however.   See, for example, the constitution of Nebraska,
Art. III, Sec. 4, which requires for adoption of an amendment not only that a majority of
the votes cast on the amendment must be favorable to it, but also that these favorable
votes must be at least thirty-five per cent of the total number of votes cast at the election.

[42] See pp. 132–137.

[43] Constitution, Art. XIV, Sec. 1.

[44] Constitution, Art. XI, Sec. 3.

[45] Constitution, Art. XIX, Sec. 1.

mental law. Their text often indicates careless or inexpert drafts-
manship. It is not at all surprising, therefore, that complete constitutional revisions are necessary from time to time. As already
suggested, specially chosen conventions are best fitted for this purpose.[46] Unhampered by the routine of ordinary legislation, they can
bend all their energies to the single task of framing a satisfactory
scheme of government. Six state constitutions specifically declare
that the question of holding a constitutional convention shall be submitted to the people at periodic intervals, ranging from seven to
twenty years. In the other states conventions may be called when
necessary; but the legislature determines in the first instance whether
such necessity exists. In a few states the legislature's decision is conclusive; much more commonly, however, the voters must also approve
the suggestion that a convention be called.

**Preliminary steps.** When a proposal to hold a constitutional convention is made and approved, numerous details must be agreed upon,
unless they have been prescribed in advance by the constitution.
The number of delegates and the manner of their choice; their qualifications and compensation; the rules of procedure that are to guide
their deliberations—these things cannot be left to chance. Only
three state constitutions, those of Michigan, Missouri and New York,
cover these matters so completely that all need for supplementary
legislation is eliminated, but the constitutions of a number of other
states deal with one or more phases of the convention and its work.
Details not included in the constitution are commonly prescribed by
law, though such matters as procedure may be left to the judgment of
the convention itself.

Prior to the gathering of the delegates it is customary, in the more
progressive states, to compile a considerable amount of necessary information: the present constitution of the state, clause by clause, together with judicial interpretations, governors' veto messages, and
opinions of attorneys-general; constitutions of other states, with necessary comments; pamphlets dealing with important problems that are
likely to occupy the time of the convention.[47] There are many states,

---

[46] There have been a few instances, however, of practically complete constitutional revisions prepared by legislative action. In 1928 the people of Virginia approved a new
constitution framed in this manner. The legislature of New Jersey, sitting as a constitutional convention by express authorization of the voters, drafted a new constitution
in 1944, but this document was defeated at the polls.

[47] Among the states that have recognized the need for preliminary collection of information are Illinois, Massachusetts, Michigan, Missouri, Nebraska, New Hampshire,
New York, and Ohio.

however, in which no work of this sort has ever been attempted, so that the constitutional conventions called from time to time are seriously handicapped. The delegates cannot possibly take time from their deliberations to collect the comparative data on which their judgments should be based, and the lack of this essential information inevitably leads to unfortunate mistakes that could easily have been avoided.

The members of a constitutional convention are popularly elected. Usually they are chosen by districts, the districts established for the selection of state senators or state representatives being used for this purpose; but election at large, either for all the members or some of them, is not unknown. They may be chosen along party lines, or on a non-partisan ticket. Elimination of the party ballot would seem to be desirable, for it is obvious that the constitution of a state should not be framed in the interest of any political party. Experience has shown, however, that even the so-called *non-partisan* election of delegates does not assure the elimination of political considerations. More than one *non-partisan* convention has redistricted the state for the benefit of deserving Democrats or reliable Republicans.

**Organization procedure.** When the members of the convention meet at the state capitol, their first task is to organize for business. Invariably they sit at a single body; the fact that every state legislature is composed of two houses has not led to a demand for similar organization of constitutional conventions. Nor is it at all difficult to explain the apparent inconsistency of the popular attitude in this respect. The argument most commonly advanced in favor of bicameral legislatures is that each house will act as a check upon the other and thus prevent hasty and unwise action. In some states, it is true, legislative acts must be submitted for popular consideration under certain circumstances, but the bills actually referred to the people form a very small percentage of the total legislative output. Moreover, most states make no provision for popular approval of ordinary legislation.[48] The belief that two houses of the legislature are necessary, so that each may correct the mistakes of the other, is probably without sound foundation; [49] yet it is widespread, and has influenced the organization of all state legislative bodies. The same reasoning does not apply to constitutional conventions, however. In nearly every case,

[48] For a more detailed consideration of the referendum as applied to ordinary legislation, see pp. 133–134.

[49] The arguments pro and con are given on pp. 161–165.

when the convention has completed its labors, the finished product is submitted to the people, and approved by them before it takes effect.[50] The popular vote thus becomes a very effective check upon the work of the convention, and any additional safeguard, such as separation of the membership into two chambers, is deemed unnecessary.

**Committees.** The convention varies in size from a membership of one hundred to three hundred or even more, the number usually bearing some relation to the number of members of the state legislature. Regardless of these variations, however, the convention is always too large to permit intensive examination of every proposal by all the members. Committees, in which most of the work of the convention is done, are therefore necessary; and one of the first tasks of the convention, after it has chosen a president or speaker and other necessary officers, is to divide its membership into appropriate committees. Although there should be one committee for each important subject considered, which usually means a total of about twenty, the number, in actual practice, has varied from four to thirty-nine. Each member of the convention is usually assigned to two or more committees. There is a general tendency to make committees too large; committees of twenty or even twenty-five members are not uncommon. The inevitable result is an impairment of their efficiency.

The personnel of committees may be determined by the presiding officer, or by a specially selected committee on committees. Each committee considers in detail its allotted subject—education, suffrage, the judiciary, or whatever it may be. Many public hearings are held. It is in committee meetings that most important decisions are made, and most of the provisions of the new constitution are welded into form. The committees of a constitutional convention, however, are not usually given complete power of life and death over proposals, as are many legislative committees, but generally must make a report to the convention on every proposal. As a result, committee members have no opportunity to dispose of suggestions that they dislike by the simple process of dropping them into the wastebasket.

CONSIDERATION OF COMMITTEE PROPOSALS. As each proposed article reaches the floor of the convention it is considered in some detail and amended as many times as may seem necessary. Adequate opportunity for discussion at this stage of the proceedings is desirable, and constitutional conventions usually begin their deliberations with virtually no restrictions on debate. If the minority resorts to obstruc-

---

50 For the exceptions to this general statement, see p. 81.

tive tactics, however, freedom of debate is likely to be limited. At best a convention cannot hope to complete a thorough overhauling of the constitution in less than two or three months, and considerably more time may be needed. Quite naturally, therefore, dilatory tactics are frowned upon.

EDITORIAL COMMITTEE. At some time during the course of the proceedings every proposal that seems at all likely to receive the approval of the convention should be referred to an editorial committee, so that it may be drafted in proper form. Though virtually every convention has such a committee, its importance varies. In some cases it acts as a central clearing house for all suggestions, ruling out inconsistencies in thought as well as carelessness and awkwardness in phraseology. In other instances its work is restricted virtually to proofreading. Members of some conventions have expressed the fear that the editorial committee may seize too firmly the reins of power and mold the new constitution to its own desires under the guise of eliminating clumsy phrases and contradictory ideas. Nevertheless, the experiences of a number of states demonstrate clearly that a convention without a powerful, well-organized, and well-informed editorial committee can seldom hope to produce a satisfactory constitution.

**Popular approval of constitution.** It has already been pointed out that the finished work of the convention is customarily submitted to the people for their approval, even though fewer than half of the state constitutions require this procedure. In a number of the Southern states, it is true, constitutional revisions are still adopted from time to time without any formal expression of popular opinion; this was done in Louisiana in 1913 and again in 1921. But such instances serve only to emphasize how nearly universal has become the practice of securing a vote of the people. Usually the convention's work is submitted as a whole to the voters; sometimes, however, it is presented in the form of a series of amendments, so that an expression of popular opinion may be obtained on each separate proposal.

## INCREASING LENGTH OF STATE CONSTITUTIONS

The men who framed the earlier state constitutions, and also the Constitution of the United States, clearly understood that the fundamental law should be restricted to *fundamentals,* and not choked with details. Chief Justice Marshall stated the matter quite simply when he declared: "A constitution, to contain an accurate detail of all the subdivisions of which its great powers admit, and of all the means by which they may be carried into execution, would partake of the prolixity of a legal code, and could scarcely be embraced by the human mind. It would probably never be understood by the public. Its nature, therefore, requires that only its great outlines should be marked, its important objects designated, and the minor ingredients which compose those objects be deduced from the nature of the objects themselves." [51] But this principle has long since been forgotten. Present-day constitutions have indeed acquired almost "the prolixity of a legal code." They are filled with wearisome details that should be left to the discretion of the legislature. Every decade they become longer and more involved.[52] And thus they become virtually unintelligible to all except the constitutional lawyers.

**Transitory nature of many provisions.** To some slight extent the increasing length of state constitutions can be traced to the development of modern civilization. The urgency of regulating new means of transportation, new businesses, new professions; the necessity of assigning to the state functions formerly performed by private initiative, or not at all—these things have led naturally to constitutional expansion. In some instances, also, new social policies have been written into the fundamental law to prevent the courts from declaring them unconstitutional. But the overwhelming majority of new articles, new sections, new clauses serve only to interfere with the normal functions of the legislature. They deal with matters that are not fundamental and certainly not permanent. Thus the constitution of Oregon, authorizing the use of the state's credit for the purpose of lending money to owners of farm lands, specifies the maturity of the bonds to be issued, the rate of interest that they shall bear, and even the denominations in which they shall be offered to the public; it states explicitly the persons to whom loans shall be made and the purposes to which the money may be put; it describes in detail the procedure that must be followed in securing a loan and the exact manner of repayment; and it establishes an ex officio board to administer these provisions. About six hundred words are required to deal with this single phase of state finance.[53] Compare this article with the simple words of the federal Constitution: "The Congress shall have power . . . to borrow money on the credit of the United States." [54]

[51] McCulloch *v.* Maryland, 4 Wheaton 407 (1819).
[52] See p. 25.
[53] Constitution of Oregon, Art. XIa.
[54] Art. I, Sec. 8, Cl. 2.

Other states have written into their constitutions detailed provisions dealing with the conduct of elections, the inheritance of property, the rules of evidence in civil and criminal cases, the compensation of public officials, the conditions of labor in private employment and in the service of the state—to select only a few from the long list. And the result has been, as anyone might have predicted, that changing conditions have rendered many of these provisions obsolete soon after their adoption. Other clauses have required still further amendment to make clear their exact meaning. It is not surprising, therefore, that state constitutions permitting of easy change have been altered with bewildering frequency. The constitution of California, an extreme example, has been amended more than two hundred times since its adoption in 1879. In some states, of course, the amending process is so difficult that frequent change is practically impossible. Proposals written into the constitutions of these commonwealths are therefore assured of some degree of permanence; but no assurance can possibly be given that they will continue to meet the need that led to their adoption. Many present-day constitutional provisions are simply reminders of conditions long past—ghosts whose fingers wrap themselves inexorably about the throat of progress until they choke it into insensibility.

As a rule the state constitution contains a schedule—an article making detailed arrangements for putting the new scheme of government into effect. This article is merely of temporary importance,[55] and for that reason it might seem advisable to place it after the ratification clause, so as to keep it entirely separate from those articles that deal with more permanent things. But instead it commonly becomes the concluding section of the constitution, thus burdening the fundamental law with additional matters of transitory concern.

## SELECTED REFERENCES

Anderson, W., and Lobb, A. J., *History of the Constitution of Minnesota*, University of Minnesota Studies in the Social Sciences, No. 15, 1921.

Bridgmen, R. L., *The Massachusetts Constitutional Convention of 1917 . . .* , 1917.

Dealey, J. I., *Growth of American State Constitutions*, 1915.

[55] In some constitutions, however, permanent matters are improperly placed in the schedule. Thus the schedule of the Illinois constitution provides (Sec. 18) that "All laws of the State of Illinois and all official writings, and the executive, legislative, and judicial proceedings, shall be conducted, preserved and published in no other than the English language." Certainly this clause is intended to have more than temporary effect.

Dodd, Walter F., *Revision and Amendment of State Constitutions,* Baltimore, Md., 1922.

Erdman, Charles R., Jr., *The New Jersey Constitution of 1776,* Princeton, 1929.

Faust, Martin, *Manuals for the Constitutional Convention of Missouri,* Columbia, 1943.

Frothington, Louis Adams, *A Brief History of the Constitution and Government of Massachusetts,* 1925.

Green, Fletcher Melvin, *Constitutional Development in the South Atlantic States, 1776–1860; A Study in the Evolution of Democracy,* Chapel Hill, N.C., 1930.

Hicks, John D., *The Constitutions of the Northwest States,* University of Nebraska Studies, Vol. XXIII, Nos. 1 and 2, 1925.

Hoar, R. S., *Constitutional Conventions; Their Nature, Powers, and Limitations,* 1917.

Illinois Legislative Council, *Problems of Constitutional Revision in Illinois,* Springfield, 1942.

Illinois Legislative Reference Bureau, *Constitutional Convention Bulletins,* Nos. 1, 3, 15, Springfield, 1920.

Kettleborough, Charles, *Constitution-Making in Indiana: A Source Book of Constitutional Documents, with Historical Introduction and Critical Notes,* 3 vols., Indianapolis, 1916–1930.

———, ed., *State Constitutions,* Indianapolis, 1918.

McCarthy, Sister M. Barbara, *The Widening Scope of American Constitutions,* Washington, D.C., 1928.

O'Rourke, Vernon A., and Campbell, Douglas W., *Constitution-Making in a Democracy,* Baltimore, 1943.

Shambaugh, B. F., ed., *The Constitution of Iowa,* Iowa City. 1935.

Swisher, Carl Brent, *Motivation and Political Technique in the California Constitutional Conventions, 1878–1879,* Claremont, 1930.

Wallace, D. D., *The South Carolina Constitution of 1895,* Bulletin No. 197, Columbia, 1927.

# Chapter Five 〜〜 NOMINATIONS AND ELECTIONS

THE first step in the election of public officials is the nomination of candidates—usually by the regular political parties or by other organized groups. This step is very important—in part because it weeds out the candidates and eliminates from the final ballot the names of those who have no appreciable support, and in part because it enables the various groups of voters to unite in support of persons who seem best fitted to represent them.

## THE CAUCUS SYSTEM

Even in the first days of American independence, when government was a far less complicated process than at present, candidates were nominated in advance of the regular election. The nominating methods of that early period conformed to no set plan, however. Most commonly a little group of community leaders would meet at some private home a short time before election day and informally indorse certain men for public office. In time this gathering of the leaders became known as the *caucus*. The word was derived from the Caucus Club of Boston, which met regularly in the garret of one Tom Dawes for the purpose of discussing public issues and nominating local candidates. Every town had its caucus—its informal conference of the "best" people.

Gradually, however, the caucus lost some of its earlier aspects. It became a meeting of the party heads, and most of its original informality disappeared. From this stage it was but a step to the legislative caucus, or gathering of the party representatives in the legislature. Because roads were poor and journeys difficult in those early days, the party leaders gave up the attempt to meet for the purpose of making nominations to state offices, and permitted the legislators to make the nominations instead. Each party would hold its caucus separately, of course; the Whig members of the legislature would unite upon Whig candidates, while the legislature's Democrats made their selections. No attempt was made to determine the wishes of the people throughout the entire nominating process, and no one was greatly disturbed by the omission. Democracy was still a questionable experiment, even in the United States, during the first two decades of the nineteenth century.

## THE CONVENTION SYSTEM

**Increase in democratic control.** But the period from 1820 to 1835 witnessed a widespread and constantly increasing demand for democratic control of government. The masses of the people, whose fathers had been content with the assurance that their interests were carefully safeguarded by the "governing class," now began to insist upon reversing the process and doing their own safeguarding. Democracy was in the air. It was not the polite, cultured democracy of Thomas Jefferson, but the raucous, untutored democracy of Andrew Jackson. In 1828 Jackson was elected president, and set out to interpret literally the rhetorical statement of the Declaration of Independence that "all men are created equal." His ideas proved extremely popular. Rotation in office became the order of the day. In most states the remaining barriers against white manhood suffrage were swept away. Men became equal—politically, at least—to the extent that the law could make them so. Of course, Negroes were excluded from the benefits of this movement. Few of those who prated at great length about the equality of man ever intended to include black men or yellow men in their generalization; equality as they understood it was equality *within the white race*.

**Rise of party conventions.** One of the results of the widespread adoption of the Jacksonian creed was the general abandonment of the caucus system. The caucus did not entirely disappear; as a gathering of the party voters it is still used in Connecticut and Rhode Island for making nominations to certain offices. But it had become generally unpopular long before 1840, and in that year it ceased to be a factor of any importance. Its place was taken by the convention system, which was designed to vest control of the selection of candidates more securely in the hands of the people. Under the convention plan the voters of each party choose delegates to a party convention; these delegates then meet prior to the election and make the party's nominations. Thus the part played by the people is indirect; instead of naming their candidates they merely empower others to do so.

**WEAKNESSES.** On its face the convention system is a reasonably accurate means of gauging public opinion. It affords the voters of each party an oportunity to elect delegates who will faithfully represent their wishes. When first introduced it was hailed as a triumph of democracy—a certain way to make the people masters of their government. But the passing of years revealed unexpected weaknesses. The triumph of democracy seemed less sure. For the professional politicians had devised and perfected means of controlling the conventions through delegates who could be counted on to vote "right." Usually they managed to have their friends and henchmen chosen as delegates; but if the voters, in an unusually independent mood, cast so many votes in opposition that even ballot box stuffing and fraudulent counting would not avail, then other methods were adopted. The unexpectedly successful delegates were exposed in turn to flattery, argument, promises of position or money, and intimidation. If, at the end of this time, some delegates still remained unmoved, their credentials were contested as soon as they arrived at the convention, and they were speedily excluded. Because practices of this sort violated no law and carried no danger of a jail sentence, they became a generally accepted part of the great game of politics.

REGULATION. It must be remembered that the convention system, as originally developed, was merely an unofficial device for securing the opinions of party members. The law did not regulate it—in fact, did not even recognize it. Therefore it became the great proving ground for all sorts of tricks and malpractices that would have been punishable with fines and imprisonment if used in regular elections. In time arose the demand that the states regulate the party conventions in the interest of fair play, and a number of states, led by California in 1866, took this step. These early statutes were crudely drawn. They prohibited only certain glaringly unfair practices, and applied only to those parties that chose to accept their provisions. But optional laws gradually gave way to mandatory, and virtually all fundamental aspects of the convention system came under state regulation. By 1900 the plan of regulated conventions was well established. It never had a fair chance to prove its worth, however, for almost immediately it was discarded in favor of the direct primary.

The unregulated convention system had been a complete failure; on that point all fair-minded persons were agreed. So something had to be found to take its place. Some students of government devoted their time and attention to improving the convention plan and bringing it under state control. Others, however, completely abandoned their faith in conventions as a means of selecting candidates for public office, and proposed instead the use of the direct primary, a system by which the voters of each party might make their nominations directly in party elections. Through such elections they hoped to determine accurately the wishes of the voters of each party, and secure party nominees who would represent the rank and file of the party members instead of the party leaders. They hoped to break the strength of the party organizations. And they hoped, too, to improve the calibre of party nominees.

### THE DIRECT PRIMARY

The direct primary was certainly used as early as 1868, and one writer finds evidence of its adoption in a Pennsylvania county in 1842.[1] Its spread was slow, however, and it did not become a part of a comprehensive, state-wide, mandatory system until 1903, when Wisconsin set the pace for the other states. Oregon followed a few months later; in 1907 six states enacted reasonably satisfactory primary laws; by 1909 the total number of direct primary states had risen to eighteen. Since that time the movement has continued to spread rapidly, and today candidates for public office are nominated by means of primary elections in forty-six states.[2] The two exceptions—Connecticut and Rhode Island—still rely solely on conventions, or on a combination of conventions and caucuses.

**Conduct of the primary.** A primary is conducted for the most part like a general election, with the same regulations and safeguards. The polling places are commonly the same, and the same persons usually serve as presiding officers. The ballots are nearly always furnished by the state, and the cost of the primary is met from public funds. The date of the primary election is fixed by state law, which generally provides that all parties must hold their contests at the same polling places as well as at the same time.[3] Each party has a separate ballot; in nearly half of the states distinguishing colors are used. The winners at the primary become the official nominees of their respective parties, and the candidates at the following general election.

**Requirements for nomination.** The laws of the several states vary

---

[1] See Brooks, R. C., *Political Parties and Electoral Problems* (1933 ed.), p. 261.

[2] It must not be assumed, however, that the primary is the sole method of making nominations in all forty-six states. Five states permit the use of primaries or conventions at the discretion of the political parties, and five others retain the convention for certain offices or under certain conditions. Utah restricts the use of the direct primary so narrowly that it is commonly listed among the states retaining the convention system.

[3] A few of the Southern states provide exceptions to these statements.

widely concerning the manner in which an aspirant for public office may have his name placed on the primary ballot of his party. In four states [4] a simple declaration of candidacy is sufficient; ten others specify that the declaration must be accompanied by a fee. Usually the fee does not exceed twenty-five or fifty dollars, except for the most important state offices. Fees as high as two hundred dollars, even for the office of governor, are unusual. Those states that do not make use of the declaration plan, with or without fee, rely instead on nominating petitions. Every nominating petition must be supported by the signatures of a given number or percentage of party voters. The required number or percentage varies with the importance of the office and also with the state. There is a general tendency to fix this requirement so low that it will not interfere with anyone who seriously desires to be a candidate for nomination, but this tendency has not prevented Illinois from specifying one thousand signatures as the minimum for a valid nominating petition to the office of governor. In a few states nominating petitions are combined with fees. California has an unusual arrangement whereby every petition of candidacy must be filed by a certain number of "sponsors"—the number ranging from ten to one hundred. These sponsors do not assume any responsibility for the private or public acts of their candidate, but they must swear that they know him personally and consider him "qualified mentally, morally, and physically" for the office he seeks to fill.

**Open versus closed primary.** There is considerable discussion concerning the relative merits of the *open* primary—which is open to all qualified voters without regard to party membership, and the *closed* primary—so called because the primary of each party is closed to everyone save the party's duly qualified members. When the open primary is used, every voter at the primary receives the ballots of all the parties. He casts one of these ballots and deposits the others in a blank ballot box, thus escaping the necessity of revealing his party affiliation.[5] Under the closed primary system the voter is asked to declare his party allegiance—perhaps to meet some test of party membership. He then receives only the ballot of his own party.

[4] Delaware, Indiana, Oklahoma, West Virginia.

[5] In Washington, where the primary is "open" to the fullest extent, the voter receives a single ballot containing the names of all candidates for all party nominations for all offices. There is no obligation to conform to a single party throughout; therefore the voter may aid the Republicans in nominating their candidate for governor and help the Democrats to select their nominee for senator.

The declaration of party affiliation, an essential feature of the closed primary, is objectionable to many men and women. Some of them desire to hold aloof from partisan groups and factions, and to cast their vote with the Republicans at one election and unite with the Democrats at the next. The very thought of party organization and party discipline may be distasteful to them. Or they may resent the necessity of stating in public how they usually vote. Such persons naturally prefer the open primary, with the complete secrecy that it assures. Yet the open primary system has had a very uneven history. At one time it was used by twelve states, and seemed to be gaining in popularity; then the number gradually shrank to two. More recently open primary legislation has been enacted by a number of other commonwealths, bringing the present total to eleven.

The opponents of the open primary complain chiefly of its failure to prevent the political trick known as "raiding the primary." When one party is united upon a single candidate, it may be able to spare the votes of hundreds or even thousands of its professional and semi-professional workers at the primary election. These surplus votes can then be used to secure the nomination of the weakest candidate of the rival party, especially in a close contest. One year the Republicans may "capture" the Democratic primary and dictate the selection of the Democratic nominee; the next year, under changed circumstances, the Democrats may be able to return the compliment. This constant shifting of voters in the primary is possible under the open primary plan because every voter has the ballots of all the parties and is free to vote for whatever set of candidates his fancy may dictate.

The closed primary is supposed to prevent the too frequent severance of party ties, thus making primary raiding impossible. The extent to which it actually does so, however, depends upon the provisions of the primary law concerning changes in party allegiance. There are a few states whose laws are so lenient in this respect that they might almost be classed with the open primary group. In Vermont, for example, a voter need merely indicate the party ballot he desires, and this selection constitutes his declaration of party affiliation. There is nothing in law or custom to restrain him from changing his party at every primary election. At the other extreme are several Southern states which empower the party committees to set up tests of party membership; the tests thus established are intended to discourage frequent transfers. Generally speaking, the tendency is to impose a moderate requirement of some sort—to ask the voter to declare that he habitually supports the candidates of the party in whose primary he desires to participate, or that he has not supported the candidate of any other party for at least two years. Failure to meet a test of this sort, it must be understood, does not prevent a qualified voter from casting a ballot in the final election, but merely excludes him from the party primary.

**Plurality principle almost universal.** Plurality choice is the general rule in both primary and final elections. The candidate who receives the greatest number of votes at a primary becomes the nominee of his party, and if he receives the greatest number of votes at the final election he is declared elected, even if the combined votes of his opponents exceed his own total by a considerable margin. Most students of government defend the plurality principle. Though admitting the desirability of securing an absolute majority whenever possible, they point out that it is usually impossible, except by artificial means, to secure an absolute majority in a field of several candidates. In most cases the voters do not prefer one candidate to all the others combined, and any attempt to create the appearance of a united majority that does not in fact exist is certain to produce disappointing results.

Yet a number of states make use of various devices for securing majority choice. Provision is made in nine Southern states [6] and Utah for second or "run-off" primaries, involving only the two highest candidates, in case no one receives an absolute majority on the first balloting. Such an arrangement adds to the expense and complexity of the election system and to the already heavy burden imposed upon the voters; therefore it is scarcely known outside of the South, where the dominance of one party makes the primary more important than the final election. Under the laws of two states—Iowa and South Dakota [7]—the highest candidate for an office must receive at least thirty-five per cent of his party's primary vote; otherwise the nomination to that office is made by a post-primary convention.

Eleven states have experimented with preferential voting [8] in primary elections, but the only state that still retains this system is Maryland.

---

[6] Alabama, Arkansas, Florida, Georgia, Louisiana, Mississippi, North Carolina, South Carolina, Texas. Tennessee also makes provision for a second primary, but only in case of a tie.

[7] In South Dakota the law applies only to candidates for governor, United States senator, and congressman.

[8] Preferential voting is briefly described on pp. 155-156.

**Non-partisanship:** NOMINATION BY PETITION. Although a candidate for public office usually tries to secure the endorsement of one of the political parties at the primary election, it is not necessary for him to do so. Instead he may be nominated by petition, and thus have his name placed on the ballot that is presented to the voters at the final election. The procedure is exactly the same as if he were merely a candidate for nomination, except that more signatures are commonly required. An independent, unwilling to affiliate himself with any political party, commonly secures nomination in this way. Most states require the filing of the petition at some time subsequent to the primary, and several of them attempt to prevent defeated party candidates from suddenly becoming "independents" by specifying that persons failing of nomination at the primary may not be candidates at the final election. It is also customary to prohibit voters who participated in the primary from signing any nominating petitions that may subsequently be circulated, since this form of nomination is reserved for those who are not regular party members.

RECENT ADOPTIONS OF THE PRINCIPLE. In recent years the principle of non-partisanship has been accepted for judicial, school, and local offices in a number of states. The names of all candidates for these offices are placed on the primary ballot by petition—minus party designations, of course—and the two highest candidates become the nominees. Their names then appear on the ballot at the final election.[9] A large number of cities, especially those operating under the commission or manager forms of government,[10] have adopted the non-partisan method of choosing all their elective officers. In some instances the non-partisanship is genuine; in others it is a convenient mask for party activities. But even strong party organizations often have difficulty in maintaining their full vigor when candidates are chosen by petition and party designations are omitted from the ballot. Professor Salter, in his careful study of non-partisanship in certain Pennsylvania cities, found that "the partisanship that did exist was subject to the more or less constant criticism and protests of different newspapers and civic agencies. It was furtive; it could not be openly defended in the light of day. It was often tolerated but rarely accepted by everyone. There was a realization that both the letter and the spirit of the law were being violated."[11]

[9] A few states specify, however, that any candidate receiving an absolute majority of all the votes cast in a non-partisan primary shall be declared elected.

[10] See Chap. Thirteen.

[11] Salter, J. T., *The Non-Partisan Ballot in Certain Pennsylvania Cities*, p. 234.

**Attacks on the direct primary.** The direct primary has become the generally accepted method of nominating candidates for public office, yet there is no general agreement as to the desirability of retaining it. Some persons contend that primary elections should be supplemented by pre-primary conventions, at which the names of "pre-nominees" would be voted upon. This plan is used by Colorado and Massachusetts, and was in effect for a time in South Dakota, but is so cumbersome that its widespread adoption is unlikely. Much stronger, however, is the movement for a return to the ordinary convention system that was commonly used before the direct primary came into vogue. In 1921 New York re-established the convention system for nomination to state offices. A bill that would have restored conventions in Vermont was defeated in 1925 by the deciding vote of the lieutenant-governor in the state senate, and the following year a similar measure failed of passage by a single vote in the New Jersey legislature. Proposals to repeal the primary laws have received more or less serious consideration in over half of the states. On the other hand, the people have consistently voted to retain the direct primary system whenever the question has been presented to them at the polls. Idaho, which adopted the direct primary in 1909 and abandoned it in favor of the convention plan ten years later, again joined the primary states in 1931.

**Merits and defects of the direct primary.** The merits and defects of the direct primary are not easily determined. To a large extent they seem to be a matter of opinion. Thus the friends of the primary system contend that it has improved the calibre of public officials, whereas its opponents assert with equal assurance that it has had exactly the opposite effect. Yet no one has explained how it is possible to measure the relative capacities of the men nominated for public office by conventions and by primaries. In many instances popular political leaders have managed to secure election under both systems. Nor is there any satisfactory way of determining the validity of the charge that the direct primary results in larger campaign expenditures. The sums spent to secure nominations and elections are undoubtedly excessive in many instances—especially in the more populous states, where large numbers of voters must be reached. But money must be spent under the convention system also, and probably with greater likelihood that it will be spent secretly for dishonest purposes.

The direct primary tends to weaken the position of the political parties; whether this fact is an argument for or against it depends largely upon the point of view. Those who favor the primary speak of the necessity of crushing the political machines and restoring control to the people. Those who desire a return to the convention system lament the destruction of party responsibility. But both groups agree that the primary method of making nominations gives the independent—especially the wealthy independent—a somewhat better chance of success.

There is one argument in favor of the direct primary that cannot be successfully refuted: it places a powerful weapon in the hands of the voters. It enables them to secure control of their respective parties whenever they seriously desire to do so. It permits them to brush aside the secret agreements and private understandings of the professional politicians, and nominate for public office the men who hold their confidence. It makes the people the masters of their government—provided, of course, that they are sufficiently interested to assume control. Usually they are not sufficiently interested. Year after year they stay at home on the day of the primary election, thus proclaiming their complete indifference. It is a matter worthy of more than passing mention when one half of the men and women who are eligible to participate in a primary actually go to the polls and vote. Very seldom does a primary contest engage the attention of so large a portion of the electorate. Occasionally, however, the people may be roused to action by some unusual circumstance, such as the exposure of widespread corruption in the state government. Their habitual apathy may be transformed into a temporary desire to act. After all, the public commonly votes its indignation rather than its approval. Under such circumstances the primary lends itself readily to the popular mood. It enables the people to name their candidates directly instead of through the complexities of party conventions.

### ELECTIONS

The election machinery conforms roughly to a standard pattern in all states. Although there are numerous minor variations, the broad outline is everywhere the same. The area of a state is divided into a large number of election districts or precincts, with a polling place in each district. One district for every four or five hundred voters is a common arrangement. The number of voters is supposed to be approximately the same in every election district; actually there are wide discrepancies. Some states use public buildings—schools, police stations, and the like—as polling places. This is a growing tendency, but has not yet been generally adopted. It saves expense, assures a proper environment, and simplifies the voter's problem of finding the building where he is to cast his ballot. When public buildings are not used, the common practice is to rent private shops, garages, or other quarters for the day of the election. Some years ago saloons were often selected. The choice of the private structures to be rented for polling places rests with the agency in charge of the election—the county commissioners or board of supervisors in most cases, but a special election board in more than one of the large metropolitan centers. Since the rental paid by the county or city is generally ten or fifteen dollars a day, and sometimes even twenty-five, for each polling place, the election officials thus possess a considerable amount of petty patronage. They can rent the polling places from those faithful followers who seem most likely to yield a small harvest of votes in return. Or, if they are sufficiently unscrupulous, they can demand for themselves a share of the rental. Election investigations occasionally unearth such scandals.

**Election boards.** The conduct of the election at each polling place is under the direction of a district or precinct election board. This board commonly consists of three members, though the number varies from two to four, according to the law of the state. Not more than two members—in the case of a three-member board—may belong to the same political party.[12] The obvious purpose of this provision is to prevent the dominant party from obtaining complete control of the board and manipulating the election in its own favor. Actually, however, bipartisan boards have not been very effective in eliminating fraud. In some instances the majority party has proved so powerful that it has been able to dictate the selection of minority party representatives as well as its own board members; in other cases the two major parties have agreed to a "rational" distribution of the spoils of office on the basis of their normal voting strength and have then proceeded to declare certain candidates of each party elected in accordance with a prearranged schedule—entirely without regard for the preferences actually expressed by the voters at the polls.

The members of the district board are known as inspectors or judges of elections. Usually they are selected by the county com-

---

[12] Except in the Southern states, where the Democratic Party normally assumes complete control.

missioners or the municipal election board. In a few states, however, they are appointed by the judge of the county court or by the court clerk, and in one state—Pennsylvania—they are elected by the party members of the district. They are commonly assisted by poll clerks. Since the election inspectors are generally selected from lists of persons who have applied for appointment and since the remuneration is too small to attract men and women of ability, it almost invariably follows that second-rate politicians—men whose honesty is questionable and whose ignorance is beyond doubt—are usually named. To this generalization there are many exceptions, of course—especially in the smaller communities; but it remains true none the less that most inspectors of elections are poorly fitted for their task. They are not required to have any special qualifications, other than the qualifications of an ordinary voter plus the ability to read and write.[13] They should be familiar with the election laws, of course, but unfamiliarity is not usually a bar to appointment.

**Watchers.** In order to minimize the likelihood of fraud, the several political parties represented at the election—and sometimes the individual candidates—are permitted to have duly accredited watchers at the polling places. These watchers are present from the original inspection of the ballot boxes or voting machines, prior to the opening of the polls, until the counting of the votes is over. They have the right to challenge any voter and to examine all the records of the election. A great deal may depend upon their knowledge of the law, their experience, and their ability to withstand intimidation.

**Corruption.** It is astonishing how many ways can be devised by corrupt politicians to insure the election of their friends. "Let the boys have their fun," an old-time New York political leader once advised his followers as they watched the independent voters cast a heavy vote for independent candidates. "Let 'em cast their ballots the way they please. After all, we do the counting." In many communities this attitude still prevails. The full extent of corruption at the polls is not known, and probably never will be known, because the heavy penalties prescribed by state law make it advisable to proceed with caution. Yet the charges of dishonesty are too common and too widespread to be entirely without foundation. Quite frequently these charges are proved in the courts, and election inspectors or other election officials are sent to the penitentiary. Every year brings fresh

[13] New York election inspectors are required by law to have a knowledge of their duties, but this requirement is not enforced.

rumors, and sometimes fresh evidence, of election frauds in widely scattered communities.

**Polling hours.** The polls usually remain open for a period of twelve hours, though there is considerable variation. Thus the Michigan law prescribes nine hours, while fifteen hours is the rule in the cities of Minnesota. The opening hour is usually early in the morning—six or seven o'clock—so as to permit laborers to vote on their way to work.

**Identification of qualified voters.** When a person appears at the polls claiming the right to vote, he is generally given a ballot and directed to one of the voting booths. Any member of the election board or any voter may challenge him, however, on the ground that he lacks the qualifications for voting established by law or that he is not the person he claims to be. The effect of such a challenge is not everywhere the same, but in most states the suspect may still cast his ballot if he takes oath that he is legally entitled to do so. Subsequently he may be convicted of perjury or impersonation; it is then too late, however, to identify his ballot and cast it out.[14] The most effective way to identify a voter is to require him to sign the registration record when registering, and also to sign when he receives his ballot on election day. The signatures can readily be compared by the election officials. This system is now used in California, in Des Moines, Iowa, and in the larger cities of New York and Minnesota.

**Counting the votes.** Immediately following the closing of the polls the count begins, and frequently continues until the early hours of the following morning.[15] It is a complicated process, except in those communities that use voting machines, for paper ballots give rise to all sorts of questions that must be answered without delay. What shall be done with ballots on which preferences are indicated by check-marks or circles, instead of the customary crosses? If a cross apparently intended for one candidate sprawls partly across another candidate's space, shall it be counted? If a facetious voter writes in the name of a comic strip character for one office, shall the entire ballot be declared invalid? Is a large ink stain across the face of the ballot sufficient reason for refusing to count it? One by one these questions are decided by the election board as the count proceeds.

[14] Except in a very few states, where the ballots are numbered.

[15] Double election boards, which are now used in about one fourth of the states, facilitate the process of counting the votes. The members of the second board arrive a few hours after the opening of the polls and maintain a continuous count of the ballots while the election is in progress.

Eventually all the votes are counted and entered on the official tally sheets.    The ballots are then placed once more in the boxes, which are padlocked and taken to some central place for safekeeping.    A contested election may necessitate a re-examination of the ballots at some subsequent time; otherwise they are destroyed after a proper interval.

**Election results.**    Upon completion of the count the election officials affix their signatures to the tally sheets—the official record of the election returns in the precinct.    From these figures the newspapers estimate the total city or state vote, so that the final result of the election is usually known by the following morning—or by afternoon at the latest.    Election results are not official, however, until the returns from the several precincts have been canvassed,—that is, until the votes for each candidate have been totaled.    The canvassing, which takes place several days or even a week later, is done by the county commissioners, the judges of the county court, or some other agency designed by law.    For officers elected on a state-wide basis there must be an additional convass—a totaling of the county figures by the state canvassing board.    Certificates of election are then issued to the successful candidates.    These certificates are only *prima facie* evidence of the right to hold office, however; they do not prevent defeated candidates from contesting the election on the ground of fraud or error.

### THE BALLOT

The form of the ballot deserves at least passing mention at this point.    During the greater part of the nineteenth century the party organizations printed and distributed their own ballots—that is, the lists of their own candidates—and no one questioned this arrangement.    Official ballots, printed by the state, were unknown; state law went no further than to provide that white paper must be used, and perhaps also to specify the size.    Because these elementary precautions were insufficient to preserve the secrecy of the ballot or to prevent wholesale ballot box stuffing, recourse eventually was had to the so-called "Australian" ballot—a blanket ballot containing the names of the candidates of all parties, printed at state expense, and distributed at the polls by state election officials.    Such a ballot, which had long been used in Australia, made its first appearance in the United States at the Louisville municipal election of 1888.    A few months later it was adopted by Massachusetts.    Within a short time it had received general acceptance; today it is used by every state except South Carolina.

**Present types of ballots.** The original Australian ballot, as borrowed from Australia and first used in the United States, contained no party designations. The candidates for each office were grouped together, and a separate mark was required for each preference the voter desired to indicate. Under American influence, however, the Australian ballot began to assume new forms. Its essential features —secrecy and official preparation and distribution—were preserved, but in other respects it differed radically from the original model. First, Massachusetts printed the party affiliation of each candidate after his name. A little later, Indiana rearranged the ballot so as to place the names of all the candidates of a party in the same column, and specified that a cross at the top of any column would be considered a vote for that party's entire slate of candidates. Although it was possible under this plan for the voter to divide his allegiance, it was much easier for him to vote a straight ticket, for splitting the ticket meant placing a cross after the name of every candidate favored, whereas straight voting necessitated only a single mark. Indiana's party-column ballot thus encouraged party regularity, and for that reason it was enthusiastically received by the professional politicians. Today it is used—with occasional variations—in thirty states. Most of the others have adopted the Massachusetts or office-group ballot. Nebraska and Pennsylvania, however, have modified this type of ballot by adding the party square or circle for the benefit of those who desire to vote a straight ticket, thus offering the very inducement to party regularity that is characteristic of the Indiana plan.

**Voting machines.** It has already been indicated that voting machines are now used by some communities in place of paper ballots. These machines are operated by means of pointers and levers. Across the face of a machine the names of the candidates are placed, each name with its separate pointer, and the voter is directed to turn down the pointers that indicate his preferences. Or, if the policy of the state is to encourage straight voting, the machine may be so arranged as to make possible a vote for all the candidates of a party by a single turn of the party's lever. The voter is carefully protected against mistakes; it is mechanically impossible for him to express too many choices or turn the pointers the wrong way. When he finally pulls the lever that records his vote, the curtain that has concealed him from the election officers and watchers is automatically drawn back, thus making it impossible for him to vote a second time without everyone's knowledge.

First introduced in 1896, voting machines have been used rather widely for several decades, and have proved markedly superior to paper ballots. They save voting time, insure absolute secrecy, eliminate the chance of error, and, despite their heavy initial cost, actually result in reduced election expenses. Still more important, they greatly diminish the likelihood of fraud. Successful tampering with the machines is almost impossible, so that correct returns are assured if there is even one honest election official or watcher in the polling place. The speed of the count is also an important factor. Votes are automatically tabulated as they are cast; therefore the final result of an election can often be announced within one or two hours after the polls are closed.

Most of the arguments against voting machines are invalid, or of minor consequence. It is sometimes said, for example, that they are apt to break down—perhaps at the voting peak—thus leaving the voters without any means of expressing their preferences. Yet the dependability of the better grade of machines has been amply demonstrated over a considerable period of years. References to their unreliability are generally the result of ignorance or deliberate malice. Troubles due to defective workmanship have not been common since the experimental period at the beginning of the present century. Moreover, it is a simple matter to keep one or two machines at some central point, ready for any possible emergency. Objection to voting machines on the ground of excessive cost can readily be met by indicating the savings made possible—fewer election officials, because of the automatic count; larger election precincts, as a result of quicker voting; no printing cost, through the elimination of paper ballots. In Maryland it was argued that voting machines were a violation of the Constitutional mandate that "all elections shall be by ballot." But the supreme court of the state rejected this contention, declaring that "a constitution is to be interpreted by the spirit which vivifies, and not by the letter which killeth." [16] The only valid objection to voting machines—that they were not adapted to the requirements of proportional representation elections—has now been removed by the development of suitable instruments. Because of their numerous advantages, voting machines have been widely adopted.

[16] Norris *v.* Mayor and City Council of Baltimore, 192 A. 531 (1937).

They are used extensively in nine states—especially in the larger cities; and twenty other states also permit their use. They have been installed in more than three hundred cities.

**Need for reform.** Students of government agree that the most necessary reform in the election systems of the several states is a substantial reduction in the number of offices filled by popular vote. Since the days of Andrew Jackson there has been a widespread belief that popular election is the one certain cure for all the ills of government, and the complete failure of this theory has only slightly diminished its popularity. In thousands of elections the people have demonstrated conclusively that their ability to discriminate among candidates and select wisely is in inverse ratio to the number of choices they are required to make, yet ballots are still filled with long lists of offices and longer lists of office-seekers. In the average state the voters are asked to choose a veritable horde of state officers—governor, lieutenant governor, secretary of state, attorney-general, treasurer, auditor, superintendent of education, legislators, and members of the judiciary, plus perhaps a few board members—in addition to such local officers as mayor, sheriff, coroner, prosecuting attorney, treasurer, recorder of deeds, registrar of wills, city clerk, and members of the city council and the county board of supervisors. Nor does this partial enumeration include the officers of school districts, park or water districts, or other special areas of local government. Likewise, it omits the elective officers of the national government—president, vice president, and members of both houses of Congress.

Small wonder, therefore, that the voter cannot make intelligent selections. He has neither the time nor the inclination to study the records of hundreds of candidates for scores of offices. Concerning a few outstanding men he may have very definite views; the other names on the ballot are meaningless to him. Yet the law specifically states that numerous minor offices are to be filled by his vote, and the societies for getting out the vote inform him that it is his patriotic duty to express preferences he does not have. Faced with such a problem, many voters conclude that the most satisfactory solution is to remain at home on election day. Those who actually go to the polls pursue the one rational course that is open to them: they vote the straight ticket of their respective parties in the hope that the party selections have been wisely made. Thus they play directly into the hands of the boss—the man who controls the dominant party organization and dictates the selection of public officials. Their votes are merely a ratification of his choice. The fault is not with them, however; it is with the system that makes any other result impossible.

THE SHORT BALLOT AS A REMEDY. Fortunately, a remedy for the long lists now appearing on ballots is at hand. It is the short ballot— a ballot that contains only the names of candidates for outstanding public offices. Other offices must then be filled by appointment. In the field of state government only the governor, the lieutenant governor, and the members of the legislature should retain their elective status.[17] With this reform accomplished, the people could reasonably be expected to shoulder their lighter burden more willingly and to exercise greater discrimination in the selection of their representatives. And the actual choice of minor officials would be transferred from the boss—an irresponsible despot—to the governor—a responsible leader.

The short ballot movement is a product of the present century. Prior to 1900 there had been a number of suggestions for the transfer of specific offices from the elective to the appointive class, and some of these suggestions had borne fruit. But there was no organized plan of attack on the old order until 1909, when the National Short Ballot Organization was formed, with Woodrow Wilson as its first president and Richard S. Childs, the mainspring of the movement, as secretary-treasurer.[18] Since that time the short ballot has been endorsed by leading statesmen, publicists, and scholars. It has received the support of every sincere friend of good government. It has proved its effectiveness, and has not been weakened by a single valid criticism. As Theodore Roosevelt told the Ohio Constitutional Convention of 1912: "You cannot get good service from the public servant if you cannot see him, and there is no more effective way of hiding him than by mixing him up with a multitude of others so that they are none of them important enough to catch the eye of the average work-a-day citizen."

Yet the progress of the short ballot movement has been slow, especially in state government. Though a few states, such as New York and Virginia, have substantially shortened their ballots in recent years, most states still encumber their ballots with the names of candidates for minor offices, so that intelligent voting is impossible. In the cities of the United States the short ballot has met with greater favor.

[17] If the auditor is not chosen by the legislature he should be added to this list, for it is necessary to maintain his independence. See p. 222.

[18] In 1921 the National Short Ballot Organization consolidated with the National Municipal League.

It has been adopted by a considerable number of the metropolitan centers, and by hundreds of smaller communities. Cities with commission or manager forms of government have accepted it as fundamental, and even the mayor-council cities have amended their charters in many instances for the purpose of reducing the number of elective officials. The short ballot has become a prime tenet in nearly every recent campaign for charter revision. Only the national government has remained entirely unaffected. Since the adoption of the Constitution in 1789 it has had a short ballot *par excellence,* and has served as a convenient illustration of the successful operation of the short ballot principle.

## WHO MAY VOTE?

**Constitutional limitations.** Every state constitution prescribes the qualifications necessary for voting at state and national elections. Therefore the qualifications that are required—even to vote for the president and vice president of the United States and for members of Congress—vary with the state in which the voter has his residence. The federal Constitution imposes only two limitations upon the power of the states to establish suffrage requirements: no citizen of the United States may be deprived of the right to vote on account of race or color,[19] or on account of sex.[20] In addition, there is an unenforced clause of the federal Constitution: "When the right to vote at any election for the choice of electors for President and Vice President of the United States, Representatives in Congress, the Executive and Judicial officers of a State, or the members of the Legislature thereof, is denied to any of the male inhabitants of such state, being twenty-one years of age, and citizens of the United States, or in any way abridged, except for participation in rebellion, or other crime, the basis of representation" of the state in the federal House of Representatives "shall be reduced in the proportion which the number of such male citizens shall bear to the whole number of male citizens twenty-one years of age in such State." [21]

The political consequences of an attempt to enforce this section on reduction of representation might be serious. Moreover, it would be necessary to reduce the Congressional representation of *every* state that imposed voting restrictions on its adult male citizens, regardless

19 Fifteenth Amendment.
20 Nineteenth Amendment.
21 Fourteenth Amendment, Sec. 2.

of the purpose of those restrictions. Therefore New York, Massachusetts, California, and other states whose literacy requirements are designed to improve the standard of intelligent voting would suffer equally with the states of the "solid South," where Negro voters are excluded *en masse*. The "reduction of representation" clause was never intended to have any such effect. Adopted in 1868, its obvious purpose was to force the extension of the suffrage to the newly enfranchised Negro population of the South. So the leaders of both major parties have tacitly agreed that the wisest course is to permit it to remain a dead letter.

**State qualifications.** The voting age is twenty-one years in every state except Georgia, which lowered it to eighteen years in 1943, on the theory that "the best training in citizenship is participation in the rights and obligations of citizenship." Every state has residence requirements, also—usually one year within the state, two or three months within the county, and a shorter time within the election precinct where residence is maintained at the time of voting. Citizenship is now universally required, though this policy has been adopted by a number of states within the last three or four decades. Just prior to the outbreak of the First World War nine states extended the suffrage to aliens who had declared their intention of becoming American citizens. Tax-paying as a qualification for voting has lost much of its early popularity, though it is still found in a number of states. Most common is the poll tax—a head tax of fifty cents or one dollar on every person, or on every person who does not meet some other requirement, such as payment of taxes on real estate. This tax is used by seven Southern states,[22] its purpose being to prevent Negroes from voting.

DISFRANCHISEMENT OF NEGROES. Of course, the poll tax is not the sole means—nor even the most important means—of disfranchising the black race. The white people of the South have displayed astonishing ingenuity in this respect. Thus at one time the constitution of many a Southern state contained a so-called "grandfather clause," which extended the suffrage to persons who lacked prescribed tax-paying or educational qualifications, *provided their fathers or grandfathers, or any of their ancestors, were voters in 1867, or had served in the Union or Confederate forces.* Obviously no black man

---

[22] Alabama, Arkansas, Mississippi, South Carolina, Tennessee, Texas, Virginia. In 1943 the legislature of Tennessee abolished the poll tax, but the state supreme court declared that this repeal was unconstitutional. Biggs *v.* Beeler, 173 S.W. (2nd) 144 (1943).

could benefit by this waiver of voting restrictions. But poor, illiterate whites could and did benefit; they lost no time in enrolling as voters. This discrimination was so obvious a violation of the federal Constitution that in 1915 the Supreme Court of the United States, considering Oklahoma's grandfather clause, declared it unconstitutional.[23] Since that time increasing reliance has been placed on unofficial party action prescribing the qualifications for voting at the party primaries; Negroes are then excluded by party rules from the Democratic primary, which is normally the equivalent of a final election in the far South. In 1935 the United States Supreme Court upheld this arrangement, on the ground that the discrimination was a party—not a state—action, and therefore outside the protection of the Fifteenth Amendment.[24] Nine years later, however, the Court specifically reversed its stand, declaring that Negroes might not be excluded by party rules.[25] But there are other ways of barring Negroes from the polls. One effective device is the literacy test. The constitutions of a number of Southern states specify that every elector must be able to read and write, or read the constitution of the state, or read any portion of the constitution "and give a reasonable interpretation thereof." To give an interpretation that will satisfy the white election inspectors is not a difficult task for a white man, but virtually impossible for a Negro. Still other plans will undoubtedly be devised if necessary. Southern whites will not readily grant the right of Negroes to equality at the polls. They point to Negro ignorance and political indifference as a justification of their stand.

LITERACY TESTS. It has already been indicated that literacy tests for voting are not confined to the South. They are now used by twenty-three states, representing every section of the country. Their obvious purpose, in the North and West, is to deny the franchise to the group that is least likely to use it intelligently. The ability to read and write is not in itself an assurance of intelligent voting, but it may well be considered a prerequisite. Illiterates are not usually well informed concerning public affairs. To them the happenings outside their own little world are necessarily a closed book. Objection is sometimes made to literacy tests on the ground that they are "undemocratic." It is said that they establish an aristocracy of education to replace the aristocracy of wealth that vanished with the disap-

---

[23] Guinn *v.* United States, 238 U.S. 347 (1915).

[24] Grovey *v.* Townsend, 295 U.S. 45 (1935).

[25] Smith *v.* Allwright, 321 U.S. 649 (1944). See also United States *v.* Classic, 313 U.S. 299 (1941), in which the right of Congress to regulate congressional primary elections was upheld.

pearance of property requirements for voting. But this argument is scarcely entitled to serious consideration. It rests on the untenable premise that democracy can best be served by a multiplication of votes, regardless of the qualifications of the voters. The real trouble is not with the theory of the literacy requirement, but with its enforcement. Usually it is administered by local election officials, whose concept of literacy often varies with the hour of the day, the state of their digestion, and the party affiliation of prospective voters. Only one state—New York—has taken the test out of the hands of the election officials. Under the New York plan it is administered by the state department of education. Persons who can give proof that they have completed the fifth grade of the grammar school receive certificates of literacy without further formality; others are required to pass the department of education's examination before they may be enrolled as voters. In no year has the percentage of failures been less than ten; twice it exceeded twenty.

### REGISTRATION OF VOTERS

**Fraudulent voting.** When a state prescribes qualifications for voting, it should also take steps to prevent ineligible persons from participating in elections. Otherwise large-scale frauds are likely to result. Aliens may cast their ballots unchallenged; the dead may come to life through the magic of unscrupulous politicians; professional "repeaters" may visit precinct after precinct, voting under a different name at each polling place. Such practices are not common in rural communities, where every man is known and attempts at impersonation would speedily be detected. But in the cities, with their congestion and rapidly shifting populations, another story must be told. Men do not know even their immediate neighbors, and therefore the opportunities for election fraud are vast.

REGISTRATION LISTS. Some means must be found of enabling the election officials to identify voters, so that persons not properly qualified may be excluded from the polls. Years ago, when this problem first became serious, some states attempted to solve it by making provisions for the preparation of lists of eligible voters, to which reference could be made when necessary. But the lists were carelessly prepared, and no effort was made to keep them up-to-date. Therefore they proved of little value, and fraud continued to be practically as prevalent as before. "The colonization of voters was quite common.   Hoodlums were rounded up and lodged for a night or so in various lodging houses and cheap hotels and then registered from all of them.   On the day of the election, gangs of 'repeaters' were hauled from precinct to precinct and voted under different names.   Sometimes the same persons would vote several times at each precinct, changing coats or hats between times.   The early registration lists were often padded with bogus names or the names of persons who had died or moved away, and these names were voted by 're- peaters' on the day of election or were checked off and voted by the corrupt precinct election officers without the necessity of providing 'repeaters.' " [26]

PERSONAL REGISTRATION.   In 1866 California and New York took an important step toward the elimination of such conditions by pro- viding for the personal registration of voters.   Every person desiring to vote was required to appear before a registration board at some time prior to election day and establish the fact that he possessed the necessary legal qualifications.   Failure to have his name placed on the list of eligible voters in this manner automatically operated to deprive him of the right to cast a ballot at the next election.   Personal regis- tration gradually came into popular favor; it is now used by forty-six states—either on a state-wide basis or for the larger cities only.   The constitution of Arkansas prohibits registration of voters; and the Texas constitution permits it only in cities whose population exceeds ten thousand.[27]

As used in the several states, personal registration assumes a variety of forms.   The most important difference is the length of time for which a voter's registration remains valid.   The election laws of some states require all voters—or at least all voters in the larger cities, where fraud is most likely to occur—to register every year.   This arrange- ment is found in New Jersey and in the cities of New York.   It places a very heavy burden on the electorate, since it requires two trips to the polls—one to register and one to vote—for every election.   More- over, it adds materially to the expense of the election system.   Bien- nial and quadrennial registration are correspondingly less expensive and less burdensome, but in the metropolitan centers, unless extreme care is taken to purge the voters' lists by striking out the names of

[26] Harris, Joseph P., *Registration of Voters in the United States*, p. 6.   Reprinted by permission of the Institute for Government Research.

[27] See the third edition (1939) of Joseph P. Harris' *Model Registration System*, pre- pared for the National Municipal League.

persons who have died or moved away, they lead naturally to fraud. Nebraska has registration every six years in certain cities, and in South Carolina decennial registration is the rule throughout the state.

*Permanent registration.* Most common, however, is permanent registration, which is used by thirty-nine states.[28] Under this plan a voter is permitted to register at any time during the year, and is not limited to two or three registration days prior to the election. His name, once placed on the list of qualified voters, remains there until he dies or moves to a new address. Permanent registration has certain obvious advantages. It is very cheap, and offers a maximum of convenience to the electorate. Unless coupled with an effective means of revising the voters' lists at frequent intervals, however, it is an open invitation to fraud. For this reason it was formerly regarded as unsuitable for the larger cities. But improved means of purging the lists have been developed in recent years, and therefore the trend has been toward permanent registration—even in cities of metropolitan proportions, such as Philadelphia, Detroit, Los Angeles, Cleveland, Boston, San Francisco, Milwaukee, and Minneapolis.

By far the best way to clear the voters' lists of names that should be removed is to conduct a house-to-house canvass. This task is performed by election officials or the police. In addition, it is an extremely simple matter to secure a copy of the official death reports and to cancel the registration of every voter who has died. An effective system for recording transfers of registration within a city or county is also important. In a few cities the proprietors of lodging houses, rooming houses and hotels are required to file lists of their permanent guests. A number of states cancel the registration of an elector who fails to vote at two or three successive elections. This action does not disfranchise him, but merely necessitates another registration. These various devices for purging the lists have proved so satisfactory, when given even a reasonably fair trial, that they have completely destroyed the only valid argument against the use of permanent registration in large cities—its tendency to encourage fraudulent voting.

#### ABSENT VOTERS

Many voters are away from home on election day, and therefore unable to go to the polls and cast their ballots. The laws of most states, however, permit them to vote *in absentia.* Usually this is done by

---

[28] Not necessarily on a state-wide basis, however. Thus Nebraska's permanent registration applies only to Douglas County, which includes Omaha.

issuing ballots in advance to those who expect to be absent on election day; the ballots are then mailed to the local election boards in time to be counted. A few states vary this procedure by permitting an elector who is absent from the precinct in which he resides to cast his ballot in any other precinct of the state. The privilege of voting without going to the polls is most commonly extended to all voters, but a few states limit it to those who are sick or disabled, and several other states provide that it shall apply only to members of the armed forces in time of war.

In the spring of 1944, with several million young Americans in the armed services in all parts of the world, and a presidential election only a few months away, absent voting suddenly became a major issue. Some leaders of public opinion, emphasizing the inadequacy of many of the state laws, urged federal legislation guaranteeing to American troops the right to vote for president and vice president and members of Congress. Opposition to this proposal was based on the undeniable right of the states, rather than the federal government, to control elections. Finally, after prolonged controversy, Congress passed a compromise law authorizing the preparation of a federal ballot to be used by overseas troops. This ballot might not be used by any voter, however, unless the governor of his own state certified that it was acceptable under state law. Furthermore, it might not be used unless the voter first applied for a state ballot, and failed to receive it by a given date. Only twenty states agreed to accept the federal ballot, and as a result more than half of the troops overseas were unaffected by the law of Congress.

Sound absent-voting legislation is desirable, not only in wartime, but also in days of peace. Men and women should always be encouraged in every legitimate way to express their political preferences. It must be confessed, however, that laws facilitating absent voting have had slight effect on the habits of the electorate. The overwhelming majority of persons who are ill or away from home fail to exercise their absent-voting privilege.

## NONVOTERS

Far more serious, however, is the problem of the chronic nonvoter —the man who stays away from the polls, though he lacks the excuse of illness or absence from home. Just how many qualified electors habitually fail to vote cannot be stated with assurance, but it is certain that the number is excessively high. Even in a presidential year, when popular interest is usually at its peak, the total number of votes scarcely ever exceeds sixty-five per cent of the number of citizens of voting age. Usually the percentage is far lower. Of course, some citizens are denied the franchise on account of illiteracy, failure to pay taxes, or inadequate periods of residence. But due allowance for these factors does not change the obvious truth that a large part of the American public deliberately abstains from voting. In state and municipal elections the citizens who vote are usually less numerous than those who do not.

There are many reasons why men and women stay away from the polls but indifference is by far the most important. The rank and file of the electorate, faced with the task of making an intelligent selection among hundreds of candidates for dozens of offices, in addition perhaps to passing upon constitutional amendments, charter changes, and ordinary legislative proposals, frequently become discouraged. And their interest in public affairs is further dampened by such hurdles as rigid annual registration laws, unnecessary taxpaying requirements, frequent regular and special elections.

It may fairly be said that widespread nonvoting is the natural and almost inevitable result of our general scheme of government. If we wish to draw larger numbers of voters to the polls, we must first simplify our election machinery and then shorten our ballots to the point where intelligent voting can reasonably be expected. It is quite fashionable at the present time to speak of the "slacker vote," as if every person who stayed away from the polls on election day had shirked an important civic duty. But many leading students of public affairs are of the opinion that uninformed voting is quite as dangerous as nonvoting, and that good government cannot be obtained by a mere multiplication of ballots. They urge that the real need is for an enlightened citizenry, and that the first step is the elimination of needless complexities so as to bring government within the comprehension of the average man.

### COMPULSORY VOTING

Compulsory voting is used with varying degrees of success in a number of foreign countries. Every qualified elector is required to appear at the polls and cast a ballot on election day. If he fails to do so and can show no good reason for his neglect of duty, he must pay a fine. European experience has led to the suggestion that compulsory voting be adopted in the United States. In fact, the constitutions of

Massachusetts and North Dakota authorize the legislature to prescribe penalties for failure to vote. But the penalties have not been imposed, and in other states compulsory voting has received scant consideration. It is contrary to the American political tradition. It transforms the privilege of participating in elections—or the "right," to use the phraseology of the federal Constitution [29]—into an obligation. And it does not in any way stimulate the public's interest or add to the public's knowledge of governmental affairs. It increases the number of ballots, of course—but that is a matter of small consequence.

## SELECTED REFERENCES

Albright, S. D., *The American Ballot,* Washington, D.C., 1942.

Brooks, R. C., *Political Parties and Electoral Problems,* 3rd ed., Chaps. X, XII, XV, XVIII, 1933.

Council of State Governments, *Soldier-Sailor Voting,* 2nd ed., 1944.

Glassman, Benjamin, *A.B.C. of the Direct Primary Law,* 3rd ed., 1938.

Harris, Joseph P., *Election Administration in the United States,* Washington, D.C., 1934.

———, *Registration of Voters in the United States,* Washington, D.C., 1929.

Illinois Legislative Reference Bureau, *Constitutional Convention Bulletins* Springfield, Ill., *Nos.* 2, 5, Springfield, 1920.

Key, V. O., Jr., *Politics, Parties, and Pressure Groups,* Chaps. XVIII–XXI, 1942.

Kies, Harry B., and McCandless, Carl A., *Manual on the Bill of Rights and Suffrage and Elections for the Missouri Constitutional Convention of 1943,* Columbia, 1943.

Luce, Robert, *Legislative Principles,* Chaps. XIII, XIV, XVIII, 1930.

McCulloch, Albert J., *Suffrage and Its Problems,* University Research Monographs, No. 9, Baltimore, 1929.

Merriam, Charles E., and Gosnell, Harold F., *Non-Voting,* 1924.

———, *The American Party System,* 3rd ed., Chaps. XIII, XV–XVII, 1940.

Merriam, Charles E., and Overacker, L., *Primary Elections,* 1928.

Overacker, Louise, *Money in Elections,* 1932.

Pollock, James K., *The Direct Primary in Michigan, 1909–1935,* Ann Arbor, 1943.

———, *Election Administration in Michigan,* 1934.

———, *Party Campaign Funds,* 1926.

———, *Permanent Registration of Voters in Michigan: An Appraisal,* Ann Arbor, 1937.

Porter, K. H., *A History of Suffrage in the United States,* 1918.

Sait, E. M., *American Parties and Elections,* 3rd ed., Chaps. XVIII–XXVII, 1942.

Smith, Carl O., ed., *Book of Ballots,* Detroit, Mich., 1938.

Titus, Charles H., *Voting Behavior in the United States,* Berkeley, Cal., 1935.

Woody, Carroll Hill, *The Direct Primary in Chicago,* 1926.

[29] E.g., "The *right* of citizens of the United States to vote shall not be denied or abridged by the United States or by any state on account of sex." (Nineteenth Amendment.)

# Chapter Six ᘔᘎᘛ PARTIES AND POLITICS

GOVERNMENT is something more than a matter of constitutions and laws. Its length and breadth are not encompassed by the administrators, legislators, and judges who officially represent the people, for these public officials are chosen by the political parties, and must look to the parties for re-election or reappointment. Their political fate is decided by the party leaders, and only at rare intervals do the voters upset the leaders' plans. Government operates through political parties; in large measure it is what the parties wish it to be. Therefore the political parties are an integral part of the governmental process and any discussion of government that overlooks their function and organization is necessarily incomplete. Before examining these, however, let us consider just what is a political party, and how the system of parties developed.

## DEFINITIONS OF A POLITICAL PARTY

To give a satisfactory definition of the term "political party" is not easy. Edmund Burke once said that "a party is a body of men united for promoting by their joint endeavor the national interest upon some particular principle in which they are all agreed." This statement has been quoted many times—usually with approval, yet it furnishes no clear understanding of what parties are or why they exist. Political parties as we know them today—and as Burke should have known them—are seldom able to find any principle upon which a substantial number of their members can agree. The Republican Party, for example, includes within its membership conservatives like Robert Taft and liberals like Hiram Johnson, isolationists like Gerald Nye, and internationalists like Joseph Ball. The Democrats are similarly divided.

Some amateur students of politics are greatly distressed to find politicians of widely assorted hues wearing the same party label. "You know very well," the March Hare is reported to have said, "how the label on tomato soup must state whether preservatives or artificial coloring matter are used, mustn't it? And the label on a peroxide bottle has to say ninety-seven per cent inert matter—namely, water. And you always have to state the alcoholic contents, don't you? So it's odd that people are so particular about tomato soup and canned spinach and beer and not at all about Republicans on a Communist ticket. But if you had a law saying that a Democratic candidate for mayor must have a label saying 'Democratic Contents Not Under 23 Per Cent'—" [1]

Despite a lack of precise principles, however, both major parties continue to operate with surprising efficiency. Their leaders may not be "united for promoting by their joint endeavor the national interest," but they are held together by the hope of office and the promise of patronage. This view of political activities is less idealistic than that presented by Edmund Burke, but it conforms more closely to the facts, and for that reason is considered more satisfactory by present-day students of public affairs. It finds expression in Professor Sait's definition of a political party as "an organized group that seeks to control both the personnel and the policy of the government." [2]

There are times when it is difficult to distinguish political parties from other organized groups that also seek to control the government. Such organizations as the National Association of Manufacturers, the American Federation of Labor, the Congress of Industrial Organizations, and the American Legion have their own legislative programs, and frequently endorse or denounce candidates for public office. Their programs are usually more restricted than the platforms of the regular political parties, however, and they do not put their own slates of candidates into the field. Instead they try to win the support of the nominees of one of the major political parties—or of both major parties, if possible; and their endorsement of individuals is given without regard to party lines.

Definitions of party are found, not only in the writings of statesmen and political scientists, but also in the election laws of the several states. These legal definitions are necessary, for in most states the political parties are subject to more or less thoroughgoing regulation. The organization and functions of party committees, the collection and expenditure of party funds, and the tests of party membership are all prescribed by state law. Provision is made for party nominations of candidates for public office. Therefore the exact nature of

[1] "Topics of the Times," in *New York Times*, July 25, 1937.
[2] *American Parties and Elections*, p. 141.

party must be determined. The laws of the states do not approach the question from the standpoint of principle, as did Burke, or from the point of view of function, as do the modern realists, but on the basis of demonstrated voting strength. In New York, for example, a party is any political organization that polled at least twenty-five thousand votes for governor at the last preceding gubernatorial election. Other states use substantially the same formula, varying the required number of votes or expressing the requirement in terms of a percentage. Such tests of party have one obvious advantage; they are easily administered. But they fail to square with the facts in many cases. Thus the Socialist Party may be a legally recognized party after one election and yet sink to the level of an "independent body" two years later—merely because some of its adherents have changed their allegiance or have neglected to go to the polls. Other minor parties may never be able to acquire the legal rank of parties under state law.

### RISE OF THE PARTY SYSTEM

In the first days of American independence parties were generally regarded with disfavor. Madison, writing in the *Federalist,* urged that the Constitution should be adopted because it would tend "to break and control the violence of faction," and Washington took occasion in his Farewell Address to warn the people "in the most solemn manner against the baneful effects of the spirit of party. . . . It serves always to distract the public councils, and enfeebles the public administration. It agitates the community with ill-founded jealousies and false alarms, kindles the animosity of one part against another, foments occasional riot and insurrection. . . . There is an opinion that parties in free countries are useful checks upon the administration of the government, and serve to keep alive the spirit of liberty. This within certain limits is probably true—and in governments of a monarchical cast, patriotism may look with indulgence, if not with favor, upon the spirit of party. But in those of popular character, in governments purely elective, it is a spirit not to be encouraged. . . . A fire not to be quenched; it demands a uniform vigilance to prevent its bursting into flame, lest, instead of warning, it should consume."

But the "spirit of party" was not quenched by Washington's words; on the contrary, it burned with greater intensity after his retirement to private life. Democrats, or "Republicans," as they first called themselves, vied with Federalists for control of the government and eventually became the dominant party in American politics. About 1834 their supremacy was challenged by the Whigs, who borrowed their name from England. Then came the collapse of the Whig Party some twenty years later, the birth of the Republican Party and its rise to national power, the period of Republican supremacy, continuing until 1874, and the subsequent rivalry of Republicans and Democrats. Throughout the history of the United States, almost from the adoption of the Constitution, there have been two major parties competing for popular favor, and occasionally the struggle has been complicated by the rise and fall of "third parties."

Yet there are still many persons who believe, like Washington, that partisanship is "a spirit not to be encouraged." Their constant aim is to make all government *non-partisan*, despite the obvious fact that partisanship is merely a synonym for differences of opinion, which are certain to exist under any scheme for managing public affairs. In the cities, as previously pointed out,[3] non-partisanship has met with some success. This is not at all surprising, for good city government is largely a matter of sound administration and does not involve policy determination to any considerable extent. But state government necessitates a much greater emphasis on politics—that is (using *politics* in its proper sense), the determination of policies—so non-partisanship has proved less popular. There is non-partisan selection of judges in thirteen states, certain school officers in four others, and members of the legislature in Minnesota and Nebraska. Elsewhere, when adopted for state-wide offices, the non-partisan plan has generally been abandoned after a short trial.

### THE FUNCTION OF POLITICAL PARTIES

In every generation the party system has been a target for the heavy artillery of reform, yet it still flourishes. Political parties are accepted by the people as a matter of course and supported as a matter of principle. It is reasonable to suppose, therefore, that parties serve a useful purpose in the general scheme of government.

**Provision of a political creed.** Their function is, in fact, threefold. First, they assort the many questions of public policy and find a common ground on which large numbers of voters may unite in order to make their political beliefs effective. In other words, they make it possible to express the will of the "people"—that mystical, composite

[3] See p. 92.

deity of which every professional politician is the self-appointed high priest. Without parties—or organized groups, whatever their name —united action would be virtually impossible; the fact that few men think exactly alike on *all* public questions would be an insurmountable obstacle. But differences of opinion can often be reconciled. In many instances they relate only to minor issues or matters of detail and can readily be compromised or brushed aside as inconsequential. All that is needed, therefore, in order to present a united front, is a political creed phrased in general terms—a platform so broad that all manner of men may stand upon it without crowding. The political parties meet this need. Their platforms are often said to be evasive and platitudinous, and undoubtedly the description is accurate. But it is difficult to see how the allegiance of a majority of the voters could be won and kept with a more specific declaration of principles.

**Responsibility for candidates.** Second, the political parties provide continuous, collective responsibility. They are the guarantors of the integrity and efficiency of the men and women whom they present to the electorate as candidates for public office. When maladministration is prevalent and corruption is the order of the day, the party in power must take the blame; when efficient administration is firmly established and honesty is generally accepted as the best—and safest—policy, the party in power may reasonably claim the credit. Continuous responsibility is highly important, for without it the voters are virtually powerless to express their displeasure. They may refuse to re-elect a faithless public servant, but he may not be a candidate for re-election. They may demand his impeachment, though they realize that impeachment is a slow and cumbersome process. They may recall him if the laws of their state provide for the recall and apply it to his office. Beyond that they cannot go, unless the official's acts are of such a nature as to justify criminal prosecution. But party responsibility places a new weapon in the hands of the voters. It enables them to vent their wrath upon the party, even if the individual dies, retires or absconds. For a political party does not die or desert the field; it strives continuously to win public support and thus control the government.

The collective nature of party responsibility should also be emphasized. In the average state the whole structure of government has been designed with a view to preventing too much concentration of authority in any one person; therefore no one person can be blamed when promised reforms fail to materialize and old evils continue unabated. The governor may declare that the secretary of state and the treasurer, over whom he has no control, are at fault; or he may point out that the senate has refused to confirm his appointments, or charge that the legislature has made unwise appropriations and refused to abide by his veto. The secretary of state and the treasurer may reply that they are trying to save the state from the consequences of the governor's folly. The members of the legislature may criticize the governor's appointments and legislative recommendations. In this maze of charges and countercharges the voter is hopelessly bewildered. He has no ready way of ascertaining the truth. If he tries to select certain individuals for punishment at the next election, he is as likely to pick the innocent as the guilty. But he can make no mistake when he places the blame on the party. For every political party is collectively responsible for the public acts of the men chosen to office as its representatives. If it selects its candidates unwisely, it must be prepared to pay the price of popular disfavor.

**Information on public business.** Third, the parties perform a valuable service by informing the electorate on public questions. The information thus supplied may not always be accurate; it may be twisted and warped to meet the requirements of temporary expediency or long-established tradition. But at least the voters are apprised that important public business awaits their consideration, and if they stay at home on election day instead of playing their part in the process of government, the political parties cannot fairly be blamed. Moreover, the misrepresentations of one party will almost certainly be pointed out by the other. Arguments in favor of virtually any proposal or any candidate will be met by arguments in opposition. Thus both sides of the story are told, and the discriminating voter has an opportunity to weigh the merits of men and measures.

For these reasons the party system has become an established and essential part of democratic government. The parties do not always perform their threefold function perfectly; sometimes they do not even perform it well. Their platforms are often unsatisfactory, and their candidates unworthy of public office. Parties created to promote noble principles now function chiefly to control ignoble patronage. But these abuses do not affect the fundamentals of the party system. As long as men are permitted to express their divergent views on public questions, they will organize into political parties for the furtherance of their respective beliefs.

### DOMINANCE OF NATIONAL PARTIES IN STATE AND LOCAL ELECTIONS

The two major political parties that occupy the center of the national arena also dominate the governments of the states and of most cities. Governors, state legislators, mayors, councilmen are usually chosen on the basis of their Republican or Democratic allegiance. To many people this merger of national and local interests seems unfortunate, since it encourages disregard of local problems. Local issues are settled on the basis of national party platforms and candidates. In strict logic there is no reason why the national record of a party should bear any relation to the selection of local party representatives, but the voters are not strictly logical. They can readily be swayed by appeals to party loyalty or party prejudice, and such appeals are commonly made. Therefore mayors are elected to office because they will "support the president"—a promise they are powerless to make effective; and governors are chosen because they oppose or favor some particular variety of farm relief, though it should be obvious that their opposition or advocacy can have no effect on the policy of the national government.

But this condition of affairs should occasion no surprise. National issues are more spectacular than local questions and make a more dramatic appeal to the voters. The nation is big—as big as the forty-eight states combined, and its vast proportions endow it with a certain prestige that no state can share. Moreover, the national parties find it decidedly advantageous to control state and local governments—in part because well-trained local party organizations are extremely valuable in winning national elections, and in part because local patronage provides a convenient means of rewarding zealous party workers. It seems likely, therefore, that national affairs will continue to overshadow matters of purely local concern and that local issues will be decided along national party lines in the future, as they have been in the past.

The experience of England with separation of national and local parties may well be cited at this point. For many decades party lines were loosely drawn in local elections, and candidates were chosen for office at municipal elections without much regard to their national party affiliations. In London the Municipal Reform Party and the Progressive Party maintained their own organizations, quite separate from the national parties. To a very large extent, it must be admitted, the members of the Municipal Reform Party were recruited from the ranks of the Conservatives, while the Progressive Party drew heavily on Liberal support. There was, however, no formal alliance. But the Labor Party's rise to power completely altered the situation. Labor refused to recognize any distinction between national and local issues or national and local candidates. Thus it forced the other parties, in self-defense, to follow its lead. National and local party lines merged and have not since separated. Nor is the English experience unique. Elsewhere the union took place long ago. In most of the countries of continental Europe everyone takes for granted that local campaigns will be conducted primarily for the benefit of the national parties.

But agitation still continues in the United States for the separation of national and local issues. Those who urge this reform propose two ways of accomplishing it. First, they suggest that state and local elections be held on a different day from the national election, or in a different year. The voters would then be free to devote their undivided attention to state and local problems. But this plan has met with little favor. The other suggestion is that state and local officials be chosen without regard to party affiliation. The spread of the non-partisan movement in cities and its limited success in state government have already been discussed.[4]

## THE TWO-PARTY SYSTEM

Throughout the course of American history a number of "third" parties have been forged in a flame of revolt against the major party organizations. But in virtually every instance[5] the flame has died out, leaving the major parties still in control. Just why the two-party system should be so firmly established in the United States is a question not easily answered. Most democratic nations make use of a multiple-party system that raises every faction to the importance of a party and makes majority control by a single party virtually impossible. Government is conducted by coalitions—combinations of political groups whose tenets are not widely divergent. In France, just prior to the Second World War, there were about seven parties whose organizations extended beyond the confines of Parliament; the number fluctuated from time to time. Germany had ten or eleven

[4] See pp. 92 and 115.
[5] The Republican Party, organized at a time when the Democrats and the Whigs controlled the political field, is the only exception.

political parties before the creation in 1933 of the Nazi one-party state. Only in the United States, England, and some of the British dominions has the balance of power been divided between two major parties almost continuously for many years. The two-party scheme was British in its inception and became a natural part of America's political inheritance. In recent years the growth of the British Labor Party seemed for a time to menace the traditional two-party alignment, but the subsequent collapse of the Liberals opened the way for the Labor Party to become the defender of the liberal faith and thus one of the two major parties. It has been suggested that the development of two-party government in England and America, in contrast with world experience, is due to racial differences, to long-established habits of thought, or to constitution and legal provisions; but none of these explanations are very convincing. The problem deserves careful investigation.

The minor parties are so incompletely organized that they merit no more than passing mention in a discussion of party organization. In some states, or parts of states, they may establish fairly complete hierarchies of committees, from precinct committees to state governing bodies. The Socialist Party, for example, maintains its local organization in many of the larger cities, and tops this local setup with a national executive committee of nine members. But only the two major parties are completely organized on a nation-wide scale; for all practical purposes their organization is the organization of political parties in the United States.

### ORGANIZATION OF THE MAJOR PARTIES

**Committees.** Most important in the organization of each party is the national committee, which consists of one man and one woman from each state and territory. This committee and its work lie beyond the proper scope of a volume dealing with state government, but a few words are necessary in order to present a clear picture of party organization. The presidential and vice-presidential nominees of a party are chosen by a national convention, which also adopts the party's national platform. Upon the national committee rests the responsibility of calling the convention, organizing it, and directing its activities along the lines desired by the party leaders. After the convention, the committee is charged with the conduct of the campaign. It raises funds and spends them as it sees fit; it prepares campaign literature; it maintains a speakers' bureau for the purpose of flooding the country with oratory. In the intervals between national elections it keeps a watchful eye on political conditions in the states. Although it is the nominal superior of state and local committees of the party, it has no direct means of controlling their activities. Only through its prestige, its use of party funds, and its supervision over party speakers and workers can the national committee influence the local party organizations.

Both of the major parties also maintain Congressional committees. These committees, composed of members of Congress, have no official connection with other party committees, but co-operate with them in furthering the party interests.

State and local committees differ from the national and congressional committees in that their organization and functions are commonly prescribed by state law. The only exceptions are found in the South, where parties are still regarded as voluntary associations, and in a scattered handful of other states that still retain the convention system for the nomination of party condidates. Elsewhere parties have been recognized as essential parts of the machinery of government, and therefore have been subjected to strict public regulation.

At the head of the party organization in each state is a central or executive committee, which ranges in size from ten or eleven members to several hundred. The members of this committee are chosen by the local committees, by conventions, or, more commonly, by direct vote of the party members. Usually they serve for two years, though longer terms are coming into favor. The powers of a state central committee are seldom clearly defined, but they relate chiefly to the management of the campaign. Funds are obtained and distributed, meetings are arranged, literature is prepared and widely circulated. Deals with the rival party or with rival candidates may be arranged if circumstances warrant. The central committee is, in fact, the party's state board of strategy. It takes whatever steps may be necessary to insure victory at the polls. To a considerable extent, especially in the collection of campaign funds and the selection of campaign speakers, it supplements the work of the national committee. In some states it exercises a measure of supervision over the local committees, but such instances are exceptional. The more common arrangement leaves the local committees free to conduct their own affairs in their own way, subject only to the necessity of maintaining harmonious party relationships.

No exact description of local committee organization can be given, because it varies so widely from state to state. There are county committees, city committees, township committees, ward committees, precinct committees. Each major division of local government has its party organizations representing the two dominant parties, and perhaps one or more minor parties in addition. The local committees perform substantially the same functions as the national and state committees, though on a smaller scale. Some of them—especially the county and city committees—usually play an important part in the management of party affairs and the distribution of local patronage. Places are reserved for women on the party committees, or else separate women's committees are established. This recognition of the woman voter is, of course, a comparatively recent development.

**The precinct captain.** At the base of the pyramid of party organization is the precinct committee—or, much more commonly, a single individual who bears the title of precinct captain or leader. In a few states he is known as precinct committeeman, even though he may be the sole member of the "committee." Under state law and party rules he is generally elected by the party's voters in the precinct, but in a considerable number of states he is appointed by the ward leader or some other party officer. Regardless of statutory and other provisions the actual choice is almost invariably made by someone high in the party councils, and this choice is ratified by the voters—should ratification be necessary—as a matter of course. Comparatively few voters take the trouble to mark their ballots for the office of precinct captain; therefore the votes of the party workers, their friends and relatives, and others who can be depended on to "vote right" are sufficient to make the popular will, as expressed at the polls, coincide with the will of the ward or district leader.

The chief function of the precinct captain is to carry the precinct for his faction on the day of the primary election—and, if possible, for his party at the final election. Failure to win, especially at the primary, may cost him his leadership and wreck his political career. So he naturally regards every election as a matter of vital importance. He tries to make as good a showing as possible, even if the final result of the city- or state-wide balloting is not in doubt, because he knows that he will be judged solely on the basis of the returns from his precinct. His superiors—the men who control the affairs of the party —are not especially interested in his methods. They give him a free hand. They are not likely to question his political morality. But failure is one sin that they will not forgive.

In many rural districts, and in some of the smaller cities, the precinct leader devotes only a small part of his time to politics. Most of his working hours are claimed by some other vocation, and he regards politics as a pleasant, though somewhat exacting, diversion. He may be attracted by the excitement of the game, the opportunity for petty profit through appointment to some minor post, or the possibility of establishing friendships that will further his business interests. But he seldom considers politics a matter of life or death, and neither knows nor cares about the fine points of political technique. He is frankly an amateur—or, at most, a semi-professional. Of course, this description does not fit all rural precinct leaders. Some of them make politics their only business, and a very serious business indeed. Their methods are so unscrupulous as to cause city politicians to turn red with shame or green with envy. But they should not be considered typical; they are exceptions to the general rule.

In the larger cities, however, everything is different. The spoils of office are many times greater, and therefore worth a hard fight. And urban politics *is* a hard fight, from start to finish. It is a game for the professional, and not the dilettante. The precinct captain is almost invariably a full-time political worker. He has no spare hours for other business, and very few hours for pleasure, for he must be always within easy reach of the voters of his precinct, ready to serve them as occasion may arise. He must be prepared to give them help when they need it, regardless of whether that help takes the form of advice, information, money, food, coal, or political influence. His power rests on the solid foundation of service. After all, it would be foolish for him to use closely reasoned arguments in an attempt to convince the electors that they should support his ticket, for some other party of faction might have better arguments or better candidates, and then his time would be wasted. But when he asks the people to vote their gratitude, he can be certain of their support as long as he gives them cause to be thankful. The precinct captain is likely to hold some minor city or county position that pays reasonably well and does not take too much time from the main business of keeping in touch with the voters. He usually has a number of assistants—aspiring young party workers who secretly covet his position and hope to win it when he moves upward into the higher party councils or downward out of precinct leadership.

The methods of the precinct captain vary with the neighborhood that he controls. He must give service, of course; but the exact nature of that service is not everywhere the same. So he learns what the people want, and sees that they get it. As Plunkitt of Tammany Hall declared, he must "study human nature and act accordin'." Even in a wealthy precinct the voters are quite willing to accept favors. Some complain that the assessments on their homes are too high, and regard the captain as the proper person to intercede with the assessor. Others go to the captain with their notices to appear in court to answer charges of reckless driving, because they know that a little political pressure applied at just the right spot can usually straighten out such matters. And the captain helps them all. He is an ever-present friend in time of trouble, and he asks nothing in return except a vote on election day. The vote he desires may not be for the "right" people—but, after all, a vote is a very little thing to exchange for big favors. So the people of his precinct fall into line. Their votes can be purchased, though not quite so readily as the votes of the very poor; it is merely a question of using the proper technique. In the slums, of course, the technique is quite different. The people need the more obvious kinds of aid—food to appease their hunger, fuel to keep them warm, money to give to the landlord. They turn to their precinct captain as a matter of course, and he never fails them. His door is always open, and his bank roll always in his hand. He finds jobs for many men who are out of work and helps to support the families of those for whom no work can be found. He makes innumerable small loans and proves a very reasonable creditor when payment is due. His name heads every subscription list. He associates freely with the people and wins their confidence as a friend and neighbor. He knows the name of every man, woman, and child; he knows their hobbies and aversions, their desires and needs, and also their voting tendencies. He attends christenings, weddings, and funerals; he rejoices with those who are glad and mourns with those who are sorrowful. When any resident of his precinct gets into trouble with the police, he whispers a few well-chosen words into the ear of the desk sergeant. Or, if the matter has passed beyond that early stage, he visits the magistrate before whom the hearing is to be held. The offense may be slight—failure to procure a peddler's license, for example. So the precinct captain gets the license and pays the small fine that is imposed. But if the offense is serious and the accused is guilty beyond reasonable doubt, the precinct captain still intercedes, and his word usually carries a great deal of weight.

It is obvious that an energetic precinct captain must spend in the course of a year many times the amount of the small compensation that he may receive from some minor government position. This does not indicate, however, that he must be a man of independent means. Money—an abundant supply—will always be available for his use if he demonstrates his ability to distribute it effectively. Nor will he be questioned too closely concerning his expenditures. If some of the gold sticks to his own fingers as it passes through, that is no one's business but his own. The city and county committees, which are usually responsible for local finances, are not inclined to quarrel over a few dollars. Their task is to win elections, and they will be generous to the point of prodigality with anyone who can produce results on election day.

### SOURCES OF REVENUE FOR STATE AND LOCAL MACHINES

**The underworld.** It may well be asked where the money comes from to finance the party machines that dominate the political life of most big cities. There are many sources of revenue. First, and among the most important, is the underworld. The gambling dens, the speakeasies, the houses of ill repute—these places must be free from police interference if they are to survive, and they are willing to pay for "protection." Every week they turn over a portion of their profit to the policeman on the beat, or to a special agent of the police captain. The money passes through several hands on its way to the top, and some of it evaporates along the way. But a considerable part eventually finds its way into the treasury of the corrupt political machine and is ready for distribution to the ward and precinct leaders.

**Public utility corporations.** The public utility corporations also contribute large sums. In many instances their contributions are forced from them so flagrantly that the transactions can best be described as blackmail. A bill is introduced imposing unreasonable burdens upon a utility corporation, and the corporation's officials are advised to take quick action to prevent its passage. The "action" consists in writing out a check for an amount sufficient to dull the consciences of those councilmen who intended to vote in the affirmative, and delay only increases the size of the check that must be written. Some public utility officials, after a few experiences of this sort, decide that the cheapest plan is to buy the government outright—not openly, of course, but through whispered negotiations. After a time the story leaks out that the president of the street railway or the electric light and power company is the real boss of the city—the man from whom all the minor politicians take orders. But very few people know what to believe, and still fewer care. So "government with the consent of the governed" becomes a polite myth, and government by the utilities becomes the order of the day.

**Other businesses.** It must not be assumed, however, that the utility corporations are the only businesses that contribute to the support of the political machine. They are very likely to be in the forefront, because they have special privileges from the government which must be protected. But other businesses have privileges also—alleys occupied for storage purposes contrary to law, old buildings that should have been condemned long ago by the building inspector, restaurant kitchens that are operated in an unsanitary (but cheap) manner without protest from the health department. Usually it costs less to buy from the politicians the right to keep these privileges than to comply with the law, so deals are readily arranged.

But it is unfair to picture business as essentially corrupt. There are many business men who do not pay a single dollar to the political machine, or who pay only in order to escape petty persecution. The number of forms that such persecution may take is surprising. *No parking* regulations may be rigorously enforced against the loading and unloading trucks of the merchant who refuses to make his contribution to "the cause," though the trucks of other merchants remain unmolested. Statutes and ordinances of every description—many of them hoary with age and almost forgotten—may be unearthed and held in readiness to cause maximum annoyance. Adequate police protection may be deliberately withheld at times when it is vitally necessary. Several months of such treatment are usually sufficient to convince a business man that he should pay for the privilege of being let alone.

**Public works construction.** Contracts for the construction of public works are also a profitable source of the machine's revenue. State laws and city charters and ordinances commonly provide that every contract shall be awarded to the lowest responsible bidder, but this requirement is easily evaded. The favored contractor's bid is almost invariably found to be the lowest, and this miracle is performed by means of a secret agreement assuring lax inspection, or by some other trick, such as the specification of patented materials that no other contractor can obtain or the omission of important features that are subsequently to be added as "extras" at excessively high prices. The contractor then shares his huge profit with the politicians who made it possible.

In the years immediately following the close of the Civil War, when the infamous Tweed Ring of New York City was at the height of its power, the construction and equipment of the county court house became a scandal of vast proportions. "When designed in 1868 its cost was estimated at $250,000. Before the end of 1871 a sum variously estimated at from $8,000,000 to $13,000,000 had been expended upon it, and it was still unfinished. This was effected, as was afterwards proved in judicial proceedings, by the simple method of requiring the contractors, many of whom resisted for a time, to add large sums to their bills, sums which were then appropriated by Tweed, Connolly, and their minions or accomplices." [6] Bills submitted by contractors and approved by the city auditor included $404,347 for safes and $7,500 for thermometers. Today the corrupt politicians who control the destinies of many American cities handle such matters less blatantly, and somewhat less crudely. But their methods have not altered radically in nearly three quarters of a century.

**Political assessments.** Considerable sums are also obtained from the political assessment of officeholders. Some years ago, when the spoils system was a part of the accepted order and virtually every person in the public service held his position by reason of his ability to control votes, political assessments were accepted without question. It was considered quite proper that public officials and employees, selected through the influence of the dominant party, should show their gratitude by contributing to the party's campaign fund. Failure to contribute the required amount—two per cent of each month's salary, or four per cent, or even ten per cent, as the case might be— would result in speedy removal from office. Thus the parties used their control of government to obtain funds that could be used for the purpose of making their control of government still more secure. It was a vicious circle. More recently the merit system has made considerable headway. The people have learned to regard public office as a public trust, and to demand that positions in the public service be filled without regard to party affiliation. It follows naturally, therefore, that officeholders should not be required, under pain of dismissal, to contribute to party campaign funds. In theory, at least, they have been selected because of their special fitness for the positions

[6] Bryce, James, *The American Commonwealth* (1914 ed.), Vol. II, p. 390.

they hold, and not through political influence.   So they owe nothing to either party.   Conforming to this modern viewpoint, state statutes and city ordinances now commonly prohibit the political assessment of public officials and employees, and impose heavy penalties for violations.   Yet assessments are still levied in many state and city governments, and those who are forced to pay dare not complain.   Sometimes the demands of the party organization are thinly veiled as requests, but everyone understands what is meant.

### BOSS CONTROL

The nominal head of the party within a state is the chairman of the state central committee.   Within a city the chairman of the city committee is supposed to possess similar authority.   It often happens, however, that the titular chief is not the chief in fact.   Instead, actual authority may rest in someone who is merely a member of the committee, or who does not hold any party or public office.   His name may not be connected with the government of state or city in any formal way; his words may have no binding effect in law.   Yet he is the boss—the absolute master of the government!   Like the centurion of old he is able to say: "For I am a man under authority, having soldiers under me: and I say to this man, Go, and he goeth; and to another, Come, and he cometh; and to my servant, Do this, and he doeth it." [7]   Governors, mayors, state legislators, municipal councilmen, and a host of minor officers do his bidding, for they know that their political fate is in his hands.   Some years ago, when George B. Cox was asked if he were boss of Cincinnati, he unhesitatingly replied in the affirmative.

"Of course," remarked his interrogator, "you have a mayor, and a council, and judges?"

"I have," Cox admitted, "but"—he pointed with his thumb back over his shoulder to the desk—"I have a telephone, too." [8]

Usually the boss shuns important public office and even chooses a minor rôle in the party organization, for he knows full well that official position brings responsibility.   And he prefers, naturally, to hold the substance of power without being held accountable for its use.   His method is to arrange the election of puppet governors, mayors, and others, who will dance when he pulls the strings and take the blame

[7] Matthew VIII, 9.
[8] Steffens, Lincoln, *Autobiography*, pp. 483-484.

when trouble arises. Of course, there are some exceptions—some bosses whose vanity has led them to seek public office despite the obvious disadvantages of such a course. But most bosses prefer to remain in the background.

This discussion of bosses and their habits should not lead to the assumption that every state or every city has its boss—its irresponsible despot who holds undisputed sway and is recognized by everyone as the unofficial head of the government. There are many states that have never known the evils of bossism, or have remained unbossed for long periods. Even in the industrial states and in the great cities, where the large spoils of office draw the corrupt politicians as sugar attracts a swarm of flies, dozens or even scores of aspiring political workers may strive in vain against one another for undisputed leadership. There may be ward bosses, even though no one is firmly established as boss of the city; or there may be city bosses vying for state control. Generally speaking, bossism is less prevalent in the states than in the cities. Even a small state has a relatively large area and many diverse interests that cannot readily be reconciled.

**The function of bosses.** The structure of American government —state and municipal [9]—lends itself readily to boss control. In most instances it is still based on the theory of checks and balances; it rests on the assumption that concentration of power is dangerous and must be avoided at any cost. Thus it virtually destroys the possibility of effective leadership under the constitution and laws. And, since legal leadership is prohibited, extra-legal leadership takes its place. The boss assumes the control that is denied to the governor and the mayor. He takes the many loose ends of government and weaves them into clear design. Scores or even hundreds of nominally independent officials acknowledge his authority.

Richard Croker, boss of New York for many years, saw very clearly the source of his power. One day he was asked: "Why must there be a boss, when we've got a mayor and—a council and—"

"That's why," he broke in. "It's because there's a mayor *and* a council *and* judges *and*—a hundred other men to deal with. A government is nothing but a business, and you can't do business with a lot of officials who check and cross one another and who come and go,

---

[9] The council-manager form of government and, to some extent, the commission plan, are exceptions to this general rule. For a discussion of these schemes of municipal government, see Chap. Thirteen.

there this year, out the next. A business man wants to do business with one man, and one who is always there to remember and carry out the—business." [10]

The surest way to strike at bossism, therefore, is to remove the need for it. When the state constitution or the city charter provides specifically for a responsible leader, irresponsible leadership is less likely to flourish. The experience of the federal government is in point. The federal Constitution recognizes the president as the leader of the nation by placing broad authority in his hands; and it is interesting to note that *there has never been a national boss.*[11] Similar concentration of power in the chief executives of states and cities would not work an immediate transformation. Political machines created with infinite care during a long period of years would not crumble overnight. The spoils of office—the life-blood of politics—would still attract the politicians. But bosses and their machines would no longer be an essential part of government, and thus the first step would be taken toward their ultimate elimination.

### SELECTED REFERENCES

Beals, Carleton, *The Story of Huey P. Long*, 1935.
Binkley, Wilfred E., *American Political Parties; Their Natural History*, 1943.
Bruce, Harold R., *American Parties and Politics*, 3rd ed., 1936.
Chambers, Walter, *Samuel Seabury; a Challenge*, 1932.
Christensen, A. N., and Kirkpatrick, E. M., *The People, Politics, and the Politician*, 1941.
Cousens, Theodore, *Politics and Political Organizations in America*, 1942.
Dimock, Marshall E., *Modern Politics and Administration*, 1937.
Gosnell, Harold F., *Machine Politics: Chicago Model*, 1937.
Harris, Thomas O., *The Kingfish; Huey P. Long, Dictator*, New Orleans, 1938.
Herring, Pendleton, *Politics of Democracy*, 1940.
Kent, Frank R., *Great Game of Politics*, rev. ed., 1936.
Key, V. O., Jr., *Politics, Parties, and Pressure Groups*, Chaps. XVIII–XXI, 1942.
Lasswell, Harold D., *Politics: Who Gets What, When, How*, 1936.
Logan, Edward B., ed., *American Political Scene*, rev. ed., 1938.
Lynch, Denis T., *Boss Tweed*, 1927.
McKenzie, Charles W., *Party Government in the United States*, 1938.
Merriam, C. E., and Gosnell, H. F., *The American Party System*, 3rd ed., 1940.
Minault, S. Sydney, *Corrupt Practices Legislation in the Forty-Eight States*, 1942.
Myers, Gustavus, *The History of Tammany Hall*, 2nd ed., 1917.

10 Steffens, Lincoln, *op. cit.*, p. 236. Reprinted by permission of Harcourt, Brace and Company, Inc.
11 Mark Hanna has sometimes been called the "boss of the United States." But he owed his influence solely to his close personal relations with President McKinley, and not to control over a national political machine.

Myers, William Starr, *The Republican Party; a History,* 1928.

Odegard, Peter H., *Pressure Politics,* 1928.

———, *The American Public Mind,* 1930.

———, and Helms, E. A., *American Politics,* 1938.

Riorden, W. L., *Plunkitt of Tammany Hall,* 1905.

Sait, E. M., *American Parties and Elections,* 3rd ed., Chaps. XVIII–XXVII, 1942.

Salter, John T., *Boss Rule,* 1935.

———, *The Republican Organization of Philadelphia,* 1933.

Schattschneider, E. E., *Party Government,* 1942.

Steffens, Lincoln, *The Autobiography of Lincoln Steffens,* 1931.

Stoddard, Theodore Lothrop, *Master of Manhattan,* 1931.

Zeller, Belle, *Pressure Politics in New York,* 1937.

Zink, Harold, *City Bosses in the United States; a Study of Twenty Municipal Bosses,* North Carolina, 1930.

# Chapter Seven ❧ DIRECT LEGISLATION
## AND THE RECALL

THERE are many times when the work of the legislature fails to reflect accurately the popular will. Every session of every legislature provides instances of such misrepresentation. Measures that would almost certainly receive the disapproval of the voters are passed by overwhelming majorities, while other proposals that have been given many evidences of popular favor are sidetracked for indefinite periods. In other words, elected representatives do not always represent. Sometimes downright dishonesty is responsible for their failure to respect the wishes of their constituents; much more commonly ignorance of the true state of public opinion is to blame. But whatever the reason, no one can deny that there is often a wide gap between the popular preference and the legislative product.

Some persons contend that the best way to correct this weakness in our governmental system is to permit the voters to enact their own laws, and a number of states have accepted this point of view. In those states, therefore, the voters are authorized to take matters into their own hands whenever they believe that their interests have not been properly protected. They may veto any legislative acts of which they disapprove. They may write their own laws and put them directly on the statute books when their elected representatives prove too slow or too indifferent. As thus stated, the theory of direct legislation is beyond reproach. There can be no quarrel with the results it seeks to achieve.

### THE INITIATIVE AND REFERENDUM

Direct legislation assumes two forms—the initiative and referendum. The initiative provides a means whereby any voter or group of voters may propose a measure and, after securing a sufficient number of endorsements, submit it to the electorate. The first step is to put the proposal into the form of a bill, so that it may be ready for enactment; then a petition must be prepared to accompany the bill.[1]

---

[1] In California there must also be a summary of the proposed measure prepared by the attorney-general of the state upon the written request of the measure's sponsors.

When the petition has been signed by the requisite number of voters, ranging from five per cent in California, South Dakota, and Utah to ten per cent in Arizona, Nevada, and Washington, it is filed with the proper official. From this point the procedure varies considerably, according to the laws of the several states. Nine states [2] specify that the measure shall without further formality be placed on the ballot at the next regular election or at a special election; this form is known as the direct initiative. Under the indirect initiative, as found in six states,[3] a popularly proposed bill does not go to the electorate unless it fails of passage at the next session of the legislature. Three states [4] complicate the matter still further by making provision for both the direct and indirect initiative, and requiring a larger number of signatures or earlier filing of the petition if the direct form is used. Three other states [5] permit the legislature to submit a rival proposal to the people if it cares to do so. Regardless of these details, the fundamental principle is the same: the fate of the measure as placed upon the ballot is determined by the voters at the polls.

The referendum is designed to secure an expression of popular opinion concerning measures that have been passed by the legislature. In its earlier form, as applied to ordinary legislation, it merely authorized the submission to the people of such proposals as the legislature might care to place upon the ballot; it was an optional referendum—so called because the option rested with the legislature of submitting pending legislation to a popular vote or of withholding it. More recently the obligatory referendum has become the generally accepted type; under its provisions a certain percentage of the voters —usually five per cent, but ranging as high as ten per cent in Nevada, New Mexico, and Utah—may compel the legislature to submit to the electorate any newly enacted measure.

The laws of those states that have adopted the obligatory referendum provide that bills passed by the legislature shall not go into effect immediately, under ordinary circumstances, but shall remain inoperative for a certain period—usually ninety days. During this period of suspension the opponents of any proposal have an opportunity to draft a referendum petition and secure the requisite number of signatures; if they are successful in their efforts the measure is then

[2] Arizona, Arkansas, Colorado, Missouri, Montana, Nebraska, North Dakota, Oklahoma, Oregon.

[3] Maine, Massachusetts, Michigan, Nevada, Ohio, South Dakota.

[4] California, Utah, Washington.

[5] Maine, Michigan, Nevada.

placed on the ballot, and its fate is decided by the voters. Certain laws designed to meet specific emergencies cannot remain inoperative for ninety days, however, without entailing considerable hardship. In recognition of this obvious fact, "emergency" measures are permitted to go into effect as soon as they have been duly enacted. This provision is necessary, yet it leads to serious abuses. The legislature has the power to determine what constitutes an emergency, so it usually places in the emergency category every enactment that is likely to arouse popular disapproval. The number of such "emergencies by definition" is astonishingly large. Many states have tried to correct this evil, but without much success. Their constitutions commonly require a three-fifths, two-thirds, or even three-fourths vote of both houses of the legislature in order to make an emergency declaration valid. But an extraordinary majority for this purpose can usually be obtained without the slightest difficulty. Thus state legislators ignore the spirit of the fundamental law.

The initiative and the referendum are separate devices, and it is quite possible to have one without the other. In fact, there are many states that do not have the initiative, and yet regularly refer proposed constitutional amendments to the voters. Two states—Maryland and New Mexico—have adopted the referendum for ordinary legislation without making provision for the initiative. Generally speaking, however, the initiative and referendum as instruments of ordinary lawmaking go hand in hand.

The first state to authorize the initiative and referendum for ordinary legislation was South Dakota, in 1898. Other states soon followed its example—Utah in 1900, Oregon in 1902, Montana in 1906. By 1918 the total had risen to eighteen, and two other commonwealths had adopted the referendum only. In addition, the voters of Idaho and Mississippi had approved constitutional amendments directing the legislatures of their respective states to establish systems of direct legislation, but the Idaho legislature failed to carry out this mandate, and the supreme court of Mississippi declared the amendment invalid. Since 1918 no state has been converted, and none has deserted.

**Merits and defects of direct legislation.** Many merits are claimed for direct legislation. According to its proponents, it takes ultimate control from the professional politicians and makes the people the real masters of their government. Certainly this is "a consummation devoutly to be wished," but there is reason to doubt that it is achieved by the initiative and the referendum. For the forces that mold public opinion—the "pressure groups" that dominate the legislative programs of state and nation—seem to operate quite as successfully in states that have direct legislation as in other commonwealths. They simply modify their technique to meet the changed situation. After all, it is idle to speak of the people as the authors of any proposal. "The people" do not draft a measure, frame a petition, go from door to door for signatures, and stimulate the necessary enthusiasm. These things are done by organized interests—manufacturers' associations, labor federations, farm bureaus, utility corporations, war veterans' organizations. Signatures are obtained by professional canvassers; there are a number of companies that make a business of securing signatures to proposals of any sort, charging five or ten cents a name for this service. When the petition has been duly filed, more money is spent in "accelerating public opinion." And the final result, registered at the polls, is apt to be a triumph of good advertising and masterful showmanship, masquerading in the guise of self-government. Sometimes the questions placed on the ballot by means of initiative or referendum petitions are of such a nature that the people may reasonably be expected to have intelligent opinions concerning them. Frequently, however, this is not the case. Highly technical questions are submitted to the electorate, as well as many non-technical measures of obscure purpose and uncertain result. Fortunately the voters have grown wary of such proposals. In self-defense they have generally adopted the maxim: "When in doubt, vote no!" Therefore the negative of any question enjoys a certain advantage at the polls.

It is often said that direct legislation stimulates popular interest in government. When all the laws are made at distant state capitals by representatives who commonly misrepresent and are approved by governors who habitually misgovern, the inevitable result is general indifference to the legislative product. The people know that their wishes will probably be ignored, regardless of the party in power, so they gradually acquire a cynical disregard for all parties and all agencies of government. They need, but do not have, some means of correcting the mistakes of the legislature. Direct legislation supplies that need. It enables the voters to enact the laws that they desire and set aside the proposals of which they disapprove. Thus popular interest quickens, and popular enthusiasm is aroused. So runs the argument. Unfortunately, it does not fit the facts. The people are actually less concerned with the proposals placed upon the ballot for their consideration than with the men who offer themselves as candidates for public office. As a rule the total vote for candidates exceeds the total vote for and against measures by at least twenty-five or thirty per cent—frequently by forty or fifty per cent. This means that a substantial portion of the electorate, though sufficiently interested in the choice of candidates to go to the polls and vote, is too indifferent or too uncertain of the right course to mark the part of the ballot reserved for initiative and referendum measures. Occasionally there are exceptions to this rule, but they serve only to emphasize the plain fact that the initiative and the referendum do not stimulate the interest of the people.

Other claims are also made for direct legislation—it produces more carefully drafted laws, because the sponsors of an initiative measure are more conscious of their need for trained assistance than are the almost equally ignorant legislators; it permits the proponents of a reform to go directly to the people, instead of accepting perforce the emasculating amendments of the legislative assembly; it eliminates the need for detailed constitutional limitations upon the power of the legislature, and thus leads naturally to shorter constitutions. But there is little reason to believe that these highly desirable results have actually been achieved.

The objections to direct legislation are numerous. It is "government by minorities," because so many important questions are decided by a minority of the voters. It weakens legislative responsibility, and thereby discourages able men from seeking seats in the legislature. It ignores the increasing complexity of governmental problems and the increasing difficulty of solving such problems by popular vote. The validity of these arguments is not easily determined. Direct legislation may be minority legislation, but so is lawmaking by legislative assemblies. All government is, to a large extent, the handiwork of minorities. As to the charge that direct legislation has an unfortunate effect upon the calibre of legislators, the only possible retort is that no one really knows. At every election the people select some incompetents to represent them in the legislature, as well as some men of outstanding ability; but they did not always choose wisely before the advent of direct legislation. The initiative and the referendum were adopted because of popular dissatisfaction with the work of the legislative body. The argument that present-day legislation is often too technical for popular consideration is difficult to refute.    Many questions appear on the ballot that cannot be intelligently decided without careful investigation of intricate data—detailed information that the public does not possess and would not know how to use. Eight states [6] attempt to overcome this objection by mailing to every voter a publicity pamphlet containing the text of each proposal plus arguments pro and con.[7]    These arguments may be officially prepared, as in California, or prepared by private persons who are sufficiently interested to pay for space in the official pamphlet, as in Oregon.    The value of the publicity pamphlet is uncertain.[8]

By far the most serious objection to direct legislation is its conflict with the short ballot movement, to which reference has already been made.[9]    Both reforms propose to make democratic government more effective, but they strive to reach this goal by opposite routes.   The short ballot is predicated on the theory that the voter is already over-burdened, that he cannot do a great deal and do it well, and that his effective participation in government depends upon his release from the multitudinous tasks imposed upon him by a long ballot.   Direct legislation, on the other hand, postulates that the voter's capacity for participation in government is infinite, that he can and will assume other burdens in addition to those already placed upon his shoulders, and that his failure to elect suitable representatives can best be cured by permitting him to make his own laws.

Between these two points of view there seems to be no tenable middle ground.   Yet thousands of so-called liberals and progressives— many of them prominent in public life—constantly reaffirm their advocacy of direct legislation *and* the short ballot with no realization of the inconsistency of their stand.    In defense of direct legislation it is sometimes said that it is not used to excess; seldom are more than three or four proposals placed on the ballot at a single election.    But there are some exceptions.    California is notorious for its excessive use of the initiative and referendum; at a recent election the people of San Francisco were asked to pass upon sixty-one questions—constitutional amendments, charter amendments, ordinary legislation.

---

[6] Arizona, California, Massachusetts, North Dakota, Ohio, Oregon, Utah, Washington.

[7] Nebraska achieves approximately the same result by publishing this information in the newspapers.

[8] For a recent analysis of official publicity pamphlets, see William L. Josslin's article, "Oregon Educates Its Voters," in the July, 1943, issue of the *National Municipal Review*, pp. 373-379.

[9] See p. 132.

## THE RECALL

Frequently associated with direct legislation is the recall, because these two reforms first sprang into popularity at about the same period. Both are concerned with the improvement of government, but the specific evils they seek to correct are very different. The recall is a device for making public officials continuously responsible to the electorate. The first state to adopt it was Oregon, in 1908, though it had been made a part of the Los Angeles charter five years earlier. It is now used by eleven states.[10]

The recall provisions of state constitutions vary somewhat in detail, but fundamentally they are much the same. They authorize the removal of a public official by an adverse popular vote at any time after the first few months of his term. The first step is the preparation and circulation of a petition for the officer's removal. This petition, which states the reasons—or at least the alleged reasons—why its sponors desire to have the officer recalled, must be signed by a certain percentage of the voters of the state. The required percentage ranges from ten in Kansas to thirty in North Dakota, but twenty-five is by far the most common. To secure the signatures of twenty-five per cent of the voters of a state is no easy task; it almost invariably necessitates a large expenditure of money. Therefore the recall cannot be put in operation by every disgruntled group that disapproves of the management of state affairs. When the necessary signatures have been obtained, the petition is filed with the secretary of state, who certifies that all legal requirements have been met. The question of the officer's removal from office is then placed on the ballot for the voters to decide. Usually their decision is registered at an election held for this special purpose, but if a general election is close at hand the matter may be postponed until that time.

There is no general agreement as to the proper form of the recall. In some states the two questions—whether the officer shall be removed, and who will succeed him in the event of removal—are placed side by side upon the ballot. In other states the voters merely express their opinions on the question of recall. The officer's successor, if any, is then chosen at a subsequent election, held usually within thirty days. Some state constitutions permit the officer whose removal is

---

[10] Arizona, California, Colorado, Kansas, Louisiana, Michigan, Nevada, North Dakota, Oregon, Washington, Wisconsin. The constitution of Idaho was amended in 1912 to provide for the recall, but the legislature has never taken the steps necessary to make this amendment effective.

sought to be a candidate for re-election. Under such circumstances it is quite possible for a public official to be recalled from office and at the same time re-elected to complete the remainder of his term. Even though a majority of the voters express their disapproval of him, their failure to agree upon his successor may enable his adherents to secure for him a substantial plurality over rival candidates, and thus return him triumphantly to power. In order to prevent such a farcical result, a number of states exclude the name of the involved official from the list of candidates. While this arrangement accomplishes its purpose, it offers no safeguard against another danger—the possibility that an unpopular official will be replaced by someone whom the voters desire even less.

An illustration is necessary to make the matter clear. Governor A is recalled from office because fifty-five per cent of the voters express a desire to be rid of him. The other forty-five per cent of the electors may be his stanch adherents, but they cannot vote to return him to power, because his name is excluded from the ballot. So one of the rival candidates is chosen to complete the remainder of the term. The winner's plurality may be small; he may be able to secure the support of but twenty per cent of the electorate. But twenty per cent is sufficient, *if it is larger than the vote cast for any of the other aspirants.* Seventy or even eighty per cent of the voters may be definitely opposed to the successful candidate. They may consider him far less desirable than the man whom they have just voted to remove. They have no effective means of expressing their dislike, however, unless they resort to another recall election as soon as the new governor has taken office. Although a number of forms of the recall are in operation, therefore, no one of them is entirely satisfactory. The problem is not easily solved.

**Merits and defects of the recall.** The recall has been a stormy petrel of American political life ever since its introduction four decades ago. It has been warmly defended and bitterly denounced. Actually it has not accomplished one tenth of the good claimed for it, nor has it produced one tenth of the evil so freely predicted. Its effect on the conduct of public affairs has been very slight. The most obvious merit of the recall is that it permits the immediate removal of unpopular or unfaithful public servants. Without it, a governor elected for four years would probably continue in office until the end of his term, even though he had completely lost the confidence of the people by repeated displays of gross inefficiency, blatant partisanship, or even downright dishonesty. Impeachment proceedings could be brought against him at any time, of course, but impeachment trials are inevitably slow, awkward, and uncertain. The recall, on the other hand, is direct and sure. It produces results when results count. It enables the people to rid themselves promptly of public officials whose popularity has waned.

It should not be forgotten, however, that the recall can be twisted and warped to serve partisan ends quite as readily as it can be used to secure higher standards of efficiency and honesty. It can be used to embarrass high-minded public officials in the proper performance of their duties. Sometimes it is so used. Bird and Ryan, in their careful monograph on *The Recall of Public Officers*, report the case of a state senator who was recalled because of his aggressive fight against the vice interests,[11] and of a city manager who lost his office by popular vote "because he was an outsider, because he stepped on the toes of certain more or less powerful men in Long Beach, and because the local populace was unenlightened as to the nature and requirements of the office." [12] Professor Barnett's *Operation of the Initiative, Referendum, and Recall in Oregon* repeats the same story with infinite variations. Only occasionally do the people know the real motives that prompted the circulation of a recall petition.

An argument commonly advanced in favor of the recall is that it forces public officials to consider the public welfare at all times, instead of just prior to election day. It is said that unless the threat of removal from office is ever present, many officials will disregard the desires and interests of their constituents, trusting to luck and their own facile tongues to justify their misconduct when the day of accounting arrives. But if they know that they may be recalled at any time, they will be much more likely to keep to the straight and narrow path. Their direct responsibility to the people is continuous, and not periodic. It might also be added that this continuous responsibility not only reduces the likelihood of improper partisanship or actual dishonesty, but at the same time compels all public officials to keep in close touch with the electorate. When impeachment is the only method of removal, the honest, efficient governor who happens to be more interested in the science of administration than the art of politics may neglect to keep the public sufficiently informed concerning the work of the state. Secure in the knowledge of his own in-

11 Pp. 275–279.
12 Pp. 224–226.

tegrity and ability, he may forget that the voters will not take these qualities for granted. But if he is subject at any time to the recall, he cannot afford to wait for the ultimate justification of his policies. He must take the people into his confidence, and explain the reasons for every important decision. Thus the recall possesses a definite educational value; it increases the opportunities of the voters to learn about their government.

Of course, this is purely deductive reasoning. No one knows whether the adoption of the recall has actually reduced corruption in government. No one can say with assurance that public officials have really been forced to lay greater emphasis upon the task of informing the electorate. In fact, it might be argued with equal plausibility that the recall has virtually destroyed the possibility of far-sighted planning in matters of state. In those commonwealths where it has not been adopted, a governor or other officer is free to use the methods that seem to him best suited to the solution of each problem, even though the reasons for his choice are not immediately apparent to the casual observer. He knows that he will not be required to give an accounting until election day, and that the intervening months or years will make the wisdom of his course apparent to all except the blindest partisans. But the governor who is subject to the recall is not so fortunately situated. He must consider the immediate political effect of every action. He must shift his course to meet every passing gust of public fancy. His policies must be determined largely on the basis of their momentary popularity. In other words, expediency must replace constructive statesmanship. It is easy to over-emphasize this danger; perhaps it has little foundation in fact. But it is doubtless quite as real as the danger that public officials will loot the public treasury or heedlessly pursue their haughty way merely because they do not have to fear a recall election.

A very strong argument in favor of the recall is that it leads naturally to longer terms for public officials. Students of government agree that terms of office are too short, generally speaking, and for many years they have constantly advocated longer tenure. They have urged, for example, that the governor be given a four-year term, instead of the two-year period of office that was typical of the large majority of states until quite recently. But the people have been slow to sanction longer terms. They have been loath to sacrifice their opportunity of calling public officials to account at frequent intervals. They have not forgotten the old adage that unchecked power soon degenerates into tyranny. The introduction of the recall, however, has undoubtedly lessened the popular opposition to longer terms. The voters have become more willing to trust their governors and other representatives with power for long periods, because they can now remove them from office at any time without waiting until some far distant regular election day.

In all fairness, however, it should be pointed out that the recall, though it leads naturally to longer terms, at the same time destroys their chief advantage. Longer tenure is desirable because it gives officeholders a fair chance to become familiar with their work and demonstrate their ability before they are forced to campaign for re-election. For a reasonable period they are placed in authority, with the understanding that at some definite time in the future they must accept full responsibility for the results of their work. But the recall robs them of any reasonable opportunity to prove the merit of their plans, free from popular interference. They must be prepared to undergo the ordeal of trial by ballot *at any time*, on the assumption that democracy is thus better served.

The original proponents of the recall advocated its adoption, in part, on the ground that it would be a weapon of last resort, to be used only in cases of extreme urgency. It would be a safety valve, they said, and not merely another fly-wheel added to the already complicated machinery of government. For the most part this prediction has proved correct. Only one governor,[13] and a mere handful of other state officers, have ever been recalled from office. Even in local elections the recall has been used sparingly. While it has "become a part of the established political technique" in some jurisdictions,[14] such instances are not typical.

One of the objections commonly raised by the foes of the recall is that it places an added burden on the voter. The average citizen already has more political obligations than he cares to assume. He is asked to vote at national, state, and local elections; to choose among hundreds of candidates for scores of offices; to pass upon the merits of proposed bond issues, constitutional amendments, and perhaps ordinary legislation as well. At best he performs these several tasks indifferently, and quite frequently he neglects them altogether. An election for state officers seldom attracts more than half of the elector-

---

[13] Governor Frazier of North Dakota, in 1921. Subsequently the people of the state elected him to the United States Senate.
[14] Bird and Ryan, *op. cit.*, p. 259.

ate to the polls. Therefore it would seem desirable to reduce the number of elections instead of increasing them. In this respect, at least, the recall is a step in the wrong direction. It imposes additional responsibilities. This objection is not serious, however, because recall elections are so infrequent.

Much more to the point is the contention that the recall is an unsound remedy for the political ill it seeks to cure. If the public invariably chose virtuous, efficient men for public office, recall elections would never be necessary. But everyone recognizes that some of the men chosen to public office are neither virtuous nor efficient. The public has erred; its judgment has been faulty. And in order to correct these mistakes of the people, the friends of the recall propose that the people be permitted to try again. If they guessed wrong the first time, perhaps they will guess right on the second or third attempt! To suggest more democracy as a means of correcting the defects of democracy is like prescribing more whisky for the drunkard or gold for the spendthrift.

As applied to appointive officials, the folly of the recall is especially obvious. The men and women who hold important appointive positions in the state administrative service are, for the most part, technical experts. The public does not understand the details of their work and cannot intelligently pass upon their qualifications. That is why their offices have been made appointive instead of elective. But if the electorate is incapable of determining the qualifications of these officers at the time of their selection, how can it hope to exercise greater discrimination when the question of removal is raised? The proper remedy for proved corruption or inefficiency on the part of an appointed officer is dismissal by the appointing authority. Recognizing this fact, three of the states [15] that have adopted the recall apply it only to elective officers. The other eight make no such distinction.

The recall presents special problems when applied to members of the judiciary; these problems are considered in a later chapter.[16] It might be well to add at this point, however, that only three [17] of the eleven states using the recall exempt judges from its operation.

### SELECTED REFERENCES

Barnett, J. D., *The Operation of the Initiative, Referendum, and Recall in Oregon*, 1915.

[15] Arizona, California, Colorado.
[16] See pp. 237–239.
[17] Louisiana, Michigan, Washington.

Bird, F. L., and Ryan, F. M., *The Recall of Public Officers; A Study of the Operation of the Recall in California,* 1930.

Crouch, Winston W., *The Initiative and Referendum in California,* rev. ed., Los Angeles, 1943.

Hall, Arnold B., *Popular Government,* 1921.

King, Judson, *The American Voter as Lawmaker,* Washington, D.C., 1923.

———, *The Initiative and Referendum Elections of 1926,* Bulletin No. 107 of National Popular Government League, Washington, D.C., 1927.

Oberholtzer, E. P., *The Referendum in America,* 1912.

Pollock, J. K., *Direct Government in Michigan,* Ann Arbor, 1940.

———, *The Initiative and Referendum in Michigan,* Ann Arbor, 1940.

Zeitlin, J. V. P., *Initiative and Referendum; A Bibliography,* Los Angeles, 1940.

———

Commonwealth Club of California, "Direct Legislation," *Transactions,* XXV, 409–450, March, 1931.

Cottrell, E. A., "Direct Legislation in California," *Public Opinion Quarterly,* III, No. 1, 30–46, January, 1939.

Crouch, Winston W., "The Constitutional Initiative in Operation," *American Political Science Review,* XXXIII, No. 4, 634–645, August, 1939.

———, "The Initiative and Referendum in Cities," *American Political Science Review,* XXXVII, No. 3, 491–504, June, 1943.

Ewing, Cortez A. M., "Sufficiency Certification of Initiative Signatures in Oklahoma," *American Political Science Review,* XXXI, No. 1, 65–70, February, 1937.

Radin, Max, "Popular Legislation in California," *Minnesota Law Review,* XXIII, No. 4, 559–584, April, 1939.

Schumacher, W., "Thirty Years of People's Rule in Oregon; An Analysis," *Political Science Quarterly,* XLVII, No. 2, 242–258, June, 1932.

Selig, John M., "San Francisco Voters Prove Sound 'Lawmakers,'" *National Municipal Review,* XXXII, No. 9, 486–492, October, 1943.

Warner, Sam B., "Criminal Responsibility for Statements in Recall Charges," *National Municipal Review,* XV, No. 2, 97–104, February, 1926.

EVERY state has a legislature, which is almost invariably composed of two houses. During the early years of American independence three states experimented with single-chambered legislatures; but Georgia abandoned the unicameral plan in 1789, after using it for a little more than a decade, and Pennsylvania followed its example the following year. Vermont retained its unicameral legislature for nearly half a century, finally discarding it in 1836. The bicameral principle was not again successfully challenged until 1934, when Nebraska approved a constitutional amendment creating a one-house legislature.

The nomenclature of the forty-eight legislative bodies varies somewhat from state to state. *Legislature* is the term most commonly used, but *general assembly* has been adopted by nineteen states. Three states [1] prefer *legislative assembly*, while Massachusetts and New Hampshire retain from colonial days the name *general court*. The upper house is invariably called the *senate*. Although the lower house is generally known as the *house of representatives*, there are a number of exceptions. Three states [2] use instead *house of delegates*; four prefer *assembly*; [3] and one—New Jersey—calls the lower chamber the *general assembly*, disregarding the fact that nearly half the states of the Union reserve this name for the entire legislative body. Nebraska's one-house legislature is officially known as the *senate*. These differences in terminology do no serious harm, but at times they produce unfortunate confusion.

### SIZE OF LEGISLATURES

Wide differences are found in the size of the state legislatures. The senate varies from a membership of seventeen in Delaware and Nevada to sixty-seven in Minnesota; the lower house has an even greater range —from thirty-five in Delaware to four hundred and forty-three in New Hampshire. The average membership is slightly less than forty for the senate, and about one hundred and twenty for the house of

[1] Montana, North Dakota, and Oregon.
[2] Maryland, Virginia, and West Virginia.
[3] California, Nevada, New York, and Wisconsin.

145

representatives.    Most state senates, therefore, are small enough to be
genuine deliberative bodies.    In a group of forty or forty-five persons
it is possible for everyone to participate in debate and take a reasonably
active part in shaping group policies.    But it can scarcely be said that
the lower houses of the state legislatures are true deliberative bodies.
Most of them are entirely too large to permit full expression of opinion by the rank and file of the members, and for that reason they
possess some of the characteristics of a mob.    Little cliques of seasoned
veterans find it relatively easy to secure control and bend the majority
to their will.    As pointed out in *The Federalist* [4] nearly a century and
a half ago: "In all legislative assemblies the greater the number composing them may be, the fewer will be the men who will in fact direct
their proceedings.    In the next place, the larger the number, the
greater will be the proportion of members of limited information and
of weak capacities. . . . The people can never err more than in sup-
posing that by multiplying their representatives beyond a certain
limit, they strengthen the barrier against the government of a few.
Experience will forever admonish them that, on the contrary, after
securing a sufficient number for the purposes of safety, of local information, and of diffusive sympathy with the whole society, they will
counteract their own views by every addition to the representatives."

**Argument for large legislative bodies.**    It is sometimes argued that
large legislative bodies are necessary to secure adequate representation of every shade of public opinion.    When the membership of a
deliberative assembly is restricted to forty or fifty, it is said, many a
small group finds itself without a spokesman.    Its views may deserve
serious consideration, yet they will probably never come to the attention of those who control the destinies of the state.    But if the
legislature contains two or three hundred members, or even more,
every group and every locality is reasonably certain to have a share in
the determination of public policies.    Local conditions will be better
understood, and local opinion will be more effective.    The legislator
who represents but a few constituents doubtless knows them all.    He
is familiar with their desires and their needs, and therefore can speak
with assurance when he presents their viewpoint.    But the legislator
who must act as spokesman for thousands or even hundreds of thousands of persons cannot truly be said to *represent* them.    He may
speak in their name, yet he can do no more than reflect his own views,
or the beliefs of those with whom he comes in close contact.    Within

[4] No. 58.    It is uncertain whether Hamilton or Madison penned these lines.

his constituency many conflicting opinions and interests will inevitably exist; no one man can adequately represent them all.

FALLACIES IN ARGUMENT. So runs the argument. It is plausible, but not entirely convincing, for no one has yet satisfactorily explained why one representative is needed in a state legislature for every three or four thousand people, whereas a member of the federal House of Representatives speaks for nearly three hundred thousand. If great cities like Detroit, Cleveland, Boston, Baltimore, and Los Angeles—all having populations in excess of three-quarters of a million—can conduct their public affairs with councils of twenty-five or less, why do states with even smaller populations require legislative assemblies four or five times as large? [5]

The truth of the matter is that nearly every decision as to the size of a legislative body is purely arbitrary. Population and area are not the determining factors; there is no proportionate relationship between the size of a state or the number of its inhabitants and the size of its legislature. It is merely by chance that Delaware and Nevada, states with small populations, have the two smallest bicameral legislatures; for New Hampshire and Vermont, only slightly more populous, have two of the largest. The argument that a minimum of one hundred or two hundred members is necessary to secure adequate representation does not deserve serious consideration. Should the membership of the assembly be increased to eight hundred or even one thousand, there would still be conflicting opinions and interests within every district. No representative could hope to express the views of *all* his constituents on *all* subjects. And anything that might be gained in securing a more representative viewpoint would be lost in efficiency. The time of the legislature would be wasted, and the conduct of the public business made immeasurably more difficult. Judge Story, who presided over the Massachusetts house of representatives at a time when it had a very large membership, expressed the belief that "in no proper sense could it be called a deliberative assembly. From the excess of numbers deliberation became almost impossible; and but for the good sense and discretion of those who usually led in the debates, it would have been impracticable to have transacted business with anything like accuracy or safety." [6]

It should not be forgotten that undue emphasis upon the representa-

---

[5] There are thirteen states whose populations are below the 750,000 mark. The average membership in the lower house of their legislatures is 106.

[6] *Massachusetts Convention of 1820*, p. 293, quoted in Robert Luce's *Legislative Assemblies*, p. 89. Chapter V of Mr. Luce's book contains an admirable discussion of the size of legislative bodies.

tion of local interests is likely to lead to neglect of matters of general concern. There is real danger that the man elected from a small district will be a small man—small in mentality and lacking in vision. Because he has long focused his attention upon his local community and its needs, he may be unable to see the broader horizon of state affairs. Every proposal for the betterment of the state may be measured in terms of its effect upon local conditions. The general welfare may be sacrificed for lack of competent defenders, and the legislative process may degenerate into a game of bargaining—each representative seeking to secure as many special privileges as possible for his own locality. These dangers are not theoretical; they menace every legislative assembly. And the larger the legislature becomes, the greater is the likelihood that their mischievous influence will be felt.

### THE MEMBERS OF THE LEGISLATURES

**Terms.** In the early days of statehood, when the memory of English tyranny was still fresh, annual elections were considered essential, in order that government might be kept close to the people, and that elected representatives might be constrained at frequent intervals to remember the source of their authority. The first constitutions of the thirteen original states provided, with only one exception,[7] that members of the lower house should hold office for but a single year, and several of them specified that state senators should also be elected annually. Belief in frequent elections was so strong that the principle was written into several bills of rights and has not since been deleted from some of them. Thus the present constitution of Maryland declares that "elections ought to be free and frequent."[8] New Jersey still retains annual elections for members of the lower house. At the other extreme, four states [9] provide four-year terms. The other forty-three states elect the members of the house of representatives or house of delegates—whatever it may be called—for two-year periods. Terms of four years for state senators are now found in thirty-one states, while virtually all the others fix the terms of senators at two years.[10] The old notion that annual elections are a necessary part of free government has practically disappeared.[11]

---

7 See p. 17.

8 Declaration of Rights, Art. 7.

9 Alabama, Louisiana, Maryland, and Mississippi.

10 New Jersey, with its three-year term for state senators, is the only exception.

11 On pp. 150 and 151 is a chart giving detailed information concerning legislators' terms and salaries.

Since state senators are commonly chosen for longer terms than the members of the lower house, and therefore are better able to familiarize themselves with the process of government, it is sometimes thought desirable to insure a measure of continuity in their service of the state. This is done by providing that only one-fourth or one-half of the entire membership of the senate shall retire at each election, instead of permitting the terms of all the members to expire simultaneously. The plan has been adopted by nearly half of the states. While it acts as a check upon capricious and ill-considered reversal of public policy, it has the serious disadvantage of retaining in office men who may have lost the confidence of the people. Thus a newly elected house of representatives, with a fresh mandate from the voters, may find difficulty in carrying out its program because of the opposition of senators whose party has been severely defeated at the polls.

**Qualifications.** Every state constitution specifies that members of the legislature must be residents of the state, and of the district from which they have been chosen. The minimum period of state residence ranges from one to seven years; one to two years meets the district residence requirement. American citizenship is also required —sometimes in explicit terms, but more commonly by implication. Age limits vary from twenty-one to thirty years for members of both houses. Twenty-one years is the most common minimum for members of the lower house, however, and twenty-five years for members of the senate. Eight states exclude atheists.[12] Persons convicted of crime are commonly denied the right to hold any public office.

**Salaries.** The salaries of state legislators are ridiculously small. Twenty-five states pay by the day, the compensation for each day of the legislative session ranging from three dollars in Kansas and Michigan to ten dollars in a considerable number of generous states. Five or six dollars is most common. In a few commonwealths even this small salary automatically diminishes, or stops altogether, after sixty or seventy days of the legislative session.[13] Seventeen states provide a fixed salary for the entire two-year period that normally represents a single session of the legislature. The other six pay by the year, but in two of them the legislature meets annually. Usually the compensation is one thousand dollars or less for the biennium; New Hampshire fixes the pay of its legislators at two hundred dollars, and Connecticut

[12] Arkansas, Maryland, Mississippi, North Carolina, Pennsylvania, South Carolina, Tennessee, Texas.
[13] See p. 166.

## LEGISLATIVE TERMS, SALARIES AND SESSIONS

Based on information in the 1943–1944 edition of the *Book of the States*.

| State | Length of Term — Senate | Length of Term — House | Salary Fixed by Statute | Sessions — Time | Sessions — Limit | Salary — Regular Session * | Salary — Special Session | Allowances (Per mile for one round-trip per session—unless otherwise stated.) |
|---|---|---|---|---|---|---|---|---|
| Alabama | 4 | 4 | | Bien. | 60 days | $10 per day | $10 per day | 10c |
| Arizona | 2 | 2 | x | Bien. | 60 days | $8—60 day limit | $8—20 day limit | 20c one way |
| Arkansas | 4 | 2 | | Bien. | 60 days | $1,000 for 2 years | $6 per day | 5c |
| California | 4 | 2 | | Bien. | None† | $2,400 for 2 years | ..... | Mileage |
| Colorado | 4 | 2 | | Bien. | None | $1,000 for 2 years | ..... | Traveling expenses |
| Connecticut | 2 | 2 | | Bien. | 5 months | $300 for 2 years | ..... | 10c |
| Delaware | 4 | 2 | | Bien. | 60 days | $10 per day | $10—30 day limit | 10c |
| Florida | 4 | 2 | | Bien. | 60 days | $6 per day | $6 per day | 10c |
| Georgia | 2 | 2 | | Bien. | 60 days | $7 per day | $7 per day | 10c |
| Idaho | 2 | 2 | | Bien. | 60 days | $5 per day | $5—20 day limit | 10c |
| Illinois | 4 | 2 | | Bien. | None | $5,000 for 2 years | ..... | 5c. $50 for stationery |
| Indiana | 4 | 2 | | Bien. | 61 days | $10 per day | $10—40 day limit | 20c one round trip |
| Iowa | 4 | 2 | x | Bien. | None | $1,000 for 2 years | $10 per day | 5c |
| Kansas | 4 | 2 | | Bien. | None | $3 per day | $3—30 day limit | 15c |
| Kentucky | 4 | 2 | x | Bien. | 60 days | $10 per day | $10 per day | 15c |
| Louisiana | 4 | 4 | | Bien. | 60 days | $10 per day | $10 per day | 10c per trip—not over 3 trips |
| Maine | 2 | 2 | x | Bien. | None | $600 for 2 years | $5 per day | $2 for ten miles |
| Maryland | 4 | 4 | | Bien. | 90 days | $1,000 per year | $5—90 day limit | 20c limit. $25 for stationery |
| Massachusetts | 2 | 2 | x | Bien. | None | $2,500 per year | Determined at session | $4.20 per mile one way |
| Michigan | 2 | 2 | | Bien. | None | $3 per day for term of office | ..... | 10c |
| Minnesota | 4 | 2 | x | Bien. | 90 days | $1,000 for 2 years | Mileage only | 10c, limit $200 |
| Mississippi | 4 | 2 | x | Bien. | None | $1,000 for 2 years | $10 per day | 10c |
| Missouri | 4 | 2 | | Bien. | None | $125 per month | $125 per month | Traveling expenses. $30 for postage |

| | | | | | | | | Traveling expenses |
|---|---|---|---|---|---|---|---|---|
| Montana | 4 | x | 2 | Bien. | 60 days | $10 per day | $10—60 day limit | 7c |
| Nebraska | 2 | : | 2 | Bien. | None | $1,744 for 2 years | None | Traveling expenses |
| Nevada | 2 | x | 2 | Bien. | 60 days | $10 per day | $10—20 day limit | 10c |
| New Hampshire | 2 | : | 2 | Bien. | None | $200 for 2 years | $3—15 day limit | 10c a mile |
| New Jersey | 3 | : | 1 | Ann'l | None | $500 per year | | Free railway transportation |
| New Mexico | 4 | : | 2 | Bien. | 60 days | $5 per day | $5—30 day limit | 10c |
| New York | 2 | : | 2 | Ann'l | None | $2,500 per year | | $1 for 10 miles |
| North Carolina | 2 | : | 2 | Bien. | None | $600 per year | $8—20 day limit | 10c |
| North Dakota | 4 | : | 2 | Bien. | 60 days | $5 per day | $5 per day | 10c |
| Ohio | 2 | x | 2 | Bien. | None | $2,000 per year | | Round-trip fare weekly |
| Oklahoma | 4 | : | 2 | Bien. | None | $6 per day; $2 after 60 days | $6 per day | 10c |
| Oregon | 2 | : | 2 | Bien. | 50 days | $8 per day | $8—20 day limit | 10c |
| Pennsylvania | 4 | x | 2 | Bien. | None | $3,000 for 2 years | $500 | 5c. $150 for postage—$50 in special session |
| Rhode Island | 2 | : | 2 | Ann'l | 60 days | $5 per day | | 8c |
| South Carolina | 4 | : | 2 | Ann'l | None | $10—40 day limit | $10—40 day limit | 5c. $5 for postage |
| South Dakota | 2 | : | 2 | Bien. | 60 days | $5 per day | $5 per day | 5c. $200 for living expenses |
| Tennessee | 2 | : | 2 | Bien. | None | $4 per day | $4—20 day limit | $4 for 25 miles |
| Texas | 4 | : | 2 | Bien. | None † | $10 per day. $5 after 120 days | $10 per day | $2.50 for 25 miles |
| Utah | 4 | : | 2 | Bien. | 60 days | $4 per day | $4—30 day limit | 10c |
| Vermont | 2 | x | 2 | Bien. | None | $400 for 2 years | $6 per day | 20c |
| Virginia | 4 | x | 2 | Bien. | 60 days ‡ | $720 for 2 years | $360—30 day limit | 10c |
| Washington | 4 | : | 2 | Bien. | 60 days | $5 per day | $5—60 day limit | 10c |
| West Virginia | 4 | : | 2 | Bien. | 60 days ‡ | $500 per year | | 10c |
| Wisconsin | 4 | x | 2 | Bien. | None | $2,400 for 2 years | | 10c |
| Wyoming | 4 | x | 2 | Bien. | 40 days | $12 per day | $10 per day | 8c |

* In states paying on a yearly or biennial basis, the salary *per year* is shown if annual sessions are held—the salary for *two years* is shown if sessions are biennial.

† Divided session—first part limited to 30 days.

‡ Session may be extended: In West Virginia by 2/3 vote in each house, in Virginia by 3/5 vote in each house for not more than 30 more days.

gives only three hundred. At the other end of the scale, however, are a few states whose legislators' salaries seem generous by comparison—California and Wisconsin, with twenty-four hundred dollars for the two-year period; Massachusetts, with twenty-five hundred; Pennsylvania, with three thousand; and Illinois and New York, with five thousand.[14] In addition to their salaries, members of the legislature are almost invariably given allowances for traveling expenses. The travel contemplated in this connection is between the legislators' homes and the state capital. Ten cents per mile is most common. Six states [15] also make modest provision for stationery, postage, or other supplies. South Dakota allows two hundred dollars for living expenses. But none of these extras suffices to raise the total compensation to the level of an adequate salary. It is not at all surprising that the most generous provisions are made in those states that leave the matter of compensation for the legislature itself to determine, instead of specifying in the constitution what the salaries of legislators shall be.

VIEWPOINTS REGARDING COMPENSATION. There have always been two points of view concerning salaries for members of legislative assemblies. One of these is the so-called "country squire" theory—the viewpoint that had become traditional in England by 1700, and was not seriously questioned by that country until the present century.[16] According to this doctrine, the privilege of public service is its own reward; therefore no additional compensation is needed. Membership in the legislature is a signal honor—a distinction that many may covet, but few may hope to win. Salary is not necessary to attract competent candidates; many men of wealth and leisure will always be glad to contribute their talents to the public service. In fact, the payment of salaries to legislators is positively destructive of the highest standards of statesmanship, for it attracts men of mediocre ability, lacking in public spirit, whose sole purpose is to use public office for their private gain. "As every freeman to preserve his independence (if without a sufficient estate) ought to have some profession, calling, trade or farm, whereby he may honestly subsist, there can be no necessity for, nor use in establishing offices of profit, the usual effects

14 New York, however, splits this sum into annual payments of twenty-five hundred dollars, since the legislature meets yearly in regular session.

15 Delaware, Illinois, Maryland, Missouri, Nevada, Pennsylvania.

16 In 1911 the members of the House of Commons received pay for their services for the first time in modern English history. Members of city councils still serve without regular salaries.

of which are dependence and servility unbecoming freemen, in the possessors and expectants; faction, contention, corruption, and disorder among the people." [17]

The obvious answer to this argument is that public office carrying with it no compensation is closed, in most cases, to all except the well-to-do. The man of average wealth, however public spirited he may be, cannot afford to neglect his private affairs in order to serve the state. He must of necessity earn his living. If the public is unwilling to pay for service rendered, then he must leave the conduct of public affairs to the favored few whose private fortunes permit them to serve without compensation—the "country squires," the landed gentry, the successful manufacturers, merchants, professional men. To withhold salaries from members of the legislature is to impose the requirement that legislators shall be wealthy.

The other theory concerning legislators' salaries might well be called the "fair wage" doctrine. It rests upon the assumption that the legislator is worthy of his hire. Those who accept this point of view contend that the only way to secure efficient service, in public or private life, is to pay for it. In the words of one writer: "We must rely for the most part on men who cannot afford to sacrifice their own interests to those of the public, or at least cannot afford to do so for a succession of years, as is necessary if the state is to reap the advantage of their previous legislative experience. The salary of the legislator should therefore be a reasonable return for the sacrifice which an ordinary citizen would be called upon to make." [18]

DRAWBACK IN SMALL SALARIES. Between these two conflicting viewpoints the people of the United States, generally speaking, have steered a middle course. They have rejected the "country squire" theory and have provided compensation for the members of their legislative assemblies. On the other hand, they have been unwilling to pay a fair wage. The miserable stipends that they have seen fit to offer have served chiefly to attract miserable men, to whom the prospect of even a small wage, coupled with opportunities for illicit gain, has proved alluring. Most honest men in moderate circumstances have felt that they could not afford the financial sacrifices entailed by service in the legislature, and most honest men of independent means have hesitated to brave the unpleasantness of a political campaign

[17] This quotation is from Pennsylvania's constitution of 1776. The document further declared, however, that "if any man is called into public service, to the prejudice of his private affairs, he has a right to a reasonable compensation."

[18] Jones, Chester Lloyd, *Statute Lawmaking*, p. 8.

in competition with second-rate politicians interested solely in private profit. Mediocre salaries have begotten mediocre legislators; no other result could reasonably have been expected. The payment of adequate compensation would not in itself guarantee a higher standard of legislative efficiency, but it would remove one of the major causes of inefficiency.

**Selection of legislators.** The members of both houses of the legislature are popularly elected in every state. A state is divided into senatorial and assembly districts, and from each district one or more members are chosen. Many years ago—even before the end of the eighteenth century—it was discovered that districts could be laid out in such a way as to strengthen the influence of the dominant political party. The plan was quite simple—to combine as many minority party voters as possible into a comparatively few districts, where they would do the least harm. Those districts, of course, would return landslide votes for minority party candidates at every election, but the other districts of the state would furnish comfortable majorities for the dominant party unless large numbers of voters deserted their normal party allegiance.

GERRYMANDERING. When this scheme became general practice, the rearrangement of districts degenerated into a sort of jig-saw puzzle, with districts of every conceivable shape resulting from the attempt to concentrate, and thus waste, the strength of the minority. Not until 1812, after it had long been in vogue, did the custom receive a name. In that year the General Court (legislature) of Massachusetts passed an act revising the boundaries of state senatorial districts in such a way as to insure the retention of power by the Republicans. Elbridge Gerry, then governor of the state, was opposed to the measure and signed it with reluctance. He seems to have been blamed for the Republican trickery, however, for when a map showing the two distorted districts of Essex County was jokingly described as a salamander, someone instantly remarked: "Better call it a Gerrymander." [19] The name stuck. Today the practice is accepted as an almost inevitable incident of partisan politics, and everywhere it is known as *gerrymandering*. Attempts have been made from time to time to put a stop to it, but without much success. A number of state constitutions contain provisions designed to insure the creation of districts composed of "compact and contiguous" territory, and in some in-

[19] Luce, Robert, *Legislative Principles*, pp. 397–398.

stances the courts have invalidated the legislature's redistricting.[20] Yet abundant examples of gerrymandering are still to be found— "shoestring," "saddle-bag," "belt-line," "dumbbell" districts, into which large numbers of opposition voters have been crowded.

THE PLURALITY PRINCIPLE. The plurality principle is generally accepted in choosing members of the legislature—that is, the candidate receiving the greatest number of votes is declared elected, even though the number of ballots cast for him may be smaller than the combined vote for his opponents. The injustice of this rule, which frequently leaves a majority of the voters without representatives of their choosing, is freely admitted; but most people sanction its use on the ground that it is a practicable, if not entirely fair, method of selecting candidates. To require a majority vote for election would be to make the selection of any candidate impossible in most cases, unless the number of contestants were arbitrarily limited to two.

PREFERENTIAL VOTING. It has been suggested that genuine majority choice might be obtained by some form of preferential voting, such as the Bucklin [21] plan which has been used by Grand Junction, Colorado, since 1909. Under this scheme the voter is permitted to express one first choice, one second choice, and as many third choices as he sees fit. If no candidate has a majority of first choices, first and second choices are added together. The election then goes to the man receiving a majority of first and second choices combined. If necessary to secure a majority, third choices are also added. It sometimes happens that even the addition of third choices does not establish a clear majority for any one candidate, so that the person with the largest plurality must be declared elected. The most serious objection to the Bucklin plan, however, is not its occasional failure to establish a *nominal* majority, but its habitual failure to create a genuine majority. For it produces results by giving second and third choices, when added, exactly the same weight as first preferences. Obviously this is not in accord with the wishes of the voter, whose first choice indicates that he prefers one candidate to all the others. Other forms of preferential voting vary the Bucklin formula somewhat by giving greater weight to the first choice than to second and third choices. The Ware plan, which is based on an entirely different principle, provides for the successive elimination of the lowest candidates and the

20 See, for example, the case of State *v.* Cunningham, 81 Wis. 440 (1892).
21 Named for James W. Bucklin, who devised the scheme.

transfer of their ballots to second or subsequent choices. But no system of preferential voting can create a majority that does not exist in fact.

INADEQUATE MINORITY REPRESENTATION. Probably the most serious objection to the ordinary method of selecting legislators is that political parties and organized groups of voters seldom receive representation in exact proportion to their numerical strength. The minority may receive more than its share of the total number of representatives; much more commonly it receives far less than its share. It all depends on the distribution of party strength. In a normally Republican state, for example, forty per cent of all the voters may be Democrats, yet so evenly distributed that they constitute a minority of the voters in every assembly district. Under such circumstances they will be unable to elect even one of their candidates, and the entire legislature will be composed of Republicans. Such an extreme state of affairs is unusual, of course, but it commonly happens that the minority party, with forty or even forty-five per cent of the state's voting strength, secures control of but fifteen or twenty per cent of the legislature's membership.

THREE PROPOSED ELECTORAL REMEDIES. A number of remedies for inadequate minority representation have been proposed—limited voting, cumulative voting, proportional representation. Limited voting is so called because each person's vote is limited to a number of candidates less than the full number to be elected. If three members of the legislature are to be elected from a given district, for example, each voter may express his preference for but two candidates. The obvious result of this arrangement is to give two seats to the majority party, and one to the strongest minority group. Minority representation is thus assured, but without any reference to actual party strength. It is a crude device and has never been tried for members of a state legislature, though it has long been used in Pennsylvania to select certain state and county officials.

For nearly three-quarters of a century Illinois has made use of cumulative voting. Three members of the lower house of the state legislature are chosen from each assembly district. Each elector has three votes, and may distribute them as he sees fit. He may give one to each of his three favorite candidates, or he may concentrate two or even three votes on one man. The result of this plan has been to give the two major parties legislative representation in very close proportion to their numerical strength as indicated at the polls. Less powerful minority groups, however, have seldom been able to elect a single representative to the legislature. The scheme has strengthened party lines and has necessitated highly developed party organizations.[22] Three states [23] have sought to copy the Illinois plan of cumulative voting, but have been restrained from doing so by action of the voters or the courts. The Illinois constitutional convention of 1920–1922 recommended the abolition of the system. The constitution that this convention submitted to the voters, however, met defeat at the polls, so cumulative voting remains.

The plan that seems most likely to secure representation of every shade of public opinion in direct proportion to its numerical strength is known as proportional representation. There are two forms of this system, but the one that has made the stronger appeal to English-speaking people is the Hare plan, named for the Englishman who perfected it. Under the Hare system the voter is told to express as many choices as he pleases. In fact, the number of his preferences is limited only by the number of candidates. He places a figure 1 on the ballot opposite the name of his first choice, a 2 opposite his second, a 3 opposite his third, and so on until he has no additional preferences to express. When the ballots are first counted, only first choices are considered. As the count proceeds, however, it soon becomes clear that some candidates have more than the number of votes necessary for election, while others are hopelessly out of the running. Therefore, the surplus votes cast for those elected on the first count, plus all the votes for those who have been declared defeated, are transferred to the second choices—or, if these aspirants have already been eliminated or elected, to the third choices. So the transferring process continues, until every vote is made effective for some candidate. The Hare plan is sometimes described as the system with the single transferable vote. No matter how many preferences a person may express, he has only one vote, and it is transferred from candidate to candidate until it actually helps to elect someone.

Although this thumb-nail description gives only a hazy notion of how the Hare system actually works, a more detailed analysis would be out of place in the present volume because the plan has never been

[22] For a careful analysis of the results of cumulative voting in Illinois, see Blaine F. Moore's *The History of Cumulative Voting and Minority Representation in Illinois, 1870–1908.* See also No. 8 of the *Constitutional Convention Bulletins* of Illinois, 1920.

[23] Michigan, Ohio, South Dakota.

adopted by any state of the Union.[24]   It is now used in eleven American cities,[25] however, and has found considerable favor in Eire, Australia, New Zealand, and Canada.   There seems to be little doubt that it has accomplished its purpose of securing representation for every group in almost exact proportion to voting strength.   Yet its adoption by American states will doubtless come slowly, if at all, for a number of court decisions indicate that constitutional amendments would be necessary in some commonwealths to permit its use.[26]   Another form of proportional representation, known as the "list" system because it is based on lists of candidates prepared by the political parties, has been adopted, with several variations, by many countries of Continental Europe.   Its excessive emphasis on party regularity makes is seem less desirable than the Hare plan for American use.

CONTESTED ELECTIONS.   State constitutions commonly provide, in language that varies but slightly from state to state, that "each House shall be the judge of the qualifications and elections of its members." Therefore every contested election of a member of the legislature is passed upon by the house concerned.   Usually there is a committee on contested elections, and a great show is made of judicial impartiality.   Actually, however, party feeling runs strong, and contests are almost invariably decided on a partisan basis unless the majority party is so strong that it can afford to be impartial.   It is said that Thaddeus Stevens, while serving as a member of a committee on elections, came to the committee room one day during the course of a hearing and asked one of his colleagues to tell him the point of the case.   "There is not much point to it," was the answer.   "They are both damned scoundrels."   "Well," said Stevens, "which is the Republican damned scoundrel?   I want to go for the Republican damned scoundrel."  [27]

[24] By far the most thorough description of the Hare system may be found in Hoag and Hallett's *Proportional Representation*. See also Geo. H. Hallett, Jr.'s *Proportional Representation: The Key to Democracy*. The value of proportional representation is challenged vigorously by Prof. F. A. Hermens in his *Democracy or Anarchy?*

[25] Yonkers and Long Beach, New York, and New York City; Cambridge and Lowell, Massachusetts; Cincinnati, Toledo and Hamilton, Ohio; Coos Bay, Oregon; Wheeling, West Virginia; and Boulder, Colorado.

[26] Wattles *ex rel*. Johnson *v*. Upjohn, 179 N.W. 335 (1920); and People *ex rel*. Devine *v*. Elkus, 211 Pac. 34 (1922).   But see also Reutner *v*. Cleveland, 141 N.E. 27 (1923); and Hile *v*. Cleveland, 141 N.E. 27 (1923).   The favorable decision of New York's highest court in Johnson *v*. City of New York, 9 N.E. (2nd) 30 (1937), was followed two years later by an unfavorable advisory opinion from the supreme court of Rhode Island, and some time afterward (1941) by a Massachusetts decision upholding proportional representation in that state.   See Moore *v*. Election Commissioners of Cambridge, 25 N.E. (2nd) 222 (1941).

[27] Luce, Robert, *Legislative Assemblies*, pp. 202-203.

It has been suggested many times that election contests be transferred to the courts for final settlement, but this proposal has received scant consideration.

## UNDERREPRESENTATION OF CITIES IN LEGISLATURES

Throughout the entire course of American history there have been two conflicting viewpoints concerning the proper basis of representation in the state legislature. Some persons have held that representation should be strictly on the basis of population. One man—one vote; to many this proposition has seemed almost axiomatic. Others have urged, however, that *territory* as well as *population* should be considered in determining representation, and this opinion has generally prevailed. Today there are thirty states whose constitutions definitely recognize territory as a basis of representation. Sometimes this is done by specifying that the senate shall be composed of one representative from each county, regardless of population, as in New Jersey. Sometimes it is accomplished by providing that every county or every town shall have *at least* one representative in the senate or the house, or both. Pennsylvania follows this plan. The constitution of New York declares that "No county shall have more than one-third of all the senators," [28] and a number of other state constitutions contain similar provisions. Still other devices, some of them highly complex, are used for the purpose of preventing representation strictly according to population.

These clauses serve to neutralize the political effect of city growth, and enable the rural districts to retain control of state legislatures despite the decline of rural population. New York City's representatives, for example, are permanently in the minority in the state legislature, though the metropolis contains more than half of the state's population. Chicago, Philadelphia, Cleveland, Baltimore, St. Louis, and most of the other large cities of the United States are the victims of similar discriminations. In the New Jersey senate it is possible for eleven rural counties, with a population not greatly in excess of half a million, to outvote ten urban counties whose total population almost reaches the three-million mark. One rural vote in Illinois carries as much weight as three Chicago votes.

The underrepresentation of Chicago in the state legislature has not been accomplished by constitutional restrictions, however, but by failure to obey a clear mandate of the fundamental law. Representa-

[28] Art. III, Sec. 4.

tion is fixed on a straight population basis, and the legislature is directed to reapportion the state every ten years, following the federal census.　No reapportionment has been made since 1901.　During the intervening decades Chicago's population has more than doubled, while the remainder of the state has grown only thirty per cent.　But Chicago's representation in the state legislature is still fixed in accordance with the census figures of 1900.　Although the constitution specifies in no uncertain terms that the legislature *must* reapportion the state every ten years, there seems to be no way of enforcing this command.　The supreme court of the state has declared that while the legislature's duty is "clear and unmistakable," it is a political obligation, and does not fall within the scope of judicial review.[29] Missouri has also failed to make a reapportionment since 1901.　For nearly thirty years Seattle's representation in the state legislature was based on 1900 census figures, but reapportionment was finally forced upon an unwilling legislature by a popularly initiated law.　A very few states, distrustful of their legislative bodies, vest the power of reapportionment in the governor or other officials, but there seems to be no general trend in this direction.

Whatever the merits of territorial representation may have been in a day when great urban centers of population were almost unknown and differences in population were less marked, they seem to be unrelated to modern conditions.　Voting distinctions based on wealth have entirely disappeared; religious discriminations are regarded as a relic of the past; the suffrage is no longer denied because of race or color, except in a few Southern states—and there it is done in defiance of the federal Constitution.　The theory that every man's vote is as good as his neighbor's has won general acceptance, save only when urban and rural voters are compared.　Yet many persons still contend quite seriously that "justice and equality" can best be secured by giving the farmer two or three times as much voting power as the city dweller.　"I insist . . . ," said Elihu Root to the New York constitutional convention of 1894, "that the small and widely scattered communities, with their feeble power comparatively, because of their division, shall, by the distribution of representation, be put upon an equal footing, so far as may be, with the concentrated power of the cities.　Otherwise we never can have a truly representative and a truly republican government." [30]　This is the generally accepted

29 Fergus *v.* Marks, 324 Ill. 513; 152 N.E. 557 (1926).
30 Quoted in Robert Luce's *Legislative Principles,* p. 366.

rural viewpoint. Nearly every constitutional convention, except in those states where great cities have not developed, is called upon to decide whether representation shall be based upon population or cow pastures. So far the cow pastures have had the better of the argument.

## BICAMERAL OR UNICAMERAL?

**Early history of bicameralism.** It has already been pointed out that every state except Nebraska has a legislature composed of two houses.[31] In the early years of American independence most states accepted the bicameral principle almost as a matter of course. They had been accustomed to two-chambered legislative bodies during the colonial period and could see no good reason why the time-honored tradition should be abandoned. It might have been argued, of course, that each house of a colonial legislature represented separate and distinct interests; the council was virtually the mouthpiece of the crown, while the assembly championed the cause of the people. But the upper and lower houses of the first state legislatures were also the representatives of distinct and ofttimes conflicting groups. The senate represented aristocracy, wealth, privilege. Relatively high property qualifications were established for senate membership, and also for the privilege of voting for senators. The house, on the other hand, was the more democratic chamber. Its members were the spokesmen of the masses, even more clearly than during the colonial era.

**Present-day conditions.** This distinction, however, has long since passed into history. Senate and house are equally democratic and equally responsive to manifestations of the popular will. Members of both houses are chosen by the same electorate and represent the same groups and interests. Though senators are commonly chosen for a somewhat longer period, and though the senate is a somewhat smaller body, these differences are unimportant. To borrow a phrase from the jargon of photography, the house is merely an enlargement from the same negative.

**Defects of bicameralism.** It may well be asked, therefore, whether two houses are still a necessary part of the legislative machinery. There can be no doubt that the bicameral system produces unwholesome friction, irritating delays, and a constant shifting of responsi-

[31] See p. 145.

bility from one house to the other.    Does it possess merits that out-weigh these evils?    Many politicians and publicists think that it does, and advance a number of arguments in support of their belief.    Most common is the statement that each house acts as a check upon the other and thus prevents hasty, ill-considered legislation.    The members of a single house may be swept off their feet by a burst of oratory; under the stimulus of strong emotion they may vote for measures that could not win their approval in more sober moments.    Or through sheer carelessness they may pass bills of uncertain meaning or awkward phraseology.    But no harm is done if there is a second chamber of the legislature, ready to correct the errors of the first.    Impassioned oratory will not defeat hard logic a second time, and carelessly worded phrases will not twice escape detection.    If the upper house were abolished, however, there would be no adequate safeguard against sudden caprice.

That is the substance of the argument.    It is commonly urged in rebuttal that disagreement between the two houses is quite as likely to obstruct the passage of necessary laws as to prevent the enactment of unwise legislation.    Delay is the essence of a bicameral system, and the forces of modern civilization have transformed government from a repressive into an active agency—one that can ill afford delay.    Serious problems demand immediate solution and cannot await the bargaining and compromising that inevitably characterize the proceedings of two-chambered legislatures.    If a check upon unwise legislation is necessary, it may be found in the veto power of the governor and the power of the courts to declare laws unconstitutional.    Moreover, experience has shown that the bicameral system sometimes actually facilitates the enactment of ill-considered measures, instead of preventing their passage.    Each house feels less responsible for the legislative product because it shares its accountability with the other chamber.    Thus it frequently happens that an unwise but popular bill is passed by the house in which it originated in the belief that it will certainly be defeated by the other house.    When it reaches the other chamber, however, the fear of popular clamor may be sufficient to secure its enactment there, also.    The members of the second house are likely to reason that after all the bill was not of their making, so that the blame does not lie primarily at their door.    If the legislature were a unicameral body, such evasion of responsibility would be impossible.

Within the last twenty-five years a number of careful studies have been made of individual state legislatures for the purpose of determining the extent to which each house really acts as an effective check upon the other.[32] They show that a certain percentage—ranging from seven or eight to twenty-five—of the bills passed by one house suffer defeat in the other; that measures reaching the second chamber are quite commonly enacted by it without amendment; that most bills fail of enactment in the house of their origin and never receive the consideration of the other house; that few major changes in policy are due to the operation of the bicameral system. These facts can scarcely be made the basis of a convincing argument in favor of bicameral legislatures.

It is sometimes said that two houses in a legislature can be used to divide the work, with a consequent saving of time. A measure rejected by one house need not occupy the attention of the other. Two chambers are also urged on the ground that they present an obstacle to the operation of corrupting influences. It is more difficult, and more expensive, to buy control over two houses than one. Both of these contentions are quite plausible, though actual experience has not tended to confirm them. More important than any closely reasoned argument, however, in persuading the states to retain their bicameral legislatures, has been the appeal to tradition. State legislatures, with but a few exceptions, have always been composed of two houses. The Congress of the United States has been a bicameral body since the adoption of the Constitution. Most of the countries of the civilized world have accepted the bicameral principle in setting up their legislatures. To many conservative persons, therefore, disregard of these precedents would seem the sheerest folly. The bicameral system has acquired sanctity with age; to disturb it would be sacrilege.[33]

---

[32] Colvin, David L., *The Bicameral Principle in the New York Legislature;* Fletcher, Mona, "Bicameralism as Illustrated by the Ninetieth General Assembly of Ohio," in the *American Political Science Review,* Feb., 1938, pp. 80–85; Grant, James A. C., *The Bicameral Principle in the California Legislature;* Hall, John E., "The Bicameral Principle in the New Mexico Legislature," in the *National Municipal Review,* Vol. XVI, pp. 185–190, 255–260; Schaffter, Dorothy, *The Bicameral System in Practice;* Wood-Simons, May, "The Operation of the Bicameral System in Illinois and Wisconsin," in the *Illinois Law Review,* Vol. XX, pp. 674–686. See also A. E. Buck, *Modernizing Our State Legislatures;* E. C. Buehler, ed., *Unicameral Legislatures;* Daniel B. Carroll, *The Unicameral Legislatures of Vermont;* Alvin W. Johnson, *The Unicameral Legislature;* Thos. Rousse, *Bicameralism v. Unicameralism;* John P. Senning, *The One-House Legislature;* Chas. W. Shull, *American Experience with Unicameral Legislatures;* and Harrison B. Summers, *Unicameralism in Practice.*

[33] For a spirited defense of bicameralism, see the article by Frank E. Horack, Jr., entitled "Bicameral Legislatures are Effective," in *State Government,* April, 1941, pp. 79–80.

**Unicameralism in Nebraska.** Since Nebraska is the only American state to make use of the unicameral principle within the last century, it should be worth while to inquire whether the experiment has been successful—whether it has fulfilled the hopes of its supporters or justified the fears of its opponents. The answer seems to be that unicameralism has proved highly satisfactory in practice. It has produced legislators who are better equipped than their predecessors in ability, training, and legislative experience. Most of the members of the 1944 legislature, for example, were college-trained men, and were generally regarded as civic leaders in their respective communities. Legislative procedure has been greatly simplified, and the time-honored device of manipulating the rules for political purposes has been virtually abandoned. Public hearings are mandatory for all bills, and measures are seldom enacted without adequate consideration. The number of bills introduced in each session has been reduced about fifty per cent since the establishment of the one-house legislature. The last-minute rush has been practically eliminated.

When unicameralism was first considered in Nebraska, its opponents loudly expressed their fears that a small, one-house legislative body would not be truly representative of the state's economic interests. But these fears have proved unfounded. The change from two houses to one has left substantially unchanged the ratio of farmers, business and professional men. As Professor Senning so aptly points out, "Multiplying men of the same occupational interest will not improve the representative character of the legislature." [34]

Most of the present criticisms of Nebraska's legislative body are directed at relatively unimportant details. It is sometimes said that committees should be smaller, that salaries should be larger, that a four-year term should replace the present term of two years. But very few impartial Nebraskans now challenge the unicameral principle. It has made many converts since its adoption.

It should be pointed out that the rest of the world is by no means unanimous in its approval of two-chambered legislatures. The provincial assemblies of Canada are nearly all unicameral, as are the law-making bodies of the Swiss cantons. So, too, are the national legislatures of several minor European nations. The unicameral principle is generally accepted for city councils in Europe, as well as

---

[34] "Unicameralism Passes Test," *National Municipal Review,* February, 1944, p. 61. See also Harry T. Dobbins' *National Municipal Review* article, "Nebraska's One-House Legislature," September, 1941, pp. 511–514.

in the United States. It is worth noting that most American cities began with councils of two houses and finally abandoned the bicameral system only after giving it a very thorough trial. They found that two houses inevitably bred delay and inaction, and as a result they shifted, one after another, to the unicameral plan. At least six state governors [35] have advocated the adoption of unicameral legislatures, and constitutional amendments providing for this change have been submitted to the voters of four states, though without avail.[36]

Years ago Benjamin Franklin, in urging the retention of Pennsylvania's single-chambered legislature, quoted the fable of the snake who had two heads and one body. "She was going to a brook to drink, and on her way was to pass through a hedge, a twig of which opposed her direct course; one head chose to go on the right side of the twig, and the other on the left; so that time was spent in the contest, and, before the decision was completed, the poor snake died with thirst." [37] The story is not without value for the present-day student of government.

## LEGISLATIVE SESSIONS

**Curbs on legislative activity.** The men who framed the first state constitutions were firmly convinced of the necessity for frequent meeting of the legislature. In colonial days the failure of royal governors to convene the provincial assemblies had been a source of much bitterness; and when England's political yoke was broken, the leaders in the revolutionary movement took care to provide for regular and frequent legislative sessions. The constitution of Massachusetts, adopted in 1780, declared that "The legislature ought frequently to assemble for the redress of grievances, for correcting, strengthening, and confirming the laws, and for making new laws, as the common good may require." [38] In most of the states annual sessions were held, and a few states provided for two sessions a year.

BIENNIAL SESSIONS. In 1796, however, Tennessee specified that its legislature should meet at two-year intervals. Its example was not generally followed at first, but after a time the biennial idea began to prove extremely popular. Men had found to their sorrow that legis-

[35] The governors of Arizona, Kansas, Massachusetts, Minnesota, South Dakota, Washington.
[36] Arizona, Missouri, Oklahoma, Oregon.
[37] *Works of Benjamin Franklin (Bigelow ed.)*, V. X, p. 188.
[38] Declaration of Rights, Art. XX.

lative assemblies could be guilty of tyranny and folly, not to speak of downright dishonesty. They had learned that every legislative session was likely to be marked by the passage of unwise and unnecessary laws. And so they reasoned, somewhat illogically, that the way to reduce the quantity of undesirable legislation was to cut in half the number of legislative sessions. With only half as much time at its disposal, the legislature could do only half as much harm. This was a counsel of despair, but it made a strong appeal to the popular imagination and has become a maxim of present-day politics. In forty-four states the legislature now meets in regular session at two-year intervals; the other four states [39] still retain annual sessions.

OTHER RESTRICTIONS. Not content with limiting regular sessions to alternate years, twenty-five states further restrict legislative activity by limiting the length of the session to a specified number of days, ranging from forty in Wyoming to one hundred and fifty in Connecticut. A sixty-day limit is most common. Sixteen states endeavor to curb legislative enterprise by specifying that legislators' salaries shall be reduced, or stopped altogether, after a certain number of days. Usually this wage restriction applies only to special sessions; sometimes, however, it refers to regular sessions as well.

Although it has been possible to limit the number of days in a legislative session, it has proved totally impossible to restrict the number of matters requiring legislative action. Every year has brought additional governmental problems and increased need for governmental regulation; at the same time state legislatures have been compelled to complete their work in fifty, sixty, or ninety days. The result of this policy is well stated by Robert Luce: [40] "Everywhere it has produced bad work, slovenly, slipshod, hurtful. Whatever theory one who has had no experience in a legislature may evolve, as a practical matter it proves impossible for such a body in a brief time to organize, appoint committees, accustom its large proportion of new members to the routine of procedure, hold hearings and executive sessions of committees, report on one or two thousand propositions, give approved measures all their readings, reconcile the views of two branches—in brief, operate the necessarily ponderous machinery of legislation, and do it right in forty, fifty, sixty, or even a hundred days. . . . Putting on a time limit is perhaps the most preposterous device men ever conceived for the remedy of political ills. No railroad, banking, or

[39] New Jersey, New York, Rhode Island, South Carolina.
[40] *Legislative Assemblies*, pp. 142, 145.

manufacturing corporation would be so silly as to try to improve an inefficient directorate by a vote compelling directors' meetings to adjourn after two hours or restricting such meetings to two months in the year. If the administration of justice became conspicuously defective, nobody would risk his reputation for sanity by advising that the courts should sit only from New Year's Day to Easter."

**Attempts to overcome evils of legislative curbs:** SPECIAL SESSIONS. Since regular sessions of most state legislatures may be held but once in two years, and even then are narrowly restricted as to length, special sessions have inevitably become more numerous, though by no means the rule except in a very few states. Even with regard to special sessions, however, popular distrust of the legislature is evident. Usually such sessions may be held only at the summons of the governor, and in some states they are limited to twenty or thirty days. Arkansas has a fifteen-day limit. Seven states permit the legislature to determine the necessity for a special session,[41] but three of them require an extraordinary majority for this purpose.[42] In addition to permitting the governor to determine whether a special session shall be called, thirty states authorize him to specify the subject or subjects requiring legislative action. The legislature, while in special session, is then prohibited from considering any other matter.[43] Under this plan, therefore, the governor can prevent the enactment at special sessions of legislation that he dislikes; but he cannot compel acceptance of his own legislative program.

The constitutional prohibition against legislative consideration of matters not presented by the governor is generally considered to apply only to the function of lawmaking. So it would be quite proper for a legislature summoned in special session for the express purpose of considering the problem of unemployment to turn its attention to the approval of appointments or the impeachment of state officials, since appointments are an executive matter, while impeachment is a judicial act. Within the last thirty years two state governors have been impeached, tried, convicted, and removed from office at special sessions of the legislature that they called to consider important pro-

---

[41] Connecticut, Louisiana, Massachusetts, Nebraska, New Hampshire, Virginia, West Virginia.

[42] Two thirds of all the members in Louisiana and Virginia, and three fifths of all the members in West Virginia.

[43] Alabama, Arkansas, and Florida, however, permit the legislature, by an extraordinary vote, to proceed to a consideration of other matters. Mississippi expressly excludes impeachments from this limitation.

posals for new legislation.   Profiting by their experience, perhaps, the governor of Mississippi announced in 1931 that he would not call an urgently needed special session of the state legislature unless a majority of the members pledged themselves in advance not to impeach him.   It is highly improbable that such a pledge could be enforced.

LEGISLATIVE COUNCILS.   In 1933 Kansas attempted to overcome some of the evil effects of infrequent legislative sessions by creating a legislative council—a body of fifteen representatives and ten senators holding at least quarterly meetings after the legislature's adjournment —whose chief duty was declared to be the preparation of a lawmaking program for the succeeding legislature.   This council was also authorized to study problems of state-wide interest and to collect information on all pertinent subjects.   Before the close of 1933 Michigan also established a legislative council—a somewhat smaller body than the Kansas council, but organized in the same manner and vested with similar functions.   The act creating the Michigan council has since been repealed, but similar statutes have been enacted in Connecticut, Illinois, Kentucky, Maryland, Nebraska, Rhode Island, and Virginia. Connecticut has partially corrected a serious weakness of the legislative council plan—namely, its failure to recognize the important part played by the governor in formulating general policies—by naming the governor as chairman of its council.   Kentucky has gone one step further, establishing a council of sixteen legislators and five heads of administrative departments.   The administrators are named by the governor.   Three other states have variations of the legislative council plan.   Wisconsin has set up an "executive council," composed of legislators and administrators; while Colorado and New Mexico have established interim committees, which perform some of the functions of legislative councils.   But the agencies in these three states scarcely deserve to be included in the list of councils, because they maintain no paid research staffs and therefore lack the factual background necessary for intelligent planning of legislation.

THE SPLIT SESSION.   Partly for the purpose of reducing the congestion and overcrowding that so generally mark the closing days of a legislative session [44] and partly to secure a more careful examination of bills by legislators and the public, California adopted a scheme in 1911 that has since become known as the *split session*.   As its name indicates, the split session is a legislative session divided into two parts.

[44] See pp. 190-192.

During the first part of the session bills are introduced and referred to committees. Some hearings are held. A few bills may even be enacted into law, but the theory of the plan is that this period shall be used solely for the purpose of setting the legislative machinery in motion. A recess of about thirty days is then taken. Legislators returning to their homes should be able to give every proposal leisurely consideration and also learn the wishes of their constituents. When the legislature reconvenes after this period of supposed meditation, the introduction of new bills is discouraged, though not absolutely prohibited. In California no member may introduce more than two bills, and in order to introduce even one he must have the consent of three fourths of the members of the house to which he belongs.

West Virginia adopted the split session plan in 1920, but abandoned it eight years later. Since 1918 the constitution of Massachusetts has authorized split sessions, but the General Court has preferred to carry on its business in the old way. The Alabama legislature, on the other hand, has occasionally split its sessions without express constitutional authorization, and in New Jersey the legislature regularly adjourns for about ten days immediately after organizing, in order to give the party leaders time to develop their legislative programs. Texas has divided the legislative session into three parts since 1930. The first thirty days are devoted chiefly to the introduction of bills; then comes a thirty-day period of committee hearings; and during the remaining sixty days bills are debated and passed. There is no legislative recess, however. In 1933 the constitution of Georgia was amended to provide for two sessions in each regular legislative year—a ten-day session in January and a longer session, limited to sixty days, in July.

The results of the split session system have been very disappointing. The mass of unfinished business has not been materially reduced, and bills still continue to pile up at the end of the session. Proposals introduced during the first part of the session are subsequently so amended that in many instances they become essentially different legislation. Very seldom do the people show any genuine interest in the measures they are supposed to examine during the legislature's recess; the layman who understands the exact nature of a single bill is probably exceptional. A careful student of the West Virginia situation declared in 1928: "Viewed from the standpoint of results achieved, it is unquestionably true that the split session has proved a dismal failure. It has not prevented the enactment of bad legislation; it has not accomplished the enactment of good legislation." [45]

## RESTRICTIONS ON THE POWER OF THE LEGISLATURE

**Constitutional provisions.** The powers of the state legislature have never been completely listed. In fact, they defy exact enumeration, for the legislature possesses residual authority. It may do anything that is not prohibited by the federal Constitution or the constitution of that state. In the first era of American national life this principle of legislative supremacy was virtually important; it enabled the legislative body to control virtually every phase of state activity. But the passing years have witnessed an ever-increasing number of limitations upon the power of the legislature, so that today it is almost impossible to enact a law on any important subject without regard to constitutional provisions that specify in great detail what may be included and what must be omitted; how the statute must be phrased and when it may go into effect; who may be included within its terms and who must receive exemption. So numerous and so minute have these restrictions become that the doctrine of legislative supremacy is now little more than a legal fiction.[46] Limitations on the frequency and duration of the legislature's sessions have already been discussed.[47] Reference will be made in the next chapter to restrictions on legislative procedure.[48] Direct legislation, which narrows the scope of the legislature's powers by giving the people the right to frame and adopt their own laws and also to veto unsatisfactory legislative enactments, has been examined in some detail.[49]

STATE FINANCE; SPECIAL LEGISLATION. At this point, however, mention should be made of two other classes of limitations on the powers of the legislature that are commonly found in state constitutions. One of these relates to state finance. Taxes must be uniform, or uniform within certain classes of property; exemptions from taxation shall not be made except in specified cases; state money shall not be appropriated to religious institutions; state credit shall not be loaned to private corporations; state loans may not exceed moderate

---

[45] Faust, Martin L., "Results of the Split-Session System of the West Virginia Legislature," *American Political Science Review*, Feb., 1928. See also Thomas S. Barclay's article, "The Split Session of the California Legislature," in the *California Law Review*, Nov., 1931, pp. 42–58.

[46] See pp. 21 and 82.

[47] See pp. 165–167.

[48] See pp. 182–183, 188–189.

[49] See pp. 132–137.

limits, unless authorized by popular vote. In the past, state legislatures have often been guilty of squandering public funds with little or no regard for the public welfare, and the financial limitations in state constitutions are designed to prevent a recurrence of such waste. The other class of restrictions deals with so-called "special legislation." A great deal of energy has been dissipated, and a great many unjust proposals have been enacted into law, as a direct result of the common legislative practice of passing laws affecting only one person, one corporation, or one community. Obviously the legislature does not have time to give serious thought to the individual needs of every person, every corporation, and every community, and its attempt to do so has prevented the proper consideration of matters of more general importance. Even worse, it has meant the passage of special laws on the recommendation of selfish vested interests or at the behest of uninformed zealots. In order to prevent evils of this sort, most state constitutions prohibit the enactment of special legislation when general laws can be used instead, or in certain enumerated cases. Restrictions on special legislation are rather easy to evade, especially if the state courts do not insist upon too literal an interpretation of the constitution; but they have unquestionably checked some abuses of legislative power.[50]

SPECIFIC GRANTS OF POWER. Since the legislature may exercise all authority not prohibited to it by the constitutions of nation or state, it would seem unnecessary to confer upon it any specific grants of power. Yet every state constitution makes particular mention of some matters that are declared to be within the scope of legislative power. Some of these detailed grants have been inserted with no other purpose than to round out a phrase, or indicate the truly liberal spirit of the constitutional convention. As interpreted by the courts, however, they have actually become limitations upon the authority of the legislature. The courts have said repeatedly that any clause empowering the legislative body to act in a particular manner must be construed as a denial of its right to act in any other manner. Thus an amendment to the constitution of California authorizing the legislature to enact a certain type of direct primary legislation was held to forbid the passage of any other kind of direct primary law. Similarly, a flowery provision of the New Hampshire constitution empowering the general court, or legislative body, to establish wholesome and

---

[50] For a more detailed consideration of the effects of special legislation as applied to cities, see pp. 256–260.

reasonable laws was declared to be in effect a prohibition against unwholesome and unreasonable legislation; the supreme court of the
state then set itself up as final arbiter of the wholesomeness and reasonableness of the legislature's acts.    Scores of other illustrations could
be given, but they would all point the same moral: that seemingly
harmless superfluities in a constitution may do a great deal of damage.
It should be added, however, that some grants of power that serve to
restrict the scope of legislative authority have been placed in the constitution for that express purpose.

Sometimes an explicit statement of certain powers of the legislature
must be placed in the constitution to counteract the effect of unpopular court decisions.    For example, the courts may interpret the
"due process" clause or the guarantee of free speech in a way never
intended by the framers of the constitution or by the people.    The
effect of their decision may be to restrain the legislature from exercising some power that it has long used as a matter of course.    Under
such circumstances the only way to restore the legislature's prerogative
is to amend the constitution, specifically bestowing upon it the power
denied by the courts.    A considerable number of constitutional
amendments containing particular grants of legislative authority have
been adopted for this reason.

### THE LEGISLATURE'S NON-LEGISLATIVE FUNCTIONS

Although the legislature is primarily concerned with the enactment
of laws, it often possesses various powers that are not directly related
to law-making.    Judges of certain courts are appointed by the legislature in four states,[51] and in six states [52] certain executive officials are
similarly chosen.    Most of the governor's important appointments
must be ratified by the state senate,[53] and in a number of commonwealths dismissal of state officers must also receive the senate's approval.    The legislature is often empowered to remove from office the
judges of the state courts, a two thirds or three fourths vote generally
being necessary in such cases.    Virtually every state [54] vests authority

[51] Rhode Island, South Carolina, Vermont, Virginia.

[52] Maine, Maryland, New Hampshire, New Jersey, Tennessee, Virginia.

[53] The advisability of requiring senate confirmation of gubernatorial appointments is
discussed in Chaps. Ten and Fifteen.    See pp. 201 and 322.

[54] Oregon is the only state that does not permit impeachment of its public officials.    Its
constitution provides (Art. VII, Sec. 6) that "incompetency, corruption, malfeasance or
delinquency in office may be tried in the same manner as criminal offenses."

in the legislature to remove executive and judicial officers by process of impeachment.

**Impeachment.** It should be noted at this point that impeachment is not the equivalent of conviction, but is merely the presentation of formal charges. The lower house nearly always has the sole right to impeach. Any member of that body may offer a resolution of impeachment, which is at once referred to an appropriate committee. The report of the committee, though not binding on the house, usually determines in large measure what action will finally be taken. If a majority of the members of the house indicate their belief that the accused official has been guilty of serious misconduct or neglect of duty, formal charges are thereupon prepared and adopted. The senate sits as a court for the trial of these charges,[55] and a specially chosen committee from the lower house prosecutes the case. The accused official is permittted to employ counsel and produce witnesses in his behalf, just as if he were on trial in an ordinary court of law. Usually a two-thirds vote of the senate is necessary for conviction; the punishment does not extend beyond removal from office, or perhaps in addition disqualification from holding further office under the state or its civil subdivisions. Impeachment and conviction for a criminal offense, however, do not render the convicted official immune from subsequent arrest and trial in the criminal courts of the state.

### Selected References

See references at end of Chapter Nine.

[55] In New York the judges of the state court of appeals sit with the senate. The Missouri constitution of 1945 directs the supreme court to try impeachment cases, unless the governor or members of the supreme court have been impeached, in which case the trial takes place before seven eminent jurists chosen by the senate.

# Chapter Nine ❧ THE LEGISLATIVE PROCESS

THE first few days of a legislative session are commonly devoted to the task of organizing for business. Presiding officers must be chosen, rules adopted, committees named. Actually these matters do not require so much time as might be supposed. Usually it is known well in advance of the session who will occupy the speaker's chair. The rules of the preceding session are commonly adopted without debate. Certain well-recognized factors, such as previous service, factional allegiance, residence, and special qualifications, determine committee membership to a very large extent. In a comparatively short while, therefore, the preliminaries are completed and the legislature is ready to begin its regular routine.

## ORGANIZATION OF THE LEGISLATURE

**The lieutenant governor.** Usually the lieutenant governor, the "fifth wheel of the coach of state," presides over the deliberations of the senate.[1] His powers are strictly limited; he is commonly though not invariably prohibited from participating in debate, and may vote only in case of a tie. Five states deny to him even this limited voting power.[2] He is presumed to be an impartial presiding officer, and as a rule he takes no active part in shaping legislation. In sixteen states, however, he appoints the regular standing committees and thus is a real factor in the legislative process.[3] The senate chooses from among its own members a president *pro tempore,* who presides during the absence of the lieutenant governor or in case of his elevation to the governorship. There are twelve states that make no provision for the office of lieutenant governor, and in those states the senate selects its own permanent presiding officer. Regardless of the method of choice, the presiding officer of the senate is known as the "president"

[1] In Nebraska the lieutenant governor presides over the single chamber of the legislature. A speaker, chosen by the legislature from its own membership, presides in his absence.

[2] Louisiana, Michigan, Minnesota, New York, Wisconsin.

[3] In three of these states—Idaho, Mississippi, and Washington—the lieutenant governor's committee appointments must be approved by the senate. In Mississippi and Washington special provision is made for the composition of the rules committee.

of that body in every state except Tennessee, where "speaker" is preferred.

**The speaker:** HIS AUTHORITY AND POWER. In the lower house the regular presiding officer is invariably a speaker chosen by the house from its own membership. It is scarcely necessary to add that he is selected for this important post because he is the recognized house leader of the majority party. As speaker he wields a large measure of authority; his office is generally considered the second most important in the whole field of state politics, ranking next to the governorship. Unlike the lieutenant governor, he is not supposed to preserve an attitude of judicial impartiality during the course of debate. On the contrary, he is expected to use the power of his office for the purpose of battering down the opposition and forcing the adoption of measures that have the support of his party. Speakers have not been slow to use the authority entrusted to them; quite frequently, however, they have given greater weight to the views of a little clique of party leaders than to the opinions of a majority of the members.[4]

*Appointment of standing committees.* One of the important sources of the speaker's influence is his power to appoint the standing committees. Forty-six states place this power in his hands,[5] and thereby enable him to control to a very considerable extent the political career of every member of the lower house. The influence of a state legislator depends largely upon the committees to which he is assigned, and only a man who is supremely confident of his ability to play a lone hand or completely indifferent to the course of his political fortunes will dare to risk oblivion by deliberately and persistently ignoring the speaker's wishes. It must be understood, however, that the speaker dares not use his appointing power in purely arbitrary fashion. He is restricted in a number of ways, and though these restrictions are not embodied in statute or formal legislative rule, but are merely the outgrowth of custom or the result of political necessity, they must be respected by every speaker who wishes to retain his prestige. First, other influential members of the party must be consulted, and their suggestions given some weight. Every shade of opinion sufficiently powerful to make its influence felt at the polls

[4] A somewhat similar development in the national House of Representatives led to the so-called "Revolution of 1911," in which Progressive Republicans united with the Democrats to deprive the speaker of some of his arbitrary power. In the states, however, the speaker of the house still retains his authority and prestige.

[5] The two exceptions are Nebraska and Oklahoma.

must be accorded some measure of recognition. Then, as already pointed out,[6] there must be geographical representation on the committees. Every section of the state must be made to feel, if possible, that it has received fair treatment. Moreover, the members who have served in other sessions of the legislature—and they are almost invariably in the majority—expect to continue as members of important committees to which they were previously appointed. To fulfil their expectations and utilize their experience is sound government and also sound politics—assuming, of course, that the electors have returned to power the same political party.

It is apparent, therefore, that the speaker is not free to make appointments according to the dictates of his own fancy. To some extent he can use his power of appointing committees for the purpose of rewarding his adherents and punishing his adversaries, but if he carries this practice too far he will speedily find himself in trouble. For the speaker, despite the broad scope of his authority, holds his office by virtue of the votes of his fellow legislators, and he knows quite well that he must rely on their favor to continue as speaker during succeeding sessions.

*Right of recognition.* Another source of the speaker's power is his right of recognition. In some state legislatures the schedule of debate on each bill is arranged long in advance by the party leaders, a certain amount of time being assigned to each member who desires to speak. Under such circumstances the speaker does little more than follow the typewritten list before him and refuse to recognize any member who tries to speak out of turn or without first securing permission to express his views. Much more commonly, however, the speaker is virtually free to recognize whom he will; he is thus in a position to guide the course of debate by recognizing his supporters and refusing to recognize those who dispute his rule. The leaders of the minority must be given adequate opportunity to express their views, of course; that is part of the unwritten law. But rebels within the ranks of the majority party need not be accorded a similar courtesy.

*Rulings on points of order.* The speaker also passes on points of order, and in so doing he is sometimes able to interpret the rules of the house in such a way as to give his friends an unreasonable advantage. Bills that he favors may be hurried to a vote, and proposals that he dislikes may be prevented from reaching the stage of general

---

[6] See p. 174.

discussion. He may twist and warp not only technical points of parliamentary law, but also questions of fact. Rulings of the speaker may be appealed to the house, but since the speaker is the chosen representative of a majority of the members, his decisions are not likely to be reversed. It must not be assumed, however, that the rules of the house are regularly misinterpreted for the purpose of gaining partisan advantage, and that questions of fact are commonly decided in the light of their political effect. On the contrary, the extreme examples of abuse of power that have just been cited are very rare; in most state legislatures they are totally unknown. The speaker always has a large number of rules and a vast body of precedents on which his decisions must be based, and usually he follows those rules and precedents with care. "Anything like habitual distortion either of special rules or general parliamentary law would result in chaos, and chaos is not characteristic of our assemblies." [7]

*Reference of bills to committees.* The other power of the speaker that is commonly cited as tending to give him absolute control over legislation in the house is his power to refer bills to committees. A bill that has been introduced in the house finds its way to the speaker's desk, and from there is sent to some committee for detailed consideration. Usually the assignment of bills to appropriate committees is a routine task; the subject matter of the bill determines in advance where it is to be sent. Some measures, however, are considered so important that the speaker feels justified in making purely arbitrary use of his power of reference. He greatly facilitates their passage, or else condemns them to certain oblivion, according to his wishes, by referring them to committees that are considered "reliable." The extent to which the presiding officers of state assemblies actually use their power to refer bills for the purpose of shaping legislation to their own desires varies from state to state.

*Voting and debating rights.* Unlike the lieutenant governor, the speaker is a member of the house over which he presides. Therefore he has a right to vote on all measures. He is not permitted to break a tie, however, by casting a second vote. The speaker commonly refrains from participating in debate, though sometimes he takes part in the discussion when the house is sitting as a committee of the whole.[8] In a few state legislatures the speaker even participates oc-

[7] Luce, Robert, *Legislative Procedure*, p. 463.
[8] For a discussion of the organization and purpose of the committee of the whole, see p. 187.

casionally in the formal debates—leaving the chair for the purpose, of course; but this is not the rule.

**Other legislative officers and employees.** In addition to the speaker, each house of the legislature also chooses other officers and attendants, including a clerk, a chaplain, and a sergeant-at-arms. A great deal of clerical, stenographic, and other help is necessary to handle the vast amount of business requiring the legislature's consideration, yet nearly always the number of senate and house employees greatly exceeds even the large number actually needed. In some states every member of the senate and house is entitled to a private secretary, and the drain on the public treasury from this source is surprisingly heavy. Some years ago a newly elected governor of Kansas found that over one hundred persons were carried on the payroll of the legislature as assistant superintendents of ventilation. Their total pay exceeded three hundred dollars a day, and their only task was to regulate a thousand windows in the capitol building. Other examples of reckless distribution of public funds without a thought of benefit to the public could be given *ad nauseam*.

REACTION AGAINST PATRONAGE. Most state legislatures quite frankly use their power to hire employees as a form of patronage; they employ an astonishingly large number of persons and select them on the basis of party loyalty and party service, with little or no regard for such a trivial matter as personal qualifications for the work that is to be assigned. Some attempts have been made to remedy this abuse, but without great success. A few states have limited by constitutional provision the number of legislative employees, or the total expenditure for their salaries. But these restrictions on legislative payrolls have remained unchanged while the volume of the legislature's business has multiplied at an almost unbelievable rate, so that their principal effect is now to hamper the legitimate work of lawmaking. Several commonwealths have specified that the number and pay of legislative employees must be established by law, thus making it necessary for each house to secure the consent of the other to the creation of unnecessary positions and the payment of excessive salaries. Consent has been given almost as a matter of course, however; each house has hesitated to question the other's demands lest its own practices be subjected to embarrassing scrutiny. All too often the two houses of the legislature have proved to be houses of glass, whose inmates have found it safer not to throw stones. More promising has been the gradual development of the merit system for the selection of legislative employees. A very few state legislatures now choose their clerical and other help solely on the basis of fitness for the task, and voluntarily renounce this source of patronage. Growing self-respect among legislators or the increased pressure of public opinion may eventually force other state legislatures into line.

**The committee system.** So great is the number of proposals placed before every legislature that some means must be found of sorting the wheat from the chaff—disposing of unwise, unnecessary, or unpopular bills as quickly and quietly as possible, and focusing attention upon those measures that should be enacted into law. The means invariably adopted is the committee system.

NUMEROUS COMMITTEES. Both the senate and the house of every state legislature are organized on a committee basis, every member being assigned to several committees. Special committees are appointed from time to time to make special investigations and deal with special problems, but the normal routine of business is carried on by the regular standing committees. The number of these standing committees is surprisingly large. Twenty or more committees are almost invariably found in the lower house,[9] the average being well above thirty. Three houses of representatives each have more than sixty standing committees, while fourteen others have more than forty apiece. In the senate the number of standing committees is somewhat smaller, though still very large. There are eight state senates having forty committees apiece, and only four senates with fewer than twenty.

*Many useless committees.* It may well be asked why so many committees are necessary. Several partially satisfactory answers to this question can be given, but the answer that best explains the situation is that such a large number is entirely unnecessary. In most state legislatures the total number of standing committees could be reduced at least one third without adversely affecting the process of lawmaking. Many committees that seldom or never meet, and have virtually no business to transact, have been created chiefly for the purpose of rewarding ambitious party workers who have not yet earned the right to important assignments on the major committees. A young man without powerful friends is usually glad to receive any sort of committee chairmanship, regardless of the committee's prominence. It

---

[9] Rhode Island, with fourteen standing committees in the lower house, is an exception. So, too, is Nebraska, whose unicameral legislature has but sixteen standing committees.

establishes his position among his constituents, to whom all committee chairmanships doubtless seem alike; and it entitles him to the clerical help—or, better still, allowance for clerical help—that accompanies the position.

The list of useless committees should include not only those created for politics and patronage, but also those once-functioning committees that are now *retained* for political reasons, or merely because of inertia, long after their work has become a matter of purely historical interest. Thus Pennsylvania still has a senate committee on canals and inland navigation, and the Maryland house retains a committee on currency. Quite frequently the number of committees is needlessly increased by the establishment of a new committee for every new field of legislation and every new phase of administrative activity. There may be one committee on the state school for the blind, another on the state school for the deaf; one on the boys' vocational school, another on the girls' vocational school; and so on through a long list.

SIZE OF COMMITTEES. Not only are the committees of state legislatures very numerous; they are also very large. Most students of government think that they are too large. The average number of members assigned to senate committees varies from three in New Jersey to twenty-three in Illinois; in the lower house the range is from slightly less than five in Nevada to more than thirty-five in Georgia. Extremes tell the story better than averages, however. Illinois has seven senate committees and fifteen house committees whose membership exceeds thirty-five. At a recent session the house committee on the judiciary was composed of forty-two members, and forty-four members were assigned to the committee on roads and bridges. Ten committees of the lower house of the Georgia legislature have from fifty to seventy-five members apiece. While it is true that certain committees must necessarily be large in order to secure adequate representation from every section of the state, it is equally certain that many legislative committees have so many members as to interfere with their careful and orderly procedure. A committee of thirty-five or forty members acquires some of the characteristics of a regular legislative body; it is too large to permit free, informal discussion, too large to encourage active participation by every member, too large to escape the necessity of formal rules. Its size lessens the probability of prompt and regular attendance, and tends to destroy the intimate personal interest of each member.

Large committees have another serious weakness, also; they make it necessary to assign every member to a considerable number of committees, thus diffusing his time and interest. In half of the states the average senator serves on seven or more committees, ranging to a high point of eighteen committees in Illinois; the average house member in half of the states serves on four or more committees.[10] Even after sufficient allowance has been made for committees that meet infrequently or not at all, it is obvious that most members of state legislatures are placed upon entirely too many committees. Some committee meetings conflict as to day and hour and make a certain amount of nonattendance inevitable. Thus nearly every committee is composed in part of some members who are too busy to come to its meetings and others who contribute little more than their physical presence. It should be pointed out, however, that a few states— notably Idaho, Nebraska, New York, Rhode Island, and Wisconsin— keep the number of committee assignments per member within reasonable limits, thus making it possible for each senator and representative to devote his serious attention to a restricted quantity of proposed legislation without neglecting other tasks of equal importance.

MAJORITY CONTROL. In most state legislatures it is customary to give the majority party control of every committee, though the minority party receives representation in every instance. Almost invariably the chairman of a committee is a member of the majority party; usually he is the majority member who has served on the committee the longest time continuously. This seniority rule has frequently been attacked on the ground that it keeps the younger men in subordinate posts, regardless of their ability or training; but state legislatures give no indication of abandoning it.

JOINT COMMITTEES. Three New England states—Connecticut, Maine, and Massachusetts—conduct most of their business through joint committees, which are composed of both senate and house members. House members usually outnumber senators on these committees, but only because the house is a larger body. A few other states also make use of joint committees for certain purposes, such as investigations and ceremonies, but most of their legislative affairs are managed by separate committees of each house. The merit of the

10 Most of the information concerning committees has been obtained from C. I. Winslow's careful monograph, *State Legislative Committees*, published as No. 2 of Series XLIX of the *Johns Hopkins University Studies in Historical and Political Science*.

joint committee system is that it eliminates some of the delays of the legislative process, and reduces the likelihood of disagreement between the two houses. It is surprising that the plan has not found more widespread acceptance.

SELECT COMMITTEES. Although the regular standing committees that have been described in the preceding pages carry on the bulk of every legislature's work, they are not the only committees of the legislature. There are also select committees, specially created from time to time to perform specific tasks and discharged when the tasks have been completed. For example, a select committee may be appointed to welcome a distinguished visitor, to investigate charges of fraud or inefficiency in one of the administrative departments, or to examine at first-hand living conditions in a strike-ridden area. The work of such committees is only temporary, and that is why they are not established on a permanent basis.

## PROCEDURE IN ENACTMENT OF LEGISLATION

Each house of the state legislature adopts its own rules of procedure. Some procedural details are quite commonly prescribed in the state constitution, but ways of evading these requirements are generally found without difficulty. The rules, as adopted at an early meeting of each legislature, are practically certain to be the preceding legislature's rules without alteration of any kind. Usually they are antiquated, cumbersome, needlessly detailed, and difficult to comprehend. It might be supposed, therefore, that the older members who sponsor their adoption would propose instead a simpler and clearer method of procedure. The truth of the matter is that these veteran legislators who dominate senate and house activity actually welcome complex, verbose, ambiguous rules. Such rules may be called into service at will by the initiated, to the astonishment and discomfiture of the unwary. It takes a long while for a newly elected member to learn all the tricks of the parliamentarian's trade; in the meantime he is at a serious disadvantage.

**History of a bill.** Perhaps the best way to obtain a clear picture of the entire legislative process is to take a single bill and trace its history from the time it is first introduced until it is officially proclaimed a law by the secretary of state. A bill may be introduced in either house by any member of the house or by any standing committee. Since the standing committees scarcely ever initiate legislation, the vast flood of proposals that threatens to swamp most legislative sessions comes from the individual members. Many bills are introduced "by request," which means that the members who offer them for the consideration of the house wish to renounce all responsibility for them. Such measures are foredoomed to an early grave, of course, but the mere fact of their introduction enables many a legislator to assure his constituents that he did everything possible.

FIRST READING. A member introduces a bill by placing it in the hands of the clerk, who reads its title and thus gives it the official "first reading." Virtually every state requires three readings on three separate days for every measure enacted into law; thirty states have written this requirement into their constitutions, while the others have commonly inserted it in senate and house rules. At one time three readings may have been necessary to prevent unseemly haste in the passage of legislation desired by special interests. Today, however, in view of the growing tendency to supply all members with printed copies of bills before final voting,[11] the requirement of three readings is considered an unreasonable restriction upon legislative procedure, and is generally evaded or ignored.

REFERENCE TO COMMITTEE. After a bill has had its "first reading," it goes to the presiding officer for reference to a committee. The extent to which the presiding officer's choice of an "appropriate" committee may determine the final fate of the measure has already been indicated.[12] Many a state assembly has a "graveyard" committee, whose chief purpose is to give decent burial to undesired proposals. Its true nature is always cloaked, however, by some imposing title such as *Special Committee on Judiciary* or *Committee on Legislative Procedure*.

An active committee receives so many bills in the course of a single session that it cannot possibly give them all serious consideration. Therefore it must select those proposals that deserve careful study. In making its selections it is influenced very largely by the wishes of the chairman, who normally acts as spokesman for the little group of "elder statesmen" controlling legislative affairs. Though legislative rules do not require committee hearings, except in a very few states, hearings are usually held on all important measures. Taxpayers, lobbyists, experts, non-experts, those who urge adoption and those who object—all are permitted to appear and express their views, sub-

11 See p. 187.
12 See p. 177.

ject to the narrow time limits necessarily imposed. The next step is committee deliberation—usually behind closed doors, though Nebraska admits representatives of the press. Every bill that progresses this far is examined clause by clause, amended to any extent that may seem desirable, and finally adopted or rejected by committee vote.

RETURN OF BILL. The power of committees to suppress or pigeonhole bills that fail to meet their favor varies from state to state. The rules of some state legislatures make the committees virtually supreme in this respect; bills need not be reported on the demand of an extraordinary majority of the house. More common is the provision for return upon a simple majority vote, but since every committee is dominated by the majority party its decision to bury a bill is not usually questioned. Some states place the power to recall a bill from committee in the hands of the author, or any member of the house, or a small part of the total house membership. Even more stringent is the requirement that all bills must be reported after a given number of days, or by a certain date, without the necessity of affirmative action by the house or any of its members. These provisions for automatic return of bills are found in the rules of one or both houses of six legislatures.[13] In some states, such as Massachusetts, they are obeyed with scrupulous care; a committee would not think of attempting to influence legislation by failing to make a report. In other states, such as Pennsylvania, they are frequently disregarded. The general tendency in state legislatures is to vest primary responsibility in the standing committees; a bill that receives committee disapproval is not likely to go beyond the committee stage.

FURTHER CONSIDERATION AND PLACE ON CALENDAR. Even committee approval, however, is not sufficient to guarantee consideration by the house. A bill reported from committee is at once placed upon the house calendar of business, but hundreds of other bills may be ahead of it, awaiting their turn. Unless a proposal has the active support of the party leaders it is apt to stay on the calendar indefinitely, remaining "unfinished business" at the end of the session. Some way must be found, therefore, to select the more important measures and obtain prompt consideration for them. The two agencies commonly charged with this dual function are the steering committee and the rules committee. In a few states the steering or sifting committee is recognized by legislative rule; much more commonly, however, it is

[13] They are found in both houses of the Massachusetts, North Dakota, and Vermont legislatures; in the lower houses of Texas and Utah, and in the Pennsylvania senate.

an informal and extra-legal body composed of the majority party leaders in house or senate. Its task, whether assigned by rule or merely self-imposed, is to examine the mass of proposed legislation and choose the bills that should receive preferred treatment. The rules committee is then expected to propose rules that will expedite their passage. It has no difficulty in doing so, for it is a privileged committee with the right to report at any time and to demand that its report receive the immediate consideration of the house. Whenever it sees fit to take action in behalf of any bill, therefore, it proposes a "special rule." This rule may specify the exact day and hour at which the house shall take up the bill; it may limit debate; and it may even prescribe the time at which the final vote shall be taken. A majority vote is sufficient to adopt this rule; the favored bill thereupon moves to the top of the calendar, even though it may formerly have occupied a place somewhere near the bottom.

*Powers and organization of rules committee.* The powers of the rules committee vary somewhat in nature and extent, but they are always sufficiently broad to insure a large measure of control over legislation. In the Georgia senate the rules committee arranges the daily calendar during the last fifteen days of the session, and no change in its program may be made save by a three-fourths vote. The rules of the Arizona senate authorize the rules committee, plus four other senators appointed by the president, to present rules during the closing days of the session "designating the order in which bills or measures shall be considered by the Senate or the Committee of the Whole, which rules shall in all cases be deemed standing rules of the Senate." [14] Unlike the steering committee, the rules committee is almost invariably a recognized part of the formal committee organization. Its members are the party leaders. In twenty states the speaker is chairman; in six others he is a member. Twenty-seven states include the president of the senate or the president *pro tempore,* or both, in the membership of the senate rules committee. Usually the committee is much smaller than other legislative committees, the number of members ranging between three and five in many of the states. There are some few exceptions, however, such as the rules committee of the Georgia house, which has a membership of thirty-nine.[15] In view of the fact that the rules committee must facilitate the enactment of bills selected by the steering committee, it is important that these

---

14 Rule X, Section 10, Senate Rules of 1929.
15 Winslow, C. I., *op. cit.,* p. 31.

two committees work together in perfect harmony. Frequently the membership is interlocking to a very considerable extent, the same men dominating the activities of both committees. In a few states the steering committee is unknown, even as an informal gathering of the party leaders, and the rules committee assumes the twofold duty of sorting bills and guiding their passage.

THE PARTY CAUCUS ON LEGISLATION. The Congress of the United States relies on caucus action to a very considerable extent to insure the enactment of important legislation. The caucus is a meeting of the Senate or House members of a party for the purpose of securing a united front on matters that vitally affect the party's welfare. Ostensibly it aims to discover the wishes of the members, so that the party leaders will know how to act. Actually it is a very effective device for forcing the leaders' views upon the rank and file, for the decisions of the caucus are usually forced upon it; and, once made, they become binding on all members. Anyone who dares to disregard the mandates of his party's caucus is likely to find himself in serious trouble. Important committee appointments will doubtless pass him by, and his re-election will be at best a matter of indifference to those who control the party campaign fund. A few men have successfully defied the caucus either occasionally or habitually, but they have been unusual men in unusual times. Their experience should not be considered an indication that the power of the caucus is on the wane.

In the state legislatures, however, the party caucus has never had a development corresponding to its growth in Congress. Barring the experience of a very few states, the caucus meets but seldom except at the beginning of the session for the nomination of officers, and its occasional decisions on legislative matters are not so seriously regarded as in Congress. Caucus measures are invariably given careful study, however, even if frequently denied united support.

SECOND READING. When the house proceeds to the consideration of a bill reported from committee, this stage is known as second reading. The bill is debated, amended, and finally voted on. Its friends try to force a vote as quickly as possible, unless uncertain of the outcome; in the meantime its opponents offer dilatory motions in quick succession, hoping to accomplish their purpose by parliamentary strategy if not by weight of numbers. During second reading a bill may be considered section by section or as a whole, according to the nature of the subject matter, the number of days before the close of the legislative session, and the wishes of the party leaders. It is common practice to supply every member with a printed copy of the bill before debate is begun.    At least a dozen states, however, merely require the printing of a bill and its amendments *before final passage—* that is, in most cases, after the debate has been concluded; and a few commonwealths make no provision for printing bills unless specially authorized.    Massachusetts, at the other extreme, is one of a small number of states that print every bill upon introduction.

*Debate.*    The course of debate in every state legislature is necessarily very formal.    Freedom of discussion is often narrowly restricted. Rules designed to save time and prevent obstructive tactics are rigorously enforced.    In order to permit less formal consideration of bills and afford the average member somewhat greater freedom of expression, the rules of nearly all legislative bodies authorize the use of a procedural contrivance known as committee of the whole.    A few state legislatures employ this device rather freely; the large majority, however, use it infrequently or not at all.    The committee of the whole, as its name indicates, is the entire membership of the chamber sitting as a committee.    In appearance one of its sessions does not differ from a regular meeting of the house, except that the speaker's chair is occupied by one of the other members.    But the regular rules are greatly relaxed, and debate is considerably freer.    When the committee of the whole has discussed and adopted a bill, it immediately reports its action to the house—that is, practically speaking, to itself. The speaker resumes his place as presiding officer, and puts the question as to whether the action of the committee of the whole shall be made the vote of the house.    This question is almost invariably answered in the affirmative, of course; but there have been instances of legislative bodies that reversed their informal opinions—and probably their honest convictions—when called upon for a formal vote.

*Acceptance of committee recommendations.*    The members of state legislatures are guided very largely by committee recommendations in making their decisions.    Dr. C. I. Winslow, in an excellent monograph previously cited,[16] points out that in recent sessions of the Pennsylvania and Maryland legislatures the action of the committee became substantially the action of the house in at least four instances out of five.    More exactly, the committee viewpoint was the determining factor eighty-three per cent of the time in Pennsylvania, and ninety-two per cent in Maryland.    A few state legislatures display greater independence, but the Pennsylvania-Maryland situation is

[16] *State Legislative Committees.*

typical of the vast majority. The predominance of committees in the legislative process need occasion no surprise. The members of a committee have—or are supposed to have—time to become reasonably familiar with the bills entrusted to their care. They have opportunity to hear the conflicting views of interested persons whenever hearings are held. Presumably, therefore, they are better qualified than their colleagues to pass upon the merits of these proposals. So their recommendations are normally followed by other legislators, who believe that committee reports, however inadequate or biased, are the safest guide. Certainly some guide is needed; the tremendous volume of proposed legislation makes it utterly impossible for every member of the senate or house to consider every bill introduced.

THE FINAL DRAFT. After a bill has been amended and passed on second reading, it is engrossed—that is, prepared for final passage. A new copy is drafted, if necessary, so as to incorporate the changes that have been ordered by the house. This task is commonly assigned to a committee on engrossed bills, whose duty is to present to the house an accurate draft of the original bill and its amendments. On some occasions surprising additions and omissions have "accidentally" been made at this time; interested members find it well worth their while, therefore, to read the engrossed bill before casting their final vote.

THIRD READING. When a bill comes before the house for its third reading it is frequently passed without debate. To propose amendments at this stage requires unanimous consent, which is not commonly given; therefore the measure must be accepted or rejected as a whole. A few states vary the customary procedure by making the second reading quite as meaningless as the first, and deferring opportunity for debate and amendment to the third reading.[17] A bill that has been passed on third reading is then sent to the other house, where the details of procedure already described must be repeated. There must be reference to some committee, generally followed by committee hearings; three readings must be given, including the usual opportunity for discussion and amendment; and the final vote must be taken.

DISREGARD OF RULES OF PROCEDURE. It may cause astonishment

---

[17] In Nebraska the procedure is somewhat different from that herein outlined, and has been adopted by the unicameral legislature to provide a careful check against too hasty enactment of laws. Every bill is considered in detail by the legislature on two separate occasions before final passage. A "constitutional reviewer," appointed by the legislative council, may be called upon at any stage in the progress of a bill to give his opinion as to its validity.

that such time-consuming procedure does not prevent the enactment of virtually all legislation. That it has no such effect is quite evident, however; every legislative session witnesses a fresh deluge of laws added to the hundreds of thousands already crowded between the covers of the statute books. Forty or forty-five thousand pages of statutes are enacted by the legislatures of the states every biennium, and even yet legislators are not convinced that the point of diminishing returns in the field of lawmaking has been reached. The chief reason why cumbersome rules of procedure do not decrease the legislative output to any considerable extent is that they are commonly ignored or evaded whenever short cuts seem necessary—especially during the closing days of the session. Robert Luce quotes this choice passage from the Iowa *Manual of Legislative Procedure:* "Bills are seldom engrossed, but the rules are suspended and they are considered engrossed. Likewise, a bill may not be given a third reading; but the rules being suspended, a reading given for information is considered a third reading. Another rule frequently suspended is the rule which provides for a second and third reading on the same day; in fact any rule can be suspended in either House by a two-thirds vote of the members present." [18] Constitutional provisions concerning legislative procedure deserve greater respect than mere senate or house rules, but even they are often brushed lightly aside. In determining whether the legislature has obeyed the letter of the constitution the courts usually refuse to go further than the written record of the senate and house journals, so that violations can readily be concealed by appropriate entries.

CONFERENCE COMMITTEES. Unless a bill is passed by both houses in exactly the same form, the differences must be straightened out before it may be submitted to the governor. A compromise must be found that will be acceptable to the members of both chambers. To prepare such a compromise is the task of a conference committee, which usually consists of three senate members appointed by the president of that body and three house members appointed by the speaker. There are some variations, however. Colorado conference committees consist of two senators and three representatives; Connecticut reduces the number to one senator and two representatives; Iowa prefers four from each house; and a few states make use of other combinations. Occasionally conference committee members are chosen by one of the standing committees or by ballot. In every state

[18] *Legislative Procedure*, p. 210.

legislature conference committees are special committees; a new committee is chosen for every bill that goes to conference.   In most states the committee is limited to a discussion of the points of difference between the two houses, but this is not invariably the case.   Quite a number of state legislatures authorize their conference committees to make any changes that may seem desirable, even to the point of including new subject matter.

Regardless of the scope of its power as defined by legislative rule, the conference committee is always a vital factor in the process of law-making.   Although its decisions may be rejected by one or both houses, they are not likely to be.   Each chamber usually welcomes any compromise that seems likely to receive the approval of the other, and adopts the conference report without close scrutiny.   To do otherwise in the closing hours of the session—the time when conference committees usually complete their work—would be to invite almost certain defeat for the bill so treated.   Thus it often happens that the conference committees, nominally the agents of senate and house, actually acquire the whip hand and re-write disputed measures according to their own desires.

When a bill has received the final approval of both houses, a new copy is made incorporating all changes.   The preparation of this copy is known as enrolment.   The signature of the presiding officer of each house is then affixed, and the bill goes to the governor for his consideration.   In every state except North Carolina the governor has the power of veto, though his veto may be overridden in most cases by action of the legislature.[19]   The vote required to overcome the governor's veto ranges from a mere majority of those present, as in Connecticut, to a two-thirds majority of the total membership of each house, as in nearly half of the states.

**Congestion at the end of the session.**   Almost without exception is the tendency of state legislatures to postpone the enactment of legislation until the closing days of the session.   The first few days are spent in organizing and getting down to business.   Then committee meetings consume the serious attention of members for weeks at a time.   The legislature may meet but a few hours each day, and only three or four days a week.   Few significant decisions are made.   At last, with only a week or ten days of the session remaining and virtually no important measures enacted into law, the need for quick action becomes apparent.   Committee reports pour in at the rate of fifty or one

19 For a more detailed consideration of the governor's veto power, see pp. 209–210.

hundred a day, and the legislative calendars become hopelessly crowded. Some reports are purposely delayed by the leaders in the hope that the majority will give a hasty assent to proposals that could never pass if carefully examined, but in most cases committee tardiness is simply an indication of the natural tendency to procrastinate. Whatever the cause, the result is almost hopeless confusion. Many bills—especially those involving appropriations and administrative routine—must be passed in order to save the state government serious embarrassment. Many others must also be adopted if specific campaign pledges are to be fulfilled, and even campaign promises acquire some significance when it is remembered that election day is a day of reckoning.

Seldom is it possible, however, to give any measure the consideration it deserves. In most cases it is totally out of the question to follow the forms of procedure specified by the constitution or legislative rule, or both. To read every bill at length twice, or even once, and to call the roll in orderly fashion, would be a physical impossibility within prescribed time limits—even assuming complete elimination of debate. So the rules are brushed aside, and the legislature sometimes enacts more laws in two hours than it did in two weeks at the beginning of the session. Under such circumstances the quality of the legislative product inevitably suffers. Many laws bear evidence of the haste with which they have been enacted. Crudely and ambiguously phrased, they sometimes defy the efforts of the administrative officials, the courts, and the public to determine their real meaning. Some years ago, after a typical session of the legislature, the Governor of Kansas stated that two chapters of laws "duplicated two others; one chapter of old law was repealed three times; a new chapter was immediately amended by the succeeding chapter; an old chapter repealed by a new one was amended and repealed by another. A bill" awaiting his approval contained "a negative reversing its purpose. Two bills were exact duplicates. A number of bills passed both houses without any enacting clauses." [20]

Nor are such conditions found only in those states that restrict the length of the legislative session. Several state legislatures that are unhampered by time limits are among the worst offenders. They heedlessly permit week after week to slip by without positive action, only to crowd hundreds of vital measures into the last few days or hours. Some states have tried to correct this situation by means of constitu-

[20] Luce, Robert, *Legislative Assemblies*, pp. 155–156.

tional prohibitions against the enactment of legislation on the last day or the last two days of the session; but the only effect of such restrictions has been to shorten the session for legislative purposes by one or two days. The final twenty-four or forty-eight hours are devoted to correcting the journals and passing resolutions and memorials.

The experience of Massachusetts, and also of Wisconsin and Nebraska to a considerable degree, indicates that the last-minute rush so characteristic of state legislatures is totally unnecessary. In Massachusetts all committee reports must be submitted to the legislature before a specified date, well in advance of the probable close of the session,[21] and the introduction of bills is limited to the first few days of the session except under very unusual circumstances. In part the success of Massachusetts in avoiding congestion at the end of the session is due to these excellent rules of procedure; in part it is the result of sound legislative tradition.

### LEGISLATIVE REFERENCE BUREAUS

**Unwise legislation.** Legislators are amateurs. Most of them have no special qualifications as lawmakers, no special training for public service, no special knowledge of public affairs. Few of them, prior to election, ever gave serious thought to government or its problems. Many are lawyers, but their legal training serves chiefly to foster a false sense of familiarity with governmental matters. Although most of them are professional or semi-professional politicians, their previous efforts have been confined largely to getting out the vote on election day and performing routine tasks for the party organization between elections. They are the chosen representatives of the people, of course, but they are wofully ignorant of even the fundamentals of sound public policy. Ability to win an election does not necessarily indicate extraordinary wisdom or profound legislative skill.

Every session of every state legislature witnesses its share of freakish proposals. From time to time legislative committees have been asked to consider bills forbidding school textbooks to be changed oftener than once in ten years, prohibiting locomotives from running backward, penalizing the exposure of bare legs on the stage, compelling every cigar store to display a wooden Indian. Some years ago a North

---

[21] It has already been pointed out that this rule, although found in several states, is not so scrupulously respected by other legislatures as by the general court of Massachusetts. See p. 184.

Carolina legislator introduced a bill making it a misdemeanor for any unmarried woman to refuse a bachelor's offer of marriage. Such suggestions are usually sidetracked without receiving serious consideration, but they indicate the low levels of legislative capacity. Some foolish bills actually become law. Thus one statute prohibited the use by hotels of soiled sheets or pillow cases, without establishing any criterion by which their soiled condition was to be determined. Another solemnly decreed that "when two trains meet at a crossing they shall both come to a full stop, and neither shall start up until the other has passed over."

**Work of the reference bureaus.** Increasing recognition of the very obvious fact that legislators are not experts, and need technical assistance of some sort, has led to the establishment of legislative reference bureaus or similar agencies in forty-three states.[22] Thirty-two of these states have separate divisions or departments whose time is devoted exclusively to legislative reference activities; the others merely increase the duties of some already existing agency—usually the state library. Legislative reference work, in its proper sense, includes two main functions: to secure for members of the legislature such information as they may require for the performance of their duties, and to put the substance of legislators' proposals into form suitable for passage. Some reference bureaus, however, are limited to one of these activities; while a few bureaus at the other extreme are charged not only with research and bill drafting but also with a considerable number of miscellaneous functions such as co-operation with legislative investigating committees, preparation for constitutional conventions, and assistance to universities and colleges. In nineteen states the task of bill drafting for members of the legislature is assigned to the attorney-general's department.

The legislative reference bureau does not, as a rule, attempt to evaluate material collected for members of the state legislature. It simply secures requested information, permitting interested legislators to interpret this information in any way they desire. The Wisconsin bureau, which passes upon the significance of facts it has compiled and supplies legislators and legislative committees with briefs and arguments, is an outstanding exception. Bill drafting is a purely technical function; the reference librarian does not attempt to decide the wisdom of proposed legislation, but merely considers its con-

[22] The only exceptions are Delaware, New Mexico, North Dakota, Tennessee, and Utah. New Mexico established a legislative reference bureau in 1937, but abolished it in 1941.

stitutionality, its consistency with existing law, and its probable interpretation by the courts. Any other course would simply invite
charges that the reference bureau was "playing politics"—charges that
even now are not entirely unknown.[23]

The first reference bureau was established in New York State in
1890 as a branch of the library at Albany. Two years later the Massachusetts legislature first made an annual appropriation of one thousand dollars to the state library "for preparing an index to current
events and other such matters contained in the newspapers of the day
as may be deemed important by the trustees and the librarian." But
when Wisconsin adopted the reference bureau idea in 1901 it organized its new bureau so thoroughly and with such good results that it
has generally been credited with stimulating other states to follow its
example. In 1931 the Interstate Reference Bureau, sponsored by the
American Legislators' Association, was set up in Chicago. It has
prepared useful digests of important legislative problems and has
aided some of the smaller and newer state bureaus to perform their
functions in an adequate manner. It is designed to become a central
clearing house that will place the results of every reference bureau's
research at the service of every other reference bureau, thus preventing needless duplication and wasted effort.

## THE LOBBY

According to the express declarations of state constitutions, bills
may be introduced only by the members of either house. It must not
be assumed, however, that every bill is the brain-child of some legislator. On the contrary, many an important proposal owes its existence to persons or groups of persons whose contacts with the legislative body are at best extra-legal, and sometimes illegal. They
conceive it, nourish it from a fugitive thought into a full-blown plan,
couch it in suitable phraseology, secure its introduction in senate or
house, marshal witnesses in its behalf at committee hearings, bring
pressure to bear upon individual members of the legislature who seem
unconvinced or hostile, and finally urge upon the governor the importance of permitting it to become a statute. The legislators who

[23] A very complete description of legislative reference bureaus and their work may be
found in John H. Leek's *Legislative Reference Work: A Comparative Study*. This monograph is now somewhat out-of-date, but a more recent statistical summary may be found
in the *Book of the States, 1943–1944*, pp. 151–155. See also Edwin E. Witte's article,
"Technical Services for State Legislators," in the Jan., 1938, issue of the *Annals of the
American Academy of Political and Social Science*, pp. 137–143.

introduce it in their respective houses can scarcely be called its authors, unless the customary meaning of the word is discarded. Rather they are its stepfathers, and they commonly uphold the time-honored step-father tradition by displaying complete ignorance of its fundamental purpose and entire indifference to its probable effects.

In every state capital are large numbers of men and women, not connected with the state government in any official capacity, whose task is to influence legislation in behalf of the groups or interests they serve. A few of them work without compensation; their fight for child labor laws, anti-cigarette legislation, or equal civil rights for all classes is a glorious adventure, tinged with the religious fervor of a crusade. But the large majority are paid, and they command large salaries. They have no illusions as to the nature of their work. They must accomplish the enactment of laws desired by their employers, and the defeat of undesired proposals. Fair means of producing results are always preferred, but are not used exclusively. These men and women swarm through the corridors of the state capitol, and even find their way into the lobbies of the assembly chambers. Thus they have come to be known as lobbyists, and their activities have been given the name of lobbying.

So successful have the lobbyists been in their efforts to control legislation that they are frequently called the "third house" of the legislature. Sometimes it seems that their influence is greater than that of the two regularly constituted houses. When the late Robert M. La Follette was governor of Wisconsin he pointed out that the school-book lobby had suppressed or defeated laws menacing the school-book monopoly; that a paid lobbyist of the telephone interests had prevented the enactment of a bill to establish competitive service; and that an effective railroad lobby had defeated every proposal to increase railroad taxes or establish a rate commission. Frequently repeated was the boast of a railway lobbyist that in sixteen years no measure objectionable to the railroads had passed the legislature.

**Methods.** The methods employed by lobbyists several decades ago were very crude, though admittedly successful. They consisted largely in spending money "judiciously"—that is, purchasing for cash the support of the members of the legislature. When one vested interest had procured a dependable majority in this way, it often leased its control to others whose position was less secure. Millions of dollars changed hands secretly, without vouchers or receipts. Franchises and other valuable privileges were literally presented to private corporations without any attempt to protect the rights of the people. In that era of shamelessness there were some who actually boasted of their knavery.

Today, however, direct bribery is uncommon. The methods now employed by lobbyists are more subtle, and no less effective. They include assistance to legislators in the preparation of bills—a service that is likely to prove more thorough and complete than that of the legislative reference bureau; dinners and other social activities that draw new legislators into the exclusive inner circle of society at the state capital; and friendly gestures of every sort that can be made without giving offense. They include, also, such indirect forms of lobbying as the publication of editorials and biased news in friendly or controlled newspapers; personal work among the voters for the purpose of inducing them to write or telegraph their wishes—that is, the lobbyists' wishes—to their wavering representatives in the legislature; and contributions to the campaign funds of favored candidates.

**Need for regulation.** It is always a difficult task to distinguish between those lobbyists who use questionable means to produce questionable results and those who merely try in straightforward fashion to protect the legitimate interests of their employers. The insurance companies take considerable pride in the work of their lobbyists, which has at times prevented the enactment of laws imposing unreasonable burdens. The utility, manufacturing, and banking interests declare that justice cannot be done unless their viewpoint is made entirely clear to the members of the legislature. The labor unions boast of their share in the preparation and passage of legislation eliminating sweatshops and child labor, improving working conditions, minimizing tenement house work, and establishing sound systems of workmen's compensation. Lobbying has unquestionably produced good results as well as bad, and any attempt to abolish the entire system root and branch would be foredoomed to failure.

There can be no doubt, however, that effective regulation of lobbyists and their activities is urgently needed. Laws designed to prevent the abuses of lobbying have been enacted in thirty-five states, but most of them have proved virtually worthless. Lobbyists are commonly required to register, giving the names of their employers, the term of their employment, and the special subjects, if any, to which their employment relates. In some states the employers are directed to submit itemized statements of their lobbying expenditures, such statements to be filed shortly after the close of the legislative session. The methods that lobbyists may properly employ, such as appearance before committees, newspaper publicity, and the like, are generally enumerated. Personal solicitation of members is forbidden. The penalties prescribed in the several state laws include fines, imprisonment, and disbarment from the lobbying service.

Although a few states, of which Wisconsin is the most notable example, have thus eliminated some of the most flagrant abuses of the lobbying system, their small measure of success should not be regarded as typical. Most of the states have accomplished little or nothing, and lobbyists continue to operate as before without molestation.

### LEGISLATIVE RECOMMENDATIONS BY THE GOVERNOR AND HEADS OF ADMINISTRATIVE AGENCIES

This chapter would be incomplete if it did not include some reference to so-called "administration measures." Every state constitution requires the governor to inform the legislature concerning the affairs of the commonwealth. This he does by sending a formal message, which usually contains specific recommendations as to necessary legislation. Many a governor, anxious to facilitate the adoption of his proposals, even has them drafted into proper form for legislative consideration. These bills are then introduced by friendly members of the legislature, and are known informally as administration measures. They receive prompt committee consideration and favored places on the calendar. Their enactment into law is by no means assured, however; much depends on the governor's ability as a political leader.

Reference should be made, also, to the part played by the numerous state administrative agencies in the process of lawmaking. The heads of these departments, bureaus, and offices are recognized as experts in their respective fields, and are frequently asked to testify before legislative committees. They supply individual legislators with information whenever requested to do so, and sometimes provide the arguments heard on the floor of the assembly. When, therefore, they make suggestions concerning the context of proposed legislation, it is not at all surprising that their words should receive respectful attention. When they ask legislators to introduce bills directly related to the work of their several agencies, they are seldom refused. In a recent year more than half of the bills enacted into law by the legislature of New York State were originally proposed by the state administrative departments or by the agencies of local governments.[24] All these measures were formally introduced by members of the legislature, of course, but their origin was an open secret.

Participation by department heads and bureau chiefs in the lawmaking process is not necessarily the same thing as executive leadership. The governor of the state is the chief executive; he supplies whatever executive leadership may be forthcoming. He may or may not consult his subordinates in the state administration before recommending the enactment of new laws. And, conversely, his subordinates may or may not secure his approval before placing their pet projects in the hands of friendly legislators. There is, of course, little likelihood that department heads or bureau chiefs will sponsor legislation directly contrary to the governor's announced program, but they may reasonably expect a free hand with regard to those matters that have never claimed the governor's attention.

### SELECTED REFERENCES

Buck, A. E., *Modernizing Our State Legislatures,* 1936.

Buehler, Ezra C., ed., *Unicameral Legislatures,* 1937.

Chamberlain, Joseph P., *Legislative Processes: National and State,* 1936.

Childs, Charles, *The Oregon Legislature,* Portland, 1937.

Commonwealth Club of California, *The Legislature of California,* San Francisco, 1943.

Farmer, Hallie, *Legislative Apportionment,* University, Ala., 1944.

Illinois Legislative Council Research Department, *Reapportionment in Illinois: Congressional and State Senatorial Districts. Research Report No. 3,* Springfield, 1938.

Johnson, Alvin W., *The Unicameral Legislature,* Minneapolis, 1938.

Kneedler, Grace M., *Legislative Councils and Commissions,* Berkeley, Cal., 1939.

Laurent, Eleanore V., *Legislative Reference Work in the United States,* 1939.

Leek, John H., *Legislative Reference Work: A Comparative Study,* 1925.

Luce, Robert, *Legislative Assemblies,* 1924.

————, *Legislative Procedure,* 1922.

————, *Legislative Problems: Development, Status, and Trend of Treatment and Exercise of Lawmaking Powers,* 1935.

Manning, J. W., *Unicameral Legislation in the States,* Lexington, Ky., 1938.

Mason, Paul, *Manual of Legislative Procedure for State Legislatures and Other Legislative Bodies,* Sacramento, 1937.

McKean, Dayton O., *Pressures on the Legislature of New Jersey,* 1938.

---

[24] Scott, Elisabeth McK., and Belle Zeller, "State Agencies and Lawmaking," in the Summer, 1942 issue of the *Public Administration Review,* pp. 205–220. See also Miss Scott's article, "State Executive Departments Play Growing Part in Lawmaking," in the November, 1943 issue of the *National Municipal Review,* pp. 529–534.

Moore, B. F., *The History of Cumulative Voting and Minority Representation in Illinois, 1870–1919*, 2nd ed., Urbana, 1919.

Pound, Merritt B., *State Legislature, Two Houses or One?*, Athens, Ga., 1938.

Rousse, Thomas A., *Bicameralism vs. Unicameralism*, 1937.

Schaffter, Dorothy, *The Bicameral System in Practice*, Iowa City, 1929.

Senning, John P., *The One-House Legislature*, 1937.

Shull, Charles W., *American Experience with Unicameral Legislatures*, Detroit, Mich., 1937.

Smith, T. V., *The Legislative Way of Life*, 1940.

Walch, J. W., *A Complete Handbook on the Unicameral Legislatures*, 1937.

Willoughby, William F., *Principles of Legislative Organization and Administration*, 1934.

Winslow, C. I., *State Legislative Committees*, 1931.

THE Constitution of the United States declares that "the executive power shall be vested in a president. . . ." [1]  State constitutions do not go so far, however; they merely vest in the governor the *supreme* or *chief* executive authority.   This distinction is more than a matter of terminology.   It indicates a fundamental difference between the offices of president and governor.   The president of the United States possesses all the executive power of the national government; he appoints the administrative officers, including heads of departments; he supervises their work to the extent that time and inclination permit; and he dismisses them at his pleasure.   Although the confirmation of the Senate is necessary for most important appointments, it is not required for dismissals.   Thus the president wields a tremendous influence over the conduct of national affairs.   In administrative matters his word is law.

## THE GOVERNOR

**Restrictions on his administrative powers.**  In contrast with the president, the governor of a state finds the scope of his executive power narrowly restricted.   He is commonly forced to share control over state administration with a number of other officials who, like himself, are popularly chosen.   This group is generally composed of the secretary of state, the treasurer, the auditor or controller, the attorney-general, and the superintendent of public instruction; sometimes others are also included, while in a few states the list of independently elected officers is materially reduced.   These officers are not responsible to the governor.   They owe him no debt of gratitude for their selection; and they have no fear that he will remove them, since their tenure of office is fixed by the constitution.   Occasionally they co-operate with the governor for the sake of party harmony or administrative efficiency, but much more commonly they disregard his wishes, and he has no way of compelling obedience.   Some state constitutions authorize the governor to require regular reports from the heads of the independent administrative departments, and a few gov-

[1] Art. II, Sec. 1, Cl. 1.

ernors have tried to mold this power into a real instrument of control by demanding detailed statements of expenditures and complete accounts of activities. In most cases, however, the reports received have been so vague that they have proved practically worthless from the standpoint of effective supervision. Moreover, the few defects occasionally revealed by such reports have usually remained uncorrected, because the elected department heads have flatly refused to accept gubernatorial leadership.

APPOINTMENTS. In recent years the appointing power of the governor has been materially increased. Although the elective administrative offices have been retained in most states, a large number of additional departments, boards, and commissions have been created by constitutional amendment or, more commonly, by statute; and the power to fill these offices has usually been vested in the governor. New activities of state government have led to new state agencies, so that the list of offices filled by appointment of the governor is now quite long. Yet even this measure of appointing authority is subject to certain restrictions. Senate confirmation of important nominations is required in most states, though not in all. Fixed and overlapping terms, sometimes extending beyond the governor's own term of office, often make it impossible for him to appoint a majority of board and commission members. Thus the governor is hampered at every turn, even in the selection of subordinates who are supposed to carry out his wishes.

REMOVAL OF ADMINISTRATIVE OFFICERS. With regard to the removal of administrative officers the governor is even more seriously handicapped. He has no general power of removal, such as inheres in the office of president of the United States, but only the authority that may be vested in him by the state constitution or by statute. Usually he is not permitted to remove the elective department heads; they may be removed from office solely through the cumbersome process of impeachment.[2] Officers appointed by the governor may be removed by him in many states, but often this power is so hedged with restrictions that its value is nearly destroyed. Senate approval may be required, with the possibility of making a political issue out of every case; or officers and employees may be guaranteed the right of formal trial before dismissal, thus transforming every such incident into a public spectacle. The limited removal power of the governor

---

[2] Those few states that permit the governor to remove or suspend elective state officers commonly require the approval of the senate.

is one of the chief causes of his inability to control state administration. Lacking any effective means of getting rid of inefficient or disloyal subordinates, he must necessarily accept their half-hearted service.

THE RESULTS OF DIVIDED RESPONSIBILITY. So restricted are the administrative powers of the governor that he cannot fairly be held responsible for the management of state affairs. Except in the few states that have thoroughly overhauled their administrative organization, only a part of the administrative machinery lies within his control. The remainder is under the direction of independent or semi-independent boards, commissions, and individuals. The inevitable results of such hydra-headed administration are lack of co-operation, wasteful duplication, neglect or omission of necessary services—in a word, inefficiency; and also divided responsibility which makes it virtually impossible to fix the blame for unsatisfactory conditions. The natural tendency is to hold the governor responsible when things go wrong. He is declared by the constitution to be the *chief executive* of the state; he is the head of the government in name, if not in fact. Uninformed persons consider him virtually omnipotent, and expect him to control matters that lie entirely beyond the scope of his authority.

In the course of a year the governor of any state receives thousands of requests that he could not possibly grant, even if he were so minded. Some of them are quite unreasonable and serve only to display the ignorance or stupidity of the petitioners. Thus one governor was asked to end Japanese aggression in China, the appeal coming from simple-minded folk who feared for the safety of their relatives in the combat zone and looked to the governor as the protector of those in danger. The governor of another state was urged to establish a state currency that would compete with the currency of the national government. But many of the requests are reasonable and proper; the governor's inability to comply indicates only the pitiful impotence of his position. When he is asked to remove obviously incompetent subordinates, or at least compel them to adopt generally accepted methods of procedure, he may be forced to reply that they are protected by constitutional or statutory position and that he has no power to act in the matter. When he is requested to enforce state laws that the legislature has duly enacted and that bear his signature as evidence of his approval, he may be compelled to admit that the indifference of popularly elected prosecuting attorneys makes enforcement impossible.   The governor has the responsibility, but not the authority; his is the kingdom and the glory, but not the power.

*Inefficient administration.*   While such conditions exist it is un-reasonable to expect efficient state administration.   Evasion of re-sponsibility is too easy.   Every official accused of incompetence places the blame at another's door.   Other officers will not co-operate, and there is no way of compelling them to do so; the legislature's appro-priation is niggardly and shows a deficient understanding of the work to be done; the requirement of senate confirmation of appointments makes necessary the selection of inefficient subordinates for political reasons; or the red tape connected with dismissals virtually prevents any improvement in personnel.   These and a hundred other explana-tions are advanced whenever things go wrong; some of them, at least, are doubtless correct.   Just before election the air is usually filled with charges and counter-charges.   The public does not know whom or what to believe.   It can see the evidences of inefficient administra-tion, such as poorly paved highways, mismanaged charitable and cor-rectional institutions, and crowded courts where miscarriage of justice is common; but it has no ready way of knowing who is at fault.   So the election is usually decided on the basis of old voting habits and life-long traditions of party loyalty.   Even those persons who are most resentful of political interference in administrative matters find it virtually impossible to fix the blame.

THE NEED FOR CONCENTRATION OF RESPONSIBILITY.   The only satis-factory solution of the problems is to concentrate control over state administration in the hands of the governor.   He should be per-mitted to select his subordinates without interference, to supervise them in his own way, and to dismiss them at will.   The secretary of state, the treasurer, the attorney-general, and other administrative officers who are now chosen directly by the people should be brought within the scope of his appointing power.   The requirement of senate confirmation, even for important appointments, should be abolished.   The governor would then possess *the executive power* of the state and not merely an emasculated portion of that power.   He would be in a position to produce results.   And, should he fail, there would be no valid excuse.   He could not shift the blame to others. It is an axiom of government that authority and responsibility go hand in hand.   When authority is divided among many persons, responsibility is similarly diffused.   It cannot be otherwise.   But concentration of authority makes possible concentration of responsibility. A governor who has been given complete control over his state's administrative affairs can fairly claim the credit for satisfactory results; conversely he must accept the blame for slipshod administration.

Within the last three decades several states have accepted to a considerable extent the principle of concentrated responsibility and have vested a large measure of executive authority in the hands of the governor. In these states the number of elective administrative offices has been greatly reduced, and the governor's appointing power has been correspondingly broadened. Boards and commissions that formerly enjoyed virtual independence have been placed under his effective control. Some states, such as Minnesota, Pennsylvania, and Vermont, have accomplished these results more or less completely by statute, without amending their constitutions. Other commonwealths—New York and Virginia, for example—have adopted the constitutional amendments necessary to overhaul their administrative systems. Administrative reorganization is a vital part of any comprehensive plan for the reform of state government. It deserves detailed consideration, and for that reason it will be treated at length in a later chapter.[3]

*Opposition arguments.* Although the movement for concentration of authority in the hands of the governor is gaining momentum, it still encounters bitter opposition. Many persons contend that the scheme is undemocratic, "un-American," autocratic. It vests too much power in one man. Concentration of power, they urge, leads naturally to abuse of power. The governor who can dominate the entire state administration may do so merely to gratify his personal whims, or to enrich himself at public expense. No guarantee is offered that he will use his authority wisely, or even honestly. He may become a veritable tyrant, and no feasible way is provided to check his excesses. One-man control is inherently dangerous, and it is especially dangerous when the administrative activities of an entire state are involved.

Briefly, this is the argument of those who support the *status quo*. They favor the distribution of authority among a number of officers—the governor, the secretary of state, the treasurer, and others—so that no one of them can influence unduly the conduct of state affairs. Each will act as a check upon his colleagues and prevent arbitrary

³ See pp. 319–328.

usurpation of power. Reduced to its simplest terms, this line of reasoning is about as follows: "Any person vested with authority is likely to abuse that authority. Therefore, in governmental matters, the only safe course is to divide the sum total of power into so many parts and distribute it among so many persons that no person will be able to do anything of importance. It naturally follows that since everyone is denied authority to act, no one can possibly act in a manner injurious to the state. The remedy for unwise action is in-action!"

*Changed conditions today.* In an earlier day, when the tasks of government were few and relatively simple, the widespread acceptance of this doctrine produced no serious consequences. Government was chiefly an agency of repression, and few people really cared that the governmental mechanism moved slowly and ponderously, or not at all. Wendell Phillips expressed a generally prevailing viewpoint when he wrote: "Government is only a necessary evil, like other go-carts and crutches. Our need of it shows exactly how far we are still children."

But the development of modern civilization has transformed the rôle of government, and made necessary a new theory to fit the new facts. To the growing list of state activities it constantly adds new functions. The state has now assumed complete or partial responsibility for the construction of highways, the development of rail and water facilities, the prevention and treatment of communicable diseases, the conservation of child life, the regulation and inspection of financial institutions, insurance companies, and public service corporations, the improvement of agriculture, the conservation of natural resources, the administration of civil and criminal justice, the establishment and maintenance of educational standards—to select at random only a few state services. It has become responsible for some functions that were formerly left to private initiative, in addition to many others that were not performed by any agency, public or private. Today, therefore, the imperative need in state government is for action. Any doctrine or formula that breeds delay must be discarded. Authority must be concentrated in the governor, for in no other way can results be obtained. It is useless to argue that concentration of power may lead to abuse of power. That danger will always exist, but it is far less serious than the danger of inaction. The only satisfactory remedy for abuse of power by the governor is an aroused public opinion that will insist upon the use of his authority solely for the public good. To fetter him with constitutional and legal restrictions is simply to invite the breakdown of state administration.

**Selection and qualifications of the governor.** In virtually all the states the governor is now chosen by direct vote of the people.[4] A plurality vote is commonly sufficient, but Georgia, Maine, Mississippi, and Vermont provide that the winning candidate must receive a majority of all the votes cast. In these states, if no person obtains a majority, the governor is selected by the lower house of the legislature or by the two houses in joint session.[5]

Every state constitution establishes certain qualifications that the governor must possess. He must be a citizen of the United States, and usually he must have resided within the state for a period of years, varying from two to ten. A five-year residence requirement is most common. As a rule he must also have attained a certain age; thirty years is generally accepted, though the range is from twenty-five to thirty-five. In a few states the constitution is silent with regard to age and residence, but the omission has no practical significance, for custom decrees that the governor must be a resident and a person of maturity. Religious qualifications have largely disappeared, though eight states still deny to atheists the right to hold any public office.[6]

**Tenure and salary of the governor.** In recent years the governor's term of office has been materially lengthened. One-year terms, which were once the rule, have entirely disappeared. Massachusetts, the last state to elect its governor annually, made the change in 1918. At present the states are almost evenly divided between two-year and four-year terms, with the trend toward the longer period. Twenty-five states elect for four years, and twenty-two for two; New Jersey has a three-year term. Only a very few commonwealths prohibit the

[4] Mississippi, the sole exception, has a peculiar arrangement that somewhat resembles the method prescribed by the federal Constitution for selecting the president of the United States. Each county or legislative district is assigned a number of electoral votes equal to its representation in the lower house of the state legislature, and the candidate who receives the largest popular vote in a county is given that county's total electoral vote. To be elected governor, it is necessary to secure a majority of the electoral votes and also a popular majority. If no candidate meets this twofold requirement the house of representatives makes the selection. The overwhelming predominance of one political party in Mississippi prevents closely contested elections, and for that reason the system produces exactly the same result as direct popular choice. But if the Negro population of the state should ever become potent politically, the scheme might prove an effective means of assuring white supremacy. That is why it was adopted.

[5] The two houses in joint session make the choice in Georgia and Vermont. The lower house selects in Maine as well as in Mississippi.

[6] See 149, n. 12.

governor from serving two terms consecutively, yet re-election is the exception rather than the rule.[7]

The salary of the governor ranges from three thousand dollars a year in South Dakota to twenty-five thousand dollars in New York. Only three other states pay less than five thousand dollars,[8] and the average is about seventy-eight hundred. An allowance for expenses is sometimes added, and more than one state supplies an executive mansion for the governor's use. Although the salaries of governors are large, as compared with the salaries of other officers in the state service, they seldom equal the expenses of the office. A governor is the ceremonial head of his state; he must of necessity live in a rather expensive manner. He is expected to entertain frequently and lavishly. It becomes his duty to welcome distinguished visitors from other states and from foreign countries, and while he is their host he must furnish accommodations befitting their rank. Many a governor thus finds it necessary to supplement his official salary, either by drawing on his private resources or by taking advantage of some of the questionable opportunities for profit that are quite certain to come his way.

**Removal of the governor from office.** The governor may be removed by process of impeachment. It is customary, however, to use this power only when some very serious offense is charged—flagrant abuse of authority, for example, or downright dishonesty. Mere inefficiency is not enough to justify the presentation of charges. As a result, only four governors have been removed from office on impeachment charges since the troubled days of reconstruction following the Civil War. One of the four—James E. Ferguson of Texas—was subsequently "pardoned" by the state legislature, and then announced his candidacy for the governorship, despite the specific provision of the Texas constitution that an officer convicted in an impeachment trial should be disqualified "from holding any office of honor, trust, or profit" under the state.[9] The Texas supreme court promptly declared the legislature's amnesty act unconstitutional.[10] This case is of more than local interest because most state constitutions similarly

---

[7] On the basis of past experience, a governor's chance of re-election seems to be not quite one in three. Yet Governor Hunt of Arizona was elected for seven terms, and Governor Smith served New York for four terms.

[8] North Dakota and Tennessee, where the governor's salary is fixed at four thousand dollars a year; and Maryland, where it is forty-five hundred.

[9] Art. XV, Sec. 4.

[10] Ferguson *v.* Wilcox *et al.*, 28 S.W. (2nd) 526 (1930).

prohibit office-holding by persons who have been impeached and convicted. Removal of the governor by means of a recall election is almost unknown, as previously pointed out.[11]

**Powers of the governor.** The powers of the governor, though much more narrowly restricted than the powers of the president of the United States, are extensive and important. In administrative matters the governor is most seriously handicapped; in the field of legislation, on the other hand, his authority and influence are considerable, and constantly growing. Most of the governor's administrative powers have already been mentioned. He fills by appointment many important state offices, though his nominations must usually receive the confirmation of the senate. He is sometimes authorized by the constitution or by statute to suspend or remove from office persons whom he has appointed. He exercises at least a nominal power of supervision over the entire sphere of state administrative activity. The state constitution usually imposes upon him the duty to "see that the laws are faithfully executed." This clause means very little, however, except to the extent that the governor can make it effective through his powers of appointment, supervision, and removal.

HIS LEGISLATIVE PROGRAM. Although the voters have been loath to extend the administrative authority of the governor, they have looked with increasing favor in recent years upon his leadership in legislative matters. They have learned to expect a "governor's program" of legislation, and to judge the success of each governor on the basis of his ability to secure the legislature's support for his proposals. Quite naturally, therefore, the governors of most of the states have decided that the way to become a successful "chief executive" is to spend less time on executive affairs and more on legislation. Their legislative powers have been strengthened by constitutional amendment, by law, and also by custom; and these powers are usually exercised to the fullest degree.

The legislative program of the governor is usually embodied in his message to the legislature. If he belongs to the same party as a majority of the members of both houses, his road should be comparatively smooth. Some pressure upon party leaders may be necessary; some bargaining may be inevitable; but the governor can usually secure a reasonable degree of co-operation. An open break would benefit no one except the opposition. If the governor and the

11 See p. 142.

legislature are of different political faiths, however, it may be necessary to go directly to the people over the heads of the legislators. Some governors have done this very effectively. They have supplemented formal messages to the legislature with widespread newspaper and radio appeals, and have succeeded in arousing popular sentiment to such a point that the members of senate and house have deemed it wise to fall into line.

His veto power. The governor's power to call special sessions of the legislature has already been discussed.[12] So, too, has his veto power,[13] but a more complete description of the gubernatorial veto is necessary. Except in North Carolina, where the veto power does not exist, every bill passed by the legislature goes to the governor for his approval. He has a certain number of days to make his decision; during the legislative session this number varies from three to ten, but five days is most common. Should the governor fail to act within the specified period, the bill becomes law without his signature—*if the legislature is still in session.* A bill on which the governor has written the word *veto* (I forbid) is returned to the legislature for further consideration.

But when the legislature adjourns before the governor has had time to decide what his course of action will be, a different set of rules prevails. In four states [14] he is required to return every disapproved bill with his objections to the legislature at its next session; bills that are not approved and not returned become law automatically. Most of the other states place a definite time limit, which varies from three to thirty days, upon the governor's post-adjournment deliberations. During this period his veto is final. But failure to act also defeats a bill in some states, whereas in the others inaction is regarded as equivalent to approval. Those commonwealths that permit the governor to veto legislation by the simple process of ignoring it follow the example of the federal government. The federal Constitution confers a similar power upon the president.[15] A veto by inaction is known as a "pocket" veto; the president or governor disposes of distasteful legislation by pocketing it.

If proposed laws flowed from the legislature to the governor in a steady and fairly uniform stream throughout the legislative session, the governor's absolute veto over bills received just prior to adjourn-

12 See p. 167.
13 See p. 190.
14 Alabama, Maine, Mississippi, South Carolina.
15 Art. I, Sec. 7, Cl. 2.

ment would not be especially significant. But the legislature's habit of procrastination, which results in postponement of final action on nearly all important measures until the last few days or hours of the session,[16] has greatly enhanced the governor's veto power. Except in a few states it has given him absolute power of life and death over the major part of the legislative program.

*Veto of specific appropriation bill items.* The president of the United States has no authority to veto portions of bills; every bill must be vetoed outright, or not at all. In thirty-nine of the states, however, the governor is empowered to veto specific items of appropriation bills. He can thus eliminate excessive, wasteful appropriations without jeopardizing the safety of appropriations that are essential to the proper conduct of state affairs. Lacking this power, many a governor would face the unpleasant alternative of vetoing entire appropriation bills because of certain objectionable features, thus incurring the enmity of the legislative leaders and probably necessitating an extra session of the legislature, or of accepting the good with the bad and signing bills that did not have his wholehearted approval. In a few states the governor not only strikes out unwelcome appropriation items but even reduces items that he deems excessive. The amount of the reduction rests entirely in his discretion. Usually his action is final, since the legislature has a habit of adjourning as soon as all necessary appropriations have been made. This plan has worked badly in most states where it has been adopted. It has encouraged legislators to please their constituents by voting for appropriations far in excess of total anticipated revenues, thus forcing the governor to make the inevitable reductions and incur the wrath of the interests adversely affected. In 1889, when Washington was admitted to statehood, its constitution contained an interesting innovation: "If any bill presented to the governor contains sections or items, he may object to one or more sections or items while approving other portions of the bill." [17] This was, in effect, an extension of the item veto principle to all legislation. South Carolina adopted a similar provision six years later. Ohio, the only other state to try the plan, abandoned it in less than a decade.

His EXECUTIVE BUDGET. In recent years a substantial majority of the states have placed upon the governor the responsibility for preparing an annual program of state expenditures and revenues, and

[16] See pp. 190–192.
[17] Art. III, Sec. 12.

sponsoring his program before the legislature. This executive budget, as it is commonly called, has greatly increased the governor's control over fiscal legislation, and in some states has made him virtually a fiscal dictator. The various forms of the executive budget, and their effect upon state organization and activities, are discussed at length in a subsequent chapter.[18]

ORDINANCE-MAKING POWER. One of the important sources of the governor's influence is his ordinance-making power. Many of the laws that he is supposed to enforce require supplementary regulations to make them effective. The legislature has purposely left out many details and has authorized the governor to supply these omissions by means of executive orders. Such decrees, when issued, have all the force of law. They are called *ordinances* to distinguish them from the *statutes* or formal acts of the legislature, but statutes and ordinances are alike in their binding effect.

When the legislature enacts a law providing for the payment of state funds to local school districts, it may specify that state payments shall be conditional upon the maintenance of school standards to be established by the governor or one of his subordinates. When the legislature decides upon a policy of conservation of wild animal life, it may authorize the governor to prescribe from year to year the length of the hunting season, the animals and birds that must not be molested, and other related matters. Thereupon the governor—or more commonly, some officer acting in his name and with his approval —issues the necessary regulations. Frequently the executive ordinances supplementing a statute are much more voluminous than the law itself. In many cases they are much more important, because the law is phrased in general terms.

Many state legislatures have acquired the habit in recent years of enacting statutes that contain the barest framework of governmental policy—skeleton or outline laws, as they are often called. The governor or other administrative officers then fill in the details. This method of lawmaking has several marked advantages over the older and still generally used plan of detailed legislation. It conserves the time of the legislature; it insures more flexible administration, because ordinances can be changed to meet changing conditions or to recognize necessary exceptions much more readily than statutes; and it materially reduces the number of unworkable laws, since the details of each statute are fixed through administrative decree by the officer

[18] See pp. 348–356.

responsible for its enforcement. Yet the legislative assemblies of the states do not make the fullest possible use of the system. They still busy themselves with numerous minor matters that could be handled much more quickly and effectively by ordinance.

The courts have said repeatedly that the ordinance-making power of the governor and other administrative officers is not a power to legislate, but merely to determine the best means of enforcing the law. They have established the constitutional principle that the legislature may not delegate its essential legislative function to any other branch of the government. Therefore if executive officers go so far as to determine broad outlines of policy, even when specifically authorized to do so by the legislature, their decrees are void and unenforceable because the legislature is without authority to delegate its lawmaking power. But if executive ordinances are issued merely for the purpose of applying principles that the legislature has established, they will be sustained by the courts. That is sound constitutional theory. In actual practice, however, it is virtually impossible to draw a clear line of demarcation between the establishment of principles and their application. At what point does any question of public interest cease to be a matter of policy and become merely an administrative detail? What tests can be used to distinguish the substance of legislation from matters of procedure?

Some years ago the Ohio legislature created a board of censors and authorized it to prohibit the showing of motion pictures that were not "in the judgment and discretion of the board of censors of a moral, educational or amusing, and harmless character." It would seem that this statute conferred upon the board of censors the right to determine policy—in other words, to perform an essentially legislative function, for no standards of any sort were established by the legislature. The board was given complete freedom to accept pictures or reject them, according to whatever rules it might see fit to adopt. But the Supreme Court of the United States, in refusing to void the act of the Ohio legislature, declared that the board of censors was exercising merely administrative discretion and not legislative power.

The scope of administrative descretion must not be too closely restricted; otherwise "the many administrative agencies created by the state and national governments would be denuded of their utility, and government in some of its most important exercises become impossible." [19]   This case shows how far the courts are willing to go in supporting the work of administrative bodies.   They insist upon retaining the doctrine that legislative power may not be delegated; sometimes, in fact, they make it the basis for invalidating state legislation that exceeds reasonable limits.[20]   But they willingly concede to administrative officers a very large measure of discretion.   Thus they facilitate the orderly evolution of efficient government.

CONTROL OF THE MILITIA.   In every state the governor is the recognized head of the state militia—the National Guard, as it is now known—unless these troops are temporarily in the service of the United States.   He is not expected to take personal command, of course; the constitutions of Kentucky and Maryland specifically prohibit him from doing so without the consent of the legislature.   Instead he merely exercises a measure of general supervision.   He is authorized to call out the militia in order to execute the laws, suppress insurrection, and repel invasion; and for other purposes also in a very few states.[21]

*Replacement of National Guard by State Guard.*   Whenever war makes it necessary to call the National Guard into the service of the nation for months or even years, the states are left without organized militia to handle possible emergencies, unless special forces can be recruited to take the place of the National Guard units.   In October, 1940, after most of the state forces had already been mustered into the federal service, Congress amended the National Defense Act to permit the states to organize emergency militia forces, and many of the states —especially those having strips of seacoast to protect—promptly established State Guard units, composed largely of business and professional men who volunteered for part-time duty.   The federal government supplied the necessary arms and equipment.   Later, as the danger of invasion by enemy troops became increasingly remote and regular army patrol became increasingly efficient, many State Guard units were disbanded or neglected.

In the early days of American independence state troops were frequently called into service to deal with Indian troubles, and as a result the governor's military power was of considerable importance.

---

[19] Mutual Film Corporation *v.* Industrial Commission of Ohio, 236 U.S. 230 (1915). See also Gaine *v.* Burnett, 4 A. 2nd 37 (1939).

[20] See, for example, Holgate Bros. Co. *v.* Bashore, 200 A. 672 (1938).

[21] See, for example, the constitution of Oklahoma, which authorizes the governor to call out the militia to protect the public health. Art. VI, Sec. 6.

But the disappearance of frontier conditions has greatly reduced the need for military activities; today the militia is seldom used except to preserve public order during industrial disputes. Even when mobs of strikers threaten life and property the governor seldom acts until the local authorities admit their inability to handle the situation and appeal to him for aid. This is not invariably the case, however; the governor is the sole judge of the existence of a state of insurrection [22] and may order the militia to assume control despite the protests of local officials.

Occasionally a governor uses his position as commander-in-chief of the state's military forces for the purpose of exercising virtually dictatorial power. Governor Walton of Oklahoma, for example, called out the state militia in 1923 to prevent the members of the legislature from meeting in the state capitol.[23] In 1931 Governor Sterling of Texas and Governor Murray of Oklahoma placed most of the oil wells of their respective states under marital law in an attempt to increase the price of crude oil. And three years later Governor Long of Louisiana directed the state militia to seize and stand guard over the New Orleans voting lists, thus insuring the triumph of the Long political machine. Other governors have used state troops for a variety of questionable purposes, such as the prevention of tax resales by county officers. But such abuses of the military power are exceptional—and sometimes they fail to hurdle the barrier of constitutionality. Thus the Supreme Court of the United States invalidated Governor Sterling's use of the militia to raise oil prices. "If this extreme position could be deemed to be well taken," said the Court, "it is manifest that the fiat of a state governor, and not the Constitution of the United States, would be the supreme law of the land; that the restrictions of the federal Constitution upon the exercise of state power would be but impotent phrases, the futility of which the state may at any time disclose by the simple process of transferring powers of legislation to the governor to be exercised by him, beyond control, upon his assertion of necessity. Under our system of government, such a conclusion is obviously untenable. There is no such avenue of escape from the paramount authority of the federal Constitution." [24]

---

[22] *In re* Moyer, 35 Colo. 159; 85 Pac. 190 (1904); Haley *v.* Cochran, 31 Ky. L. Rep. 505; 102 S.W. 852 (1907).

[23] As a result of this controversy the governor was subsequently impeached and convicted.

[24] Sterling *et al. v.* Constantin *et al.,* 287 U.S. 378 (1932).

PARDONING POWER. Until the middle of the nineteenth century the governor had virtually unrestricted power to pardon persons convicted of crime. This had been a prerogative of the English crown and was given to the chief executives of the states and the nation as a matter of course. Since 1850, however, the restrictions on the governor's pardoning power have become increasingly numerous. In many states he has been compelled to share his authority with a pardon board; in others he has become merely a member of the board; and in a few he has lost all control over the granting of pardons.[25]

**Previous experience of the governor.** Most of the men who have been elected governors of American states have possessed considerably more than average ability and training. In recent years, at least, more than half of them have been college graduates. Most of them have stood quite high in the occupational scale—as lawyers, educators, merchants, manufacturers. They have been fairly representative of the better class of business and professional men in their respective communities. A large majority have held other public office before ascending to the governor's chair. Few have had administrative experience, however, either in public or private life. This is unfortunate, for it leads naturally to a neglect of administrative duties. The last few years have witnessed an increasing recognition of the importance of efficient state administration, and it may be that governors of the future will be chosen with greater regard for their proved administrative capacity.

**The governor's council.** In four state—Maine, Massachusetts, New Hampshire, North Carolina—the governor's council still exists as a relic of colonial days. It is composed of a number of persons, ranging from four to nine, whose duty is "to advise the governor in the executive part of government." [26] The functions that it actually performs are not very important. In the three New England states its approval is required for certain appointments, and in addition it deals with some judicial matters. The North Carolina council of state, as it is called, is a purely advisory body. The members of the governor's council are popularly chosen in Massachusetts and New Hampshire; in Maine they are chosen by the legislature; and in North Carolina four state officials serve *ex officio*.

Iowa also has a so-called "executive council," composed of *ex officio*

---

[25] The pardoning power is considered at greater length in a subsequent chapter. See p. 433.

[26] Constitution of Maine, Art. V.

members, but this body does not attempt to advise the governor. Instead it performs a number of miscellaneous functions, from compilation of the state census to supervision of building and loan associations. It serves also as a central purchasing agency. In 1931 Wisconsin adopted the idea of an advisory governor's council, modifying it to meet present-day conditions. An executive council of twenty members was created to advise the governor on important matters of public policy. This body has been given authority to investigate the affairs of all the administrative departments and to make studies of governmental problems. As reorganized in 1939, it has six legislators in addition to the department heads. Unfortunately it lacks a trained research staff and therefore cannot adequately perform its important duties. Kentucky, as previously pointed out,[27] has a legislative council whose membership includes administrative officers, and has provided competent technicians for the council's research activities.

## THE LIEUTENANT GOVERNOR

**His duties.** Thirty-six states make provision for the office of lieutenant governor. The others do not, and the omission seems to occasion no inconvenience. After all, the duties of the lieutenant governor are unimportant. He has been described as an administrative officer with legislative functions, but even his legislative functions —which consist solely in presiding over the state senate and casting a vote in case of a tie [28]—scarcely justify the maintenance of a separate office in the state government. By far the most important duty of the lieutenant governor is a contingent one and seldom exercised. It is the duty of serving as governor of the state in case of the governor's death, disability, resignation, removal from office, or absence from the state.

The exact meaning of "disability," as used in this connection, is not easily determined. A few governors, with health shattered, have continued to exercise their authority through trusted subordinates instead of admitting their infirmities and relinquishing the reins of power. Nor is it certain, in most jurisdictions, just how long a governor must be absent from the state before the lieutenant governor may exercise gubernatorial authority. Some lieutenant governors have seized upon a few hours' absence as an excuse for signing bills and pardoning convicted criminals. Only Alabama attempts to solve this

[27] See p. 168.
[28] See p. 174.

problem by specifying exactly how long the governor may be out of the state without being temporarily out of office; under the provisions of its constitution the lieutenant governor acquires the power and authority of the governor's office if the governor is absent for twenty days.

Quite frequently the lieutenant governor is made an ex officio member of numerous boards and commissions; like most ex officio members, however, he usually contributes but little to the work of these bodies. Unless the office of lieutenant governor can be made to fill a more useful place in the general scheme of state government, it should be abolished. A successor to the governor in case of emergency could be provided in some other way. Most of the twelve states that have no lieutenant governors vest the succession in the secretary of state or the president of the senate.

**His qualifications and tenure.** The qualifications prescribed by state constitutions for the office of lieutenant governor are the same as for the office of governor—quite naturally, since the lieutenant governor may succeed to the governorship. The term of office is also the same. The lieutenant governor is elected by the people of the state on the same ballot as the governor and normally belongs to the same political party. Factional rivalries, however, may result in the selection of a governor and lieutenant governor whose political tenets are greatly at variance, even though both men wear the same party label. Thus, if the conservative element of a party is sufficiently strong to dictate the nomination of its candidate for governor, it may gladly agree to the nomination of a liberal lieutenant governor for the sake of retaining liberal support. It is this possibility of discord between governor and lieutenant governor that has led some observers to suggest that the governor's successor, in case of death, disability or removal, should be an officer whom the governor has appointed.

## THE SECRETARY OF STATE

The deep-rooted distrust of the governor, which was a prime tenet of American political life for many years, led naturally to the plan of choosing by popular vote most of the important administrative officials of state government. More recently the governor's prestige and influence have greatly increased, but he must still share with elective officers, in most states, the authority that should properly be concentrated in his hands. One of the most important administrative officers is the secretary of state, who is popularly elected in thirty-eight states, and chosen by the legislature in three others.[29]

**His duties and selection.** Aside from the keeping of state records and the countersigning of proclamations and petitions, there is no general agreement among the states as to what his duties should be. Usually these duties are prescribed by statute rather than by the constitution, and in recent years they have increased rapidly. Some states, whenever faced with the necessity of undertaking new activities, assign most of the routine work connected with these activities to the secretary of state. As a result, this officer is now charged with a wide variety of duties, few of which bear any logical relationship to one another. He may be the custodian of certain state buildings and grounds, responsible for their maintenance and repair. He may be charged with the administration of the state's election system. He may be the official who issues charters to cities and to private corporations, and he may be responsible for the enforcement of laws controlling the sale of securities. He may supervise the issue of automobile licenses. Almost certainly his office will involve *ex officio* membership on numerous boards and commissions. In every state he performs some of these functions; in many states he performs them all.

His work involves little or no discretion; he merely complies with constitutional or statutory provisions. It may well be asked, therefore, why the secretary of state should be popularly chosen. The election of policy-determining officers can readily be justified on the ground that they are expressing the will of the people and therefore should be selected in a manner best calculated to secure a direct expression of the popular will. But the secretary of state is not a policy-determining officer, no matter how this phrase may be stretched. His only task is to execute state policy, and for that reason he should be made directly responsible to the state's chief executive—the governor.

**His tenure and salary.** In half of the commonwealths the secretary of state has a four-year term; in most of the others his term is two years. His salary ranges from two thousand dollars a year in Maryland to twelve thousand dollars in New York, with an average of about four thousand.

---

[29] The three states in which the legislature does the choosing are Maine, New Hampshire, and Tennessee. In seven other states—Delaware, Maryland, New Jersey, New York, Pennsylvania, Texas, and Virginia—the secretary of state is appointed by the governor, with senate approval.

## THE ATTORNEY-GENERAL

**His duties and selection.** The attorney-general is the governor's legal adviser. He also furnishes legal advice to other state officers and to the legislature and prosecutes or defends cases in which the state has an interest. A few states give him a measure of supervision over the activities of the local prosecuting attorneys. He is an extremely important cog in the machinery of state administration, for his opinions on constitutional and legal questions often play a decisive part in determining the actions of the governor and other administrative officers. Thousands of legal problems that are passed upon by the attorney-general never find their way into the courts; in such instances his judgment is conclusive. Many state agencies—especially the semi-independent boards and commissions—prefer, however, to have their own legal counsel instead of relying on the attorney-general for advice and assistance. While such an arrangement is sometimes necessary because of the volume of legal business handled by certain agencies, or the highly specialized nature of the problems involved, there can be no doubt that it is often carried to unjustifiable extremes. The resultant duplication is unfortunate.

Equally unfortunate is the practice of electing the attorney-general, yet the constitutions of forty-two states provide for his selection in this manner.[30] A former governor of Indiana forcefully stated the case for appointment when he declared: "The attorney-general is necessarily the legal arm of the executive; upon him must the governor depend for carrying forward many of the acts of his administration, and the appointment should be made by the governor. . . . I do not believe that we will be treading on dangerous ground if we give to the next chief executive of Indiana . . . the right to choose his own legal adviser, a right enjoyed by every citizen of our land, a right accorded the mayor of every city in our state and by every other executive officer from the president of the United States down to the most unassuming county commissioner."[31]

**His salary and tenure.** The compensation of attorney-generals is relatively high. Five states pay annual salaries of ten thousand dollars or more, and the average for all the states is about six thousand.

[30] Four states—New Hampshire, New Jersey, Pennsylvania and Wyoming—provide for appointment by the governor, with the advice and consent of the senate. In Maine the choice is made by the legislature, and in Tennessee, by the Supreme Court.

[31] Quoted in *Illinois Constitutional Convention Bulletins*, p. 694.

Terms of office are longer than for most administrative officers. Tennessee provides a term of eight years; two other states [32] specify five years; and more than half of the others have established four-year terms.[33]

### THE TREASURER

**His duties.**   The state treasurer is the custodian of state funds; he has no important policy-determining functions.   He pays out state money from time to time, but only in accordance with law, and elaborate safeguards have been set up to prevent him from making improper disbursements.   Every expenditure must be authorized by some administrative official, and in addition must be approved by the auditor or controller, who makes certain that a sufficient sum has been appropriated by the legislature for this purpose, that the appropriation has not already been spent, and that all necessary formalities have been observed.   Thus the treasurer has no discretion in the matter; he merely pays out money from the state treasury when directed to do so by proper authority.   Virtually his only opportunity to exercise discretion is in the selection of banks as depositories of public funds.

**His selection.**   Since the treasurer's duties are chiefly ministerial and routine, there seems to be little justification for his election by the people.   The line of reasoning that justifies gubernatorial appointment of the secretary of state and the attorney-general applies with equal force to the state treasurer.   If the governor is to exercise a reasonable measure of control over state administration, he must certainly be the dominant figure in the field of state finance, for administrative control without financial control is virtually a contradiction in terms.   Yet only one state—Virginia—authorizes the governor to appoint the state treasurer, and even in this state the change from election to appointment was approved as recently as 1928.   Five commonwealths—Maine, Maryland, New Hampshire, New Jersey, Tennessee—provide for selection by the legislature, and in New York a department of taxation and finance performs the treasurer's functions; elsewhere the treasurer is chosen by popular vote.   Virtually every proposal to make him an appointive officer is met with the argument that so great concentration of authority in fiscal matters

[32] New Hampshire and New Jersey.

[33] The information concerning salaries, terms and method of selection of attorney-generals, as well as many other state officials, is obtained from the *Book of the States,* *1943–1944.*

would be dangerous. The governor and the treasurer could conspire to defraud the public without any likelihood of detection, and state funds might readily be diverted to private uses. Obviously this reasoning is based on fear and distrust of the governor; it assumes that he will probably prove unworthy of the voters' confidence. It could be answered by a reiteration of the declaration that present-day government, with its imperative need for action, must be based on faith instead of fear. But another rejoinder is also at hand—a rejoinder that should prove more satisfactory to those who doubt the efficacy of administrative integration as a cure for the ills of state government. It may be stated briefly: the likelihood that misuse of state funds will be more common under an appointive system than under the present plan of electing the state treasurer is very small indeed, if only because dishonest practices are so common at the present time. Control by the governor ought to improve the situation materially; it could scarcely make matters worse.

Professor Faust, in his careful study of *The Custody of State Funds,* writes of "repeated revelations of the misuse of state funds and their gross mismanagement by the officials charged with their custody. . . . Exposures during recent years indicate that misfeasance in the treasurer's office is a chronic condition. Colorado, Connecticut, Idaho, Illinois, Indiana, North Dakota, Oklahoma, Pennsylvania, South Dakota, and Texas all report incidents of treasury malpractices and misappropriations during the last ten years." [34] Banks have been selected as depositories of state funds for personal or partisan reasons; interest on public funds has been applied to private uses; actual embezzlement of state money has been all too common. In the light of such unpleasant facts, it seems little short of absurd to argue that the treasurer must be elected, so that the people may be quite certain they are choosing an honest man to act as custodian of the money they pay into the public treasury.

### THE AUDITOR

**His duties and selection.** Some provision must be made for auditing the accounts of state officials, so as to reduce the likelihood of peculation and insure proper respect for the usual constitutional declaration that "no money shall be drawn from the treasury except in pursuance of an appropriation made by law." This task of auditing state accounts is commonly assigned to an officer known as the

[34] Pp. 2–3.

auditor or controller.    Only three states fail to provide for such an officer; in two of them—Oregon and Wisconsin—the secretary of state performs the auditor's functions, while in New Hampshire certain members of the executive council annually serve as an auditing committee.

It is generally recognized that the auditor should be permitted a considerable degree of independence and that he should not be dependent for tenure or salary on the governor or other administrative officers whose records he must examine.    After all, an audit of executive accounts by someone politically subservient to the chief executive would smack too strongly of self-audit.    Nearly all the states have attempted to solve the problem of securing adequate independence for the auditor by providing that he shall be popularly chosen; in two states [35] his term of office is longer than that of the governor.    Maine, New Jersey, Tennessee, and Virginia—the four exceptions to the general rule of popular election—specify that the auditor shall be chosen by the legislature.    In Great Britain and most of the countries of continental Europe the auditing officials hold office on the basis of judicial tenure, but no state of the American Union has been willing to go so far.

**Administrative functions.**    No valid objection to the auditor's freedom from gubernatorial control can possibly be made, if the auditor continues to devote his entire time and attention to his primary task of investigating accounts.    His duties in this connection are inquisitorial rather than administrative, and their proper performance should not be endangered by the possibility of unreasonable interference.    In recent years, however, has appeared an unfortunate tendency to burden the state auditor with a number of additional functions that are quite clearly administrative.    Thus some states make him responsible for the supervision of banks and building and loan associations, while others direct him to administer the inheritance tax law, dispose of swamp and other undesirable public lands, and serve as an *ex officio* member of numerous administrative boards and commissions.    The governor has an interest in the proper performance of these additional functions of the auditor, because they are an integral part of the administrative activities of the state; yet he is denied the right of supervision on the ground that the auditor is an investigator whose independence must be protected.    The remedy for this anomalous situation is not to place the auditor under guber-

[35] Minnesota and Ohio.

natorial control, but to take from the auditor his administrative duties and permit him to devote his entire time to his main task of inspecting public accounts.

**Duplicate auditing by governor.** A few states, recognizing the need for centralized financial control, have vested in the governor authority to make his own inspections of the accounts of state officials; these inspections necessarily duplicate the work of the auditor. Thus the State of Arizona has an examiner appointed by the governor with senate approval, in addition to the popularly chosen auditor. Montana and Wyoming have also adopted this plan. In Washington, where the governor is authorized to conduct an investigation of the financial practices and transactions of any state office, the law provides that the expense of every such inspection must be defrayed by the agency that is being investigated from its current salary appropriation. Under such circumstances the right of investigation may become a powerful weapon of coercion, and the governor of Washington has not hesitated to use it for the purpose of forcing recalcitrant elective officials into line. The office of the land commissioner, for example, has been repeatedly investigated without disclosing serious irregularities; one such investigation required about eleven months for its completion, and cost nearly eight thousand dollars.

## THE SUPERINTENDENT OF PUBLIC INSTRUCTION

**His duties and selection.** Every state has an officer who is known as superintendent of public instruction, superintendent or commissioner of education, or something of the sort. Regardless of the title, his duties are always much the same—to administer the school laws of the state, apportion the state school funds among the local jurisdictions, and exercise a measure of supervision over local school authorities. In thirty-three states he is chosen by the voters. Seven states [36] provide for his appointment by the governor, and in the other eight [37] he is selected by the state board of education—a board whose organization and work are discussed in a later chapter.[38]

The folly of permitting the electorate to select an officer whose work is chiefly advisory, supervisory, and clerical, and whose technical qualifications are of the highest importance, should be obvious; yet the

[36] Maine, Massachusetts, New Jersey, Ohio, Pennsylvania, Tennessee, Virginia.
[37] Connecticut, Delaware, Maryland, Minnesota, New Hampshire, New York, Rhode Island, Vermont.
[38] See pp. 468–469.

superintendent of public instruction remains an elective officer in more than two thirds of the states. The objections to choosing him in this manner are well stated in a bulletin of the United States Bureau of Education: [39]

"1. This method of selection limits the field from which to choose, as the superintendent must be a citizen of the given state. In states where the superintendent is appointed by the state board of education or by the governor, this official may be selected from the country at large. Such freedom of selection is clearly in the interest of better service.

"2. Where the state superintendent is selected by popular vote the salary is fixed by law. The salary cannot be adjusted to fit the person desired; but a person must be found to fit the salary.

"3. Where the state superintendent is elected by popular vote the term of office is short—two to four years; and re-election is uncertain. This lack of continuity in the service is a serious handicap to the superintendent, however capable.

"4. This method of appointment makes the office political and subjects it to all the fluctuations of party and factional politics."

## OTHER ADMINISTRATIVE OFFICERS AND AGENCIES

Every state has a considerable number of administrative officers in addition to the secretary of state, the attorney-general, the treasurer, the auditor, and the superintendent of public instruction. Among the more common are the adjutant-general, the director of public health, the director of welfare, the director of public works, and the director of agriculture. The picture is further complicated by numerous boards and commissions dealing with virtually every phase of state activity. These various agencies differ so widely from state to state with regard to organization, functions, and jurisdiction that no attempt will be made to describe them at this point. Some are appointed by the governor; many are not. The general result is unco-ordinated, headless administration, wofully defective according to sound standards of organization and procedure.

## AN EXECUTIVE CABINET

In the federal government, the heads of the major departments usually meet with the president at regular intervals for a discussion of im-

[39] *A Manual of Educational Legislation for the Guidance of Committees on Education in the State Legislatures*, 1919, p. 11.

portant public policies. This group—the president's cabinet, as it is called—is a purely advisory body, whose opinions the president is free to accept or reject; but its combined wisdom often proves valuable in the solution of complicated problems of government. A similar gathering of state department heads at frequent intervals should be an outstanding feature of state government; in the majority of states, however, it cannot readily be arranged, because the heads of the most important departments are independent of the governor, and in many cases are not even on friendly terms with him. A number of states have recently reorganized their administrative systems, vesting in the governor authority to select the heads of nearly all departments, and thus making possible a governor's cabinet.[40] The governors of most of these states regard the cabinet idea with indifference, however, and scarcely ever call their department heads together for joint discussion. In Ohio, for example, where the desirability of a political cabinet was one of the points stressed by the proponents of administrative reorganization, the second governor chosen under the reorganization code definitely abandoned the cabinet idea, and it has not since been revived. The best example of an executive cabinet in state government is found in New York State, where fortnightly meetings are held without express statutory sanction, but at the direction of the governor.

## Selected References

Alexander, M. C., *Development of the Power of the Executive in New York,* Smith College Studies in History, Northampton, Mass., 1917.

Barth, Harry A., *Financial Control in the States with Emphasis on Control by the Governor,* 1923.

Black, Henry Campbell, *The Relation of the Executive Power to Legislation,* Princeton, N.J., 1919.

Cheek, Roma S., *The Pardoning Power of the Governor of North Carolina,* Durham, 1934.

Council of State Governments, *Emergency War Powers of the Governors of the Forty-eight States,* 1942.

Faust, Martin L., *Manual on the Executive Article for the Missouri Constitutional Convention of 1943,* Columbia, 1943.

Friedman, J. A., *The Impeachment of Governor William Sulzer,* 1939.

Governors' Conferences, *Proceedings,* 1909—(published annually).

Illinois Legislative Reference Bureau, *Constitutional Convention Bulletin No. 9,* Springfield, 1920.

Jensen, Christen, *The Pardoning Power in the American States,* 1920.

[40] See pp. 323–328.

Lipson, Leslie, *American Governor from Figurehead to Leader,* 1939.

MacMillan, Margaret B., *The War Governors in the American Revolution,* 1943.

Porter, Kirk H., *State Administration,* Chap. II, 1938.

Rohr, Charles James, *Governor of Maryland; A Constitutional Study,* Baltimore, 1932.

Ruscowski, Casimir W., *The Constitutional Governor,* 1943.

Smith, Alfred E., *The Citizen and His Government,* Chap. IV, 1935.

United States Army Service Schools, Ft. Leavenworth, *Military Aid to the Civil Power,* 1925.

White, L. O., *Public Administration,* rev. ed., 1939.

THE courts are specialized agencies for the enforcement of law.   They settle disputes between private persons, and also controversies between private persons and the state.   They determine the innocence or guilt of persons accused of crime.   They protect the rights of the individual, as guaranteed by federal and state constitutions.   They prevent the executive and legislative departments from overstepping the bounds of their authority.

In addition to their judicial acts the courts commonly perform a number of essentially administrative functions that have been assigned by the constitution or by law.   Thus they appoint and supervise certain public officers in a number of states, and in some instances they also have the right of removal.   School boards, for example, are judicially appointed in several jurisdictions.   The supreme court of Tennessee selects the attorney-general.   Many city and county officials may be removed by court action.   Some control over elections is also exercised by the courts in a number of states, and occasionally they are empowered to pass upon applications for various kinds of business licenses.   The estates of deceased persons are administered by the regular trial courts—or, in the more populous communities, by special probate courts; and this work differs in no essential respect from the activities of many administrative departments of the state government, which also handle a great deal of property.   The courts appoint receivers to manage the property and affairs of bankrupt persons. These various administrative duties, which are becoming constantly more numerous, consume a great deal of time, and tend to interfere with the primary function of the courts—the conduct of litigation. The suggestion is often made, therefore, that they be reduced to an absolute minimum, and that new administrative duties be assigned to administrative officers wherever possible.   But only a few states have acted on this principle.

### CIVIL AND CRIMINAL CASES

The cases that come before the courts for adjudication may be divided into two classes—civil and criminal.   A civil suit arises when one person seeks legal redress from another person for an alleged private wrong or *tort,* such as the violation of a contract. The state has no interest in the outcome of such a case, other than to insure fair play. Its function is solely that of impartial arbiter. A criminal suit, on the other hand, grows out of a public wrong—an offense against the state. The laws of each state enumerate and define these public wrongs, and prescribe the penalties to be imposed upon guilty persons. They also provide for public prosecution of persons whose probable guilt has been established by some formal process, such as indictment or information. Most of the public wrongs or crimes defined by law are acts against persons, and to that extent they resemble torts. Homicide, kidnaping, burglary, and arson, for example, are wrongs against individuals. But they are such serious matters that it has seemed wise to take them out of the category of private wrongs and declare them to be offenses against the state. In many instances a wrongful act gives rise to a criminal prosecution and also to a civil suit. Thus assault and battery may be a breach of the peace and, in addition, an invasion of the injured person's rights that leads naturally to civil action. The criminal prosecution and the civil suit are separate proceedings, however, and are separately tried. Frequently they go before the same court, but in such cases the court clearly indicates whether it is sitting in a criminal or civil capacity. Or the court may have separate divisions, established by law, to handle the two classes of cases.

## ORGANIZATION OF THE COURTS

**Justices of the peace:** JURISDICTION. At the base of the judicial pyramid, in the small towns and rural districts, are the justices of the peace. Almost invariably they are popularly chosen, and their terms of office are short—usually two years. They are not required to be learned in the law, and as a result they seldom have any special preparation for their important work. Their jurisdiction, though narrowly restricted by constitutional and legal provisions, extends to both civil and criminal matters. In civil suits it is limited by the sum in controversy or the amount of damages demanded; thus the state law may fix fifty or one hundred dollars, or even five hundred dollars, as the maximum. Suits involving larger sums may not be tried before a justice of the peace, but must go to a higher court. In criminal cases the justices of the peace have two distinct functions. First, they exercise summary jurisdiction over minor infractions of the law, such as breaches of the peace, traffic law violations, disregard of health ordinances, and the like. With regard to such matters they issue warrants when necessary, hold hearings, determine innocence or guilt, and impose suitable sentences. But their power does not extend beyond the imposition of small fines and imprisonment for short periods. Moreover, their decisions may almost invariably be appealed to some court of superior jurisdiction. The second important function of the justices of the peace in connection with criminal matters is the preliminary hearing of serious complaints. They determine whether sufficient evidence exists to warrant holding accused persons for further action by the grand jury or other authorities; and, if bail is required, they fix its amount.

DEFECTS UNDER PRESENT-DAY CONDITIONS: *Lack of legal training.* To entrust these important duties to persons without legal training, whose chief qualification is their ability to control votes, is little short of absurd. In earlier times, when life was far less complicated, and the controversies of rural Americans could best be settled by a proper application of common sense, the justice of the peace system gave reasonably satisfactory results. The justice knew every man in the community; he understood the situations that gave rise to lawsuits and breaches of the peace, and frequently he could give words of friendly advice that would be worth more than long citations from statutes and court decisions. But that day is past. The justice of the peace is no longer a community patriarch, dispensing Solomon-like justice through his superior wisdom. He is an agent of the state for the enforcement of state law, and he cannot possibly hope to give reasonable satisfaction in the performance of his duties without adequate legal training. Even for laymen, according to the old maxim, ignorance of the law is no excuse. For justices of the peace such ignorance is utterly inexcusable.

*The fee system.* Some of the worst abuses of the justices' court arise in connection with the fee system. Justices of the peace receive no stated salaries, except in a very few jurisdictions,[1] but instead rely on the fees that they are able to collect. Therefore their incomes bear a close relationship to the volume of business that they can attract to their courts. Within a single county there are usually several justices of the peace exercising concurrent jurisdiction, and each of them strives to secure a larger number of cases than his competitors. For this reason the decision in a civil case is likely to favor the plaintiff,

---

[1] Arizona, California, Louisiana, Nevada, and South Carolina are exceptions.

regardless of the circumstances; the plaintiff's attorney is thereby encouraged to supply additional customers. In some parts of the Chicago metropolitan area "various devices are resorted to in order to increase business. Advertising is frequent. By the use of cards and stationery, justices conspicuously announce their business and the extent of their jurisdiction. About ten per cent of the regional justices appear in classified telephone directories, and some advertise as collection agents. Shingles and window signs blare forth 'Justice of the Peace,' and there is frequently added the teaser, 'collections of all kinds.' At the entrance of an office building in a large Fox River Valley city one is faced by a confusing sign with the strange mélange of announcements, 'Justice Court, Auto Licenses here. We Remodel, Reline, Repair Men's and Women's Garments, Fur and Cloth, 2nd floor.' When competition is keen, some justices advertise by making personal visits to merchants to whom they promise quick service and certain justice." [2] The average justice of the peace welcomes a large number of arrests, since every arrest means an additional fee. Small wonder that such conditions have inspired the phrase—"injustices of the peace"!

*Need for reform.* The justice courts have long been regarded as a defective branch of the American judicial system. Nearly twenty years ago the New York State Crime Commission declared: "Probably the most unsatisfactory feature of the criminal law is the obsolete and antiquated institution known as the justice of the peace. Thoughtful students of the subject have for some years past realized fully that this was an unsatisfactory form of organization, and nothing but the expense of providing adequately trained lawyers to man these minor courts has prevented remedying the situation." [3] This criticism is as valid today as when it was written. Many reforms have been suggested, ranging from the abolition of the fee system to the complete elimination of the justice courts and the substitution of district courts presided over by judges selected from the legal profession. But none of these proposals have received widespread favor.

**Magistrates' courts.** In the cities the lowest tribunals are commonly known as police or magistrates' courts. The men who preside over these courts do not differ in any essential respect from the justices of the peace, except that they are commonly on a salary basis. They

[2] Lepawsky, Albert, *The Judicial System of Metropolitan Chicago*, pp. 145–146. Reprinted by permission of the University of Chicago Press.

[3] Annual Report, 1927, p. 44.

are chosen by the voters in most cities, which is merely another way of saying that they are selected by the dominant political machine. Their salaries are low—so low as to attract only the poorer grade of politicians. They are constantly reminded that they owe their positions to the favor of the boss, and they are expected to retain this favor by using their authority for such purposes and in such manner as the boss may direct. Since they are not learned in the law, the intricacies of constitutions and statutes present no difficulties, and they can readily arrive at any conclusions that fancy or political wisdom may dictate. Of course, a right of appeal from their decisions exists in nearly all cases. But appeals are tedious, costly, and uncertain, so it usually happens that justice—or injustice—is finally done in the magistrates' courts.

**Special police courts.** Many cities have attempted to solve some of their more difficult problems in the administration of justice by creating special courts—juvenile, domestic relations, small claims, traffic, and others. These courts are presided over by judges who are presumed to be specialists in the various fields to which they have been assigned.

TRIAL PROCEDURE. The procedure is adjusted to the nature of the business at hand; usually the formality of the court room is swept aside in the interest of efficient justice. In a juvenile court case, for example, everything is done to put the boy or girl at ease and to ascertain all the facts without creating the impression that a trial is in progress. More important than the fact that a criminal act has been committed is the reason for that act, and the treatment that may be necessary to prevent the young delinquent from becoming a confirmed offender. Other problems connected with the family—legal separation of husband and wife, divorce, support, the custody of children—also require special consideration and are generally handled in domestic relations or family courts. Here, too, the procedure is informal, since the purpose of the court is to bring about a reconciliation whenever possible and a friendly settlement when reconciliation is out of the question. It has been proposed that the juvenile and domestic relations courts be consolidated, on the ground that virtually every problem affecting the child is necessarily a family problem. This suggestion is logical, and its general adoption would eliminate many perplexing questions of conflicting jurisdiction.

Special court procedure is also necessary to handle small claims—perhaps for amounts less than twenty-five or fifty dollars. In such cases the sum in controversy is often but a fraction of the cost of an ordinary trial, including a lawyer's fee. Therefore some way must be found to give substantial justice simply and cheaply. It is absurd to declare—as the laws of every state did declare until a few years ago, and as most state laws still provide—that such matters as a twenty-dollar claim for unpaid wages or a bill of seven dollars for groceries cannot be adjusted judicially without an expenditure of approximately one hundred dollars. The small claims court offers the most satisfactory solution of this difficult problem. As established in seven states [4] and in a number of the larger cities,[5] it eliminates all unnecessary formality, discourages the participation of lawyers, reduces court costs to a nominal figure, and narrowly restricts the right of appeal.

Traffic courts also deserve at least passing mention. Their function is to handle all cases of alleged violations of the motor vehicle laws, so as to secure prompt and uniform treatment of offenders. Poor organization, however, has prevented them from attaining maximum efficiency in most of the cities where they have been established.

**The unified municipal court.** One of the most important reforms of recent years in the American judicial system is the unified municipal court. Such a court, if properly organized, has complete original jurisdiction, both civil and criminal, over all matters arising under state law or municipal ordinance within the city's limits. Its work is divided among a number of branches—small claims, traffic, domestic relations, and the like—but complete responsibility is centered in the chief justice of the court, who assigns his colleagues to the divisions for which they are presumably best fitted.

To a large extent the municipal court determines its own organization and makes its own rules. Thus it is able to modify its procedure whenever necessary to obtain greater efficiency. Cases may be transferred from one judge to another, in order to distribute the work equally and prevent congested dockets. This, then, is a unified municipal court—as properly organized. But very few courts conform to this ideal pattern. So-called "unified" municipal courts have been established in five of the six largest cities of the United States, and in a number of other metropolitan centers, including Baltimore,

---

[4] California, Idaho, Iowa, Kansas, Massachusetts, Nevada, South Dakota.

[5] Chicago, Cleveland, Philadelphia, Portland, Oregon (Multnomah County), Spokane, and others.

Buffalo, Pittsburgh, Cincinnati, and Milwaukee. Most of them are defective in some particular, however. They usually lack complete original jurisdiction or adequate rule-making power.

**County or circuit courts.** Above the justice and police courts, in every state, are the trial courts, where most litigation originates and most persons accused of crime are brought to trial. These courts are called by various names. In some states, where there is one such court in each county, they are known as county courts. More commonly they are designated as district or circuit courts, since the laws of approximately two thirds of the states combine counties into judicial districts or circuits. Under this plan two or three counties comprise a district, and in each county a session of the district court is held at regular intervals. The number of judges assigned to a district varies with the population and the volume of litigation, but one judge to a district is generally regarded as a satisfactory arrangement, except for the larger cities. The jurisdiction of the trial courts—by whatever name they may be known—is very broad. They usually handle all civil suits, without restriction as to amount.[6] Such suits may be begun in the trial courts, or may come on appeal from the justice or police courts. Original jurisdiction is exercised in virtually all criminal cases, other than the minor misdemeanor cases handled by the justices of the peace and the magistrates. Separate courts may be established for civil and criminal matters, or merely separate divisions of the same court. It has already been indicated that the trial courts commonly perform a number of administrative duties, such as the management of the estates of deceased persons and the appointment and supervision of certain county officials.[7] In thirty-seven states the judges of these courts are elected by the people.[8] Four-year terms are most common.

**Appellate courts.** Above the trial courts, at the apex of the state's judicial pyramid, stands the state supreme court. More than one third of the states have found it necessary, however, to interpose courts of appeal between the trial courts and the supreme court, in order to lighten the burden of the highest tribunal. These intermediate courts are called by various names—courts of appeal, district courts of appeal, superior courts. In New York the "supreme" court is really

[6] In a few states, however, a limit of one or two thousand dollars is imposed.

[7] See p. 227.

[8] The other eleven states are Connecticut, Delaware, Florida, Maine, Massachusetts, New Hampshire, and New Jersey, where the governor appoints; and Rhode Island, South Carolina, Vermont, and Virginia, where the choice is made by the legislature.

an intermediate appellate tribunal, inferior to the highest court, which is known as the court of appeals. The "supreme" court of New Jersey is subordinate to the court of errors and appeals. The intermediate courts of the states vary almost as widely in jurisdiction as in nomenclature. In general, they handle cases that come to them on appeal from the trial courts. Their jurisdiction is final in some matters, but subject to an appeal to the supreme court in others. The laws of a few states confer original jurisdiction upon them for certain important subjects of controversy, such as contested elections. Within a single state there may be but one intermediate court of appeals, as in Pennsylvania, or several such courts, as in California, or several divisions of one court, as in New York. Each court has from three to nine judges, who sit as a body and render decisions by a majority vote.

**The supreme court.** Every state constitution, save that of New Hampshire, provides for a supreme court (though not always by that name), and in New Hampshire a supreme court has been created by act of the legislature. The number of members ranges from three to sixteen, and a majority vote is necessary in each case. The chief function of the supreme court is to hear and decide cases from the lower courts. In eleven states it has only appellate jurisdiction,[9] and in thirty-three others its original jurisdiction is limited to the issuance of certain writs. The constitutions of the remaining four states [10] confer original jurisdiction in certain important cases—for example, cases in which the state is a party. The supreme court of a state is the final interpreter of the state's constitution and laws. No appeal from its decisions may be taken to the Supreme Court of the United States unless a so-called "federal question" is involved—that is, unless the case hinges upon the meaning of the federal Constitution or a federal law or treaty. State supreme court judges are generally chosen by the people.[11] Their salaries are relatively high,[12] and their terms of office fairly long. More than one third of the states provide six-year

[9] Arizona, Connecticut, Georgia, Indiana, Kentucky, Maryland, Mississippi, New Hampshire, New Jersey, New York, Tennessee.

[10] Massachusetts, Nebraska, North Carolina, Pennsylvania.

[11] The manner of selection is the same as for judges of the trial courts (see footnote on p. 233 except in two states—Florida and Maine. In Florida the members of the supreme court are popularly elected, though minor judges are appointed by the governor; and in Maine this plan is reversed.

[12] Only four states—Idaho, North Dakota, South Dakota, and Utah—pay less than six thousand dollars a year. One third of the states pay ten thousand dollars or more.

terms, and three New England states [13] have accepted the principle of tenure for life or during good behavior. Vermont, on the other hand, still retains a two-year term.

## SELECTION OF JUDGES

Students of government and members of the bar are generally agreed that the judges of all courts should be appointed by the chief executive, and not forced to engage in the hurly-burly of an election campaign. "Popular election" is likely to be synonymous with "political selection"; therefore judges chosen by popular vote may reasonably be expected to be cogs in the dominant political machine. Judges should be experts—technicians of the highest order; but experts cannot be obtained by popular election, except at rare intervals and under unusual circumstances. It is an axiom of public administration that appointment should be used when skill is desired, and that election should be employed only to secure representation. The more progressive states, in reorganizing their agencies of administration, have generally recognized this principle, at least to some extent.[14] But election by the voters still remains the generally accepted method of choosing the judiciary. Selection by the legislature seldom, if ever, gives better results than popular choice; it diffuses the responsibility for improper selections, and opens the way to secret deals.

An interesting experiment has been tried in New Jersey, where the seven vice-chancellors of the court of chancery are appointed by the head of the court, who is known as the chancellor. The high calibre of the vice-chancellors chosen under this plan has led to the suggestion that the chief justice of the supreme court in each state be vested with authority to appoint all other members of the judiciary. Appointment of inferior court judges might, perhaps, be made subject to the approval of the other justices of the supreme court. Such a proposal, if seriously considered, would undoubtedly be attacked on the ground that it was "un-American"—that is, contrary to customary American procedure. But it seems to have only one serious disadvantage—the danger that so much "patronage" in the hands of a judicial officer might transform him into a political officer and make him a storm-center of state politics. Even this danger may not be great. In England, where all judges of courts of record are appointed on the recom-

---

[13] Massachusetts, New Hampshire, Rhode Island.
[14] See pp. 319–328.

mendation of the lord chancellor, the charge of partisan politics in appointments is never heard.

**Proposals to improve calibre of judges.** For some years to come, at least, popular election is likely to remain the generally accepted method of choosing state judges in the United States. All federal judges are appointed by the president, with Senate approval, but this long-standing [15] federal practice has had little effect upon state government, and is still generally disregarded when state constitutions are amended or rewritten. It is worth while, therefore, to inquire whether some way can be found to improve the calibre of the judges chosen by popular vote.

Two important suggestions, both designed to accomplish this purpose, have been made. One of these is that the bar association of each state assume responsibility for nominating suitable candidates. This proposal has already been adopted in a number of states and in most of the larger cities, with varying degrees of success. In Wisconsin, where popular election of judges has produced unusually good results, the bar association is generally given the credit. The other plan to obtain a better judiciary was set forth in 1922 in the recommendations of the Cleveland Survey of Criminal Justice: "Judges in first instance should be elected as they are now. Their first term should be comparatively short, six years. At the end of that time they should run for re-election for a longer term of, say, ten or twelve years, and for this purpose they should run *against their own record,* not against a motley group of other candidates. In other words, the voters decide a plain issue: Shall the judge be retired or shall he be retained? The third term should be even longer and consist of, say twenty years. In the event of the retirement of a judge a special election, in which he could not be a candidate, would be held. Such a plan will reduce the amount of electioneering and the constant interruption of judicial work thereby occasioned. For a judge to run against his own record is infinitely less degrading than the scramble for votes in the open field. The question of re-election or retirement will be an issue of moment and on it all the responsible agencies in the community can focus their attention." [16]

This scheme, or modifications of it, were promptly considered in a number of jurisdictions, but did not pass beyond the discussion stage

[15] Since the adoption of the Constitution in 1789.

[16] *Criminal Justice in Cleveland*, p. 365. Reprinted by permission of The Cleveland Foundation.

until 1934, when the voters of California approved a constitutional amendment permitting judges to run solely against their own records, instead of forcing them to campaign against rival candidates. Under the provisions of this California plan any incumbent judge may, just prior to the end of his term, indicate his desire to retain his office. His name is then placed on the ballot, and the voters are asked merely to decide whether he shall be retained—not whether they prefer him to a number of other candidates. An unfavorable vote causes a vacancy, which is then filled by gubernatorial appointment. The governor does not have a free hand in the matter, however; his selection must be approved by a commission on qualifications, consisting of the state supreme court's chief justice, another judge of a high court, and the attorney-general. Moreover, the voters must give their approval at the next election. If they again vote in the negative, another vacancy occurs; and so the process continues until everyone is satisfied.[17] This plan is a marked improvement over the ordinary scheme of popular election, but proposals for its adoption in other states have received little support.

## REMOVAL OF JUDGES

**Impeachment and joint address.** Almost as important as the selection of judges is the matter of their removal. Every state constitution provides that judges, as well as other civil officers, may be removed by process of impeachment. In most states a two-thirds vote of the senate is necessary for conviction. Moreover, state constitutions customarily limit the use of impeachment to very serious cases, in which criminal misconduct is charged. Nearly half of the states authorize removal of judges by joint address of the two houses of the legislature —that is, by passage of a concurrent resolution. This method does not partake of the judicial nature of impeachment; it is a purely legislative act and not suitable for determining the innocence or guilt of any person charged with an offense so serious as to warrant his removal from public office. Fortunately, joint address has been hedged about with so many constitutional restrictions that it is scarcely ever used.

**The recall.** It is obvious, therefore, that removal of judges by the ordinary processes of government is extremely difficult. Impeachment—the means universally provided—is cumbersome, tedious, and

[17] See Charles Aikin's article, "A New Method of Selecting Judges in California," in the June, 1935, issue of the *American Political Science Review* pp. 472-474.

suitable only for extreme cases. Therefore a judge may and sometimes does remain in office long after his period of usefulness is past. He may suffer from physical infirmities that seriously interfere with his judicial duties, yet refuse to resign. He may acquire an arbitrary and unreasonable attitude that prevents even-handed dispensation of justice in his court, yet continue in office because no ready way can be found to get rid of him. Such cases have actually occurred, though infrequently, and have given rise to a demand for some easier way of removing judges who have become infirm, unreasonable—or unpopular. The scheme most commonly advocated is the recall. The constitutions of eight states [18] now provide for the recall of judges, and in two other states judges have been exempted from the provisions of the recall by the narrow margin of a few votes.

Many leaders of the bench and bar believe, however, that the recall provisions of state constitutions should not be applied to judges under any circumstances. They cite the usual arguments against the recall [19] and stress also the necessity of maintaining an independent judiciary. Judges must be independent, because they must be free to enforce the law as they find it, without fear or favor. They are charged with the protection of the rights of the individual, and in the performance of their duties they may frequently find it necessary to safeguard minority rights, guaranteed by federal and state constitutions, against the momentary desires of a majority of the voters. Thus they are the representatives, not merely of the dominant element in the commonwealth, but of every element. And their decisions must be based on law—not on popular notions of right and wrong. This theory—of an independent judiciary—is the basis of the American judicial system. The recall, however, as applied to judges, is predicated upon an entirely different assumption. It implies that judges shall be the representatives of the majority and subject to majority rule, since they may be removed from office at any time by a vote of the majority of the voters. Fortunately, in those states where the recall has been adopted it has been used with great moderation. But it is an ever-present menace to judicial independence.

Of course, there is another side to the story. It can be argued, with reason, that secure tenure for judges operates to the benefit of the incompetent as well as the competent, and sometimes keeps men on the bench who have amply demonstrated their unfitness for public

---

[18] Arizona, California, Colorado, Kansas, Nevada, North Dakota, Oregon, Wisconsin.
[19] See pp. 139–143.

office. But the danger of keeping some judges too long seems less serious than the danger of rendering the entire judiciary subservient to the whims of popular fancy. And no way has yet been found to make good judges independent, while subjecting bad judges to the constant necessity of retaining the support of the voters.

## NEED FOR COURT REFORM

**Defects in the judicial system:** DELAY IN THE ADMINISTRATION OF JUSTICE. For many years the American judicial system has been condemned as thoroughly unsatisfactory by statesmen, publicists, jurists —in fact, by virtually everyone qualified to express an opinion on the subject. Delay is one of the most common causes of complaint. A certain amount of delay is inevitable; it is, in fact, desirable. It is inevitable because many things must be done in preparation for a case. Facts must be ascertained, witnesses located and subpoenaed, evidence assembled, and the case listed for trial. Moderate delay is desirable because it materially lessens the likelihood of injustice. It affords an accused person reasonable opportunity to prepare his defense. As the Supreme Court of the State of Pennsylvania said in an important case: "The 'law of the land,' like 'due process of law,' requires timely notice and an opportunity to defend. It is vain to give the accused a day in court, with no opportunity to prepare for it, or to guarantee him counsel without giving the latter any opportunity to acquaint himself with the facts or law of the case." [20] The National Commission on Law Observance and Enforcement reports the case of a person accused of arson who was put on trial three hours after entering his plea, despite the fact that his attorney had just been appointed and was totally unprepared.[21]

*Injustice of delay.* At times, therefore, undue haste may produce very unfortunate results. But when delay extends beyond a reasonable period, objection may well be raised. Cases that drag on for months or even years before final settlement are productive of nothing but evil. In many instances they amount to a substantial denial of justice. Witnesses die, move away, or forget. In a civil suit, attorneys' fees grow until they sometimes equal or exceed the amount of damages awarded. A poor person, badly in need of money and impatient with the apparent procrastination of the courts, may finally agree to accept a small sum in full payment of a large debt, rather than

[20] Commonwealth *v.* O'Keefe, 298 Penna. 169. 148 Atl. 73 (1929).
[21] Report No. 11, on *Lawlessness in Law Enforcement*, p. 274.

undergo a further period of uncertainty. In such cases, delay is a form of unfairness that should not be tolerated. Frequently cited as an extreme example of faulty justice is the case of the injured railroad brakeman whose suit for damages was tried seven times, and finally decided twenty years after the accident occurred. Some time ago two young men spent one hundred and seven days in an Ann Arbor jail, awaiting trial for simple larceny, and were finally convicted and sentenced to the maximum penalty of ninety days. Thereupon the judge credited them with seventeen days apiece on the next sentences they might receive. Such happenings are not typical, but they occur frequently enough to create a serious problem.

*Causes of delay.* It may well be asked, therefore, why civil suits and criminal prosecutions are not handled more expeditiously. The answer, at least in part, is that the courts are not properly organized to handle the large and increasing volume of business imposed upon them by the complexities of modern civilization. Court dockets are congested. In many jurisdictions new cases are placed on the calendar more rapidly than old cases can be disposed of, and every year the problem of delay becomes more serious. New discoveries, new inventions—in fact, a new world—have vastly broadened the field of human relationships, and therefore have made more litigation almost inevitable. Thousands of new laws dealing with hundreds of new subjects have defined as criminal many acts that were formerly regarded as beyond the scope of the law and in this way have increased the number of "criminals by definition." So it is not at all surprising that the judicial system, designed in another day to meet the requirements of a simple mode of life, should be unsuited to the tremendous task of dispensing justice swiftly and surely in this modern world.

A major cause of delay is the abuse of the right of appeal. This right must be preserved, of course; otherwise there would be no way of correcting the injustices that naturally result from human ignorance, indifference, carelessness—or worse. But it should be restricted within narrow limits. It should not be permitted to become a device for defeating the plain provisions of the law. Unfortunately, it has reached that low level in every American state. Wealthy persons carry civil suits that have been decided against them to court after court, perhaps without shadow of moral right, in the hope of exhausting the physical and financial resources of their opponents. Professional criminals, assisted by clever attorneys who know every trick of the legal trade, often succeed in having their convictions set aside on technical grounds entirely unrelated to the main issue of innocence or guilt. The only remedy for this unwholesome state of affairs is a modification of judicial procedure whereby appeals will be limited to those cases in which substantial injustice seems to have been done.

UNCERTAINTY OF PUNISHMENT. One of the most serious defects of the American judicial system is the uncertainty of punishment. When a person commits a crime—anywhere in the United States— the chance that he will be apprehended, convicted, and punished is fairly remote. Crime may properly be listed among the safer professions, provided one steers clear of murder. And even murderers, in this country, enjoy a comparative safety that is unknown in the progressive nations of western Europe. This state of affairs cannot be charged wholly against the judiciary. The police, who are primarily responsible for the apprehension of persons accused of crime, are often inefficient, and sometimes corrupt. Prosecuting attorneys, swayed by personal or partisan motives, frequently fail to press serious charges against politically powerful persons, preferring to make impressive records by forcing confessions from poor wretches who have neither money nor friends. But a great many miscarriages of justice in the United States can be traced directly to the obsolete judicial system. Their recurrence can be prevented only by thoroughgoing changes.

JUDICIAL REFORM PROPOSALS. Hundreds of reforms of the court system have been suggested. Some are highly conservative, amounting merely to slight changes in procedure. Others are extremely radical, contemplating a complete revision of judicial organization and methods. Many of the moderate proposals have already received more or less widespread acceptance. Many others, also, though not in actual operation, deserve serious consideration. In this volume, however, only a limited amount of space can be devoted to judicial reform; therefore attention will be centered on a few outstanding proposals.

*Court unification.* Most comprehensive, perhaps, is the plan of court unification advanced by a committee of the American Bar Association nearly four decades ago, and since indorsed by statesmen and publicists. According to this suggestion, the entire judicial power of each state, "at least for civil cases, should be vested in one great court, of which all tribunals should be branches, departments, or divisions. The business, as well as the judicial administration, of this court should be thoroughly organized so as to prevent not merely waste of judicial power, but all needless clerical work, duplication of papers and records, and the like, thus obviating unnecessary expense to litigants and cost to the public." [22]   The lowest courts would be known as county courts, and would have exclusive jurisdiction over all petty matters.   Above them would be the superior courts, exercising original jurisdiction over controversies in which larger sums were involved and separated into appropriate divisions for the several types of business.   At the top would be the supreme court—a single ulti-mate court of appeals with its necessary branches.   The chief justice of the supreme court, or a council presided over by him, would have power to assign judges to branches or communities as needed, to assign or transfer cases in order to equalize the amount of court work, and to establish court procedure within the limits fixed by law.   Thus au-thority would be concentrated in one man, or a small group, and responsibility could readily be fixed if the court system failed to oper-ate smoothly and efficiently.

This scheme is in marked contrast to the present organization—or disorganization—of the courts.   If adopted, it would eliminate over-lapping and conflicting jurisdiction, simplify appeal procedure, per-mit judges to specialize in particular classes of legislation, and produce a co-ordinated judicial system.   It seems to have virtually no dis-advantages worth mentioning.   Yet it has not been written into the constitution of a single state.   It is a sharp departure from present practice and therefore not likely to win strong support overnight.

*Judicial councils.*   Less ambitious than court unification, but also designed to improve court organization and procedure, is the judicial council movement.   Ohio led the way in 1923.   Its statute creating a judicial council was carefully drafted but the necessary appropriation was not made; therefore the council was able to accomplish virtually nothing.   The next year, however, Massachusetts enacted suitable legislation and also provided adequate funds.   Since 1924 the move-ment has grown steadily.   There are now judicial councils in twenty-nine states, though three of them are inactive, and five others are obliged to function without appropriations.

The primary function of judicial councils is to study the court sys-tem and recommend desirable changes.   For this purpose they con-duct a continuous survey of the volume and condition of business in the various state courts and also observe the result of experiments in other jurisdictions.   They devise ways of simplifying judicial pro-cedure and handling cases more expeditiously.   Proposals for im-

[22] American Bar Association *Reports,* 1909.

proved organization and methods are submitted to the legislature and occasionally to the judges of the courts. Special investigations are made from time to time at the legislature's request. In most instances, therefore, a judicial council merely investigates and recommends. It is without power to compel the adoption of any of its suggestions. It has no final authority. But in a few states of which California is the most notable example, it has a certain measure of control over the court system. The California judicial council assigns judges to care for crowded calendars and also makes rules of procedure that supplement the rules established by state law. Usually a judicial council is composed of nine or ten members, though the number varies from six in Rhode Island to fifty-two in Kentucky. One or more members are chosen from the state supreme court and several from the lower courts. In addition, it is customary to appoint one or two practicing attorneys who hold no public office.

*Revision of rules of procedure.* One reason for excessive delays and congested court dockets is the antiquated set of rules under which virtually every state court is obliged to operate. These rules, which prescribe judicial procedure in minute detail, have been enacted by the legislature and may not be altered except through legislative action. Many of them serve chiefly to hamper the courts and prevent the efficient administration of justice. Nor should this result occasion surprise. Legislators are laymen—amateurs elected to public office because of personal popularity or political power. They do not know the needs of the court system, and cannot be expected to understand the problems involved. Even though many of them are lawyers, they exceed the limits of their capacity when they attempt to frame suitable codes of judicial procedure. In recent years, therefore, the suggestion has frequently been made that the courts be given authority, within broad limits, to establish their own rules and to make such changes from time to time as may seem desirable. In defense of the proposal it is urged that cumbersome rules could be swept away with ease, that greater flexibility would inevitably result, and that the overburdened legislature would be relieved of a task for which it is poorly fitted. The American Bar Association believes that the courts should make their own rules of procedure and has appointed a committee to foster the movement. About one fourth of the states have already conferred more or less extensive rule-making powers upon the judiciary, and several other states have given the matter serious consideration. There is some disagreement as to whether the rules of procedure should be prepared by the state supreme court, by the judges of the supreme court plus other judges selected from some of the inferior courts, or by the judicial council. For a number of reasons, however, the judicial council method seems likely to give best results.

*Increase of judge's authority.* The part played by the judge in the conduct of a trial varies somewhat from state to state, but not a single state of the American Union empowers him to assume a commanding position, like the judge of an English court, and guide the trial to a proper conclusion. Instead, the American judge, at least in the state courts, is merely an umpire, enforcing the rules of the game and unconcerned as to the result. The judicial codes of many states, though permitting him to instruct the jury as to the law applicable to each case, specify that the statement of law must be abstract. Therefore the jurors are utterly without guidance in their attempt to apply legal principles that they but half understand. In other respects, also, the judge is greatly handicapped. Usually he is forbidden to comment on the facts, or to express his opinion concerning the credibility of witnesses. The effect of all these restrictions has been to reduce— almost to the vanishing point—the influence of the one disinterested person in the courtroom whose training and experience fit him to direct a search for justice. Thus a present-day trial in a state court becomes a sort of judicial duel, with the opposing attorneys as chief participants. The obvious remedy for this state of affairs is to increase the authority of the judge, so that he may direct the course of the trial with a firm hand. But the states seem disinclined to enact the necessary legislation.

**Defects in the jury system.** Blackstone once declared that "trial by jury ever has been and I trust ever will be looked upon as the glory of the English law . . . and the most transcendent privilege which any subject can enjoy or wish for." [23] In present-day America, however, the "glory of the English law" shines less brightly, reflecting only the light of a time long past, and the ancient and honorable institution of jury trial has been subjected to a great deal of sharp criticism.

SELECTION OF JURORS. A number of factors are responsible for the present widespread dissatisfaction with the jury system. In the first place, modern conditions are not well suited to a scheme of fact-finding by twelve "good men and true, drawn from the vicinage." In

[23] *Commentaries*, Book III, p. 379.

urban communities, especially, men scarcely know their neighbors, and their slight familiarity with neighborhood happenings is valueless at a trial. Moreover, any prospective juror who has first-hand knowledge of the facts of a given case, or has given time and thought to the published accounts, is immediately challenged and declared ineligible to serve. Thus we find that the ancient practice has been completely reversed. Whereas jurors were once selected from the immediate vicinity so that their knowledge of local men and events might lead to a fair verdict, now jurors with pertinent knowledge of either men or events are excluded, and ignorance is made virtually a prerequisite of jury service.

Further, the methods commonly employed for the selection of jurors result in serious delays. Any prospective juror may be challenged by the prosecution or the defense "for cause"—that is, because of alleged prejudice or incompetence—and will be dismissed if the challenge is sustained by the court. In addition, the law always permits a certain number of challenges without assignment of cause— peremptory challenges, as they are called. But it is the abuse of the right of challenge for cause that chiefly produces delay. In a hotly contested case, with a judge who is disposed to allow virtually all challenges, an almost unbelievable amount of time is often wasted. The selection of the jury may take days or even weeks, and involve the examination of hundreds of prospective jurors. Moreover, the jury laws of every state authorize presiding judges to relieve persons from jury service, if it appears that such service would impose a serious hardship. Judges usually grant exemptions liberally, for they realize that jury duty places a heavy burden on busy men and women who are engaged in important business and professional activities. Thus the better elements in the community are weeded out, and the only persons available for jury service are "the ignorant, narrow, prejudiced, unfit, and untruthful. . . . Around every court house there are professional jurors, able to qualify by giving the proper answers for any case. Most of these professionals are peanut politicians in their precincts or wards during election times and appreciate the little fees and regard it as an honor to serve on a jury." [24]

JURY VERDICTS. The mere fact that jurors are not trained in the law would seem to be a sufficient reason why they should not be permitted to determine the law under any circumstances. Yet in a number of states the jury is made the judge of both law and fact. The

[24] Fuller, Hugh N., *Criminal Justice in Virginia*, p. 133.

results are usually distressing to anyone interested in an impartial judicial system. In some types of cases—complicated breach of contract suits, for example—the jury is not even a good judge of the facts. The exact meaning of abstruse documents, couched in formal legal terminology, must be determined, and the jurors are completely ignorant of the rules that should guide them. Even in less technical cases, where sound judgment is the chief requisite, juries are easily swayed by racial, religious, or class appeals. The stirring words of a clever attorney may prove more effective than unrefuted evidence. Then, too, it is generally recognized that jury decisions are often compromises—not the honest opinion of all the jurors, but merely a means of reaching a formal agreement. If some members of the jury desire conviction, while others hold out for acquittal, the only way to reach a verdict may be to find the accused guilty of some offense less serious than that charged. Substantial injustice may result, but the fiction of unanimous agreement is preserved. It should be pointed out, also, that the danger of jury tampering is always rather serious. One or two dishonest jurors, with bribe money in their pockets, may successfully prevent a fair verdict. Of course, bribery of judges is not unknown, but it is certainly far less common than the unwholesome practice of tampering with juries.

PROPOSALS FOR CHANGES. The foregoing charges constitute a serious indictment of the jury system. The system itself is on trial today in the United States. Some persons maintain that it should be modified to meet modern conditions; others contend that it should be abolished root and branch. Virtually no one urges its retention without changes of some sort. A number of plans to improve the jury system have been proposed, and most of them have been tried in certain states.

It has been suggested that the size of the jury be reduced from twelve—the traditional number—to five, six, seven, or, at most, eight. A smaller number of persons should be able to reach an agreement more readily, with no greater likelihood of doing injustice. This plan has been adopted by twenty states for civil suits, and by eight states for criminal cases not involving the death penalty. The usual requirement of a unanimous verdict is also under fire. Many persons believe that a verdict rendered by a substantial majority of the jury would often be much fairer than a so-called "unanimous" agreement. Real unanimity of opinion seldom exists, in juries or elsewhere, and constitutional provisions that fail to recognize this important fact simply place an unreasonable amount of power in the hands of one juror or a small minority. In recent years a number of states have amended their fundamental laws to permit jury verdicts by less than unanimous vote, especially in civil suits. Criminal cases are less frequently included, and no state has abolished the unanimity requirement for capital cases. A three-fourths vote is usually necessary for a verdict, though two-thirds suffices in Montana, and also in Idaho for minor offenses. Another proposal is to place the responsibility for selecting jurors primarily on the court, where it properly belongs.

Striking at the very heart of jury inefficiency is the suggestion that persons accused of crime or engaged in civil suits be permitted to waive their right of jury trial if they so desire. The right to waive trial by jury in civil suits is now found in virtually all states, having been granted by constitutional amendment, statutory provision, or judicial action. Forty states permit waiver in misdemeanor cases. With regard to more serious offenses, however, only fifteen states [25] have abandoned the outworn custom of compulsory trial by jury without regard to the wishes of the accused. Moreover, in some of these states the right of waiver has no practical significance, since it is virtually never used by persons accused of crime.[26] But in other commonwealths trial of felonies by the judge without jury has become the rule.

**Three widely used judicial reforms:** DECLARATORY JUDGMENTS. Three important judicial reforms remain to be considered. One of these, the declaratory judgment, is designed to provide a judicial interpretation of statutes, contracts, and the like before lawsuits actually arise. The persons involved are thus saved time and money, and the cost of administering civil justice is reduced. In order to produce this desirable result, however, it is necessary to modify the well-established rule that the courts will not pass upon any legal question until it is presented to them in the course of ordinary litigation. But modification is needed, for the rule often works hardship. It compels business men to guess at the exact meaning of a contract unless one of them breaks it and the other sues. It forces them to grope blindly through a maze of legislative "Thou shalt nots," without any certain knowledge of their legal rights.

Quite naturally, therefore, practical men long ago wearied of such a method of interpreting the law, and asked why it would not be

[25] California, Connecticut, Illinois, Indiana, Maryland, Massachusetts, Michigan, New Jersey, Ohio, Oklahoma, Oregon, Rhode Island, Virginia, Washington, Wisconsin.

[26] In Ohio and Rhode Island, among others.

feasible to permit the courts to determine in advance of litigation, when requested to do so, the exact meaning of statute or ordinance, or a written instrument such as a contract, a will, or a deed. The only answer was that tradition and precedent would be seriously disturbed. So in recent years "declaratory judgment" statutes have been enacted in three fourths of the states, and the Conference of Commissioners on Uniform State Laws has drafted a model law on the subject which is urged for general adoption. Under the provisions of such an act, the courts are authorized to issue binding declarations of rights—declaratory judgments, as they are called—that will enable interested persons to determine their rights and duties under a written instrument or statute without the unpleasant necessity of engaging in litigation. It must be clearly understood, however, that the courts cannot be compelled to issue declaratory judgments; they exercise a wide discretion in the matter. Thus the declaratory judgment statutes of the several states usually contain some such provision as the following: "The court may refuse to exercise the power to declare rights and to construe instruments in any case when a decision under it would not terminate the necessity or controversy that gave rise to the action, or in any case where the declaration or construction is not necessary and proper at the time under all the circumstances." Dissipation of the time and energy of the courts is thus prevented.

CONCILIATION AND ARBITRATION. The two remaining judicial reforms—conciliation and arbitration—are so closely related that laymen frequently fail to distinguish between them. Both aim to settle disputes by less formal methods than the ordinary processes of litigation. But conciliation is an attempt by a third person—usually a court official—to induce the interested parties to settle their differences, whereas arbitration is the submission of a dispute by the interested parties to a third person whom they have jointly selected and whose award they agree to accept.

Conciliation has not been used in the United States to any extent until recent years. Since 1913, however, when Cleveland led the way, the municipal courts of a number of the larger cities [27] have established conciliation branches or have made provision for special conciliation procedure. In 1921 North Dakota adopted a state-wide conciliation act. The general features of conciliation are the same in all jurisdictions where it is employed. When a civil suit is begun, it may be taken first—usually at the discretion of the plaintiff—to the concilia-

[27] Including New York City, Minneapolis, and Des Moines.

tion branch. Here the presiding judge attempts to find a way of satisfying both contestants. He points out the expense and trouble of prolonged litigation and suggests a reasonable settlement. His proposals have no binding effect, however, but depend upon the good will and good faith of the parties to the dispute. Yet many cases are quickly and cheaply settled by means of the simple process of conciliation.

Arbitration is much more common in the United States. In fact, arbitration laws are found in virtually every state, though most of these laws are inadequate and totally unsuited to modern conditions. A few commonwealths—especially California, Massachusetts, New Jersey, New York, and Oregon—have recently enacted effective, statewide arbitration acts, and therefore offer the best examples of satisfactory arbitration procedure. When a dispute arises—perhaps as to the exact meaning of a clause in a contract—the parties select an arbitrator, and agree to abide by his decision. This arbitrator then studies every aspect of the case, and makes an award that may be enforced like any court judgment. An appeal from the arbitrator's award may be taken to the courts, but, in the more progressive states, only to determine whether the arbitration procedure was in accordance with the law. The civil codes of these states specify that the facts, once determined, may not again be challenged. In many jurisdictions, however, appeals are permitted on questions of fact as well as questions of law, so that arbitration necessarily loses much of its effectiveness. Moreover, state arbitration laws are limited in most instances to disputes that have already arisen, because of the old theory that a man should not be permitted to bargain away, in advance, the right to his traditional "day in court." The courts long held the view that it would be contrary to public policy to compel any person to arbitrate, even if he had agreed in advance to do so. But the New York law of 1920, which specifically authorized agreements to arbitrate future disputes, was upheld by the Supreme Court of the United States in the important case of Red Cross Line *v.* Atlantic Fruit Company.[28] This decision opened the way for the passage of similar laws in other states, but very few states have acted.

## JUDICIAL REVIEW

**Invalidation of laws.** One of the fundamental principles of American government is the doctrine of judicial review. The need

[28] 264 U.S. 109 (1924).

for review arises when the legislative body enacts a law that is alleged
to conflict with the constitution. Some person or group must then
determine whether the disputed law is actually contrary to a constitutional provision, or whether apparent differences can be reconciled.
The decision might well be left to the legislature; in fact, most nations
have solved the problem in this way.[29] The United States, however,
is a noteworthy exception. In this country the courts—both state
and federal—will pass upon the constitutionality of any law if the
question is properly presented to them in the course of ordinary litigation. They will not consider the constitutional issue if the case can
be decided on some other point; nor will they accept an unconstitutional interpretation of a law if a constitutional interpretation can be
found. But when necessity arises they will invalidate any legislative
act that, in their judgment, violates the supreme law—the constitution. It has already been pointed out that the supreme court of a
state is the final interpreter of the state constitution.[30] Disputes involving the federal Constitution, however, may be appealed to the
Supreme Court of the United States. Whether the framers of federal
and state constitutions intended to confer upon the courts the power
to declare laws unconstitutional has long been a matter of dispute.[31]
Certainly this power is not expressly granted, but has been assumed by
judicial interpretation. And, in the final analysis, the intention of
the fathers is not vitally important. The courts have exercised the
right of judicial review for so many years that they could not be deprived of it except by constitutional amendment.

**Proposals for limiting judicial review.** The courts have long declared that they will not invalidate properly enacted laws, however
unwise or inexpedient such laws may seem to be. This is a proper
point of view, for policy determination is a function of the legislature,
and not of the judiciary. Legislators decide what is to be done, and
the task of the courts is to enforce the law in specific disputes. In
recent years, however, many cases have arisen in which the courts have
adopted the rôle of policy makers and have set aside legislative acts as
"unreasonable"—that is, undesirable. Most of these cases have been
concerned with "due process of law." Judicial interpretation of the

29 In England, for example, the courts have no authority to invalidate an act of Parliament.

30 See p. 234.

31 The best discussion of the matter is found in the revised edition of *The American
Doctrine of Judicial Supremacy*, by Chas. G. Haines.

due process clause, as previously pointed out,[32] has given to the courts a broad power to pass upon the wisdom of legislation. This power has sometimes been used to thwart the popular will and to substitute the wishes of the judiciary for the wishes of the people, as expressed through their chosen representatives. Not unnaturally, therefore, considerable popular opposition to unrestricted judicial supremacy has developed within the last few decades, and a number of proposals designed to limit judicial power have received serious consideration. Thus it has been suggested that an extraordinary majority—perhaps three-fourths, or all but one or two—of the members of the supreme court be required to declare a duly enacted law unconstitutional. With such a rule it would no longer be possible for a single judge to set aside the handiwork of the legislature—a state of affairs that occasionally arises when a statute is declared invalid by a four-to-three or five-to-four vote. This plan has been adopted by three states.[33] The recall of judges should also be mentioned at this point, since it provides a means of getting rid of judges who invalidate popular legislative enactments.[34]

Deserving of mention, also, is the recall of judicial decisions, a scheme advocated by Theodore Roosevelt in 1912. "When a judge decides a constitutional question," he said, "when he decides what the people as a whole can or cannot do, the people should have the right to recall that decision if they think it is wrong." A short time afterward he elaborated his scheme. "I am proposing merely that, in a certain class of cases, involving the police power, when a state court has set aside as unconstitutional a law passed by the legislature for the general welfare, the question of the validity of the law . . . be submitted for final determination to a vote of the people, taken after due time for consideration."[35] This novel plan, intended to make the people the final interpreters of the provisions of state constitutions, was adopted by one state—Colorado—but was set aside nine years later by the state supreme court as contrary to the federal Constitution.[36]

Quite different from any of these schemes, but directed toward the

[32] See pp. 44–45.
[33] Nebraska, North Dakota, Ohio
[34] For a discussion of the recall as applied to judges, see pp. 238–239.
[35] Quoted by Chas. G. Haines in *The American Doctrine of Judicial Supremacy*, rev. ed., p. 483.
[36] People *v.* Western Union Telegraph Co., 70 Colo. 90 (1921), People *v.* Max, 70 Colo. 100 (1921).

same goal, is the proposal to simplify the process of amending state constitutions. The growth of the movement for easier amendment has been considered in an earlier chapter.[37]  As this movement gains momentum, and the fundamental law ceases to be a document made for all time, judicial review will inevitably become a matter of minor concern. If the people dislike the supreme court's interpretation of a clause of the state constitution, they will have little difficulty in amending the disputed clause to meet their desires.

### ADVISORY JUDICIAL OPINIONS

When a bill of doubtful constitutionality is introduced in the legislature, the natural tendency is to turn to the supreme court to learn whether the measure, if enacted into law, will be upheld. The governor, also, may desire some specific assurance before he affixes his signature. In the large majority of states, however, the courts refuse to give advance information; they insist that their function is merely the settlement of specific disputes. So the only way to determine whether a proposal is constitutional, in these states, is to put it on the statute books and then wait until some injured person challenges its validity. Years may pass before a test case reaches the courts; in the meantime no one really knows what the final outcome will be. To obviate unsatisfactory conditions of this sort, ten states [38] have adopted constitutional or statutory provisions directing the justices of the supreme court to render advisory opinions upon all important questions of law presented to them by the governor or the legislature. Except in Colorado,[39] an advisory opinion is merely a statement of the views of the individual justices, and therefore lacks the binding effect of a formal court decision resulting from ordinary litigation. But it is commonly accepted by the governor and the legislature as the final word on any constitutional question, for experience has shown that the courts, as official bodies, are not likely to reverse the opinions of their individual members. Advisory opinions have proved an effective means of reducing the uncertainties incident to law making, and

---

[37] See pp. 76–77.

[38] Colorado, Florida, Maine, Massachusetts, New Hampshire, North Carolina, Rhode Island and South Dakota have made provision in their constitutions for advisory opinions. Two other states, Alabama and Delaware, rely on statute. In Minnesota, however, a law directing the supreme court to render advisory opinions was declared unconstitutional; and in New York, North Carolina, Nebraska, Oklahoma and Pennsylvania, where advisory opinions were once given without constitutional or statutory authorization, the practice has long since been discontinued.

[39] In Colorado, advance opinions have the authority of final court decisions.

of preventing many unnecessary lawsuits. There seems to be no valid reason why they should not be authorized in every state.

## SELECTED REFERENCES

Aumann, F. R., *The Changing American Legal System*, Columbus, Ohio, 1940.

Beattie, Ronald H., *A System of Criminal Judicial Statistics for California*, Berkeley, 1936.

Borchard, Edwin M., *Declaratory Judgments*, rev. ed., Cleveland, 1941.

Callender, C. N., *American Courts, Their Organization and Procedure*, 1927.

Fuller, Hugh N., *Criminal Justice in Virginia*, Charlottesville, 1931.

Haines, C. G., *The American Doctrine of Judicial Supremacy*, rev. ed., Berkeley, Cal., 1932.

Hannan, W. E., and Csontos, M. B., *State Court Systems*, 1940.

Harris, S. A., *Appellate Courts and Appellate Procedure in Ohio*, Baltimore, Md., 1933.

Haynes, Evan, *The Selection and Tenure of Judges*, 1944.

Hays, A. G., *Trial by Prejudice*, 1933.

Jensen, Christen, *The Pardoning Power in the American States*, 1922.

Lepawsky, Albert, *Judicial System of Metropolitan Chicago*, 1932.

Lou, Herbert H., *Juvenile Courts in the United States*, Chapel Hill, N.C., 1927.

Martin, Kenneth J., *Waiver of Jury Trial in Criminal Cases in Ohio*, Baltimore, Md., 1934.

Miller, B. R., *The Louisiana Judiciary*, Baton Rouge, 1932.

National Commission on Law Observance and Enforcement, Report No. 4, *Prosecution*, Washington, D.C., 1931.

Osborn, Albert S., *The Mind of the Juror*, Albany, 1937.

Pound, Roscoe, *Criminal Justice in America*, 1930.

———, *Organization of the Courts*, 1940.

President's Research Committee on Social Trends, *Recent Social Trends in the United States*, Vol. II, Chap. XXVIII, 1933.

Robinson, Edward S., *Law and the Lawyers*, 1935.

Ulman, J. N., *A Judge Takes the Stand*, 1933.

Warner, Florence M., *Juvenile Detention in the United States*, 1933.

Warner, Sam B., and Cabot, H. B., *Judges and Law Reform*, Cambridge, Mass., 1936.

Waite, John B., *Criminal Law in Action*, 1934.

# Chapter Twelve ❧ STATE CONTROL OVER LOCAL GOVERNMENTS

A CITY, in law, is defined as a municipal corporation. It possesses a charter granted by the state, conferring upon it certain rights and privileges and also imposing certain obligations. To some extent, therefore, it resembles a private corporation, which is also chartered by the state and given certain rights and duties. But the resemblance between municipal and private corporations is only superficial, for private corporations receive a measure of protection against arbitrary state action that is commonly denied to cities.

## STATE AUTHORITY OVER LOCAL GOVERNMENTS

The courts have said repeatedly that municipalities are merely the creatures of the state, called into being for the express purpose of doing the state's will and exercising such powers as the state may choose to confer. Therefore the state possesses broad authority over the structure and functions of municipal government; and, in the absence of constitutional provisions to the contrary, this authority is exercised mainly by the legislature. While it is undoubtedly true that cities have been given considerably broader powers of self-government in recent years and that to this extent the state legislature has relinquished its control, these recent changes have not altered the fundamental proposition that in most states, and for most purposes, the legislature molds the destiny of every city within the state boundaries.

Counties and townships are in an even less fortunate position. They, too, are regarded as creatures of the state, subject to the will of the legislature, but they are not accorded even the status of municipal corporations.[1] Instead, the courts commonly describe them as quasi-corporations and declare in no uncertain terms that their rights and privileges—and, in fact, their very existence—are subject to the pleasure of the legislature, except so far as constitutional provisions

[1] Some exceptions must be made to this statement, however. The counties of a number of states, including Indiana, New York, Oklahoma, Texas, and Wyoming, are specifically designated as municipal corporations by constitutional provision or judicial decree.

limit legislative control. "Municipal corporations," said the Supreme Court of Illinois in a recent decision, "are those called into existence either at the direct request or by consent of the persons composing them. Quasi-municipal corporations, such as counties and townships, are at most but local organizations, which are created by general law, without the consent of the inhabitants thereof, for the purpose of the civil and political administration of government, and they are invested with but few characteristics of corporate existence. They are, in other words, local subdivisions of the state created by the sovereign power of the state of its own will, without regard to the wishes of the people inhabiting them. A municipal corporation is created principally for the advantage and convenience of the people of the locality. County and township organizations are created in this state with a view to carrying out the policy of the state at large for the administration of matters of political government, finance, education, taxing, care of the poor, military organization, means of travel and the administration of justice." [2]

**Legislative control.** In the early days of American independence the state legislatures were given complete freedom to manage municipal affairs as they saw fit. Constitutional restrictions on legislative control of cities were practically unknown. At first there was a tradition of local self-government that prevented excessive state interference with local matters, but this tradition disappeared with the passing of years, and then state legislatures proceeded to regulate every minute detail of municipal activity. Sometimes their interference was prompted by a sincere desire to protect the people of the cities against the machinations of scheming municipal politicians; sometimes, in fact, it came as a direct result of requests made by the "better" elements of the urban population, who were disgusted with municipal inefficiency and corruption and desired state protection from further excesses; but in most instances the chief motive was the desire of the state legislators to seize for themselves greater power, prestige, and patronage.

BAD RESULTS. Whatever the motives for state interference with municipal affairs, the results were almost invariably bad. State legislators soon proved that they were as inefficient and corrupt as city councilmen and far less familiar with city needs. Almost everywhere the legislature was dominated by the voters of the rural sections—a condition of affairs that has continued to the present day, despite the

2 Cook County *v.* City of Chicago, 142 N.E. 512 (1924).

stupendous growth of American cities; [3] therefore control of cities by the state legislature meant control by the country districts. Every agency of city government was forced to pass in review before the critical and somewhat unfriendly view of the farmers' representatives, and requests by city officials for additional authority to deal with pressing problems were frequently denied without serious consideration. The legislature seemed to consider itself the keeper of the municipal pocketbook and the municipal conscience. It specified the exact number of administrative officers and employees that each city might have; it prescribed their powers and duties, stating precisely how each power should be exercised and each duty performed; it imposed rigid limits on municipal taxing and borrowing. Some of these restrictions appeared in the charter, as framed by the legislature; others took the form of special laws, which were enacted at every legislative session. In either case, the members of the legislature habitually displayed little or no regard for local sentiment.

**Reaction against special legislation.** Such arbitrary use of power inevitably produced a reaction against state control. The people of the cities began to demand a larger share in the management of their local affairs. Having learned from bitter experience that the legislature could not be trusted to use its authority wisely, they united to secure the adoption of constitutional amendments restricting that authority. At the outset this movement took the form of an attack upon special legislation. In every state the legislature had acquired the habit of dealing separately with each municipality, and each additional grant of power was made the subject of a special law. No two cities were treated alike. This differential treatment might have been advantageous if it had borne some relationship to the widely different problems and needs of the cities affected. Actually, however, such a relationship seldom existed.

State legislators had neither time nor inclination to acquire a reasonable understanding of municipal affairs, and in many instances they voted additional grants of power or additional limitations of power for individual cities with only the faintest notion of what they were trying to accomplish. Sometimes they acted because of the insistence of interested local groups; sometimes because of a hazy belief that cities should be restrained; and many times because of mere caprice. So those who favored a larger measure of municipal self-

---

[3] The various methods by which the rural sections maintain their supremacy in the state legislatures have already been discussed. See pp. 159–161.

government naturally pointed to the evils of special legislation. They urged that all cities should be treated alike. All men were equal before the law; why, they asked, should not cities also be placed on an equal footing? Although this change would not entirely prevent legislative interference, it would probably put an end to the worst abuses of legislative power. If properly enforced, it would compel the legislature to impose its will in general terms, and leave the cities free to determine all the details of their government and administration. For general laws, applying alike to cities of five thousand population and cities of five hundred thousand population, could not possibly be made to cover more than the broad outline of legislative policy. They could not specify, for example, the size of the police force or the salary of the police chief; if designed to meet the needs of the large metropolitan centers, they would prove unenforceable in small communities.

ITS PROHIBITION. Ohio was the first state to prohibit special legislation. In 1851 it adopted a new constitution which provided that "the general assembly shall pass no special act conferring corporate powers." [4] This clause was not the product of the movement for municipal self-government, however; on the contrary, it was designed especially to secure equal treatment for *private* corporations, and the inclusion of municipal corporations was largely a matter of chance. But other state constitution makers, copying the Ohio provision, were directly concerned with the protection of cities. Thus the framers of the Illinois constitution of 1870, after specifying that all corporations must be created by general law, then proceeded to forbid the enactment of local or special laws "incorporating cities, towns, or villages, or changing or amending the charter of any town, city, or village." [5] Somewhat similar restrictions, applying directly or indirectly to cities, have now been written into the constitutions of three fourths of the states. Usually they take the form of an unqualified prohibition of special legislation, but in some instances they permit the exercise of legislative or judicial discretion. Thus the constitution of Michigan declares that "The legislature shall pass no local or special act in any case where a general act can be made applicable, and whether a general act can be made applicable shall be a judicial question." [6]

Popular resentment against state interference with local affairs has

[4] Art. XIII, Sec. 1.
[5] Art. IV, Sec. 22.
[6] Art. V, Sec. 30.

been limited almost entirely to the cities, especially until the last few decades. The demand for local self-government, as previously indicated,[7] has been made chiefly by the people of the urban centers. In nearly every state the counties have been judicially recognized as state agencies peculiarly subordinate to the legislative will, and this attitude of the courts has aroused no widespread opposition. Constitutional prohibitions against special legislation for corporations do not apply to counties as a rule because of the generally accepted doctrine that counties are not corporations. Yet a number of state constitutions have been amended to forbid special legislation for counties as well as for cities. The constitution of Kentucky, for example, specifically declares that special laws may not be enacted for "any city, town, district, or county," [8] and several other constitutions use substantially the same phraseology.

*Classification as a means of evasion.* Even the most absolute prohibitions against special legislation, whether for cities or counties, have proved rather easy to evade and therefore have afforded a much smaller measure of protection against legislative abuses than their language would seem to indicate. One very effective method of evasion, regularly employed by most state legislatures, is to classify the cities of a state on the basis of population, and then enact laws applying to all the cities *within a single class.* This is general legislation, according to the legislatures; and the courts of every state except Ohio agree. There is, in fact, a great deal to be said for the principle of classification. It is a recognition of the differences in local needs arising from the very fact of differences in size. Great metropolitan centers have little in common with small, semi-rural municipalities. Therefore, if all cities of approximately the same size are treated alike, the result should be substantial justice.

Once the principle of classification has been accepted, however, difficulties immediately arise. What is to prevent the legislature from setting up fifty or one hundred classes—or as many classes as there are cities? And, with every city in a separate class, what is to prevent the enactment of different laws for every class—that is, for every city—under the guise of general legislation? Solemn humbuggery of this sort has been practiced more or less extensively in many states, and still serves a useful purpose for legislatures intent upon defeating the spirit of the constitution. In California, where

[7] See pp. 255–256.
[8] Sec. 60.

classification has been reduced to an absurdity, the fifty-eight counties of the state have been placed in fifty-eight classes. Counties of the forty-sixth class—to cite a single provision of the law—are defined as those whose populations are in excess of 7,750 and less than 7,790; thus Tuolumne County becomes the "counties of the forty-sixth class." This is legislative madness, of course, and most states have at least attempted to prevent such excesses. Some state constitutions have been amended to prescribe the maximum number of classes that may be established. The constitution of Pennsylvania contains such a provision: "The legislature shall have power to classify counties, cities, boroughs, school districts, and townships according to population, and all laws relating to each class . . . shall be deemed general legislation within the meaning of this constitution; but counties shall not be divided into more than eight classes, cities into not more than seven classes, school districts into not more than five classes, and boroughs into not more than three classes." [9] In other states excessive classification has been prevented by court decisions.

But neither constitutional provisions nor court rulings have served to keep the legislature from abusing its authority. If only four classes of cities are permitted, each of the three largest cities is generally accorded the doubtful honor of occupying a separate class, and all the smaller municipalities are grouped together indiscriminately. The legislature is then free to deal with the largest cities as it sees fit. It can no longer prescribe every detail of government for the cities of the lowest class because these cities vary too widely in population. But that is a minor restriction, as most legislators see it; for the spoils of office are concentrated largely in the great metropolitan centers, with their large public payrolls and vast taxable wealth.

*Other means of evasion.* Classification is the most common method of evading the requirement that state regulation of affairs shall be by general law, but it is not the only way. Sometimes laws can be so phrased as to be general in form, though in fact they apply only to a single municipality or county. Often the plain purpose of the constitution can be nullified by the creation of special districts, such as school or highway districts, charged with a single function of government. Such districts can be multiplied indefinitely, and each district accorded separate treatment, in the absence of an express constitutional provision to the contrary. Thus the legislature that is prohibited from passing special laws concerning the educational sys-

9 Art. III, Sec. 34.

tems of counties may often regulate the educational systems of school districts in any way that it pleases, even though county and school district boundaries are practically identical.

## MUNICIPAL HOME RULE

Even under most favorable circumstances, constitutional prohibitions against special legislation are merely a protection against the worst abuses of legislative control. They do not assure any substantial measure of local self-government. Therefore the people of the cities have been forced to seek other devices to secure control of their own affairs.

**Its first constitutional establishment.** Before the close of the Civil War it was suggested that municipal charters should be home-made, instead of coming as a gift from the legislature; but this proposal did not bear fruit until 1875. In that year Missouri adopted a new constitution that contained an epoch-making clause: "Any city having a population of more than one hundred thousand inhabitants may frame a charter for its own government . . ." Thus the principle of municipal home rule was recognized for the first time. The constitution then specified the manner in which this unprecedented power of self-government should be exercised. A board of freeholders should be chosen by the qualified voters of the city; this board should prepare a charter for the voters' approval; and the charter should go into effect when approved by four sevenths of those voting at the next general or special election. Legislative consent was not required, but the constitution contained two provisions designed to insure continued state control over matters of state concern. One of these clauses declared that the charter adopted by the urban voters should "always be in harmony with and subject to the constitution and laws of the state." The other specified: "Notwithstanding the provisions of this article, the General Assembly shall have the same power over the city and county of St. Louis that it has over the other cities and counties of this state." St. Louis was the only Missouri city with a population in excess of one hundred thousand at that time, and therefore the only city qualified to frame its own charter.

Just what the framers of the Missouri constitution thought they accomplished by adopting these several clauses is not certain. What they actually did was to create a serious legal tangle that threatened to nullify the principle of home rule. Even a cursory reading of the provisions concerning local self-government for St. Louis should have made clear this ambiguity. If the city's charter must always be "in harmony with and subject to the constitution and laws of the state," and this clause were interpreted literally, "home rule" would speedily degenerate into a meaningless shibboleth. For the legislature would be free at any time to enact statutes at cross purposes to the charter of St. Louis; it might, in fact, indirectly repeal nearly every charter provision; and the charter would necessarily be subordinated to state law. Perhaps the men who framed the constitution of 1875 meant to say that the charter of St. Louis should be in harmony with the constitution and general laws—that is, laws dealing with matters of general concern instead of purely local affairs. But certainly they gave no indication of such an intention. On the contrary, they seemed to be intent on establishing beyond question the supremacy of the state legislature. Otherwise, why would they have adopted the further provision that "the General Assembly shall have the same power over the city and county of St. Louis that it has over the other cities and counties of this state"? The general assembly's power over other cities and counties was almost plenary; therefore its authority over the affairs of St. Louis must likewise be practically complete. And, under such circumstances, what did the grant of home rule mean—if, indeed, it meant anything? Only the courts could decide.

A charter framed by a group of freeholders was adopted by the people of St. Louis in 1876, only one year after the adoption of the new constitution, and the courts were speedily afforded an opportunity to produce judicial order out of constitutional chaos. This they did, after a series of involved and ofttimes contradictory decisions, by interpreting the several clauses of the constitution to mean that the St. Louis charter should be "in harmony with and subject to" *those state laws dealing with matters of state-wide concern,* and that the general assembly should have complete control over the city and county of St. Louis, *except with regard to local affairs.* Thus they read into the state constitution important limitations on legislative power that most certainly were not placed there by the men who drafted it, but they succeeded in saving for St. Louis a small measure of local self-government. Later, Kansas City qualified for home rule, and in 1945 all Missouri cities with populations in excess of ten thousand were given the privilege of framing and adopting their own charters.

**Spread of the movement.** In 1879 California became a convert to the new gospel of municipal home rule. At the outset San Francisco was the only city authorized to establish its own framework of govern-

ment, but subsequently this privilege was extended to all municipalities with populations of more than ten thousand. The home-rule
clause of the Missouri constitution was copied practically verbatim,
with no regard for its ambiguities and downright contradictions.
Within a few years, therefore, California municipalities operating
under their own charters were enmeshed in countless legal difficulties.
A constitutional amendment and a long series of court decisions were
necessary to determine the exact meaning of home rule, but the final
result was to confer upon the cities of California considerably greater
powers of self-government than had been gained by the cities of
Missouri.

For more than a quarter of a century after California's adoption of
home rule the movement lagged. Only three states made the necessary changes in their constitutions during this period,[10] and popular
agitation for local self-government was not widespread. Between
1906 and 1915, however, municipal home rule became a vital force.
It was adopted by Oregon in 1906, by Oklahoma and Michigan in
1908, and by Arizona, Ohio, Nebraska, and Texas in 1912. In 1915
Maryland adopted county home rule and extended the provisions of
this amendment to the City of Baltimore. Since that time there have
been but four adoptions—New York in 1923, Wisconsin in 1924, Utah
in 1932, and West Virginia in 1936, bringing the total number of
municipal home-rule states to seventeen. It should be noted, however, that twenty-one of the thirty largest American cities [11] are in
these seventeen states.

**Division of authority between states and municipalities.** The
problem of maintaining a reasonable degree of state control over cities
in matters of state concern, while giving them a free hand in the
management of their purely local affairs, has always been difficult to
solve. Other states profited somewhat by the experiences of Missouri
and California, as shown by the terminology of their constitutional
amendments granting home rule; yet every home-rule amendment has
required numerous judicial interpretations to make clear its meaning.
To some extent, of course, this uncertainty might have been avoided
by the use of more explicit language; but it has arisen in part from the
natural complexity of the subject. For any division of authority between state and city, involving municipal control over municipal

10 Washington (1889), Minnesota (1896), and Colorado (1902).
11 Excluding Washington, D.C., which is under the jurisdiction of the federal government. The residents of the national capital have no voice in their governmental
affairs.

functions and state authority over matters of state-wide importance, necessarily implies a more or less clear-cut recognizable distinction between state and local functions. And such a distinction, while it does actually exist, is neither clear-cut nor readily recognizable. Virtually every governmental activity within municipal boundaries affects the residents of the municipality and also affects the people of the entire state to some extent. When a state constitution specifically provides, therefore, that cities shall have authority to exercise all powers of local self-government or all municipal powers—and such clauses are typical of home-rule amendments—the courts must decide what matters are in fact matters of local concern. The framers of the New York amendment tried to remove this difficulty by enumerating a considerable number of functions that should be considered essentially local and therefore subject to municipal control; and, to prevent undue restriction of the scope of municipal authority, they added that this enumeration should not be considered final or complete. "The legislature may by general laws confer on cities such further powers of local legislation and administration as it may, from time to time, deem expedient." [12] Although this plan has removed some of the uncertainties surrounding the exact meaning of home rule, it has by no means prevented extensive litigation.

**Variations in autonomy.** The measure of self-government actually enjoyed by so-called "home-rule" cities varies considerably from state to state. In California and Michigan, for example, the cities manage their own affairs, largely free from state interference, whereas in Texas and Washington the control of the legislature over municipal matters is almost as complete as before the adoption of home rule.[13] These differences are due partly to variations in the phraseology of the home-rule clause of the state constitution and partly to variations in judicial interpretation. The attitude of the legislature is important, also. If the legislature of a home-rule state desires to obey the spirit as well as the letter of the constitution in matters of local self-government, the cities have no cause to fear the loss of their autonomy. If, on the other hand, the legislature is determined to re-

---

12 Constitution of New York, Art. XII, Sec. 5.

13 During 1932 the *National Municipal Review* published a series of articles under the caption: "What Municipal Home Rule Means Today." Note especially the articles by Edwin A. Cottrell, "California" (January); Arthur W. Bromage, "Michigan" (March); Chester C. Maxey, "Washington" (April); and Frank M. Stewart, "Texas" (July). Note also Joseph D. McGoldrick's important contribution, *Law and Practice of Municipal Home Rule, 1916–1930*.

tain control of municipal affairs, it can find ways to evade more or less completely the home-rule section of the constitution, just as it has commonly found ways to defeat the purpose of the prohibition against special legislation.

In recognition of this fact, the constitutions of a few states make the grant of home rule dependent on legislative action. Thus the Michigan constitution declares: "The legislature shall provide by a general law for the incorporation of cities, and by a general law for the incorporation of villages . . . Under such general laws the electors of each city and village shall have power and authority to frame, adopt, and amend its charter." [14] Although the legislature is clearly directed by this section of the constitution to enact a general home-rule law, there is no power that can compel it to do so. In fact, the Pennsylvania legislature has completely ignored the provisions of a 1922 constitutional amendment concerning home rule. But in every other state where legislative action under the home-rule section of the constitution has been necessary, the legislature has acted promptly and fairly, though not always generously.

**Legislative grants of self-government.** The legislatures of six states,[15] in the absence of definite constitutional authorization, have conferred upon cities more or less extensive power of self-government. Iowa took this step in 1858—seventeen years before the beginning of constitutional home rule. Most of these "home-rule" laws have proved virtually worthless because of legislative hesitancy to renounce a single important power; the Mississippi statute, however, vests broad authority in the cities of the state and shows that home rule by legislative grant need not be a contradiction in terms. In a few states, when the legislatures have attempted to grant municipal home-rule powers, they have been blocked by adverse court decisions.[16] Otherwise this method of increasing municipal powers might have acquired a considerable degree of popularity.

**Steps in adoption of home-rule charter.** Municipal home-rule procedure, as established by constitutions and laws, follows the same general lines in all states, though varying somewhat in certain details. The city charter is framed by a commission especially chosen for this

---

[14] Art. VIII.

[15] Connecticut, Florida, Iowa, Louisiana, Mississippi, South Carolina.

[16] See, for example, Elliott *v.* City of Detroit, 121 Mich. 611 (1899); and State *ex rel.* Mueller *v.* Thompson, 149 Wis. 488 (1912).

purpose.[17]   Usually the members of this commission are chosen by the voters, but in Minnesota they are appointed by the district court. When the commission's work is finished, the charter goes to the voters, and must be approved by them—a bare majority usually sufficing for this purpose.   Three states—Arizona, Michigan, and Oklahoma— specify that every home-rule charter must receive the approval of the governor before taking effect; and California requires the assent of the state legislature.   But these restrictions on local self-government are not serious, because California's legislature and the governors of the other three states regularly give their assent to charters that have received popular approval.   Amendments to home-rule charters are proposed by city councils, or by the people through initiative petitions.

**Arguments against municipal home rule.**   The municipal home-rule movement is opposed as a matter of course by those rural politicians who consider it a direct menace to their control of city patronage.   It is opposed, also, by some students of government who urge that the field of strictly municipal affairs is too narrow to deserve serious consideration, and that, even within this narrow field, cities need the firm hand of the state to protect them from the corruption and inefficiency of their own officials.   These arguments are scarcely worthy of rebuttal.

INCONSISTENCY OF OPPOSITION.   The list of governmental functions in which the local interest is paramount cannot fairly be called narrow or unimportant.   It includes the structure of city government, the salaries, terms, and qualifications of city officials, the methods of awarding contracts, ordinance procedure, the enforcement of charter and ordinance provisions, street cleaning and lighting, fire protection, recreation, water supply, ownership and operation of municipal utilities, zoning, housing, and the construction and maintenance of local streets.   Although some persons might debate the propriety of assigning paramount interest to the city in a few of these functions, other persons would insist that the list was not sufficiently long—that it should include also such functions as taxation for local purposes, the use of eminent domain, the settlement of claims against the city, and the organization and jurisdiction of local courts.   Without attempting to settle controversies involving specific functions or to define exactly the proper sphere of municipal authority, it may safely be

---

[17] A few states permit city councils to frame new charters. provided the voters approve this arrangement.

reiterated that a broad field exists for the exercise of home rule. And the assertion that state control is needed, even in matters of local concern, is a flat denial that local self-government is possible. Although it is true that city officials are sometimes inefficient and corrupt, the assumption should not be made that state officials are always efficient and incorruptible. State legislatures sometimes prevent city councils from using city property and funds for unwise or dishonest purposes, but at other times state control becomes a dangerous instrument of oppression in the hands of unwise or dishonest legislators. Honors— and dishonors—are probably about even.

**Arguments for municipal home rule:** THE PRINCIPLE OF SELF-DETERMINATION. There are many arguments for municipal home rule, but the strongest point in its favor is that it is based upon the generally accepted principle of self-determination. The people of the cities have many interests that they do not share with the people of the rural districts, and simple justice would seem to demand that they be given the right to control those interests in such manner as they may see fit. The opponents of home rule for cities contend, with some force, that the principle of self-determination can readily be abused—that it can be used to justify the establishment of a separate government for every dissatisfied ward within a city, or every precinct within a ward. But this danger of abuse does not in any way invalidate the principle. Almost every desirable reform would prove undesirable if carried to extremes. Cities are "natural" units for the exercise of governmental functions—"natural" in the sense that they have commonly been created by the play of economic forces. They are legal entities, too—municipal corporations, as they are designated by law; and sometimes the boundaries established by charter are quite different from the boundaries of the economic area. But, all things considered, the city is an important unit for the solution of local problems and the satisfaction of local needs, and its right to control its own affairs should not be denied or abridged.

**Arguments against county home rule.** County home rule is sometimes advocated as a desirable reform. The sponsors of this movement usually reason by analogy: municipal home rule is a proper recognition of the right of local self-government; therefore county home rule is also a proper recognition of that right. But such an argument ignores the fundamental differences between counties and cities. Counties are not natural units created by economic forces, nor is the legislature's demarcation of their boundaries merely a recogni-

tion of existing fact. Instead, counties are local areas established by
the state for the performance of state functions. Their boundaries
have been fixed more or less arbitrarily. Their purely local functions
have been assigned largely as a matter of convenience. Therefore the
home-rule argument loses a great deal of its force when applied to
counties. "It seems open to question," in the opinion of two careful
students of the field of county government, "whether home rule should
be granted to counties to the same degree that it has been granted to
cities. In the case of counties any home-rule grant should stress their
freedom to select the form of government organization rather than
freedom in the exercise of governmental powers. The position of
the county as a state agent makes it advantageous to have some degree
of uniformity throughout the state. There are certain officers, as
sheriffs and judges, whose duties are such that the state should retain
some degree of control over them. They are primarily state officers,
engaged in carrying out state law, and for the benefit of the state at
large." [18]

Perhaps such considerations have retarded county home rule. At
any rate, it has been adopted by but six states—California in 1911,
Maryland in 1915, Ohio and Texas in 1933, New York in 1935, and
Missouri in 1945.[19] A constitutional amendment conferring a measure of local self-government upon Arkansas counties was invalidated
by the supreme court of the state in 1925. Even in the so-called
"home-rule" states local self-government means less freedom for counties than for cities. Thus the section of the California constitution
conferring home rule on counties—a section of about four thousand
words—specifies a number of matters that must be included in every
county charter and even prescribes certain details of organization and
procedure. The county home-rule section of Ohio's constitution has
been seriously weakened by judicial interpretation.

**The optional charter plan as a substitute.** A device for permitting
the people to take some part in their local government, without an actual grant of home-rule powers, is known as the optional charter plan.
The legislature offers to the cities or counties of the state a certain
number of charters, ranging from three to six, which generally include
the more important forms of governmental organization. Thus, for
cities, the choice may lie among commission government, council-

---

[18] Fairlie, John A., and Kneier, Chas. M., *County Government and Administration*,
p. 76. Reprinted by permission of D. Appleton–Century Company.
[19] The county home-rule provision of Missouri's constitution applies only to those
counties having more than eighty-five thousand inhabitants.

manager government, the weak-mayor plan, and the strong-mayor plan. Each of these charters is fully drawn, and the people of the city or county have no discretion beyond designating the charter that they desire. Amendments must be made by act of the legislature—the customary procedure when home rule has not been granted.

WEAKNESS OF THE PLAN FOR CITIES. Clearly this scheme is a poor substitute for home rule—at least in cities, where home rule is a vital need. The plan affords an opportunity for each community to determine its structure of government, but nothing more. Local powers and duties are prescribed by the legislature, often with little regard for local sentiment. The first state to offer a reasonably complete list of municipal charters from which the people of the cities might choose was Ohio, in 1913. Several other states promptly followed suit—New York in 1914, Massachusetts in 1915,[20] and Virginia and North Carolina in 1917. As early as 1907 Iowa had extended the option of commission government to its first-class cities,[21] and a number of other states have since adopted the optional principle in part for certain cities or classes of cities. But the optional charter plan, as it concerns municipal government, is rapidly losing whatever significance it may have possessed.

SUITABILITY FOR COUNTIES. In the field of county government, however, it still serves a definite purpose. It conforms to the previously quoted specifications set up by Professors Fairlie and Kneier—that any grant of power to counties "should stress their freedom to elect the form of governmental organization rather than freedom in the exercise of governmental powers." [22] Six states [23] have adopted the optional charter plan for counties, and the constitutions of a number of other states permit its use.

**Veto by cities of special legislation.** In 1904 Illinois amended its constitution to confer upon the people of Chicago the right to veto special legislation relating to that city. "No [special] law . . . affecting the municipal government of the City of Chicago," declared the amendment, "shall take effect until such law shall be consented to by a majority of the legal voters of said city voting on the question at any election." [24] New York had adopted a somewhat similar plan

20 The provisions of the Massachusetts optional charter law were not extended to Boston.
21 That is, cities whose population exceeded fifteen thousand.
22 See p. 267.
23 Illinois, Missouri, Nebraska, North Carolina, North Dakota, Virginia.
24 Art. IV, Sec. 34.

ten years earlier, but the power of veto had been vested in municipal officials instead of the people, and the legislature had been authorized to override the local veto by a simple majority vote. In Illinois, of course, the people of Chicago were given the final word. This "Illinois plan," as it is sometimes called, was heralded as a sure way to end the constant wrangling between Chicago and the farm-controlled state legislature, but it has failed to meet early expectations. The legislature seldom submits proposals that are acceptable to the metropolis; Chicago voters seldom accept the measures that are offered by the legislature; and the result is usually a deadlock.

## EXPANSION OF STATE CENTRALIZED CONTROL

**Reasons for the movement.** During the last few years the movement for a greater degree of local self-government has run counter to a more recent movement for extending the scope of state supervision and control of local affairs. One state restricts the sphere of city or county authority while another expands it. Even within a single state cross-purposes are at work. The reasons for the comparatively new development of interest in state supervision are fairly obvious. First, many governmental functions are outgrowing municipal boundaries and require some larger unit of control. The county is seldom properly equipped to assume additional responsibilities; moreover, even county boundaries may be restricted too narrowly to permit adequate performance. Therefore the state must take charge unless it can place complete responsibility in some agency specially created for regional government.[25]

To some extent, at least, the movement for state control has arisen from the desire of local property owners to escape from the crushing tax burden on real estate. As pointed out in a subsequent chapter, the general property tax—essentially a tax on real property, because most forms of personalty escape—is still the mainstay of local governments, whereas the states have developed many new sources of revenue.[26] Therefore a transfer of control from city or county to state, provided it involves a transfer of financial responsibility as well, is likely to lead to a rearrangement of the tax system and some reduction of property taxes. Tax relief has been the avowed goal of the proponents of a number of recently adopted constitutional amendments increasing state control over certain functions. While it is doubtless

[25] For a discussion of such agencies, see pp. 274–275.
[26] See p. 363.

true that general property bears an unreasonably heavy share of the total tax burden, this fact should have no weight in deciding the important question of the proper distribution of governmental powers. Tax relief for real estate could be accomplished equally well by unconditional distribution of state-collected funds in greater amounts among the local units of government. This suggestion does not imply elimination of state supervision over such local functions as are generally conceded to require such supervision; it is merely a proposal to separate two logically unrelated subjects—tax relief and state control.

In many instances state control of city and county finances has been established to counteract the more disastrous effects of excessive local borrowing and local mismanagement of public funds. State legislatures have been unwilling to permit the weakening of state credit by insolvent local units, and have taken some drastic steps to forestall such a development. In North Carolina a local government commission, created in 1931 for the primary purpose of exercising control over local debts, has greatly facilitated the task of refinancing local bond issues. Kansas has a state municipal accounting board, set up in 1935 which controls the auditing of accounts in the larger cities. In 1937 Iowa adopted the plan—long established in Indiana—of permitting state review of local budgets. The same year Maine established an emergency municipal finance board and authorized it to take over the fiscal management of virtually bankrupt cities. Kentucky set up a county debt commission in 1938. In New Jersey a state department of local government has been created, with broad general powers of supervision over city and county finance and additional authority to regulate defaulting local governments. Many of these laws authorizing state financial control were the product of the economic depression; some of them were said to be temporary. But there has been no general tendency to repeal them since the end of the depression. On the contrary, state control has been strengthened in a number of states.

**Increase in administrative control.** Probably the most important reason for the recent development of state control is the improvement of control technique. Authority to supervise and direct local affairs is being vested increasingly in administrative departments or boards, rather than in the state legislature, though legislative control is still the rule. Under the plan of administrative control the legislature prescribes merely the broad outlines of policy, leaving the determination of details to administrative officers who presumably possess special qualifications for the task.

ADVANTAGES OF ADMINISTRATIVE CONTROL. The advantages of administrative control are obvious. First, it supplies an element of flexibility that is urgently needed in state control of local affairs. It permits separate consideration of each local problem, rather than general treatment under a general law. Local variations may be approved on the basis of differing local needs. Absolute uniformity of treatment, which may result in the grossest inequalities, need no longer be insisted upon, for every exception to the general policy is approved by administrative officers who have time to examine the facts of the case. The legislature has neither the time, the inclination, nor the ability to examine the requirements of each city, and any variations that it might permit would be based on favoritism or caprice rather than actual need. The other important advantage of administrative control is that it is—potentially, at least—control by experts. Local health matters are passed upon by the state board of health; local educational programs are scrutinized by the state board of education. In other words, the power of supervision is vested in those persons who ought to be most competent to use it properly. Of course, no scheme of government provides an absolute guarantee that properly qualified men and women will be chosen to public office; incompetents may often be appointed to important administrative posts through personal or partisan influence. But administrative control at least makes possible government by experts, whereas legislative control definitely assures government by amateurs. For no legislative body, however well informed its members, can possibly possess an adequate working knowledge of every administrative activity; and without such knowledge its attempts at detailed regulation must necessarily be amateurish and bungling.

The widespread use of legislative control in the relation of American states with their local units is often contrasted with the virtual disappearance of such control in Europe. The nations of Europe, without exception, rely almost entirely upon administrative control of local activities. The central government grants broad powers to the cities—and usually to the local rural areas; but it appoints its own representatives to supervise local affairs, and make certain that these broad powers are not misused. Even in England, where Parliament is supreme and grants of power to the boroughs are made piecemeal, the actual responsibility for passing upon borough activities rests with administrative officers of the national government. In the states of the American Union, though legislative control is still generally used, it has already lost considerable favor. The pages of this volume are filled with examples of supervision of city and county functions by state boards, commissions, or administrative departments,[27] and this type of supervision may completely replace the legislative variety some day. But reforms move slowly—especially administrative reforms that lack the dramatic quality of great moral issues.

### CITY-COUNTY RELATIONS

**Duplications and conflicts of services.** This chapter would be incomplete without at least a passing reference to the relations of county and city. Whenever a city acquires a large population and multiplies its functions to correspond to the growing needs of its citizens, it soon finds that it is duplicating certain functions already performed by the county. Moreover, conflicts of authority develop. City and county officials often fail to co-operate, with consequences that are disastrous to efficient administration. In the fields of law enforcement, finance, health, and poor relief these duplications and conflicts are especially noticeable. The county sheriff may interfere with the work of the municipal police in the solution of a crime that is receiving wide newspaper publicity, though usually he pursues a hands-off policy; county and city assessors may conduct separate assessments of all property within the city limits and arrive at very different conclusions as to property values; county health regulations may conflict with municipal health ordinances; some poor families may receive relief from both county and city workers because the two welfare agencies fail to exchange necessary information.

REMEDIAL MEASURES. A number of schemes have been attempted to correct these evils. None have proved entirely satisfactory. Separation of city and county was tried as early as 1851, when the City of Baltimore was established as a political unit entirely distinct from the county in which it had formerly been situated. It was, in fact, both a city and a county, performing both city and county functions, though never given official county status. Three years later the area of the City of Philadelphia was made coterminous with the county area, and most county functions were transferred to the city government. Several county offices with independent authority were retained, how-

[27] See, for example, p. 454 (welfare); 468–474 (education); 482 (health); 502–504 (highways).

ever, and this anomalous situation has continued to the present day. There have been a number of other instances of city-county consolidation or separation—San Francisco in 1856, New Orleans in 1874,[28] St. Louis in 1875, and Denver in 1903. Certain county functions are performed by the city government of Boston—an arrangement dating from 1821; and New York City has carried on important county activities since 1898, though the five counties originally comprising the area of Greater New York still remain as districts for the administration of justice.

*City-county consolidation.* The constitutions of a number of states permit city-county consolidation—usually with the approval of the people of both city and county and the consent of the legislature. Thus the Michigan constitutions specifies that "when any city has attained a population of one hundred thousand inhabitants, the legislature may organize it into a separate county without reference to geographical extent, if a majority of the electors of such city and of the remainder of the county in which such city may be situated voting on the question shall each determine in favor of organizing said city into a separate county." [29] Under these various constitutional provisions a number of proposals for city-county consolidation have been made during the past two decades, but all have been defeated at the polls. Therefore the creation of the City and County of Denver in 1903 remains the most recent successful attempt to combine all city and county functions in a single unit of government.

Obviously city-county consolidation—or separation—is not a cure-all. The combination of city and county activities has given reasonably satisfactory results in some instances, and not in others. Legal obstacles, popular opposition, especially from the less populous parts of the county, and numerous other difficulties have usually prevented the fulfilment of many of the promises made by ardent reformers during the heat of campaigns for consolidation. All factors considered, "city-county consolidation can hardly be expected to offer a solution to the difficulties confronting most of the metropolitan regions today. All that can be hoped of it is that it will eliminate one source of confusion—the duplication of city and county governments within the central city. But the obstacles that stand in the way of city-county consolidation are so great, as attested by the failure of

---

[28] The consolidation of city and county governments in New Orleans was not complete.

[29] Art. VIII, Sec. 2.

all efforts made during the past twenty years, that prudence should suggest other lines of attack." [30]

*Expansion of county authority.* Various other schemes for completely eliminating, or at least minimizing, the duplication of effort and conflict of authority of city and county have likewise proved but partially successful. One of these schemes—the expansion of county government to meet metropolitan needs, while permitting the city government to carry on most of its usual functions without change —faces a number of difficulties at the outset. County boundaries seldom coincide with the limits of the metropolitan area. Even in those rare cases where the area of the county, as defined by the legislature, corresponds roughly to the area of the metropolis, as defined by economic forces, the county government is almost invariably so poorly organized and so inefficient that it cannot safely be entrusted with additional responsibilities. Moreover, the people of the city are likely to look with disfavor upon any expansion of county authority; they prefer the extension of municipal boundaries, if only to make a better showing in the census records. It is not surprising, therefore, that only one American county—Los Angeles County, California—has reconstructed its government and multiplied its activities in fairly complete recognition of metropolitan needs. A number of other urban counties have undertaken some additional functions, paying special attention to highways, park systems, and health; but they have gone only a short distance along the path of complete reorganization.

*Creation of metropolitan districts.* Since neither the multiplication of county functions nor the extension of city boundaries has seemed to offer an adequate solution of the problem, some states have tried the experiment of taking control of certain functions away from both city and county and vesting authority in specially created metropolitan districts. Usually a metropolitan district is responsible for but a single function—sewerage, as in the case of the Chicago Sanitary District, or park development, as in the case of the Cleveland Metropolitan Park District. Its authority can readily be expanded to include a number of activities, however; thus the Massachusetts Metropolitan District controls water supply, sewerage, and parks for the Boston metropolitan area, though originally it was merely a sewerage district. A considerable number of such metropolitan districts have been created to serve the needs of the great urban centers. Their

[30] National Municipal League's Committee on Metropolitan Government, *The Government of Metropolitan Areas,* p. 215.

boundaries are supposed to conform more or less closely to regional lines, disregarding both city and county limits. Usually their officials are appointed by the governor of the state. Some excellent results have been achieved under this plan. Even better results would probably follow, however, if two important changes were made—first, if the boundaries of every metropolitan district were redefined, wherever necessary, to correspond exactly to the economic area it is designed to serve; and, second, if every metropolitan problem were placed under metropolitan district control. The proper manner of choosing the officials of metropolitan districts has long been a disputed subject. Many students of government believe that the method of selection now used in most cases—appointment by the governor of the state—is an unreasonable violation of the right of local self-government. It must be admitted, however, that any plan of local selection is certain to encounter serious opposition because of the conflicting interests of the residents of the city and the residents of the outlying areas included within the region.

## SELECTED REFERENCES

Anderson, William, and Lehman, Bryce E., *An Outline of County Government in Minnesota*, Minneapolis, 1927.

Barclay, Thomas S., *The Movement for Municipal Home Rule in St. Louis*, 1943.

Betters, Paul V., ed., and Others, *State Centralization in North Carolina*, Washington, D.C., 1932.

Brannon, Victor D., *State Auditor and Fiscal Control in Missouri Counties*, Columbia, 1940.

Carr, Robert K., *State Control of Local Finance in Oklahoma*, Oklahoma City, 1937.

Committee on Intergovernmental Fiscal Relations, *Federal, State and Local Government Fiscal Relations*, Senate Document No. 69, Washington, D.C., 1943.

Crouch, Winston W., *State Aid to Local Government in California*, Berkeley, 1939.

Fairlie, John A., and Kneier, Charles M., *County Government and Administration*, Part II, Chaps. IV, V, VI, 1930.

Ford, Robert S., and Goodrich, Kenneth S., *State Supervision of Local Borrowing*, Ann Arbor, Mich., 1942.

Jacoby, Neil H., and Others, *State-Local Fiscal Relations in Illinois*, 1941.

Kilpatrick, Wylie, *State Supervision of Local Budgeting*, 1939.

———, *State Supervision of Local Finance*, 1941.

Leland, S. E., ed., *State-Local Fiscal Relations in Illinois*, 1941.

MacCorkle, Stewart A., *State Financial Control Over Cities in Texas*, Dallas, 1937.

McBain, H. L., *American City Progress and the Law*, 1918.

———, *Law and Practice of Municipal Home Rule*, 1916.

McGoldrick, Joseph D., *Law and Practice of Municipal Home Rule, 1916–1930,* 1933.

McQuillin, Eugene, *Law of Municipal Corporations,* 2nd ed., Cumulative Supplement, 1943.

Pontius, Dale, *State Supervision of Local Government; Its Development in Massachusetts,* Washington, D.C., 1942.

Reed, Thomas H., *Federal-State-Local Fiscal Relations,* 1942.

Schulz, Ernest B., *Effect of the Contract Clause and the Fourteenth Amendment upon the Power of the States to Control Municipal Corporations,* Bethlehem, Pa., 1938.

Shavely, Tipton Ray, Hyde, Duncan Clarke, and Biscoe, Alvin Blocksom, *State Grants-in-Aid in Virginia,* 1933.

Tharp, Claude R., *State Aid in Michigan,* Ann Arbor, 1942.

Van de Woestyne, Royal S., *State Control of Local Finance in Massachusetts,* Cambridge, 1935.

Wager, Paul W., *County Government and Administration in North Carolina,* Chapel Hill, 1928.

Wallace, Schuyler, *State Administrative Supervision over Cities in the United States,* 1928.

———

MacCorkle, Stewart A., "Theory of State-Municipal Purchasing Arrangements," *Southwestern Social Science Quarterly,* XIX, 233–247, December, 1938.

Marion, John H., "State Supervision in New Jersey over Municipalities in Unsound Financial Condition," *American Political Science Review,* XXXVI, No. 3, 502–508, June, 1942.

Maxey, Chester C., "What Municipal Home Rule Means Today, IV—Washington," *National Municipal Review,* XXI, No. 4, 229–231, April, 1932.

McGoldrick, Joseph D., "What Municipal Home Rule Means Today, X—New York," *National Municipal Review,* XXI, No. 12, 601–605, October, 1932.

McMillin, Frederick N., "What Municipal Home Rule Means Today, IX—Wisconsin," *National Municipal Review,* XXI, No. 10, 601–605, October, 1932.

Pate, James E., "State Supervision of Local Fiscal Officers in Virginia," *American Political Science Review,* XXV, No. 4, 1004–1008, November, 1931.

Porter, Kirk H., "County Government and State Centralization," *National Municipal Review,* XXI, No. 8, 489–492, August, 1932.

Senning, John P., "What Municipal Home Rule Means Today, VIII—Nebraska," *National Municipal Review,* XXI, No. 7, 564–568, September, 1932.

Stewart, Frank M., "What Municipal Home Rule Means Today, VII—Texas After Twenty Years," *National Municipal Review,* XXI, No. 7, 434–441, July, 1932.

Wager, Paul W., "State Centralization in North Carolina," *American Political Science Review,* XXV, No. 4, 996–1003, November, 1931.

# Chapter Thirteen ⚜ CITY GOVERNMENT

THE history of the United States has been a history of unbroken urban growth. As in virtually all modern civilized nations, there has been a steady population shift from farm to city, and this trend seems likely to continue. When the first census was taken, in 1790, only about four per cent of the people were city dwellers; today this percentage is at least fifty-six. New York, the largest city in 1790, with a population of thiry-three thousand, now has a population not far short of the seven and one-half million mark. Nearly three hundred present-day American municipalities are more populous than the New York of the post-Revolutionary period.

## MOVEMENT FOR MUNICIPAL REFORM

**Tremendous increase in functions of city governments.** Together with the growth of cities has come an amazing multiplication of the functions performed by city governments. Public works, police and fire protection, public health and sanitation, street paving and lighting, water supply, and other matters that were once left to private initiative or else entirely neglected have become commonplaces of municipal administration. Serious problems of traffic regulation and control have been created by the automobile. Many kinds of inspectional services have become necessary. The list of present-day municipal activities ranges from street cleaning to the maintenance of community centers; it includes such widely diverse subjects as smoke abatement, maternity work, snow removal, band concerts, education of the blind. Almost every phase of modern urban existence is affected by some aspect of city government.

**New governmental organization.** It is important, therefore, that municipal affairs be conducted with at least a reasonable degree of efficiency. The modern movement for efficient city government began about 1900. Prior to that time the efforts of reformers had been directed chiefly toward the nomination and election of honest city officials, on the assumption that honesty would be sufficient to insure good government. But bitter experience finally drove home the lesson that even honest men might be poor administrators, and that even good administrators, however honest, could make little progress if hampered by outworn state laws and charter provisions. So a determined effort was made to improve the framework of city government, and also to develop more satisfactory administrative technique. At the outset greater emphasis was placed on framework, and new schemes of governmental organization became popular. Galveston adopted the commission form of government in 1901, and its success inspired hundreds of other communities to abandon their obsolete charters in favor of new charters of the commission type. In 1908 Staunton, Virginia, took an important step by originating the city manager plan, and six years later the plan received nation-wide attention when its adoption transformed Dayton, Ohio, from a badly governed city into a well-governed community almost overnight. Municipalities in every section of the United States followed Dayton's example. Although the mayor-council form of government, descended with many modifications from colonial days, continued to be by far the most widely accepted scheme of municipal organization, it was materially strengthened by the adoption of the short ballot and the expansion of the mayor's authority.

**Improved administrative technique.** Meanwhile, as the movement for improved governmental organization gathered momentum, the importance of perfecting administrative technique became more generally recognized. Men and women interested in the cause of municipal reform joined together to finance privately controlled municipal research bureaus. The first of these—the New York Bureau of Municipal Research—was organized in 1906 [1] and was instrumental in the establishment of similar agencies in many other cities. Because the directors and staffs of these research bureaus were trained technicians, familiar with the problems of municipal administration, their influence was profound. "It may be said that the government research movement is in no small measure responsible for the origin or development of scientific budget methods in this country, the intelligent development of public accounting and reporting, the systematic approach to public purchasing, the application of standards in public personnel, the short ballot and responsible governmental organization, and the expansion of American political science to include practical administration. . . ." [2]

[1] At first it was known as the Bureau of Civic Betterment, but it assumed its present name in 1907.

[2] Governmental Research Conference, *Twenty Years of Municipal Research*, p. 15.

American city government, therefore, is no longer a conspicuous failure, as Bryce once pictured it. Some municipalities have been conspicuously successful in the conduct of their affairs, and the government of the average city has been vastly improved since the beginning of the present century. Much remains to be accomplished, of course. Except in the more progressive cities, faulty governmental structure must be swept away, and concentrated authority must replace diffusion and irresponsibility. Administrative technique must be perfected. Corruption must be materially reduced. The spoils system, with its inevitable tendency to corrode and destroy efficient government, must be eliminated. But a great deal has already been done toward the fulfilment of these ideals.

### FORMS OF AMERICAN MUNICIPAL ORGANIZATION

**The mayor-council plan.** A wide diversity exists in the forms of American city government. The strong-mayor plan, the weak-mayor plan, and variations of these two; commission and council-manager government—all have found favor in some municipalities. But mayor-council government, whether of the strong-mayor, weak-mayor or hybrid-mayor variety, continues to be by far the most widely used form, and for that reason it deserves first consideration.

THE COUNCIL. Under the mayor-council plan, the popularly elected council has a wide variety of powers. As the local legislative body it enacts ordinances on all manner of subjects falling within the scope of the city's powers. Sometimes it frames the budget through its finance committee, though much more commonly it passes upon the budget presented to it by the mayor or some administrative board. It grants franchises, approves large purchases, designates certain banks as municipal depositories, and fixes salary schedules not prescribed by charter. In many ways it exercises control over administrative matters. Thus its approval is generally required for all important appointments made by the mayor, and sometimes for removals as well. In some cities the actual selection of certain administrative officers is made by the council. By ordinance it usually regulates many administrative details that should be in the hands of department heads or bureau chiefs.

The city council of today is almost invariably a single-chambered body, in marked contrast to the council of the mid-nineteenth century, which generally had two houses. A few cities, of which Atlanta and Richmond are conspicuous examples, still cling to the bicameral principle, but the day of the bicameral council in American city government is clearly past. For many years the trend has been toward longer terms for councilmen, and progressive municipalities have widely accepted the four-year term as most satisfactory. Two-year terms are still generally used, however, and even one-year terms have not entirely disappeared. Salaries are low—sometimes merely nominal, especially in the smaller communities, where service is not arduous and only a small amount of time is required. In some of the large metropolitan centers councilmen receive three or four thousand dollars a year, or even more, but their time is fully occupied with council and committee meetings, the hearing of individual petitions and complaints, and the maintenance of their local political organizations. Many a big-city councilman spends several times his salary every year keeping his political fences in repair.

City councils are much smaller than formerly; today most of them range in size from five to nine. There are some marked exceptions to this generalization, however; thus the city council of Cleveland has thirty-three members, and Chicago's council has a membership of fifty. The members of the larger councils are usually chosen by wards; but most cities, with their smaller legislative bodies, have adopted the plan of electing all councilmen at large. Reference has already been made to the Hare plan of proportional representation, now found in eleven American cities.[3] Other schemes—limited voting, combinations of the ward and at-large plans, and the like—are used by a few municipalities, but are not sufficiently important to warrant separate consideration.

THE MAYOR. Under the mayor-council plan the mayor is the central figure of the municipal administration. Nominally, at least, he is the head of the city government, though in many cities he is forced to share control of the city's administrative activities with a large number of independently elected officers. The form of mayor-council government known as the weak-mayor plan, which was generally accepted fifty or sixty years ago and still finds some stanch adherents, carries this administrative decentralization to extremes. Administration is largely in the hands of independent boards and commissions, which perform their separate activities with little or no regard for duplications, omissions, and needless waste. The mayor makes but few appointments, and those few must receive the approval of the council. He has a veto over proposed ordinances, but that

3 See pp. 157–158.

veto may be overridden by the council, usually by a two-thirds vote. Obviously this plan is very similar to the scheme of state government that still persists in most American commonwealths, and its faults are the same.[4]   It is complex, inefficient, and largely unresponsive to the popular will.   Fortunately, the weak-mayor plan is no longer widely used, and seems destined to disappear eventually from the American municipal scene.

Just as the administrative reorganization movement in state government has centered around the governor, so the effort to improve the structure of city government has been directed toward strengthening the position of the mayor—except under the commission and council-manager plans, which will be described later.   Reformers have urged that the chief executive should be supreme in fact as well as in name, and that he should have full responsibility for the conduct of municipal administration.   The result of this fight for better government has been the adoption of the strong-mayor plan by a considerable number of American cities, including such metropolitan centers as New York, Detroit, and Boston.   Under this scheme the mayor has power to appoint and remove virtually all administrative officers without consulting the council.   All employees of the administrative departments are selected in his name, though usually under civil service regulations.   He has important powers in connection with the municipal budget.   His veto of proposed ordinances may be overridden only by a three-fourths—or perhaps even a five-sixths—vote.

HYBRID TYPE.   The average American city lies somewhere between the weak- and strong-mayor plans.   It has strengthened the power of the mayor and reduced the number of independent administrative agencies, yet it has not fully concentrated authority in the mayor's hands.   A considerable number of administrative officers are still chosen by the voters or by the council.   The mayor prepares the budget, but the council is free to ignore his fiscal plan if its members so desire.   The council's approval of the mayor's appointments is still generally required.   Such a scheme of municipal organization can scarcely be called either weak-mayor or strong-mayor government; it is a hybrid type that virtually defies classification.   It is wholly illogical, of course, for it follows neither the theory of checks and balances nor the doctrine of concentrated responsibility.   The trend of city government, in those cities that still cling to mayor-council government, is undoubtedly toward a stronger mayor; but the forces of

4 See pp. 200–203.

decentralization are powerful and cannot be brushed aside lightly.

**Commission government.** When commission government first acquired wide popularity during the first decade of the present century, many persons believed that the ideal form of municipal organization had at last been found.   And, at a glance, the commission plan does seem to correct the evils of excessive decentralization.   Without doubt it eliminates the complexities of weak-mayor government and greatly simplifies municipal organization.   In fact, simplicity is the essence of the commission plan.

THE COMMISSION.   Administrative and legislative authority are combined in a small commission, having five members as a rule, but sometimes three or seven.   These commissioners are the city government.   As a body they enact necessary local legislation; individually they control the several administrative departments and supervise the enforcement of the laws that they have made.   The number of departments generally corresponds to the number of commissioners, and each commissioner becomes responsible for the work of the department assigned to his care.   Commissioners are popularly chosen, usually for two-year terms, but sometimes for four.   A few city charters provide for terms of one or six years.   Salaries range from a few hundred dollars a year to several thousand.   One member of the commission is commonly designated as mayor, but he possesses substantially the same authority as his colleagues though representing the city on ceremonial occasions.

*The Galveston charter and modifications.*   Because the members of the commission are chosen by the voters, it is unreasonable to suppose that they will possess the technical qualifications necessary for the direct handling of administrative matters.   Popular election does not produce technical skill, except by chance.   The men who framed the Galveston charter of 1901 recognized this fact and made provision for appointive department chiefs to serve under the commissioners and be directly responsible to them.   The administrative duties of each commissioner, therefore, were to be purely supervisory.   But most of the cities that copied Galveston's charter promptly "improved" this part of the commission plan by eliminating the appointive department chiefs and making the elective commissioners the active heads of their respective departments.   Thus the efficiency of the commission plan was materially reduced.

Another modification of the original Galveston scheme, now found in many cities, is the nomination and election of commissioners to specific offices—commissioner of health, commissioner of finance, and the like—instead of the distribution of offices among the successful candidates after election. This change is a logical result of the theory that members of the commission should be active department heads instead of lay supervisors. Its widespread adoption has merely added to the inherent inefficiency of commisson government.

DEFECTS OF THE PLAN. When the commission plan was new, many arguments were advanced in its favor. Reformers urged its adoption on the ground that the old system of diffused responsibility would be swept away and that responsibility as well as authority would be concentrated in the hands of a small group of men directly responsible to the voters. Thus, it was thought, praise and blame could be fairly apportioned. Moreover, commission government would eliminate friction and needless delays. Independently elected department heads would no longer flout the wishes of the mayor and make coordinated administration impossible. The greater simplicity of the new scheme would enable the voters to understand their government, and the result would be an awakened interest in civic affairs.

Many of the supporters of commission government were unduly optimistic, but undoubtedly the new plan was superior to the schemes of municipal organization that had preceded it. And, in many instances, its adoption marked the beginning of an era of civic improvement. The mainspring of the movement for commission government was a widespread popular demand for reform. The voters were disgusted with the inefficiency and corruption of the professional politicians, and proceeded to sweep them out of office, replacing them with men of high caliber, many of whom accepted public office temporarily as a civic duty. Such men could have produced satisfactory results with almost any form of organization; actually they produced results with commission government, and the commission plan received the credit. Later, of course, the tide of public indignation receded, and in most cities the professional politicians again took control without serious opposition from the independents. The defects of commission government then became glaringly apparent.

Among the many weaknesses of the commission plan is its failure to concentrate responsibility sufficiently. Its friends contend that concentration of responsibility is its chief merit; that it sweeps away a large number of independent boards, commissions, and departments, and puts in their place an all-powerful commission—usually having but five members. Even the elimination of many independent agencies does not produce unity, however, if control is still divided among co-equal members of a commission. Five men may disagree, and American experience with commission government has proved that they often do. Five men may shift responsibility from one to another, and experience has further demonstrated the likelihood that such evasion will actually occur. Commission government, therefore, stops short of its declared objective; it goes only part way along the path of administrative centralization. Instead of concentrating authority in the hands of one man, it provides a five-ring circus with an all-star cast.

It has already been pointed out that commission government is necessarily government by amateurs. The members of the commission are elected by the voters for relatively short terms, and their continuance in office depends upon personal popularity rather than technical skill. In nearly every instance, therefore, they are masters of the art of winning votes. Their spare time is usually devoted to additional vote-getting rather than additional study of public works or personnel programs, for they realize that the commission plans subordinates good administration to good politics.

Other defects of commission government should also receive at least passing notice. The commission, usually composed of five members, is too small to serve as a legislative body, especially in the larger communities. The many shades of opinion that inevitably divide the voters of a great city cannot be adequately represented. On the other hand, the number of commissioners cannot be multiplied indefinitely, because of the necessity of assigning to each commissioner one of the departments of the city government. Closely akin to this weakness is another defect: the arbitrary grouping of all municipal activities into five or some other specified number of departments, without regard to local needs. The framers of a commission type of charter do not survey the administrative activities of a city for the purpose of determining how many departments are required and then fix the number of commissioners accordingly. Instead they agree that the commission shall have five—or possibly three or seven—members, and then proceed to establish five—or possibly three or seven—administrative departments. If this scheme of administrative organization happens to coincide with the city's activities, so much the better. But no effort is made to insure such a result.

RISE AND FALL IN POPULARITY. The heyday of commission government is past, but for a number of years it spread at a rapid rate, and seemed destined to replace government by mayor and council. In 1904, three years after Galveston first gave the plan nation-wide publicity,[5] it was adopted by another Texas city—Houston. Five other Texas municipalities fell into line in 1907, and also two Iowa cities —Des Moines and Davenport. After that adoptions came very rapidly. Twenty-eight cities discarded their mayor-council charters in favor of commission charters during 1909, and the following year forty-four municipalities became converts. By 1911 the number of commission-governed cities was one hundred and fifty-five; by 1917 it was nearly five hundred. Since 1917, however, there have been few new adoptions, and many cities have abandoned commission government to return to the mayor-council type of organization or, much more commonly, to accept the newer council-manager plan. Even yet, however, commission government is used by several hundred American cities,[6] including such large metropolitan centers as Newark, New Orleans, Jersey City, St. Paul, and Portland, Oregon. Buffalo and Oakland, formerly commission-governed cities, can no longer be included in the list.

**The council-manager plan.** When Dayton adopted the council-manager plan in 1914 and made it a conspicuous success, friends of good government in every section of the country began to urge its adoption by their communities. Within two years thirty-eight municipalities had followed Dayton's example. By 1920 the number of manager cities had risen to one hundred and sixty-two; by 1930 it was slightly in excess of four hundred. In 1944, according to the official list of the International City Managers' Association, there were five hundred and sixty-two manager cities.[7] Among them were Cincinnati, Kansas City (Missouri), Rochester, Oakland, and Dallas. Only a scattered handful of cities have abandoned the manager plan, though the list of abandonments includes Cleveland, the largest city that ever operated under a manager charter.

THE DUTIES AND POWERS OF THE COMMISSION OR COUNCIL. At the outset the manager plan was scarcely regarded as a new form of municipal organization, but rather as a development of commission gov-

[5] Galveston does not deserve the credit, which it often receives, for originating commission government. This scheme of municipal organization was adopted by Sacramento in 1863, and by a number of other cities prior to 1900. But most of these early experiments were abandoned after a few years, and there is no evidence that they affected the course of municipal history.

[6] The exact number is not known. In fact, no careful enumeration has ever been made.

[7] *Municipal Year Book, 1944*, pp. 575–578.

ernment.   The name "commission-manager plan" was widely used.
The popularly elected commission of five members was generally retained, but its functions were considerably modified.   No longer were
its members to supervise the details of municipal administration; instead they were to select a manager who would become the city's chief
administrator, choosing his own subordinates to serve as department
heads and holding them strictly responsible for the conduct of municipal affairs.   Thus the commission would become purely a legislative body, without control over administrative matters except through
its right to dismiss the manager.   Many a manager charter now specifically declares that the members of the local legislative body shall
deal with the administrative service solely through the city manager,
and even goes so far as to provide penalties for violation of this requirement.   None the less legislative interference with administrative matters occurs occasionally in nearly all manager cities, and
habitually in a few.

Since the commission was not intended to be an administrative
agency under the manager plan, but a purely deliberative or policy-
making body, there was no reason why its membership should be
limited to five.   On the contrary, the need for adequate representation of different shades of opinion was a sound reason for increasing
the number of members.   Gradual recognition of this fact led to
the establishment in some cities of legislative bodies having nine,
eleven, or fifteen members, or even twenty-five, as in Cleveland under
its city manager charter.   Most of the largest cities operating under
the plan have found nine an adequate number.

The name *commission,* as applied to the legislative body of city
manager government, has generally been discarded in recent years,
and *council* used in its place.   More than a matter of terminology
is involved, for the change indicates that the new scheme of governmental organization is something more than a variation of the commission plan—that it is, in fact, something very different from commission government.   The council, as organized under a manager
charter, is *not* a commission.   It is a legislative body, with just two
major functions—the determination of municipal policies and the
selection of a manager to execute those policies.   Quite naturally,
therefore, the *commission-manager plan* has become the *council-
manager plan.*

The term *council-manager* indicates the position of the council in
the new scheme of government.   Its members, under the strict theory

of the plan, are the only elective city officials. They form the connecting link between the public and the administration. Although they are expressly denied any part in the management of administrative matters, they employ the manager—the city's chief administrator—and dismiss him at their pleasure. Therefore they necessarily assume responsibility, in a broad way, for successful administration. One of the members of the council is designated as mayor, but his position is not very important. He presides over council sessions and acts as ceremonial head of the city. A few manager charters, varying from the standard form, bestow additional powers upon the mayor. Sometimes he is authorized to grant pardons, to suspend ordinances temporarily, or even to exercise a suspensive veto over the legislative proposals of his fellow councilmen. These changes are unfortunate, for by strengthening the power of the mayor they establish him as a potential rival of the manager for control of the city's government. There should be no question that the manager is supreme—subject, of course, to the continued approval of the council.

THE MANAGER AS AN ADMINISTRATOR. The manager is chosen for an indefinite term and holds office as long as he gives satisfaction. Usually he may not be removed except upon presentation of formal charges and after a public hearing. Some charters even provide that charges may not be presented during the first six months, so that the manager will be assured of an opportunity to prove his worth. The obvious purpose of these various clauses is to attract trained technicians —career men who will devote their lives to the city manager profession, instead of using the managership as a steppingstone to political fame. Technical requirements for the office of manager are not precisely specified, but many charters declare that the manager must be "a qualified administrator" or "possessed of business and executive ability." Although such clauses are merely the expression of a pious hope, they indicate a new attitude toward public administration. They emphasize the need for administrative skill in the municipal service.

Even more important than the insistence upon "competence" in the manager is the omission of a residence requirement. Many charters state directly that residence is not necessary. Thus the council is free to select the best man for the job, wherever he can be found. It may go beyond the boundaries of the city or the state. It may select a trained manager on the basis of his record in other cities, just as German municipalities choose their burgomasters. On the other hand, there is nothing except the pressure of public opinion to prevent it from awarding the managership to some local politician in exchange for votes duly delivered on election day. But no form of government can insure good appointments—especially if bad men are in control; and the manager plan goes much farther than any other in making possible the selection of trained administrators.

Experience with the manager plan has proved that this advantage is not purely theoretical. Many cities go outside their own borders to select their managers, and the result has been the development of a group of trained administrators, who serve city after city as their records in small communities lead to more tempting offers from larger municipalities. The list of city managers includes the names of scores of men who are serving their second, third, or even fourth cities. Engineers predominate, and many managers have had wide administrative experience in various phases of private industrial activity. While managers are sometimes chosen without regard to administrative capacity and sometimes with direct reference to political availability, the general level of manager appointments is surprisingly high. Managers' salaries are high, also, in marked contrast to the salaries paid by American municipalities to their chief executives under the mayor-council plan. More than a score of cities pay their managers ten thousand dollars or over.

THE MANAGER NOT A POLITICAL LEADER. Despite the signal success of the manager plan, it has been bitterly opposed by many persons. The professional politicians are usually lined up solidly against it because it simplifies the structure of municipal government and makes boss control more difficult. Other groups join the opposition for various reasons—most commonly because they do not understand the theory of the manager plan or its practical operation. The argument most commonly advanced against manager government is that it is essentially undemocratic because it vests the selection of the city manager in the hands of the council instead of directly in the hands of the people. The fallacy of this line of reasoning is obvious. It assumes that the chief executive of a city must be a political leader, whose time is devoted largely to framing policies. But efficient city government is not primarily a matter of making wise decisions on important political questions; instead it is concerned chiefly with the satisfactory performance of day-by-day administrative routine. Persons must be protected against violence; homes must be protected against fire; streets must be kept clean; water supplies must be kept pure. These activities, and most of the other matters that properly occupy the time of a municipal executive, require efficient administrative technique rather than the ability to guide public opinion. City government is at least ninety per cent administration, and it is for this reason that the leaders in the fight for good city government advocate the method of selecting the chief executive best calculated to secure administrative skill.

Since the manager is expressly denied the rôle of popular leader, the necessary leadership must come from the council. It is the popularly elected branch of the city government, and its members must inevitably accept the task of guiding public opinion. But this is a responsibility to which the council is not accustomed. For half a century it has looked to the mayor for leadership and has done little more than pass upon his suggestions. Small wonder, therefore, that most councils in manager cities have proved unequal to the task of formulating sound policies! Opponents of the manager plan have seized upon this weakness and urged it as a reason for returning to the mayor-council system. American experience has proved, however, that the solution of the difficulty is not popular election of the chief executive but the development of a tradition of leadership within the council. Much more time is required to develop such a tradition than to change a charter provision, but the result is certain to be infinitely more satisfactory.

*Unfortunate results of manager's political activities.* Some managers, wearied by the stupidity or ignorance of councilmen, attempt to supply the leadership so obviously lacking in municipal affairs. According to the theory of the manager plan the manager is only the paid employee of the council—a glorified employee, with broad powers, but none the less subordinate to the legislative body. He may urge the council to act upon his recommendations; but, once the council has decided upon a course of action, he is obligated to support that course, even though it runs counter to his own ideas. But why should a competent manager, sure of the wisdom of his proposals, hesitate to appeal directly to the people? Why should he not go over the heads of the councilmen in an effort to win popular support? If obstinate councilmen will not accept his point of view, why should he not ask for their defeat and the election in their place of other councilmen who will pledge themselves in advance to support his policies? The answer, written large in the history of American city government, is that virtually every attempt by a manager to play the part of a popular leader has resulted eventually in his resignation or dismissal from office and in the weakening of the manager plan.

Nor is this at all surprising. The manager who regards himself as a professional administrator, dissociated from the highly controversial issues of public policy, may well hope for permanent tenure and the opportunity to devote himself without interference to his administrative duties; but the manager who advocates policies must be prepared to stand or fall by them. Sooner or later he will almost certainly find himself on the unpopular side of some important issue, and then he will be morally obligated to resign. His place must be taken by someone who can better express the popular will. Under such circumstances the manager ceases to be a permanent, non-political officer, and becomes instead a political officer, concerned only incidentally with the problems of administration. He does not differ in any substantial way from the mayor of mayor-council government, save that he is appointed instead of elected. And, if he remains a political officer, that difference will surely disappear, for American voters will insist upon choosing their policy-determining officers. The necessity of divorcing the manager from political leadership is recognized by the International City Managers' Association in its code of ethics: "Loyalty to his employment recognizes that it is the council, the elected representatives of the people, who primarily determine the municipal policies, and are entitled to the credit for their fulfilment."

ACCEPTANCE AND EFFECTIVENESS OF THE PLAN. Very few city charters are adopted today without serious consideration of the manager plan, and there is strong probability that in time it will become the accepted form of municipal government in the United States. Much depends on the type of managers chosen, however, and on their willingness to keep clear of policy determination. Equally important is the willingness of the council to avoid interference with administrative matters. The manager plan may not be the final word in municipal organization, but undoubtedly it is the most effective scheme yet devised.

### IMPROVEMENT OF MUNICIPAL ADMINISTRATION

As previously pointed out,[8] the municipal reform movement has not been concerned solely with the structure of government, but has been directed also toward the improvement of administrative technique. Thus, in the field of finance, the budget system has been

[8] See pp. 278-279.

developed and perfected until, in the more progressive cities, it provides an effective means of planning expenditures and balancing them against income. Half a century ago the budget system was unknown in American cities; today it is used, at least nominally, by every large municipality and by most of the smaller urban centers. In many instances, of course, the so-called budget system is merely a cloak for haphazard spending, but everywhere the desirability of budgeting is recognized. Some of the better-governed municipalities, with long-term financial programs, have even applied the budget principle to their capital expenditures.

The merit system, also, has made steady progress. Virtually all the large metropolitan centers have established civil service commissions, and at least pay lip worship to the merit principle in the selection of their employees. In many smaller communities, also, the spoils system has been officially pronounced dead, though the corpse may occasionally show signs of life. Central purchasing, mechanical valuation of real estate, city planning and zoning, and other desirable reforms have similarly made forward strides. The improvement of municipal government through the adoption of better administrative methods is inevitably a slow process, but a great deal has been accomplished in recent years.

## Selected References

Griffith, Ernest S., *Current Municipal Problems,* 1933.
——, *The Modern Development of City Government in the United Kingdom and the United States,* 2 vols., London, 1927.
——, *History of American City Government,* 1938.
Hoan, D. W., *City Government,* 1936.
Hodges, Henry G., *City Management: Theory and Practice of Municipal Administration,* 1939.
Horlacher, J. P., and Phillips, J. C., *City-State Relations,* 1937.
Institute for Training in Municipal Administration, *The American City and Its Government,* Chicago, 1937.
International City Managers' Association, *Government in Small American Cities,* 1938.
——, *Selection of a City Manager,* 1937.
Jones, Victor, *Metropolitan Government,* 1942.
Kneier, Charles M., *City Government in the United States,* 1934.
——, *Illustrative Government and Administration,* 1939.
MacCorkle, Stuart, *Municipal Administration,* 1942.
Macdonald, Austin F., *American City Government and Administration,* 3rd ed., 1941.
Munro, William Bennett, *Municipal Administration,* 1934.

National Institute of Municipal Law Officers, *Municipalities and the Law in Action*, rev. ed., Washington, D.C., 1944.

National Resources Committee, *Urban Government*, Washington, D.C., 1939.

Pfiffner, John M., *Municipal Administration*, 1940.

Reed, Thomas H., *Municipal Management*, 1941.

Stone, Harold A., and Others, *City Manager Government in the United States*, 1940.

Taft, Charles P., *City Management: the Cincinnati Experiment*, 1933.

Wells, Roger H., *American Local Government*, 1939.

White, Leonard D., *The City Manager*, 1927.

Zink, Harold, *Government of Cities in the United States*, 1939.

---

The *Municipal Year Book*, published by the International City Managers' Association, contains a wealth of information concerning city government and administration. Another useful annual, the *Municipal Index*, is published by the *American City Magazine*.

FORTY-SEVEN of the forty-eight states are divided into smaller governmental units known as counties, and the lone exception—Louisiana—has corresponding units called parishes.   The number of counties varies widely from state to state; thus Delaware has only three counties, whereas Texas has two hundred and fifty-four.   Marked variations exist, also, in the area and population of counties and in the organization and functions of county government.   Generalization, therefore, is difficult, but any brief description of county government and administration must necessarily be in general terms.

## ORGANIZATION OF COUNTY GOVERNMENT

**Its varying functions.**   Everywhere the county plays an important part in the administration of justice.   Some states use it as a judicial district, with one trial court in each county.   Other states combine counties to form judicial districts, which is the more common plan by a wide margin; [1] but even under such circumstances the prosecuting attorney, the sheriff, and the clerk of court are usually county officers.   County courthouses expedite judicial business, and county jails hold those persons who are awaiting trial as well as those who have been sentenced to short terms of imprisonment.   Poor relief administration, also, is in the hands of county officials in most states. Highway construction and maintenance, public health work, and education, including vocational training specifically designed to improve agriculture, are generally regarded as matters in which the county should take a part.   Almost everywhere the county is an important unit of fiscal administration, levying and collecting taxes for its own purposes and often for state and municipal purposes as well.   The election system of the state commonly utilizes the county as a major unit.   These are the more important county functions, but if the list were extended to include all activities performed wholly or partly by county officials in any state, it would be a most impressive enumeration.   It would include the development of park systems, the establish-

[1] See p. 233.

ment of other recreational facilities, such as gymnasiums, swimming pools, and public baths, the maintenance of libraries, and the development of airports. It would include, also, rural housing—a movement greatly stimulated by federal aid.

ITS CHAOTIC STRUCTURE. The governmental structures established in the three thousand-odd [2] counties of the United States closely resemble one another in one important respect—they violate, almost without exception, every sound principle of organization. They are headless and formless. Authority is scattered among a large number of elective officers, who usually pursue their separate ways with little or no thought of effective co-operation. No one person, corresponding to the mayor or manager of a city or the governor of a state, exercises supreme executive power. No one person can be held responsible for the lack of effective, co-ordinated administration. Even the so-called legislative body of the county has very limited legislative powers and can determine county policies only within certain narrowly limited fields. Administrative and judicial functions are often combined in the same officer or group of officers. The inevitable result of such a governmental jumble is chaos, and *chaos* accurately describes the present state of county government in the United States.

A few counties are predominantly urban, the cities within their borders having grown to metropolitan proportions. Such counties present special problems that have already received passing notice.[3] A much larger number of counties contain cities of medium size and therefore face some of the same problems. Duplication of county and city activities must be reduced or completely eliminated, if possible; co-operation between county and city authorities must be fostered. But these matters are not typical county problems, for the average county is still a predominantly rural area, existing as a unit of local rural government and designed, however crudely, to meet rural needs. Most of the state legislation for counties is for rural counties, and most of the proposals for the reform of county government are based on rural conditions.

**The county board.** The chief governing body of the county—or, more accurately, the body that most nearly deserves to be called *chief* among the numerous independent and unrelated agencies of county government—is the county board,[4] generally known as the board of

[2] There are 3,050 counties, including the Louisiana parishes.
[3] See pp. 272–275.
[4] Rhode Island is the only state where the county board is unknown.

supervisors or board of county commissioners, but sometimes called the board of revenue, fiscal court, or board of chosen freeholders.

ITS FUNCTIONS. The county board performs both legislative and executive functions, contrary to the traditional and commonly accepted doctrine of the separation of powers. Its legislative functions are narrowly restricted, covering only a few matters that the legislature or, less commonly, the framers of the state constitution have seen fit to place under county control. The constitutions of a few states, such as California, specifically empower the county commissioners to make necessary local regulations not in conflict with the general state laws; and in a few other states, such as New York, the legislature is authorized to confer such power of local legislation as it may deem expedient. But even these narrowly restricted grants or potential grants of authority represent an attitude of extreme liberality. In most states the legislative powers of the county board, aside from its power to tax and to appropriate for specific purposes, are scarcely worthy of enumeration.

As an administrative agency the county board is more important. It manages county finances and property, supervises the construction of public works other than highways, and sometimes highway construction as well,[5] maintains court-houses and jails, administers the county poor relief program, and supervises the conduct of elections. Its financial powers generally include examination and approval of the budget, which its finance committee sometimes prepares, and also equalization of property assessments among the townships of the county—or, in some states, among individuals.[6] Effective management of county affairs is virtually impossible, because the county board shares responsibility with a large number of independently chosen officers, such as the sheriff, the coroner, and the assessor, whose acts are largely beyond its control. Only a few minor county officers are appointed by the county board in most states. The list usually includes the superintendent of the poor and the superintendent of the workhouse. Sometimes, though rarely, it includes an important county officer—the treasurer.

ITS ORGANIZATION. The organization of county boards varies widely from state to state. Two general types of boards may be distinguished, however, though with many exceptions and modifications. One of these general types is the large board, ranging in size from fifteen mem-

[5] In most states the county boards at least locate the more important county roads.
[6] See p. 368.

bers to one hundred or even more. The members of such a board are commonly chosen by the voters of their respective townships, and individually have supervision of township affairs; therefore the board is known as a board of supervisors. New York, Michigan, and Wisconsin make use of this plan, and Illinois has adopted it in part. The other general type of county board is the small board, with a membership seldom in excess of seven, and more commonly three or five. This is called a board of county commissioners; its members are usually though not invariably elected at large from the entire county. It is popular in most of the states of the South and Far West, where township organization is unimportant or non-existent. Townships do not necessitate large county boards, however, as shown by the experience of a number of states. Thus Pennsylvania, Ohio, Indiana, and most of the New England states combine township or town organization with small county boards. On the other hand, large boards are found in Arkansas and Tennessee, which have no townships. Moreover, the states do not follow a consistent scheme of nomenclature. Some of them use the term *board of supervisors* for the small county board, even if there are no townships to be supervised.

*Attemps to improve efficiency.* Neither large nor small boards have proved wholly satisfactory because of the various—and, to some extent, conflicting—functions that county boards are called upon to perform. As legislative bodies they should be fairly large, in order to secure adequate representation for the many shades of opinion that exist in virtually every community. Three men, or five, cannot be expected to legislate with due regard for all the interests that are entitled to consideration. And yet, when county boards are enlarged to permit adequate representation, they immediately become too unwieldy for administrative bodies. They spend their time in discussion when action is needed. They adopt formal rules of procedure, and these rules delay still further the normal functioning of the administrative machinery. Some of the large county boards in a number of states have tried to overcome the difficulty by creating small standing committees to handle the details of administration, but this plan has proved generally unsatisfactory. The committees usually show very little desire to co-operate with one another, and there is no way of compelling them to do so. The result is a still further disintegration of county administration. Moreover, all important committee actions must receive board approval, and most county boards are not disposed to accept committee recommendations, except in rare instances, without prolonged debate. Therefore the saving of time under the committee plan is more apparent than real.

Devices intended to improve the efficiency of county government by separating to some extent the functions of legislation and administration include the establishment of a county council in addition to the county board, as in Indiana, and the creation of a chief county administrative officer, as in some of the counties of New Jersey. In most instances, however, the chief county administrative officer possesses very limited powers and cannot be considered the county equivalent of a city manager. A handful of counties have adopted the manager plan, but these experiments are discussed in another part of this chapter.[7]

MEETINGS AND COMPENSATION. When the county board is a large body, it usually meets at infrequent intervals; in some states three or four meetings a year are the rule. The small board usually holds meetings more often—every week or every fortnight, in some of the more populous counties. Members of county boards are commonly paid by the day, the compensation ranging from three to eight dollars, plus an allowance for mileage. This arrangement is often coupled with some sort of limitation on the number of days that the board may meet or the number of days that salary may be drawn. A few of the large counties in several states pay their board members by the year rather than by the day, thus removing the temptation to delay the public business in order to obtain a slightly larger salary.

SHARED RESPONSIBILITY. As previously indicated, the county boards share responsibility for the management of county affairs with a large number of independently chosen officers. One of these is the sheriff, the peace officer of the county, who enforces the law, serves court processes, and keeps the county jail. Another is the coroner, whose task is to investigate cases of violent death. The public prosecutor, also, is usually though not invariably a county official. A few counties have public defenders as well as prosecutors. Since the work of these several officers will be described in a later chapter,[8] nothing need be added at this point.

**The treasurer:** SELECTION AND TENURE. Nearly every county has a treasurer, who receives, holds, and disburses county money according to law. Usually he is elected by the voters, but he may be chosen by the county board, as in Connecticut and New Jersey, or by the

[7] See pp. 303–306.
[8] Chap. Twenty. See pp. 400–408.

governor, as in South Carolina. The term of office of the treasurer is generally fixed at two years, and in many states he is forbidden to serve two consecutive terms. Such provisions concerning tenure, though designed to insure strict examination of county funds at frequent intervals, as each new treasurer takes office, actually accomplish no useful purpose. On the contrary, they put a premium on ignorance by excluding men from office as soon as they have had an opportunity to gain experience.

BONDING AGAINST DEFALCATION. Virtually everywhere the treasurer is placed under heavy bond to protect the county against possible defalcation. The county is also protected against poor judgment in the selection of depositories, under the court decisions of some states, which hold that the treasurer is liable for the safe-keeping of all funds placed in his custody. The effect of these decisions is to permit the county, in the event of a bank failure, to recover directly from the treasurer to the extent of his personal resources, even though no evidence of bad faith appears. The numerous bank failures during the years 1930, 1931, and 1932 worked serious hardship upon many honest county treasurers, and have led to a number of modifications of the rule. Eventually, in all probability, the deposit of county funds will be regarded universally as a matter to be regulated by law, and the treasurer will not be held liable unless he violates some statutory provision. This more rational plan has already been adopted by a majority of the states.

DISBURSEMENTS. With regard to disbursements the treasurer exercises but slight discretion. He must pay every lawful claim allowed by the county board and approved by the auditor. If, however, the claim is for a purpose not authorized by law, he may refuse payment. In fact, it is his duty to do so. County treasurers, therefore, should know all the lawful objects of expenditure, so as to be able to pass upon the legality of claims presented to them. But in practice they seldom possess such knowledge, relying instead on the auditors or corresponding officers to reject unlawful claims.

**The auditor.** Every county needs some officer to examine bills and claims and determine their validity. Even though these bills and claims are approved by the county board before payment, a separate audit by some person not a member of the board is highly desirable. Many counties, however, make no provision for such an audit. Many others assign this task to the county clerk, with reasonably satisfactory results. There is, in fact, little justification for both a county auditor and a county clerk, except in very populous counties. But separate county auditors have been established, regardless of need, in about one-third of the states.

They are chosen in a variety of ways—by the county board, as in New Jersey; by the county's members of the state legislature, as in Connecticut; by the judges of the courts, as in Vermont; by the governor, with senate approval, as in South Carolina; or by the voters at the polls, as in at least ten states. One auditor to a county is the rule, but a few states prefer boards of auditors as a further check upon possible dishonesty. In addition to passing upon bills and claims against the county, some auditors are empowered to examine the accounts of other county officers at regular intervals. Such periodic examinations are necessary, of course, though often neglected in county government. But they should be made, in the opinion of most students of public administration, by some state agency with broad powers of audit rather than by any county officer, however chosen.

**Assessors.** The locally elected assessors, sometimes county officers and sometimes officers of the town or township, are poorly qualified to perform the difficult task of determining the value of property for purposes of taxation. A few states have amended their constitutions to provide for assessors appointed by the governor, and this plan has usually proved more satisfactory. But some politically minded governors have used this additional appointing power to strengthen their own political machines, and these unfortunate experiences, coupled with the long-standing American fear of concentrated authority, have been sufficient to prevent widespread adoption of the appointive plan. In Kentucky, one of the many states where assessors are still chosen by popular vote, the names of candidates are not placed upon the ballot until they have demonstrated their fitness by appearing before the state tax commission and passing an examination. This scheme, or some modification of it, has been tried by a number of metropolitan centers in several states and has proved infinitely superior to the usual method of popular election without any attempt at prequalification.

**The clerk of the court and the county clerk.** Two other county officers whose duties are sufficiently important to deserve special mention are the clerk of the county court and the county clerk. The clerk of the county court opens court sessions and adjourns them, keeps the official record of all court proceedings, dockets all cases for trial, and issues necessary processes and writs. The county clerk acts as secretary to the county board; in addition, he has a wide variety of miscellaneous functions, ranging from the preparation of ballots to the issuance of marriage licenses. In no two states are his duties exactly the same; often they include the examination and approval of claims, in case there is no separate auditor, or the registration of voters, if no other officer has been assigned that task. The offices of clerk of the county court and county clerk have been considered jointly because in many states they are combined in one official, who usually bears the title of court clerk. Popular election and short terms are the rule, for no better reason than that most county officers are popularly elected and serve for short terms.

**The register of deeds.** In many states the clerk of court or county clerk maintains a public record of deeds, mortgages, and other documents affecting the title to real estate. More than half of the states, however, have assigned this duty to a separate officer whose title is recorder or register of deeds. This officer is elected by the voters, and as a rule his term is two years. Like other county officials, therefore, he is an amateur charged with a task requiring professional skill. In most instances he makes use of the old-fashioned methods inherited from his predecessors in office. Documents are copied tediously in longhand—or, more rarely, on the typewriter. Only a few of the more progressive recorders' offices make full use of available printed forms, and modern photostat recording is practically unknown, except in some of the large metropolitan centers. Filing systems are antiquated. The inevitable result, in nearly every county, is a set of records whose accuracy is open to serious question. Private interests have taken advantage of this situation to establish companies for the purpose of searching the records and guaranteeing the title to property. A few states have adopted the so-called "Torrens system" [9] of land registration, which eliminates the dangers of possible flaws in the title at comparatively small cost to the purchaser. Under this system title is awarded by court decree after a public hearing, and may not be clouded by valid claims presented at a later date. These claims are not ignored, however; instead they are settled by cash payments from an assurance fund built up from the fees charged for registration.

**The surveyor.** Nearly every county has a surveyor—an elective officer whose duty is to make surveys of land upon the request of private owners or the order of the court. He has no fixed salary, but instead receives his compensation in the form of fees. Today his office is unimportant, because property lines have been precisely fixed

---

[9] Introduced in Australia by Robert Torrens.

in most communities. Some surveyors still play a part in the construction of highways, and in a few states this is their principal function. But modern road building is a task for trained engineers, and county engineers are rapidly replacing surveyors as the directors of highway construction programs. A considerable number of states have combined the duties of the county surveyor and the county engineer, and this arrangement has generally proved satisfactory.

### DEFECTS IN COUNTY ORGANIZATION AND ADMINISTRATION

This, then, is the usual form of county government: a board with limited powers, responsible in a general way for policy determination and also for the administration of county affairs, but forced to share its control over county administration with a large number of independently elected officers who follow their separate paths unchecked, utterly heedless of the need for effective co-ordinated action. By every adequate theory of government such a theme should be a complete failure—and, by every practical test, it is. All students of public affairs agree that county organization must be thoroughly overhauled before it can function effectively under modern conditions. The literature of county government is filled with recitals of inefficiency and waste until the story becomes monotonous through repetition. Professors Ogg and Ray declare "that, in general, the county has been largely untouched by the reform movements which have wrought so effectively for better government in city and state; that no state in the Union has worked out a thoroughly satisfactory system of county government; that, almost everywhere, cumbersome governmental machinery and antiquated business methods persist, and divided, diffused, and diluted authority and responsibility prevail. . . ." [10]

Official reports and unofficial surveys, both new and old, are in the same vein. Only a few years ago the *National Municipal Review* editorialized: "Almost all counties . . . seem to present a uniformly depressing picture of political control at its worst, serene adherence to the spoils system, wasteful inefficiency, lack of administrative organization, diffusion of responsibility to the point where there is virtually none, accompanied by an amazing indifference on the part of the voters." [11] Recent years have witnessed increasingly sharp attacks by students of government upon county inefficiency, and increasing interest by taxpayers in the possibility of economizing through improved

[10] *Introduction to American Government,* 7th ed., p. 894.
[11] February, 1939, p. 78.

county organization and more efficient county administrative technique. Some changes have actually been made—largely as a result of pressure by state legislatures and state administrative agencies. But the reforms so far adopted do not change the picture in any material respect. County government is still bad government by almost any test.

**Lack of a responsible executive.** The chief—and most obvious—defect in the organization of county government, as previously pointed out,[12] is the lack of a responsible executive. The county does not have a president, governor, mayor, or any other officer to exercise supreme executive authority. "None of the county officers has any appointive power beyond his own deputies, clerks, etc. The board of supervisors holds the purse strings and the other officers must come to it, hat in hand, once a year for the money, but they come strong in the knowledge that their salaries or fees are fixed by law anyway, and, in fixing the appropriation, the supervisors have little discretion. Indeed it is more usual for each officer to run his own office according to his own lights, and his only contact with the supervisors may be when vouchers, covering expenditures already made, are presented for the supervisors' audit and approval, such piecemeal action being about as near to a budget and an appropriation as a typical county board ever gets. Individual supervisors have power to annoy the other county officers and it pays the latter to keep friendly, but the board as a whole would be helpless and ineffective if it attempted to utilize its power of the purse to enforce economy and efficiency among its independently elected associates. Moreover, being a board—a board that meets once a month or once a quarter—it is quite unable to operate as an executive or follow its resolutions through to secure whole-hearted compliance. When there is a controversy between county officers, their only common superior to which appeal may be made is the remote legislature which, by special law, may for example settle the issue of what salary the sheriff may pay his wife for services as cook in the county jail." [13]

Failure to vest complete authority and responsibility in a single executive is due in part to the opposition of local politicians, who regard any proposal to change the existing governmental structure as a threat aimed directly at their freedom of action. In part, too, popular indifference is responsible. The average voter is not interested in the

12 See p. 295.
13 Childs, Richard S., *The County Manager Plan*, pp. 3–4.

government of the county in which he happens to live, unless his pocketbook is directly and obviously affected. But other factors are also to blame. Thus the constitutions of most states indirectly prohibit the establishment of unified executive control by imposing a long ballot on all counties. In Texas, for example, the list of elective county officers—by constitutional mandate—includes the county judge, the justice of the peace, the clerk of the district court, the constable, the county commissioner, the county clerk, who serves *ex officio* as recorder, the county attorney, the tax collector, the assessor, the treasurer, and the surveyor. And Texas is not an especially serious offender in this respect; its constitutional provisions concerning counties are typical of the provision found in many state constitutions. Amendment of the constitutional clauses imposing a long ballot is possible, of course, but in most states amendment is a slow and difficult process. So those interested in the reform of county government often give up the fight in despair, and the old, inefficient organization continues to function in the same old, inefficient way.

A few county governments have been altered to provide for a popularly elected executive possessing a certain general power of supervision over a county administration. Thus Cook County, Illinois, has a county president, elected as a member of the county board and authorized to appoint those county officers—mostly of minor rank— who are not chosen by direct vote of the people. He exercises a limited veto over the acts of the board. In certain counties of New York, New Jersey, and Virginia a popularly chosen chief executive officer is partly responsible for the co-ordination of county administration. But such schemes are far from satisfactory. First, they go only a short distance along the path of reform. Though recognizing in part the need for concentrated authority, they still diffuse power among a considerable number of independently chosen officials. Second, they rely on an elective officer, who is therefore necessarily an amateur, to direct the technical details of administration.

DESIRABILITY OF THE COUNTY MANAGER PLAN. The next step, logically, is the adoption of the manager plan by counties. County government—perhaps even more than city government—is chiefly a matter of administration. Only occasionally does an important question of policy require consideration. Therefore the head of the county should be an administrator; he should be chosen with regard to technical qualifications and not on the basis of ability to get votes. In other words, he should be appointed, because this method of choice is much more likely to produce technical skill than any scheme of popular election. The appointing body should be the county board, representing the voters; and board members should understand clearly that they are no longer responsible for the details of administration. All officers and employees in the administrative service of the county should be appointed by the manager and hold office at his pleasure; thus the ballot for county officers would become a short ballot *par excellence.*

Despite the obvious merits of the manager plan for counties, it has made but slight progress, in marked contrast to the rapid spread of manager government in the municipal field. Only seven American counties [14] make use of the orthodox manager plan, though a number of others have accepted hybrid schemes that divide authority between a so-called manager and the chairman or clerk of the county board. In Los Angeles County, California, the board of supervisors appoints a chief administrative officer, who supervises the activities of nearly all county departments, but has no power to appoint or remove department heads. The slowness of counties to adopt the manager plan can be explained in part by the fact that constitutional or statutory provisions quite generally prevent such a step and that these restrictions must be cleared away before the voters can indicate whether they desire a change from the ramshackle form of county government that has so long served as a barrier to progress.

Although most qualified persons accept the point of view presented in these pages—that the manager plan is desirable for counties and should be generally adopted by them—there are a few careful students who express strong disagreement. They contend that the functions of the county are primarily matters of state concern and should be brought under direct state control, until little or nothing is left for a manager to manage. "The problems of county government in the rural areas are so elementary and the areas so poor," wrote Professor Howard M. Kline a few years ago, describing conditions in Maryland, "that a modern streamlined executive could neither be fully occupied nor easily afforded. . . . The state has already assumed primary responsibility for improved standards of administration in the basic functions of justice, health, schools, roads, welfare, and police. Here local responsibility has been narrowed to the administration of these

[14] Albemarle, Arlington and Henrico Counties, Virginia; Butte and Sacramento Counties, California; Petroleum County, Montana; and Monroe County, New York. Two other county manager charters have been invalidated by the courts. San Mateo County, California, abandoned the plan in 1938 after a brief trial.

## CHART SHOWING MODEL COUNTY GOVERNMENT

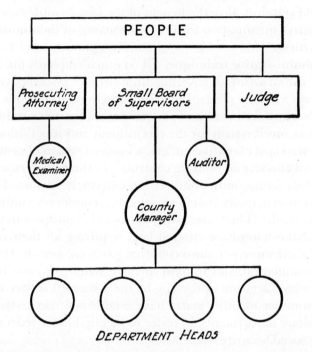

PEOPLE

Prosecuting Attorney — Small Board of Supervisors — Judge

Medical Examiner — Auditor

County Manager

DEPARTMENT HEADS

Reprinted from Richard S. Childs' *The County Manager Plan,* with the permission of the National Municipal League.

functions under state supervision with exclusive responsibility in relatively few matters." [15]

This line of reasoning is plausible, but it rests on the highly questionable assumption that expanding state control will reduce the importance of counties until they become little more than agencies for the performance of state functions. As a matter of fact, the counties in most states have by no means reduced the number of their functions. Loss of control of some activities has been matched by the assumption of new services. County planning, unknown ten years ago, has already become a vital force in a number of states. County libraries are rapidly becoming commonplace, and county recreational facilities are far from rare. Some counties maintain airports; some accept responsibility for the prevention of forest fires; some have assumed important new obligations in the fields of education, health and housing. Un-

[15] "No Job for a County Manager," in the *National Municipal Review,* May, 1939, p. 364.

less counties cease to function as separate agencies of government—and there is no indication that such a radical change is in prospect—they should certainly have the benefit of the best possible type of local administrative organization for the performance of their multifarious local activities.

**Poor administrative technique.** Too much emphasis must not be placed on the structure of government, however. Good government is more than a matter of managers or supervisors; it depends in large measure on the development of adequate administrative technique—a satisfactory merit system for the recruitment and supervision of employees, a standard executive budget, a modern system of central purchasing, and effective accounting control. In these matters, as in governmental structure, most counties are extremely backward. Thus the time-honored spoils system of selecting employees continues almost unchecked. There are, however, some bright spots in the dark picture. Nine states have enacted laws requiring all their counties, or at least their more populous counties, to choose personnel by competitive examination, and in most of these states provision has been made for administration of the law by the state civil service commission. A number of other states have established merit systems for county welfare departments, in order to be eligible for federal grants under the Social Security Act.

County budgets are now required by law in more than half of the states, but many of the statutory provisions concerning county budgetary procedure are so poorly phrased as to be practically worthless. Not more than one county in ten has established a system of central purchasing. Modern methods of keeping accounts have been adopted by many counties in recent years; this improvement has been effected largely by changes in state laws making the use of improved, standardized accounting methods mandatory. State supervision of county accounts, including the preparation of standard forms by the state auditor for county use, is rapidly increasing in popularity, and bids fair to solve the problem of slipshod county accounting.

### COUNTY CONSOLIDATION

One of the most serious obstacles to efficient county government, in many states, is the excessive number of counties. Poor counties, with small populations, totally unable to support expensive governmental organizations or to find a sufficient number of competent officials, are required by state law to have substantially the same form of government as wealthy counties with large populations. In many parts of the United States the county organization exists chiefly for the benefit of empty acres. The most obvious solution of this problem—though not the most satisfactory, according to some critics—is the consolidation of counties to form units of government sufficiently rich and sufficiently populous to support adequate governmental organizations. The pioneer in this field was Tennessee, which consolidated two counties in 1919. More recently there have been proposals for extensive consolidation in other states, but the only concrete result has been the recent union of two small counties in Georgia with Fulton County, of which Atlanta is the county seat. Much more popular is a plan of "county co-operation," whereby two or more counties join in the conduct of certain administrative services, though retaining their separate entities as governmental units. In the field of poor relief, for example, the Virginia county almshouse is rapidly disappearing; as many as eight counties, in some instances, co-operate to maintain a district poor home. Many other states have authorized similar arrangements concerning police, fire, and health protection, public utility services, construction and maintenance of public improvements, and other services.

### FUNCTIONAL REALIGNMENT

Some students of county government, dissatisfied with the slow progress of reform and the indifferent results achieved by many reform programs, urge the creation of special districts for the performance of certain functions now placed under county control. These districts would not be the same for all functions; on the contrary, each separate activity would involve the division of the state into new districts, presumably on the basis of the work to be done. Thus, within a single state, there might be fourteen judicial districts, twenty districts for school administration, and forty districts for the assessment of property. Presumably the officers of these various districts would be state-appointed and state-controlled; any other arrangement would lead to serious complications. The proponents of this plan are pleased to call it *functional realignment,* because they believe that the new governmental areas would be created solely on a functional basis. Whether the most suitable administrative areas could be determined with any degree of accuracy, and whether, once found, they would be utilized by politically minded state legislatures or constitutional conventions, are questions that lie within the realm of speculation.

## SELECTED REFERENCES

Alderfer, H. F., *Pennsylvania Local Government Survey*, 1935.

Anderson, William, *Local Government and Finance in Minnesota*, Minneapolis, 1935.

Andrews, Columbus, *Administrative County Government in South Carolina*, Chapel Hill, N.C., 1933.

Bradshaw, William L., *County Government Manual for the Missouri Constitutional Convention of 1943*, Columbia, 1943.

Bromage, Arthur W., *American County Government*, 1933.

Carleton, R. L., *Local Government and Administration in Louisiana*, University, La., 1935.

Crouch, W. W., *State Aid to Local Government in California*, Berkeley, 1939.

Euler, H. L., *County Unification in Kansas*, 1935.

Fairlie, John A., and Kneier, Charles M., *County Government and Administration*, 1930.

Georgia University Institute of Public Affairs, *Round Table on County Government*, Athens, Ga., 1934.

Jay, C. A., *County Reorganization in Texas*, Dallas, 1934.

Kilpatrick, Wylie, *County Management*, Charlottesville, Va., 1929.

Lancaster, Lane W., *Government in Rural America*, 1937.

Manny, T. B., *Rural Municipalities*, 1930.

Murphy, W. C., *County Government and Administration in Texas*, Austin, 1934.

Porter, K. H., *County and Township Government in the United States*, 1922.

Reed, Thomas H., *Twenty Years of Government in Essex County, New Jersey*, 1938.

Rosenthal, Edgar P., *The County Unit of Local Government*, Mineral Point, Wis., 1941.

Schmit, Edward Benjamin, *County Consolidation*, Lincoln, Neb., 1934.

Snider, Clyde F., *County Government in Illinois*, Springfield, 1942.

Sorrell, V. G., and Stuart, James R., *County Consolidation in New Mexico*, Albuquerque, 1934.

Wager, Paul W., *County Government and Administration in North Carolina*, Chapel Hill, 1928.

Wisconsin Historical Records Survey, *County Government in Wisconsin*, 3 vols., Madison, 1941.

Works, George A., and Lesser, Simon O., *Rural America Today*, 1942.

Wright, M. A., *Administrative County Government in South Carolina*, Chapel Hill, N.C., 1934.

*Part Two*

STATE ADMINISTRATION

# Chapter Fifteen ∽ STATE ADMINISTRATIVE ORGANIZATION

ONE of the outstanding characteristics of modern state government—and of all modern government, for that matter—is the sharp increase in the number of its functions. The rapid expansion of the field of human knowledge and the important inventions that have marked our machine age have combined to make modern civilization an exceedingly complicated affair. Automobiles and airplanes have replaced the simpler conveyances of another day. Great skyscrapers—modern towers of babel whose sheer walls extend upward from the shadows of city streets to the sunshine of city skies—have been substituted for the more modest office buildings of an earlier generation. Equally startling transformations have taken place in the fields of medicine, surgery, and public health. Business organization has developed through successive stages from the simple partnership to the corporation, the trust, the holding company—until value is pyramided upon value, and only a few know where responsibility really rests.

## MULTIPLICATION OF ADMINISTRATIVE AGENCIES

Truly, this is a new and ever-changing world. And every change—whether in modes of living or techniques of satisfying human wants—has necessitated new governmental activities. Matters formerly left to private initiative, such as the establishment and maintenance of schools, or left undone, such as the conservation of public health, have become an accepted part of the work of the state. Businesses and professions have been subjected to rigorous regulation that would not have been tolerated a century ago, but is now regarded as essential. Research laboratories dealing with a wide variety of problems have been established in the more progressive states and are now maintained with public funds.

Such development is inevitable. But efficient state administration has suffered from the unfortunate, and by no means inevitable, practice of making every new activity the excuse for a new agency to administer it—a department, board, or commission, as the case might be.

The result has been the multiplication of the agencies of state government to a point where they cannot possibly be supervised intelligently by any one person.   Prior to administrative reorganization California, Illinois, New York, and Pennsylvania had more than one hundred separate administrative agencies apiece, and Massachusetts had over two hundred; all these agencies were largely independent of one another and performed their several functions with little or no regard for the work of other branches of the state government.   Many of them were responsible to the governor, at least in part.   But such responsibility meant virtually nothing.   It was idle to expect the governor to exercise a reasonable measure of supervision over seventy-five or one hundred separate agencies; faced with such a task, the average governor promptly abandoned it, and permitted the several departments, offices, boards, and commissions to manage their own affairs according to their own ideas of proper administration, while he devoted his attention to the more promising field of legislation.   The administrative reorganizations in California, Illinois, Massachusetts, New York, and Pennsylvania have materially improved this situation in these commonwealths, and similar reorganizations in a number of other states have likewise accomplished a great deal.[1]   But most states still struggle under the handicap of disintegrated administration, with the responsibility for the proper conduct of their administrative affairs scattered among sixty, seventy, or even eighty independent agencies.

### INDIVIDUALS OR BOARDS?

Whenever a state undertakes a new function, it must decide whether the task of administering that function will be entrusted to a single individual or to a group of individuals who exercise authority jointly. The single-headed department or bureau has certain obvious advantages.   To put control in the hands of one person is usually to get action.   Moreover, responsibility is more easily fixed.   If the work of a single-headed department is improperly done, everyone knows where to place the blame.   There is no possibility of evasion.   And, conversely, the credit for good work can readily be fixed and rewarded. When a board or commission assumes control, however, everything is changed.   Responsibility is no longer centered in one person, but is diffused among five, six, or a dozen—as many persons as the commission has members.   It is impossible to determine who is to blame for maladministration.   Another good reason for preferring individuals

[1] See pp. 319–328.

to boards is that the single-headed department plan is more likely to
lead to the performance of administrative duties by technical experts.
Even though a board is composed of laymen who admittedly have no
understanding or appreciation of the problems involved and must
therefore hire a trained administrator to carry on the day-to-day routine, there is seldom a disposition to give the administrator a free hand
in the performance of the work for which he has been employed.   The
members of the board, forgetful or careless of their ignorance, are
likely to interfere with every detail.   They may, and often do, insist
upon examining the persons whom the administrator has selected as
subordinates—or, worse still, appointing their friends and followers
to important positions.   This is not just a theoretical danger; long
and bitter experience has shown that it is a common trend in the
field of American public administration.

Here, then, is the case for the single-headed department.   But there
are many arguments that can be advanced in favor of boards and commissions.  , One of these arguments weaves itself naturally about the
time-tested belief that many heads are better than one when important decisions are to be made.   "In a multitude of councilors there is
wisdom," said Solomon, and throughout the centuries this opinion has
been generally accepted.   The work of any state agency involves the
execution of policy, of course; but first the policy must be formulated.
One man cannot be trusted to reach sound conclusions; the truth must
be revealed, if at all, through the give and take of debate.   Plausible
errors will be corrected, and the combined judgment of all the board's
members will prove superior to the judgment of any one member.
Of course, this line of reasoning is frequently challenged.   It is said
in rebuttal that the legislature, rather than any board, should settle
all questions of policy.   It is urged, too, that the "give and take of debate" is largely a myth.   Board members may give and take, but they
usually give votes and take patronage.   They determine basic questions of public policy by bargaining among themselves, each for his
own gain, instead of considering the public welfare.   These charges
are true in many cases, without doubt.   Small men are often chosen to
office, and inevitably they decide big problems in a small way.   But
no amount of controversy can destroy the fundamental fact that for
certain purposes—for determining policy, for example—the views of
many are preferable to the views of one.

Another argument in favor of boards is that they make possible continuity of policy.   When an activity of state government is controlled

by one man, serious consequences may follow his death, resignation, dismissal, or promotion to another post. His successor may have neither the desire nor the knowledge to carry on the old program. Time and money expended on one set of policies may be entirely wasted when a new set of policies comes into fashion. This condition of affairs can readily be corrected, it is said, by taking control out of the hands of one man and vesting it in a board. Not every board brings with it a reasonable assurance of continuity of policy; that is obvious. But if the members of the board have overlapping terms, so that only one or two new members are chosen at any given time, while the experienced members continue in the majority; and if, in addition, the governor is denied the right to remove members and appoint new members in their place at his pleasure, then it is reasonable to suppose that the plans and practices of the board will not be subjected to sudden fluctuations following every election. This reasoning is sound as far as it goes, but many persons urge that it does not go far enough. It gives no indication of the dangers and disadvantages inherent in a board so constituted and so freed from gubernatorial control. The members of such a board are not responsible to the governor; they are not responsible to the people, except indirectly and at infrequent intervals; they are, in fact, responsible to no one but themselves. They are under no obligation to carry out the policy of the state, as determined by the state's chief executive; instead they may substitute any whims or fancies of their own. Such a scheme is a flagrant violation of the essential principle of concentrated responsibility, because it is based on diffused control. It may well be asked whether continuity of policy is not being purchased at too high a price.

One of the reasons for the establishment of boards is that they permit the representation of different interests—economic, social, political. Some of the activities of state government are of vital concern to widely diverse groups. The administration of the pension system, for example, affects the rank and file of state employees quite as directly as those in authority—even more directly, some would say, especially if contributions are compulsory; and therefore it can be argued quite logically that both groups should be given a voice in the management of the system. The easiest way to accomplish this result is to establish a pension board, with some of its members appointed by the governor or another state official and the other members selected by the employees. With regard to elections, also, a representative board may be useful. But this argument must not be taken to justify the establishment of bipartisan boards for all state activities—health, welfare, highway construction, and the like. Partisanship, which is the essence of an election (even a so-called nonpartisan election), has no place in state administration. However much the Democrats and the Republicans may disagree on matters of policy, they should present a united front with regard to the fundamental principles of public administration.

**Distinction between boards and commissions.** This discussion of boards versus single-headed departments has not, thus far, distinguished between *boards* and *commissions;* it may have created the impression that the two terms are synonymous. As a matter of fact, there is a considerable and important difference between boards and commissions. This distinction is not always recognized by legislators and public administrators; sometimes it is ignored by writers on governmental subjects; but it is quite significant, both theoretically and practically.

Loose thinking and writing in the field of government are often due to the failure of political scientists to define their terms. Properly speaking, a commission is a group of persons who have been assigned to the full-time task of administering some activity. Other duties may, perhaps, be assigned to them; but this primary job for which the commission has been created calls for virtually all their working hours and carries with it full-time compensation. The members of a commission are presumed to be expert technicians whose special training fits them to carry on the commission's work; otherwise they are unfit to serve as commissioners. A board, on the other hand, is a group of persons who serve only part-time in the performance of the specific duty for which the board has been created, and entrust the actual details of administration to a full-time technician whom they hold responsible for results. The members of the board, therefore, need not be technicians; their board duties may require but a few hours a week, or a few afternoons a month. They are paid but little, in view of their light duties; sometimes they serve without compensation.

A good example of a commission is the public service commission, whose members devote their entire time to the task of regulating public utilities—hearing complaints, taking testimony, making necessary investigations, passing upon requests for increased rates or fares. The board of education is typical of board organization; its members are laymen, serving ex officio in many instances, who act in an advisory capacity or determine broad outlines of policy, but presumably take no part in administrative routine. As previously indicated, state legislatures do not always respect this distinction in establishing the various agencies of government. Sometimes they create commissions and call them boards; sometimes they create boards and call them commissions. Occasionally they even provide for the establishment of a board of port commissioners or a board of prison commissioners—although a "board of commissioners" is a curious contradiction in terms. But in most instances they follow the line of demarcation here indicated.

**Differing functions of individuals and boards.** Although reference is made to boards and commissions versus single-headed departments, it must not be assumed that these separate types of administrative organization are mutually exclusive. It is not at all necessary, or even desirable, for a state to depend entirely on individual department heads or to put its trust completely in boards and commissions. Concerning any one function of government, a choice between an individual and a board or commission may be necessary; but when the manifold activities of state government are considered, it may seem best to entrust some of them to boards and commissions and others to departments presided over by individuals. In every instance the test lies in the nature of the agency's work. Its task may be quasi-legislative—that is, resembling the work of the legislature. In other words, it may find itself concerned chiefly with the determination of policies, in the form of rules and regulations that do not differ greatly from the statutes enacted by the legislature at every session. Therefore it should be organized for deliberation rather than for action; its work should be entrusted to several persons instead of to one. Another agency of the state government may perform quasi-judicial functions— functions that resemble those of a court. It may sit as a court, hear witnesses, take testimony, and render decisions. A workmen's compensation board or a public utility commission answers this description perfectly. True, the findings of such a board or commission are subject to review by the courts, but this fact does not alter the judicial character of its work. The decisions of courts of first instance are also subject to review. Now, an administrative agency that is performing quasi-judicial functions also lends itself readily to the commission type of organization; impartial justice can best be secured by the meeting of trained minds. But the majority of state agencies are not concerned chiefly with the performance of quasi-legislative or quasi-judicial duties. Their most important task—often their only task—is to execute the policies that they receive ready-made. Obviously they should not be hampered by the needless discussions and delays that characterize board administration. Action is their primary need, and they should be organized to produce results promptly. That is simply a way of saying that individuals, rather than boards or commissions, should be placed in control.

FAILURE OF STATES TO RECOGNIZE DIFFERENCES. Few states have made any serious attempt to apply the general principle that a board or commission should be used for deliberation and a single-headed department for action. Usually they have accepted a very different premise: "When in doubt, establish a board or commission." The result has been a veritable epidemic of multiple-headed agencies—an epidemic that has spread from coast to coast and has not yet been brought under control by the advocates of sound administrative organization. The disease has assumed a more malignant form in some states than in others, of course, but nearly every state has placed under board control some activities that could be better administered by single-headed departments. And, strangely enough, there are relatively few instances of departments with individual heads administering functions that ought properly to be assigned to boards or commissions. The states have pinned their faith to the board idea. Time after time that faith has been rudely shaken. Government has stood still while some board deliberated, or merely waited for a quorum; it has suffered from the mistakes of board members who did not understand their rôle as amateurs. But always the faith in boards has risen triumphant above the lessons of experience. For the people of the United States, despite their oft-repeated boast that they are practical men and women, find it extremely difficult to change their theories of government.

**Types of boards:** UNIPARTISAN BOARDS. There are various types of boards charged with the supervision or control of state administration. The oldest type—still widely used—is the unipartisan board, so called because all its members belong to the same political party. Some years ago, when even the clearest thinkers failed to make any sharp distinction between politics and administration, and positions in the administrative service were universally regarded as suitable rewards for faithful partisan service, the unipartisan board was accepted as a matter of course. It was a device whereby the true believers might gather and preserve the fruits of their victories. And if the fruits were mostly political plums, no one saw any reason to object.

BIPARTISAN BOARDS. The passing of years has made the unipartisan board somewhat less popular than formerly, however. Public administration has been differentiated from politics, at least in part. Public administrators have begun to acquire a professional status. And these changes have led to an appreciation of the rather obvious fact that no administrative agency can produce satisfactory results if it is dominated by a political machine. The public has begun to demand nonpartisanship in administrative matters. Frequently, however, it assumes that the way to secure a nonpartisan board is to provide for the representation of at least two political parties. *Bipartisanship* is thus confused with *nonpartisanship*. Yet it ought to be clear that the selection of representatives of two parties will not result in a board whose members represent no party. Bipartisanship does not destroy the baneful effects of politics in public administration; it merely forces the politicians to barter with one another.

NONPARTISAN BOARDS. Genuinely nonpartisan boards—boards whose members have been chosen without regard to political affiliations—are now found in a number of states. Their work is more consistently satisfactory than that accomplished under any other type of board organization. Sometimes such boards are composed, at least in part, of expert technicians who are willing to devote a small part of their time to the service of the state as a matter of public duty. Since little or nothing is paid for such service, the state obtains the advice of high-grade consultants practically without cost. This method of drawing the best talent into the service of the state is widely used in Germany and, to some extent, in England; but American public officials have as yet no real appreciation of its possibilities.

EX OFFICIO BOARDS. One of the most ineffective devices yet conceived for the performance of administrative duties is the ex officio board—that is, a board whose members serve by virtue of holding certain designated offices. The state board of pardons, for example, may be composed of the governor, the lieutenant governor, the director of welfare, and the attorney-general. Some states make widespread use of ex officio boards, apparently regarding them as a cheap means of carrying on necessary administrative activities. The governor is frequently made a member of numerous boards—probably on the assumption that the state's chief executive ought to be in direct contact with all state activities. If he takes the obligations of board membership seriously, he is likely to find a major portion of his time consumed by board meetings. His efficiency as an executive inevitably suffers. If, on the other hand, he consistently absents himself from board meetings and takes no part in the determination of board policies, he cannot fairly complain that the other board members have ignored his wishes. And every board of which he is a member is handicapped by his absence. We expect too much of the governor when we ask him to serve on boards of every description in addition to his other numerous duties; we make it literally impossible for him to do everything well. The same reasoning applies to other state officials, though less obviously. They too have been assigned numerous duties by constitution or statute, and ought not to be overburdened with ex officio board membership. There is still another objection to ex officio boards: members cannot be chosen with special reference to their fitness for the work to be done. Thus the lieutenant governor may be required to serve on the board of health, the pension board, the board of education, and a dozen others—not because he knows anything about public health or pensions or education, but because his other public duties consume only a small portion of his time. The ex officio board is at best a haphazard means of administering state affairs; at worst it results in flagrant partisan interference with public administration.

### THE ADMINISTRATIVE REORGANIZATION MOVEMENT

The need for reorganization of state administration has been emphasized repeatedly in these pages. All students of government recognize this need, and many studies and investigations have been made of the requirements of individual states. For more than a quarter century the reorganization movement has been gaining momentum. In 1909 a group of Oregon reformers, who called themselves the People's Power League and whose principal purpose was to fight the predatory activities of certain utility interests, proposed a rearrangement of state administration that would vest in the governor the power to appoint all administrative officers except the auditor. This plan was defeated by the voters of Oregon, but it is significant as a pioneer attempt to reorganize state administration. The next year Governor Hughes of New York proposed the consolidation of existing departments and the strengthening of the governor's power in the interest of greater efficiency. Soon afterward it became the fashion to create committees or boards for the purpose of studying state administrative organization and recommending needed changes. Studies have now been made and reorganization plans submitted in more than three fourths of the states. Usually the official, committee or board charged with the task of making the survey has employed a group of technicians to do the actual work, or at least to act in a consulting capacity. The Institute of Public Administration (New York), for example, has conducted a number of surveys of state administration.[2] Some reorganization plans have been proposed without adequate preliminary investigations, but fortunately they are not typical.

More than half of the proposals for state administrative reorganization have fallen on barren ground. Sometimes they have encountered the opposition of the governor, as in New Jersey, where Governor Larson in 1930 protested that the transfer of the work of the state's seventy-two boards and commissions to a smaller number of centralized departments would be a violation of the principle of "representative government." At times they have been declared unconstitutional by the courts, as in Indiana and Louisiana.[3] Occasionally they have been defeated by the voters, as in Oregon in 1930, when the issue of "democracy versus autocracy" was successfully raised. Much more commonly, however, they have failed to secure the necessary support in the legislature, as in Arizona, Arkansas, Missouri, New Mexico, Texas, and a considerable number of other states. Even if the legislature is not openly hostile to all proposals for reorganization, it frequently modifies carefully drafted plans in the interest of political expediency, so that the final result leaves much to be desired.

**Standards of administrative reorganization.** The suggestions for state administrative reform that have been made during the last twenty-five years, and the discussions that they have aroused, have led to the development of certain standards of reorganization. These standards have been shaped into a definite reorganization program, which receives the approval of most students of government. The program is concisely stated by Mr. A. E. Buck: [4]

"*1. Functional departmentalization of administrative agencies.* All offices, boards, commissions, and agencies of the state government

[2] The three other important professional survey organizations in the United States are Griffenhagen and Associates (Chicago), the Institute for Government Research of the Brookings Institution (Washington, D.C.), and the Public Administration Service (Chicago).

[3] Tucker, Secretary of State, *et al. v.* State *et al.,* 35 N.E. (2nd) 270 (1941); Graham *et al. v.* Jones *et al.,* 3 So. (2nd) 761 (1941).

[4] *Administrative Consolidation in State Governments,* 5th ed., pp. 5–6.

should be consolidated and integrated in a few orderly departments, each of which comprehends a major function of the government, such as finance, agriculture, public welfare, or public works. The number and character of the departments should be determined by the conditions within the state government and the scope of its existing activities. However, the total number of departments in any state government ought not to exceed twelve or fifteen. Closely related work within each department should be grouped under appropriate bureaus and divisions.

"2. *Fixed and definite lines of responsibility for all departmental work.* Each department should be headed by a single officer appointed and removable by the governor. This arrangement places beyond question the responsibility for the administrative work of the government and makes the governor in fact, as well as in theory, the responsible chief executive of the state. The department heads should constitute a cabinet to advise with the governor in matters of administration and to assist him in budgeting. Responsibility for the work of each bureau or division should be placed on a single officer directly accountable to the head of the department. The bureau heads should, as a general rule, be appointed by the department heads under which they work.

"3. *Proper co-ordination of the terms of office of administrative officials.* The term of office of the governor should be at least four years, and the terms of the department heads, if they are to be definitely fixed, should be carefully adjusted with reference to that of the governor. The department heads should not have longer terms than that of the governor. It seems preferable to have them serve at the governor's pleasure. . . .

"4. *Boards undesirable as purely administrative agencies.* Boards in this capacity are generally found inefficient owing to division of powers and absence of initiative and responsibility. Ex officio boards are almost never effective. Whenever there are quasi-legislative, quasi-judicial, advisory, or inspectional functions within a department, a board may with advantage be attached to the department to perform any one of these functions."

More recently Mr. Buck has added the following standards:

"5. *Co-ordination of the staff services of administration.* The responsibility of the governor ordinarily relates more to efficiency and economy in the operation of the state administration as a whole than to the performance of the highly technical services by the various operating units. In other words, the staff services concern the governor a great deal more than do the operating or line services. These staff services have to do mainly with budgeting, accounting and reporting, purchasing, and personnel. There are several advantages to having them properly co-ordinated and, if possible, brought together in a single staff department.

"*6. Provision for an independent audit.* A complete separation of the functions of financial control and accounting from those of independent auditing (postauditing) and review is necessary in order to obtain the most satisfactory results. The control and accounting functions are executive in character and therefore belong to an officer —a controller—directly responsible to the governor. Such functions are part and parcel of the system of budgeting and financial management by which the governor is enabled to control the state's business. To remove them from the governor by placing them under an independent officer is to hamstring his authority over the state administration. On the other hand, the functions of postaudit and review belong to the legislature. They are implied in the powers of the legislature to appropriate money to the executive and the administrative departments to carry on the activities of the state government. They are the means of enforcing financial accountability upon the governor and his department heads—a highly important, but almost neglected, duty of the legislature under the centralized form of state government. Power and authority commensurate with full responsibility for all administrative operations may be accorded the governor as long as the legislature brings him to complete accountability for his acts." [5]

To this list of standards should probably be added abolition of the requirement of senate approval for appointments made by the governor. This requirement is a part of the system of checks and balances in which the American people have placed—or misplaced—so much confidence. It is based on the fear that the governor may make wrong appointments, and the hope that the members of the senate will keep him in the straight and narrow path, and also the path of wisdom. Unfortunately, its principal result has been to force the governor along the path of least resistance. Faced with the necessity of winning support for his legislative program, many a governor has purchased that support by appointing to office the friends of influential senators. Thus members of the senate have come to regard the selection of ad-

---

[5] Buck, A. E., *The Reorganization of State Governments in the United States*, pp. 21, 23-24.

ministrative officers as one of their inalienable rights; they unite in open hostility to the occasional governor who dares to flaunt their wishes by appointing men to office solely on the basis of merit. This vicious arrangement should be destroyed. The governor should be given the right to appoint his subordinates, free from senate interference—not because his appointments will necessarily be good, but because under existing conditions they are much more likely to be bad. Unfortunately, no state has yet abolished the requirement of senate confirmation.

**Growth of administrative reorganization.** Although a number of studies of state government and proposals for administrative reorganization along the lines of consolidation and fixed responsibility were made during the years immediately following the unsuccessful Oregon campaign of 1909, nothing of importance was accomplished until 1917. In that year Illinois led the way by adopting a comprehensive plan of administrative consolidation. Under the leadership of Governor Lowden the civil administrative code was drafted and adopted. More than one hundred statutory offices, departments, boards, commissions, and agencies were abolished, and their functions consolidated under nine departments—finance, agriculture, labor, mines and minerals, public works and buildings, public welfare, public health, trade and commerce, registration, and education. Each department was placed in charge of a director appointed by the governor, with senate approval, for a four-year term. A number of boards and commissions were created within the departments for the performance of quasi-judicial and quasi-legislative duties, but each board and commission was made a component part of the department to which it was assigned. Under the provisions of the administrative code the lines of responsibility were made to extend from the division and bureau chiefs through the heads of departments directly to the governor.

The Illinois reorganization of 1917 was epoch-making. It established a uniform and simplified administrative system. It paved the way for the adoption of consolidation schemes by other states. Yet it fell far short of the complete reorganization program desired by careful students of public administration. It failed to measure up to the highest standards of administrative reform. Though it greatly increased the authority and prestige of the governor, it did not give him complete control over state administration. It left untouched the constitutional provisions for popular election of the secretary of state, the attorney-general, the treasurer, and the superintendent of public instruction. It did not attempt to interfere with the elective state board of equalization, though this board was subsequently abolished and its functions transferred to a small tax commission under the department of finance. It did not alter the statutory requirement that the trustees of the University of Illinois should be chosen by the voters of the state. Since the creation of nine consolidated departments in 1917, two additional departments have been established. And yet, despite these handicaps, the reorganization plan has fully justified its adoption. In the words of an impartial investigator: "It continues to stand out in sharp contrast to the old order of things. That it has given the people of Illinois better service than they formerly got, and at less cost, there can be no doubt." [6]

In 1919 Idaho followed the example of Illinois by abolishing more than fifty offices, boards, and commissions, and creating in their place nine consolidated departments. New Jersey had already completed a partial reorganization. During 1919 Nebraska and Massachusetts also adopted consolidation schemes, the 1919 act of the Massachusetts general court following the voters' approval of an amendment to the state constitution that authorized administrative reorganization. Washington, Ohio, Michigan, and California followed in 1921, although the California reorganization was not made even reasonably complete until 1927. Then came Maryland in 1922, Pennsylvania, Tennessee, and Ve mont in 1923, Minnesota and South Dakota in 1925, New York and Virginia in 1927, Georgia, Maine, and North Carolina in 1931, Colorado and Indiana in 1933, Kentucky in 1934, Rhode Island in 1935, Connecticut and Wisconsin in 1937, Louisiana in 1940, and Missouri in 1945. In 1939 Idaho and Minnesota enacted laws designed to make their reorganization schemes more effective, and two years later Colorado and North Carolina followed suit. The Indiana and Louisiana statutes were invalidated by the courts in 1941, but shortly afterward the legislature of Louisiana passed another reorganization law designed to overcome the supreme court's objections.

THE REASONS FOR INADEQUATE CHANGES. Thus twenty-seven states have accepted and retained the principle of administrative consolidation, though some of them have been content to accept the principle without making any serious attempt to put it into practice. A number of the reorganization schemes finally adopted and now in effect are so complex—so far removed from the ideal of departmental consolidation and concentrated responsibility—that an understanding of earlier

[6] Buck, A. E., *Administrative Consolidation in State Governments*, 5th ed., p. 11.

conditions is necessary in order to realize that progress has actually been made.

*Compromise.* Not one of the states has adopted an entirely adequate scheme of administrative reorganization. Failure to go the entire distance along the path of reform is due in part to the need for compromise. Every reorganization movement has a multitude of enemies. Those who seem likely to lose prestige, positions, or patronage by the change combine with those who honestly believe that the proposed plan will not serve the public interest; the ultra-conservatives —the defenders of the sacred *status quo*—also join the ranks of the opposition. These various groups, diverse in viewpoint but united by a common purpose, must be dealt with in some way. Often it becomes necessary to purchase their partial support with partial abandonment of a carefully devised program. Thus the plan of reorganization as finally adopted is usually a curious compromise—an amalgam of conflicting ideas. Small wonder that it so frequently proves a disappointment to everyone!

*Statutory instead of constitutional reform.* Another reason for the inadequacy of consolidation schemes is the general preference for statutory reform, instead of reform through constitutional amendment. Statutory reform, it must be admitted, has marked advantages. It is more easily accomplished, since it requires only favorable action by the legislature and the approval of the governor. Unlike an amendment to the constitution, it cannot be blocked by a persistent legislative minority. It requires no formal expression of approval by the voters and thus eliminates the need for an expensive campaign of civic education. It can be put into effect more quickly—a matter of considerable importance to the governor who is trying to make an impressive showing before the expiration of his short term. Quite natural, therefore, is the tendency to rely on statutory changes. Only four states—Massachusetts, Missouri, New York, and Virginia—have changed their constitutions in order to facilitate administrative consolidation; the others have left the fundamental law unaltered. This unwillingness to change the constitution may be good politics. Statutory consolidation may be an effective means of securing half a loaf of reform from an otherwise bare cupboard. But the fact remains that thorough administrative reorganization is virtually impossible without constitutional amendment. State constitutions, almost without exception, scatter the administrative functions of government among a number of independently elected offices, and nothing short of the elim-

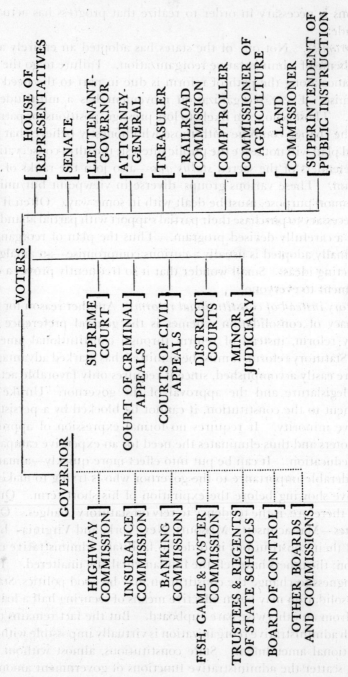

GOVERNMENT UNDER A TYPICAL STATE CONSTITUTION*

VOTERS

HOUSE OF REPRESENTATIVES
SENATE
LIEUTENANT-GOVERNOR
ATTORNEY-GENERAL
TREASURER
RAILROAD COMMISSION
COMPTROLLER
COMMISSIONER OF AGRICULTURE
LAND COMMISSIONER
SUPERINTENDENT OF PUBLIC INSTRUCTION

SUPREME COURT
COURT OF CRIMINAL APPEALS
COURTS OF CIVIL APPEALS
DISTRICT COURTS
MINOR JUDICIARY

GOVERNOR

HIGHWAY COMMISSION
INSURANCE COMMISSION
BANKING COMMISSION
FISH, GAME & OYSTER COMMISSION
TRUSTEES & REGENTS OF STATE SCHOOLS
BOARD OF CONTROL
OTHER BOARDS AND COMMISSIONS

LEGEND
———— Elected
·············· Appointed

* Chart prepared for the Committee by Robert S. Bourn, University of Texas. Although based upon the Texas Constitution, the set-up is typical of those states whose constitutions provide for a considerable number of popularly elected commissions and heads of departments.

# GOVERNMENT UNDER THE MODEL STATE CONSTITUTION*

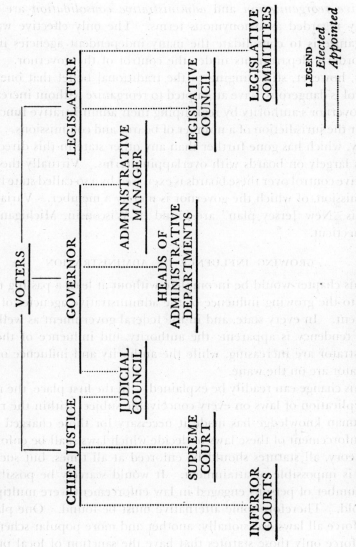

LEGEND
Elected
Appointed

VOTERS
GOVERNOR
LEGISLATURE
CHIEF JUSTICE
SUPREME COURT
INFERIOR COURTS
JUDICIAL COUNCIL
ADMINISTRATIVE MANAGER
HEADS OF ADMINISTRATIVE DEPARTMENTS
LEGISLATIVE COUNCIL
LEGISLATIVE COMMITTEES

• Chart prepared for the Committee by Robert S. Bourn, University of Texas.

ination of those offices or their subordination to gubernatorial authority can produce a completely consolidated administrative system.

*Fear of one-man control.* In the field of state government, *administrative reorganization* and *administrative consolidation* are commonly regarded as synonymous terms. The only effective way to reorganize is to consolidate the many independent agencies into a few orderly departments under the control of the governor. Four states, however, still clinging to the traditional belief that one-man control is dangerous, have attempted to reorganize without increasing the governor's authority by regrouping their administrative functions under the jurisdiction of a number of boards and commissions. New Jersey, which has gone further than any other state in this direction, relies largely on boards with overlapping terms. Virtually the only effective control over these boards is exercised by a so-called state house commission, of which the governor is merely a member. Variations of this "New Jersey plan" are found in Wisconsin, Michigan and Connecticut.

### GROWING INFLUENCE OF ADMINISTRATION

This chapter would be incomplete without at least a passing reference to the growing influence of the administrative agencies of government. In every state, and in the federal government as well, the same tendency is apparent: the authority and influence of the administrator are increasing, while the authority and influence of the legislator are on the wane.

This change can readily be explained. In the first place, the rapid multiplication of laws on every conceivable subject within the realm of human knowledge has made it necessary for those charged with the enforcement of these laws to decide which laws shall be enforced. In theory, all statutes should be enforced at all times, but such an ideal is impossible of attainment. It would scarcely be possible if the number of persons engaged in law enforcement were multiplied fiftyfold. Therefore some alternative must be found. One plan is to enforce all laws occasionally; another and more popular scheme is to enforce only those statutes that have the sanction of local public opinion. Laws that are rigidly enforced in some jurisdictions are deliberately ignored by the law-enforcement authorities of other communities; in each case popular sentiment, as interpreted by administrative officers, is the deciding factor. The legislators write the law, but the administrators interpret and enforce it; and every good lawyer knows that interpretation and enforcement are infinitely more important than the mere words of which statutes are made.

Another important explanation for the growth of administrative supremacy has been the passage of considerable skeleton or outline legislation, to which reference has already been made.[7] This system of legislation has developed because the subjects of legislative enactment are so numerous that even the most progressive members of legislative assemblies cannot possibly acquire the knowledge necessary for detailed legislation. To meet this inadequacy, the legislature enacts much legislation which indicates merely broad outlines of policy and leaves the details to be filled in by administrative decree. As a result the regulations made in pursuance of the legislature's avowed policy are frequently more important than the policy itself.

As a final explanation, it must not be forgotten that the administrative officers of the state are chiefly responsible for the day-to-day conduct of state business. The legislature meets infrequently—perhaps sixty or seventy days every second year. And much of the time of those sixty or seventy days is spent in organizing for business, taking brief recesses, and jockeying for political advantage without giving thought to the enactment of a sound legislative program. But the administrative agencies of government are at work every week of the year; they do not adjourn *sine die*. And their constant availability is an important source of their power. Long after the legislators have completed their work and gone home the administrators are still on the job, interpreting the law and enforcing it in the way that seems to them best.

### SELECTED REFERENCES

Benson, G. C. S., and Litchfield, Edward H., *State Administrative Board in Michigan*, Ann Arbor, 1938.

Brookings Institution, Institute for Government Research, *Report on a Survey of the Organization and Administration of State and County Government in Mississippi*, Jackson, 1932.

Buck, Arthur Eugene, *Reorganization of State Governments in the United States*, 1936.

Bureau of Government of the University of Michigan, *Administrative Organization of State Government in Michigan*, Bulletin No. 5, Ann Arbor, 1936.

Bureau of Government Research of the University of Louisiana, *The Reorganization and Consolidation of State Administration in Louisiana*, Baton Rouge, 1938.

[7] See pp. 211–213.

Carleton, R. L., and Others, *Reorganization and Consolidation of State Administration in Louisiana*, Baton Rouge, 1937.

Coleman, James Karl, *State Administration in South Carolina*, 1935.

Graham, George A., and Reining, Henry, eds., *Regulatory Administration*, 1943.

Institute of Public Administration, *Report on a Survey of the Organization of the State Government of New Jersey*, 1930.

———, *Survey of the Organization and Administration of the State Government of Maine*, 1931.

Kansas Legislative Council Research Department, *Legislative Functions of Administrative Agencies*, Topeka, 1938.

Leiserson, Avery, *Administrative Regulation*, 1942.

Martin, Roscoe C., *The Growth of State Administration in Alabama*, University, Ala., 1942.

Nebraska Legislative Reference Bureau, *Organization of the State Government of Nebraska*, Lincoln, 1938.

Pennsylvania General Assembly Joint State Government Commission, *Report on the Organization and Administration of Pennsylvania's State Government*, Harrisburg, 1941.

Porter, Kirk H., *State Administration*, Chap. I, 1938.

Short, Lloyd M., and Tiller, Carl W., *The Minnesota Commission of Administration and Finance*, Minneapolis, 1942.

Taylor, Clyde W., *Public Administration in Arizona*, 1942.

White, Leonard O., *Introduction to the Study of Public Administration*, rev. ed., 1939.

# Chapter Sixteen ❧ PERSONNEL

THE number of full-time state employees, according to a recent estimate carefully prepared by the Division of State and Local Government of the Bureau of the Census, is almost four hundred thousand—an increase of fifty-two per cent in twenty years; and the combined annual payrolls of the states amount to more than six hundred millions of dollars.[1] The states, therefore, are employers of labor on a very large scale, and the efficiency of their labor forces determines in large measure the efficiency of their administrative systems. Unfortunately the methods used by many states for the recruitment, supervision, promotion, and dismissal of their employees do not differ radically from the methods of a century ago, when positions in the public service were quite frankly distributed among the faithful after each election as a reward for services to the victorious political party.

## GRADUAL ABOLITION OF SPOILS SYSTEM

Until the latter part of the nineteenth century the spoilsmen completely dominated every phase of governmental activity. Few persons dared to make the radical suggestion that the public's business should be conducted for the benefit of the public, instead of serving as a means of strengthening party organizations. But the last fifty years have witnessed a remarkable change in public sentiment. The spoils system is now quite generally regarded as an evil to be uprooted and cast aside. Civil service reform is a part of practically every general program for the improvement of state government. Yet most state employees are still selected with but scant regard for their special fitness. Administration is definitely subordinated to politics. Some technical positions are given to technically trained experts, because government has become so highly specialized that the amateurs cannot control it without the aid of the specialists. There must be physicians to direct public health activities, educators to supervise the school system, engineers to plan and execute construction programs. But in most states the professional administrators take orders from the

[1] The Census Bureau figures are conveniently summarized in the *Book of the States, 1943–1944*, p. 222.

professional politicians, even in such matters as the selection of their subordinates.

**Beginnings of national merit system.** The first victory of the friends of the merit system was won in 1883, when Congress passed an act providing for the selection of some federal employees by means of competitive examinations. This law was very inadequate; it applied to but a small percentage of the total number of persons in the federal service. Of necessity it was a compromise between those who desired a complete recognition of the merit principle and those who wished to continue unchecked the operation of the spoils system. But it was a beginning, and its influence was destined to be far-reaching.

**State civil service laws.** A few months after the passage of the federal act the State of New York established a civil service commission, with authority to prepare and administer tests for the selection of persons in the state service. Massachusetts followed in 1884. After that, for more than twenty years, these two states were the sole exemplars of the merit principle in state government. Early in the present century, however, a new era of civil service reform began. In 1905 Wisconsin and Illinois set up civil service commissions, and provided for the selection of state employees on a merit basis. Colorado and New Jersey did likewise two years later. Subsequently other states fell into line—Connecticut, California, and Ohio in 1913, Kansas in 1915, and Maryland in 1920. After that there were no further converts for nearly two decades, though California and Wisconsin materially strengthened their civil service laws in 1929. But in 1937 interest in the merit system suddenly revived. Four states—Arkansas, Maine, Michigan, and Tennessee—enacted statutes placing their administrative services on a merit basis; and Connecticut, which had repealed its earlier law in 1921, again adopted the merit principle. Between 1939 and 1942 six states—Alabama, Indiana, Louisiana, Minnesota, Rhode Island, and Virginia—joined the ranks. Kansas, which had returned to the spoils system, was reconverted to the merit principle in 1941. Meanwhile, however, Arkansas repealed its civil service law. Thus twenty states now specifically provide for the recruitment of all, or substantially all, their employees on a formal merit basis. Moreover, the other twenty-eight states have enacted civil service laws applying to workers in certain departments.[2]

---

[2] In 1939 Congress adopted an amendment to the Social Security Act, requiring all state departments co-operating under the act to recruit their employees on a merit basis. For this reason nearly all the state welfare agencies now function under civil service rules.

Many states, however, accept the merit principle in name only. Interference with the intent of the civil service law takes a wide variety of forms, ranging all the way from crude tampering with examination scores to "refined" devices, such as the inclusion in examinations of questions so highly specialized as to baffle those who have not been told in advance what to expect. Temporary appointments without examination, which are regularly permitted, are used to draw political favorites into the service of the state, and the "temporary" appointees soon become permanent fixtures, notwithstanding express provisions of the law to the contrary. On the other hand, a number of states that have no civil service laws have succeeded fairly well in establishing the custom of making appointments on a merit basis.

PREFERENCE LAWS FOR VETERANS. In recent years the task of selecting and retaining efficient employees has been made more difficult by the widespread enactment of laws giving preference to war veterans. Some states had legislation of this type at the beginning of the present century, but the trend did not become widespread until after the First World War. The Second World War complicated the problem still further by increasing greatly the number of persons entitled to receive preference. Under the laws of the several states veterans are favored in various ways. Thus in Massachusetts they need only receive a passing grade in examinations to have their names placed above all other candidates on the eligible list, and in a number of other states their earned ratings are increased five or ten per cent—a bonus that gives them a marked advantage over competitors.

*Disregard of merit.* Those persons who advocate such preference legislation obviously ignore the merit principle in government. They regard public employment as a reward for services already performed; and, to that extent, they reason in exactly the same manner as the professional politicians. Their purpose, of course, is to reward service to the state, whereas the politicians' purpose is to reward service to the party or faction; but in either case the result is the same. Men are placed on the public payroll for reasons that bear little or no relation to their training, skill, or experience, and the efficiency of public administration is thereby reduced. In defense of preference legislation it is often said that war veterans should be rewarded for their sacrifices during a national emergency. Friends of the merit system do not deny that some reward may be entirely proper, but they insist that it should not take the form of employment in the public service.

For they know from bitter experience that appointments made on any other basis than proved merit are apt to be disastrous.

## STATE CIVIL SERVICE COMMISSIONS

**Supervision of local governments.** Six states—California, Colorado, Louisiana, Michigan, New York, and Ohio—have written the merit principle into their constitutions; the civil service systems of the other fourteen states are based on statute. There is no general agreement as to the desirability of extending state jurisdiction in personnel matters over the local units of government—the cities, counties, towns, and villages. A few states restrict the activities of the civil service commission to the personnel of the state service, but most of them permit a certain amount of supervision or control over their civil subdivisions, though the extent of this supervision or control is not the same in any two states.

In Massachusetts the state commission still handles the recruitment of both municipal and state employees, though this arrangement has caused considerable local discontent.[3] The New Jersey commission also conducts examinations for the municipal service, but only in those cities that have voted to accept its jurisdiction. Maryland has a similar plan. The cities of New York and Ohio have their local civil service commissions; in each of these states, however, the state commission has a measure of authority over local activities. The New York commission may, by a unanimous vote and with the governor's approval, remove a local civil service commissioner for incompetence, neglect of duties, or other sufficient cause. It may also amend or rescind any rule made by a local commission. In Ohio the state civil service commission may direct the mayor of any city to remove one or more members of the municipal civil service commission, subject to an appeal to the courts.

**Administration of laws.** The civil service law of a state is usually administered by a three-member commission appointed by the governor. In Ohio, however, a commission of two members has been established; New Jersey and Massachusetts have five-member commissions; and three states—Maryland, Tennessee, and Connecticut— have adopted the interesting experiment of vesting control in the hands of one person—a state personnel director.[4] The Connecticut per-

---

[3] See Geo. C. S. Benson's excellent monograph, *The Administration of the Civil Service in Massachusetts.*

[4] California adopted the one-man plan in 1925, but re-established a commission of three members in 1927.

sonnel director, who serves during good behavior, is chosen by the governor from a list of eight eligible persons prepared by the Advisory Personnel Committee—a group of state department heads whose duty is to "advise and assist the personnel director in the formulation of rules and regulations . . . and in the establishment and maintenance of procedure and technique relating to personnel administration." This committee is not a civil service commission in the usual sense.

**Control over commission activities.**  Power to appoint the civil service commission—or, in its absence, the director of personnel—is vested in the governor, usually with senate consent.  Yet the governor's control over civil service activities is very slight.  The civil service commission is still regarded as a part of our system of checks and balances—an agency to prevent the governor and other administrative officers from doing something wrong; and the laws that determine its composition and powers reflect this point of view.  In nearly every state the civil service commissioners are given longer terms than the governor—usually six years.  In addition, provision is generally made for overlapping terms.  The governor's power to remove civil service commissioners is seriously restricted; in California, for example, the removal power is given to the legislature, and a two-thirds vote of each house is required.

Although most of the states cling to the idea of a plural executive for personnel matters, they are beginning to recognize the rather obvious fact that most of the work of the personnel agency is detailed administration, rather than rule-making.  Such work can be done much more effectively by one person than by a group.  For this reason California has created the office of director of personnel, and retains its civil service commission only as a rule-making and disciplinary body.  A somewhat similar arrangement is found in Wisconsin.

**Selection of employees.**  By far the most important task of the civil service commissions is the recruitment of persons for the state service.  Examinations must be prepared for different types of positions and administered to applicants as the need arises.  An alert civil service commission usually keeps on hand lists of eligibles who have passed previous examinations but failed of appointment, so that it can submit suitable names to the appointing authority promptly whenever a vacancy occurs.  It also takes care to obtain due publicity for its examinations by such means as bulletin board notices, news stories to newspapers and trade journals, occasional advertisements, and circular letters to carefully selected groups.  Otherwise it might fail to reach the very persons who were best fitted for the jobs to be filled.

EXTENSION AND IMPROVEMENT OF EXAMINATIONS. Formerly large numbers of state employees were outside the classified service—that is, they were appointed without examinations of any sort. Some of them, such as private secretaries, were placed in the unclassified group on the ground that their work was confidential. Every important state officer, it was said, should be permitted to have one or more employees chosen without restrictions—men or women in whom he had complete confidence. Other employees, especially those holding high-salaried positions in the state service, escaped the necessity of passing examinations because of the widespread belief that no examination questions could be devised to measure with any degree of accuracy their fitness for important posts. Still others were placed in the unclassified service for lack of suitable examinations or because tests were deemed unnecessary; skilled and unskilled laborers were in this group. The passing years have witnessed a great improvement, however, in the technique of the merit system. Trade tests now determine with accuracy the fitness of skilled laborers such as plumbers, bricklayers, and electricians. Even more important, ways have been found to measure the suitability of applicants for high-salaried positions. Of course, the examinations given to these candidates differ radically from the tests used in selecting clerks or typists. Much greater emphasis is placed on training and experience, and personal fitness as determined by interviews may be a factor of considerable importance. An examination for an important state position is likely to be of the *non-assembled* variety—in other words, an examination in which the applicants are not required to assemble at one time and place. It may even be a *non-competitive* examination, designed merely to ascertain whether the person selected for the post by higher officials has the necessary qualifications.

POLITICAL OPPOSITION. Although the development of civil service technique has made possible the extension of the merit principle to nearly everyone in the administrative service of the state, this extension has been delayed by the professional politicians. Loath to relinquish the patronage that has helped to maintain their power and prestige, they have fought the merit system at every turn—secretly, in most cases, but desperately. Despite their efforts thousands of state employees have been transferred from the unclassified to the classified service; but thousands of others who should also be chosen on a merit basis are still selected without examinations of any sort.

CERTIFICATION FOR APPOINTMENT. While the civil service commission administers the examinations to applicants for positions in the state service, it does not make appointments. Instead, in most states that have adopted the merit system, it certifies to the appointing authority the names of the three persons who stood highest in the examination, and from these three the appointing authority makes his selection. Thus it frequently happens that the candidate with the highest score is brushed aside, and one of the others chosen in his place. This arrangement is justified on the ground that it provides the appointing authority with necessary discretion. If the highest person on the list possesses undesirable traits not revealed by the examination—anything from a bad temper to a habit of wearing soiled linen—he may be kept out of the state service despite his arithmetical average. The professional proponents of the merit system have frequently pointed out, however, that the certification of three names opens the door to partisan interference. They contend, with reason, that if the highest candidate may be refused appointment because of his bad temper, then he may also be ignored because he does not possess sufficient political influence. For this reason they constantly urge that the law be changed in every state to provide for the appointment of the highest person on the eligible list. Their proposal is based on distrust of state officials, instead of the newer foundation of confidence, but in all fairness it must be admitted that the high officials of most states have done very little to justify confidence in their impartial administration of the civil service laws. A few states require the appointment of the candidate receiving the highest grade. One commonwealth—Maryland—at the other extreme, permits the certification of the five highest names to the appointing authority.

CLASSIFICATION OF POSITIONS. The civil service system cannot produce satisfactory results unless a classification has been made of the positions in the state service. Lacking such a classification, it is inevitable that persons performing the same work in different departments will have different titles and widely varying salaries. The first step in the preparation of such a classification is the collection of all necessary information concerning the duties of each position. Then the positions with similar duties must be grouped together, and each group given an appropriate title, an accurate description, and a suitable compensation schedule. Only in this way is it possible to prevent gross salary discriminations, with resultant dissatisfaction throughout the entire administrative service.

**Supervision of employees.**   Most civil service commissions devote their time and attention chiefly to the task of *selecting* employees for the public service.   It is natural that they should do so, for the civil service movement had its inception in a desire to "keep the rascals out of office."   Honest and efficient men must be chosen for positions in the state service, it was said; once chosen, there was nothing more to be done.   In recent years, however, the leaders of the civil service movement have stressed the important fact that selection of employees is only one of the duties of the civil service commission, and should not receive disproportionate emphasis.   Quite as important as selection is adequate supervision.   Efficiency ratings should be kept; a sound system of promotions should be established; salaries, hours of employment, and working conditions should be standardized; training facilities for new employees should be provided; research programs should be planned and executed.

Very few state civil service commissions are in a position to perform all these functions.   They are handicapped by inadequate appropriations, by constitutional and legal provisions, by the baneful influence of partisanship, by the ignorance of commissioners, and by the inefficiency of subordinates.   Sometimes they are even handicapped by a hostile public opinion, as in their attempts to maintain efficiency ratings.   Nor is it surprising that the use of such ratings should arouse widespread cynicism.   "American experts have pushed their experiments toward an 'objective' and automatic system boldly and hopefully, but not always with adequate insight into the hazards of their venture.   Production records are reasonably objective criteria of efficiency, but all judgment ratings are subjective and are not cured of the inevitable variability of human opinion by being spread out on a graphic rating scale or in an elaborate personality inventory.   Inspired by an extraordinary faith in the validity of various schemes, they have been put to work in some jurisdictions with a thoroughness which cast caution to the winds.   Men and women have been singled out to lose their jobs, to sacrifice a part of their income, and to abandon prospect of promotion because a mathematical conversion of a series of check marks by supervisors totaled less than an arbitrary sum.   The effort to control the judgment of supervisors to this degree and to govern the fate of individuals in this way is not sound personnel policy." [5]   But this does not mean that efficiency records are value-

[5] White, Leonard D., *Introduction to the Study of Public Administration*, rev. ed., p. 384.   Reprinted by permission of the Macmillan Company.

less. They should provide a basis for mature judgment—not a substitute for it. Fortunately, a few state civil service commissions have learned this important lesson.

**Training of employees.** The need for some sort of training to keep public employees abreast of the latest developments in their respective fields has long been recognized by progressive students of government. New tools and new techniques are constantly being developed in almost every phase of public life, and public servants cannot be expected to do their work properly unless they are familiar with these changes. Government must assume the responsibility for keeping them up to date by providing the necessary courses of instruction and making them widely available. This "in-service" training —so called because it is designed for those who are already in the public service—has long been used by some states for some jobs, but its widespread development is quite recent. In 1936 Congress specified that part of the federal funds paid to the states for vocational education might be used for the in-service training of public employees, and this offer greatly stimulated the interest of state officials, even though most of the money had to come from state revenues. State after state fell into line. Today [6] thirty-seven states have vocational programs covering at least some of their workers—the forest fire fighters, the finance officers, the purchasing agents, the prison guards, or other groups. But only a small percentage of the employees needing such instruction has yet been reached. The in-service training programs of the state governments must be greatly expanded.[7]

**Dismissal of employees.** With regard to the dismissal of state workers the civil service commission acts in a quasi-judicial capacity. State laws guarantee to every employee accused of incompetence or something worse a full opportunity to answer the charges against him. The hearing often assumes the appearance of a formal trial, with the members of the civil service commission sitting as a court. The department head presents his view of the controversy, and the accused subordinate makes reply. Sometimes the subordinate is represented by counsel, since the law usually gives him this privilege. With all the evidence before it, the civil service commission then passes judgment.

This elaborate procedure is generally considered necessary to pro-

[6] 1945.
[7] See the excellent article by Wm. A. Ross, "Training for Public Servants," in the March, 1944 issue of the *National Municipal Review*, pp. 123–127.

tect employees from unwarranted dismissal—perhaps for political or personal reasons.   It compels department heads to retain their subordinates unless there are sound reasons for removal.   Some persons believe, however, that so much "red tape" protects state employees at the expense of administrative efficiency.   They contend that it weakens discipline.   And in many cases their belief is confirmed by experience.   For the department head who has had two or three unpleasant sessions with the civil service commission, trying to prove charges that by their very nature are largely matters of opinion and therefore difficult to prove—carelessness or indifference, for example —is not anxious to stir up further trouble.   After hearing department secrets dragged into the open and alleged department scandals given unwelcome publicity, he is likely to decide that a repetition of such happenings must not be permitted to occur.   So he accepts the course of least resistance and retains all his subordinates indefinitely, regardless of the quality of their work.   Under such circumstances it may well be asked whether the protection of employees by means of trials before the civil service commission is worth what it costs the taxpayers of the state. Massachusetts, especially solicitous for the welfare of accused employees, permits them to appeal to the courts.

## PENSION SYSTEMS

**Benefits.**   One of the most effective ways to raise the standard of efficiency in the administrative service of a state is to establish a sound pension system.   This is contrary to the popular belief that pensions are a form of charity, but it is a truth that has long been recognized by careful students of public administration.   A pension system is desirable, in part, because it facilitates the retirement of employees whose efficiency has been materially reduced by disease, accident, or old age.   There is a natural tendency among administrative officials, in the absence of some sort of pension scheme, to keep such employees on the payroll of the state indefinitely.   The only alternative would be to dismiss them, and peremptory dismissal is scarcely a fitting way to reward years of faithful work.   So the payrolls of the state gradually become clogged with the sick and the decrepit—men and women who are permitted to remain in the service long after their period of maximum usefulness has passed—solely because the state owes them a debt of gratitude and is not permitted by law to pay its debt in any other way.   This condition of affairs can only be remedied by the establishment of a pension system. Then the employees who have outlived their ability to serve may be retired with the assurance that they will be properly cared for, and their places may be taken by younger, more active persons. Such an arrangement is desirable from the standpoint of the superannuated workers, of course; but it is much more important as a means of improving the personnel of the administrative service of the state.

The improvement in personnel that follows the adoption of a pension system is due not only to the clearing away of human debris, but also to the recruitment of better equipped men and women. Pensions for state employees increase the attractiveness of the state service. They provide a protection against the danger of an impoverished old age. Thus they make it possible to draw into the employ of the state persons of considerable ability who would not otherwise accept the low salaries that notoriously accompany public service.

**Limited application of pension laws.** Despite the obvious advantages of pensions, only one-half of the states have adopted comprehensive pension systems applying to all state employees. Most of the others, however, maintain pension funds for certain favored groups— teachers or state police or health department employees, for example. There is no logic in such an arrangement; it is simply an indication of the political influence of the groups that are benefited. In all probability it does more harm than good, for it breeds a rankling feeling of injustice among the less fortunate employees.

**Eligibility requirements.** Retirement should be based on age rather than years of service, even if employees are required to serve ten or some other number of years before becoming eligible for retirement benefits. The earlier pension systems regularly provided for retirement at the end of a specified period of years, with the result that some persons were able to leave the public service with comfortable pensions when still in their prime, while others who had entered the service comparatively late in life necessarily remained in the public employ long after their days of usefulness had passed because they had no other means of support. Commenting on the evils of time-limit pension systems, Professor White once cited the case of a man who entered the employ of the City of Chicago at the age of twenty-two, and retired twenty years later with a pension for the rest of his life. Despite the obvious disadvantages of using years of service as the basis for retirement, several states still follow this plan. Thus

Connecticut pensions employees who have been in the state service for thirty years,[8] and both Massachusetts and Minnesota, in addition to their specific age limits, provide pensions for those who have been in state employ for thirty-five years, regardless of age.

**Methods of financing:** THE CASH DISBURSEMENT PLAN. Some of the state pension systems are financially unsound because the reserves established by law bear but slight relation to the obligations that are certain to arise. A great deal of improvement has been made in some states since the days of the first pension plans, which entirely ignored the question of reserves or else merely provided that the revenues from certain licenses and permits should be paid into a pension fund. But even today several states with pensions systems applying to all state employees make no attempt to establish adequate, scientifically determined reserves. Instead they treat all payments into the pension fund as current revenue, and all payments of pension benefits as current expenses. Those who favor this so-called "cash disbursement" plan contend that it is simple, because it requires no elaborate computation of reserves, and safe, because it leaves the money with the taxpayers until needed, instead of piling up large sums in the state treasury and thus tempting loose-moraled politicians. But such arguments cannot conceal the obvious fact that the cash disbursement plan is unbusiness-like and unscientific. Though it may work fairly well during the early years of a pension system, when relatively few employees are entitled to benefits, it usually encounters serious difficulties as the number of pensioners increases and the burden on the taxpayers becomes noticeably heavier. When the situation is further complicated by periods of economic depression, there is a strong likelihood that pensions will be reduced, or even that the pension system will be abandoned. A number of public retirement systems based on the cash disbursement plan have become insolvent in various parts of the United States during the last three decades, and their reorganization has usually worked serious hardship on pensioned employees.

THE ACTUARIAL PLAN. The only proper way to finance a pension system is to put it on an actuarial basis. The life insurance companies have statistical information concerning the expectation of life at various ages, and this information can be used by the state to determine exactly what its obligations will be. It can calculate accurately how long its employees will live after retirement, and how many of them will be incapacitated before they reach the normal retirement age.

[8] Or for twenty years, if the age of seventy has been reached.

These matters can be taken completely out of the realm of guesswork. With all the necessary information at hand the state can then establish a pension fund and provide for regular payments sufficient with compound interest to cover the benefits anticipated for each employee. Suitable provision is thus made at the outset for the heavier obligations sure to come as the pension system and the pensioners both grow older. Acceptance of the actuarial principle by California, Massachusetts, New York, Pennsylvania and others has placed the retirement systems of these states on a firm foundation.

COMPULSORY EMPLOYEE CONTRIBUTIONS. Most persons who have studied the operation of public pension systems agree that pension funds should be supported by the contributions of the employees as well as by legislative appropriations. The employees should be required by law to contribute, and the amount of their payments should be deducted from their salary checks. Compulsory contributions are sometimes opposed on the ground that they infringe the right of every worker to be as improvident as his fancy may dictate, but they are desirable for a number of reasons. First, they reduce the likelihood that the employees will make extravagant demands. Every additional benefit means additional cost, and when the workers are required to bear a portion of that cost their viewpoint is considerably modified. Then, too, compulsory contributions lead naturally to employee representation on the pension board, though they do not always produce this result.[9] It might also be added that simple justice would suggest the partial support of the pension fund by those who are the direct beneficiaries. Connecticut, Maine, and Maryland are now the only states with complete retirement systems that do not require employee contributions. Minnesota relies solely on such contributions, instead of making public appropriations to the retirement fund.

### SELECTED REFERENCES

Benson, G. C. S., *Administration of Civil Service in Massachusetts,* Cambridge, 1935.

Civil Service Assembly of the United States and Canada, *Employee Relations in the Public Service,* 1942.

————, *Employee Training in the Public Service,* 1941.

————, *Policies and Practices in Public Personnel Administration,* 1942.

————, *Position-Classification in the Public Service,* 1942.

————, *Public Relations of Public Personnel Agencies,* 1941.

[9] New York, which requires all employees to contribute, gives them no voice in the management of the pension system.

Civil Service Assembly of the United States and Canada, *Readings in Public Personnel Administration,* 1943.

———, *Recruiting Applicants for the Public Service,* 1942.

Commission of Inquiry on Public Service Personnel, *Better Government Personnel,* 1935.

Cooper, Alfred M., *Supervision of Governmental Employees,* 1943.

Egger, Rowland A., *Retirement of Public Employees in Virginia,* 1934.

Frederic, Katherine A., *Trained Personnel for Public Service,* Washington, D.C., 1935.

Hormell, O. C., *Personnel Problems in Maine: The Merit System,* Brunswick, 1936.

Joint Commission on the Merit System, *The Merit System in Illinois with Special Reference to Chicago and Cook County,* Springfield, 1935.

Marx, Fritz M., and Others, *Public Management in the New Democracy,* 1940.

Meriam, Lewis, *Public Personnel Problems from the Standpoint of the Operating Officer,* Washington, D.C., 1938.

———, *Public Service and Special Training,* 1936.

Mosher, William E., and Kingsley, J. Donald, *Public Personnel Administration,* rev. ed., 1941.

Pois, Joseph, Martin, Edward, and Moore, Lyman S., *The Merit System in Illinois,* 1935.

United States Bureau of the Census, *Financing State and City Pensions,* Washington, D.C., 1941.

———, *Retirement Systems for State and Local Government Employees,* Washington, D.C., 1943.

White, Leonard O., *Introduction to the Study of Public Administration,* rev. ed., 1939.

———, *Government Career Service,* 1935.

———, and Smith, T. V., *Politics and Public Service,* 1939.

Wilmerding, Lucius, *Government by Merit,* 1935.

# Chapter Seventeen   ~~~   STATE EXPENDITURES

FOR many years state expenditures have been mounting at a rapid rate.   In 1915 the cost of state government for all forty-eight states was slightly less than half a billion dollars; by 1930 this cost had mounted to more than two and one-half billions—an increase of over four hundred per cent.   Then came industrial depression, with a corresponding reduction in the taxpaying capacity of the nation.   But state expenditures did not decrease; on the contrary they continued to mount by leaps and bounds.   By 1937 they had climbed to three and one-half billions—a six hundred per cent increase over 1915. During the subsequent war era they still rose rapidly, and by 1943, the most recent year for which complete figures are available, they had reached the staggering total of almost six billion dollars.   State expenditures were sixty-eight per cent higher in 1943, therefore, than in 1937, and nearly eleven hundred per cent higher than in 1915.

## ANNUAL EXPENDITURES SINCE 1915

**Causes of upward trend.**   A number of factors have combined to produce these tremendous increases in the annual totals.   First, the level of prices has moved generally upward, despite a drop during the depression.   Second, the population of the nation is now about thirty per cent larger than in 1915.   Third, and most important by a wide margin, the states have assumed a great variety of new functions, and at the same time they have adopted higher standards of performance for functions already undertaken.   Highways—a notable example— have represented huge additional outlays.   The cost of public welfare has increased ninefold within the past decade.   Public health work has expanded rapidly.   The importance of public conservation and development of natural resources has become generally recognized. In the field of education new and expensive experiments have been tried, and higher standards of teacher training have been established. In fact, virtually every phase of governmental activity has felt the effect of the demand for improved services involving, in most instances, the expenditure of considerably larger sums.   Students of govern-

345

ment may reasonably assume, therefore, that the tax rate will continue to rise—at least for another decade. There is no sign of a counter-trend.

**Items.** The three most important items of state expenditure are education, welfare, and highways. Together they account for more than fifty per cent of the total. Debt redemption and interest on outstanding indebtedness represent another fourteen per cent. Smaller sums are spent for hospitals, protection of person and property, development and conservation of natural resources, and general government. The following table shows the per capita cost of operating and maintaining the general departments of the several states in 1943 (the most recent year for which the United States Census Bureau has yet released comparable figures), and also provides a comparison with 1932: [1]

PER CAPITA EXPENDITURES FOR OPERATION OF STATE GOVERNMENTS, 1943 AND 1932

| | | 1943 | 1932 |
|---|---|---|---|
| General government ................................ | | $1.28 | $0.98 |
| Public safety ..................................... | | 1.01 | .70 |
| Conservation of health: ........................... | | .46 | .21 |
|     Apportionment to minor civil subdivisions (1943) | $0.04 | | |
|     All other (1943) .............................. | .42 | | |
| Development and conservation of natural resources: | | .94 | .58 |
|     Apportionment to minor civil subdivisions (1943) | .04 | | |
|     All other (1943) .............................. | .90 | | |
| Highways: ........................................ | | 4.18 | 2.46 |
|     Apportionment to minor civil subdivisions (1943) | 2.41 | | |
|     All other (1943) .............................. | 1.77 | | |
| Public welfare: ................................... | | 6.86 | .88 |
|     Apportionment to minor civil subdivisions (1943) | 2.80 | | |
|     All other (1943) .............................. | 4.06 | | |
| Hospitals, and institutions for the handicapped .... | | 1.82 | 1.26 |
| Correction ....................................... | | .56 | .51 |
| Education: ....................................... | | 8.25 | 4.78 |
|     Schools: (1943) ............................... | 8.23 | | |
|         Apportionment to minor civil subdivisions (1943) | 6.18 | | |
|         All other (1943) ......................... | 2.05 | | |
|     Libraries (1943) .............................. | .02 | | |
| Recreation ....................................... | | .06 | .06 |
| Miscellaneous .................................... | | .38 | .09 |
|     Total ....................................... | | $25.80 | 12.51 |

[1] Summarized from *State Finances, 1943*, a publication of the United States Bureau of the Census.

## PAYMENTS TO LOCAL GOVERNMENTS

Every state government pays large sums to its local units—chiefly the counties—in the form of subsidies or grants-in-aid. The largest payments, as indicated on the above table, are made for education, welfare, and highways, but health and other functions are also subsidized in many of the states. Usually this money is apportioned on the basis of need. The various states have their own peculiar methods of measuring need, however, and most of the methods now used are very crude. Some subsidies are conditioned upon the adoption of minimum standards established by state officials, and thus provide a means of improving governmental services in the less progressive communities. The grants for education,[2] health,[3] and highways,[4] which have special problems connected with them, will be considered in some detail in later chapters.

Other money is paid from the state treasury to the counties and cities —not as a subsidy, but as the local share of taxes that have been imposed, assessed, and collected—or at least directly controlled—by state officials. This money may be apportioned on the basis of need or on the basis of the tax yield in each local district; it may be given with or without conditions; but in any event it differs from a subsidy in that it varies with the amount of tax collections. It is not a definite sum fixed by legislative action. An illustration may serve to make clear this distinction. When the legislature appropriates one million dollars to be apportioned among the counties of the state for the purpose of developing community health centers, it grants a subsidy; but when it specifies that the counties shall receive twenty per cent of income tax revenues, even if the money must be used for health centers. it merely shares a tax with its local subdivisions. Many state-administered taxes are thus distributed among the counties and cities of the several states. Every one of the forty-eight commonwealths now distributes some state-administered taxes among its counties and cities. Gasoline tax receipts are commonly paid in part to the local communities; so, too, are motor vehicle license revenues and the receipts from various corporation taxes. Other taxes, involving smaller sums, are apportioned in many states. The practice of sharing state tax money with counties and cities is becoming increasingly common; it

2 See pp. 464–466.
3 See p. 482.
4 See pp. 499 and 503–504.

has, in fact, been growing constantly since the beginning of the present century.

## STATE BUDGET SYSTEMS

The vast sums collected and spent by state governments make necessary some kind of fiscal plan—in other words, a budget system that will correlate expenditures and revenues. Thirty-five years ago not a single state had a budget system. Comprehensive planning of expenditures and revenues was unknown. There was no way of telling in advance whether a fiscal year would end with a surplus or a deficit. Former Governor Young of California has drawn a typical picture of conditions in pre-budget days: "When I first entered the legislature in 1909, there was little short of chaos as far as any orderly provisions for state expenditures were concerned. There had been no audit of the state finances for over twenty years. The finance committees of the two houses were scenes of a blind scramble on the part of the various institutions and departments of the state in an endeavor to secure as large a portion as possible of whatever money might happen to be in the treasury. Heads of institutions encamped night after night in the committee rooms, each alert for his own interest regardless of the interests of other institutions. Logrolling and trading of votes on appropriation bills was the common practice among members of the legislature." [5]

**Differences among systems.** Fortunately, the last few years have witnessed a material change in fiscal procedure. Every state now has a budget system—or something that goes by that name. Some of these systems are models of careful planning; they present an accurate and complete statement of co-ordinated expenditures and revenues. Others are far from satisfactory—the omission of certain proposed expenditures from the budget document is authorized; the legislature is permitted to make as many additional appropriations as it desires; or other ways are found to defeat the real purpose of budget legislation by allowing expenditures in excess of revenue. But even the least effective budget systems are several steps in advance of the generally accepted practices of 1910. The importance of budgeting is universally recognized.

THREE DESIRABLE FEATURES OF A BUDGET. The budget of a state is its fiscal plan—the means whereby it proposes to balance its expenditures and revenues over a given period—usually a biennium. A new

[5] Quoted in A. E. Buck's *Public Budgeting*, p. 12.

budget is adopted for each fiscal year by the federal government, and cities commonly make use of annual budgets also. But most state governments are obliged to budget their activities for two years at a time, since the legislature, whose affirmative action is necessary to make the budget plan effective, meets in regular session but once in two years. According to foremost authorities, a budget should contain three main parts—a budget message, a detailed fiscal plan, and drafts of the statutes required to make the plan effective. The budget message comes first; it is a summary of the detailed estimates comprising the bulk of the budget. Its purpose is to present clearly and concisely, with the aid of a few simple schedules and charts, a bird's-eye view of the state's fiscal policy. Then follows the detailed plan, together with all the information on which it is based. This portion of the budget should contain all the data necessary for a complete understanding of the fiscal condition of the state. It is not enough, however, merely to present a program for the consideration of the legislature and the public. That program can only be put into effect by the passage of appropriation and revenue acts; therefore carefully prepared drafts of these acts should be included. Unfortunately, not many state budgets contain all these features. Three fourths of them omit the budget message altogether, substituting for it a letter of transmittal from the budget-making authority that neither summarizes nor interprets the detailed estimates, and therefore permits them to remain a mystifying mass of apparently unrelated figures. Most state budgets also omit the drafts of necessary legislation. These bills, if prepared by the budget-making authority, are separately submitted and are referred to appropriate committees for separate consideration. A few states—especially New York, New Jersey, and Washington—are notable exceptions to this general rule.

**A gradual development.** It is difficult to fix an exact date as marking the beginning of budgetary legislation in the states. Some of the first statutes that might conceivably be called "budget laws" were so crudely drawn and so deficient in the fundamentals of sound budget procedure that they scarcely deserve the name. Public budgeting has been a gradual growth. But if a date is desired, 1911 is probably as good as any. In that year California and Wisconsin established fiscal agencies—the Board of Control in California and the Board of Public Affairs in Wisconsin—that were charged with the duty of making certain estimates of expenditure in advance of the legislative session. The following year Massachusetts passed a law containing some provisions that were preliminary to budget procedure. In 1913 budget legislation was enacted in three states—Arkansas, Ohio, and Oregon. Seven other states fell into line in 1915. By the end of 1919 forty-four states had set up budget systems of some sort. Then came Indiana and Florida in 1921, and Pennsylvania in 1923. Rhode Island, displaying once more the conservatism that had made it the last to ratify the federal Constitution, was the last to adopt a budget plan. In 1926 it made the list of states complete. Most of the state budget systems have been established by legislative action. But in seven states, beginning with Maryland in 1916, and subsequently including West Virginia, Massachusetts, Nebraska, Missouri, California, and New York, the budget systems are based on constitutional amendments. Most of these amendments are brief and are supplemented by detailed legislation.

## PREPARATION OF THE BUDGET

Students of government are generally agreed that the governor should be vested with complete responsibility for the preparation of the budget. The people look to him for leadership, and in the shaping of the state's fiscal policy leadership is especially important. The need for gubernatorial control was not clearly recognized at first, however; seven of the first twelve budget laws placed control in the legislature or, more commonly, in a board. But shortly afterward came a pronounced swing toward budget systems of the executive type. Most of the states that enacted budget legislation after 1915 accepted the theory of executive responsibility.

Today [6] thirty-eight states—more than three fourths of the whole number—vest budget responsibility in the governor. In nine states [7] the budget is prepared by a board, whose membership usually includes the governor and the more important state administrative officers, especially the treasurer and the auditor. Members of the legislature are also included in a few instances. [8] The usual reason for placing a board in charge of the budget is that the nineteenth century fear of gubernatorial authority has not yet disappeared. The old theory of checks and balances makes its appearance in a new form. If the governor has complete control over the budget he may use his power to suggest expenditures that are inimical to the common welfare, and

[6] 1945.

[7] Connecticut, Delaware, Florida, Indiana, Mississippi, Montana, North Dakota, South Carolina, Texas.

[8] This arrangement is found in Indiana, North Dakota, and South Carolina.

a weak-willed legislature may enact his proposals into law. The only safe plan, therefore, according to those timid souls who accept this line of thought, is to associate other officers with the governor at the time the state's fiscal plan is formed, so that unwise suggestions will be detected and cast aside. Of course, board administration of the budget system has not produced the results that its adherents claimed for it. Its chief accomplishment has been to force the adoption of an ambiguous and ofttimes confusing fiscal policy instead of a carefully integrated plan. Quite naturally, therefore, the board budget plan is losing in popularity. Not a single state has adopted it since 1921, whereas eleven states have abandoned the board plan since 1921 in favor of the executive budget system. Only one commonwealth —Arkansas—has a so-called "legislative" budget; here the budget is prepared by the finance committees of the two houses of the legislature.

**Assistance of staff agencies.** Although the governor is responsible for the preparation of the budget in most states, it must not be assumed that he actually administers all the details of budgetary procedure. His time and attention are inevitably divided among a great variety of activities, and the only part he can reasonably be expected to play in budget-making is to make important decisions with regard to the general scheme of the fiscal plan. Moreover, he seldom possesses the technical training necessary to enable him to prepare the budget document properly. He must have expert assistance, and this assistance should take the form of a permanent staff agency. In one third of the states, however, no such agencies exist; the governors of these commonwealths are obliged to rely on such temporary help as they can obtain at budget-making time from the several administrative departments of the state government or from private sources. The permanent staff agencies that have been created assume a variety of forms. In some states they are known as departments of finance or departments of administration and finance, and exercise broad powers of supervision over the accounts and expenditures of the other administrative departments. Budget-making, therefore, is but one of their functions. Much more common are budget bureaus or offices charged solely with the preparation of the budget, or perhaps made responsible also for the administration of the budget plan. The head of such a bureau or office is generally appointed by the governor and reports directly to him. No state that still clings to the board type of budget authority has set up a formal budget agency.

**Collection of estimates.**   The first step in the preparation of the budget is the collection of the estimates of expenditure for the ensuing year or biennium.   These estimates, based on actual expenditures of previous years, are made on standard forms by the heads of the several departments and agencies of the state government.   From the heads of departments they go to the budget officer, whose task is to harmonize them with the estimate of revenue furnished by the auditor, the treasurer, or some other officer or group of officers.   Almost invariably the department estimates of expenditure exceed the amount of anticipated income—sometimes by a wide margin.

**Harmonizing estimates of expenditures and receipts.**   After estimates of expenditures are collected, unless the governor is willing to propose new means of raising revenue, some way must be found to cut down the department requests.   The simplest way to bring proposed expenditures within the limit of probable revenue is to slice a uniform percentage from all department estimates, regardless of conditions or needs.   This method produces grossly unfair treatment of some departments, of course; it illustrates the old maxim that equality may be the worst form of discrimination.   But it can be done quickly and requires no highly specialized knowledge of budgetary procedure or intimate acquaintance with the details of state administration. Quite naturally, therefore, it appeals to the busy administrator who has been designated as ex officio budget officer in addition to filling the post of auditor, examiner of accounts, or purchasing officer.   If no adequate staff of assistants is provided by the state, the temptation to rely on a scheme of uniform cuts—tempered only by political expediency—is all the stronger.   No state that has established a permanent budget staff agency, with proper personnel and equipment, makes use of such a slipshod method.

The only way a budget officer can hope to produce satisfactory results is to subject each department's estimates of expenditure to an item-by-item scrutiny.   Many department requests will doubtless seem excessive; their propriety must be determined by interviews with department heads.   After all, the heads of the several departments of the state government are more familiar than the budget officer with their respective projects and needs, and they can best indicate where necessary reductions will cause the least harm.   They cannot measure the needs of their own departments in relation to the needs of other agencies of the state government; that is a task primarily for the budget officer and ultimately for the legislature and the governor.   But they possess information that the budget officer must have, and any budget scheme that neglects to secure their co-operation is foredoomed to failure. There is no simple formula for reducing department estimates and harmonizing their total with the total of expected revenues. The task is extremely difficult and quite delicate; its proper performance requires extensive experience, broad knowledge, and infinite tact.

## LEGISLATIVE BUDGETARY APPROPRIATIONS AND REVENUE BILLS

When the budget has been nicely balanced and arranged in a form satisfactory to the governor or other budget-making authority, it is submitted to the legislature, where it is referred to the appropriate committees of each house. Two or more committees in the senate usually consider separate portions of the budget plan, and the work of these senate committees is duplicated by two or more committees of the house of representatives. Attempts to co-ordinate the work of these several committees have generally proved ineffective, though a few states have obtained satisfactory results by establishing joint committees or by providing for joint sessions of corresponding committees.[9] Committee metings on the budget are generally held behind closed doors, but in a few states open sessions are required. Some legislative committees still regard the budget as a heaven-sent device to enable them to see the state at state expense. They contend that the propriety of institutional requests for state funds can only be determined by visiting these institutions, which are widely scattered. Thus budget time becomes vacation time for the fortunate committee members. Fortunately, however, such practices are rapidly passing into disfavor.

**Disregard of executive recommendations.** When the committees have finished their work, they report their recommendations to their respective houses. Early consideration is assured. In the overwhelming majority of states the legislature is free to amend the budget plan according to its desires. It may strike out, increase, or reduce items of expenditure recommended by the governor, or it may add new items. But there are some exceptions. In Maryland, New York,[10] Nevada,[11] and West Virginia the appropriation recommendations of the budget may only be reduced or struck out; they may not

[9] For a discussion of joint committee systems, see pp. 181–182.

[10] In New York items may be added under some circumstances, however.

[11] The Nevada restriction is imposed by statute, and therefore may be amended or abolished by the legislature at any time. In practice, however, the legislature has been careful to respect its self-imposed rule.

be increased, nor may new items be added. Separate appropriations not contemplated in the budget plan may be made in these four states, but such appropriations are hedged about with numerous restrictions. In the absence of such restrictive provisions—or, in some states, despite their existence—large numbers of appropriation bills are usually enacted at every legislative session. Twenty-five, fifty, or even one hundred special appropriations approved by a single legislature at its regular biennial session are not at all uncommon. The inevitable result is to destroy in large measure the effectiveness of the budget system. Of what use is a fiscal plan that carefully provides for balanced expenditures and revenues, if one branch of the state government persistently ignores its provisions and makes appropriations greatly in excess of anticipated income? Under such circumstances a sound fiscal system in state government is closely akin to faith as defined by Saint Paul—"the substance of things hoped for, the evidence of things not seen."

**The budget bills.** The budget, as such, has no binding effect. It is merely a series of proposals that require legislative action to give them the force of law. So when the legislature has concluded its budget debates and has agreed upon all changes that are deemed necessary it makes the budget effective by passing the necessary appropriation and revenue measures.

LUMP SUM AND SEGREGATED APPROPRIATIONS. There is considerable difference of opinion among state officials as to whether the appropriation bill should merely provide for lump sum payments to the several departments and independent spending agencies of the state government or should specify instead in exact and very minute detail just how every appropriation is to be spent. The "lump sum" plan assumes that the heads of departments will allocate their appropriations to the bureaus and divisions under their control according to some carefully devised work program. The so-called "segregated" plan, on the other hand, is dedicated to the belief that department heads cannot be trusted, and that the only way to prevent them from squandering public money is to state in the appropriation act exactly how every dollar is to be spent.

Some years ago nearly all state appropriations were of the lump sum variety. Department heads were given a large measure of discretion, and many of them abused it. In conformity with the spirit of the times they made contracts with professional politicians for work that was not needed and used unexpended balances to hire their partisan followers just before election day. The most obvious way to prevent abuses of this sort was to limit the discretionary power of all spending officers. So state after state abandoned the lump sum plan of making appropriations, and proceeded to enact appropriation laws that set forth minutely the purposes for which state funds were to be used. These segregated appropriation acts put a stop to the worst abuses of administrative discretion. On the other hand, they introduced a new and undesirable element of rigidity into the state administrative system. They made it impossible for unused surpluses in one bureau to be transferred to other bureaus. They prevented department heads who were honest and efficient from using their money to the best advantage. They fixed the exact mold of state administration for at least one year, and usually two, without providing an opportunity to make changes in accord with changing conditions and changing needs.

ALLOTMENT METHOD OF APPROPRIATIONS. Careful students of government were not slow to recognize these serious defects of the segregated appropriation plan. They soon came to the conclusion that the proper way to prevent abuses of the lump sum method was not to abolish the method but to provide effective supervision and control of all state administrative activities by the governor. Therefore they urged the adoption of a scheme that has now become generally known as the allotment method. This method is merely the lump sum system plus direct control by the chief executive. The fiscal year is usually divided into four quarters, and at the beginning of the year each department head is required to submit to the governor or to the budget agency a work program showing just what is to be done during each quarter and the probable cost of each operation. This work program, when approved, becomes the basis of allotments to the several departments. Appropriations are made by the legislature on a lump sum basis, usually for two years, but the heads of departments receive their funds in quarterly allotments according to their scheduled needs. Each new quarter provides an opportunity to revise the work programs of the several departments, to examine the condition of department finances and to make certain that deficits will not occur. A few states make allotments monthly instead of quarterly. The allotment method is vastly superior to the segregated appropriation plan, because it permits the exercise of necessary administrative discretion; it is preferable to the original lump sum method because it places squarely on the governor the responsibility for preventing the abuses that are likely to accompany unsupervised lump sum appropriations. Only about a dozen states, however, led by Illinois in 1917, use the allotment plan. Most states still cling to the system of segregated appropriations that has long hampered the development of efficient administration.

TIME OF PASSAGE. The appropriation and revenue bills necessary to make the budget effective are usually passed by the state legislature prior to the beginning of the fiscal year or biennium to which they apply. Occasionally, however, the failure of the majority to agree upon a budget program or the obstructive tactics of an obstinate minority may prevent the enactment of necessary legislation. In some states the budget bills are chronically late because the legislatures do not meet until the fiscal period has begun. The situations thus created prove serious at times. Failure to vote the regular appropriations may render the administrative departments virtually impotent. Some states solve the problem very simply by refusing to make payments of any sort—even for salaries—during the period between the beginning of the fiscal year and the passage of the appropriation acts. But there are other ways of overcoming the difficulty that are more satisfactory. The administrative departments may be authorized, as in Massachusetts, to continue spending money on the basis of their old appropriations until such time as the legislature may act; or they may be permitted, as in Rhode Island, to spend temporarily at the rate provided in the budget in case legislative action is delayed.

## CENTRAL PURCHASING

Hand in hand with the development of budgetary reform has gone the movement for centralized purchasing. At the beginning of the present century it was the almost universal practice for every agency of a state government to buy its own supplies. Virtually no attempt was made to exercise central supervision of any sort over the method of making purchases or the prices paid. The results may be imagined. Goods of standard quality were obtained by different departments at prices that varied as much as three or four hundred per cent. Favoritism was rife, and matériel for the state service was commonly bought from those who possessed the strongest political influence. Even the few state officials who refused to respect the open alliance of business and politics and insisted upon trying to obtain maximum value with the public's money seldom knew how to achieve their desire. Frequently they purchased at needlessly high prices through sheer ignorance. Moreover, departments competed against one another, and the advantages of large-scale purchasing were lost.

In 1897 Iowa established a board of control with power to supervise all purchases for the state's penal and charitable institutions, and two years later Texas adopted a somewhat similar plan. But no other state recognized the principle of central purchasing until 1910, when Oklahoma established a state board of affairs and authorized it to buy the supplies of most of the state departments, boards, and agencies. This was the first instance of a fairly complete central purchasing system in state government. Soon afterward, however, the movement gained considerable popularity. Vermont fell into line in 1912, New Hampshire in 1913, and Alabama, California, and West Virginia in 1915. Forty-two states now make use of central purchasing systems to obtain all or a considerable part of their materials, supplies, and equipment.[12]

**Exemptions.** Some kinds of supplies are commonly exempted from the jurisdiction of the state purchasing officer. Perishable goods are placed in this group as a rule, and also certain technical apparatus and equipment. To such exceptions there can be no legitimate objection. All too frequently, however, the principle of exemption is carried still further to include *all* the purchases of those state agencies whose political influence is sufficient to keep them clear of the general purchasing scheme. Educational institutions are frequently permitted to do their own buying; so, too, are highway departments. In a few states the exempted agencies are so numerous that the value of the central purchasing system is seriously impaired.

**Standardization.** One of the most perplexing problems of central purchasing arises in connection with the standardization of supplies and equipment. Every department, board, and commission demands its own particular grade of paper, its own favorite brand of automobile tire, its own accustomed quality of soap. Reasons for insisting upon one grade or brand or quality are always forthcoming, but the real reason in many cases is simply the unwillingness of department heads to break away from old habits. Under such circumstances the purchasing officer is unable to secure the lower prices that accompany large-scale purchasing. Usually he is without authority to override the judgment of department heads as to the needs of their respective departments; and if they will not agree upon a small number of brands

---

[12] The exceptions are Delaware, Florida, Mississippi, Nevada, New Mexico, and South Carolina.

and grades, he cannot compel them to do so. But there are a few exceptions. In Massachusetts, for example, the purchasing agency formulates and adopts standard specifications that become binding upon all departments when approved by the governor and council. Minnesota has adopted a somewhat similar plan. New York has a bureau of standards, whose tentative specifications are submitted to all using agencies for their approval. Nearly all the states that have adopted central purchasing systems have given some attention to the matter of standardization. Many of them have created standardization committees, composed of the heads of the administrative departments; usually these committees are merely advisory bodies.

**Organization of agency.** There is no general agreement among the states as to the proper organization of the purchasing agency. Seven states place control in a separate department, whose head is selected by the governor; eighteen others assign the function of purchasing to some department that has been given other duties also—usually the finance department; the remaining states that have adopted central purchasing systems rely on boards—appointive, ex officio, or mixed. It need scarcely be added that the board type of administration is not best suited to this kind of work.

**Advantages.** The advantages of central purchasing have been summarized by a careful student of the subject as follows: [13]

1. Reduction in overhead cost through reduction in personnel.
2. Lower unit costs and better delivery service.
3. Reduction in the volume of "paper work."
4. Standardization and the adoption of standard specifications.
5. Centralized supervision over
    (a) Inspection of deliveries;
    (b) Storage and distribution of stock; and
    (c) Interdepartmental transfers and sales of surplus stock.
6. Closer accounting control over expenditures.
7. Saving of discounts through prompt payment of invoices.
8. Employment of a full-time purchasing staff
    (a) Improves buying technique; and
    (b) Tends to eliminate graft and favoritism.
9. Simplification of the vendor's problem through
    (a) Solicitation of business from one purchasing office;
    (b) Reduction in the number of orders and deliveries; and
    (c) Reduction in account-keeping with the government.

[13] Forbes, Russell, *Governmental Purchasing*, p. 10. Dr. Forbes' book is now somewhat out-of-date as to facts, but its principles remain unchanged. This quotation is reprinted by permission of Harper and Brothers.

Of course, not all these advantages accrue to every state that has adopted a central purchasing system. The state systems are all defective in one or more respects; they do not provide for sufficient standardization, or they fail to insure prompt payments, or they apply only to certain departments. In a number of states graft and favoritism have not been eliminated. Even at its worst, however, central purchasing is an improvement over the old methods of buying supplies. At its best it is a highly important phase of efficient state administration.

## SELECTED REFERENCES

Buck, A. E., *Public Budgeting*, 1929.

———, *The Budget in Governments of Today*, 1934.

Buehler, Alfred G., *Public Finance*, rev. ed., 1940.

Cline, D. C., *Executive Control over State Expenditures in New Jersey*, Princeton, 1934.

Forbes, Russell, *Government Purchasing*, 1929.

Groves, H. M., *Financing Government*, 1939.

Hansen, Alvin H., and Perloff, Harvey S., *State and Local Finance in the National Economy*, 1944.

Hutchinson, Ruth G., *State Administered Locally-Shared Taxes*, 1931.

Kilpatrick, W., *State Supervision of Local Budgeting*, 1940.

———, *State Supervision of Local Finance*, 1941.

Porter, Kirk H., *State Administration*, Chap. VI, 1938.

Pfiffner, John M., *Public Administration*, Chaps. XIV, XV, XVI, 1935.

Reed, Thomas H., *Federal-State-Local Fiscal Relations*, 1942.

Schultz, William J., *American Public Finance*, 3rd ed., 1942.

Snavely, Tipton R., Hyde, Duncan C., and Biscoe, Alvin B., *State Grants-in-Aid in Virginia*, 1933.

Sundelson, J. Wilner, *Budgetary Methods in National and State Governments*, Albany, N.Y., 1938.

Tharp, C. R., *State Aid in Michigan*, Ann Arbor, 1942.

Van de Woestyne, Royal Stewart, *State Control of Local Finance in Massachusetts*, Cambridge, 1935.

Williams, John H., *The Flexible Budget: How to Use It*, 1934.

Williams, Mrs. Juanita K., *Grants-in-Aid Under the Public Works Administration*, 1939.

# Chapter Eighteen ◆◆◆◆◆ STATE REVENUES

STATE revenues, like state expenditures, have risen rapidly. They amounted to four dollars and sixty-six cents per capita in 1915; by 1932 they exceeded seventeen dollars; and by 1943—the most recent year for which complete figures are available—they exceeded forty-seven dollars per capita. Gasoline taxes and motor vehicle license fees together represented nineteen per cent of the 1943 total; unemployment compensation taxes represented eighteen per cent; and taxes on sales and incomes each accounted for another ten per cent. The following table shows the various sources of state revenue in 1943, and also in 1932: [1]

### PER CAPITA STATE REVENUES, 1943 AND 1932

|  | 1943 | 1932 |
|---|---|---|
| **Taxes:** | | |
| General property | $1.23 | $2.58 |
| Selective property | .71 | — |
| Income: | | |
|     Corporation | 2.55 | .38 |
|     Individual | 2.20 | — |
| Inheritance | .81 | 1.15 |
| Poll | .04 | .04 |
| Severance | .56 | — |
| Sales: | | |
|     Motor fuel | 5.84 | 3.35 |
|     General sales and use | 5.04 | — |
|     All other | 5.29 | — |
| Business license and privilege | 1.98 | — |
| Non-business license and privilege: | | |
|     Motor vehicles | 2.97 | 2.14 |
|     All other | .08 | — |
| Unemployment compensation | 8.80 | — |
| All other | .14 | 3.40 |
| **Non-taxes:** | | |
| Grants-in-aid | 6.28 | 1.84 |
| Earnings of general departments | 1.68 | 1.23 |
| Contributions from public service enterprises | .72 | — |
| All other | .23 | 1.14 |
| Total | $47.15 | $17.25 |

[1] Summarized from the U.S. Census Bureau's publication, *State Finances, 1943.*

The 1943 figures differ widely from those of 1932, not only in total revenues, but also in the relative importance of specific sources. General sales taxes have been widely adopted and now play an important part in state revenue systems. Payroll taxes to cover the cost of unemployment insurance have become the largest single state tax. New kinds of business taxes have been imposed. The gasoline sales tax rates have been sharply increased in many states. Individual income taxes have been adopted quite generally. And grants from the federal treasury have more than tripled within the brief span of eleven years.

## TAX CONFLICTS BETWEEN THE FEDERAL GOVERNMENT AND THE STATES

One of the most unfortunate effects of the rising cost of government, with its resultant demand for increased revenues, is the frantic attempt of both the nation and the states to collect maximum taxes from every possible source—frequently from the same source. Congress imposes taxes on personal incomes or liquor sales or motor vehicles, and state legislatures follow a similar course, though perhaps with little or no regard for what Congress has already done; the result is often a pyramiding of the tax burden until it becomes almost unbearable. In some cases, to be sure, Congress deliberately imposes a light tax in order to leave a specific source of revenue primarily for the use of the states. It has adopted this policy with regard to gasoline sales taxes. But some states take full advantage of this arrangement, while others do not. Therefore the price of gasoline varies widely from state to state—a situation that inevitably encourages gasoline bootlegging and greatly increases the cost of efficient tax administration. The competition between the federal government and the states for additional revenue works serious hardship upon the states, because of their smaller areas and more limited jurisdiction. Commonwealths maintaining relatively high levels of taxation have found no effective way to prevent the emigration of persons and corporations to other states that collect less revenue and provide fewer or poorer services.

State income is derived chiefly from taxes. Fines, permits, and private donations are of relatively minor importance as revenue producers. Grants from the federal treasury, which now represent more than thirteen per cent of the total income of state governments, have already been considered in some detail.[2] This chapter, therefore,

---

[2] See pp. 36–40.

will deal largely with state tax systems and the problems of taxation. At the outset it must be confessed that these problems cannot be solved by the adoption of a few obvious reforms. Certain reforms are very obvious and very necessary, but even their general acceptance would by no means guarantee an equitable tax system. Wide divergence of thought exists concerning the exact meaning of "equitable" as applied to taxes. Every person tends to view new tax proposals in the light of their effect upon his individual interests or the interests of his group. Moreover, there is considerable uncertainty as to the true incidence of certain taxes, so that legislators do not know, in many instances, who will actually bear the burden of the taxes they impose. Under the circumstances, no system of taxation is likely to command the allegiance of all classes.

### THE CANONS OF SOUND TAXATION

Adam Smith, a famous English economist of the eighteenth century, set forth certain principles that he deemed essential to the establishment of a sound tax system, namely: [3]

"1. The subjects of every state ought to contribute towards the support of the government, as nearly as possible, in proportion to their respective abilities; that is, in proportion to the revenue which they respectively enjoy under the protection of the state.

"2. The tax which each individual is bound to pay ought to be certain, and not arbitrary.

"3. Every tax ought to be levied at the time, or in the manner, in which it is most likely to be convenient for the contributor to pay it.

"4. Every tax ought to be so contrived as both to take out and to keep out of the pockets of the people as little as possible over and above what it brings into the public treasury of the state."

These four principles—equality, certainty, convenience, and economy—are generally accepted as axiomatic. They form the usual point of departure for studies of tax revision, even if those making the studies do not always depart in the same direction. The real difficulty arises when Adam Smith's maxims are applied to specific tax proposals. Does a given tax—the gasoline tax, for example—conform sufficiently to the principle of ability to pay? And, in the last analysis, who really bears the tax? Is it borne by the dealers who originally pay it, or passed on to the consumers of the product? Concrete evidence on these points is seldom available, and the whole problem

[3] *The Wealth of Nations*, Book V, Chap. 11, Part II.

is complicated by the fact that every new tax is superimposed upon an already complicated network of taxes whose incidence can be determined only with the greatest difficulty, if at all. Moreover, even if it could be demonstrated beyond a shadow of doubt that the gasoline tax bears no relation to ability to pay, would that fact be sufficient to justify the states in abandoning its use? Or should they be influenced instead by the fact that the gasoline tax possesses other highly desirable characteristics, such as ease of collection and economy of administration? After all, there is probably no tax that conforms exactly to all four of Adam Smith's maxims. Convenience must be sacrificed to economy, or equality to certainty. Every tax system is a compromise.

## THE GENERAL PROPERTY TAX

During the nineteenth century the general property tax was the main source of state revenue. As recently as 1902 it represented more than half of the state income from taxes. But almost every year since 1902 has witnessed a steady decline in its relative importance; in 1943 it accounted for less than three per cent of the tax revenue of the several states. But this does not mean that property owners are escaping their fair share of taxes, or even that they have found substantial relief from a heavy tax burden. Far from it. State governments have largely abandoned this source of revenue for just one reason: to clear the field for the counties, cities, and other local units of government, which have few other available tax sources. So property owners still pay their taxes and still complain about excessively high rates. But the money goes chiefly into local treasuries. Today, therefore, the general property tax retains its major importance in the American tax scheme because it is the mainstay of local government.

**Wasteful duplication of assessments.** The first step in the taxation of property is to determine its value by means of assessments at regular or irregular intervals. Most assessments are in the hands of local officials. In twenty-four states assessment is regarded as a county function; in seventeen it is entrusted to the towns, townships, or districts; while in the others the counties and towns make separate assessments, thus duplicating a vast amount of work. Cities frequently possess the power to make separate valuations and usually insist upon doing so instead of accepting county assessment figures. There is no logical reason why two sets of officials, working independently of each other, should place their separate valuations upon thousands or hundreds of thousands of pieces of property merely because the property is to be taxed by state, county, and town or city. One valuation should serve for all purposes of taxation.[4]

Some of the evils of local assessment of real estate are avoided by placing the assessment of certain realty in the hands of state officials. Most states follow this plan with regard to the property of all public utilities, but a few states, such as Nebraska and Texas, limit its application to railroads, while a number of others, including Kansas, Mississippi, and North Dakota, use it only for railroads and telephone and telegraph companies. The state agency charged with the task of making these assessments is the state tax commission or board of equalization. In those states that still rely upon local assessors to value the property of statewide utility corporations, every tax district is virtually free to follow its own whims, and the widest variations inevitably result.

Incompetence of assessors. Local assessors—the officers who determine the value of property for purposes of taxation—are commonly chosen by popular vote. Except in a few of the more progressive metropolitan centers, technical qualifications are neither required nor expected. The inevitable result is that property valuations are made largely on the basis of political influence or guesswork. A few jurisdictions have made the office of assessor appointive, and this plan has usually produced better results. But the voters of most communities still seem to prefer the elective plan; there is a widespread feeling that such an important matter as property assessment, which directly affects the pocketbook of every property owner, should not be entrusted to persons who are one step removed from direct popular control, however competent they may be. So the inherent popular distrust of appointive officers is made to serve the interests of the professional politicians, and the farce of popular election of incompetents to important technical positions continues.

Personal property: Tangible personalty. One of the most serious defects of the general property tax arises from the attempt to tax personal property. The attempt is foredoomed to failure in large measure, for no known method exists of measuring tangible personalty with even approximate accuracy, and intangibles escape detection almost completely. Certain kinds of tangible personal property, such as automobiles, may be assessed rather easily, since the state has a rec-

---

[4] Cities sometimes insist upon separate valuations because their tax and debt limits are based upon the assessed value of property within their borders, and county valuations would fix these limits too low. If all property were assessed at full value instead of a fraction of actual value, this difficulty would disappear.

ord of each registration. But what of household goods? Assessors cannot be expected to go from door to door, making inventories of tables, chairs, beds, and radios, nor to fix the value of the articles they find. And what of jewelry, which combines high value with ease of concealment? Obviously it cannot be reached unless its abnormally conscientious owners decide to reveal its existence. Faced with such stupendous practical difficulties, some counties, cities, and towns simply abandon the attempt to tax household effects, even if not authorized by state law to take this step. Other local jurisdictions solve the problem by varying the amount of the personal property assessment with the character of the neighborhood, each family in a neighborhood being assessed at the same rate. It is possible, of course, to require taxpayers to declare under oath the nature and value of their personal property; and this plan is used in nearly all states. Heavy penalties for false returns are provided by law, yet virtually everyone submits a deliberately falsified statement, knowing full well that his neighbors will do the same. Taxpayers' oaths have become meaningless in all American communities, and public opinion regards this particular form of perjury as entirely harmless—in fact, rather commendable. The occasional man who deliberately shoulders his neighbors' tax burdens by telling the truth about his personal property is considered a fool.

INTANGIBLE PERSONALTY. The difficulties in the way of finding and valuing tangible personalty, though sufficient to baffle the ablest assessor, seem scarcely worthy of mention when contrasted with the difficulty of reaching intangibles. Bonds, stocks, mortgages, and the like readily escape their share of the local tax burden, and there seems to be no way of preventing this evasion under the general property tax. Moreover, according to generally accepted economic doctrine, taxation of intangibles is a particularly objectionable form of double taxation. Stocks, for example, are merely evidences of wealth, and the tangible property that they represent is required to bear its separate tax burden. Mortgages are evidences of debt; to tax them is, in Professor Seligman's words, to tax liability instead of ability. Of course, these difficulties and inequalities have not passed unnoticed. The literature of taxation, from the writings of cloistered academicians to the official reports of state and local tax commissions, is filled with condemnations of the general property tax—especially as applied to personalty—and with proposed remedies. Some of these proposals, such as the classification of property and the exemption of intangibles, have already been made effective in certain jurisdictions. Their effect is considered in another part of this chapter.[5]

**Real estate.** Even as applied to real estate, the general property tax is far from satisfactory. It does not conform to the cardinal principle of taxation—that the tax burden should fall on all members of the commonwealth in proportion to their ability to contribute to the cost of government. For the extent and nature of a man's real estate holdings are at best a poor indication of his net income. He may be literally "land poor"—owning a large amount of real property yet unable to make it yield a dollar above taxes and repairs. Or he may invest his savings in stocks or bonds instead of real estate and thus escape the real property tax entirely except so far as he pays a higher rental for his home. Under the general property tax the poor are sometimes taxed more heavily than the rich—not only relatively, but absolutely; and in almost every instance they bear more than their proportionate share of the tax burden.

INEQUALITIES OF ASSESSMENT. Although the real estate tax is admittedly an inequitable tax and could not under any circumstances be made to conform to a sound theory of taxation, some of its worst features could be eliminated by the adoption of proper administrative methods. The methods now used in most American cities to determine the value of real property are thoroughly bad and lead inevitably to glaring inequalities. For one thing, real estate is generally assessed at a fraction of its actual worth, as measured by selling price. This fact would be of little importance if all property within a state were assessed at some uniform percentage, whether thirty, fifty, or one hundred. Actually, however, the greatest variations exist among the counties, cities, towns, or other assessment areas. Some communities habitually value real estate at one half of its actual worth, while others use one fourth or three fourths of fair value as the basis of their assessments. These local assessments, with or without some attempt at equalization by the central authorities, then become the basis of a state tax. Equalization is seldom completely effective, and thus the communities whose assessments are nearest actual value make the heaviest proportional contributions to the cost of state government. Even within a single county or city wide variations appear. The tax burdens of some property owners are shifted to other property owners —sometimes inadvertently and sometimes as the result of political pressure—through a process of unequal assessments. Although the

[5] See pp. 369–370.

general level of assessments may be fixed at fifty per cent of full value, the variations on individual pieces of property may range from twenty to one hundred per cent, or even higher. Every student of assessment procedure complains of the inequalities that generally exist. Every thorough investigation of conditions in a specific city or county reveals injustices that should not be permitted to continue. If every piece of property were assessed at its fair market value, then deviations from this standard could be discovered and corrected without great difficulty. But when the level of assessments is "said to be" about sixty per cent, or some other arbitrary percentage, widespread unfairness almost invariably results.

*Mechanical valuation as a remedy.* Some of the larger cities, including New York, Cleveland, Detroit, Baltimore, and Newark, have developed systems of so-called "scientific" or "mechanical" valuation of real estate. These systems are mechanical in the sense that they involve the application of certain definite rules to all pieces of property, but they do not in any way eliminate the factor of human judgment. Land and buildings are valued separately. Front foot values are obtained for all land within the city limits; and, with this information at hand, the assessed value of any piece of ground can be obtained simply by multiplying its front foot value by the number of front feet —assuming, of course, a lot of standard depth. Special rules must be applied to lots that are longer or shorter than the accepted standard, as well as to irregularly shaped lots. Corner lots, of course, also present special problems. The assessment of buildings is based upon a number of factors, of which the cost of construction is most important, though not controlling in every instance. Depreciation tables for different types of structures have been prepared by a number of authorities. Mechanical valuation is unquestionably the most satisfactory plan yet devised for assessing real estate. In the hands of competent assessors it can be made to produce highly satisfactory results. If administered by persons who are politically minded or feeble-minded, it is no more likely to give satisfaction than the methods now in general use. But every administrative device depends for its success upon able administrators.

**Review and equalization of assessments.** After the assessments of property have been completed, opportunity must be provided for persons who think that they have been unjustly treated to seek redress. For this purpose boards of review or equalization are maintained by the towns or counties, or both. If the original assessments have been prepared by town officials, appeals usually go to a town board of review, and from that body to a county board. Under such circumstances the county board may perform two separate functions: the hearing of individual appeals and the equalization of town assessment rates. From the decisions of the county board appeals are sometimes permitted to the state tax commission, but more commonly to the courts. The state commission is generally concerned with the equalization of assessments among counties rather than the examination of individual property owners' complaints. Other duties of the state tax commission are considered in a later part of this chapter.[6]

The most significant aspect of the entire process of review of assessments is its almost universal failure to accomplish any worthwhile result. No effort is made to secure specially qualified persons as members of the local boards of review; in fact, most of these boards are composed of ex officio members, who devote only a small part of their time to assessment hearings. Since these men know virtually nothing about the valuation of property, they are forced to rely for their opinions almost entirely upon the judgment of the assessors whose work they are reviewing—unless they substitute partisan considerations or personal caprice. Occasionally an honest, intelligent board of review makes a determined and successful effort to judge each case on its merits and correct injustices that have developed during the process of preparing the assessment rolls, but such cases are exceptional.

**Exemptions from tax:** PREFERENTIAL TREATMENT OF REAL ESTATE. Many persons have long believed that too much property is exempted from the operation of the general property tax. Despite this widespread belief the list of exemptions constantly grows longer. In nearly all jurisdictions it includes real estate used for religious, educational, or charitable purposes. Federal property cannot be taxed by the states or their civil subdivisions because of the implied prohibition in the federal Constitution, as interpreted by the United States Supreme Court.[7] State property is commonly exempted from local taxation. More than one third of the states exempt growing crops or the products of domestic agriculture. Exemption is sometimes granted to factories that produce farm machinery, and a few states exempt all manufacturing establishments. One of the many unfortunate effects

[6] See pp. 378–379.
[7] McCulloch *v.* Maryland, 4 Wheaton 316 (1819). It might perhaps be argued, however, that the United States Supreme Court's decision in Graves *v.* New York, 306 U.S. 466 (1939), opens the door for state taxation of federal property and federal taxation of property owned by the states. See pp. 49–50.

of the depression has been the growing tendency to grant complete or partial tax exemption to "homesteads," or private homes. Texas set the example in 1933 by exempting from state taxation the first three thousand dollars of assessed value of homes, and shortly afterward West Virginia made provision for preferential treatment, though not complete exemption. Then, in 1935, Florida exempted homesteads, to the assessed value of five thousand dollars, from all *state and local* taxation. Thirteen states [8] now grant more or less complete exemption—or at least special consideration—to private homes.

*Need for curtailment of preferential treatment.* The inescapable effect of such preferential treatment is to narrow the tax base and shift the burden of taxation to those whose property has not been placed in the exempt class. Thousands of property owners are thus compelled by constitution or statute to pay the taxes on their neighbors' homes, or to contribute to the support of churches they do not attend, manufacturing establishments whose products they do not buy, and private schools whose very existence is unknown to them. Even though it be granted that religious, educational, and charitable institutions are performing valuable community services, or that agricultural and manufacturing development are essential to community welfare, the propriety of this particular form of encouragement is open to serious question. Certain property must remain exempt from the operation of the general property tax because of constitutional limitations or administrative difficulties, but the quantity of tax-exempt property in virtually every community could be materially reduced. It *must,* in fact, be substantially lowered in some commonwealths, if cities and counties are to be saved from virtual bankruptcy through the disruption of their tax rolls.

THE PROBLEM OF PERSONAL PROPERTY TAXES. The most serious complaints against the general property tax arise from the attempts to include personal property. Quite naturally, therefore, some of the most important attempts at reform are directed at the relief of personalty from its heavy tax burden. One proposal receiving serious consideration is that intangibles be taxed at a lower rate than other property, on the theory that taxpayers will thereby be induced to declare their intangible wealth. This plan has been adopted more or less completely by more than half of the states. Many of the other commonwealths are prevented from granting preferential treatment

---

[8] Alabama, Arkansas, Florida, Georgia, Iowa, Louisiana, Minnesota, Mississippi, Oklahoma, South Dakota, Texas, West Virginia, Wyoming.

to intangibles by constitutional restrictions, such as the provision of the Mississippi constitution that "Taxation shall be uniform and equal throughout the state." The results of low-rate taxation of intangibles have been generally disappointing. While more intangible wealth has been brought to light than under the uniform tax plan, a large percentage still escapes. Apparently the only way to solve the problem, therefore, is to grant complete exemption from the general property tax to all the more important forms of intangible personalty, relying on other taxes to reach this wealth. A few states have adopted this scheme *in toto,* and a number of others have accepted it in part. Although it runs counter to the general plan for reducing the number of exemptions under the general property tax, most students of taxation believe that it is a step in the right direction. Nothing is to be gained by insisting upon the assessment of any form of property that assessors have repeatedly demonstrated their complete incapacity to discover.

## THE STATE INCOME TAX

Three fourths of the states have enacted income tax legislation.[9] This action represents a comparatively new movement. Virginia had an income tax as early as 1843, but no general interest was manifested in this form of taxation until Wisconsin, by its law of 1911, demonstrated that the most serious administrative difficulties could be removed. The severe industrial depression following the stock market crash of 1929 caused a frantic search by state legislatures for new sources of revenue and added fresh impetus to the income tax movement. During 1931, 1932, and 1933 the tax was adopted by thirteen states, and during the next four years it was accepted by eight others. As a rule it covers both individual and corporation incomes, but three states[10] limit its application to incomes of individuals, while three others[11] apply it only to incomes of corporations. In the computation of the net income subject to taxation, certain deductions and exemptions are always permitted. Individual incomes are usually taxed at progressive rates—that is, at rates that increase with the amount of the income. Thus persons in the large-income brackets pay more—proportionately as well as absolutely—than persons in the small-income groups, in recognition of the generally accepted theory

[9] The twelve exceptions are Florida, Illinois, Indiana, Maine, Michigan, Nebraska, Nevada, New Jersey, Ohio, Texas, Washington, and Wyoming.
[10] Delaware, New Hampshire, and West Virginia.
[11] Connecticut, Pennsylvania, and Rhode Island.

that proportionately greater contributions from the rich involve no greater sacrifice. The rates of the federal government's income tax are much more steeply progressive than state rates, and this feature has been especially noticeable in recent years; but there is a tendency to strengthen the progressive feature of state income taxation.

Most students of public finance agree that the personal income tax should have an important place in the tax systems of the several states because it conforms perfectly to the principle of taxation in proportion to ability to pay. Some of the earlier writers expressed the opinion that this tax should be left to the federal government exclusively because of the administrative difficulties involved. But most of these difficulties have been removed, at least by certain states, and there is no apparent reason why all states should not be equally successful.

### THE INHERITANCE TAX

**General state acceptance.** Inheritance taxes have long played a part in the general scheme of state finance, though yielding a comparatively small revenue. Pennsylvania taxed inheritances as long ago as 1826, and Virginia and Maryland enacted similar legislation before 1850. These early laws, however, were aimed at collateral inheritance; not until 1891, when New York set the fashion, did any state levy a tax upon direct heirs. In recent years the inheritance tax principle has been greatly extended, and direct as well as collateral heirs have been made subject to taxation in most states, though direct heirs are commonly given the benefit of a lower rate.[12] The inheritance tax is now used by every state except Nevada and includes direct heirs in every state except Maryland, New Hampshire, and Texas. The rates adopted by most commonwealths are mildly progressive. In 1925 New York modified its inheritance tax law to provide for the exemption of intangible personalty belonging to residents of other states, but only on condition that other states grant a similar exemption to the estates of New York residents. This reciprocal provision, which has since been written into the laws of nearly all the other commonwealths, has virtually solved a serious problem of double taxation that formerly caused gross injustice in many instances.

**Congressional action to force tax uniformity.** For many years the wide variations in the inheritance tax laws of the several states, coupled with the failure of some states to make provision for inheritance taxa-

[12] The only states that make no distinction between direct and collateral heirs are Georgia, North Dakota, and Utah.

tion of any sort, aroused unfavorable comment from many quarters. It was pointed out that wealthy men could establish their legal residence in some commonwealth, such as Florida, that did not tax inheritances, and that in this way they could escape death levies upon their estates.   In 1926 Congress set out to remedy this situation by enacting a federal inheritance tax law, and including a proviso that any inheritance tax paid to a state government might be credited against the federal tax, up to eighty per cent of the total.   The obvious intent of this statute was to secure some degree of uniformity in the taxation of inheritances.   It was a plain announcement to the states that they must tax the estates of decedents, or have the federal government impose the tax instead.   And, obviously, if the tax were levied by the federal government, all money collected would be paid into the federal treasury.   The State of Florida promptly brought suit to have this law set aside on the ground that it was an unconstitutional interference with state affairs, but the Supreme Court of the United States refused to accept this point of view.   "The contention that the federal tax is not uniform because other states impose inheritance taxes while Florida does not," said the Supreme Court, in upholding the federal statute, "is without merit.   Congress cannot accommodate its legislation to the conflicting or dissimilar laws of the several states nor control the diverse conditions to be found in the various states which necessarily work unlike results from the enforcement of the same tax." [13]   As a direct result of this decision Florida levied an estate tax in 1930, including in the law a provision that limited the tax in all cases to the amount of the federal exemption.

### BUSINESS TAXES

**Special corporation levies.**   A considerable part of the total state tax revenue is derived from taxes on business corporations.   For the most part these taxes are special levies imposed upon corporations *per se,* and separate from the property taxes that corporations must pay as owners of real estate.   The justification commonly given for such special taxation is that the corporate form of business organization confers special privileges denied to individuals: corporations have perpetual or long-term existence; their stock may be transferred at will; and their stockholders enjoy a limited liability fixed by law. These privileges have been created by state law; therefore they may reasonably be made the basis for special taxation.   In recent years,

---

[13] Florida *v.* Mellon, 273 U.S. 12 (1927).

however, corporation taxs have become increasingly heavy, and many persons believe that this form of taxation has been carried to excess. The state usually imposes one tax for the privilege of becoming a corporation—or, in the case of a foreign corporation, the privilege of coming within state boundaries. Another levy is made for the privilege of doing business as a corporation. Other special taxes are placed on utility corporations for the privilege of doing business in a special way—in many instances, making use of public property. Banks and insurance companies are also subject to heavy taxation. These taxes on corporate enterprise assume a variety of forms—taxes on capital stock, taxes on gross earnings, taxes on net earnings (already considered under the head of income taxation), and "corporate excess" taxes.

The corporate excess tax. The theory of the corporate excess tax is that every profitable business undertaking has a going value higher than the appraisal value of its property assets—a value created by the union of these property assets under a single effective management. The problem is to measure this going value for purposes of taxation. Most of the states that impose corporate excess taxes solve this problem by ascertaining the market value of each corporation's capital stock and then subtracting the value of its property already reached by the general property tax. The difference between these two figures is supposed to be the corporate excess. Thus the corporate excess tax is really an extension of the general property tax, designed to uncover the residuum of value that the general property tax fails to touch.

**License taxes.** Although corporations are taxed more heavily than unincorporated businesses, the latter do not escape taxation. On the contrary, they are required to bear a considerable portion of the tax burden—not only through the general property tax, but also through license charges levied on particular occupations and trades, as well as license taxes imposed on all manufacturers and merchants. Some of these special license charges affect all businesses, whether incorporated or unincorporated, and thus place a still heavier tax load on corporations.

**Unemployment insurance taxes.** Every state now imposes a payroll tax on employers in order to permit regular payments, for a limited period, to workers who have lost their jobs. Wisconsin adopted this plan in 1932, but no state followed its example until 1935, when the national Congress virtually compelled state action by levying a three per cent payroll tax and simultaneously offering to credit against the federal tax any amounts paid to the states for unemployment insurance, up to ninety per cent of the total. Congress also offered to provide federal funds to cover the cost of administering the state laws. The immediate result was a flood of state legislation. Five states accepted the federal government's terms in 1935; twenty-eight others enacted suitable laws in 1936; and all the other commonwealths fell into line before the end of the summer of 1937. Although the states must meet certain conditions imposed by Congress, they are still free to establish, within broad limits, the kind of job insurance that seems best suited to their individual needs. Smaller businesses are commonly exempted from payment of the tax; so are employers of certain types of labor—for example, domestic servants and agricultural workers. The social effects of unemployment insurance are considered at some length in another chapter.[14]

**Sales taxes:** TAXES ON SPECIFIC COMMODITIES. Among the more common business taxes are the so-called sales taxes—levies on the sale of specific commodities and also general sales taxes affecting virtually all goods. Taxes on the sale of specific articles are by far the more common form. Thus the gasoline tax, which is discussed in greater detail in a subsequent chapter,[15] has been adopted by every state. Twenty-nine states levy taxes on the sale of cigars, cigarettes, and other forms of tobacco. Laws imposing taxes on liquor have been generally adopted since the repeal of the Eighteenth Amendment. Other specific commodities are singled out for "honorable mention" in certain state tax lists. There seems to be a definite trend toward this form of taxation.

GENERAL SALES TAX. Equally significant, in view of the widespread discussion that it has aroused, is the general sales tax, which is a tax at uniform rates upon the sale of all commodities, or a wide variety of selected commodities, as well as the sale of property and the use of personal services. Strictly speaking, a "general" sales tax should apply to every business transaction, but the name is used to describe a broad tax on sales, even if some specific exemptions are authorized. Thus the West Virginia business and occupation tax is commonly accepted as a good example of a general sales tax, though it does not apply to the sale of professional services. The general sales tax may be levied upon all sales—that is, upon sales by manufacturers, wholesalers, and

14 See pp. 586-588.
15 See pp. 508-509.

retailers, with the effect of taxing most commodities a number of times before they reach the ultimate consumers; or it may be levied only upon sales by manufacturers or retailers.

The first state to adopt the general sales tax as an important part of its fiscal scheme was West Virginia, in 1921. Several other states had long made use of levies that might be classed as general sales taxes —for example, Pennsylvania, with its mercantile license tax of 1821, and Virginia, with its merchants' license tax of 1887. But the rates of these older taxes were very low, and it was not until West Virginia had demonstrated the feasibility of the general sales tax as a substantial producer of revenue that other states fell into line. Even then they were forced to act by the serious crisis in state finance resulting from the industrial depression of the 1930s, and in several states the general sales tax was treated strictly as an emergency measure. Thus Georgia enacted an "occupation privilege sales tax" in 1929, but did not re-enact it two years later.

Opposition to the tax is intense and comes from many sources. Manufacturers and merchants insist that it imposes an unreasonable and well-nigh intolerable burden upon industry and, in fact, upon every form of human activity; that it is a "tax upon the swaddling clothes of the newborn infant; upon the medicine that alleviates human suffering; upon the instruments of surgery and the bandages that bind its wounds; upon the plow that furrows the field; upon the pot that boils the midday meal; upon the coffins that encase our dead; and upon the spades that dig their graves." [16] Economists agree, for the most part, that the general sales tax is regressive, since it imposes a heavier burden upon the poor than it places upon the rich. Nevertheless this tax has been accepted by twenty-six states, plus New York City, as an established feature of their revenue systems; and it has received serious consideration in many states that have not yet adopted it, because it has been found to yield a large and reasonably certain revenue even in periods of economic depression. Professor Alfred D. Buehler, whose careful study of general sales taxation is an important contribution to the literature of the subject,[17] accepts the usual theory that the tax is regressive and unfair, at least when considered by itself; but he believes that in times of emergency, when revenue is the primary consideration, the general sales tax may properly have a place in state tax programs.

[16] *Congressional Record*, 72nd Congress, 1st Session, v. 75, p. 6332.
[17] *General Sales Taxation.*

**Severance taxes.** Twenty-three states [18] impose so-called severance taxes—that is, taxes upon the utilization of natural resources. As these resources are severed from the land they cease to be a part of the natural wealth of the state; therefore it is not at all surprising that the state should levy a tax upon the process. In some states the tax applies only to coal or to coal and iron ore; in others it affects only oil and gas or only forest products. The severance taxes of Arkansas and Louisiana are designed to reach all natural resources.

## OTHER TAXES

**The poll tax.** The poll tax, an arbitrary annual levy of a flat sum —usually one, two, or three dollars—on all persons, all able-bodied persons, all males, or all males between certain age limits, such as twenty-one and seventy, is a common feature of state or local tax systems. It is forbidden by but four [19] state constitutions, and required by ten [20] others. As a rule the tax is levied and collected by local officials, and paid into local treasuries. Under no circumstances can it be made a satisfactory tax, and its evils are accentuated when payment is made a prerequisite to voting.[21]

**License fees.** Motor vehicle license fees are an important source of state revenue, as pointed out in a later chapter.[22] Hunting and fishing licenses, dog licenses, and other miscellaneous license fees yield additional small sums. The money obtained from these various license fees is commonly placed in special funds, to be used exclusively for the support of the various licensed activities. Thus motor vehicle license revenues are generally devoted to road construction and maintenance, and hunting and fishing license fees defray the cost of wild life conservation.

## USE OF TAXATION FOR REGULATORY PURPOSES

The state's power of taxation is used chiefly to provide revenue. There are many instances, however, of state taxation with the primary

[18] Alabama, Arkansas, California, Colorado, Idaho, Illinois, Kentucky, Louisiana, Michigan, Minnesota, Mississippi, Montana, Nevada, New Mexico, Oklahoma, Oregon, South Carolina, South Dakota, Texas, Utah, Virginia, Washington, Wisconsin.

[19] Maryland, Ohio, Oregon, Utah.

[20] Arkansas, California, Delaware, Nevada, North Carolina, Rhode Island, South Carolina, Virginia, West Virginia, Wyoming.

[21] The relationship between poll taxes and voting has already been discussed. See p. 104.

[22] See pp. 507–508.

intent of regulation, and many businesses or types of business organization are encouraged or restricted by the use of the taxing power. An excellent example of state regulation under the guise of taxation arises in connection with the development of chain stores. Many persons, especially the independent merchants, are opposed to this type of selling. They contend that it amounts to unfair competition, because the chain stores secure the business as long as purchasers are able to pay cash, whereas the independents secure their turn after the customers' supply of cash has been exhausted and credit must be extended.

The legislatures of twenty-one states [23]—more than half of them in the South—have decided that chain-store selling is undesirable and have attempted to discourage it by especially heavy taxation from which single-unit stores are exempt. Thus the Indiana statute, which is typical, forbids the operation of any store in the state without a license and fixes steeply progressive fees for stores operating "under the same general management, supervision, or ownership." The fee for one store is three dollars; for two to five stores it is ten dollars for each additional store; and so the fee mounts until it becomes twenty-five dollars for each store in excess of twenty. Shortly after the enactment of this law the owner of a chain of grocery stores in Indianapolis sought an injunction to restrain its operation, on the ground that it arbitrarily discriminated against him and thus deprived him of the equal protection of the laws guaranteed by the federal Constitution. Though admitting that the state legislature might establish classifications for taxing purposes, he urged that chain stores did not differ from independent single-unit stores in any way that would warrant proportionately heavier taxation. The state board of tax commissioners, in arguing for the validity of the statute, tried to show that important differences between chain stores and independents did actually exist. When the case reached the Supreme Court of the United States, the law was upheld. "It is not the function of this court in cases like the present to consider the propriety or justness of the tax, to seek for the motives or to criticize the public policy which prompted the adop-

---

[23] Alabama, Colorado, Delaware, Florida, Georgia, Idaho, Indiana, Iowa, Kentucky, Louisiana, Maryland, Michigan, Mississippi, Montana, North Carolina, South Carolina, South Dakota, Tennessee, Texas, West Virginia, Wisconsin. The list originally included five other states, but Arizona and Maine repealed their laws, Minnesota and Wisconsin permitted their statutes to expire, and in California the chain-store tax was repealed by a popular referendum.

tion of the legislation," said Justice Roberts, speaking for the Court. "Our duty is to sustain the classification adopted by the legislature if there are substantial differences between the occupations separately classified. Such differences need not be great." [24]

### SPECIAL ASSESSMENTS

A small part of state revenue is derived from special assessments— that is, special charges levied against the owners of real estate on the assumption that some special benefit has been derived from services performed by the state government. Thus, when a new highway is built, there is certainly reason to believe that the owners of abutting property receive a special benefit in the form of higher property values. Why, then, should they not be made to bear all or a portion of the construction cost? In theory there is no valid objection to the prin- ciple of special assessments. Certain practical administrative difficul- ties sometimes arise, however. One of these is the difficulty of measur- ing the area of benefit and determining the exact extent to which benefit has been conferred. Should special assessments be levied only against the owners of abutting property, or also against other neighbor- ing property owners who secure an advantage? Should property owners bear the entire cost of permanent improvements involving the use of special assessments—assuming, of course, that the cost does not exceed the benefit actually conferred—or should a part of the burden be borne by the entire taxpaying public? These questions have been answered in a variety of ways by the states that have accepted the special assessment principle. Some states levy assessments up to the full value of the property; others fix the limit for special assessments at fifty per cent. The assessments for certain types of permanent improvements, such as highways, are commonly restricted to abutting property, but some other special assessments are spread over a considerably wider area. Almost never, however, is any attempt made to employ scien- tific principles in determining just how far benefit actually extends. Guesswork is the rule, and one man's guess is as good as another's. Nearly three fifths of the states make use of special assessments, but only about a dozen obtain any substantial revenue from this source. Municipalities, on the other hand, use special assessments extensively.

---

[24] State Board of Tax Commissioners *v.* Jackson, 283 U.S. 527 (1931). For a careful study of the economic effects of chain-store taxation, see *The Chain Store Problem,* by T. N. Beckman and H. C. Nolen.

## STATE TAX COMMISSIONS

The agency chiefly concerned with the administration of the tax laws is the state tax commission. Iowa was the first state to establish such a commission, in 1851. But other states followed slowly, and by the beginning of the present century only ten tax commissions had been set up. More recently, however, the need for central control of local assessments and the rapid multiplication of separate state taxes have combined to make some central agency virtually a necessity, with the result that every state except Florida now has a tax commission or similar agency.

Nearly half of the states have adopted the plan of vesting control in a single officer, whose title is commissioner of taxes, superintendent of taxation, or director of finance; the other commonwealths still cling to the commission plan. The membership of the commissions ranges from three in twenty-seven states to six in Nevada. Terms of office are rather long—rarely less than four years, and six or eight years in many states. Appointment by the governor is the most common method of selection, though popular election has not been entirely abandoned. As previously indicated,[25] the state tax commission plays an important part in the supervision and equalization of local assessments and usually assumes direct responsibility for the assessment of public utility properties. In addition, it administers a wide variety of state taxes; sometimes the list includes inheritance and income taxes, gasoline and tobacco taxes, motor vehicle license taxes, and taxes on incorporated and unincorporated business enterprises. Efficient administration of the state tax program can best be served by placing the state tax commission—or, preferably, the director of finance—in charge of all state tax collections. Most of the states, however, still divide responsibility for the collection of taxes between the tax commission and other agencies.

### SELECTED REFERENCES

Beckman, Theodore N., and Nolen, Herman C., *The Chain Store Problem; A Critical Analysis,* 1938.

Blakey, Roy G., and Johnson, Violet, *State Income Taxes,* 1942.

Buehler, Alfred G., *General Sales Taxation, Its History and Development,* 1932.

Clark, Kenneth R., *Inheritance and Estate Taxes on Life Insurance,* 1935.

Crawford, Finla G., *The Gasoline Tax in the United States,* 4th ed., 1937.

Critz, Maurice, *The Use Tax; Its History, Administration, and Economic Effects,* 1941.

[25] See pp. 364 and 368.

Federation of Tax Administrators, *Recent Trends in State Revenues*, 1943.

Hansen, Alvin H., and Perloff, Harvey S., *State and Local Finance in the National Economy*, 1944.

Jacoby, Neil H., *Retail Sales Taxation*, 1938.

Lee, Maurice W., *Anti-Chain Store Tax Legislation*, 1939.

Leonard, J. M., and Mohaupt, Rosina, *Exemption of Homesteads from Taxation*, Detroit, 1937.

National Association of Assessing Officers, *Exemption of Institutional Real Property from Taxation*, 1939.

Nichols, E. R., and Others, *The State Sales Tax*, 1938.

Simpson, Herbert D., *Effects of a Property Tax Off-set Under an Income Tax*, 1932.

——, *Tax Racket and Tax Reform in Chicago*, 1930.

——, *The Tax Situation in Illinois*, 1929.

South Carolina State Planning Board, *Is New Industry Tax Exemption Effective?* Columbia, 1943.

Tax Institute, *Wartime Problems of State and Local Finance*, 1943.

Tax Policy League, Inc., *Tax Exemptions*, 1939.

——, *Tax Relations among Governmental Units*, 1938.

Tobin, Charles J., Hannan, W. E., and Tolman, L. L., *Exemption from Taxation of Privately Owned Real Property Used for Religious, Charitable, and Educational Purposes in New York State*, Albany, 1934.

Tuller, Walter K., *Treatise on the Taxing Power with Particular Application to State Income Tax*, 1937.

Twentieth Century Fund, Committee on Taxation, *Facing the Tax Problem: A Survey of Taxation in the United States and a Program for the Future*, 1937.

Woolsey, John B., *State Taxation of Banks*, Chapel Hill, N.C., 1935.

MOST state programs are financed in part by borrowing. Some temporary indebtedness is incurred to cover unforeseen shortages arising from emergencies or to tide over the period between the beginning of the fiscal year and the date for the payment of taxes, but this form of borrowing is relatively unimportant. The bulk of state indebtedness is represented by long-term bonds, issued to cover the cost of permanent improvements.

In the early days of American history borrowing was unpopular except for war purposes. The functions of government were few and comparatively simple. Needed funds were often obtained from the sale of public lands. In 1820 the expenditures of Pennsylvania's state government amounted to only four hundred and forty thousand dollars—just about enough to meet its present-day expenses for seven hours. Yet Pennsylvania spent considerably more than the average state. It is easy to understand, therefore, that the states had no real need to borrow substantial sums. Their modest tax revenues were quite adequate.

### THE NINETEENTH CENTURY TO THE CIVIL WAR

**Reckless borrowing.** Shortly after 1820, however, the picture began to change. More extensive public improvements were undertaken, and their cost could not be borne out of current revenues. So the states began to borrow extensively—almost lavishly. They turned their attention particularly to means of transportation between the established East and the newly settled Middle West. Canals and roads were built at a rapid rate, and sometimes without sufficient regard to the costs involved. The success of the Erie Canal, which was completed in 1825 at a cost of seven million dollars, inspired similar projects in a number of states. Nearly all the money came from borrowing. Pennsylvania, whose debt had been nominal in 1820, issued ten million dollars' worth of bonds during the next ten years. New York borrowed even more, and Ohio was not far behind. A little later the development of the railroads necessitated additional capital outlays. It was uncertain for a time whether the railroads would take the place of the canals, and some states made large expenditures for both purposes, increasing their indebtedness accordingly.

Between 1835 and 1838 the states borrowed more than one hundred million dollars—a very substantial sum, in terms of their revenues at that time. Such reckless financing would have been bad enough, if the money had been spent wisely and the debt had been properly administered. Unfortunately, however, neither of these conditions generally prevailed. "Loans were incurred for questionable purposes, money was spent without restraint, and there was much downright fraud. Frequently no provision was made for the payment of interest and principal of the loan; but, instead, new loans were incurred for their payment. Thus debt was pyramided upon debt." [1]

The prevailing interest rate was five per cent in some states, and six per cent in most of the others. As a rule no attempt was made to adjust the official rate to market conditions. The legislature would decide—perhaps six months in advance of the actual sale—that a new issue of bonds should be offered at six per cent. And as a result the bonds might command a handsome premium or might have to be sold instead at a substantial discount. Seldom did the official rate correspond to the market rate. If the bonds yielded a premium, state officials frequently used this surplus to make interest payments, thus concealing the real burden of the debt that had been incurred. Prosperity was in the air, and few persons questioned the wisdom of further borrowing.

**Results of business depressions.** It should have been obvious, however, that there must be a day of reckoning. The first sign of impending disaster was the severe panic of 1837. But this warning had little effect on state borrowing. "In the first place, the states were in the midst of their programs of internal improvements. Generally the canal and railroad systems were not completed, and brought in little, if any, revenue. The states had to complete these projects or lose everything. Secondly, there were many who refused to accept the panic at its true value; they regarded it as merely a financial phenomenon which would not affect the economic situation." [2] And so the states continued to plunge even more deeply into debt. Between 1838 and 1841, when borrowing should have been sharply curtailed, the total of state indebtedness actually increased ten per cent. Then

[1] Studensky, Paul, *Public Borrowing*, p. 37.
[2] Ratchford, B. U., *American State Debts*, p. 86. This authoritative work deserves the attention of every student of public finance.

came another financial crisis and severe industrial depression. Some of the states lost heavily through bank failures, and their tax revenues declined sharply. State legislators had little inclination to improve the situation by imposing heavier taxes; on the contrary, many of them actually yielded to the demand for tax reduction, in order to relieve the financial burden on the masses of the people. Under such circumstances, it is not surprising that some of the states could find no better way to solve their difficulties than to stop paying the interest on their outstanding bonds. Before the end of 1842 nine states [3] had defaulted on their interest payments. One of them—Mississippi—eventually repudiated a large part of its indebtedness.

**Constitutional restrictions on borrowing.** Public confidence in the integrity of the state governments was badly shaken, as well it might have been. The voters of many states came to the conclusion that they could not trust their representatives in the legislature to use the borrowing power wisely and moderately, and so they took steps to check further abuses. Constitutional limitations on borrowing were quite generally written into state constitutions. Rhode Island was the first state to take this step; it amended its constitution in 1842 to prohibit the legislature from incurring debts in excess of fifty thousand dollars, without the consent of the voters, "except in time of war, insurrection, or invasion." Within the next decade and a half eighteen other states followed Rhode Island's example, and eventually similar restrictions on borrowing were written into nearly all the state constitutions. These limitations have proved singularly ineffective, however, in checking unwise borrowing. For they operate as a restriction only upon the legislature—not upon the voters. And whenever public opinion regards large-scale borrowing as a desirable method of financing permanent improvements, nothing can prevent a substantial increase in indebtedness.

**Continued debt increases.** It might be supposed that the unhappy experiences of the 1840s would have had a sobering effect upon the American public and would have prevented further large-scale borrowing, at least for several decades. But the memory of a democratic people is notoriously short, and so it proved in this case. Business conditions improved after 1845, the credit of many states was restored, and soon there was a determined demand for improved railroad facilities, to be financed largely through the use of state credit. The pres-

[3] Arkansas, Florida, Illinois, Indiana, Louisiana, Maryland, Michigan, Mississippi, Pennsylvania.

sure was strongest, of course, in those states that had not borrowed in the earlier period and had thus kept their credit unimpaired. But New York, which had indebted itself almost to the point of repudiation between 1820 and 1840, increased its debt another fifty per cent before the outbreak of the Civil War. Total state indebtedness, for all thirty-three states of the Union, soared to a quarter of a billion.

## THE CIVIL WAR AND RECONSTRUCTION

**War financing.** The Civil War forced new financial burdens upon the states, and most of them resorted to additional borrowing. Some issued bonds in the early days of the war for the purpose of equipping troops. Some borrowed in order to supplement the pay of soldiers and aid in the care of their families. Money was needed, also, to stimulate enlistments by the payment of bounties. Later, when Congress decided to draft the men needed for the army, the states continued to pay bounties to substitutes and even to those who were drafted. Many years afterward Congress reimbursed the state governments for a considerable part of these expenditures, but in the meantime state indebtedness continued to grow. The Confederate states, of course, were in a particularly difficult position. At the outset they had to shoulder most of the financial responsibility for the war, because their central government was in process of organization. Even after it had been firmly established, it lacked both the power and the will to tax extensively. Nor did the states increase their taxes to any appreciable extent. They obtained necessary funds by issuing paper money and by floating long-term bonds. The central government followed their example. The war ended with both the paper money and the bonds worthless.

**Postwar borrowing in the Confederate states.** In the period immediately following the Civil War the plight of the former Confederate states was desperate. Their governments were practically without funds and unable to pay for badly needed public improvements. Negroes and "carpetbaggers" from the North were in control of the state governments, and they permitted or encouraged systematic looting of state treasuries. It was under such conditions that large new bond issues, totaling more than one hundred million dollars, were floated by the Southern states in the decade after 1865. The ostensible purpose of most of this borrowing was to aid the railroads; its real purpose was to line the pockets of the crooked manipulators. Most of the white people of the South were outraged, and many leading citizens declared in no uncertain terms that the new debts would never be honored. The men who uttered these warnings had been disfranchised, and they were powerless to stop the borrowing orgy, but they could still raise their voices in protest.

REPUDIATION OF DEBTS. Under such circumstances it is surprising that purchasers could be found for the new bond issues. Unusual inducements were necessary. Some of the bonds were offered at sixty cents on the dollar or even less, but they speedily declined to thirty or forty, despite interest rates of seven or eight per cent. Professor Ratchford tells how North Carolina bonds taken to New York were "hawked about the streets like stale fish from the market." [4] Eventually, of course, the Southern whites regained control of their state governments, and one of their first acts was to repudiate—at least in part—the debts incurred by carpetbagger administrations. In some instances they even extended the principle of repudiation to certain debts incurred before the Civil War, but this was not a common practice.

**Debt reduction up to 1900.** During the latter part of the nineteenth century state borrowing was generally unpopular. Most of the states of the North and West financed their activities from current revenues and even managed to reduce the amount of their indebtedness. In the South the borrowing habit persisted, for the most part, but there were some exceptions.[5] The net result, for all parts of the United States, was an actual reduction in the total of state debt between 1860 and 1900, despite the admission of fifteen additional states and an increase of one hundred and fifty per cent in the nation's population.

## THE TWENTIETH CENTURY

**Resumption of borrowing.** At the beginning of the present century came the automobile, bringing with it an urgent demand for the construction of good—and expensive—roads. The states began to borrow once more, and on a scale that made previous borrowing seem extremely modest. Within a dozen years after the turn of the century state indebtedness had increased forty-two per cent. It rose another twenty-seven per cent within the next three years. But that was only a beginning. The per capita net debt of the forty-eight

---

[4] Ratchford, B. U., *History of North Carolina Debt*, p. 190.
[5] Louisiana paid off a substantial part of its state debt before 1900; so did North Carolina.

states was three dollars and seventy-five cents in 1915; in 1930 it stood at sixteen dollars—an increase of three hundred and twenty-five per cent. The states borrowed and borrowed, using their credit freely to obtain the funds for the permanent improvements demanded by the voters. Most of the money, as indicated in a later chapter,[6] was spent on highways, but substantial sums were used to pay bonuses to veterans of the First World War and to aid them in a variety of other ways.

**Mounting indebtedness.** The years of industrial depression following 1930 witnessed some deceleration in the rate of increase, but state debts continued to mount. In 1937 they totaled nearly nineteen dollars per capita. Most of these newer bond issues were specifically approved by the voters at regular or special elections; otherwise constitutional debt limits would have been exceeded many times. Unemployment relief was one of the major reasons for borrowing during this period. Only fifteen states [7] incurred indebtedness for this purpose, but they borrowed nearly one-half a billion dollars. Large quantities of bonds were issued, also, for harbor improvements, for aid to local governments, and for additional road building. Although excessive borrowing and inept debt administration had been characteristic of state government for many years, the situation did not reach a climax until 1932 or 1933. By that time the depression had seriously affected state revenues, and some states found themselves on the brink of financial disaster. But only one state—Arkansas—actually defaulted on its obligations and it later resumed interest payments after refunding some of its bond issues at lower rates of interest.

**Debt reduction during the Second World War.** When the United States entered the Second World War in 1941, the net indebtedness of the states was at an all-time high of slightly more than twenty dollars per capita. The war years brought unparalleled prosperity to the state governments. Revenues mounted by leaps and bounds. Individual and corporation income taxes, general sales levies, and business taxes of all kinds swelled the total, more than compensating for a drop in the yield of the gasoline tax. The states took advantage of this opportunity to reduce their indebtedness. In 1942 the net state debt dropped to nineteen dollars and seventy cents per capita,

6 See pp. 510–511.

7 California, Illinois, Maryland, Massachusetts, Minnesota, Nevada, New Hampshire, New Jersey, New York, Pennsylvania, Rhode Island, Tennessee, Texas, Vermont, Washington. New York borrowed more than forty per cent of the total.

and the next year it went down to seventeen dollars and forty-three cents—the lowest figure in ten years.

**The postwar era.** Whether this trend will continue is uncertain, but there is some reason to believe that it will not. In the first place, state revenues will almost certainly be smaller, unless reinforced by new taxes or higher tax rates. Then, too, the postwar era will witness a widespread demand for additional public services, which cannot be financed out of current revenue without considerable sacrifice. Highway systems will require extensive improvement. New school buildings will be badly needed. Various forms of aid to returning war veterans will involve the expenditure of large sums. Social security systems will be greatly expanded. One student of the problem offers his opinion "that we have entered a new phase in the development of public finance, in which state debts are to play a more important part than in the past." [8] On the other hand, the vast proportions of the war-swollen national debt may possibly cause state officials to hesitate before proposing new bond issues.

**Wide debt variations among states.** It should be pointed out, in all fairness, that not all forty-eight states have resorted to large-scale borrowing. Two of them [9] have no long-term obligations, and a number of others have only nominal debts. At the other end of the scale are six commonwealths [10] that have issued more than one half of all the state bonds outstanding. New York alone accounts for one fifth of the total. As a group, the Southern states are in a particularly unfavorable position. Their per capita indebtedness is far above the national average, while their capacity to pay is far below. But even in this group there are some outstanding exceptions, such as Florida, Georgia, Kentucky, and Virginia.

### BORROWING PRACTICES

**Terms of bonds.** One of the worst features of state borrowing is the long terms for which bonds are issued. Twenty-five- and thirty-year bonds are common, and fifty-year bonds are by no means rare. The excesses of the past have led to the adoption of numerous constitutional provisions concerning the term of loans; these clauses are designed, for the most part, to restrict the term of each loan to the probable life of the improvement for which it is issued. Some states

---

[8] Ratchford, B. U., *American State Debts*, p. 584.
[9] Florida and Nevada.
[10] Arkansas, California, Illinois, Louisiana, New York, Pennsylvania.

go even further; the constitution of Maryland, for example, specifies that no indebtedness may be incurred for a longer period than fifteen years.

DESIRABLE RELATION TO LIFE OF IMPROVEMENT. Many students of public finance look with disfavor upon the widely accepted theory that the terms of loans should be related directly to the estimated life of improvements. Admitting that this test might be acceptable if each state were faced with the necessity of financing but one permanent improvement, they contend that it breaks down when applied to vast and varied construction programs. Total indebtedness, they point out, rises rapidly in peace years; interest charges become increasingly burdensome; and eventually the states may be confronted with such a mountain of debt that they will be almost compelled to repudiate their obligations. The only escape from this dilemma, therefore, is to pay off state debts as rapidly as possible, and well within the limit of the probable life of improvements. At the same time, attention should be given to the possibility of financing a considerable part of the construction program by means of taxes instead of relying solely on borrowing.

**Inclusion of call feature.** It is important that states issuing new bonds reserve the option of calling them at or slightly above par after an initial period of perhaps five years. More than half of the states failed to take advantage of this elementary principle during the era of heavy borrowing that followed the First World War, and as a result they found themselves saddled with long-term obligations on which they had agreed to pay interest of four or four and one-half per cent, while the interest rate on new issues was dropping steadily. By 1936 any state that had maintained sound credit could borrow at two and one-half per cent. So the states that had been sufficiently foresighted to include the call feature in their earlier bond issues simply floated new loans at the new low interest rates, and used the proceeds to pay off the older bonds. Thus they made substantial reductions in their interest charges, to the benefit of the taxpayers.

**Redemption of bonds.** When a state issues bonds it must make some provision for redeeming them at maturity. In the past the generally accepted method was to establish a sinking fund, paying into the fund each year from current revenue a sum which, together with earned interest, would be sufficient to meet the principal when it came due. But this plan has fallen into disfavor in recent years because of the difficulty of preventing political manipulations of the sinking fund. Neither constitutional limitations nor statutory restrictions seem to offer a sufficient guarantee that the fund will be honestly and efficiently administered. So sinking fund bonds are gradually disappearing, and serial bonds are taking their place. Under the serial bond plan there is no need for a fund. A certain number of the bonds mature each year, in equal or practically equal instalments, until at the end of the period they have all been paid off.

**Importance of a capital budget.** Students of government have long emphasized that state borrowing should follow some consistent plan, carefully considered and prepared well in advance. Budgeting is just as important for capital outlays as for operating expenditures. Therefore every state should prepare a capital budget, showing what permanent improvements it plans to make during the next six or eight years and how it proposes to finance them. This capital budget should be revised annually or biennially in order to keep it up to date, for modifications will be necessary regardless of the care with which the original plans are laid. No person or group of persons can say with absolute certainty what the needs of a state will be after six or eight years. No person or group of persons can foresee the changes that may be wrought by war or industrial depression or population movements. But everyone understands that modifications will be made from time to time. Every new legislature will insist upon the right to revise the plans of its predecessors. This fact does not lessen the importance of a capital budget. Without such a plan, borrowing is likely to be haphazard; with it, borrowing can be orderly. The proper place of any one bond issue in the whole fiscal picture can readily be understood. A number of the more progressive states fully realize the importance of long-term financial planning and have entrusted the task of preparing and maintaining capital budgets to their planning commissions or other agencies.

### SELECTED REFERENCES

Buehler, Alfred G., *Public Finance*, rev. ed., 1940.
Fowler, John F., *Revenue Bonds*, 1938.
Groves, Harold M., *Financing Government*, 1939.
Hansen, Alvin H., and Perloff, Harvey S., *State and Local Finance in the National Economy*, 1944.
Horton, Donald C., *Long-Term Debts in the United States*, Washington, D.C., 1937.
Knappen, Laurence S., *Revenue Bonds and the Investor*, 1939.
Lutz, H. L., *Public Finance*, 3rd ed., 1936.

McGrane, Reginald C., *Foreign Bondholders and American State Debts,* 1935.

Pfiffner, John M., *Public Administration,* Chap. XVI, 1935.

Porter, Kirk H., *State Administration,* Chap. VI, 1938.

Ratchford, B. U., *American State Debts,* Durham, N.C., 1941.

Raymond, Wm. L., *State and Municipal Bonds,* rev. ed., 1932.

Schultz, Wm. J., *American Public Finance,* 3rd ed., 1942.

Studensky, Paul, *Public Borrowing,* 1930.

Taber, Norman S., and Co., *Report on a Survey of the Highway Indebtedness of Texas,* 1937.

Tax Institute, *Wartime Problems of State and Local Finance,* 1943.

Thomson, Wood and Hoffman, *The Tax Exempt Status of State and Municipal Bonds,* 1937.

Trull, Edna, *Borrowing for Highways,* 1937.

———, *Resources and Debts of the Forty-Eight States, 1937,* 1937.

The federal Constitution forbids the states to keep troops without the consent of Congress.[1]  At the same time it recognizes the need for state militia forces of some sort, and authorizes Congress "to provide for organizing, arming, and disciplining the militia, . . . reserving to the States respectively, the appointment of officers, and the authority of training the militia according to the discipline prescribed by Congress."[2]

### THE NATIONAL GUARD

The federal government does not hesitate to use the full extent of its authority over state troops. It specifies the amount and kind of training that they are to receive, and details Regular Army personnel to act as instructors and report whether federal training standards are regularly maintained.  It fixes the size of each state's military force and even prescribes the units that must be maintained.  Thus the peacetime military organizations of some states include anti-aircraft, field artillery, and other units that round out the general scheme of national defense, though not needed to maintain order.  The federal government also passes upon the qualifications of state militia officers. It requires every member of the state militia, upon enlistment, to take an oath of allegiance to the United States.  Even the name of the state military forces indicates their essentially national character. Since 1916 they have been known as the *National Guard.*

**Training.**  Strictly speaking, the federal government does not compel any state to keep troops, or train them, or officer them with properly qualified persons.  It merely offers to bear most of the cost of maintaining the National Guard, and conditions this offer upon the acceptance of federal standards by the states.[3]  But every state long ago accepted the federal proposal and met federal requirements, so that all state troops bore the mark of federal standardization when they

[1] Art. I, Sec. 10, Cl. 3.
[2] Art. I, Sec. 8, Cl. 16.
[3] See pp. 36-40.

were called into the federal service during the period of hasty military preparation that preceded American entry into the Second World War. The president is not required to wait until war threatens, however, before calling upon the National Guard. He may do so in any national emergency. Several presidents have, in fact, found it necessary to make use of state troops in the enforcement of federal laws. Usually, however, the National Guard has been held in reserve; its periods of peacetime active duty, whether in federal or state service, have been infrequent. This has necessarily been so, because the National Guard was not an organization of professional soldiers. Instead it was composed almost entirely of civilians who merely devoted a few of their spare hours to the serious business of preparing for war. National Guard training comprised but forty-eight evening drills a year, plus fifteen days of intensive training at camp during the period of summer vacation. The pay was nominal.

**Its work during emergencies.** From time to time, however, the governors of the several states have called upon their National Guard troops to enforce the law. Most commonly these calls were for the preservation of order during industrial disputes. Troops were directed to protect private property and to prevent militant demonstrations by strikers. Sometimes they did this work very effectively; quite often, however, they only succeeded in provoking bloodshed. It must be remembered that the members of the National Guard were essentially amateurs; most of them had had very little military training and no military experience. In emergencies they could not be expected to act like seasoned veterans. If taunted almost beyond endurance by the strikers and their friends and then attacked without seeming justification, they might forget their orders to hold fire. And the strikers, already irritated by the sight of soldiers among their enemies, might lose all restraint at the spilling of blood. There have been many instances of sanguinary riots that would never have occurred in all probability but for the presence of National Guard troops. Then, too, strike duty requires an excessive amount of time—an amount that the officers and men, nearly all of whom were filling positions in the business or professional world, could ill afford to spare. It necessitates prompt action, but the National Guard was not organized to act promptly. Valuable time was lost while the necessary units were mobilized. Moreover, strike duty is scarcely a military function; it is more closely akin to the regular work of the police. It has been generally unpopular, and undoubtedly retarded National

Guard enlistments. The common hostility of labor to the National Guard movement can be traced directly to the assignment of state troops to strike duty.

Although state troops have been used chiefly for the protection of property and the preservation of order during industrial disputes, this has not been the full extent of their activity. They have commonly been called into service following any great calamity, such as flood, fire, hurricane, or earthquake. At such a time they have assisted in giving necessary first aid treatment, distributing food and medical supplies, constructing temporary shelters, and guarding private property. The more progressive National Guard organizations prepared comprehensive plans for the use of troops in time of disaster; these plans included special training of officers and men and also the collection of information for each locality concerning such important matters as sources of food, water, and fuel supply, location and bed capacity of hospitals, location and ownership of buildings suitable for housing the homeless, and areas available for establishment of tent camps. Other reasons for calling out the National Guard, less commendable than the relief of distress following serious calamities, have been noted in an earlier chapter.[4]

**Gubernatorial control.** Although the governor is the constitutional head of the state militia, he does not actually assume command of his forces, as did some governors in the early days of American history. Instead, he exercises control through an adjutant-general, who is directly responsible to him for the organization, training, and work of the state troops. The governor selects the adjutant-general, but his choice is narrowly restricted by the necessity of securing federal approval. Federal standards are high, and politically minded governors experience considerable difficulty in evading them.

**Size.** It has already been pointed out that the federal government fixes the size of the National Guard;[5] the combined total of officers and men in 1940, the last peacetime year, ranged from about two hundred and seventy-five in Nevada to more than twenty-one thousand in New York. Nearly half of the states had militia organizations of three thousand or more.[6] In October, 1940, the National Guard was called into the federal service, and, as previously indicated,[7] its place

4 See p. 214.
5 See p. 391.
6 Annual Report of the Chief of the National Guard Bureau, U.S. Department of War, 1941.
7 See p. 213.

was taken by State Guard units, composed largely of part-time volunteers.

## STATE POLICE FORCES

It is generally admitted that the National Guard is poorly fitted to enforce state law; it has been used for this purpose only in emergencies. Yet in most states it has been the only agency on which the governor —the chief executive, who has sworn to execute the laws faithfully— could rely for the general enforcement of the laws of the state. He might have fish and game wardens to enforce the statutes concerning fishing and hunting, or food and drug inspectors to supervise the sale of foodstuffs and medicines; but as a rule he had no permanent body of police officers regularly exercising general police authority on a state-wide scale.

There are, however, some exceptions. As early as 1865 a number of "state constables" were appointed in Massachusetts. Their chief duty was to suppress commercialized vice, but they were given the authority usually conferred upon police officers and their jurisdiction was state-wide. Thus they became the first state police force possessing general police powers.[8] Both the organization and functions of the Massachusetts force were altered from time to time until 1920, when it became part of a department of public safety combining police and fire protection, in addition to numerous inspectional duties. No state saw fit to follow the early lead of Massachusetts until 1903, when Connecticut established a small force—so small that regular patrols could not be established. In 1905 Pennsylvania created its state constabulary—an organization that was far more effective than the forces of Massachusetts or Connecticut. The New York department of state police, set up in 1917, was based on Pennsylvania's experience. Later in 1917 Michigan established a state police force. In 1919 the Texas Rangers, a border patrol established when Texas was an independent republic, were given police powers sufficiently broad to warrant their inclusion in the list. Then came West Virginia, also in 1919, New Jersey and Maryland in 1921,[9] Rhode Island in 1925, Maine in 1929,[10]

---

[8] Texas had previously established a state police organization known as the Rangers, but the Texas force was concerned almost entirely with border patrol.

[9] The Maryland force was established for purposes of highway patrol, and is still responsible to the commissioner of motor vehicles. The members of the force have been appointed as deputy sheriffs, however, by the sheriffs of the counties of the state, and thus they possess general powers of law enforcement.

[10] In 1929 the members of the Maine highway patrol force were given general authority to enforce the laws of the state.

Oregon in 1931, Arkansas in 1935, Louisiana in 1936, and New Hampshire in 1937. Thus fifteen states now have police organizations exercising state-wide jurisdiction and responsible for the enforcement of all state laws.

This list does not include the Colorado Rangers, an emergency force subsequently abolished; nor does it include the border patrols of Arizona and New Mexico, which have also ceased to function. It takes no account of the highway patrols that have been established in all the other states for the primary purpose of enforcing the motor vehicle laws. Most of these patrols have been empowered to enforce all criminal laws,[11] but they are not equipped to do a thorough job of general law enforcement, and in practice they limit themselves almost exclusively to traffic matters. Usually they are under the direct control of the head of the department or division of motor vehicles.

**Duties.** In the fifteen states that have set up comprehensive state police systems, the forces vary widely in size. Thus Rhode Island has only about sixty state police officers, while Pennsylvania has more than twelve hundred. There is also a great deal of variation in the duties assigned. The members of all the state forces in this group are expected to serve as general law enforcement officers, and for this purpose they are given the police powers regularly possessed by sheriffs, constables, and municipal police officers; but some states require in addition the performance of numerous special duties. Thus in New Jersey, New York, Pennsylvania, and West Virginia the state policemen are designated as fire, fish, and game wardens. State policemen in Connecticut examine applicants for motor vehicle operators' licenses. These special duties tend to multiply rapidly; in some states they have already become so numerous as to interfere with the normal routine of patrol work.

INDUSTRIAL DISPUTES. Although the protection of life and property during industrial disputes is merely an incidental function of the state police, it has caused a great deal of bitterness among the wage earners of the manufacturing and mining districts. The police have proved to be much more efficient than the National Guard when assigned to strike duty; of that there can be no doubt. But friends of labor contend that they are too efficient and too ruthless. The mem-

[11] There are, however, thirteen states that specifically limit their highway patrols to the enforcement of the traffic laws. These states are Arizona, California, Colorado, Florida, Mississippi, Montana, Nebraska, North Dakota, Ohio, South Carolina, Tennessee, Vermont, and Wisconsin.

bers of the Pennsylvania state constabulary have been dubbed the "American Cossacks," and in New York and West Virginia charges of brutality are frequently heard. In some states the opposition of organized labor has prevented the establishment of state police systems; in others it has led to restrictions on the use of the state police for strike duty. In New Jersey, for example, the state force may not act to suppress riot or disorder within the limits of a city unless the city's governing body calls upon the governor for assistance in preserving the peace. Massachusetts forbids its police to participate in industrial disputes unless violence has actually occurred, and then only by order of the governor. Other states have somewhat less stringent provisions. The advisability of such limitations is questionable. While they reduce the opposition of organized labor to state police systems, they also hamper a legitimate phase of police activity more or less seriously. No amount of sophistry can alter the fact that the state is responsible for the protection of life and property, and this responsibility does not vanish at the outbreak of a strike.

LAW ENFORCEMENT. The state police organization is generally regarded as an agency for the enforcement of state law in the rural districts. Law enforcement in the cities is primarily a task for the municipal police. There are times, however, when this distinction cannot be strictly maintained. A state patrolman has authority to make arrests within the limits of a city as well as beyond its boundaries, and when he is in hot pursuit of a criminal he is not likely to stop at the city line. Nor is it reasonable to expect him to do so. Yet care must be taken not to affront local pride, for the result may be the severance of friendly relationships between state and municipal authorities. If the local police find that the area within their jurisdiction is subject to "invasion" by state forces at frequent intervals, they are almost certain to show their resentment in the one way open to them—by refusing to co-operate in the detection of criminals. The state police must definitely subordinate themselves to the local police authorities when operating within the cities, or else be prepared to play a lone hand. Usually they accept the rôle of subordinates. Thus the state policeman who enters a city on business normally reports first at city headquarters, explains his errand, and requests local assistance. Even this precaution does not invariably eliminate friction, however; the state policeman may still be considered an outsider who has exceeded the proper scope of his authority. A great deal of tact is sometimes required to establish and maintain co-operation.

The police forces of a few states are sent into the larger cities without the consent or even the knowledge of the city authorities for the purpose of enforcing the laws against commercialized vice, but this practice has not been generally adopted.

**Organization:** THE SUPERINTENDENT. There is considerable variation in the organization of state police forces. Some states—Pennsylvania, New York, and Oregon, for example—vest control in a superintendent of police appointed by the governor and removable at his pleasure. Others, such as Connecticut, Michigan,[12] and West Virginia, rely on an administrative board to direct state police activities. The board selects the superintendent of police and usually insists on interfering with every detail of his work. Thus in Connecticut it exercises a veto over all appointments to the force and passes upon questions of discipline. Within the limits of the law it fixes police force salaries, and it also prescribes uniforms and equipment. The superintendent of state police serves in a distinctly subordinate capacity. The powers of the West Virginia board of police commissioners are somewhat more narrowly restricted, and as a result the superintendent is able to produce more satisfactory results.

THE DEPUTY SUPERINTENDENT. Just below the superintendent in the scheme of organization is usually a deputy superintendent—a second in command whose task is to relieve his superior of a great deal of burdensome administrative routine. In case of the absence or disability of the superintendent the deputy superintendent normally assumes active direction of the force; his selection is therefore a matter of considerable importance. Most of the states that have established comprehensive police systems permit the superintendent to choose the deputy—in some cases, with the consent of the police board; in others, without consulting anyone. But a few states, notably Michigan, Oregon, and West Virginia, consider the deputy superintendent so important that they give the governor a voice in his selection.

HEADQUARTERS AND SUBSTATIONS. The state police force is divided into troops or companies. Each troop has its permanent headquarters and is usually assigned to the protection of a definite area. Within the troop area substations are established; these substations may be temporary or permanent. The advantage of temporary substations is that they may be moved from time to time to permit adequate patrol of all sections of the state, and also to facilitate concentration of state

---

12 The Michigan board is responsible for fire protection and inspection as well as police inspection.

troops at any spot where trouble is anticipated. Such substations are commonly located in private homes, boarding houses, or small hotels. When permanent substations are used, the troops are housed in buildings owned by the state; therefore the men are less likely to become unduly familiar with any one group of persons, and less likely to display favoritism in the enforcement of the law. On the other hand, they must of necessity neglect the more remote sections unless the force is very large or the state very small. Reserves, if any, are quartered at the main troop stations. Patrol of the rural sections is the regular work of the rank and file of the force. In some states the men are assigned to definite routes that they must follow according to a prescribed time schedule; more commonly, however, they are permitted considerable discretion as to the exact roads to be covered and the time to be spent in each community. Their work has been greatly facilitated in recent years by the equipment of patrol cars with radio facilities.

TRAINING. The amount of training provided for new recruits is far from uniform. Some states have established regular police schools, where new members of the state force are given systematic instruction for a period of weeks or even months. In other states the men receive only a little superficial training and are then assigned to patrol duty, in the hope that experience will soon teach them the things they ought to know. New York assigns recruits to regular patrol almost from the very beginning, but always in the company of experienced policemen. After several months of this probationary work the men who have proved their ability to fill regular positions on the force are sent to the state police school for highly intensive instruction.

## MUNICIPAL POLICE

**Agents of the state.** The police forces of the cities are primarily agencies for the enforcement of state law. They are concerned also with municipal ordinances and regulations, but the enforcement of state statutes is their most important task. Every serious crime is defined by state law; [13] every professional criminal deliberately challenges the state's supremacy. Quite naturally, therefore, the courts declare that municipal policemen are agents of the state.

BUT UNDER MUNICIPAL CONTROL. This doctrine has been affirmed

---

[13] Excepting, of course, those acts that are solely offenses against the federal government.

in case after case.   In Buttrick *v.* City of Lowell [14] the supreme court
of Massachusetts stated in part: "Police officers can in no sense be regarded as agents or servants of the city.   Their duties are of a public
nature . . . The detection and arrest of offenders, the preservation
of the public peace, the enforcement of the law, and other similar powers and duties with which police officers and constables are intrusted,
are derived from the law, and not from the city or town under which
they hold appointment."   Yet all the judicial decisions combined do
not provide the governor or any other state officer with the means of
controlling local police forces.   City policemen are agents of the state,
of course, but they are locally chosen, locally paid, locally disciplined,
and subject to local dismissal.   Therefore they take orders only from
their locally selected superiors, and give no heed to state policy.   They
enforce those state laws that meet with local approval, and disregard
other laws that are locally unpopular.   In a sense, therefore, municipal control of municipal police forces gives to the cities a certain
amount of self-government.   It enables them to veto quite effectively
any act of the state legislature that meets with local disfavor.   Sunday-
closing and anti-liquor laws illustrate this tendency; placed on the
statute books by farm-controlled assemblies, they are seldom effectively
enforced in the metropolitan centers.

  **Trial of state control.**   During the second half of the nineteenth
century it became fashionable to transfer the control of urban police
forces from municipal to state agencies.   New York set an example
for other states in 1857, when it created a metropolitan police district
comprising New York City and surrounding territory and gave to the
governor the power to appoint the members of the metropolitan police
board.   During the next two decades a number of other states followed suit.   Most of these changes were made at the insistent demand
of prominent citizens of the communities affected.   Locally controlled
police departments had quite generally become corrupt and inefficient, and there was a widespread belief that state control would speedily remedy this condition of affairs.   Unfortunately, however, the
belief proved ill-founded.   The police forces remained substantially
unchanged, and gradually the people of the cities awoke to the unhappy realization that corruption and inefficiency were not solely
urban products.   State officials were quite as likely as municipal
office-holders to deviate from the narrow path of wisdom or virtue.
And they were even more likely to disregard local sentiment, because

---

[14] 1 Allen (Mass.) 172 (1861).

they owed no allegiance to the people of the cities whose police forces they directed. Their responsibility was solely to the governor of the state.

After a time, therefore, the prominent citizens who had previously urged state control of the police as a remedy for civic ills began to demand that control be returned to the cities. Local self-government became the immediate goal, and as a result of this movement the states relinquished their authority over municipal police forces. State control was retained, and has continued to the present day, in only a few cities—Boston, Baltimore, and St. Louis. To the list of municipal police forces under state jurisdiction, however, must be added the police force of Providence, which was placed under a state board in 1931.

## THE SHERIFF

**His duties.** The peace officer of the county is the sheriff, whose office dates from Anglo-Saxon times. In those early days the "shire-reeve"—the presiding officer of the shire or county—was a very important person. He was the governor of the shire, the military commander of its troops, and the president of its court. But the passing years have witnessed a constant reduction of the English sheriff's powers, until at the present time the office is of very little consequence. In the United States, however, no such change has occurred. In fact, the sheriff has managed to retain most of his early powers. Not only does he conserve the peace of the county, but in addition he commonly serves court processes and writs, and executes court decrees. He is the keeper of the county jail and sometimes the executioner.

**His payment from fees:** PROCESS SERVING. As a rule he performs all these functions very badly. His time and energy are devoted mostly to serving processes and managing the jail instead of conserving the peace, because the profit is greater. The sheriff is paid on a fee basis in almost all jurisdictions—fifty or seventy-five cents, or some other fixed amount, for every court process served. So he employs his own deputies and pays them out of his earnings. He buys the automobiles needed for the work, and keeps them in running order; they are his personal property. From the county treasury he then collects his fees, and the net profit is his reward. It is a reward well worth fighting for, especially in a county with a large urban population. In such a county the sheriff's income may exceed forty or fifty thousand dollars a year after all expenses are paid.

COUNTY JAIL MANAGEMENT. A considerable part of the income of the sheriff is derived from the management of the county jail. He is allowed a certain amount for feeding the inmates; fifty or sixty cents a day for each prisoner is quite common. Since this sum is constant, regardless of the amount actually spent, it is to the interest of the sheriff to spend as little as possible for the prisoners' food. Some sheriffs have experimented with the near-starvation of jail inmates until they know exactly the minimum amount of food on which it is possible to sustain human life. They find that this minimum can be purchased for eight or ten cents a day and act accordingly. The remainder of their allowance is clear profit. In some states it is customary to permit the sheriff to sell "luxuries" to the prisoners, either directly or through concessionaires. These luxuries often consist in large measure of food that should properly be a part of the regular daily ration. The sheriff knows from experience, however, that by starving the inmates sufficiently he can induce those with funds to purchase the so-called luxuries that they actually need; thus he reaps a further gain.

LAW ENFORCEMENT. As previously suggested, the sheriff's duty to enforce the law pales into insignificance when contrasted with the highly profitable functions of jail tending and process serving. Then, too, law enforcement is a much more dangerous undertaking. So the average sheriff spends very little time apprehending criminals and justifies this neglect of duty on the ground that he cannot afford to do otherwise. He argues that the pursuit and arrest of a thief yield only an arrest fee of seventy-five cents or one dollar and that he can earn this sum much more easily and safely by serving a jury summons or a warrant. The fee system that makes possible these abuses has never been successfully defended. It is an outworn relic of another day, and continues in vogue, even on a limited scale, only because it suits the questionable purposes of the professional politicians.

**Conflict with municipal police.** An American city normally lies within the boundaries of a county.[15] Thus we commonly have two independent agencies charged with the duty of maintaining municipal peace and order—the municipal police force, which operates solely within the city's boundaries, and the sheriff, whose jurisdiction extends throughout the entire county, including both urban and rural areas. A possibility of conflict thus exists. In ordinary routine

---

[15] There are a few exceptions. The area of New York City is so great that it embraces several counties. Philadelphia is a combined city and county; so are San Francisco, St. Louis, Denver, and New Orleans.

police work this danger is not serious, however, because of the sheriff's tendency to abandon almost completely his function of crime repression. But occasionally, when an especially atrocious or spectacular crime attracts popular attention, a publicity-loving sheriff may seize the opportunity to play a dramatic part in the investigation that follows. His activities may hamper the police most seriously, but no one can deny that he is acting within his legal rights. Apparently the best way to overcome this difficulty is to provide by law that the sheriff may not act as a conservator of the peace within the boundaries of a municipality unless at the request of the municipal authorities.

**His selection.** The sheriff is an elective officer almost everywhere,[16] for no good reason save that election is the traditional method of choice. Usually the constitution or statutes of the state prohibit him from serving two consecutive terms, so that he cannot possibly hope to acquire a complete understanding of the tasks entrusted to his care. He is an amateur—not a professional; and the provision that he may not succeed himself is a sure way to preserve his amateur status. If this limitation were removed, if the method of choice were altered from election by the people to appointment by the governor, and if in addition the fee system should be discarded, there would be a considerably greater likelihood of securing men with wide experience in police administration to serve as sheriffs of American counties. Some students of the problem contend, however, that even these drastic changes would not be sufficient to fit the sheriff's office to modern conditions and present-day needs. They urge that the office be abolished, and its functions transferred to other agencies—process serving and jail management to court officers and law enforcement to the state police.

### THE PUBLIC PROSECUTOR

**His selection.** The public prosecutor—prosecuting attorney, district attorney, state's attorney, or whatever he may be called—is a very important figure in the general scheme of law enforcement. Usually he serves a single county, but this is not invariably the case. A few states combine their counties into districts, with one prosecutor for each district. Nearly everywhere the public prosecutors are popularly chosen. They are selected by the governor in four states,[17] how-

---

16 Rhode Island is the only exception.
17 Alabama, Florida, Georgia, New Mexico.

ever, and by the judges of the superior court in one.[18]   Their terms
of office range from two to six years; four-year terms are most common.

**His authority in criminal proceedings.**   The importance of the
prosecuting attorney arises from the powerful influence that he is
able to exert over the entire course of criminal proceedings.   At
every step in the conduct of a case, from the preliminary search for
clues to the conviction of the accused person, the public prosecutor
plays a leading rôle.   To some extent he derives his authority from
statute, but more largely he relies on custom.   The people look to
him for results in the unending war of society on crime, and, if he
produces results they are not likely to ask whether he has stayed within
the exact legal limit of his powers.   Thus the prosecutor constantly
faces the temptation to exceed the authority delegated to him by law,
and very frequently he succumbs.   This tendency is quite marked
in the field of criminal investigation.   The police are supposed to
conduct the inquiry following a crime; they are responsible for locat-
ing witnesses, accumulating evidence, and apprehending the person
to be accused.   Until their task is accomplished the prosecutor is
intended to be merely a gentleman-in-waiting.   But the average
prosecutor does not accept this view of his duties.   Lacking formal
authority, he nevertheless tends to dominate the police investigation
from its inception.   He forces his leadership upon the police department—chiefly by means of the party organization and the party press.

INFLUENCE WITH THE GRAND JURY.   Even more pronounced is
the prosecuting attorney's influence on the grand jury, a body
of persons chosen by lot and ranging in number from seven
to twenty-three.   Unlike the petit or trial jury, a grand jury does
not decide the innocence or guilt of persons accused of crime.
Instead, it merely determines whether there is sufficient evidence
against suspects to warrant holding them for trial.   Its presentation
of formal charges is known as *indictment;* persons who have been in-
dicted must then stand trial for the crimes of which they have been
accused.   A unanimous verdict is not necessary to indict.   Since the
grand jury is picked at random, and is composed of men and women
who presumably know little of the law or of the science of criminal
investigation, it is poorly fitted to perform its allotted task.   It has
no facilities for obtaining important facts on its own initiative, no
knowledge of the names or whereabouts of witnesses, no ready way of

[18] Connecticut.

separating the true from the false. Therefore it is virtually compelled to rely on the prosecutor for its facts, witnesses, and opinions. His attitude nearly always determines what action the grand jury will take, for he is in a position to suppress vital evidence—either favorable or unfavorable to the accused; to summon witnesses or neglect to do so; to tell the whole story or only a part. The exact nature of this arbitrary power can be understood more clearly if it is realized that grand jury proceedings are secret and wholly onesided. The suspect does not normally appear, either in person or by proxy, because he has not yet been formally accused of crime.

ACCUSATION BY FILING AN INFORMATION. Some persons, fearful lest the prosecutor use his authority to gain personal or partisan ends, have proposed that the grand jury be strengthened and developed into a more effective instrument for the determination of probable guilt. They have tried to find ways of freeing it from the prosecutor's overpowering influence. Their efforts have met with no success, however. In fact, the present trend seems to be toward the further expansion of the powers of the prosecuting attorney and the virtual abandonment of the grand jury system in ordinary criminal prosecutions. More than half of the states now specify that prosecution may be by *information* instead of indictment, at least for some offenses, and in a number of these states the grand jury is never called except by an occasional court order. Information is the presentation of formal charges by a prosecuting attorney against a person suspected of crime; these charges are filed in a court of competent jurisdiction and have exactly the same effect as indictment. The person informed against must stand trial for the crime of which he is accused. This procedure thus places responsibility squarely on the shoulders of the prosecutor.

It has proved quite satisfactory in those states that have given it the most thorough trial. By saving time and money and eliminating unnecessary technicalities it has demonstrated its superiority over the older method of fact-finding by amateurs. The mistake must not be made, however, of assuming that the grand jury has entirely outlived its usefulness. Though unsuited to the ordinary routine of separating the obviously innocent from the probably guilty, it may still prove at times an eminently satisfactory agency for investigating the alleged inefficiency, neglect, or dishonesty of public officials.

REFUSAL TO PROSECUTE. An important source of the prosecutor's influence is his power to refuse to proceed with the prosecution of a criminal case. Since prosecution is commonly the result of an information that he has filed or of a grand jury indictment that he has recommended, he is not likely to take this step. But occasionally the discovery of new facts or the pressure of influential politicians may cause the prosecutor to experience a change of heart. Thereupon he enters a *nolle prosequi* or notice that he does not intend to prosecute; this he may do before or after the trial has begun. The court is free, technically, to proceed with the case even after the prosecutor's support has been withdrawn, but the probability that it will do so is very remote.

NEGOTIATIONS WITH ACCUSED. The public prosecutor frequently bargains with persons accused of crime. He may, for example, agree not to prosecute one member of a gang in return for a full confession that can be used against the other members. He may accept a plea of guilty to a crime carrying a lighter penalty than that charged in the information or indictment in order to be certain of securing a conviction. He may even enter into informal agreements for more personal reasons if he chances to be unscrupulous. The law makes no provision for bargaining of any sort with criminals, regardless of additional evidence or additional convictions that may be obtained; but public prosecutors do not wait for express authorization. They regard the power of negotiation as one of the most important weapons in the arsenal of crime prevention, and they use it freely. That it is subject to abuse does not disturb them in the least.

When the trial of an accused person ends in conviction, the judge then pronounces sentence. In so doing he may impose whatever penalty, within the limits of the law, that seems to him best suited to the circumstances. He may even suspend sentence, in many instances, and place the convicted person on probation. His decision as to the proper measure of punishment is final, except for the possibility of appealing certain cases to the higher courts. In practice, however, a judge does not usually rely solely on his own opinion, but turns to the prosecuting attorney for guidance, for he knows that the prosecutor or one of his assistants is supposed to have studied each case carefully and should be in possession of all the facts. Thus the power of the prosecutor is still further increased.

CONFLICT IN PROTECTION OF THE INNOCENT. It is a maxim of the law that the prosecutor's duty is to ascertain the truth in every case that comes within his jurisdiction. He is legally responsible for the protection of the accused, and it is his task to make certain that no unfairness is practiced. Therefore the acquittal of the innocent should be his goal quite as much as the conviction of the guilty. But legal maxims cannot alter the plain fact that the prosecutor is *not* the protector of the innocent, except at rare intervals and under unusual circumstances. His success or failure is measured in terms of convictions, and every ambitious prosecutor sets out to secure as many convictions as possible. To save from prison those who are falsely accused is noble, but not likely to lead to political preferment.

### THE PUBLIC DEFENDER

Some persons, convinced that the prosecutor's office can never be transformed into an agency for the protection of the rights of the accused as long as it performs its primary function of trying to secure convictions, urge that a separate office be established in every county or district for the defense of persons held on criminal charges. This plan has already been adopted by a number of cities and counties throughout the United States, including Los Angeles County, San Francisco, St. Louis, Indianapolis, Omaha, Columbus, Portland (Oregon), Cook County (which includes Chicago), Minneapolis, New Haven, and Bridgeport. The public defender, as the head of this office is called, ranks equally with the prosecutor. The facilities of the state are at his disposal for the purpose of proving men innocent, just as they are at the disposal of the prosecutor for the purpose of proving men guilty. Thus many of the abuses common to criminal trials are curtailed, and every person is given a reasonable assurance of fair treatment.

**Weakness of assigned counsel system.** In those jurisdictions—the overwhelming majority—that have not provided for public defenders, it is customary for the court to assign counsel to the defense of poor people who cannot afford to hire the attorneys they need. This plan is practically worthless, however, because the fees paid from the public treasury for the defense of accused persons are so small as to attract only recent law school graduates who are badly in need of experience and shyster lawyers who hope to augment the regular compensation by means of various unsavory tricks. A number of states make no provision for the payment of counsel assigned to the defense. The weaknesses of the assigned counsel system are of no consequence to the professional criminals, who can usually afford to pay for the best legal talent; nor do they trouble the wealthy, whether innocent or guilty. But they have serious consequences for the poor man accused of crime.

## THE CORONER

**His duties.** The office of coroner is also a part of the machinery of law enforcement, and therefore deserves mention at this point. The coroner is a county officer, elected by the people in most states, and virtually free from state supervision. His task is to investigate cases of violent death and to hold inquests to determine how death occurred. Customarily every case of sudden death unattended by a physician also comes within his jurisdiction, even if violence is not suspected. The coroner is empowered to call a jury whenever the circumstances surrounding a death are unusual, and this so-called *coroner's jury,* which is usually composed of six persons chosen at random, then makes the decision as to the cause of death. In some jurisdictions coroners' juries are frequently sworn in; in others they are used scarcely at all.

In the entire structure of American government—federal, state, and local—there is probably no officer who is more poorly qualified than the coroner to perform his assigned duties. There are some outstanding exceptions, of course, but the average coroner is a political worker who has been rewarded in this manner for long years of amenability to party discipline. Sometimes he is an undertaker with strong political connections; this arrangement is epecially undesirable from the standpoint of the public because of the business advantages that accrue from office-holding under such circumstances. Almost invariably the coroner lacks the requisite specialized medical and legal training.

HIS LACK OF QUALIFICATIONS. His methods are the layman's methods—crude, blundering, ineffective. Yet there is probably no phase of governmental activity that requires greater knowledge or skill in order to produce satisfactory results. Accurate determination of the causes of death is extremely difficult in many cases; it calls for highly specialized information and a carefully developed technique. The specialist in this field should have a comprehensive knowledge of medicine, surgery and law. He should be familiar with firearms and with the exact effect of bullets on the human body, and should be able to recognize powder marks and burns. He should understand the methods employed in testing stains made by blood, semen, and other substances. A practical knowledge of botany is essential to the proper performance of his work, for he must at times examine dust and other foreign matter upon the clothing of suspects, and must also examine the contents of the intestines for particles of food. He should know as much as possible about poisons. On the legal side he should have at least a clear understanding of the rules of evidence. To ask an elected coroner to meet all these requirements is virtually to ask the impossible.

In some counties it is customary to have one or more physicians attached to the coroner's staff. While the degree of M.D. does not necessarily imply a knowledge of all the specialized subjects that fall within the province of the coroner, it assures a technical training that is of considerable value. A physician on the staff of the coroner can usually make the inquest less of a guessing contest and more of a scientific inquiry. But if the physician is politically appointed, as is often the case, he is likely to take his responsibilities rather lightly.

**Steps to eliminate weakness.** A few states, impressed with the weaknesses of the coroner system, have abandoned it altogether. In place of the coroner's office they have established the office of medical examiner and vested it with responsibility for determining the causes of death. Massachusetts took this step in 1877. The law passed in that year provided that the governor should appoint as medical examiners in the several counties of the state "able and discreet men learned in the science of medicine." The judicial functions formerly performed by the coroner were transferred to the district attorney, and the coroner's jury was abolished. Subsequently Maine and New Hampshire followed Massachusetts' example; New York City has had an appointive medical examiner since 1915. A number of other states, though retaining the office of coroner, have tried to strengthen it by abolishing the coroner's jury, as in Indiana, or by specifying that the coroner must be a physician, as in Louisiana.

## THE STATE FIRE MARSHAL

Thirty-four states have state fire marshals or officers with similar titles. The functions of the fire marshal, which vary somewhat from state to state, commonly relate to the prevention of fire and the enforcement of the state's fire laws. Every serious fire—other than a forest fire—is investigated, and an attempt made to determine its cause. Fires that bear evidence of incendiary origin are studied with especial care for the purpose of finding clues that may lead to the guilty persons. The fire marshal also enforces the laws of the state concerning the storage, sale, and use of combustibles and explosives, and in many states he examines buildings to make certain that they are provided with proper exits and fire escapes and contain no prohibited fire hazards. Educational campaigns designed to reduce the fire loss are commonly directed by the fire marshal; he supervises the systematic instruction of school children in ways of preventing fire and also appeals to the adult population by means of such devices as "Fire Prevention Week." Forest fire protection lies beyond his jurisdiction, and is commonly assigned to the state forester.[19] Generally speaking, the fire marshal operates in the smaller cities and the rural districts, since there is no reason to duplicate the educational and inspectional activities of the metropolitan fire departments.

## SELECTED REFERENCES

Beckwith, Edmund R., and Others, *Lawful Action of State Military Forces*, 1944.

Chadbourn, J. H., *Lynching and the Law*, Chapel Hill, N.C., 1933.

Fairlie, John A., and Kneier, Charles M., *County Government and Administration*, Chap. XIII, 1930.

Heiges, R. E., *The Office of Sheriff in the Rural Counties of Ohio*, Findlay, 1933.

Heinberg, J. G., and Breckenridge, A. C., *Law Enforcement in Missouri; a Decade of Centralization and Central Control in Apprehension and Prosecution, 1931–1941*, Columbia, 1942.

International Association of Chiefs of Police, Committee on Uniform Crime Records, *Uniform Crime Reporting*, rev. ed., [c.1929].

Monroe, David G., *State and Provincial Police*, Evanston, Ill., 1941.

National Commission on Law Observance and Enforcement, Report No. 4, *Prosecution*, Washington, D.C., 1931.

———, Report No. 11, *Lawlessness in Law Enforcement*, Washington, D.C., 1931.

Olander, Oscar G., *Michigan State Police; a Twenty-Five Year History*, Lansing, 1942.

Porter, Kirk H., *State Administration*, Chap. IV, 1938.

Schultz, Oscar T., and Morgan, E. M., *The Coroner and the Medical Examiner*, National Research Council Bulletin, Washington, D.C., 1928.

Smith, Bruce, *Rural Crime Control*, 1933.

Vollmer, August, and Parker, A. E., *Crime and the State Police*, Berkeley, Cal., 1935.

Wood, Sterling, *Riot Control by the National Guard*, Harrisburg, Pa., 1940.

19 See pp. 520–521.

# Chapter Twenty-One  CORRECTION

THE treatment of criminals—those who have violated the rules that society regards as essential for its protection—is one of the most perplexing problems of state administration. The difficulties arise chiefly from the fact that the causes of crime are shrouded in uncertainty. Certain mental, physical, and environmental stimuli predispose men to anti-social conduct; that much is definitely known. Yet many persons who are subjected to those stimuli remain law-abiding citizens. Why, then, do men become criminals? And, lacking a definite answer to that question, how can criminal tendencies be corrected? How is it possible to transform lawbreakers into properly behaved members of society without a knowledge of the reasons for their criminal behavior?

## CAUSES OF CRIME

It must be confessed that most state officials are not greatly concerned with these questions. Their philosophy is simple: Man has a free will and is capable of telling right from wrong. If he elects to do wrong instead of right, he must be punished for his obstinacy and his refusal to respect the rules of the established social order. Punishment will doubtless make him realize the error of his ways and may deter others from following his example. Therefore the only function of penology is to determine the punishment best suited to each crime—having due regard, of course, for the best interests of society.

Unfortunately, crime is not so simple and obvious a problem, nor is a satisfactory solution so readily achieved. The doctrine of free will, which is the sole justification of punishment for crime, has long since been discarded by careful students. It was seriously questioned as long ago as the fourth century, though the discussion at that early date centered around ecclesiastical matters. And in recent years a large number of scholarly investigations have established man's utter dependence on his physical equipment and his environment. He may choose to steal rather than to work, but *why* does he make this choice? Perhaps physical or mental defects dull or warp his intellect and give him a false sense of values; perhaps he comes from a home where stealing has been considered a proper way to make a living. Certainly the problem cannot be dismissed with the assertion that the man is wicked. That is merely a re-statement of the case, and not an answer.

Even climatic conditions have a bearing on crime. In warm countries, and during the warmer months in all countries, crimes against the person attain a relatively high rate. Crimes against property, on the other hand, seem to be related to cold. Barometric pressure, humidity, wind velocity—all these things apparently influence human conduct and partly determine the amount of criminality. Just why these relationships exist is still an unsolved problem. But no one can doubt that man is profoundly affected by forces over which he, as an individual, has little or no control.

To list the more important factors involved in criminality is a simple matter. To determine their relative significance in the case of an individual criminal, however, is often virtually impossible. Physiological, mental, social, and economic factors may be so blended that they can scarcely be unraveled. Here, for example, is a man arrested for stealing a watch. Investigation reveals that he pawned the watch and bought food for his family. Since he has been out of work for some months, the cause of his conduct seems clear. But further inquiry may show that he has been without a job because of his inability to remain sober for more than two weeks at a time and that he has stolen on previous occasions. It may bring to light his childhood in a degenerate home, his early contacts with professional criminals, his lack of education. Careful tests may reveal a poor physique and the mental intelligence of a nine-year-old child. Glandular activity may be abnormal. What, then, is the cause of this man's criminality? To ask this question is to suggest the impossibility of a clear-cut answer.

It is obvious, however, that any serious attempt to understand crime and to remove its basic causes must begin by discarding the theory of moral responsibility. Man is not the master of his fate and the captain of his soul—the poet to the contrary notwithstanding; he is the creature of internal and external forces that mold his destiny. It is necessary, therefore, to know what these forces are and how they affect human conduct. Only by controlling them can crime be reduced to a minimum, and criminology be made a fairly exact science.

**Physical and mental factors.** First to be considered as the causes of criminal acts are the physical and mental factors. Is it true that certain physical and mental characteristics predispose men to crime and require only the proper set of circumstances to produce actual criminality?   Some of the earlier criminologists contended that virtually all criminals were radically different from normal men and women—that they were atavistic beings with the ferocious instincts of wild beasts.   Cesare Lombroso, the noted Italian whose great work, *L'Uomo delinquente,* appeared in 1875, pictured the criminal as a half-animal with "enormous jaws, high cheek-bones, prominent superciliary arches, solitary lines in the palms, extreme size of the orbits, handle-shaped or sessile ears found in . . . savages and apes, insensibility to pain, extremely acute sight, tattooing, excessive idleness, love of orgies, and the irresistible craving for evil for its own sake, the desire not only to extinguish life in the victim, but to mutilate the corpse, tear its flesh, and drink its blood." [1]   That Lombroso overstated his case is evident.   Many of his theories have since proved untenable. But he performed a valuable service by calling attention to the physical factors involved in criminality.

Physical defects, such as poor teeth, poor eyesight, or poor hearing, tend to prevent normal reactions.   Almost every form of bodily weakness or disease likewise tends to impair the normal functioning of body and mind.   Abnormal conduct may result, and under certain circumstances that conduct may assume a form that we call criminal. Physical deformities, especially, seem to bear a logical relationship to crime.   They are a serious handicap in the struggle for a living; in addition, they may fill the mind with bitter thoughts.   One investigator, studying the problem of juvenile delinquency, observes: "The frequency among juvenile delinquents of bodily weakness and ill health has been remarked by every recent writer.   In my own series of cases, nearly seventy per cent were suffering from such defects and nearly fifty per cent were in urgent need of medical treatment. In London I find that defective physical conditions are, roughly speaking, one and one-fourth times as frequent among delinquent children as they are among nondelinquent children from the same school and street." [2]   Other students, however, are less certain of a definite relationship between poor health and criminality.   Some of them offer evidence that, in their judgment, "may be fairly utilized as negating certain older ideas that delinquents and criminals were the malnourished, the underdeveloped members of society, exhibiting thus the

[1] Introduction by Cesare Lombroso to Guglielmo Ferrero's *Lombroso's Criminal Man,* p. xiv.

[2] Burt, Cyril, *The Young Delinquent,* p. 239.

effects of poverty. Rather the charts show surprisingly good conditions of development and nutrition for a very large share of our cases." [3] In view of such conflicting evidence it is impossible to form definite conclusions. Poor health undoubtedly produces delinquency and criminality in certain cases, but it cannot be regarded as a specific cause of crime unless it leads naturally, in most instances, to criminal conduct.

Mental defects of every description, from feeble-mindedness to insanity, and including all sorts of border-line neurotic conditions, are closely related to criminality. Some writers, after exhaustive investigations, have declared their belief that at least fifty per cent of all criminals are mentally defective. [4] This estimate may be entirely too high. It "is very far from the truth," declares Dr. East, [5] after making a comprehensive survey of four thousand male adolescents. Some students even regard the criminal group as of superior intelligence. [6] But no one can doubt that feeble-mindedness is a contributing factor in hundreds of thousands of cases of delinquency and criminality. Mental aberrations also play an important part.

Still more closely related to crime, in the judgment of many criminologists, are glandular disturbances. Two enthusiastic converts to this theory declare their belief that "the vast majority of all criminals, misdemeanants, mental deficients, and defectives are the products of bodily disorders, that most crimes come about through disturbances of the ductless glands in the criminal or through mental defects caused by endocrine troubles in the criminal's mother. . . . Criminal actions are in reality reactions caused by the disturbed internal chemistry of the body." [7] And it must be admitted that there is a wealth of evidence to prove the connection between glandular disorders and criminality. In many cases the professional murderer, though of average or even superior intelligence, is found to be an emotional defective of the interstitial-suprarenal group. The woman thief is often the victim of periodic glandular disturbances. The sex pervert probably suffers from excessive glandular activity. Thus it becomes clear that

---

[3] Healy and Bronner's *Delinquents and Criminals*, p. 132. An excellent discussion of the physiological factors involved in criminality may be found in Report No. 13 of the National Commission on Law Observance and Enforcement (*Report on the Causes of Crime*), Vol. I, Chap. II.

[4] See, for example, Henry H. Goddard's *Feeble-Mindedness, Its Causes and Consequences*, p. 9.

[5] East, W. Norwood, *The Adolescent Criminal*, p. 209.

[6] See, for example, Carl A. Murchison's *American White Criminal Intelligence*.

[7] Schlapp and Smith's *The New Criminology*, pp. 28–29.

the difference between vice and virtue—between criminality and good citizenship—may be nothing more than a difference in internal chemistry. "The diffident, the gentle, the unselfish, the refined, and the sensitive are creatures not of the will but the helpless mechanical products of inner secretion; . . . the insatiable and irrepressible adventurers and conquerors of the earth are nothing more; . . . cowardice and courage, dullness and genius, sloth and aspiration are alike only chemical sublimates." [8]

**Social and economic factors.** But it would be a mistake to explain the commission of criminal acts solely in terms of physiological and mental forces operating within the individual. These forces merely produce tendencies; whether the tendencies will develop into criminal activity depends upon dozens of environmental factors, such as training, home life, companions, recreational opportunities. Therefore any well-rounded consideration of the factors involved in criminality must include a discussion of the chief social and economic forces.

Home life is extremely important; perhaps it should be placed first on the list. Careful investigations now furnish a scientific basis for the long-established belief that criminals are often the product of broken, deserted, or disgraced homes, of homes overshadowed by neglect, jealousy, favoritism, or clashes of parental authority, of homes where the father is out of work or the mother is forced to work out, and the total family income is insufficient to purchase the barest necessities. Children from such homes drift quite naturally into careers of crime. Denied the opportunity of normal companionship and recreation, they become members of neighborhood gangs, and soon become proficient at the fascinating game of petit larceny. From their fellows they learn that the world owes them a living; that they need not work, if they are smart enough to steal without detection; that the police are their natural enemies—men to be hated as well as feared. They know only one commandment—*Thou shalt not get caught!* And if they prove apt pupils in this school of experience, finally graduating into the ranks of the professional thugs and assassins, society sits in solemn judgment and declares that they are wicked. It would be nearer the truth to say that they are the victims of a bad environment —remembering, of course, that defective heredity may also be partly to blame.

An inadequate education may likewise be a factor in the social process by which criminals are made. Lack of suitable recreational

[8] Schlapp and Smith, *op. cit.*, p. 99.

facilities may play a part. The inability of many of the foreign-born to adjust themselves readily to American habits and customs may lead to conduct that is contrary to the criminal laws of the state—and therefore "criminal" in the dictionary sense of the word, even though there is no intent to do wrong. For many years criminologists and other students of social phenomena accepted as axiomatic the oft-repeated assertion that the foreign-born contributed more than their share to the nation's crime record. Recent studies indicate, however, that the foreign-born actually commit considerably fewer crimes, in proportion to their numbers, than the native-born. There is some reason to think that the native-born children of foreign parents drift more readily into careers of crime, but on this point the evidence is inconclusive. All that can be said is that such children are commonly exposed to many undesirable influences that might readily produce a high rate of criminality.[9]

The records of the penitentiaries seem to indicate a rather close relationship between poverty and crime. It has been suggested that this relationship is more apparent than real—that poor people accused of crime go to jail because they have no powerful friends and no money to purchase the protection of competent attorneys, whereas rich men and women remain at liberty by hiring the best legal talent, or even by purchasing "immunity" if necessity warrants and opportunity offers. Unquestionably this suggestion contains a considerable measure of truth. The poor are at a serious disadvantage under the American system of judicial administration. But it is equally true that poverty provides an incentive to certain kinds of criminality—theft, for example—that would otherwise be lacking. And every prolonged period of depression finds the unemployed swelling the ranks of the prison population.[10] So marked is this phenomenon that it can scarcely be dismissed as merely an evidence of the inequality of the law.

## TREATMENT OF CRIMINALS

**Reasons for imprisonment.** REVENGE. From this discussion of the elements involved in criminality one fact stands out in bold relief: criminals are the helpless and hapless product of mighty forces. Viewed in this light, the folly of punishing lawbreakers becomes apparent. It is no more logical, wise, or fair to seek revenge upon those

[9] See Report No. 10 of the National Commission on Law Observance and Enforcement, *Crime and the Foreign Born.*
[10] *The Causes of Crime* (Vol. I), p. 217.

who have violated the rules of the social order than to punish those who are suffering from the ravages of disease. Both groups are the victims of circumstance; both require treatment in order that they may be restored, if possible, to normality. And treatment should be discontinued when the need for it seems to have disappeared. All this, of course, runs counter to the philosophy of the average man, who still accepts the age-old tradition of free will and moral responsibility. But it must not be forgotten that until very recently insane and feeble-minded criminals were regularly thrown into prison or put to death upon the gallows, and that only a few centuries have passed since men and women were made to suffer torture, disgrace, and death because they allegedly practiced "magic, sorcery, witchcraft, and enchantment." Modern thought moves slowly in the field of penology, but at least it is moving in the right direction. Today revenge is no longer considered a sufficient reason for putting men behind iron bars and treating them like caged animals. The idea of revenge is still present, as evidenced by the occasional pronouncements of distinguished jurists; but it is usually coupled with other motives—the desire to deter others from embarking upon a criminal career, the hope of reforming those who have violated the law (and been caught), and also the necessity of protecting society.

DETERRENCE OF OTHERS. The public has long believed that punishment of criminals will deter others from embarking upon careers of crime, despite the very obvious fact that crime still flourishes after centuries of punishment. As long ago as 1748, according to early English court records, a ten-year-old boy named William York was hanged for the murder of one of his playmates, apparently on the theory that a more merciful course might lead other English children to set about murdering their companions. The court declared that "it would be of very dangerous consequence to have it thought that children may commit such atrocious crimes with impunity. . . . And therefore, though the taking away the life of a boy ten years old may savor of cruelty, yet as the example of this boy's punishment may be the means of deterring other children from the like offenses; and as the sparing this boy, merely on account of his age, will probably have a quite contrary tendency, in justice to the public the law ought to take its course." A wholesome change of viewpoint has long since occurred in the treatment of juvenile delinquents, but men and women are still sentenced to death or long prison terms in the belief that potential criminals will thus be frightened into becoming law-abiding citizens.

REFORMATION.   Sometimes it is said that criminals must be kept behind steel bars so that they may have time to consider the enormity of their wrong-doing and repent of their evil ways.   This argument is valid to the extent that imprisonment actually results in reformation.   But virtually all the evidence points to the conclusion that prison life has exactly the opposite effect.   It hardens and brutalizes men and usually sends them out into the world with their hatred of society intensified a hundredfold.   It sends them out, also, with a broader knowledge of criminal methods and technique, gleaned from fellow prisoners in a score of illicit ways.   It unfits them for life in the outside world—the world of normal men and women; and yet imprisonment is still urged as a means of reformation.   Of course, the "reformation" argument cannot possibly be used to justify capital punishment or very long prison terms.   Society cannot be greatly benefited by the repentance of a man who must speedily lose his life, or spend a major portion of it within a prison cell.

PROTECTION OF SOCIETY AND/OR CURE.   The only valid reason for imprisoning criminals is to protect society from the effects of their abnormal conduct.   General acceptance of this theory of penology would transform the prison system of the modern world.   Men and women suffering from the social malady known as criminality would enter prison for treatment, just as men and women suffering from physical ills now enter the hospital.   Expert diagnosis would indicate the kind of treatment most likely to be effective.   And release, which would follow as a matter of course whenever a cure seemed to have been effected, would be coupled with an adequate system of parole. Such a program is radical, but radical ills require radical remedies. And it is obvious that society has long been waging a losing battle against crime.   The old methods of dealing with criminals have proved totally ineffective; certainly new methods deserve at least a trial.   As a matter of fact, the new theory has already received some recognition.   Psychopathic clinics, systems of probation and parole, habitual offender laws, and other comparatively recent developments are designed, not to make the punishment fit the crime, but to make the treatment fit the criminal.   Some of these schemes are poorly conceived; most of them are poorly administered.   But at least they point the way to a scientific solution of the problem of crime.

**Punishment before modern times.** Few people realize that imprisonment is a comparatively new method of punishing criminals. There were dungeons in Europe during the Middle Ages, but they were reserved chiefly for those who had incurred the disfavor of the king or some powerful baron. Even the jails of eighteenth-century Europe and America were used mainly for the detention of debtors, persons awaiting trial, and those convicted persons who were about to be executed or subjected to flogging or some other form of corporal punishment. Imprisonment as a means of punishment did not come into general use until the early part of the nineteenth century. For thousands of years—in fact, from earliest antiquity—torture and death were customarily meted out to anyone who transgressed against the established social order. The Bible is filled with accounts of the brutal punishment of criminals and with exhortations to kill those guilty of wrong-doing. "He that curseth father or mother, let him die the death." [11] "And the daughter of any priest, if she profane herself by playing the harlot, she profaneth her father: she shall be burnt with fire." [12] These were the standards of a primitive people, but English ideals were not much higher during medieval times. "Under the Saxon and Norman kings, common criminals were mutilated in various ways, blinded, branded, amputated of feet and hands, and let crawl about the country as a warning to others. William the Conqueror decreed such punishments with great particularity. Five hundred years later, in Tudor times, we look for but find no advance. Boiling alive was the punishment for poisoners and burning at the stake the penalty paid by traitors, by a wife who killed her husband and by a servant who killed his master or mistress. . . . Under Elizabeth a bankrupt was likely to be publicly scourged through the streets at the end of a cart, his tongue split, his nose cut off, his eyes put out, his property dispersed, and he himself finally hanged." [13] Even in colonial America death was the penalty decreed for scores of crimes. Minor offenses were punished less severely—with the branding iron the whipping post, the pillory. The ducking stool and the gag were reserved chiefly for nagging women.

**Transportation as punishment.** During the early part of the seventeenth century England began to send large numbers of convicted criminals to America, instead of hanging them. This plan had

[11] Exodus XXI: 17.
[12] Leviticus XXI: 9.
[13] Schlapp and Smith, *op. cit.*, p. 34. Reprinted by permission of The Liveright Publishing Corporation.

a number of advantages: it got the convicts out of England, where they were not wanted; it gave the colonists a supply of cheap labor; and it sometimes transformed the criminals into law-abiding citizens, provided they managed to survive the terrible sufferings of the long sea voyage. So shipments were frequent until the Revolution. Then the English government turned to Australia as a suitable place to establish convict colonies and sent shipload after shipload of criminals to the new land for more than half a century. Finally it was forced to seek other territory because of the hostility of the free settlers of Australia, who vigorously objected to having their country overrun with murderers, thieves, swindlers, and forgers. Van Diemen's Land —now Tasmania—was then used for a time, but eventually the cost of transportation combined with a number of factors to compel the complete abandonment of the system. Transportation of criminals has now practically ceased to play a part in systems of punishment.

**Capital punishment.** Reliance is now placed chiefly upon imprisonment as a means of punishing criminals, reforming them, deterring others from following their example, and protecting society against their further wrongdoing. Corporal punishment is used very little except to enforce prison discipline. Fines are reserved for minor offenses, or as a supplement to incarceration. Capital punishment is still retained for certain major crimes in forty states of the American Union, however,[14] and in seven of these states the judge and jury have no power to substitute life imprisonment.[15] The list of offenses for which the death penalty may be imposed includes murder (in every state that makes provision for capital punishment), rape (in seventeen states), treason (in fourteen), arson (in nine), and robbery, burglary, kidnaping, and train wrecking (in a scattered handful of states).

ARGUMENTS FOR AND AGAINST. Whether capital punishment should be completely abandoned is a question that has long occupied the attention of state legislatures, as well as high school debating societies. In favor of abolition it is urged that the death penalty is wrong in principle, since it snuffs out human life and makes reformation impossible. And what does society gain thereby? Certainly not an added measure of protection against criminality, for crimes are quite as numerous in states that have retained capital punishment as in those that have abandoned it. Nor does the death penalty increase

14 The eight states that do not have capital punishment at the present time are Kansas, Maine, Michigan, Minnesota, North Dakota, Rhode Island, South Dakota, and Wisconsin.

15 These seven states are Connecticut, Florida, Massachusetts, New Mexico, New York, North Carolina, and Vermont.

the certainty of punishment. Instead it is likely to have quite the opposite effect, for juries who know that a verdict of guilty will mean death are more likely to find for acquittal. The irrevocability of the death penalty is also urged as a reason for its abandonment. In more than one instance men convicted of serious crimes have subsequently been proved innocent. Such errors are sufficiently tragic under any circumstances, but society can at least make some measure of atonement if the death penalty has not been imposed. On the other hand, it is said that capital punishment is necessary to protect society against its worst enemies—those criminals whose physical or mental abnormalities prevent them from conducting themselves like normal persons. Life imprisonment is designed to accomplish the same purpose, but it is less certain. There is always the possibility of escape, commutation of sentence, or complete pardon. Moreover, the expense of maintaining irreformable criminals until the end of their natural lives is very great and imposes a burden that may well be regarded as unreasonable.

Here, then, are the two sets of arguments, and it is difficult to weigh one set against the other. There can be no doubt that many dangerous criminals deserve to die—not because they are wicked and have earned the hatred of mankind, but because their criminality is the result of indelible character traits. And yet it must be admitted that the American system of criminal justice is not well fitted to separate those who deserve to die from those who are entitled to live. It still places too great emphasis on the crime and too little on the criminal. It sends to the electric chair some men who might conceivably be rehabilitated, while merely confining in prison other men whose lives are not worth saving. Perhaps, under the circumstances, the use of the death penalty should be deferred until such time as the fundamental principles of modern criminology are better understood and more generally applied. Then capital "punishment" will no longer be looked upon as a *punishment;* it will be regarded instead as a means of protecting society—"the highest measure of social defense," to borrow a phrase from the jargon of Bolshevism.

**Imprisonment:** Unwholesome environment. Within each state are a number of different kinds of penal institutions—state prisons, county and city jails, workhouses and houses of correction, and state and local reformatories. The state prisons are reserved for those who have been convicted of serious offenses, usually involving imprisonment for more than one year. Although these prisons are generally known as penitentiaries the name is clearly a misnomer, for steel bars and brutal treatment do not make criminals penitent. Almost every aspect of the prison environment confirms the inmates in their anti-social outlook and tends to make rehabilitation a virtually impossible task, for prisons are not designed to remake men; they are designed to hold them in safety until the end of their terms. Therefore the emphasis is placed mainly on prevention of escape. Only about one third of the criminals in a penitentiary, under normal circumstances, would take desperate chances to regain their freedom, but prison architects and prison wardens find it easier to assume that all convicts are desperate. And every aspect of prison life, from buildings to discipline, reflects this assumption. Most penitentiaries are still built on the cell block plan. Most of the rules that govern the lives of the inmates are unnecessarily severe. From the outset the new convict is made to realize that he has lost his identity as a human being and has become merely a cog in a great machine that is responding blindly to the merciless decrees of a blind social order. Soon he becomes indistinguishable from his fellows. He quickly learns that any attempt to distinguish himself by exceptionally hard work is regarded suspiciously by the guards and resentfully by the other prisoners. Every one of his normal instincts is carefully repressed. And in this strange—almost unbearable—atmosphere the criminal is supposed to repent of his crimes and prepare for a new life in the outside world.

OLD VERSUS MODERN PRISON CONDITIONS. Despite its many unsatisfactory features, however, prison life in the newer penitentiaries under the higher type of prison officials is a vast improvement over the living death that awaited convicted criminals only a few decades ago. Sunlight never penetrated to the cells, and fresh air for prisoners was generally regarded as an unnecessary luxury. The food was unbelievably bad, and many men literally starved to death. Some died from the effects of the barbarous punishments inflicted upon them in the name of discipline. Little regard was paid to prison sanitation; one result of this situation was that the most malignant form of typhus fever became popularly known as prison fever. Small wonder, therefore, that popular agitation forced a change! Sanitary provisions are now much better. Suffering from extremities of heat and cold is less common than formerly, though even in the most modern prisons there is frequently a difference in temperature of 10° to 15° F. between the bottom and top tiers of cells. Many prison cells now in constant use are so designed that they never receive the direct rays of the sun, but a determined effort is being made to correct this state of affairs, for sunlight and fresh air are now recognized as necessities for convicts quite as much as for other people. In the treatment of prisoners, also, marked changes have taken place. The strict rule of early days that absolutely prohibited communication with friends and relatives has been substantially modified, though most states still limit mail privileges in various ways. Nearly every present-day prison has a fairly good library, and a number of prison newspapers have been established. Prison schools are becoming increasingly common. Interesting experiments have been made with the honor system for selected groups of prisoners, and also with various forms of prison self-government.

**Prison labor.** Persons convicted of crime and sentenced to the state penitentiary are supposed to serve their sentences "at hard labor." The idea of putting prisoners to work was originally conceived as a means of increasing the severity of their punishment, but penologists have long understood that enforced idleness is a far more drastic penalty. They point out that idleness is subversive of discipline and that it injures both the minds and the bodies of prison inmates. Long hours of dreary monotony are the surest way of incapacitating men for normal living when their sentences have expired. Therefore the importance of providing suitable work for all able-bodied prisoners can scarcely be overemphasized.

Too LITTLE WORK. Unfortunately, however, "hard labor" is little more than a meaningless phrase in many prisons, and for large numbers of prisoners. Only a few years ago the American Prison Association estimated that "out of a total population approximating 150,000 prisoners in state penal and correctional institutions, . . . possibly 15,000 are really employed in any worth-while industry; another 35,-000 are assigned to maintenance details; while perhaps 20,000 or 25,000 may be employed on institution farms and public road work, leaving 75,000 or more completely idle, or maybe a small number of them dawdling away their time at tasks where five or more men do work which could easily be accomplished without great effort by one." [16] This picture changed somewhat after the Japanese treachery at Pearl Harbor because of the sharply increased demand for foodstuffs and manufactured products. Work was found for many idle prisoners, and the products of the penitentiaries proved a valuable

[16] *Proceedings of the American Prison Association, 1938*, p. 229.

contribution to the war effort. But this improvement in prison conditions was admittedly temporary; it was a war phenomenon, unlikely
to survive the shock of peace.

*Reasons for idleness.* One may properly ask, therefore, why sufficient work cannot be found in normal times to occupy the attention
of prisoners. To some extent, at least, poor prison management is
to blame. Prison wardens are not usually selected on the basis of
their proved business ability, and all too often their ignorance or indifference prevents the establishment of even a reasonably satisfactory
labor system. Adequate workrooms, power plants, and space for
storage are lacking in many prisons. Much more important, however, as a factor in promoting prison idleness, is the attitude of union
labor. The American Federation of Labor and the Congress of Industrial Organizations both resent the competition of prison-made
goods with the products of union workmen and have succeeded in
securing the enactment of state laws that restrict prison labor in various
ways. In some states, for example, machine work by prisoners is
forbidden; in others the hours of work are limited. Prisons may be
prohibited from setting up any industry that is prominent in the state.
Not all these laws have originated with organized labor, however.
Many manufacturers have also used their influence to foster restrictive
legislation. The truth of the matter is that every group recognizes
the necessity of keeping prisoners at work, and favors—at least in
principle—some form of prison labor, but wishes to have such labor
turned into channels that do not affect its own selfish interests.

THE LEASE SYSTEM. A number of different systems of prison labor
have been devised. One of these, the lease system, was seriously
criticised for many years and seems to have been finally abandoned by
all the states. It involved the leasing of prisoners to private persons,
who paid the state a specified amount for the labor of each prisoner
and in addition assumed the responsibility of providing food, clothing,
and shelter. The state reserved the right to inspect the living and
working conditions of prisoners. But state inspection proved virtually worthless in most instances, and the cupidity of the lessees resulted
in many abuses—insufficient food, clothing unsuited to the rigors of
the winter months, and unreasonably long hours of work. The lease
system was virtually a scheme of licensed slavery, and very few people
regretted its passing.

THE CONTRACT SYSTEM. Far more satisfactory, but also open to
numerous objections, is the contract system, under which the contrac-

tor merely furnishes the necessary machinery and materials, together with necessary supervision, leaving the state to care for and guard the prisoners. Payment to the state for the prisoners' labor may be made on a per capita basis or on the basis of a fixed amount per finished article.[17] In either case the favored contractor usually gets his labor supply so cheaply that he has a marked advantage over other manufacturers, who must rely on free labor. The contract system is now prohibited by law in nearly two thirds of the states and has been narrowly restricted in the remaining commonwealths by federal legislation.[18]

THE STATE ACCOUNT SYSTEM. Another method by which goods are made in prison for the open market is known as the state account system. The state buys the raw material, directs the manufacturing process within the prison walls, and markets the finished product. Thus it conducts the prison much like an ordinary factory, assuming whatever profit or loss may result. Quite naturally the state account system is in disfavor with manufacturing and labor groups, which do not relish state competition; and it is gradually being discontinued.

THE STATE USE SYSTEM. In recent years organized labor has strongly supported the state use system, whereby the state limits its production of goods to those articles that are intended for us by the several agencies of the state government, including state institutions, and perhaps by city and county governments as well. The chief merit of this plan, from the standpoint of union labor, is that it prevents the "dumping" of cheap prison goods on the open market. It does not eliminate competition between prison-made and privately made articles, however, as some labor leaders seem to think, for state agencies now supplied with prison goods would otherwise be obliged to turn to private industry. From the public's point of view the state use system has some important advantages. It places less emphasis on the element of profit

---

[17] When the price paid by the contractor is determined by the number of finished articles, and not by the number of hours of prison labor provided, the necessity for private supervision of the prisoners' work disappears. For this reason some writers prefer to distinguish between the *contract* plan (per capita payments) and what they choose to call the *piece price* plan (per article payments).

[18] The Hawes-Cooper Act of 1929, which removes the protecting cloak of the "original package" doctrine from prison-made goods shipped in interstate commerce; and the Ashurst-Sumners Act of 1935, which makes it unlawful "knowingly to transport in interstate or foreign commerce goods made by convict labor into any state where the goods are intended to be received, possessed, sold or owned in violation of its laws." These statutes were upheld by the Supreme Court of the United States in two far-reaching decisions: Whitfield *v.* Ohio, 297 U.S. 431 (1936), and Kentucky Whip and Collar Co. *v.* Illinois Central R.R. Co., 299 U.S. 334 (1937).

and therefore increases the likelihood that the prison population will be given proper vocational guidance and training. It often leads to a considerable diversification of industry, with a greater probability of providing each prisoner with the kind of work for which he is best fitted. On the other hand, it is difficult to administer, and has led to increased idleness among the prison populations of a number of states. "In my own state of Maryland," Harold E. Donnell reported to the American Prison Association a few years ago,[19] "we have had as high as 2200 idle prisoners out of a population slightly in excess of 3000 inmates."

*Public works and ways.* A form of state use is the so-called public works and ways system, under which prisoners are employed to construct roads or buildings belonging to the state. This method is used by sixteen states,[20] at least for part of their prisoners. It can be made to give good results, especially if the convicts assigned to the work are selected with some care, put on their honor, and placed in charge of guards who are competent foremen. In California the plan works well, even with unselected groups of prisoners. But in the southern states, where prisoners are commonly turned over to the counties instead of remaining under state control, highly unsatisfactory conditions exist.

WAGES. Whether prisoners should be paid a wage for their work is a question that has not been definitely settled, but public opinion seems to incline toward payments of some sort. Only a few states, however, maintain wage scales that bear any reasonable relationship to the work performed by prisoners. Wages of ten or fifteen cents a day are common, and forty cents is well above the average. In many states the wages paid to prisoners take the form of a bonus for over-task. Some states reward faithful work by convicts with slightly reduced sentences instead of money, and the men seem to prefer this arrangement.

## LOCAL JAILS

Although living and working conditions in the state penitentiaries are unsatisfactory in many respects, they are far superior to the conditions found in most county jails, workhouses, and houses of correction, where persons serving terms of one year or less are commonly sent.

[19] *1937 Proceedings*, pp. 232-233.
[20] Alabama, Arkansas, California, Colorado, Florida, Georgia, Louisiana, Maine, Maryland, Michigan, Mississippi, New Jersey, New York, North Carolina, Oklahoma, Virginia.

Every careful study of these local correctional institutions has dwelt upon their filthiness, their lack of proper sanitary facilities, their failure to classify prisoners, and the almost universal absence of "equipment for feeding prisoners, so that meals of none too satisfactory quality have to be brought in from the outside. . . . One instance is recorded in which for a period of one week the meals of the inmates consisted substantially of spaghetti, oatmeal, bread, and coffee." [21] Epecially regrettable is the customary lack of work, because idleness leads so readily to mental, moral, and physical deterioration. Dr. Louis N. Robinson estimates that at least seventy-five per cent of all prisoners in institutions for misdemeanants are idle.[22] Since young criminals commonly make their first contacts with the county jail, rather than the state penitentiary, they are exposed to all the worst features of our penal system at the very time when they most need protection from debauching influences. Small wonder that they drift naturally into careers of professional crime! The suggestion has been made that all institutions for misdemeanants be placed under state control, so as to secure units of sufficient size to permit the classification of prisoners according to age, type of offense, personality, and number of convictions. Such a plan, if coupled with the establishment of district industrial farms in place of the present county jails, might well be expected to accomplish the rehabilitation of a fairly high percentage of misdemeanants—especially young offenders in whom the habit of crime had not yet become firmly fixed.

## REFORMATORIES

**Delinquent children.** For many years it has been generally understood that delinquent children should not be forced into intimate association with hardened criminals, but should receive separate treatment better suited to their needs. At first it was thought that special juvenile institutions would serve this purpose. As early as 1818 a privately incorporated society built a so-called House of Refuge for young offenders and received authority from the State of New York to deal with children assigned to it by the courts. In 1847 Massachusetts established the first state institution for juvenile delinquents. By 1900 the number of juvenile reformatories in the United States had grown to sixty-five. At the present time such institutions are found in nearly every state, but only a few of them provide the in-

21 National Probation Association, *1943 Yearbook*, p. 59.
22 *Should Prisoners Work?*, p. 42.

dividualized treatment and specialized training programs necessary to insure even a moderate degree of success in the reformation of wayward children.

Many reformatories are little better than small-scale prisons, their superintendents having adopted prison standards and methods, with only slight modifications, instead of developing a new technique especially designed to meet juvenile requirements. In some of the more progressive institutions, however, important changes have been made.[23] The buildings are less imposing—and more homelike. The educational program, largely vocational, is adjusted to each child's interest and capacity. Discipline is made to serve an educational purpose whenever possible. A serious attempt is made to discover the causes of delinquency in each case, and to take whatever steps may be necessary to remove those causes—unless, of course, there is some irremediable mental or physical defect. But even the best of reformatories is a poor place to rear children. Its routine, however enlightened, cannot take the place of normal home life. Therefore the modern tendency is to keep young delinquents out of institutions just as long as possible, relying instead upon probation, change of surroundings, new opportunities, and the like to produce the desired transformation.

ADULT DELINQUENTS. Nearly half of the states have established reformatories for women, where certain classes of older female delinquents are sent. Among these states, however, there is no uniform rule for determining whether women convicted of criminal offenses shall be committed to the reformatory or to prison. In some states the determining factor is age; in others it is the nature of the offense, the length of the sentence, or the previous record of convictions. A number of states leave the matter entirely to the discretion of the judge. Reformatories for men, also, have been established in many commonwealths. The obvious purposes of reformatories is to care for the inmates, train them, and fit them for useful citizenship, instead of merely punishing them for their sins. There is considerable doubt, however, that the adult reformatory movement, as at present organized, is producing satisfactory results. Many of the inmates of these institutions are feeble-minded, or at least so low in the intelligence scale that they seem incapable of learning. Many others are emotionally unstable and clearly unsuited to life in the outside world of normal men and women. To attempt to "reform" such persons by means

23 Massachusetts took the lead in this matter.

of training and discipline is a waste of time. If they were placed in separate institutions, where they could receive treatment more nearly suited to their needs, closer attention could then be paid to those whose delinquency seemed to be a product of social or economic factors. The result would almost certainly be a much higher percentage of reformatory successes.

### PRISON ADMINISTRATION

The prison systems of the several states are administered in a number of different ways. Some states use the Connecticut plan of maintaining a separate board for each penal institution—the worst possible arrangement, because it leads to rivalry among the boards of the various institutions of the state and prevents co-ordination of psychiatric, psychological, and medical work, in addition to interfering with proper parole supervision. Other states—Kansas and Texas, for example—unite all state penal institutions under a single board of control. Sometimes a single board is given control over all penal and charitable institutions, as in Minnesota, where each board member receives a salary of forty-five hundred dollars a year, or in New Jersey, where members serve without pay. In recent years a number of states have replaced their boards with single executives—a commissioner of corrections, who is responsible for all penal institutions, as in Massachusetts and New York, or a director of public welfare, whose control extends over both penal and charitable institutions, as in Illinois, Ohio, and Pennsylvania. Further variations are found in other commonwealths.

**Political appointees.** Usually the boards or commissioners are appointed by the governor, and they in turn choose the wardens of the prisons. In most states politics plays an important part in the selection of every prison official and employee, from warden to guard. Positions are commonly distributed among the faithful as a reward for votes delivered on election day, and little effort is made to obtain men who are fitted by temperament or training to deal with convicted criminals. It is difficult to arouse the public to a clear realization of the seriousness of this situation, for prison guard duty is still generally regarded as closely akin to wild animal training, in that it requires expertness with the lash and the shotgun. Repression of criminals is the keynote of the average man's philosophy. This attitude is partly responsible for the low salaries and long hours that characterize prison work. Guards in the major state penitentiaries earn, on an average, less than fourteen hundred dollars a year, and in many states they are required to work twelve hours a day. Little effort is made to acquaint them with the psychology of delinquency and the technique of prison discipline. Such a situation inevitably produces unfortunate results. Good laws are of little value without able men to administer them.

### PROBATION

Since prison life usually has a disastrous effect upon the minds and bodies of the men who are required to undergo it, any plan that can keep some convicted criminals out of prison and yet afford a reasonable likelihood of rehabilitation, together with reasonable protection for the community, deserves a thorough trial. Such a plan is probation, which originated in Massachusetts in 1878, and has since swept the country. Today it is used for juveniles in every state except Wyoming, and for adults in all but six states. As a rule, though not necessarily, it is associated with the suspended sentence. When a person convicted of crime for the first time is brought before the court for sentence, the judge who imposes the sentence may suspend its operation for a considerable period, in order to give the offender a reasonable opportunity to demonstrate his ability and willingness to live as a law-abiding citizen. During this period the offender is said to be on probation. If he is found guilty of further anti-social conduct or violates any of the conditions that the judge may see fit to impose, he is sent to jail without additional delay. But if he successfully avoids other conflicts with the law and gives promise of having abandoned his criminal ways, he is given unconditional freedom at the end of his probationary period. Such a scheme is excellent in principle, but its successful operation requires a large staff of thoroughly trained social workers to serve as probation officers. Without such a staff probation speedily degenerates into a farce. Probation work has been hampered more or less seriously in nearly every state of the Union by poor probation officers—politically chosen, poorly paid, overworked. Despite these handicaps it has produced good results in a surprisingly large number of cases and seems destined to become increasingly important as the personnel of probation staffs improves and the courts acquire a better understanding of the fundamental factors involved. The principles underlying a satisfactory probation system have been summarized clearly in a study manual recently published by the National Probation Association: [24]

1. Full power to place adult offenders on probation without hampering restrictions.
2. Complete presentence investigation in each case before probation is granted.
3. Careful selection of cases.
4. Qualified personnel.
5. Provision of men and women officers, and, for juvenile offenders, officers trained in children's work.
6. Case loads of not over fifty.
7. Intensive supervision according to sound case work.
8. Revocation of probation in case of failure or menace to society.
9. Adequate staff organization and machinery.

### PAROLE AND THE INDETERMINATE SENTENCE

Parole and the indeterminate sentence are other important modern developments in the field of penology. Though not necessarily related, they usually go together and are now found side by side in thirty-eight states.[25] Under the laws of these states prisoners are given sentences with minimum and maximum limits instead of the fixed sentences so popular a few decades ago. Any prisoner who has served his minimum term may then be released by the parole agency, provided his conduct in prison points to the likelihood of his rehabilitation.

**Regular reports.** As under the probation system, however, he is assigned to some officer and required to make reports at regular intervals, either in person or by correspondence. These reports may be the merest formality, especially if personal visits are not required. On the other hand, they may be made the means of keeping in close touch with the paroled man and guiding him along the path of good citizenship. Everything depends on the parole officer. It is rather discouraging, therefore, to learn that the methods of supervision are singularly inadequate in many states. In Colorado, for example, reliance is placed solely on the written reports of parolees. No attempt is made to check these reports, which are received by a parole officer stationed at the state penitentiary. Montana, which follows a somewhat similar plan, does not even have a parole officer; the letters of parolees are sent to the clerk of the state board of prison commis-

[24] Pigeon, Helen D., *Probation and Parole in Theory and Practice*, p. 90.
[25] Nine other states permit parole of prisoners, but lack the indeterminate sentence. Only one state—Mississippi—has neither the indeterminate sentence nor parole.

sioners. In some states the written reports are occasionally coupled with volunteer oversight. Part-time paid parole agents may be used, as in Connecticut and Maine. There are, in fact, but fourteen states that maintain regular staffs of full-time, professional parole agents. And even in these states the parole officers are usually underpaid and overworked.[26]

**Selection of parolees.** Equally unsatisfactory are the methods generally employed in the selection of the prisoners to be paroled. Parole is commonly granted by the governor or the board of pardons as a form of executive clemency, or by state or institutional administrative boards as an incidental part of their general duties. There are only a few states that have established full-time, salaried parole boards. Sometimes two separate agencies are vested with power to grant parole to the same prisoners—a situation that almost inevitably produces confusion and conflicts of authority.

**Recent developments.** An interesting development of the last few years has been the consolidation of adult probation and parole within a single agency. This plan, long used in Rhode Island and Vermont, has recently been adopted by a number of other states. Another interesting development has been the ratification by nearly three fourths of the states of an agreement to supervise one another's probationers and parolees.

### SHOULD A BOARD OF SENTENCES BE CREATED?

The suggestion has frequently been made that sentences be imposed upon convicted criminals by an administrative board—a board of sentences, or something of the sort—instead of by the judges of the trial courts. Two chief advantages are claimed for this plan. First, it would eliminate the inequalities that inevitably arise when sentences are meted out by different judges sitting in different parts of the state, each governed by his own theories of punishment and entirely independent of his colleagues. Second, it would make possible the sentencing of prisoners by skilled specialists—psychiatrists, social workers, criminologists—whose composite judgment as to the time necessary to accomplish complete rehabilitation should be of considerable value. It is no easy task to decide exactly what penalty will produce maxi-

---

[26] Probation, parole, and pardon methods of the several states are elaborately described in a five-volume work, *Survey of Release Procedures*, published by the U.S. Department of Justice in 1939. For more recent developments, see the volumes of the *Social Work Year Book*.

mum results in each case, considering the interests of the prisoner and also of society; a great deal of information is needed concerning the prisoner's mental and physical condition, emotional reactions, habits and desires, home life and companions, education, and occupational experience. The average jurist does not possess this information, and would not know what to do with it if he had it. Therefore his relation to a case should end when the fact of guilt is definitely established, and the board of sentences should assume the function of imposing a suitable penalty—or, more accurately, finding a suitable remedy. If this innovation were adopted, it would no longer be necessary for the sentence to be fixed, even within broad limits, at the time of the trial. Instead, each criminal could be sent to the institution best suited to his needs for an indefinite period of treatment and would remain until the board of sentences was convinced that his trouble had been corrected. Mental defectives, even though convicted of minor offenses, might never be granted their freedom.

Under this plan the board of sentences would assume the functions of the present-day parole board; it would not be limited by minimum and maximum terms for each type of offense, however, but would be free to fix the period of imprisonment solely on the basis of the conditions existing in each case. Of course, this proposal rests on the assumption that the board of sentences would not fall within the greedy grasp of the spoilsmen. If appointments to the board were made on political rather than professional grounds, the entire scheme would be foredoomed to failure.

### HABITUAL OFFENDER LAWS

One of the most serious aspects of the problem of crime is the tendency of certain persons to continue their criminal careers with systematic regularity, regardless of warnings, fines, and even occasional jail sentences. These repeaters—recidivists, as they are called—do not comprise a large part of the total number of lawbreakers, but they are responsible for a very large percentage of the total number of crimes committed. Apparently they have adopted crime as a profession, and lack the ability or the desire to change their habits of living. Such persons have long been subject to life imprisonment under the laws of many states, but many of them have speedily regained their freedom on parole after serving only a small part of their "life" terms. In 1926 New York amended its criminal code to prohibit the paroling of these habitual offenders—persons convicted of felonies for the fourth time; and several states have since followed its example, with certain modifications.

No fault can be found with the theory of habitual offender legislation—the theory that persons who have demonstrated beyond question their incapacity for normal, law-abiding citizenship should be compelled to spend the rest of their days in institutions, where they will do the least possible harm to others. The difficulty lies in determining just when such incapacity has been definitely proved. Certainly four convictions are not conclusive evidence, and should not be so regarded. What is needed in each case is a knowledge of the causes of the anti-social conduct, and an investigation by skilled experts of the possibility that those causes can be removed. Mention should also be made at this point of a defect that the habitual offender laws have revealed in practice—the difficulty of convicting fourth offenders. Many juries, regarding life imprisonment as too severe a punishment for comparatively minor misdeeds, have insisted on finding thrice-convicted criminals innocent in the face of overwhelming evidence of guilt.

### THE PARDONING POWER

The possibility of convicting innocent men or of treating guilty men with undue severity makes necessary the retention, somewhere in the general scheme of government, of a pardoning power. Usually this power is vested in the governor, assisted in many states by an advisory board that sifts the applications and makes recommendations. But there are many variations. Pardons issued by the governor may require the approval of the state senate, as in Rhode Island, or the approval of both the executive council and the board of pardons, as in Maine. In a few states the pardoning power is granted to a pardon board, of which the governor may or may not be a member. The movement to restrict the governor's free use of the power of pardon has resulted chiefly from the abuses of which many governors have been guilty. Some governors have granted pardons in questionable cases, without sufficient investigation, and apparently because of political pressure; others have issued pardons in such quantities as to lead to virtual jail deliveries. Not unnaturally, therefore, greater reliance has been placed on specially created boards. These boards are in a better position than the governor to make a careful examination of the facts of each case. Whether their findings should be final or merely advisory is a moot question.

## STERILIZATION

Closely related to the treatment of criminals is the sterilization of the feeble-minded and the insane. The connection between mental abnormalities and crime has already been pointed out.[27] While it is undoubtedly true that many persons of subnormal intelligence have found work and recreation suited to their capacities and are safely in the ranks of the law-abiding citizens, yet it cannot be denied that mental peculiarities often lead to anti-social conduct and intensify the problem of crime. The suggestion has frequently been made, therefore, that feeble-minded and insane persons committed to state institutions be sterilized before release, so as to spare future generations the necessity of dealing with their offspring.

A great deal can be said in favor of this plan. It is in no sense a method of punishment, but a means of preventing the progressive deterioration of the human race. Moreover, sterilization is no longer a complicated and dangerous procedure. It can now be accomplished with a minimum of inconvenience to the patient, without the removal of organs or glands and without effect on the normal sexual life. Its only effect is the primary one for which it was designed—the prevention of conception. Yet compulsory sterilization has been held unconstitutional by the courts in several cases, on the ground that it is a "cruel and unusual punishment," [28] or because it is a denial of equal protection of the laws.[29] In 1927, however, a test case came before the Supreme Court of the United States, and the principle of compulsory sterilization was unqualifiedly sustained. The case involved a feeble-minded girl named Carrie Buck, the daughter of a feeble-minded mother. The girl herself had already given birth to an illegitimate feeble-minded child, and the superintendent of the institution to which she had been sent ordered that she be sterilized. In disposing of her objections, the Supreme Court, speaking through Mr. Justice Holmes, said in part: "We have seen more than once that the public welfare may call upon the best citizens for their lives. It would be strange if it could not call upon those who already sap the strength of the state for these lesser sacrifices, often not felt to be such by those concerned, in order to prevent our being swamped with incompetence. It is better for all the world, if instead of waiting to execute degenerate

27 See pp. 413–414.
28 Mickle *v.* Henrichs, 262 Fed. 687 (1918).
29 Smith *v.* Board of Examiners, 85 N.J. Law 46; 88 Atl. 963 (1913); Osborn *v.* Thompson, 169 N.Y. Sup. 638 (1918); Haynes *v.* Lapeer, 201 Mich. 138; 166 N.W. 938 (1918).

offspring for crime, or to let them starve for their imbecility, society can prevent those who are manifestly unfit from continuing their kind. The principle that sustains compulsory vaccination is broad enough to cover cutting the Fallopian tubes. . . . Three generations of imbeciles are enough." [30]

The first state to enact a compulsory sterilization law was Indiana, in 1907.[31] Then came Washington, in the early part of 1909, and California a few months later. At the present time sterilization laws are on the statute books of twenty-nine states.[32] In a number of these states, however, there has been virtually no attempt at enforcement. California has gone further than any of the others and is responsible for more than half of the operations performed. The California law provides that no operation shall be performed unless recommended by the prison physician, and approved by the director of the state department of institutions and the director of the state department of health.[33]

## Selected References

Barnes, Harry E., and Teeters, Negley K., *New Horizons in Criminology; the American Crime Problem,* 1943.

Bates, Sanford, *Prisons and Beyond,* 1936.

Brearley, H. C., *Homicide in the United States,* Chapel Hill, N.C., 1932.

Cantor, N. F., *Crime and Society: An Introduction to Criminology,* 1939.

Carr, Lowell J., *Delinquency Control,* 1940.

East, W. Norwood, *The Adolescent Criminal,* London, 1942.

Gillin, John L., *Criminology and Penology,* rev. ed., 1935.

Glueck, Sheldon, *Crime and Justice,* 1936.

———, *Criminal Careers in Retrospect,* 1943.

———, *Juvenile Delinquents Grown Up,* 1940.

———, *Mental Disorder and the Criminal Law,* 1925.

Haynes, Fred E., *The American Prison System,* 1939.

———, *Criminology,* 2nd ed., 1935.

Hooton, Ernest A., *The American Criminal; an Anthropological Study.* Vol. 1, *The Native White Criminal of Native Parentage,* Cambridge, Mass., 1939.

[30] Buck *v.* Bell, 274 U.S. 200 (1927).

[31] This act was subsequently declared unconstitutional, however, by the state supreme court. A compulsory sterilization measure passed the Pennsylvania legislature in 1905, but was vetoed by the governor.

[32] In two of these states—Minnesota and Vermont—the laws merely provide for voluntary sterilization.

[33] For an excellent discussion of the entire problem of eugenic sterilization see E. S. Gosney and Paul Popenoe's *Sterilization for Human Betterment.* See also J. H. Landman's *Human Sterilization.* Valuable statistical information may be found in a pamphlet by James E. Hughes entitled *Eugenic Sterilization in the United States,* and published as Supplement No. 162 to the Public Health Reports of the U.S. Public Health Service.

Hooton, Ernest A., *Crime and the Man,* Cambridge, Mass., 1939.

Landman, J. H., *Human Sterilization,* 1932.

LaRoe, Wilbur, Jr., *Parole with Honor,* Princeton, N.J., 1939.

Lunden, Walter A., *Statistics on Crime and Criminals,* Pittsburgh, 1942.

MacCormick, Austin H., ed., *Handbook of American Prisons and Reformatories,* 5th ed., 1942.

Reckless, Walter C, *Criminal Behavior,* 1940.

———, *The Etiology of Delinquent and Criminal Behavior,* 1943.

Robinson, Louis N., *Should Prisoners Work?—A Study of the Prison Labor Problem in the United States,* 1931.

Sellin Thorsten, *The Criminality of Youth,* 1940.

Shaw, Clifford R., and McKay, Henry D., *Juvenile Delinquency and Urban Areas,* 1942.

Sutherland, Edwin H., ed., *The Professional Thief,* 1937.

Taft, Donald R., *Criminology: An Attempt at a Synthetic Interpretation with a Cultural Emphasis,* 1942.

Tannenbaum, Frank, *Crime and the Community,* 1938.

Tulchin, Simon H., *Intelligence and Crime,* 1939.

United States Department of Justice, *Survey of Release Procedures,* 5 vols., Washington, D.C., 1939.

Waite, John B., *The Prevention of Repeated Crime,* Ann Arbor, Mich., 1943.

Wallack, Walter M., and Others, *Education within Prison Walls,* 1939.

Weir, Eligius, *Criminology, a Scientific Study of the Modern Crime Problem,* Joliet, Ill., 1941.

White, William A., *Crime and Criminals,* 1933.

Wood, Arthur E., and Waite, John B., *Crime and Its Treatment; Social and Legal Aspects of Criminology,* 1941.

Young, Pauline Vislick, *Social Treatment in Probation and Delinquency,* 1937.

# Chapter Twenty-Two ❧ WELFARE

The care of the poor is a social problem of the first magnitude. It cannot be solved merely by good intentions and a full purse. The poet may advise "a hand open as day for melting charity," [1] but every student of social problems knows that indiscriminate almsgiving is a sorry substitute for efficient welfare work. Generosity is not enough; there must be a highly developed organization, trained personnel, and skilful technique. In other words, guesswork must be eliminated. The problem requires a scientific approach.

## SUB-STANDARD INCOMES

**Extent.** The extent of poverty cannot be determined with any degree of exactness. No one knows how many people are trying to subsist on incomes that are insufficient to maintain even a minimum standard of decent living. But extensive surveys are not necessary to show that poverty is very widespread. Evidence of dire need appears on every hand, even in prosperous times; and in periods of depression the proofs of poverty multiply with startling rapidity. Social workers used to speak of the poor as "the submerged tenth," and many writers of a few decades ago estimated that ten per cent of the people of the United States were wholly or partly dependent on public or private charity. But recent figures have undoubtedly been much higher. In 1939—the last so-called "normal" year—before preparations for war created new jobs and sharply reduced the relief rolls, more than twenty million people—fifteen per cent of the men, women, and children of the nation—were on public relief. Obviously, therefore, poverty is a serious problem demanding serious consideration.

**Causes.** Many factors predispose to poverty. To determine their relative importance in any given case, however, is extremely difficult —sometimes almost impossible. Yet little can be accomplished without an understanding of fundamental causes and a determined effort to remove them. To give poor people money, food, or shelter without at least trying to correct their social maladjustment is strongly

---

[1] Shakespeare's *King Henry IV*, Pt. II, Act. IV, Scene 4.

suggestive of bailing a tub of water without turning off the faucet that constantly brings a fresh supply. Temporary relief may be accomplished, but something more is needed for permanent results.

Among the factors that tend to produce poverty, some lie wholly within the individual. Feeble-mindedness, for example, or low normal mentality, may prevent steady employment at any regular trade. Mental instability may have the same effect. Sickness, especially for long periods, may dissipate savings and also reduce earning capacity. Physical handicaps of any sort may play a part. So, too, may an improper diet or an abuse of stimulants and narcotics. Frequently several of these factors combine to produce that condition of mind and body known—for lack of a more precise term—as shiftlessness. The person so afflicted is in need of charity more or less constantly. Any small savings that he may manage to accumulate soon disappear as a result of extravagance, or lack of sound judgment in business matters, or "unforeseen" emergencies for which provision should have been made long in advance. Every step forward is followed by a loss of the ground gained. Poverty becomes chronic. Welfare agencies are well acquainted with such persons and families, but have found no way to effect a solution of their problems. Against stupidity, it is said, the gods themselves are powerless. Not all the factors that predispose to poverty, however, lie within the individual. Inadequate natural resources or bad climatic conditions may affect whole communities. Changes in manufacturing processes or in the popular demand for certain products may throw entire groups of workers into the ranks of the unemployed and force them below the level of self-support. Periods of depression may have a nation-wide or even world-wide effect.

Obviously, therefore, no simple remedy will cure such a complex social disease as poverty. Every one of the factors involved, of which only a few have been suggested above, must be given separate consideration. Some factors can be completely eliminated or substantially modified by careful planning and proper treatment; others seem to defy solution. Whether poverty can be wiped out is a moot question; that it can be greatly reduced is beyond doubt.

### THE FORCED SHIFT FROM PRIVATE TO PUBLIC POOR RELIEF

Until recent years poor relief was largely in private hands, although the part played by the state was becoming increasingly important. Some persons urged that the government should assume primary responsibility for the care of the poor, but their proposals were met with numerous objections. Public charity, it was said, would mean an undue expansion of charity; it would probably involve an expenditure of public money out of all proportion to normal need, for public agencies would not be dependent on private generosity. They might demand, and rightfully expect to receive, their share of the revenues from public taxation. And they might forget their duty to conserve wherever possible. Moreover, large appropriations made in times of emergency might continue at the same high level with the return of normal business conditions—partly because of the voting strength of the beneficiaries and partly because of the influence of public welfare workers. Some persons objected to public poor relief because of its obvious political implications. Charity, they said, might be dispensed with a view to influencing elections. Such cases were not unknown. And it was urged, too, that public poor relief was more mechanical than private—less concerned with the personal problems and personal needs of its supposed beneficiaries. Government tended to become enmeshed in "red tape"; it commonly substituted formalism and bureaucratic indifference for personal interest and sympathetic understanding.

**The Reconstruction Finance Corporation.** There was, of course, another side of the story, but it was seldom heard until after 1930. Then depression compelled the abandonment of theoretical arguments. The rapid increase of poverty, together with the corresponding reduction in the incomes of those self-supporting persons who normally carried the burden of poor relief, made government intervention an absolute necessity. Moreover, it compelled federal intervention, for many states, counties, and cities were fast aproaching the limit of their resources. At first the federal government adopted the theory that recovery would be rapid and permanent, and it took steps to speed the process. There was to be a national business survey; industry should be asked to increase production; and "the spirit of voluntary service" should be encouraged. But these measures were of no avail, and even a marked increase in federal public works took care of but a small part of the unemployed. In 1932, therefore, the Reconstruction Finance Corporation was set up, with power to lend large sums to the states "to be used in furnishing relief and work relief to needy and distressed people and in relieving the hardships resulting from unemployment." The states were to receive these federal loans with virtually no strings attached; their own officials were to determine the exact nature of relief plans. In few cases was the money spent with maximum efficiency—a not unnatural condition of affairs, for state officials were totally unprepared to meet the crisis. Suitable agencies had to be set up, and suitable personnel had to be obtained. But relief could not await the refinement of administrative processes; it demanded immediate attention. So the money was spent, and the states thus indebted themselves to the federal government to the extent of several hundred millions of dollars. Later, however, an act of Congress waived the earlier provisions for repayment, and the loans became gifts.

**Social security legislation.** When President Roosevelt took office, in 1933, the unemployment situation was acute. At least fifteen million men were out of work, and most of them had exhausted their meager savings. Many states and cities lacked available funds for relief purposes. Federal grants had proved insufficient by a wide margin. A more comprehensive federal relief program was urgently required, and it was speedily adopted. This program had three major parts: (1) employment of young men in forest camps maintained by the federal government, (2) large direct grants (not loans) to the states, and (3) employment of large numbers of persons on federal work projects. Thus the emergency situation was met.

But something more was needed: a permanent program that would insure workers against poverty and provide systematic care for all persons in need. A Committee on Economic Security was created, and for more than a year it dealt with every aspect of the problem. In the early days of 1935 it presented its report, and seven months later Congress enacted its recommendations into law—though with substantial modifications. Thus the United States achieved a form of "social security." But many criticisms have been directed at the program. Some persons declare that it is totally inadequate. It excludes large groups from unemployment benefits; it fixes maximum benefits for many classes—dependent children, for example—at a very low level; and it makes no direct attack on the problem of poverty through illness. Then there are other persons who criticize the program for a very different reason. They say that its cost is excessive and must somehow be reduced. To these complaints others are added: the present methods of financing the plan are economically or socially unsound; the lack of proper federal supervision over related state activities is a serious weakness; numerous administrative difficulties interfere with the prompt granting of relief. Some of these objections are undoubtedly valid. Certain changes in the program have already been made. But real social security is undoubtedly much nearer for the people of the United States as a result of the legislation of 1935 and its subsequent amendments.

**State and federal responsibility.** The social security program is essentially a co-operative affair, involving both the states and the federal government. Some phases of the plan, such as old age insurance, are handled directly by the nation, but most aspects are administered by the states with the aid of federal funds and a small measure of federal supervision. Each state prepares its own program— within broad limits fixed by Congress—and uses its own staff of administrators. The federal government's grants for general relief ended in 1935, but Congress indicated its intention to provide continued work for "employable" persons by making huge appropriations to the federal works program. This arrangement threw upon the states the full burden of caring for so-called "unemployables," except those persons covered by specific legislation—aged men and women, dependent children, and the like. Whether this division of responsibility will continue permanently is uncertain, but it seems likely to do so.

**Subordination of private agencies.** Private charitable organizations still function, of course, and play an important part in the relief of human misery. The Red Cross maintains an organization, even in peacetime, that permits prompt action at the scene of every major disaster, such as earthquake, flood, or fire. The Salvation Army cares for homeless persons and attempts to rehabilitate them. In many cases it successfully bridges the gap between private need and available public funds. Dozens of other private welfare agencies still perform useful services. The annual Community Chest drive provides an excellent means of financing this private work. But private activity has been definitely subordinated to public in the field of poor relief. The old argument concerning the desirability of public participation has been settled for all time.

### INDOOR *versus* OUTDOOR RELIEF

**Advantages of each form.** The relief of the poor assumes two general forms—indoor relief, or the care of poor persons in institutions, and outdoor relief, or the care of poor persons in their own homes. Both forms of charity are used in present-day American communities. The outdoor principle has many advantages. It enables the unfortunate to receive assistance without suffering the inevitable

humiliation of life in a charitable institution.   It avoids the necessity of severing family ties or separating friends.   It is frequently
urged as an economical solution of the problem of poor relief, on the
ground that a great deal of the cost of indoor relief can be saved.
Many families are only a little below the level of self-support and
could maintain themselves with a minimum of assistance.   To insist
that they abandon their family life and go to an institution, at greatly
increased public expense, may sometimes be the height of folly.   But
other factors, which must not be overlooked, present outdoor relief
in a less favorable light.   For one thing, the absence of humiliation
that is advanced as a merit of the system often proves to be a serious
disadvantage, since it greatly increases the number of applicants.
Men and women who managed to live without charity when charity
meant the poorhouse suddenly discover that they can no longer support themselves, but must have food, fuel, or money at public expense.
Because outdoor relief is more pleasant, it is very much more popular.
Thus the savings effected in the care of each family must be used to
provide for additional families, and still larger appropriations may
become necessary.   The experience of public officials with outdoor
relief in many communities lends force to this argument.   The present trend is undoubtedly toward an expansion of outdoor relief and
a corresponding restriction of the indoor principle.   But indoor relief
is still an important phase of American charity; there is little reason
to believe that it will ever be completely eliminated.

**The almshouse.**   In most sections of the country the chief public
institution for the care of the poor is the almshouse—sometimes known
as the poorhouse, the poor-farm, the county infirmary, or the home
for the aged and infirm.   The more populous states usually have one
such institution in virtually every county, maintained with county
funds and subject to little or no state supervision.   But there is a
recent trend toward consolidation of almshouses into hospitalized institutions serving larger areas and directly under state control. In
Virginia, for example, six large district homes have replaced sixty-
eight county almshouses.

PREVIOUS CONDITIONS.   Several decades ago, before the rising tide
of public indignation compelled a change, the almshouse was almost
everything that it should not have been.   It was a filthy breeding place
of disease, a cheerless, comfortless refuge for those who had abandoned
hope, a veritable catch-all where young and old, diseased and well,
sane and insane, temperate and inebriate were forced to associate on

intimate terms. According to the report made by one board of supervisors during the closing years of the last century, only a few of the
almshouses "have been constructed for the purpose for which they
are used. In most cases a farm with a dwelling house already upon
it has been purchased, and additions from time to time, as they seem
to be required, made to the house. The building thus pieced out and
patched up is in the majority of cases inconvenient, poorly constructed,
and without any adaptation to the object to which it is appropriated.
With no convenience for a division of the inmates, or a complete
separation of the sexes. With low ceilings, small windows, no drain-
age, and oftentimes damp and cold, without means for safely heating
and properly ventilating the rooms, it fails to meet the wants and
requirements which such a building should supply." [2] Particularly
unfortunate was the plight of the insane, for whom no special provision was made. "They are neglected, abused, confined with chains,
locked up, left in nakedness and filth, caged, and not a soul has for
them a friendly word. The medical supervision of them is wholly
inadequate; they have no proper personal attendance; they are without amusement or occupation of any sort. Some of them are taken
out at long intervals for an airing or to be washed, possibly by standing them naked in a corner and throwing water upon them with a
hose pipe. Others remain in their cells or dens from one end of the
year to the other. Their mental malady is aggravated by neglect and
cruelty, and their only hope is in death." [3]

RECENT IMPROVEMENTS. In recent years, however, conditions in
the county almshouses have been vastly improved. This improvement has been made possible, in part, by the transfer of groups requiring special care to separate institutions. The sick poor are sent to
hospitals where their maladies may be treated; the feeble-minded and
insane are placed in hospitals for mental diseases. Children are placed
in separately maintained orphanages or in private homes. Cripples
are given highly specialized vocational training whenever such instruction seems likely to make them wholly or partly self-supporting.
Therefore the almshouse is more largely an institution for the care
of the aged. Other groups have not been completely weeded out, nor
is it likely that they ever will be. But at least the inexcusable herding
together and undifferentiated treatment of an earlier day have long

---

[2] Breckinridge, Sophonisba P., *Public Welfare Administration in the United States,*
p. 630.

[3] *Ibid.,* p. 640.

since been abandoned in most states.   Almshouse construction, also, has received greater attention.   First, large, dormitory-type buildings took the place of makeshift farmhouses, and these, in turn, are now being replaced, in at least a few jurisdictions, by poor homes of the cottage variety.   Greater attention is generally paid to the selection of almshouse superintendents, though much remains to be accomplished in this respect.

NEED FOR CONTINUANCE.   The introduction of old-age pension systems and other forms of social security has led to the widespread belief that public homes need no longer be maintained.   Why, it is asked, should aged men and women be sent to institutions when they can receive from the government sufficient funds to enable them to live comfortably in their own homes?   The obvious answer—entirely aside from the frequent inadequacy of public pensions—is that many old people require institutional care.   Thousands of them must have almost constant medical and nursing services that cannot be provided adequately in their own homes or the homes of relatives.   Although many institutions have closed their doors since the Social Security Act became operative, a considerable number of states, including the most populous, report that there has been little reduction in their total almshouse populations during this period.[4]

PROVISION FOR ACTIVITY.   Some provision should be made for the old people living in institutions.   This aspect of the care of inmates is often neglected, largely because the aged cannot engage in many forms of diversion that are open to younger men and women.   But it is a vital factor in making institutional life bearable for those who are obliged to accept its inevitable monotony.   Equally important is the assignment of light daily tasks to all inmates—except, of course, the incapacitated—for idleness is quite as harmful to the able-bodied inmates of homes as to the prisoners in jails and penitentiaries.   The women can assist in the housework; the men can engage in agricultural or industrial work suited to their physical condition.   Small savings in the operation of the home usually result from the adoption of such schemes of general employment.   Far more significant, however, is the effect upon the workers.   In most instances they acquire a fresh interest in life, and delight in the realization that their usefulness is not entirely past.

[4] *Social Work Year Book, 1943,* p. 223.

### THE OLD-AGE PROBLEM

In the United States, according to the most recent census figures, there are now more than nine million men and women who have passed their sixty-fifth birthdays. This group comprises nearly seven per cent of the total population. Their earning power has dropped practically to the vanishing point, yet most of them have not saved enough to buy even the barest necessities for the remainder of their lives. Many have children or other close relatives who are willing to assume the burden of support, or can be made to do so. But many others do not have relatives or friends to help them and must inevitably turn to charity. Some provision must be made for their care.

Assignment to institutions was, until recently, the plan most commonly adopted. Privately managed homes for the aged supplemented the public homes and almshouses in many communities. These private institutions aided in reducing the burden of public charity, but their usefulness was lessened by the restrictions that they imposed upon would-be inmates. Sometimes they required a flat payment of several hundred or even several thousand dollars, in addition to the deeding of any real property that the applicant might own. Quite commonly they imposed religious or racial restrictions, or accepted only persons belonging to certain fraternal groups. Most of the responsibility of caring for the aged, therefore, rested upon public institutions. And every study of this phase of poor relief emphasized the fact that public institutions—or public and private institutions combined, for that matter—were too few and too small to meet the needs of the aged poor. Moreover, the situation was constantly becoming more acute. High standards of living were making it increasingly difficult for the average wage earner to save any substantial sum during his working years despite reasonably good wages; and medical science was rapidly augmenting the proportion of old people in the general population. Recent trends in birth and death rates have by no means relieved this situation; on the contrary, they have accentuated it. The proportion of aged persons continues to increase. By 1980, according to the estimates of the National Resources Committee, 14.4 per cent of the population of the United States will be sixty-five years of age or over. The following table shows the steady increase in the number of the aged:

| Year | Percentage of the Total Population |
|------|-----------------------------------|
| 1880 | 3.5 |
| 1890 | 3.9 |
| 1900 | 4.2 |
| 1910 | 4.3 |
| 1920 | 4.7 |
| 1930 | 5.4 |
| 1940 | 6.8 |

**Old-age insurance.** When the federal government decided to establish a permanent scheme of social security in 1935, it recognized that the ultimate solution of the problem of poverty in old age must be a nation-wide retirement system. Similar systems had long been maintained by leading private corporations for the benefit of their employees, but they applied only to employees who had been in their service for twenty or twenty-five years. At most they applied to not over four million workers—a small percentage of the total number requiring protection. Nor could private industry extend the system very greatly. But the federal government, with its nation-wide jurisdiction and broad powers of taxation and control, encountered no substantial difficulties. Its old-age insurance plan was applied to all workers—with the exception of certain groups—who had been employed at least five years (though not necessarily with one employer, or for any specified minimum period during each year). A tax, beginning at one per cent and rising gradually to three per cent—was placed on the payroll of each employer, and a similar tax was imposed on the wages of each employee. From these revenues a huge reserve —reaching an ultimate total of forty-seven billion dollars, according to government actuaries—was to be created; and from this reserve workers were to receive, after retirement, regular payments which would continue until death. The amount of each worker's pension would depend in part upon the length of his service, and in part upon the amount of his earnings.

As might have been anticipated, numerous objections were raised. The new taxes were too heavy; the number of beneficiaries was too few. Most serious of the plan's weaknesses, however, was the contemplated forty-seven-billion-dollar reserve. No government in the

[5] These figures are taken from the *Statistical Abstract of the United States, 1942*, p. 9.

world's history had ever created such a fund, and no one could say with certainty what its effects would be. But most students believed that it would unsettle the investment market and that it might readily be used for purposes not originally contemplated. In order to avoid these difficulties, Congress amended the law in 1939 by advancing the year for the first payment of benefits, increasing the number of beneficiaries, holding the tax at one per cent for a number of years, and limiting the size of the reserve to three times the maximum yearly benefit payments expected in the next five years. More recently, on three separate occasions, Congress has continued to postpone the scheduled increases in the rate of the tax.

**Old-age assistance.** Old-age insurance does not completely solve the problem, however. It has no value for aged persons who never earned wages, or who retired before the insurance plan was adopted. It fails to cover many groups. Yet indigent men and women in these various categories cannot be permitted to starve. Some provision must be made for their care, despite the fact that they fall outside the scope of an insurance system. The establishment of public alms-houses was one of the earliest recognitions of this obligation. Later a number of the states granted relief to the aged poor in their own homes. Small sums, contributed regularly from state or county treasuries on the basis of need, often supplemented the money earned by the old people themselves or contributed by relatives or friends. In California, where this scheme was in operation for a number of years prior to the adoption of a regular pension system, public contributions of ten or fifteen dollars a month enabled the beneficiaries to live semi-independently in many instances, and thus retain their self-respect and escape the odium of becoming poorhouse inmates.

From this form of poor relief it was but a step to the establishment of old-age pensions, available on equal terms to all poor persons who had reached a certain age. Pension systems for the aged had long been a part of the social insurance schemes of European nations, but had received little serious consideration in the United States. An old-age pension law had indeed been enacted by Arizona in 1914, but had been declared unconstitutional by the state supreme court because of ambiguous phraseology. Then came the Montana law of 1923—the first valid old-age pension statute. Nevada followed a few months later, and Wisconsin fell into line in 1925. By 1935 the number of states with pension laws had risen to thirty, though some of the state statutes were virtually inoperative because they permitted each county to determine whether it would accept the plan contemplated by the legislature's action, at the same time placing the financial burden upon the county treasury. Most of the state laws required fifteen years of uninterrupted residence, and specified a minimum age of seventy years.

At this point the federal government entered the picture. In addition to providing old-age insurance for workers, it brought great pressure to bear on the states to set up adequate pension systems for the aged poor. The federal offer consisted in matching state funds for old-age pensions, up to fifteen dollars a month (later increased to twenty dollars). A state appropriating less than twenty dollars per person per month would thus receive from the federal government only a sum equal to its own outlay, while a state appropriating more than the twenty-dollar maximum would still receive but twenty dollars from the federal treasury. Certain conditions were attached to the federal grant: every plan submitted for federal approval must be state-wide in operation; it must provide a fair hearing for any person denied assistance; the age limit (after 1940) must not be higher than sixty-five years; the residence requirement must not exceed five years in the last ten. But no provision was made for federal supervision of state administrative activities; on the contrary, the Social Security Board was specifically directed not to interfere with state affairs. All forty-eight states have now accepted the federal offer, and established more or less satisfactory pension schemes. Pensions have been generally increased since 1940, as a result of higher living costs and improved state finances. But there are many variations in the terms of state laws and also in their administration. Many common weaknesses must be eliminated.

### THE CARE OF HOMELESS CHILDREN

Not only the very old, but also the very young, are likely to require the special consideration of the state. When parents die without making adequate provision for their dependent children; when broken homes leave the children without proper care; whenever, for any reason, young boys and girls lack the bare necessities of life— then public or private charity must assume the responsibility that the parents have failed to meet.

**Children's homes.** For many years it was believed that homeless children should be placed in institutions, where their training could be closely supervised, their habits carefully regulated, and their playtime activities guided into useful channels. Children's homes were established by public authorities, religious denominations, and fraternal orders. Today, however, most students of social problems vigously challenge the old assumption that institutions furnish a proper environment for growing boys and girls. In large measure they have convinced the public that institutional life retards initiative, produces undesirable uniformity, and tends to unfit children to take their places as normal men and women in the outside world. The result has been an increased emphasis on placement in private homes. But the "orphanage"—usually so-called regardless of whether the children in it are actually orphans—has by no means outlived its usefulness. It provides a temporary shelter for children whose normal family relationships have recently been severed. Moreover, it is still considered the proper place to rear certain kinds of children—those whose chronic physical disabilities require highly specialized training, for example, or those whose emotional reactions suggest the need of institutional discipline. Even normal children, under some circumstances, may fare better in orphanages than in private foster homes. Thus if the mother is dead and the father, although anxious to maintain affectionate relationships, is unable to make suitable provision in his own home for the children's care, an institution may be the means of preserving family ties and eventually reuniting the family when the children have reached the age of self-support.

A number of different types of institutions for the care of children have been established. In addition to the usual orphanages or children's homes, which formerly sheltered all kinds of young people without regard to their individual differences and needs, there are now industrial schools for the delinquent, special institutions for the blind, the deaf, the crippled and the feeble-minded, and receiving homes where boys and girls may be kept and studied pending final disposition of their cases. Day nurseries and nursery schools, where working mothers may leave their very young children during the day, are becoming increasingly common.

**Foster homes.** A significant development in the care of the homeless young is the growing practice of placement with private families. Sometimes this plan is used not only for homeless children, but also for children whose homes are badly disrupted or whose parents are habitually so cruel or neglectful as to forfeit the right of parental control. As a rule, children are placed in foster homes with the understanding that they will be formally adopted at some later time if the arrangement proves satisfactory to all concerned. But there are many exceptions. Some families willingly take boys or girls for long periods without any expectation of adopting them—perhaps requiring a certain amount of work as the children grow older. Other families, in exchange for regular payments by public or private agencies, assume the responsibility of caring for children who are to be returned eventually to parents or relatives.

PROPER PLACEMENT. Whatever the basis of placement, it is important to select for each child a foster home suited to his individual needs. Therefore the first step in placement proceedings is a careful investigation of the families that are applying for children. The intelligence, training, ability, and character of the would-be foster parents should be considered, as well as their financial status, home life, and attitude toward children's problems. Any adverse factors that might make the process of adjustment difficult should be brought to light by means of questionnaires and personal interviews. It must not be forgotten, however, that the placement of children in permanent foster homes creates mutual relationships. Not only must the home be good; it must be good for the child who is to become a member of the family circle. Therefore the agency responsible for selecting homes must have an intimate understanding of every child's character and a full appreciation of his needs. Proper consideration should be given to his health, habits, intelligence, family history, and early environment. Provision should be made for curing any disease and correcting any remediable physical defect.

SUPERVISION AFTER PLACEMENT. Quite as important as proper placement is careful follow-up work. There should be a staff of trained social workers whose duty is to exercise watchful supervision over the children after they have been placed in foster homes, and make certain that the experiments are turning out as planned. During the first few months, especially, misunderstandings are likely to arise. Children may feel that they are unfairly treated, and foster parents may conclude that their efforts are wasted. Under such circumstances a skilful supervisor can often straighten out apparently irreconcilable differences by bridging the gap between the viewpoints of youth and age. Periodic visits are necessary to determine also whether the children's interests are being properly safeguarded— whether health and education, for example, are receiving the attention they deserve. The foster parents may require some training in the fundamentals of their new work. After the children have been legally adopted, of course, the jurisdiction of the placement agency is at an end, although friendly relationships may still be maintained. It is important, therefore, to be quite sure that the experiment is well on the road to success before custody is judicially awarded. Every public or private agency that places homeless children with private families admits the necessity of close supervision after placement, but only a few maintain supervisory staffs that could be called adequate by any stretch of the imagination. Frequently the visitors are untrained and have no real understanding of their duties. In almost all cases they are underpaid and overworked. Thus supervision becomes largely nominal, and the success of placement becomes a matter of choice. While this is not an argument against the placement system, it is a serious criticism of the manner in which placement is being conducted in nearly every state of the American Union.

### MOTHERS' AID FOR DEPENDENT CHILDREN

It requires no elaborate discussion to show that children should be reared by their own mothers wherever possible, and not by foster mothers or workers in institutions. The home should not be disrupted if it can be held together. This principle is fundamental in social work, yet it was virtually ignored until 1911, when Missouri enacted a law authorizing regular payments from the public treasury to indigent mothers of dependent children. Illinois followed with similar legislation a few months afterward, and in 1913 mothers' aid laws were adopted by eighteen states. The movement continued to spread, and by 1934 there were but three states that made no provision of any kind for assistance to mothers. Many of the laws were practically worthless, however. They relied solely on county initiative, as in Indiana and Oregon, or authorized state appropriations that were never made, as in Virginia. The early statutes applied only to *widows* with dependent children, but most of the later laws granted financial assistance to poor mothers who were dependent on their own efforts to support their children, regardless of whether the fathers were dead, deserting, imprisoned, or incapacitated. American citizenship was not usually made a prerequisite, but residence in the state for a given period—one to five years—was almost invariably required. Moreover, nearly all the states relied on county officials to administer the mothers' aid laws, and made little attempt to supervise county activities.

But the situation changed rapidly when the federal government entered the field in 1935. Federal funds were made available to the states for mothers' aid, but with conditions that entailed liberalization of most state laws. No child might be excluded for lack of county or city residence, nor might the state residence requirement exceed one year. Assistance should be granted until children were at least sixteen years of age, and might extend to children living with close relatives other than mothers. Administration must be directly in the hands of the state. The federal funds granted under this statute are limited to one half of the amount appropriated by states and cities; and there is a further restriction that they must not exceed eighteen dollars per month for the first child in a family, and twelve dollars for each additional child. Forty-five states have accepted the federal offer, and have prepared plans meeting federal approval. The three remaining states [6] make some provision for the support of dependent children, though not in accord with federal policies.

### HELP FOR THE BLIND

The federal Social Security Act also makes provision for federal participation in state programs of financial assistance to needy blind persons. The usual conditions are attached to the federal offer: the states must participate financially; they must submit work plans acceptable to the federal government; and they must make regular reports. When this grant was first offered to the states, in 1935, only two states were able to qualify. But state laws were speedily changed in conformity with federal standards. The number of co-operating commonwealths is now forty-three. The other five states also provide some form of aid to the needy blind.

### THE ABLE-BODIED UNEMPLOYED

The problem of poverty is accentuated by the fact that many able-bodied adults are unable or unwilling to find employment. Some of the members of this group are professional or semi-professional vagrants—homeless wanderers who seldom or never work because they have reached the conclusion that charity will meet all their needs. Such men constitute a class of unemployables. Closely allied to these shirkers is a second group, occasional workers, whose periods of employment are likely to become less frequent as the lure of vagabondage proves increasingly difficult to resist. Then there is still a third group. made up of men and women who genuinely desire work but can find

[6] Kentucky, Iowa, and Nevada

none. In periods of depression the number of such persons is very large, but even in war times, when employment is at the peak, there are still some who cannot find jobs—perhaps because of changes in popular taste or the adoption of new manufacturing processes. Obviously all three classes of persons cannot be treated alike.

Just what should be done with those who seem to prefer unemployment and charity to steady work and independence is still a moot question. In some counties they are arrested as vagrants and committed to jail for a term of days or months. Other communities simply order them to leave town within twenty-four hours—a method that does not solve the problem but shifts it to other shoulders. Police stations are often used as lodgings for the homeless. A few of the more progressive communities have established public lodging houses, where destitute men may receive temporary shelter and perhaps one or two meals in exchange for a few hours' work on the wood pile.

Modern society is less concerned with the unemployable and semi-unemployable, however, than with those self-respecting men and women who have been forced into idleness by the pressure of economic forces. Their right to a job or public support can no longer be questioned. Federal work relief took care of several million such persons until the spring of 1943, when the federal program was temporarily abandoned because of the tremendous increase in private employment. But the long-run need of these jobless men and women is not relief; it is some form of job insurance, so that they will be guaranteed a means of self-support when they are thrown out of work. Unemployment insurance has long been accepted by European nations as a matter of course, but it was not generally adopted in the United States until 1935. Now it has become a major factor in the fight against poverty. Its main features are discussed in a subsequent chapter.[7]

### ADMINISTRATIVE ORGANIZATION

**Movement toward state control.** In the early days of American history the care of the poor was entrusted solely to the local units of government—chiefly the counties. State authorities did not attempt to exercise even a cursory supervision. The results were highly unsatisfactory. Diverse practices, competitive relationships, and wasteful methods characterized local poor relief. Unsuitable buildings and inadequate equipment were found almost everywhere. A de-

[7] See pp. 586–588.

mand for some measure of state supervision naturally arose, therefore, and in 1863 Massachusetts led the way by creating a state board of charities. Ohio and New York followed in 1867; then came Illinois, North Carolina, Pennsylvania, and Rhode Island in 1869. By 1913, just half a century after the establishment of the first state board of charities, thirty-eight states had set up similar agencies, and during the next twenty years the number increased to forty-five. There was a definite tendency to make the board or department of charities responsible for the administration or supervision of all state charity. But depression set in motion a counter-trend. Separate agencies were created in some commonwealths for the administration of unemployment relief, children's services, old-age pensions, and other phases of the social security program. Today [8] only about one half of the states vest responsibility for all forms of assistance in a single department or board. The state agency or agencies responsible for the various aspects of public charity usually possess a considerable measure of control over local activities. Sometimes they inspect all local charitable institutions and approve plans and specifications for new buildings, in addition to supervising the administration of local charity. Usually, however, state jurisdiction is not so extensive.

UNIFIED CONTROL. In 1917 Illinois departed from the traditional plan of board control and established the first single-headed state department responsible for charity administration. The head of the department, selected by the governor and responsible solely to him, was made a member of the newly created executive cabinet. Provision was also made for a board of public welfare commissioners, but the functions of this board were purely advisory. It was given no voice in rule-making or the preparation of department estimates; these matters, as well as general supervision of the department's work, were entrusted to the director. The Illinois department was called the *department of public welfare,* and its authority was made sufficiently broad to justify this new name. In addition to poor relief it assumed supervision over the treatment of criminals, administering the penal institutions of the state, directing parole work, and investigating applications for pardons. Establishment of single-headed departments has been opposed by many students of social problems on the ground that political influences might interfere more readily with efficient administration. The plan has made considerable headway, however, despite this stock argument against every form of unified control. At

[8] 1945.

the present time it is used, at least for some aspects of charity, by thirty states.    Almost all the newer plans of reorganization substitute *welfare* for *charities,* but this change in nomenclature does not always indicate a regrouping of functions.

BOARD CONTROL.    Among those states that still rely on the board plan of charity control, there is no general agreement as to the size of the board, its powers or duties, or the terms or salaries of its members.    In many cases the board is composed of laymen whose principal function is to select an executive officer to handle the actual details of administration.    Alabama, which employs this plan, has a six-member board of public welfare, appointed by the governor for six-year over-lapping terms.    Some states vary this scheme by providing for ex officio boards of charities or welfare.    So-called boards of control— really commissions [9]—have been established, at least for certain aspects of charity administration, in nine states.[10]    These "boards" usually have from three to five members, appointed for long terms by the governor with senate approval.    Since the members receive full-time salaries [11] they are expected to devote full time to their official duties. Individually they administer various phases of the work; as a group they formulate policies and establish rules of procedure.    They are presumed to possess special technical fitness, though sometimes their chief qualification is an ability to control votes.

### SELECTED REFERENCES

Abbott, Edith, *Public Assistance,* 1940.
Abbott, Grace, *From Relief to Social Security,* 1941.
Atwater, Pierce, *Problems of Administration in Social Work,* 1940.
Bossard, J. H. S., *Social Change and Social Problems,* rev. ed., 1938.
Breckenridge, Sophonisba P., *Public Welfare Administration in the United States;*
      *Select Documents,* 2nd ed., 1938.
———, ed., *The Family and the State; Select Documents,* 1934.
Brown, Josephine C., *Public Relief, 1929–1939,* 1940.
Clarke, Helen I., *Social Legislation,* 1940.
Clarke, John J., *Public Assistance and Unemployment Assistance,* 2nd ed., 1937.
Douglas, Paul H., *Social Security in the United States,* rev. ed., 1939.
Epstein, Abraham, *Insecurity: A Challenge to America,* 2nd rev. ed., 1939.
Grant, Margaret, *Old-Age Security; Social and Financial Trends,* 1939.
Harris, Seymour E., *Economics of Social Security,* 1941.

[9] The distinction between boards and commissions is pointed out above.    See pp. 315–316.

[10] Iowa, Kansas, Minnesota, Nebraska, North Dakota, Oregon, Texas, West Virginia, Wisconsin.

[11] Three to five thousand dollars a year.

James, Arthur W., *The State Becomes a Social Worker*, Richmond, Va., 1942.

Klein, Alice C., *Civil Service in Public Welfare*, 1940.

Lane, M. D., *America on Relief*, 1938.

Lansdale, Robert T., Long, Elizabeth, Leisy, Agnes, and Hipple, Byron, *The Administration of Old-Age Assistance*, 1939.

National Resources Planning Board, *Security, Work, and Relief Policies*, Washington, D.C., 1942.

Stevenson, Marietta, *Public Welfare Administration*, 1938.

——, and MacDonald, Alice, *State and Local Public Welfare Agencies*, 1939.

Stewart, Bryce M., and Others, *Planning and Administration of Unemployment Compensation in the United States*, 1938.

Stewart, Maxwell S., *Social Security*, rev. ed., 1939.

Street, Elwood, *The Public Welfare Administrator*, 1940.

White, R. Clyde, *Administration of Public Welfare*, 1940.

——, and Mary K., *Social Aspects of Relief Policies in the Depression*, 1937.

Woytinsky, Waldimir S., *Earnings and Social Security in the United States*, Washington, D.C., 1943.

Wyatt, B. E., and Others, *Social Security Act in Operation*, Washington, D.C., 1937.

---

Every student of welfare problems should be familiar with the *Social Work Year Book*, published by the Russell Sage Foundation.

# Chapter Twenty-Three ❧ EDUCATION

DURING the early period of American history, and even in the first years of the nineteenth century, education was generally considered a private matter. Except in New England, where public schools early made their appearance because of the close connection between church and state, free education was reserved almost exclusively for the children of paupers. It was, in fact, a form of poor relief. As one writer declares, the masses made no distinction "between putting a coat on a child's back, food into his stomach, and knowledge into his head." [1]

## SHIFT FROM PRIVATE TO PUBLIC EDUCATION

A few persons, like Thomas Jefferson in Virginia, favored universal elementary education at state expense, but they were shouted down. They were many years ahead of their time. As late as 1850, when the proposal for a system of free schools received final approval in New York State, most rural voters expressed themselves in opposition. A similar plan for Pennsylvania proved unpopular in the farming sections until the Civil War. Many persons argued vehemently that public education would foment social unrest and perhaps lead to revolution, since the poor would gain a better understanding of their burdens. It was said, also, that taxation for school purposes was a gross violation of private property rights. Why should a man be compelled to support a public school system if he chose to send his children to a private sectarian academy? But these arguments were of no avail against the trend of the times. The ideal of free, universal, compulsory education was rapidly gaining general acceptance. Today it is no longer questioned; it is a foundation of the American social structure.

**Division of responsibility for public education.** Responsibility for financing and directing public education is divided among the nation, the states, and the local units of government. The nation's part is narrowly restricted by the federal Constitution, which makes no mention of educational matters, thus reserving control of education to the

[1] Cook, Wm. A., *Federal and State School Administration*, p. 35.

457

states.[2] Yet the federal government has appropriated hundreds of millions of dollars for educational purposes. It has turned over to the states more than seventy million acres of the national domain in furtherance of public education. And it has even secured the right to supervise certain phases of the state educational systems by means of conditional grants from the federal treasury.[3] It maintains an Office of Education that collects educational statistics, conducts educational surveys, and furnishes advice to state and local school officials concerning educational problems. Until the Second World War its Civilian Conservation Corps operated an elaborate educational program; its Works Progress Administration maintained many educational projects; and its National Youth Administration provided part-time employment for hundreds of thousands of young people enrolled in high schools and colleges. Recently Congress has enacted legislation permitting many returned war veterans to complete their education at federal expense. For the most part, however, education still remains outside the sphere of federal control. Though the federal government is much more than a mere spectator of educational progress, it plays no important part in the administration of public education.

A vast number of court decisions have established beyond reasonable doubt the fact that education is primarily a matter of state concern.[4] Even in those states that have accepted the principle of municipal home rule,[5] education remains under state control unless specifically assigned by the state to the local units of government. "Authorities in control of the public or common schools, under whatever name, are mere auxiliaries or agencies of the state for educational purposes only, created by the state as a means of exercising its political powers in an orderly and systematic manner, and as such are subject to the unrestricted control and direction of the legislature in matters of internal government."[6] In nearly every state, however, the actual management of the school system rests with locally chosen officials. School expenses are met chiefly from local taxes. The state, though supreme in matters of education, generally prefers to exercise its au-

---

[2] By the Tenth Amendment. See p. 30.

[3] See pp. 36–40.

[4] See, for example, Louisville *v.* Board of Education, 154 Ky. 316; 157 S.W. 379 (1913); Associated Schools *v.* School District, 122 Minn. 254; 142 N.W. 325 (1913); MacQueen *v.* Port Huron, 194 Mich. 328; 160 N.W. 627. 630 (1916).

[5] See pp. 264–266.

[6] McQuillin, Eugene, *A Treatise on the Law of Municipal Corporations*, Supplement, Vol. VIII, pp. 8122–8123.

thority through local channels. Therefore the local units of government properly come first in any discussion of school administration.

## LOCAL UNITS OF SCHOOL ADMINISTRATION

**The school district plan.** The local unit responsible for directing the school system is not everywhere the same. It may be the school district, the town, the township, or the county. The school district plan of organization has several features worthy of mention: It was one of the earliest schemes of school management; it is unquestionably the worst; and it is still the most widely used. In early times, and under more primitive conditions, the district plan was reasonably satisfactory. But as educational standards rose and it became increasingly evident that small districts—especially districts of the "little red schoolhouse" variety—could not meet present-day requirements, a determined movement began in many states for the elimination of the school districts and the transfer of their functions to larger units of government, such as the townships or counties.

OBJECTIONS. In opposition to the district system it was pointed out that most districts were too poor to warrant the employment of suitable teachers and too small to permit the division of the student body into grades; that schools were unwisely distributed; that educational facilities varied widely from district to district because of unequal wealth and uneven interest in education; that so many school trustees—often five hundred or more in a single county—were required by the plan as to make the selection of many mediocre persons almost inevitable; and that in practice the scheme had proved inefficient, wasteful and a barrier to educational advancement. The result of this crusade, which is still in progress, has been the abandonment of the district system in many states and its modification in a number of others. It is still used in about one third of the states, however. West of the Mississippi River it is especially strong. But the district trustees have generally been deprived of several important functions, including the certification of teachers, the selection of textbooks, and the distribution of school funds.

LARGE URBAN DISTRICTS. It should be pointed out that a municipality, from the standpoint of educational administration, is simply a single school district. Even a large metropolitan center occupies this legal position. It has its own board of trustees (or board of education, as it is more commonly known) and its own teachers and schools. Usually the board of education is independent of the municipal government. It levies a separate tax for the support of the schools [7] and makes rules and regulations concerning school policy without consulting the mayor or council. Its powers are much broader than the powers of a rural board of trustees. Obviously the usual objections to the district system do not apply to the large urban districts, which maintain high standards and generally lead in educational matters.

**The township plan.** A number of states have tried to escape the disadvantages of the direct plan by adopting the township as the chief unit of school administration. Because a township is many times larger than the average rural district, this change has usually produced reasonably good results. Better teachers have been employed in many instances. Better buildings and equipment have been made possible. Township high schools have been established without the delays incident to separate district action. The merit of the township as the unit of school control is that it is large enough to wipe out some of the more glaring district inequalities. Properly applied, the township plan tends to equalize educational cost and educational opportunity *within each township.*

Results have not been uniformly good, however. Nor has the township plan always assumed the same form. In some states the township trustees exercise only a small measure of control over school affairs, while the districts within the townships continue virtually undisturbed as the primary units of educational administration. Such an arrangement scarcely deserves to be called the township plan, though it generally assumes that name; it is more nearly the district scheme behind a thin disguise. Moreover, among the several townships of a county, inequalities continue undisturbed.

**The county plan.** Quite natural, therefore, is the proposal to abolish township as well as district control of education and make the county the primary administrative unit. This plan or its equivalent is now in state-wide use in Alabama, Kentucky, Maryland, and Utah, and has been adopted by certain counties in other states.

ITS OPERATION. Control vests in a board of education chosen by the people of the county or appointed by the governor. This board supervises all the county schools, appoints all supervisors, principals, and teachers, fixes salary schedules, and determines all questions of policy concerning courses of instruction, textbooks, and other school matters, except so far as state law requires uniformity. Most im-

---

[7] In New York, Detroit, Baltimore, Buffalo, and a number of other cities, however, the school system is dependent upon the city government for financial support.

portant of all, the county board of education selects a school superintendent who acts as the administrative officer of the school system. The list of his duties commonly includes the co-ordination of the work of the schools, the approval of plans for new schoolhouses, the examination of applicants for teaching positions, the supervision of teachers, the direction of institutes for further teacher training, and the settlement of disputes that arise among members of the teaching force. As a rule the school superintendent also acts as the business officer of the county school system. Thus all the educational activities of the county are brought under a single executive. The county plan eliminates a great deal of unnecessary duplication and makes possible the use of county school funds for the benefit of all the county schools without regard to district or township boundaries. Authorities are generally agreed that its universal adoption would be an important advance along the path of educational progress.

Though only a few states look with favor upon the county as the primary unit of school administration, nearly all have established some form of county control over educational matters. County school superintendents and county boards of education are now found in forty states,[8] usually in addition to the district or township school authorities. The superintendent is commonly elected by the people of the county, though he may be chosen by the judges of the county courts, as in Tennessee, or by the state board of education, as in Virginia. His powers vary widely from state to state. In Iowa he is little more than a figurehead; in California he exercises considerable authority. The functions commonly assigned to him include general supervision of district or township school activities and auditing of local accounts. He keeps necessary records, collects and reports statistical information, and acts as intermediary between state and local officials. He is supposed to be a professional educator and an expert in school administration. All too often, however, his selection is due to partisan considerations. Popular election is a poor way to choose any technician, and county superintendents are no exception to the rule.

County boards of education also assume a variety of forms in the several states. Some of them exercise scarcely more than nominal authority. In New York, for example, each county board meets but once in five years, and its sole function is the selection of the school superintendent. The Mississippi county school board, whose mem-

[8] The only exceptions are Connecticut, Delaware, Maine, Massachusetts, Nevada, New Hampshire, Rhode Island, Vermont.

bers are appointed by the county superintendent, holds annual meetings but possesses no important powers. In Virginia, however, the county board apportions the school fund among the districts, audits the district accounts, prepares a county school budget, and makes rules governing a number of minor matters. Reference has already been made to the broad powers of the county school boards in those states that have abolished districts and townships, and adopted the county plan of school administration.[9]

**The New England town plan.** In New England, where the county has never possessed important governmental functions, the town remains the primary unit of school administration. The New England town must not be confused, however, with the township found in other parts of the United States. It is a "natural" unit of government, separated at least in part from neighboring towns by a river, a line of hills, or some other topographical feature. Usually it includes not only the central village but also a considerable area of agricultural land and perhaps several smaller villages. Each village may have its separate school, but all are managed by the town school committee, which decides questions of policy and selects a superintendent to handle the actual details of administration. In recent years, as a result of state insistence upon proper standards, it has become common practice in some of the New England states for two or more towns to join in choosing a school superintendent, whose jurisdiction extends over the "superintendency union" thus formed.

**Gradual shift to larger units.** For many years the trend toward larger units of school administration has been manifest in every part of the United States. The transfer of school control from district to township and from township to county has seldom been matched by a counter-movement favoring a return to the smaller units. School consolidation, proposed and debated in virtually every state and used effectively in many, is a reflection of the general tendency. In New England, the impracticability of developing county administration has led to closer state supervision and control. State control has been strengthened in other sections of the country, also. Professional educators agree that the small units have outlived their usefulness, and constantly urge their abolition. But such changes come slowly; the traditions of a century cannot be swept away overnight. Therefore the transition from small to large units will doubtless continue at an exasperatingly slow pace, and school districts will probably play an

9 See pp. 460–461.

important part in American educational systems for several decades to come.

## UNIFIED STATE SCHOOL ADMINISTRATION

The arguments for a county system of school administration apply with equal force to a state system of school administration. If a large unit is good, a larger unit should be better. If inequalities of educational opportunities within a county should be removed, then similar inequalities among counties should also be eliminated. The logic of this position is unassailable.

To date, however, only one state—Delaware—has attempted to organize its schools into a single centrally administered unit, and this attempt has not been completely successful. By act of 1921 the counties were deprived of all control over educational matters, and their powers transferred to the state board of education. School districts were retained, but only for administrative purposes. The state assumed the responsibility of financing the system. The City of Wilmington and the larger towns, however, were specifically exempted from the provisions of the law. In Wilmington and these towns the schools are now managed by specially created local boards, subject to general state oversight. The remainder of the state is under direct central control. In 1931 the state government of North Carolina accepted complete financial responsibility for the maintenance and support of the public schools for the six months' term guaranteed by the constitution, and later lengthened this term to eight months. The county boards of education have been retained, however, and in some respects their authority has actually been increased. They still select superintendents and teachers, and exercise considerable discretion over the business affairs of the schools. New Hampshire, though still retaining the town form of school administration, has greatly strengthened state control within recent years. Minimum local standards are fixed by the state board of education, and maintained by contributions from the state treasury wherever necessary. Local school revenues in excess of local needs are paid into the state fund. Nearly half of the area of Maine lies within territory unorganized for school purposes, and the administration of this area is under the immediate direction of the state superintendent. The laws of Rhode Island authorize the state board of education to assume control of the schools of any town, upon request of the town school committee, if satisfied that local revenues are insufficient. Apparently, therefore, a number of states are well on the road to unified state control. Other states, also, have gestured in the direction of state unification, but their gestures are scarcely worth recording.

**Inequalities in educational facilities.** During the past half century surveys of school finance have been conducted in every section of the United States. Every major fiscal problem of school administration has been considered from many standpoints. These investigations differ in many respects, but they invariably reach the conclusion that *wealth is so unevenly distributed among the local units of school administration as to preclude the possibility of maintaining reasonably uniform—or even reasonably adequate—standards without some form of state support.* Even assuming equal willingness, it would be utterly impossible for the poorer districts to support schools equal to the schools found in some of the richer sections. Taxes sufficient to provide satisfactory educational facilities would impose a very light burden on some communities but would prove virtually confiscatory if applied to others. The inequalities resulting from this uneven distribution of wealth are so glaring that they cannot be brushed aside or condoned by any person interested in the establishment of a sound educational system. In the rural sections, which are chiefly affected, and also in many poor industrial areas, boys and girls are taught for shorter periods by teachers of inferior training and experience. Equipment is inadequate or obsolete.

**State financial support.** Such inequalities in educational facilities cannot be permitted to continue indefinitely. Reform comes slowly, however, because it necessarily involves larger contributions from the state treasury—a policy at variance with the widespread idea that education is purely a matter of local concern. For many years the states have contributed to the support of the public schools, but until recently these payments never represented more than a small part of the total cost except in a very few states. Even today the local units of government—school districts, towns, townships, cities, counties— bear more than sixty-five per cent of the burden in twenty-eight of the states.

STATE SUBSIDIES. Some states have recently moved in the direction of increased state support, however. Delaware provides the most conspicuous example of state-financed education; its establishment of a state-managed school system has necessitated complete state support. Half of the cost of the Florida, Texas, and West Virginia school systems is paid from state appropriations, and in a number of states [10] the percentage of state support is even higher.[11]

In 1943 the states paid $822,000,000 to their minor civil subdivisions for school purposes—an increase of more than one hundred per cent in twelve years. A great deal of this money was distributed on the basis of the school census, each governmental unit receiving state aid in proportion to the number of children of school age resident within its borders. But many other bases were used also, such as the number of children actually enrolled in school, the number of children attending for fixed periods, the average daily school attendance. Some states paid a fixed sum for each teacher; others graduated their teacher grants according to experience, training, and salary. Still other plans were in operation—a flat sum to each school or each district; a grant to each district proportioned to its ability to finance a minimum educational program; a subsidy applying only to the poorer units. These schemes, and others, were combined by many states in various ways, with interesting but sometimes confusing results.

*Defective operation of laws.* One of the chief reasons for the faulty operation of these subsidy laws is that most of them have been enacted and are now being administered without any clear understanding of what they are supposed to achieve. Relief of the poorer districts is undoubtedly a factor, at least in many of the laws, but this purpose is often defeated by the very statutes that seek to accomplish it. Take, for example, the school-census method of apportionment, which is designed to lighten the financial burdens of the less fortunate communities. This plan "grants the same amount of aid to a district whether it maintains a school for the minimum legal term or for several months in excess of this minimum; whether it provides an adequate or an inadequate number of teachers; whether its school program is satisfactory or unsatisfactory; whether the district is exceedingly wealthy and levies a light tax or is exceedingly poor and levies a heavy tax." The result is that "this method actually perpetuates inequalities in school revenues and school burdens." [12]

[10] These states are Alabama, Georgia, Louisiana, New Mexico, North Carolina, Oklahoma, Washington.

[11] See the National Education Association's *Research Bulletin*, Vol. XX, No. 5, Nov., 1942, pp. 154–158. This issue is entitled "State School Finance Systems."

[12] Swift, Fletcher H., *Federal and State Policies in Public School Finance in the United States*, p. 212.

Thirty-eight states [13] use at least a portion of their school funds for a broader purpose than mere haphazard relief—namely, equalization of the financial burden of education among all the local units. New York, Pennsylvania, Colorado, Idaho, and South Dakota apportion all their distributive school funds with this end in view; on the other hand, such states as Maine and Wyoming devote only nominal sums to equalization. Most states lie somewhere between these two extremes. A number of different equalization schemes have been devised. Thus Michigan apportions certain funds among school districts whose property valuation per child in average school membership is less than the state average; New York grants money to cover deficits in approved local budgets; and Mississippi employs a complicated formula involving three factors—need as measured in terms of cost per teaching unit, effort as measured by the local tax rate and average daily attendance, and ability to finance a school system as measured by the taxable wealth per teaching unit. Most of these so-called "equalization" plans do not equalize, or do so only to a very limited extent. Some actually work against the poorer districts. No entirely satisfactory plan has yet been formulated, though several of the newer equalization schemes are reasonably acceptable.

*Conditions attached to apportionments.* Nearly every state apportions some of its school money to local units with certain conditions attached—conditions that must be met as a prerequisite to state aid. In Massachusetts, where this policy of stimulation has been highly developed, the local communities receive money from the state treasury in proportion to the caliber of their teachers and other school officers, as determined by salary, professional preparation and teaching experience. Thus every town is encouraged by the prospect of state aid to employ properly qualified teachers and pay them adequate salaries. The weakness of this plan is that it tends to foster inequalities. The wealthy communities, which least need state money, are best able to meet minimum state requirements.

**Proposals for federal support.** Uneven distribution of wealth, which so hampers the poorer sections in their efforts to provide a decent minimum of educational opportunity, occurs not only within the boundaries of each state, but also among the several states of the American Union. The National Education Association estimates that for every dollar raised by Mississippi for educational purposes,

[13] The only exceptions are Arizona, California, Delaware, Florida, Iowa, Kentucky, New Mexico, North Carolina, Oregon, and Virginia.

New York could raise eleven with equal ease, and Delaware could raise thirteen.[14]   Not unnaturally, therefore, many persons contend that the federal government should assume a large measure of responsibility for general education, and that it should distribute to the several states, on the basis of educational need, a reasonable part of the funds collected, presumably on the basis of ability to pay, from the people of the several states.   Such a proposal presents numerous technical and administrative difficulties, but it has been warmly supported, nonetheless, by many professional educators.   Bills authorizing large grants from the federal treasury to the states in support of general education have been introduced at every session of Congress for many years, but have invariably lacked sufficient support.

### STATE ADMINISTRATIVE ORGANIZATION

**The state superintendent.**   In the first period of American independence not a single state had a superintendent of public instruction or corresponding officer.   Nor was any such officer needed, since education rested so largely in private hands.   But as the emphasis shifted from private to public education, and local school activities began to assume more than purely local importance, the need for some state agency vested with supervisory powers over the local units in matters relating to education became increasingly clear.   In 1812 New York took the first step by appointing a superintendent of public schools. Other states followed slowly—Maryland in 1826, Vermont in 1827, and Michigan in 1829.   Several of these states temporarily abandoned the office after experimenting with it a few years, but in the meantime the movement was growing, and before the end of the nineteenth century the office of superintendent of public instruction had been established in every state.

At first the superintendent's duties were light and his powers few. He apportioned the state school grants to local communities in the manner prescribed by law, prepared rudimentary educational statistics, and furnished legal advice on educational questions.   Other duties and powers were added from time to time, however, as the state's part in the general scheme of education became increasingly important.   In many states the superintendent acquired considerable authority over the local school units—the power to supervise local

14 *Research Bulletin,* Vol. XX, No. 4, Sept., 1942, p. 135.   This issue, which is entitled "Federal Aid for Education," contains a careful analysis of the proposal to make education a federal responsibility.

finances, to issue and revoke teachers' certificates, and to control a number of other matters that will be considered at greater length in the remaining pages of this chapter.

The recent trend has been to increase still further the superintendent's powers. Little has been done, however, to attract able men. As previously pointed out, the superintendent of public instruction is still chosen by popular vote in more than two thirds of the states.[15] His salary is small—often much smaller than that paid to school superintendents of the larger cities. His term of office is short—seldom more than four years, and frequently only two years. In those states that retain popular election as the method of choosing the superintendent, re-election is the exception rather than the rule. Quite naturally, therefore, professional educators of proved ability commonly refuse to become candidates for the post of state superintendent of public instruction, and the professional politicians gladly include it among the spoils.

**State boards of education.** State boards of education, exercising varying degrees of control over general educational policy, have been created in forty-two states.[16] Sometimes they are composed solely of state officers serving ex officio, as in Oregon, where the three members of the board are the governor, the secretary of state and the superintendent of public instruction. Sometimes they are made up of persons appointed by the governor, as in California. A number of states—Georgia and Tennessee, for example—combine ex officio and appointed members. Usually the state board of education plays a minor part in the general scheme of educational administration. This is especially true in the case of the ex officio board,[17] which in some states does little more than administer certain school funds, formulate general policies on minor educational matters, and give the superintendent of public instruction advice that he is free to accept or reject. For many years, however, the tendency has been to increase the board's powers, at the same time ridding it of ex officio members. In the eight states [18] that provide for the selection of the superintendent of public instruction by the board of education, the board is the domi-

---

15 See p. 223.

16 In the six remaining states—Illinois, Iowa, Maine, Nebraska, Ohio, South Dakota—there are boards that exercise control over certain specific aspects of education, such as normal schools or vocational training.

17 The objections to ex officio boards have already been considered. See pp. 322–323.

18 Connecticut, Delaware, Maryland, Minnesota, New Hampshire, New York, Rhode Island, Vermont.

nant force in the administration of the school system. It exercises broad powers of supervision and control, though presumably leaving to its agent, the superintendent, the task of enforcing the policies upon which it has agreed.

**Original plan of local certification.** Many matters formerly left to the discretion of the local administrative units have been brought under the state control in recent years. One such matter is the certification of teachers. The necessity of determining whether prospective teachers were properly qualified was recognized as soon as education became a public function. In each community the local authorities examined applicants and issued teaching certificates to those who passed with satisfactory grades. But this plan was defective in many respects. It permitted each local unit to fix the standards of its own teaching force, regardless of how low those standards might be; it left the preparation of examination questions and the grading of papers to laymen whose fitness to serve as examiners might well have been questioned; and it limited the supply of teachers in each community to residents of that community because certificates granted elsewhere were not accepted.

**Gradual change to state certification.** Gradually, however, important changes were made in the system of certification—if the plan first adopted can be called a "system." The right to certify teachers passed from the districts and townships to the counties and from the lay officials to the county superintendents of education,who presumably were better informed concerning the maintenance of proper educational standards. Inter-county recognition of the higher grades of certificates was first made optional, and then compulsory. A little later, in the more progressive states, the lower grades of certificates were abolished by state law. The next step was state preparation of examination questions, to be used in all counties. Then some states authorized the counties to forward the papers to the state office for grading. About this time state certificates began to make their appearance, though certificates were also issued by those counties that refused to accept state control. From this point it was but a step to a complete system of state certification of teachers, with the counties completely eliminated from the picture. Not all states have passed through these several stages, however. In fact, the counties still play a part in the issuance of teachers' certificates in more than one third of the states. They grant certificates in direct competition with the state authorities, or use questions prepared by the state, or, in some jurisdictions, merely act as state agents in giving examinations. Quite frequently cities are exempted from the operation of a state certification system on the assumption that their standards are higher than the minimum prescribed by state law. But this assumption is not always justified. In some small municipalities the exemption from state supervision merely affords a welcome opportunity to avoid reasonable requirements. With the possible exception of a few great metropolitan centers, therefore, all municipalities should be compelled to conform to the state certification system. Those cities desiring to maintain still higher standards should be permitted to do so, of course; but their special requirements should be in addition to, and not in lieu of, the state certificate.

**Teacher training and salary schedules.** At one time certificates were granted to teachers solely on the basis of examinations, but the modern tendency is to place emphasis chiefly on recognized academic and professional training. Graduates of normal schools need not further demonstrate their fitness by passing formal tests. In half of the states graduation from high school is a prerequisite to certification. Professional educators agree that teachers should be certified solely on the basis of their credentials, thus eliminating the need of examinations; but there is no likelihood that this plan will be generally accepted in the near future.

Not only by certification, but by other plans as well, the states try to secure competent teachers for the public schools. State normal schools and teachers' colleges have become commonplaces.[19] Half of the states have established general plans for teacher training in the high schools, the last year of the high school course or, less commonly, a fifth graduate year being set aside for this work. Although high school teacher training is objectionable in many respects, it has undoubtedly improved the quality of rural teaching. In twenty states minimum salary laws have been enacted. Most of these laws have proved practically worthless, partly because the minimum has been placed very low and partly because the districts unable to pay even the minimum have defeated the purpose of the higher-salary-per-month requirement by keeping their schools open fewer months each

[19] These state schools have been supplemented by county normal schools in a number of states. Municipal normal schools are less common than formerly, but are still maintained by a number of cities.

year. A few states, however, have adopted carefully prepared state-wide salary schedules based on advanced teaching preparation and maintained by heavy state subsidies. Teacher pension systems have been quite generally accepted as a means of making the teaching profession more attractive to able men and women. Pension benefits are now available to all teachers in twenty-seven states and to certain classes of teachers in a number of other commonwealths.

## COMPULSORY SCHOOL ATTENDANCE LAWS

**Nation-wide adoption.** Compulsory school attendance laws are now found in every state, but their adoption was attended with a number of difficulties and opposition from many sources. When Massachusetts in 1852 declared that all children between the ages of eight and fourteen must attend school for twelve weeks each year, "if public schools so long continue," thus initiating the compulsory attendance movement in the United States,[20] a veritable storm of adverse criticism broke loose. Such legislation was declared to be un-American, an unreasonable violation of the rights of parents, a gross disregard of the sanctity of the home, and an unnecessary interference with business. Even many teachers and county superintendents voiced their disapproval. But the principle of compulsory attendance slowly gained popular support despite widespread opposition. New York followed the example of Massachusetts in 1853, and Vermont in 1867. By the end of the nineteenth century thirty-one states had enacted some sort of compulsory school attendance legislation, and the number was finally increased to forty-eight in 1918 when Mississippi, the last to fall into line, adopted a weak county-option scheme.

**Provisions.** The provisions of these laws are by no means uniform. Some fix the age limits of compulsory attendance within a narrow range; the Georgia statute, for example, applies only to children between the age of eight and fourteen. The laws of other states fix much broader age limits, as in Nevada, where the span is from seven to eighteen years. Wide variations are found, also, in the length of the required annual period of school attendance. While more than half of the state laws now require attendance for the full school term, others specify merely that children must attend school for a fraction of the term—often two thirds, or for a minimum number of days,

[20] During the early colonial period Massachusetts and Connecticut had compulsory school attendance laws, but these statutes had become dead letters long before the Revolution.

the minimum sometimes being placed as low as forty or fifty. In some states many classes of children are exempted from the provisions of the law for no good reason. Certain exceptions are necessary, of course, and have become a universal feature of compulsory school attendance statutes. But the undue multiplication of exempted groups is contrary to the spirit of compulsory attendance and leads inevitably to a breakdown of the compulsory feature of public education.

EXEMPTION OF PRIVATE SCHOOL STUDENTS. The exemption from public school attendance of children who are receiving equivalent instruction in private or parochial schools is generally recognized as proper. Proposals to abolish private education, aimed chiefly at parochial and other sectarian schools, have been made from time to time, but have won popular favor in only one state. That state— Oregon—adopted a 1922 initiative measure requiring private and parochial school children to attend public schools throughout the entire school term. The law was promptly attacked in the courts, however, and in 1925 was set aside by the Supreme Court of the United States as an unconstitutional interference with the right of parents and guardians to direct the upbringing of their children. "Rights guaranteed by the Constitution," declared the Court, "may not be abridged by legislation which has no reasonable relation to some purpose within the competency of the state. The fundamental theory of liberty upon which all governments in this Union repose excludes any general power of the state to standardize its children by forcing them to accept instruction from public teachers only. The child is not the mere creature of the state; those who nurture him and direct his destiny have the right, coupled with the high duty, to recognize and prepare him for additional obligations." [21]

**Enforcement.** Quite as important as the text of a compulsory school attendance law is the manner of its enforcement. In many states, however, enforcement is limited to occasional feeble gestures. This is true especially in the rural districts, where reliance is often placed on the sporadic efforts of constables or deputy sheriffs. Even the appointment of regular compulsory-attendance officers does not always solve the problem. These officers are commonly overworked; in some jurisdictions they receive from the school authorities reports of far more cases than they can possibly find time to investigate. Salaries are low, and appointments are often made for partisan rea-

21 Pierce *v.* Society of the Sisters, etc., 268 U.S. 510 (1925).

sons.   Provision is scarcely ever made for an accurate census of school children, with the result that the compulsory-attendance officers commonly lack the information necessary for a proper performance of their duties.   Small wonder, therefore, that thoroughly satisfactory enforcement of the compulsory school attendance law is a matter worthy of special comment!

STATE CONTROL OF OTHER EDUCATIONAL MATTERS

**Courses of study.**   The state legislature usually specifies in considerable detail the subjects to be taught in the public schools.   Sometimes it goes still further and prohibits the teaching of certain subjects or certain theories that are considered undesirable.   Thus the schools may be required to give instruction in American and local history, or forbidden to teach the theory of evolution.   A certain amount of state control over courses of instruction is justifiable, especially if it assumes the form of general requirements, leaving sufficient discretion to the teachers and the local school authorities.   Too often, however, the value of local initiative is forgotten, state regulations even going so far as to establish uniform courses of study, with uniform textbooks and uniform assignments.   While such detailed central control may at times raise the standards of instruction in the least progressive rural communities, its general effort is to prevent desirable experiments and set the curriculum of the public schools in a hard, unyielding mold.

**Textbooks.**   State-wide uniformity of textbooks is the practice in twenty-five states of the South and West.[22]   A few Western states make provision for county-wide uniformity; elsewhere the district or township is the unit for textbook adoption.   In those commonwealths having state uniformity the adopting body may be the state board of education, a separate textbook board, or the board of education plus other persons designated to sit with it when textbook adoption is being considered.   There are a number of arguments in favor of statewide uniformity, most of them centering around the factor of lower cost, but experts in educational administration generally consider such uniformity unwise.   They point out that the use of uniform textbooks hampers local initiative in curriculum construction, prevents proper recognition of differences among the school systems of the state, and often leads to the corruption of the state board by text-

---

[22] Five of these states, however, make uniform textbook adoptions for elementary schools only.   These states are Arizona, Arkansas, Nevada, New Mexico, and West Virginia.   In Idaho uniformity is limited to the rural elementary schools.

book publishers whose scruples have melted away in the heat of the fight for a large contract.[23]   At one time pupils were generally required to pay for the textbooks they used, but in recent years the trend has been toward free distribution.   Nineteen states now specify by law that free textbooks must be supplied, and twenty-two others make free distribution optional with the local communities.   California and Kansas have tried to reduce textbook costs by establishing their own printing plants and publishing the textbooks used in their schools, but the experience of these two states should not lead others to adopt the plan.

**Building construction; pupils' medical inspection.**   The physical environment of the school is regulated by the state to some extent.   A few states have enacted elaborate codes that deal with virtually every phase of schoolhouse construction, including such matters as gross structure, lighting, air supply, heating system, fire protection, cleaning system, water supply, toilet facilities, and arrangement and equipment of class and play rooms, gymnasium, and offices.   Only a few of these subjects are covered by the code of the average state, however, and in many states schoolhouse construction is still considered a purely local function.   Medical inspection of school children is generally optional with the local communities, but a few states require every local unit to arrange for periodic physical examination of all school children by qualified physicians.

**Rural school supervision.**   More than three fourths of the states exercise some degree of supervision over the work of the rural schools. This supervision may be simply a device for enforcing some of the specific state requirements already described, or it may be made an effective means of promoting desirable educational policies and inducing backward communities to adopt improved practices.   Inspirational professional guidance has largely taken the place of routine inspection in the more progressive states, and this trend will doubtless become more pronounced during the next decade.

### PRIVATE AND PAROCHIAL SCHOOLS

Private and parochial schools are required by law to provide instruction equivalent to public school instruction, but very few states

---

[23] In some states the adopting body prepares a list of four or five acceptable books for each high school course, and permits the schools to make the final selections. Such a plan avoids some of the most serious objections to state-wide uniformity, but unfortunately it lacks some of the advantages.

attempt to define "equivalent." Instead, the schools operating outside the public school system are generally permitted to teach whatever they please in any manner that they see fit. The state does not usually assume responsibility for the qualifications of teachers in these schools. Co-operation with public authorities in the enforcement of the compulsory attendance law is not commonly required. A few states have attempted to impose public school teaching standards upon the private and parochial schools by specifying that the teachers must hold public certificates. In some jurisdictions these schools are directed to make complete reports of attendance to the public school authorities, so that truancy cases may be investigated by the public compulsory-attendance officers. But these exceptions are not sufficiently numerous to warrant modification of the general statement that the state is profoundly indifferent to the quantity and quality of instruction offered by the private and parochial schools within its borders. This indifference has had a profound and unfortunate effect upon the American educational system. It has made possible the maintenance of dual standards of education, even within the same county or school district. There can be no doubt, therefore, that private and parochial schools should be subject to public supervision, though the extent of this supervision is open to debate.

### SCHOOLS FOR HANDICAPPED CHILDREN

State schools are maintained in nearly all the states for the training of handicapped children—the blind, the deaf and the dumb, the feeble-minded. Sometimes blind children and deaf and dumb children are educated at the same institution, though this arrangement is not common. Special day-class instruction for these several groups has recently been made a feature of the school systems of the larger cities. This instruction, which supplements the work of the state institutions, is usually financed in part with grants from the state treasury.

### HIGHER EDUCATION

All the states make some provision for higher education. Fortytwo of them support state universities, twenty-three of these states have agricultural colleges as divisions of the state universities, and nineteen have separate colleges of agricultural and mechanical arts. Of the remaining six states, three [24] have so-called state "colleges"

[24] Massachusetts, Pennsylvania, Rhode Island.

which are, in effect, universities.[25]　Reference has already been made to the state normal schools and teachers' colleges.[26]　The junior college movement, now rapidly gaining favor in many parts of the country, is bringing a form of higher education within the reach of many persons who could not afford to attend a distant state university.　The several public institutions of higher learning within a state may be placed under the control of a single board, as in Kansas; they may have their individual presidents and boards of trustees, though functioning as parts of a unified administrative organization, as in Montana; or they may be permitted to act with almost complete disregard of one another, even competing for legislative appropriations, as in most of the states.　The modern trend is toward some form of unified control, but this movement is progressing slowly.

## SELECTED REFERENCES

Carr, William G., comp., *County Unit of School Administration,* 1931.

Chambers, M. M., *Some Features of State Educational-Administrative Organization,* Washington, D.C., 1936.

Chism, Leslie L., *The Economic Ability of the States to Finance Public Schools,* 1936.

Cook, William A., *Federal and State School Administration,* 1936.

Cornell, Francis G., *A Measure of Tax-paying Ability of Local School Administrative Units,* 1936.

Cubberly, E. P., *State School Administration,* 1927.

Educational Policies Commission, *Education in the Depression,* 1937.

Epsy, H. G., *Public Secondary School,* Cambridge, Mass., 1939.

Frederic, Katherine A., *School Finance and School Districts,* Washington, D.C., 1936.

Graves, Frank P., *Administration of American Education,* 1932.

Hamilton, Robert R., and Mort, Paul R., *The Law and Public Education,* 1941.

Jaggers, R. E., *Administering the County School System,* 1934.

Macdonald, Mary E., *Federal Grants for Vocational Rehabilitation,* 1944.

Merrill, Julia W., *State Grants to Public Libraries,* 1942.

Morrison, Henry C., *School Revenue,* 1930.

———, *School and Commonwealth,* 1937.

Mort, Paul R., *Federal Support for Public Education,* 1936.

———, and Others, *State Support of Public Education,* Washington, D.C., 1933.

National Education Association, *Efforts of the States to Support Education,* Washington, D.C., 1936.

———, *Federal Aid for Education, Research Bulletin,* Vol. XX, No. 4, September, 1942.

[25] Every state receives a grant from the federal government for the benefit of a college of agricultural and mechanical arts, but three states—New Jersey, New York, and Vermont—give this money to privately endowed institutions.

[26] See p. 470.

National Education Association, *Financing Public Education*, 1936.

————, *State School Finance Systems*, Research Bulletin, Vol. XX, No. 5, November, 1942.

Norton, T. L., *Public Education and Economic Trends*, Cambridge, Mass., 1939.

Porter, Kirk, *State Administration*, Chap. X, 1938.

President's Research Commission on Social Trends, *Recent Social Trends in the United States*, Vol. I, Chap. VII, 1933.

Reavis, William C., Pierce, Paul R., and Stullken, Edward H., *The Elementary School, Its Organization and Administration*, 1931.

Reeder, Ward G., *Fundamentals of Public School Administration*, rev. ed., 1941.

Shepard, E. F., and Wood, W. B., *The Financing of Public Schools in Michigan*, Ann Arbor, 1943.

# Chapter Twenty-Four ❧ HEALTH

PUBLIC health work is of comparatively recent origin. The first state board of health—in the modern use of the term—was established by Massachusetts in 1869. Fourteen years previously Louisiana had created a health board with state-wide powers, but this body had been concerned chiefly with the enforcement of quarantine regulations arising from a severe epidemic of yellow fever. It may seem surprising that the public health should have been so generally neglected for so long a time, yet the explanation is simple. No one knew what health measures should be employed. The causes of disease were not understood, and therefore public officials were virtually powerless to prevent the spread of many virulent diseases that have since been brought under control. Smallpox, the worst scourge, was combated with quarantine and with valueless sanitary ordinances. In 1866, however, Louis Pasteur laid the foundation for the germ theory of disease and the modern science of preventive medicine. His investigations made possible, for the first time, the development of effective public health work based on disease prevention instead of disease suppression.

## ESTABLISHMENT OF STATE HEALTH ORGANIZATIONS

The example of Massachusetts in setting up a state board of health was soon followed by other states. California set up a state health organization in 1870, and Minnesota and Virginia fell into line two years later. Then came Michigan in 1873, Maryland in 1874, and Alabama in 1875. By 1881 twenty-five states had assumed direct responsibility for the public health. Fifteen other states created health departments before the close of the century, and in 1909 the list was made complete. This universal recognition of public health protection as a state function has not led, however, to the establishment of uniform standards of public health organizations. The effectiveness of the several state health organizations varies widely.

**Federal participation in public health activities.** The federal Constitution makes no mention of public health, thereby reserving to the states the right to protect the health of the people. Despite this restriction upon federal activity, however, a number of federal-state relationships in the field of public health are profitably maintained. Several federal agencies collect important data concerning health work, sometimes in co-operation with the state health departments, and distribute this information widely. Federal agencies also engage in scientific research dealing with health problems, and some of their findings are widely used by the health departments of states, counties, and cities. During the First World War, and for a number of years afterward, federal money was given to the states to encourage state activity against venereal disease, and in 1938 this subsidy was placed on a permanent basis. State child hygiene programs, as well as the more general aspects of public health work, are stimulated with federal funds. At least forty federal agencies are concerned directly or indirectly with some phase of the public health, though only a few of these agencies, such as the Public Health Service and the Children's Bureau, deal with health as a major activity.

### ORGANIZATION OF THE STATE HEALTH DEPARTMENT

**The executive officer.** The executive officer of the state health department is known by a variety of names in the several states—health officer, health commissioner, director or secretary of public health, chief of the bureau of health. Usually he is chosen by the governor or the state board of health, the former method being preferred by twenty-seven states.[1] The term of office of the health officer ranges from two to seven years; four years is most common. In one third of the states the health officer serves at the pleasure of the appointing authority, without definite term. The trend is toward longer tenure, thus increasing the likelihood of securing professional service. Salaries, though low, have been materially increased in recent years, and now compare favorably with the salaries paid to other state officials of corresponding rank. The legal qualifications of the health officer vary considerably, from the Colorado requirement that he must be a "citizen and a voter" to the New York specification that he must be a "physician with ten years' experience, skilled in sanitary science and public health work." Six of the forty-eight states omit the essential requirement that he be a doctor of medicine, but physicians are commonly chosen in these states despite the lack of constitutional or

[1] In twelve of these states, however, the governor's choice must be confirmed by the senate. In two others the approval of the state board of health is necessary.

statutory provisions. When the health officer is appointed by the state board of health he serves as the executive officer of the board, carrying out the general policies that have been determined at board meetings. When appointed by the governor, however, the health officer is largely independent of the state board and generally assumes full responsibility for the work of the health department.

**The state board of health.** Nearly every state [2] has created a state board of health, public health council, or similar agency. Sometimes it is an ex officio body, as in Arizona, where it is composed of the governor, the attorney-general, and the superintendent of health. Much more commonly, however, the members are appointed by the governor, usually without the necessity of securing senate approval. The state medical association plays a part in the selection of health board members in six states.[3] Members usually hold office for four, five, or six years,[4] with overlapping terms to insure reasonable continuity of policy and experience in handling board business. They are paid by the day in about half of the states and serve without compensation in the others.[5] Regular meetings are held three or four times a year except in a few states, where monthly meetings are the rule. Most of the state health boards have authority to make and enforce necessary rules and regulations concerning public health and sanitation, including proper sewage disposal, prevention of water pollution, and prevention and treatment of communicable diseases. Less frequently their jurisdiction extends to such matters as the practice of medicine, the practice of midwifery, or the sale of foods and drugs.

## LOCAL HEALTH ORGANIZATION

Although public health work is generally conceded to be a state function, many health activities are commonly performed by the local units of government. The local unit exercising jurisdiction over health matters is not everywhere the same. In some states it is the township or—in New England—the town. More often it is the county. A few states have adopted the district plan. Just as the township has proved unsatisfactory as a unit for school administration,[6] so it has produced undesirable results in the field of public health. The average township is too small and too poor to employ full-time pro-

---

[2] The only exceptions are Idaho, Nebraska, and Oklahoma.
[3] Alabama, Georgia, Mississippi, Montana, North Carolina, Tennessee.
[4] The range is from two years in Arizona, Iowa and Texas to seven years in Louisiana.
[5] Except in New York, where they receive one thousand dollars a year
[6] See p. 460.

fessional personnel; therefore it relies on a part-time health officer, who in some instances is not even a physician. Attention is devoted almost exclusively to epidemic control because this matter seems especially urgent and because a more complete public health program would be financially impracticable. The county is better fitted to serve as the primary public health unit, but little is accomplished by the mere transfer of health activities from township to county unless this rearrangement is made the basis for the establishment of a full-time county health service.

**County health activities.** As recently as 1915 there were only thirteen counties in the United States that had created effective public health organizations. Elsewhere, under the county plan, health work was generally restricted to the occasional services of a physician whose chief interest was his private practice. Thus county health work differed from township health work only in the size of the administrative unit. During the last few decades, however, more than fourteen hundred county health departments have been organized for full-time service. These departments, with trained medical health officers in charge, employ public health nurses and sanitary inspectors, in addition to necessary office assistants. Part of the cost is commonly borne by the state, which also provides consultant service in laboratory diagnosis, sanitary engineering, child hygiene, and a number of other fields.

**District health activities.** A number of states, dissatisfied with the county as a unit of health administration, have adopted the district plan. This scheme should not be confused with the district plan of school administration. Whereas the school district is a small unit within the township or county,[7] the public health district is a combination of counties. Thus Florida's sixty-three counties are grouped into eight districts, and seven districts are formed from Maine's sixteen counties. Health work is carried on by state health officers assigned to the several districts. Some health functions may still vest in township or county authorities, but fundamentally the district plan is based on the assumption of state responsibility. When this scheme is used, state health activities within each district should be unified under the control of a centrally appointed district health officer. Too frequently, however, responsibility is diffused. Different groups of state health workers operating within a district report directly to their respective bureau chiefs—sanitary engineers to the chief of the bureau of sanitary engineering, for example, and public health nurses to the

7 See pp. 459–460.

chief of the bureau of public health nursing. Thus the authority of the district health officer is reduced to the vanishing point, and the effectiveness of district health work is made to depend largely upon the voluntary co-operation of persons whose chief interest is the accomplishment of their own programs.

**State supervision and control.** There is great variation in the extent of state supervision and control over local units. State authority has been greatly strengthened in recent years, but even today some states give the counties virtually a free hand, permitting them to care for the public health in any way they may see fit. Although the counties in these states are supposed to enforce state health laws and state board regulations, no state agency has adequate authority to compel them to do so. At the other end of the scale are such states as Georgia, where the health officer of each county, though locally appointed, must be approved by the state, or Oklahoma and South Carolina, where the local health officers are appointed by the state health officer. The health departments of more than one third of the states have separate bureaus of county health work, whose duty is to supervise local health activities, and in a number of other states this task is specifically assigned to some other bureau—often the bureau of administration. Nearly every state makes some contributions from the state treasury to the local units for public health work, usually with a view to stimulating local endeavor and raising local standards. Delaware and Pennsylvania pay the entire cost of full-time county health service. Some states, especially in the South, recognize the wide variations among counties in their ability to maintain adequate public health programs, and use state money to equalize these differences, at least in part. But equalization is not a major purpose of state subsidies for public health.

### COMMUNICABLE DISEASE CONTROL

The first state health departments were organized to prevent the spread of communicable diseases. Their principal function was to fight epidemics with quarantine regulations. The value of vaccination as a means of preventing smallpox was known, but compulsory vaccination was prevented by the opposition of various ill-informed groups. Gradually, as medical science developed effective means of combating a number of major diseases, quarantine assumed a less important position in the public health program. But attention still centered on a few communicable diseases, such as tuberculosis, typhoid fever, malaria, diphtheria, syphilis, and gonorrhea. Within the last few decades, however, public health work has undergone a virtual transformation. The emphasis has shifted from communicable disease control to public health education, maternal and child hygiene, the detection and removal of physical defects, and the development in the general population of sound habits of living. Yet this change has not involved an abandonment of the fight against communicable diseases. On the contrary, most states are spending considerably more money today for the purpose of controlling these diseases than they did in 1915, though a smaller percentage of the total appropriation for public health. In a number of states communicable disease work receives less than three per cent of the health appropriation; in other commonwealths the percentage ranges as high as thirty. Virtually all state health departments have separate bureaus or divisions of communicable diseases or epidemiology, usually headed by full-time epidemiologists.

**Reports by physicians.** The first step in the fight against communicable diseases is to make certain that they are promptly and accurately reported. This principle is recognized in the laws of every state, but unfortunately these laws are far from satisfactory. Sometimes they are carelessly phrased, making evasion easy. Sometimes they omit reference to diseases that should be on the notifiable list. Even more serious, they are negligently enforced in the rural sections of nearly all the states and in every section of some states. In some commonwealths, however, physicians are required to report to the state health department at regular intervals—daily, as in Iowa, weekly, as in Indiana, or monthly, as in Nevada.

**Immunization.** Smallpox vaccination is now compulsory—usually for school children—under the laws of twelve states.[8] Twenty-one other states permit local authorities to provide for compulsory vaccination at their discretion, or under certain prescribed circumstances. Elsewhere free vaccination is generally provided by state or local health departments, and the people are taught the value of this protection against smallpox. In recent years the development of antityphoid vaccine and diphtheria toxin-antitoxin has made possible the further immunization of large groups of persons in many states. The Southern states, especially, have waged active campaigns against typhoid fever and have immunized virtually the entire populations of many communities. Immunization against diphtheria has become an

---

[8] Arkansas, Kentucky, Maryland, Massachusetts, New Hampshire, New Mexico, New York, Pennsylvania, Rhode Island, South Carolina, Virginia, West Virginia.

important part of the public health program in many sections of the country. Several states have separate appropriations for the purchase of antitoxins, vaccines, and serums. Malaria control, in those states where malaria is a problem, is frequently under a separate division or bureau, though sometimes it is entrusted to the state sanitary engineer.

**Venereal diseases.** The growth of great urban centers has made venereal disease control a problem of the first magnitude. Three fourths of the states have bureaus, divisions, or sections of venereal diseases, and the remaining commonwealths carry on the work through their bureaus of communicable diseases or central administrative staffs. Federal funds have greatly stimulated this activity. Venereal disease clinics are maintained by state or local health authorities, or through state-local co-operation. Wassermann tests [9] are made without charge or at nominal cost, and fees for treatment are reduced to a minimum. Free treatment is almost invariably provided for the indigent. Syphilis and gonorrhea are now universally declared to be reportable diseases, most states having added them to the list since the First World War. Within the last decade more than half of the states have enacted laws requiring a premarital health examination, including a blood test for syphilis. The removal of federal financial support from state venereal disease control caused a marked reduction in state appropriations for this activity after 1926. But a few states, especially those with large urban populations, ran counter to the general trend and spent considerably more money in an effort to prevent the spread of venereal diseases. Federal interest has now been aroused once more, and as a result the United States Public Health Service is leading the fight for venereal disease control.

**Tuberculosis.** At the beginning of the present century the state health departments were just beginning anti-tuberculosis work. Methods of combating the disease and preventing its spread were known, but not widely used. In 1904 the National Tuberculosis Association was formed, and through its efforts hundreds of local private organizations were established. Today more than one third of the states have separate divisions or bureaus of tuberculosis in their health departments, and practically all the commonwealths maintain public tuberculosis clinics or leave this work to their cities and counties. Public sanitariums, also, have become a feature of public health programs. State, county, and municipal sanitariums, as well as private and semiprivate sanitariums, often function within a single state.

9 The Wassermann blood test is the standard test for syphilis.

Some local sanitariums receive subsidies from state treasuries. The tendency in recent years has been to transfer a larger measure of responsibility for tuberculosis control from private to public agencies, and this movement will doubtless gather momentum as the importance of public health work is better understood.

**Other health activities.** Activities for the prevention of trachoma and various forms of blindness are carried on by a number of states. Other minor communicable diseases, as they occasionally acquire local significance, receive the attention of state or county health departments.

**Quarantine.** Although quarantine is relatively less important than in the early days of state health activity, it still remains a vital part of public health routine. In most states, however, quarantine regulations are enforced by the local health authorities. Nearly three fourths of the states have created special funds for emergencies. The use of these funds may be limited to public health emergencies—principally epidemics—or may be permitted for emergencies of any sort. In some states the emergency fund is administered by the state board of health or some other board or commission; but more often it is placed at the discretion of the governor.

#### MENTAL DISEASES

Most persons requiring hospital care are treated in private hospitals. The state may contribute to the support of these private institutions, but usually it does not accept responsibility for providing hospital facilities. With regard to the treatment of mental disorders, however, this situation is reversed. Every state maintains at least one institution for the care of persons who are mentally ill, and eighty-four per cent of all mental hospital cases are in state hospitals.[10] Such an arrangement is necessary because the treatment of mental disease is expensive and long-continued. Patients are commonly accepted on a part-pay basis, or even without charge, if necessary. Usually the state mental hospital is operated by a hospital board or commission, which is entirely independent of the health department. Mental hygiene clinics are maintained in about one half of the states. These clinics provide facilities for the early diagnosis and treatment of psychiatric disturbances, which might have serious consequences if permitted to continue unchecked.

[10] Mountin, Jos. W., and Evelyn Flook, *Distribution of Health Services in the Structure of State Government*, Public Health Bulletin No. 184, 3rd ed., 1943, Chap. VI, p. 4.

## VITAL STATISTICS

One of the most important phases of public health work is the collection of vital statistics. These statistics—the "bookkeeping" of public health—provide the only effective means of measuring health department success or failure. They point the way to future health department activities. A complete record of deaths, and of the various causes of death, serves as a crude index of the effectiveness of the several aspects of health work. Communicable disease reports furnish the basis for community health plans and forewarn against impending epidemics. Birth records enable the health department to keep in close contact with mothers during the crucial first year of their children's lives. In large part because of the efforts of the federal government, more or less complete vital statistics are now kept in all the states.

**Registrars.** A bureau or division of vital statistics in the state department of health usually supervises the collection of records. The primary registration unit, however, is the county, city, town, township, or election district. Within each unit is a registrar of vital statistics, who is generally paid a small fee for each birth and death entered on the records. There is no uniform method of selecting these local registrars. They may be chosen by the state board of health, as in Wyoming, the state health officer, as in Pennsylvania, the state registrar, as in Virginia, the local board of health, as in New Jersey, or the county commissioners, as in Utah. Or they may be elected by the voters of the community—a procedure still followed by six states. The folly of relying upon popular election to secure competent registrars is so apparent that comment is unnecessary. In a few states the justices of the peace or city clerks serve as registrars ex officio.

### PUBLIC HEALTH LABORATORIES

In 1890 Minnesota made provision for a smallpox vaccine laboratory. Four years later Rhode Island established a public health laboratory for the diagnosis of communicable diseases. From these early beginnings have developed the modern public health laboratories, now operating in every state. Sometimes the state laboratory is connected with the state university, but this arrangement is less common than formerly and is now found in only a few states.

Diagnosis of communicable diseases—the *raison d'être* of the early public health laboratories—is still one of their major activities. In addition, however, they perform a number of other functions, such as the examination of water supplies, sewage, and milk. They also manufacture or purchase biological products—antitoxins, vaccines, and the like—and distribute them to the local health departments free or at cost. The Kentucky laboratory conducts a school for laboratory technicians. In Michigan the health laboratory does technical work for the state police and the state bureau of education. More than half of the state public health laboratories devote some of their appropriations to research activities; the others are prevented from engaging in research by limited funds and personnel. Within recent years has developed a movement for branch laboratories conveniently located throughout the state, in addition to the central state laboratory. These branches, though equipped to perform only the simpler laboratory functions, have rendered a valuable service to many outlying sections. In emergencies, especially, their prompt diagnosis has sometimes prevented the spread of epidemics.

### SANITARY ENGINEERING

Nearly every state health department employs a sanitary engineer and generally places its sanitary engineering functions in a separate division or bureau. These functions have become much more numerous and important during the last two decades; they now consume ten per cent or more of the total state health appropriation in more than half of the states.

The work of the bureau of sanitary engineering is not everywhere the same, though it commonly includes the examination of water and milk supplies and the protection of lakes, streams, and harbors against pollution. State health department approval is generally required for all plans for the construction, alteration, or extension of public water supplies and sewerage systems, and these plans go to the sanitary engineer, who determines whether they meet minimum state requirements. His analysis of public water supplies is made at regular intervals—monthly, quarterly, or annually—in some states, and irregularly in others. A number of states have enacted laws requiring inspection of bottled waters offered for sale. This inspection is commonly made by the bureau of sanitary engineering, though sometimes by the food and drug division. In those states that have sanitary regulations concerning the ice industry, enforcement is uniformly entrusted to the bureau of sanitary engineering. Water supplies to be used in the production of ice are analyzed, and on the basis of this analysis permission to make ice is granted or withheld.

Camp sanitation has become a matter of considerable importance in recent years, largely as a result of the increased use of camps by motorists, and is now generally regulated by state law. In many states the camps are required to secure health department licenses, which are granted only after inspection by the bureau of sanitary engineering. The health departments of a few states, however, act merely in an advisory capacity regarding camp sanitation.

Varying degrees of control over swimming pools are exercised by the sanitary engineers of the several states. In some states swimming pool plans must be approved; in others operating permits are required. Roadside water supplies, also, are frequently subject to health department examination. Satisfactory supplies are marked with "safe water" placards. In some sections of the country shellfish sanitation has recently acquired considerable importance.

### CHILD HYGIENE

In 1921, when a federal subsidy was offered to the states for child hygiene, only a few state health departments were carrying on extensive child hygiene activities. The federal grant proved a powerful stimulus, however, and before long nearly every state had adopted a reasonably adequate program. Later, when the federal government withdrew its support, many state appropriations for child hygiene decreased, and many child hygiene activities were abandoned. But no state entirely deserted the field; and when federal funds again became available, as part of the social security program, state interest quickly revived. More than half of the states now have separate bureaus of child hygiene, and a number of others have bureaus that combine child hygiene with public health nursing.

**Prenatal care and advice.** Under the head of maternal and child hygiene, prenatal work is an important phase of public health in many states. Large numbers of permanent prenatal clinics have been established, and at these clinics expectant mothers are supplied with necessary information. Some states rely on temporary or itinerant clinics, while in a number of instances the permanent clinics are conducted by the counties or other local units as part of their general health programs. An alternative to the clinic, less effective but also less expensive, is the prenatal "conference"—a public meeting under the direction of state doctors and nurses at which questions concerning mothers and babies are asked and answered. Women who attend prenatal conferences and leave their names are placed on the mailing list of the state bureau of child hygiene, which sends out monthly letters as well as educational pamphlets and leaflets. Many—perhaps most—women reached by the health department's clinics or conferences receive no regular medical care during the prenatal period, and have no other way of learning how to care for themselves and their babies.

**Midwifery.** In certain sections of the country the supervision and training of midwives is a serious problem. While midwifery is not recognized in Massachusetts and is steadily decreasing in a number of other states, it is still very important in the South and some parts of the West. The Southern midwives, chiefly Negroes, are sadly in need of even the most elementary instruction. Their practices are often reminiscent of the days before the Civil War, when semi-savage prayers to unknown spirits were a part of the established ritual. Because of the vast differences among midwives in the several states, radically different standards have been adopted. Thus New York provides instruction through lectures and letters, and subjects all its midwives to rigid state inspection, whereas some commonwealths, though supplying short courses of training, ignore the legal requirement that all midwives must be licensed and thus permit hundreds of midwives to practice without training of any sort.

**Eye treatment for the new-born.** Legislation concerning eye treatment of the new-born for the purpose of guarding against gonorrheal infection has been enacted everywhere. Usually the law specifies that a one per cent solution of silver nitrate must be used, though in some instances a "comparable antiseptic" is permitted. In five states the law is inadequate. Thus Indiana merely declares that "all necessary precautions" must be taken, and North Dakota "urges" the use of silver nitrate. California, Massachusetts, and New Jersey distribute silver nitrate free to physicians, though not compelling its use. Most of the states with compulsory laws also provide for free silver nitrate distribution. Infant and preschool clinics, corresponding to the prenatal clinics already described, are maintained by the state health department in nearly three fourths of the states. In some of the remaining states infant and preschool clinics are directed by the local health organizations.

**Crippled children.** In 1935 the federal government offered to pay a part of the cost of medical care for crippled children, and all the states accepted the subsidy. The result has been a marked expansion in state programs, which now include diagnosis, treatment, and convalescent care. Permanent clinics for crippled children have been established in the larger population centers; elsewhere the work is carried on by itinerant staffs, which make a complete circuit of the state once or twice a year. Nurses attached to the clinics assume responsibility for finding cases, stimulating clinic attendance, and following up clinic work with home visits. Braces and other orthopedic appliances are furnished by the state if they are not available from any other source. Twelve states maintain their own orthopedic hospitals; the others rely on local hospital facilities.

**Dental inspection and care.** Nearly all the states are concerned with the possibility of improving the dental health of children. Boys and girls in the schools are taught the importance of caring for their teeth, and these lessons may be followed by regular dental inspection. Teeth found to be defective are not usually treated by the school dentist, however. Instead, the condition is called to the attention of the parents, who are urged to take their children to the family dentist at the earliest opportunity. But treatment at public expense may be provided for the indigent, or for those in the first two or three years of school.

### PUBLIC HEALTH NURSING

Public health nursing, stimulated by federal funds, has become an important phase of health work during the last few years. In most states it developed under local control and marked an expansion of local health activities. More than half of the state health departments, however, have now assumed responsibility for public health nursing programs and have created separate bureaus to deal with this work. Public health nursing is closely related to child hygiene, and the two activities are often carried on by the same nurses. In many instances women seeking information concerning the care of their babies are taught valuable lessons in health protection for the entire family. Home visits as well as public demonstrations serve to emphasize the importance of health and the necessity of obeying the simple rules of personal hygiene.

The eligibility requirements for public health nurses vary considerably. Usually they must be registered nurses with a certain amount of experience in general nursing or public health work, but some states specify merely that they must be registered nurses or even omit this basic requirement; while some states at the other extreme demand post-graduate training in public health nursing and extensive experience under supervision. Political considerations do not usually play a part in the selection of public health nurses, though there have been a few flagrant examples of partisan interference in this field.

### INDUSTRIAL HYGIENE

More than half of the states have now established bureaus or divisions of industrial hygiene, whose task is to promote the health of workers in industry. Occupational diseases are studied, and the causes removed wherever possible.[11] Efforts are made to improve the working environment by encouraging better lighting and ventilation. Workers are given medical examinations, and in many instances physical defects are corrected. Instruction is provided for factory employees concerning such diverse matters as nutrition, personal hygiene, and methods of avoiding industrial accidents. Sometimes the state health department co-operates with the department of labor—especially in accident prevention. Federal funds have been granted to the states for the development of industrial hygiene programs, and most of the nation's factory workers now receive some services in this field.

### EDUCATIONAL ACTIVITIES OF THE STATE HEALTH DEPARTMENT

It has already been indicated that nearly all the state health departments carry on educational activities. In some states these activities are widely scattered, each bureau preparing and distributing its own literature, designing and displaying its own exhibits, and making its own arrangements for radio broadcasts, without regard for the plans of other bureaus. Much more commonly, however, responsibility for health education vests in a single division—either a separate division of public health instruction or the office of the head of the department. Not all the details of the department's educational campaigns are centrally administered, but a general oversight is exercised and an attempt is made to prevent unnecessary duplication and other forms of wasted effort.

**Types of publicity.** The educational programs of the state health departments assume a variety of forms. Newspaper publicity is nearly always important, because it provides a means of reaching a maximum

[11] See p. 566.

number of people at minimum expense. About one third of the state health departments maintain regular newspaper service, with department employees assigned to the task of finding newsworthy incidents and putting them in proper form for publication. In most of the other states news stories and articles are released from time to time.

Another common form of publicity is the health department bulletin, published at regular intervals in most states. Some of the more progressive health departments issue their bulletins every week or every month; others provide for quarterly or semiannual publication. Radio talks are given on health topics. Motion picture films and projecting machines are often a part of the equipment of the state health department; in some instances the projecting machines are mounted on trucks that tour the rural sections.

**Co-operation of state department of education.** Many phases of public health education require the co-operation of the state department of education, and in most instances this co-operation is freely given. In fact, more than half of the states report some co-operative activities involving the department of education and the health department. Among the co-operative features of public health programs may be mentioned the joint management of courses in public health at teachers' institutes, the preparation by the health department of the hygiene textbook for the public schools, and the promotion of teacher training in health subjects.

**Miscellaneous duties.** A number of miscellaneous duties occupy the attention of many state health departments. Most important is the enforcement of the food and drug laws—a task entrusted to the health department in thirteen states.[12] Nearly all the other states place food and drug inspection in the department of agriculture. Among the other functions occasionally performed by the health department are plumbing inspection, inspection of weights and measures, and enforcement of sanitary regulations concerning hotels and restaurants.

### SOCIALIZED MEDICINE

One of the most marked characteristics of public health work has been its tendency to include an ever-expanding list of functions.

---

[12] California, Colorado, Indiana, Kansas, Kentucky, Louisiana, Maryland, Massachusetts, Montana, New Jersey, Oklahoma, Pennsylvania, Texas.

From its early beginning in the field of communicable disease control it has grown to comprise child hygiene, public health nursing, sanitary engineering, and a surprisingly long list of additional activities. It goes far beyond the original concept of disease suppression. From time to time the proposal has been made that public health go still further, and take as its province practically the entire field of medicine, including the suppression, prevention, and treatment of disease. Necessary medical attention might be supplied directly by the state to all the people, or to all in the lower income brackets; or, as an alternative, such attention might be supplied by quasi-public groups of physicians, who would be closely regulated by the state as to charges and quality of service.

**Recent studies and legislative proposals.** This suggestion for public medicine, in whatever form, was formerly brushed aside with scant consideration. But in 1932 the Committee on the Costs of Medical Care, a committee of eminent physicians, social scientists, and laymen whose investigations were financed by the Rockefeller Foundation, the Russell Sage Foundation, and a number of other foundations and funds, indorsed the idea of quasi-public medical service under state control. At once socialization of medicine became a live issue, and its importance was emphasized still further by the enactment in 1935 of the federal security program, which seeks to eliminate most of the major causes of economic insecurity *except illness.* Many persons have since contended that this omission is serious—that it weakens the entire program. Numerous additional studies supporting this thesis have recently been made. Bills providing for some form of public medicine have been introduced in Congress and in a number of state legislatures, and in some instances the margin of defeat has been extremely narrow. As yet, however, medicine has not been socialized in any state of the American Union. The determined opposition of the American Medical Association has undoubtedly been responsible, at least in part, for this result.

**Health insurance.** In Europe, where the masses of the people have long been supplied with free medical services at public expense, weekly benefits are regularly paid by the government to persons incapacitated by illness. Some of the proposals recently made in the United States contemplate the payment of sickness benefits in the European style, on the ground that health can be insured quite as readily as life and much more certainly than employment. But it must be understood that health insurance is not necessarily a companion of public medicine, though the arguments that can be advanced in favor of both plans are much the same.

**Recommendations for extension of medical services.**  The fundamental thesis of the Committee on the Costs of Medical Care, which studied only the availability of medical services and did not even consider the question of sickness benefit payments, was that thousands of families in the lower income groups, while suffering at least as much sickness as those with comfortable incomes, received far less medical care; and that this inequality could be removed only by distributing the cost of medical care "over groups of people and over periods of time."  The Committee offered no specific plan by which this distribution was to be effected, but it made three important recommendations: [13]

1. That medical service, both preventive and therapeutic, should be furnished largely by organized groups of physicians, dentists, nurses, pharmacists, and other associated personnel.  Such groups should be organized, preferably around a hospital, for rendering complete home, office, and hospital care.  The form of organization should encourage the maintenance of high standards and the development or preservation of a personal relation between patient and physician.

2. The extension of all basic public health services—whether provided by governmental or non-governmental agencies—so that they will be available to the entire population according to its needs.  This extension requires primarily increased financial support for official health departments and full-time trained health officers and members of their staffs whose tenure is dependent only upon professional and administrative competence.

3. That the costs of medical care be placed on a group payment basis, through the use of insurance, through the use of taxation, or through the use of both these methods.  This is not meant to preclude the continuation of medical service provided on an individual fee basis for those who prefer the present method.  Cash benefits, i.e., compensation for wage-loss due to illness, if and when provided, should be separate and distinct from medical services.

In order to attain these ends, according to the Committee, there should be at least one non-profit community medical center in every city whose population exceeds fifteen thousand.  Whether these medical centers should be publicly owned and operated, or maintained instead through private initiative, with "state regulation of the finances to assure actuarial soundness," is a moot question.  But in any event the adoption of the Committee's program would inevitably lead

[13] The recommendations of the Committee on the Costs of Medical Care are conveniently summarized by I. S. Falk, C. R. Rorem and M. D. Ring in *The Costs of Medical Care.*  See also Harry A. Millis' monograph, *Sickness and Insurance,* and Herbert D. Simpson's impartial analysis, *Compulsory Health Insurance in the United States.*

to a marked expansion of public health services—a fact recognized in the recommendations. In time medical care would probably acquire the same status as education and police protection. It would be supplied on the basis of need and financed on the basis of ability to pay. As nearly as possible, inequalities in opportunity for healthful living would be eliminated.

**Arguments against socialized medicine.** Thus stated, the merits of socialized medicine seem to exceed its defects by a wide margin. But there are a number of arguments against socialized medicine that must not be overlooked. The opponents of the scheme contend that it would lead to the establishment of a medical hierarchy in every community, without whose consent medicine could not be practiced. Arbitrary discriminations would result, and the situation might be complicated still further by the intrusion of partisan politics. Then, too, the expense of administering great medical centers and of assigning patients would be so great as to increase, instead of decreasing, the cost of medical care. Wastefulness and inefficiency, so often associated with public and quasi-public undertakings, at least in the public mind, would characterize this newest enterprise. And the final result would be a triumph of bureaucracy, to the infinite detriment of American medicine. Perhaps most serious of all, the continuous personal relationship of physician and patient, involving understanding on the part of the physician and confidence on the part of the patient, would be destroyed. The Committee on the Costs of Medical Care, recognizing this danger, specifically declares that a personal relationship must be preserved. But their scheme, according to its opponents, would make such preservation impossible.

**Conclusions.** Here, then, are both sides of a bitter controversy. The arguments against socialized medicine are potent, yet it must be admitted that they closely resemble the objections once raised against "socialized" education—that is, a system of free schools with compulsory attendance. Perhaps the public will soon decide that health, like education, is so closely related to the general welfare that it should not be left in private hands. The trend seems to be in that direction. But no one can safely predict the future of medicine in the United States.

SELECTED REFERENCES

American Medical Association, Bureau of Medical Economics, *Handbook of Sickness Insurance, State Medicine and the Cost of Medical Care,* 1935.

American Public Health Association, *Control of Communicable Diseases,* 1943.

Anderson, Gaylord W., and Arnstein, Margaret G., *Communicable Disease Control; A Volume for the Health Officer and Public Health Nurse,* 1941.

Bolduan, C. F., and N. W., *Public Health and Hygiene,* 2nd ed., 1936.

Buehler, E. C., *Free Medical Care,* 1935.

Cabot, H., *The Doctor's Bills,* 1935.

Collins, S. D., and Others, *Research Memorandum on Social Aspects of Health in the Depression,* 1937.

Currie, J. R., *Manual of Public Health Hygiene,* Baltimore, 1938.

Davis, Michael M., *America Organizes Medicine,* 1941.

———, *Public Medical Services,* 1937.

Dodd, Paul A., and Penrose, E. F., *Economic Aspects of Medical Services,* Washington, D.C., 1939.

Falk, I. S., *Security Against Sickness,* 1936.

———, Rorem, C. R., and Ring, M. D., *The Costs of Medical Care* (Publication No. 27 of the Committee on the Costs of Medical Care), 1933.

Hiscock, I. V., *District Health Administration,* 1936.

Johnsen, J. E., *Socialization of Medicine,* 1935.

Millis, H. A., *Sickness and Insurance,* 1937.

Mountin, Joseph W., and Flook, Evelyn, *Distribution of Health Services in the Structure of State Government,* Public Health Bulletin No. 184, 3rd ed., U.S. Public Health Service, Washington, D.C., 1943.

Mustard, H. S., *An Introduction to Public Health,* 1935.

Paterson, R. G., *Historical Directory of State Health Departments in the United States,* Columbus, Ohio, 1939.

Simpson, Herbert D., *Compulsory Health Insurance in the United States,* Evanston, Ill., 1943.

Smilie, W. G., *Public Health Administration in the United States,* rev. ed., 1940.

Tobey, J. A., *Public Health Law,* 2nd ed., 1939.

White House Conference on Child Health and Protection, *Hospitals and Child Health,* 1932.

———, *Public Health Organization,* 1932.

# Chapter Twenty-Five ⚶⚶⚶ HIGHWAYS

THE early American roads were chiefly from farm to market. Designed primarily to serve local needs, they were controlled by the local road districts into which the counties and townships were commonly divided. At best these roads were rutted and dusty; at worst, during the rainy months, they were virtually impassable bogs. Such road maintenance as might prove indispensable was entrusted to the residents of the district, and each man was required by law to devote a portion of his time—perhaps one or two days a year—to road work. In farming communities this requirement was not unreasonable, yet it was evaded whenever possible. Later, as trade and commerce became more important, and many men found it increasingly inconvenient to devote even a small portion of their time to road maintenance, the early laws were modified to permit the hiring of substitutes, or even the payment of cash in lieu of labor.

## ROAD BUILDING IN THE UNITED STATES

**Early federal construction.** Road building was not limited entirely to the local units of government, however, for at an early date the federal government took a hand. In 1806 Congress made an initial appropriation of thirty thousand dollars for a national road to connect Cumberland, Maryland, with Steubenville, Ohio, and this Cumberland Road, as it was generally known, eventually became an important artery of traffic. Total appropriations for its construction ultimately reached nearly seven million dollars, and the road extended as far as southern Illinois.[1] But the successful development of railroad transportation about 1840 marked the end of national highway construction, and for more than half a century the railroad was unchallenged as the principal means of long-distance travel. Wagon roads served the local communities, and the federal government did nothing to further highway construction except to continue its well-established practice of granting to the newly created states a portion of the receipts from the sale of public land within their borders, directing

[1] See p. 31, n. 4.

497

that this money be used for "highways or other internal improvements."

**Influence of the bicycle.**　About 1890 a definite movement for good roads began to take form.　This movement was given impetus by the widespread popularity of the bicycle, which had just been improved by the addition of the safety brake and the newly invented pneumatic tire.　A number of large bicycle factories were established during the nineties, and "wheel clubs" with large memberships functioned in all the principal cities.　The national organization known as the League of American Wheelmen devoted its attention largely to the task of rousing popular sentiment in favor of improved highways; its official magazine carried the good roads gospel everywhere. While many persons, especially in the rural sections, considered well-paved roads a needless luxury, the trend of the times was definitely toward better road construction and systematic road maintenance.

**Influence of the automobile.**　It was not until the advent of the automobile, however, that the phrase "good roads" began to acquire its present significance.　Motor vehicles, with their greater weight and higher speed, necessitated a more substantial type of road construction, and hard surfaces replaced sandclay and gravel along the main lines of travel.　Then came the surfacing of even the secondary roads.　Highways became more durable and more expensive.　A major revolution in methods of road building was well under way. In the four decades following 1900, as motor car registration increased from four thousand to thirty-three million, more than one and one-half million miles of American roads were surfaced in varying degrees. Highway construction became a task for skilled engineers instead of a neighborhood job dependent upon the skill and energy of the residents of each community.　And highway expenditures, mounting at an astonishing rate, became one of the major expenditures of government.

**Abandonment of toll roads.**　Toll roads, which existed in the United States in great numbers prior to the era of railroad building, eventually ceased to be profitable undertakings and were abandoned or taken over by the state.　The twentieth century renaissance in highway construction did not lead to a return of the toll road, for the public had learned to regard highways as a free means of communication and looked with disfavor upon the toll-road principle.　Today the total mileage of American toll roads is negligible—not more than one hundred and fifty miles at most.　Tolls are charged on many newly constructed bridges, however, as a means of defraying the heavy cost of these projects. Most of the present-day toll bridges are in private hands, but the charters of some operating companies provide that the bridges shall become public property after a period of years.

## HIGHWAY ADMINISTRATION

**Trend toward larger control units.** The trend in highway administration, as in most governmental activities, has long been toward larger control units. Years ago, in most states, the township took over the work of the small, inefficient road district, and more recently the township has been replaced by the county—at least in some states and with regard to some of the more important highways. Even the county has proved too small a unit to be entrusted with the construction and maintenance of the principal thoroughfares, and the state has therefore been forced to enter the field. First it subsidized the road-building activities of the townships and counties; then it coupled each grant with the requirement that materials and methods must be approved by state inspectors; and finally, in most states, it assumed full responsibility for building the main roads and keeping them in repair.

**State highways.** The first state-aid highway law was enacted by New Jersey in 1891. This statute solemnly recited that "public roads in this state have heretofore been built and maintained solely at the expense of the respective townships in which they are located," although "such roads are for the convenience of the citizens of the counties in which they are located, and of the entire state as well as of said townships"; and then made provision for payment from the state treasury of one third of the cost of road construction. The following year Massachusetts also accepted the state-aid principle for main highways connecting the cities of the state. Then came California and Connecticut in 1895, Maryland, Vermont, and New York in 1898, and North Carolina and Maine in 1901. Thirty-six states had fallen into line by 1911, and in 1917 the list was made complete. The condition of the roads had ceased to be a matter of purely local concern. As early as 1894 Massachusetts amended its state-aid law to provide for the construction and maintenance of state-aid roads by the state highway commission, the counties being required to bear their share of the total cost. This increase of state authority and responsibility was generally regarded with suspicion at the outset, but the results were so satisfactory that eventually all the other states followed Massachusetts' example and established state highway systems—usually under complete state control. In 1916 the federal government assumed a portion of the cost of road construction in exchange for a measure of supervision and control over the main roads, and a national system of highways speedily developed from the highway systems of the several states.

**Township and county road administration.** This gradual transition to larger control units has not involved all roads, however. In fact, nearly nine tenths of the rural road mileage in the United States is still under county or township control, though the other one tenth includes virtually all the main highways and most of the hard surfacing, and bears most of the motor vehicle traffic. The township is the primary unit of road administration in the states of the North and East, while the county generally serves in this capacity in the South and West.

TOWNSHIP CONTROL. Under the township plan one or more road commissioners are elected or appointed—election being the more common method—in each township. Popular favor seems to incline toward single-headed rather than group administration. Since the road commissioner is not required to possess any special qualifications for his office, he is seldom a trained engineer. Frequently he lacks even a practical working knowledge of road-building methods and is forced to rely on such gratuitous information as he can secure from various sources. He employs the road gangs who do the actual work of construction, and the foremen who supervise them. If plans and specifications are required, they are secured from private contractors on a competitive basis. Bridge and culvert work, also, may be entrusted to contractors, or may be placed under the jurisdiction of the county authorities. Thus township road construction is essentially construction by amateurs, and township road policies are merely a phase of township politics. Small wonder that the township plan is marked by waste and inefficiency in every state where it still exists!

Its continuance is due in part to the insistent demand of local politicians that government be kept "close to the people," but more largely to the relative unimportance of township roads. These roads comprise no system; they are merely the residue after national, state, and county systems have been selected. They serve only to connect the farms with the main highways. Since they are worth building and repairing, however, the way in which this work is done should not be a matter of complete indifference. Efficient administrative methods should be adopted wherever possible, and the first step in this direction should be the abolition of the township plan of road administration.   The township is too small a unit to obtain competent engineering services, except in rare instances.   Its amateur government is not competent to deal with the technical problems of road construction.   Its financial resources are usually too limited to permit any large expenditures, even with a view to ultimate savings.   The change from township to county road administration has already been made in some states, but there is little likelihood that all the states will fall into line, at least for some years to come.

COUNTY CONTROL.   The extent of county control over highways is not everywhere the same.   In those states where the township still assumes responsibility for local roads, the county's part is usually limited to construction and repair of some of the more important thoroughfares that have been designated as county highways.   There may be a certain amount of county supervision over township activities, however.   The laws of a few states specify that all township road expenditures, or township contracts for road construction and maintenance, must be approved by the county authorities.   Where the county is the primary unit of road administration, it usually exercises complete control over all roads within its boundaries, with the exception of a few main highways that comprise the state system.   In a number of states even these principal thoroughfares are entrusted to the counties, subject to state supervision.

Responsibility for county road work may be vested in the county board of supervisors, as in Maryland, or in a special county highway commission, as in Missouri.   In either case the actual direction of road building and repair is generally entrusted to a single official, who is variously known as road supervisor, road overseer, or road engineer. This official is usually appointed, though sometimes chosen by the voters of the county.   In most cases he is a politician with little or no knowledge of road-building methods.   Several states have tried to insure the selection of more competent persons by providing that every road supervisor must be "a practical road builder" or "a man well versed in practical road building" while a few states have declared that only civil engineers may be chosen.   Engineering training is highly desirable, and should be required wherever practicable.   In most states, however, there are poor counties that cannot afford to pay for skilled engineering services and must accept whatever measure of practical experience their meager salaries will attract.   One way to solve the problem of the poor county is to provide that two or more counties may join to form a highway district, though continuing to function independently in other matters. This plan has been adopted in California, Michigan, Oregon, Pennsylvania, South Dakota, and a number of other states.

**The state highway departments:** THE COMMISSION PLAN. The state plays a dual rôle in highway administration. On the one hand it constructs and maintains a system of main state highways; on the other it exercises supervision over county road building and repair. Every state now has a department of highways, usually headed by a commission of three, five, or seven members. The single-headed department is slowly winning favor, however, and has been adopted by nearly one third of the states. When the commission plan is used, the members serve only part-time; in a few states they serve ex officio. Meetings are held at infrequent intervals to consider matters of policy —especially the designation of highway routes, the approval of contracts, and the preparation of financial plans for legislative consideration. The most important task of the highway commission, however, is to select a state highway engineer, who directs the actual work of road building and repair.

THE SINGLE-HEADED DEPARTMENT PLAN. Under the single-headed department plan the highway engineer has the title of director of highways and combines the functions of engineer and commission. He is responsible solely to the governor—or, in some states, to a director of public works whom the governor has appointed. Single-headed control has generally proved more satisfactory than control by a commission because it has tended to emphasize the importance of the technical factors in highway work. In many of the states where the commission plan is used there are frequent disagreements between politically minded commissioners and professionally minded engineers. Commissioners at times interfere with the selection of department personnel, and even go so far as to override the engineer's decisions concerning the location of new roads. While such practices may be the exception rather than the rule and are no longer attempted on projects built in part with federal money, they occur with sufficient regularity in certain states to constitute a serious objection to commission control of highways. The single-headed department plan furnishes no guarantee that highway administration will escape the blighting effect of partisan politics, but experience shows that this result is more likely to ensue. The argument that a highway commission is necessary to determine policies need not be given serious consideration, for policy determination is an infinitesimal part of the work of a state highway department.

SUPERVISION AND CONTROL OF COUNTY CONSTRUCTION. State-county relations in the field of highway administration assume a variety of forms. The laws of a number of states provide that the state highway department shall furnish advice and assistance upon the request of the county authorities. This advice and assistance may be limited to the examination of general plans prepared by county road officials, or it may include the preparation of actual specifications for county roads by the state's engineering staff.

In Massachusetts the state division of highways compiles statistics concerning the public roads of counties, cities, and towns, and makes such investigations as it deems advisable, in addition to maintaining a free consulting service for local highway officials. A few states, including Arkansas, Massachusetts, Michigan, Mississippi, and West Virginia, have established road schools or institutes, where those in charge of local road building may receive practical instruction under the direction of the state highway engineer. Annual sessions are held in the several counties or at convenient places scattered throughout the state, and county road commissioners, supervisors, and overseers are required to attend. Some measure of supervision over county road-building activities is maintained by the provision that county road officials must submit annual reports to the state. A few commonwealths have gone much further along the path of state control by requiring state approval of locally chosen highway officials. Thus Illinois specifies that persons selected by the county boards must pass competitive state examinations, and West Virginia provides that county road engineers must hold certificates of efficiency from the state road commission. In Iowa the state highway commission, though unable to prevent the selection of incompetent persons as county road engineers, may remove them at its discretion. A few states, of which Wisconsin is the most conspicuous example, give the state highway department broad powers with regard to the selection of county highway systems.

Some measure of state supervision usually accompanies state aid to counties for road construction. In exchange for state financial assistance, amounting generally to one half of the total construction cost of approved projects, the counties are required to build their main roads according to state specifications—or at least to secure state approval of the specifications prepared by county engineers. Alabama is typical of a small group of states that restrict county authority even more narrowly by directing the state highway department to construct all roads financed in part with state funds.

In 1931 North Carolina tried a new and interesting experiment. The state government assumed full responsibility for the construction and maintenance of all roads, thus taking from the counties one of their most important functions. This transfer of authority followed the publication of a careful survey that showed widely varying results in county highway administration. "Some counties were maintaining their roads in good shape, others wholly inadequately. Some were using convict labor profitably, others at an uncertain cost. Some had suitable road machinery, others lacked adequate road equipment. Some had been extravagant in the purchase of machinery. Twenty-six counties had township or district road organizations either in place of or in addition to a county organization. All of the counties had large and generally mounting road debts." [2] So the state legislature dissolved all local road districts and road boards and reorganized the state highway department to enable it to perform its new duties efficiently. The following year the state government of Virginia also assumed responsibility for all roads, and some time later this plan was adopted by West Virginia and Delaware. But no other states have yet abandoned the historic division of responsibility between state and county road authorities.

THE STATE HIGHWAY SYSTEM. The state highway system, which generally comprises about ten per cent of the total road mileage of the state and bears from one half to three fourths of the volume of traffic, is under the direct control of the state highway department in most states, though occasionally built and maintained by the counties under close state supervision. The trunk highways forming this system were tentatively selected after many preliminary hearings, and then definitely chosen after additional hearings and intensive surveys by members of the state highway department's staff.

### FEDERAL AID FOR HIGHWAYS

In 1916, when the federal government renewed its early interest in good roads, there were a number of states that had no functioning highway departments. But the act offering federal funds for high-

---

[2] Wager, Paul W., "State Centralization in North Carolina," in the *National Municipal Review*, Sept., 1931, p. 528.

way construction directed the federal secretary of agriculture to co-operate with the *state highway departments,* and a subsequent statute specified that these departments must have "adequate powers" and be "suitably equipped and organized." Thus the federal government did its share to develop in every state a strong central road authority capable of dealing with the problem of main highways.

**Appropriations.** For a number of years the federal subsidy to the states for road building amounted to seventy-five million dollars a year. In 1931 the annual grant was increased to one hundred and twenty-five millions, and in 1933 an additional sum of four hundred millions was appropriated under the National Industrial Recovery Act. The 1938 grant was in excess of three hundred million dollars, but by 1941 it had dropped to one hundred and twenty-five millions. Then came the war, and the virtual suspension of the federal-aid program. Congress made no additional appropriations for this purpose, and funds available from previous years were used only for improvements having direct war significance. It must not be assumed, however, that the federal-aid highway program has been permanently abandoned. On the contrary, its principles remain unchanged, and large grants have already been authorized for the first three postwar years.

CONDITIONS OF GRANTS. Let us see, therefore, how the program functions in normal times. A somewhat complicated basis of apportionment is used, involving population, area, and mileage of rural mail delivery routes. The usual conditions are attached to the federal grant: the state legislature must specifically accept the federal government's offer; federal funds must be matched—dollar for dollar —from state or county sources; and federal approval must be given to every project before payment is made. When a state desires to improve a section of highway or construct a new road it submits to the federal district engineer [3] a project statement containing all necessary information, such as the exact route to be followed, the nature of the proposed construction, the type of paving, the grades, and the estimated cost. Federal approval of this project statement enables a state to begin construction with the assurance that it will be partially reimbursed from federal funds after the job has been finished and inspected by a federal representative. Although federal money may

---

[3] The United States has been divided into eleven districts for the purpose of administering the federal road subsidy, and each district has an engineer authorized to deal with the state highway departments.

not be used for road repairs, the federal government insists upon proper maintenance as a prerequisite to continued federal aid. Completed projects are inspected twice a year by the federal field forces, and any state failing to keep its federal aid highways in good condition is notified that it must make necessary repairs promptly or forfeit its claim to further federal funds.

**The federal-aid system of highways.** In 1921 Congress specified that subsequent federal road subsidies, and also the state money used to match them, must be expended upon a connected highway system limited originally to seven per cent of the total road mileage in each state, but with additions of one per cent permitted as the accepted program neared completion. The result has been the development of a network of main roads touching practically every city with a population in excess of five thousand. This network—the federal-aid system, as it is generally known—is composed of roads originally selected by the highway engineers of the several states and subsequently co-ordinated by the federal government. Standard route numbers, and also uniform guide and warning signs, are used on important highways comprising more than half of the system.

**Secondary road building.** During the depression years of the early 1930's highway construction was used as a device for relieving unemployment. Congress appropriated several hundred millions of dollars to aid the states in building secondary roads, on which large quantities of relief labor could readily be employed. The program of federal grants for main highways was not abandoned, but it was definitely subordinated to the new policy. Most students of highway administration assumed that this change was temporary. They reasoned that local road construction was scarcely a matter of federal concern and that congressional interest would wane as soon as the unemployment crisis had passed. But Congress showed no sign of losing interest. On the contrary, it incorporated into the regular federal aid program a provision for continued support to secondary road building. Thus it modified considerably the original purpose of the federal highway subsidy.

**Federal and state control of municipal construction.** Some years ago city streets that formed connecting links in the state highway systems were generally permitted to remain completely under municipal control, but this policy has now been virtually abandoned —largely because of congressional legislation providing for the use of federal highway funds within city boundaries. The laws of a number of states now authorize state control of trunk highways within the boundaries of all cities or all small cities and towns, and in most of the other commonwealths the grants from the state treasury to the municipalities are conditioned upon the adoption of certain types of paving material or the establishment of certain minimum pavement widths. Proper maintenance, also, is sometimes required. More than half of the states subsidize municipal street construction, but some of them distribute their funds unconditionally instead of using state aid to secure state control.

### MEANS OF FINANCING HIGHWAY CONSTRUCTION

The rapid increase in road mileage and the marked trend toward high-type construction, with many trunk highways costing more than fifty thousand dollars a mile, have created a serious financial problem. The magnitude of this problem can best be appreciated by a comparison of highway expenditures in 1903 and 1941, the last year of normal peacetime road building. The states and their local units spent about fifty million dollars for highways in 1903, this sum including the cost of construction and repair, and also payments for equipment, interest on highway bonds, and administration. By 1941 the annual state and local expenditures for highways were in excess of one billion and three-quarters—an increase of more than three thousand per cent. This stupendous increase represents in part the needs of a growing population, but chiefly it indicates the growth of highway mileage. Small wonder, therefore, that legislators have many times been hard pressed to find revenues sufficient to meet the cost of such a vastly expanded governmental activity!

**License fees.** Most of the burden of paying for the highways has been placed on the motorist, who is generally recognized as the chief beneficiary. This result has been accomplished by means of license fees and taxes of various kinds. The first state to license motor vehicles was New York, in 1901. Its fees for that year amounted to nine hundred and fifty-four dollars. By 1909 the licensing of automobiles had become general, and state revenues from this source had increased to nearly one hundred thousand dollars. Subsequent increases in motor vehicle registration and in the amounts charged per vehicle have raised the total to more than four hundred million dollars a year. Some states have established flat rates for all pleasure cars, but the more common practice is to vary the license fee according to weight, horse-power, or value. Higher rates are generally charged for trucks than for pleasure vehicles. In a few states the counties are permitted to collect license fees in addition to the fees imposed by the state government.

**The gasoline tax.** Among the taxes imposed on motorists, the gasoline tax is of prime importance. First adopted by Oregon in 1919, it spread rapidly and within a decade had been adopted by every state of the Union. At the outset the rate was one cent a gallon, but higher rates have now become universal, ranging from two cents a gallon in Missouri to seven cents a gallon in Florida, Louisiana, and Tennessee. Four cents is most common. The federal government also imposes a tax of one and one-half cents a gallon on gasoline sales, and a few states permit counties or cities, or both, to make additional levies. The highest rate is found in some of the cities of Alabama, where combined federal, state, county, and municipal taxes amount to twelve cents a gallon. Throughout the United States the state gasoline tax normally yields over six hundred million dollars a year, though this total has been reduced sharply since 1942, because of gasoline and tire rationing and the gradual withdrawal of cars from road service. The tax, is collected easily and cheaply, especially if no serious attempt is made to prevent evasion; and, within reasonable limits, it has no marked effect upon the consumption of gasoline. State officials are now beginning to learn, however, that the rate cannot be increased beyond five or six cents a gallon without creating serious problems.

APPORTIONMENT TO LOCAL UNITS. Twenty-one states distribute some part of their gasoline tax receipts among the local units of government—usually the counties, although the cities are gradually establishing their claim to a share for the paving of their streets. The portion allotted to the local units varies from forty-three per cent in Florida and forty-five per cent in Iowa to less than ten per cent in Arkansas. Thirty per cent is common. No uniformity exists as to the basis of distribution. Some states divide the money equally among the counties; some return to each county a fixed percentage of the amount collected within its borders; while others apportion the fund on the basis of area, population, highway mileage, motor car registration or assessed valuation.

USE OF GASOLINE TAX RECEIPTS. The original purpose of the gasoline tax was to defray at least a part of the cost of building and maintaining highways, and revenue obtained from this source is still commonly used for highway improvements. A few states, however, now devote a portion of the gasoline tax receipts to various activities that yield motorists, as a class, no special benefits. Thus Georgia, Illinois, Ohio, and Texas use gasoline tax money for public schools, and Alabama, Louisiana, and Mississippi set aside a portion for poor relief. On the other hand, proposals to divert gasoline tax money from its chief purpose of highway improvement have been severely defeated in a number of commonwealths, and eleven states [4] have gone so far as to write into their constitutions the provision that gasoline tax receipts may be used only for highways. Congress has entered the lists with a statutory provision withholding a part of federal aid from any state using motor vehicle tax revenues for other than highway purposes. It was once thought that the gradual completion of the main highway systems might lead to a reduction of gasoline tax rates or to a continuance of present rates and a more general use of this revenue for other purposes. But more recent increases in the potential speed of motor cars, plus the adoption of expensive highway construction methods for greater safety, seem to have destroyed the likelihood of reducing the total outlay for road building.

**Personal property and motor vehicle sales taxes.** Personal property taxes on automobiles, in addition to registration fees and gasoline taxes, are used in eighteen states, and more than half of the states impose taxes on the sale of motor vehicles. The revenues from these sources are commonly paid into the general fund, however, instead of a separate fund for the construction and maintenance of highways. Students of public finance are agreed that the personal property tax is unequitable and difficult to administer, especially when applied to *all* personal property.[5] Many forms of personal property can be concealed with ease; and if they are found, their value can be ascertained only with the greatest difficulty. But these objections do not apply to the taxation of motor vehicles. Registration makes concealment virtually impossible, and automobile trade lists make assessment of value by year and model a very simple matter.

**Real estate assessments.** A number of states, especially those of the South and West, place a portion of the cost of road construction on the owners of benefited property. The laws of these states commonly provide that whenever a new road is built, it shall be financed in part by special assessments on the real estate improved by the project. The

---

[4] California, Colorado, Idaho, Kansas, Michigan, Missouri, Minnesota, Nevada, New Hampshire, North Dakota, South Dakota.

[5] See pp. 364–366.

assessment area is fixed by the local governing body—the county or township commissioners or the road commissioners—usually without the application of any generally accepted rules. Abutting property is always included in the assessment area and bears the brunt of the burden, but other property presumed to be benefited by the improvement is also included under the laws of most states. Usually the amount that may be charged against benefited property for any single project is limited to twenty-five or fifty per cent of the actual cost of the project, and in no case may it exceed the value of the benefit conferred. Sometimes the law declares that special assessments may be imposed only on petition of the affected property owners, though this plan is gradually becoming unpopular because of its tendency to foster uneven development of road systems.

The principle upon which special assessments are based—namely, that persons receiving special benefits from government should contribute in proportion to their gain—is unquestionably sound. But the application of this principle presents a number of problems.[6] The most serious objection to the special assessment method of financing highways, aside from the difficulty of determining the assessment area, is that this method may be used to justify amateur interference in the selection of paving materials. When property owners know that they must pay a considerable part of the construction cost of a new road, they frequently demand and receive the right to specify the type of roadway. Usually their intentions are good, but their knowledge of the characteristics of paving materials is lamentably slight, and the result is likely to be more or less haphazard selection, with reference chiefly to the element of cost. It should be obvious that the choice of roadway types is a technical matter unsuited to the capacity of the rank and file of property owners,[7] but Americans are loathe to admit that any function of government is beyond the comprehension of the average man. Special assessments have lost considerable popularity in recent years, because of the default of many special assessment districts during the depression.

**Borrowing.** More than half of the states and many of their civil subdivisions have resorted to borrowing in order to finance the construction of their highway systems. The long-term debt of all the states, according to the most recent census figures,[8] is in excess of two

6 See p. 378.

7 A contrary view is expressed by Professor Geo. R. Chatburn, however, in his *Highways and Highway Transportation*, pp. 252–253.

8 1943. See the Census Bureau's annual publication, *State Finances*.

and one half billion dollars, and forty per cent of this total represents indebtedness incurred for highways. Fifteen years ago this percentage was even higher, but poor relief replaced highway construction as the chief reason for state bond issues during the 1930s—the depression decade.

Whether the states were justified in borrowing so extensively for road-building purposes during the first thirty years of the present century, when motor car registration was rising at an astounding rate and the demand for new highways was especially insistent, is a moot question. Sound financial procedure usually requires that all regularly recurring expenditures, such as road building, be met from current revenues; on the other hand, it can scarcely be denied that road building would have proceeded much more slowly on a pay-as-you-go basis. Perhaps the pressing need for new roads in a new age was a sufficient reason for the assumption of heavy state indebtedness. But pressing need can scarcely be used to justify further borrowing for highway purposes. The main routes in the highway systems of most of the states are now paved, and the most urgent demand has been met. Although it is true, as pointed out by highway officials, that large parts of the state highway systems still remain unpaved, that some of the present-day paving must soon be replaced with more substantial construction as traffic becomes heavier, and that even the finest highways, with but few exceptions, are incapable of permitting maximum speed with maximum safety, yet these facts should not lead to the conclusion that more highway bonds must be issued. The emergency stage in road building has passed.

### MEASURES TO DECREASE MOTOR CAR ACCIDENTS

An unfortunate result of increased highway travel and increased highway speeds has been the rapid multiplication of highway accidents. During the two decades from 1921 to 1941 the number of fatalities due to motor car accidents rose from twelve thousand to nearly forty thousand a year. Gasoline and tire rationing during the war caused a substantial reduction from the high mark of 1941, but this fact was accepted with qualified optimism by students of the traffic problem, who feared that increased driving in the postwar era would produce a new wave of fatalities. Regardless of the number of fatal motor car accidents in any year, it may always be assumed that non-fatal accidents are many times as numerous. Accurate information concerning the value of property damaged by motor cars is not available, but there is no doubt that this annual property loss amounts to many millions of dollars. Every state has taken some steps to reduce the number of motor car accidents, or at least to prevent further increases; and the more progressive commonwealths have approached the problem in a number of different ways—for example, by limiting the speed of motor vehicles and in other ways regulating their operation, by testing the fitness of drivers, by inspecting motor vehicles at periodic intervals, and by constructing highways with greater regard to the factor of safety.

**Speed laws.** Laws governing the speed of automobiles have been enacted in all the states. These laws usually fix maximum open-road driving speeds and also maximum speeds for residence districts, business districts, and curves and intersections. Early in 1942 state maximum speed regulations were superseded by the thirty-five-mile-an-hour limit requested by the federal government for the duration of the war. But our concern is with the peacetime functioning of the speed laws.

THE PRIMA FACIE MODIFYING CLAUSE. In some states the maximum speed limitation is modified by a so-called prima facie clause, which specifies that a driver exceeding the speed limit is only prima facie guilty of law violation and that he may introduce evidence, if arrested and brought to trial, to show the reasonableness of his speed under the road conditions existing at the time. Unfortunately, however, this plan has worked poorly. Most drivers are too busy to contest the charges brought against them, and most courts are loathe to accept refutatory evidence.

THE RULE OF REASONABLE AND PROPER SPEED. Many of the states, dissatisfied with the customary methods of speed regulation, have abolished fixed limits for open-road driving—and, in some instances, for driving in cities and towns. In place of the fixed limit has been substituted the rule that operators of motor vehicles must at all times drive at a reasonable and proper speed. This rule is a recognition of the obvious fact that safe driving is not merely a question of miles per hour, but of miles per hour in relation to driving conditions—the road surface, the weather, the volume of traffic, and a dozen other factors. At first glance, therefore, the requirement of "reasonable and proper" driving may seem to be the fairest way to limit motor car speed. But there is a practical objection—the difficulty of enforcement. The rule provides no guide for motorists or law-enforcement officers, with the inevitable result that the phrase "reasonable and proper" receives many different interpretations.

**Other state motor vehicle laws.** State laws concerning the operation of motor vehicles cover a great many matters in addition to speed. Nearly all require the use of hand signals for stopping and turning, and declare that cars must not stop on the highway. The passing of street cars on the left, or when taking on or discharging passengers, is generally prohibited. Three fourths of the states forbid drivers to overtake and pass on hills or curves if the view is obstructed. The use of stickers on windshields or rear windows is prohibited in twenty-eight states, and approximately the same number of states forbid coasting in neutral. Other regulations concerning motor car operation, such as requirements that headlights be dimmed for approaching vehicles or that a full stop be made at railway grade crossings, have been adopted less widely. The enforcement of the motor vehicle laws by state highway patrols has previously been noted.[9]

**Drivers' examinations.** In recent years increasing emphasis has been placed upon the fitness of motor car operators. The first state to require applicants for drivers' licenses to pass a test was Rhode Island, in 1908. For two decades other states followed slowly, but since 1928 the scheme has acquired considerable popularity, so that three fourths of the states now require drivers' examinations. A few of the other states have license laws applying only to chauffeurs and taxicab operators.

The examination for prospective motor car operators is generally divided into four parts: physical test, literacy test, test of knowledge of state laws, and road test. The physical examination deals chiefly with eyesight and hearing, though an attempt is made in some jurisdictions to discover any physical defects that might interfere with efficient driving. Frequently the literacy test is combined with the examination on the state motor vehicle law, the applicant being required to write answers to printed questions dealing with the provisions of the state code. The road test, involving a demonstration by the applicant of his ability to handle an automobile on the open road, is by far the most important part of the examination, and some states use it in lieu of written questions. A few states, however, go to the other extreme, relying solely on written questions—plus, perhaps, a physical examination.

[9] See p. 395.

The value of a road test depends in large measure on its administration. Some states entrust the administration of the test to the state police, without giving them any special training for the work, while others give their inspectors—police or civilians—thorough courses of training and complete instructions before assigning them to road test duty. In a few states the road test is administered by county officials who are not subject to state supervision or control, with the result that widely varying standards are found. The test means much or little, according to the diverse concepts of county inspectors. In recent years psychologists have devised numerous tests for measuring driving ability. Some of these tests are conducted in the laboratory; others simulate actual road conditions and measure the skill of motor vehicle operators in backing, turning, giving signals, and the like while they drive through a labyrinth of paths and lanes. These tests have been adopted by several large industrial establishments in the selection of their truck drivers, but state officials have evinced slight interest.

**Motor vehicle inspection.** The laws of a number of states require the periodic inspection of all motor vehicles for the purpose of eliminating serious mechanical defects that might cause accidents. Most of these laws are far from satisfactory, however. They commonly apply only to brakes or headlights, or both, instead of including such important additional factors of automobile safety as wheel alignment, steering wheel, horn, rear-view mirror, windshield cleaner, parking lights, tail light, and stop light. Moreover, inspection is not generally required once a year, as it should be, but biennially, triennially, or at infrequent intervals determined by the whim of the legislature. Still more serious, most state laws fail to make adequate provision for supplementary road examinations by members of the highway patrol, with the result that mechanical defects multiply unchecked after the formal biennial or triennial inspection.

**Elimination or protection of grade crossings.** Railway grade crossings have long created a serious traffic accident problem, and in recent years the more dangerous crossings have been steadily eliminated. Until 1935 the cost of this work was borne by the railway, the state, and, as a rule, the benefited county or township, but since that year Congress has granted several hundred million dollars to the states for grade-crossing elimination. Yet the problem is by no means solved, for new highways are constructed and new railway grade crossings created almost as rapidly as the old crossings are removed. A great deal has been done to reduce the element of danger by protecting grade crossings. Nearly nine tenths of all crossings are now marked by fixed signs, and most of the others—especially those located on the main arteries of traffic—are protected by crossing gates, watchmen, or warning devices that indicate the approach of trains.

NEED FOR OTHER SAFETY STEPS IN HIGHWAY CONSTRUCTION. During the last fifteen years the state highway departments have increasingly emphasized the factor of safety in their road-building programs, yet much remains to be accomplished. Highways should be wider, for the most part, with medial strips to separate traffic flowing in opposite directions and distinct footways for pedestrian traffic. Parking space off the traveled portion of rural highways should be provided—either continuously or at reasonable intervals. Grades should be reasonable and curves should be banked. Heavy guard rails should protect embankments, and all necessary steps should be taken to insure a clear view of approaching vehicles for several hundred yards. And adequate night lighting of highways, despite its heavy cost, should be seriously considered as an important means of reducing after-dark accidents.

**Safety education.** Nearly all the state highway departments devote some attention to educational campaigns. The need for caution on the highways is explained and emphasized by means of posters in public places, motion pictures, lantern slides, radio talks, newspaper and magazine publicity, mass meetings, and special campaigns. Schools for motorists are maintained in a few states, and privately organized safe drivers' clubs are encouraged. A number of states place strong emphasis on safety education in the schools. The task of educating the public in matters of highway safety was first undertaken by the motor clubs and later developed by safety councils and other private or semi-private groups. These various organizations are still functioning very efficiently and doing their full share to reduce the traffic accident rate, but state activity has made possible the distribution of safety propaganda among many groups not reached by private agencies.

**Accident reports and investigation.** The importance of adequate statistics concerning motor car accidents has long been recognized, and the laws of most of the states now provide a means of securing such statistics by specifying that accidents must be reported to some state agency—usually the agency vested with power to revoke operators' licenses. The law may apply only to accidents causing injury to persons, as in Maryland and Massachusetts, or it may specifically exempt accidents involving only property damage below a certain amount—often twenty-five or fifty dollars. Prompt investigation of accident reports enables the police to determine accurately the causes of most accidents and to fix the blame in many cases. In Oregon, where the investigation is unusually prompt and thorough, including an examination of the brakes and mechanical parts of damaged cars whenever possible, information has been obtained for a scientific approach to the problem of reducing traffic accidents. Most states, however, use their traffic accident records merely for the purpose of suspending or revoking the licenses of habitually reckless drivers.

**A uniform motor vehicle code.** In 1930 the National Conference on Street and Highway Safety, meeting at the national capital, revised the earlier draft of a so-called "uniform vehicle code" and offered this revision for the consideration of the forty-eight state legislatures. The code comprises five acts, covering major phases of motor vehicle regulation: (1) the registration of automobiles, and the prevention of theft; (2) the issuance of drivers' licenses; (3) civil liability for motor car accidents; (4) responsibility for highway safety; and (5) the regulation of highway traffic. Every state has adopted one or more of these five acts, at least in part or in modified form, but the goal of virtual uniformity in all vital matters of motor vehicle regulation is still far distant.

### SELECTED REFERENCES

Bateman, J. H., *Introduction to Highway Engineering*, 3rd ed., 1939.

Crawford, F. G., *The Administration of the Gasoline Tax in the United States*, 4th ed., 1936.

Dearing, Charles L., *American Highway Policy*, Washington, D.C., 1942.

De Silva, H. R., *Mechanical Tests for Drivers*, Cambridge, Mass., 1938.

Ford, Robert S., and Bacon, Marvin A., *Michigan Highway Finance*, Ann Arbor, 1943.

Hewes, Laurence I., *American Highway Practice*, 1942.

Hoffman, P. G., and Clark, N. M., *Several Roads to Safety: A Program to Reduce Automobile Accidents*, 1939.

Kennedy, G. D., *Modern Urban Highways*, Washington, D.C., 1944.

Key, V. O., Jr., *The Administration of Federal Grants of the States*, 1937.

Macdonald, Austin F., *Federal Aid*, 1928.

McGalliard, H. W., *Guides to Highway Safety*, Chapel Hill, N.C., 1935.

National Conference on Street and Highway Safety, *Manual on Street Traffic Signs, Signals and Markings*, Washington, D.C., 1930.

———, *Model Municipal Traffic Ordinance*, 1930.

———, *Report of the Committee on Maintenance of the Motor Vehicle*, 1930.

———, *Report of the Committee on Protection of Railroad Grade Crossings and Highway Intersections*, 1930.

National Conference on Street and Highway Safety, *Report of the Committee on Uniform Traffic Regulation,* 1930.

——, *Uniform Motor Vehicle Code,* 1930.

——, *Ways and Means to Traffic Safety,* 1930.

Owens, W., *A Study in Highway Economics,* Cambridge, Mass., 1934.

Stocker, H. E., *Motor Traffic Management,* 1938.

Tripp, H. A., *Road Traffic and Its Control,* 1938.

Trull, E., *Borrowing for Highways,* 1937.

Tucker, Harry, and Leager, Marc C., *Highway Economics,* Scranton, Pa., 1942.

Walker, J. E., *Highway Tax Costs,* Washington, D.C., 1938.

# Chapter Twenty-Six 🖋 NATURAL RESOURCES

UNTIL almost the beginning of the present century the natural resources of the United States were considered practically inexhaustible. They were exploited as rapidly as possible without the slightest attempt to prevent waste; in fact, many resources were wantonly destroyed in the process of facilitating the nation's development. By 1895, however, a number of scientists and statesmen were pointing out the folly of heedless waste, and gradually during the next two decades conservation became a national slogan.

The masses of the people realized for the first time that gas, oil, and coal supplies were rapidly diminishing and could not be replaced. They began to understand the relationship between forest lands and a constant water supply. So they demanded legislation that would encourage the proper utilization of the nation's wealth and prevent careless or extravagant methods of development. As a result, every state now devotes some attention to the conservation and development of its natural resources. Generally speaking, state programs are far from adequate. The conservation laws are sometimes needlessly repressive or, much more commonly, needlessly lenient. Enforcement is often lax. Resources that should be included are frequently omitted. But public responsibility for the public's natural wealth is universally recognized, and sound principles of conservation have been developed by the more progressive commonwealths.

## STATE CONSERVATION AGENCIES

Nearly three fourths of the states have created conservation commissions or departments, whose official task, phrased in slightly varying terms, is "to protect, conserve, and replenish the natural resources of the state." In this field the commission (properly, board) form of administration is popular. Usually the members are appointed by the governor for overlapping terms and serve without pay.

**Varying duties and functions.** Their principal duty is to select an executive officer to handle the actual details of administration. Matters of policy are decided at regular monthly or quarterly meetings.

The functions of the several conservation commissions, departments, and divisions vary widely from state to state. Almost all are responsible for the prevention of forest fires and the protection of forest resources; many enforce the fish and game laws and manage the state parks; some supervise the development of water power and mineral resources; and a few administer the laws against stream pollution. The Massachusetts department of conservation is empowered to control, prevent, and suppress contagious diseases in domestic animals, and the Indiana conservation commission to control plant diseases and insect pests. The Maryland department of conservation plants oyster shells on rocks in the tributaries of Chesapeake Bay. In not more than six states, however, can the principal conservation agency claim to have even an approximation of complete responsibility for the protection and development of natural resources. Usually it must share this duty with a number of other bodies. Fortunately, however, the recent trend seems to be in the direction of greater centralization.

### FORESTRY

Forty-two states [1] are actively engaged in some form of forest protection or development, though the nature of this work varies considerably. Some states are mainly interested in fire prevention; some devote most of their forest funds to tree planting; while others consider the prevention of insect or fungus attacks most important. Much depends on local conditions, local finances, and local sentiment. A number of the states, recognizing forestry as a major governmental activity, have developed practically every phase of forest conservation; their well-trained organizations include foresters, rangers, guards, and nurserymen.

**Federal subsidies.** State interest in foresty has been greatly stimulated during the last thirty-five years by annual grants from the federal treasury. As under most of the other subsidy laws, the states are required to accept the federal offer, match federal money dollar for dollar, and prepare plans for federal approval. The first federal forestry subsidy law, enacted in 1911, limited federal funds to "protection from fire of the forested watersheds of navigable streams," but subsequent legislation has broadened materially the scope of federal aid. All "timbered and forest-producing lands" have been brought

---

[1] The exceptions are Arizona, Missouri, Nevada, New Mexico, Utah, and Wyoming. In Arizona, Nevada, Utah, and Wyoming the work is handled by the United States Forest Service. The other two states do not have large forest areas needing protection.

within the terms of the federal offer; moreover, additional federal funds have been appropriated to aid the states in growing and distributing trees and in stimulating popular interest in tree growing. Nearly all the states have accepted the federal government's terms and now co-operate with the United States Forest Service.

**Fire protection:** ORGANIZATION. Over three hundred million acres of state and private forest lands are afforded more or less systematic protection from fire. Unfortunately, another one hundred and twenty million acres are practically without protection, though this state of affairs is being corrected gradually. State organization for forest fire protection has assumed three main forms, with a number of variations. Most common is the scheme of centralized administration, which vests complete authority and responsibility in the state forester. This officer selects his staff of fire fighters, and directs their work. Another plan is generally used in New England; there each town [2] assumes the obligation of protecting its own forests. The town fire wardens are locally chosen, with the almost inevitable result that wardens from neighboring towns often fail to co-operate in fighting serious conflagrations. The state forester has no way of compelling co-operative action. In the heavily forested states of the Northwest, where the large timber owners had developed efficient private fire-fighting organizations before the state governments became interested in forest protection, the work of the states centers around this private activity. Some states entrust the entire task of fire protection and fire fighting to the private associations, paying them with public funds and supervising their work closely.

LEGISLATION. Most states have enacted legislation designed to reduce the forest fire hazard. The burning of brush in or near woodland is generally prohibited, or at least restricted in various ways. Some state laws specify that a permit must first be secured. Penalties are provided for lack of proper care in handling camp fires and for carelessness or malicious intent in starting fires on public or private property. The laws of a few Western states declare that any person burning brush or grass on his own land during the dry summer months must notify his neighbors some time in advance. The timber companies and others engaged in logging operations are required to dispose of slash—that is, the leftover tops and limbs of trees—before a

---

[2] It must be remembered that the New England *town* is not merely an urban community, but commonly includes rural territory also. Many New England towns are almost entirely rural.

sufficient quantity accumulates to constitute a serious fire risk. Spark-arresting devices are commonly prescribed for locomotives and other engines operating near forest land. Many of these state laws were enacted years ago, and are now badly in need of revision. Even more serious is the general laxity of enforcement. The state forester's office often lacks adequate authority and usually lacks adequate funds; and local enforcement has proved a failure in nearly every state where it has been tried.

**Educational programs.** The federal government's offer to aid in financing educational field work in forestry has been accepted by thirty-seven states. This field work consists of practical demonstrations and projects conducted on the farmers' own land. The importance of timber is emphasized, and farmers are shown how their woodlands can be made to yield increased returns. Boys and girls are taught the essentials of forest planting, woods care and management, and fire protection. The federal appropriation for this activity is so small that most of the cost is necessarily borne by the states, yet state programs are regularly submitted to the federal government under the terms of the co-operative agreements.

**State forests.** Laws providing for the permanent retention of state forest lands as state forests have been enacted in forty-one states. These forest areas vary greatly in size. Thus Georgia has only a few acres, while the area of Pennsylvania's twenty-four state forests totals nearly two thousand square miles. Most of the large state forest areas are found in the Western states because these commonwealths originally received substantial grants of timberland from the national government. In many cases, however, this land was given for the purpose of resale—the money thus obtained to be used for specific purposes, such as common schools, institutions of higher learning, penal and charitable institutions, or public buildings. Moreover, the bulk of the land, even if free from such restrictions, was in widely scattered sections that could not readily be administered as state forests. In recent years, however, the federal government has encouraged consolidation of state forest holdings by offering to exchange timberland with the states, and many exchanges have been effected. Federal funds have recently been made available to help complete state forest systems, the states agreeing to repay these loans as they derive revenue from the sale of forest products and the use of forest lands. A number of states have formulated the general policy that all state lands chiefly valuable for timber or for watershed protection shall be "forever dedicated to the public welfare." Large bond issues have been floated in some states for the acquisition of wooded areas suitable for state forests, whereas in other states bond issues for this purpose are prohibited.

**Reforestation.** More than five sixths of the states, under co-operative agreements with the United States Forest Service, maintain nurseries for the production of planting stock. Millions of young trees are distributed to farmers each year. Usually a nominal charge is made, but the laws of a few states provide for free distribution. This activity is so closely related to other phases of forestry that it is generally administered by the state forester. In some states, however, the growth and distribution of forest trees have been entrusted to the state agricultural college, whose numerous contacts with the farmers through the county agents [3] greatly simplify the task of arousing popular interest in reforestation.

Most of the timberland of the United States is in private ownership. When it is cut over its immediate commercial value is destroyed, and its owners usually abandon it. Taxes on the land become delinquent, and after a time the state or county comes into possession of cut-over forest areas that have become a liability instead of an asset. Of course, the private owners are not to blame. Their sole interest is in the timber, and after that is gone they cannot afford to pay heavy taxes for many years while slow-growing crops of fresh timber replace the trees that have been cut down. Yet some way must be found to reforest these areas, for the forests of the United States are being cut four times as fast as they are grown.

It is obvious, therefore, that if private owners could be induced to retain their cut-over land and grow new timber, and to pay taxes and contribute to the cost of fire protection during the years required for the new crop to mature, the states would be spared the necessity of undertaking reforestation at public expense. More than half of the states have offered the inducement of materially lower taxes, or even tax exemption, on cut-over lands devoted to new forest crops. On the other hand, a number of states have been prevented from granting preferential treatment by "uniform tax" clauses in their constitutions. Whether the inducement of a lower tax—or no tax at all—will lead to widespread reforestation of private lands is a question not yet decided. Some states seem to have obtained fairly satisfactory results, but others have been less fortunate.

**Forestry research.** The movement for conservation of the nation's

3 See pp. 526–528.

forest resources has suffered a severe setback as a result of the war. Huge demands for lumber and high prices have greatly increased the drain upon available supplies. Production in 1944 was twenty-five per cent higher than in 1936. Large quantities of young second growth were cut prematurely. But public interest in the problems of forest conservation did not wane. In fact increased appropriations were made for the eleven forest experiment stations that have been established in various parts of the United States. These stations are administered by the federal government, but close relationships are maintained with the state foresters and the state agricultural colleges. Many of the experiments are made co-operatively, the states supplying money, equipment, or personnel, and sharing in the results. These experiments include nursery and planting investigations, studies of the best methods of forest cutting, studies of forest growth and productivity, and investigations of forest relationships to climate, grazing, and fire. Tree insects and diseases are studied, these inquiries necessitating the assistance of specialists in entomology and plant pathology. A few experimental forests are being developed in connection with some of the stations.

## FISH AND GAME

**Protective legislation.** Every state has enacted more or less complete legislation designed to protect its wild life. The federal government, also, has acted to safeguard wild animals and birds, and its laws supplement the state statutes. While there is considerable variation in detail from state to state, the general principles of all the state fish and game laws are substantially the same. Open and close seasons are fixed, with perhaps no open season for certain kinds of game that seem threatened with extinction or no close season for other kinds that have proved too prolific. Hunting and fishing licenses are required, usually with higher fees for non-residents. Bag and possession limits are established. Prohibitions are generally placed on the sale of protected game and also on its exportation from the state except under certain specified conditions. Certain methods of killing fur animals, such as the use of poison or of traps that unnecessarily inflict torture, are forbidden.

**Commissions.** These fish and game laws, which far antedate the modern conservation movement, were originally enforced by the local sheriffs and constables as a part of their general duties of law enforcement. But this arrangement never produced satisfactory results, and during the latter half of the nineteenth century it was abandoned by most of the states in favor of the appointment of special officers.    The first state to take this step was Maine, and it made the change even before the middle of the century—in 1843.    The governor was authorized to appoint three county fish wardens and also, a few years later, a number of county moose wardens.    Fish commissions were established in Massachusetts and New Hampshire in 1865, and shortly afterward in Connecticut and Vermont.    Other states fell into line rapidly, creating agencies for the protection of fish or game.    After the reorganization in 1878 of the New Hampshire fish commission as the board of fish and game commissioners, it soon became customary to place fish and game protection under a single agency.

ACTIVITIES.    Commissions, boards, departments, bureaus, or divisions of fish and game are now found in every state, though under a variety of names.    Louisiana has a division of fur and wild life, while a game, fish, and oyster commission functions in Texas.    The commission may have jurisdiction over parks, as in Nebraska.    It has already been indicated that in some states the department of conservation enforces the fish and game laws.[4]    The fish and game commission —by whatever name it may be called—ranges in size from three members in Arizona and eight other states to nine members in New Jersey. Usually the members are unsalaried, though there are some exceptions.    The executive officer, chosen by the commission, directs the daily administrative routine.    He selects a number of wardens, whose primary duty is to police the state and apprehend violators of the fish and game laws.    In the more progressive states the wardens perform a number of other important functions also.    They aid in solving the conservation problems of their respective districts, and in planning and constructing fish ponds.    They lead many local movements for the conservation of wild life.

Although the state fish and game commissions were created merely as agencies of law enforcement, their activities now include virtually every phase of wild life conservation.    Most of them carry on extensive programs of propagation and restocking, involving the operation of fish hatcheries and rearing ponds, from which various species of fish are distributed to the public lakes and streams; and also the operation of game farms where birds and animals are reared and kept until ready for distribution.    In addition, game refuges are maintained by more than one third of the states.    They furnish sure rest and feeding

4 See p. 519.

grounds for protected birds and animals, and thus play an important part in the general plan to increase the game supply. Predatory animal control is also an important function. Most of the states try to secure the protection of game by offering bounties for the skins of such predatory animals as wolves or mountain lions. In addition, a few states employ trained hunters whose task is to trap and kill these beasts of prey.

. Educational work is almost invariably a part of the fish and game commissioner's program. Motion pictures of wild life are prepared and distributed, lecturers are provided at the request of many organizations, and schools are aided in their conservation studies and exhibits. Other common methods of arousing popular interest, such as newspaper publicity and the publication of reports and bulletins, are regularly used. Some states issue periodicals devoted to fish and game, distributing them without charge or at the cost of printing.

Within the last few years many of the states have made co-operative agreements with their neighbors, or have adopted uniform regulations, concerning the conservation of wild life. Co-operative agreements usually cover such matters as hunting and fishing seasons, bag and possession limits, issuance of reciprocal licenses, and joint policies of stocking and policing wild life areas.

**Relief from wild life overpopulation.** The movement for the protection of our wild animals and birds has been so successful that many states are now faced with the problem of wild life overpopulation. Deer and elk are so numerous in some sections that they seriously damage crops. Pheasants, also, have multiplied so rapidly in many areas that they present a grave menace to agriculture. Today the United States has more bears, rabbits, ducks, and other forms of wild life than it has had in many decades. The bison is no longer in danger of extinction. The war has focused attention on the problem of a wild life surplus, partly by making it difficult for hunters to get their usual supplies of fuel and ammunition and partly by creating a demand for larger quantities of meat. Even the most ardent conservationists are willing to concede that wild game might be made a valuable supplementary source of food. Many states have recognized this fact by permitting longer hunting seasons, increasing bag and possession limits, and otherwise relaxing the game laws. There seems to be little danger that these temporary changes will impair the long-run policy of protection.

### AGRICULTURAL EXTENSION WORK

**Farmers' institute.** The states have long recognized their obligation to improve the standards of American farming by acquainting the people of the rural sections with the best farming methods. As early as 1852, when the Massachusetts state board of agriculture was established, the secretary was directed to "visit the various agricultural districts of the state and deliver lectures on the practice and science of agriculture." Eleven years later the board made provision for annual meetings of the leading agriculturalists of every farming community for the purpose of discussing common problems. Other states followed with so-called "farmers' institutes," and before 1890 the movement had spread to more than half of the states. By 1910 practically every state was included, the one- or two-day sessions of the institutes drawing hundreds of thousands of people. The railroads ran special trains to all the more important institutes. In 1914, when the institute movement was at its peak, the total attendance in all states exceeded three million. Farmers were vitally interested in the discussion of their problems by experts. About this time, however, it became clear that a still better way of reaching the rural population of the United States had been found, and after 1914 the farmers' institutes declined rapidly in importance. Today their influence is negligible.

**County agents.** The better way to reach farmers is the county agent system, now employed by every state. This system had its inception in Texas in 1906. The federal government had established a number of demonstration farms in various parts of the South for the purpose of teaching better methods of crop production and had succeeded in persuading many farmers to cultivate some of their own land under government supervision. Federal agents were assigned to the task of supervising these co-operative enterprises and pointing out mistakes. Pleased with the results obtained, the farmers in one Texas county requested the full-time services of a federal agent, offering to pay part of his salary. Their request was granted, and the county's share of the agent's salary was raised by popular subscription. Other counties soon made similar arrangements, and by 1914 the number of "county agents," as these men were generally called, had risen to nine hundred. In that year Congress recognized the importance of the work by making a grant of several million dollars to the states for the purpose of providing "instruction and practical demonstrations in agriculture and home economics to persons not attending" the state agricultural colleges. This statute was a typical piece of subsidy legislation, including the usual stipulations that the state must accept the federal offer, that it must match federal money with money from state or local sources, and that it must submit plans acceptable to the federal administrative officials. The state agricultural colleges direct the work of the county agents, and assume responsibility for the effectiveness of extension work.

Although the county agent is paid from federal and state sources as well as from county funds and must possess the qualifications established by the state with federal approval, he is primarily a county employee. His title clearly indicates that he is chiefly responsible to the county he serves. He is chosen by the county supervisors, though usually from a list of names submitted by the state director of extension work, and in most states he may be dismissed by the supervisors for any reason that they deem adequate. Dismissal from a county does not necessarily involve dismissal from the extension service, for the state director who desires to place a dismissed agent in another county can usually do so without difficulty. But chronic inability to give satisfaction is certain to destroy an agent's usefulness and force him from the service after a period of years.

ACTIVITIES. The county agents carry their message to the farmers by means of actual demonstrations on the farmers' own land wherever this method of instruction is practicable. Their activities are numerous and varied. They teach soil improvement through the increased use of fertilizers and the introduction of nitrogenous crops such as sweet clover, soy beans, and cow peas. They emphasize the use of higher grade seed. The importance of tree crops is a part of their message. They encourage the breeding of better live stock and lead the fight on animal diseases. Land improvement is a part of their program, whether the land needs terracing, draining, irrigating, or clearing. They teach the use of dynamite. Nor is the work of the county agents restricted to improving methods of production. Better marketing is emphasized. The farmer who keeps bees, for example, is shown how to grade his honey and how to pack it attractively. In many states, emphasis is placed on co-operative marketing. Through another important phase of the work—instruction in farm management—farmers are taught how to keep accurate records of their transactions. As a result, cost accounting is becoming more generally understood and used.

Although some of the poorer rural counties, unable to bear the financial burden of extension work, have never had county agents, or have abandoned extension activities after a short trial, many a county has two or more agents. The work of the male county agent is often supplemented by the work of a female home economics agent, whose task is to teach farm women how to make their homes more attractive, how to use time- and labor-saving devices, and how to safeguard the health of their families. Club agents, who deal exclusively with children, helping them to form pig clubs, cotton clubs, or other juvenile organizations where the use of proper farming methods can be stressed, are found in some of the wealthier counties. Usually, however, boys' and girls' clubs are developed and supervised by the county agricultural agents, who accept this task as a part of their regular duties. A few Southern counties employ Negro extension agents to carry the message of improved agriculture to the members of their own race, but in most cases the white agents serve all the families in their respective counties, without regard to race or color.

The federal government prescribes minimum educational standards for county agents, including successful completion of a four-year college course in agriculture and practical farming experience. Some states, however, have gone considerably beyond the federal minimum. and have thus been able to secure agents of unusually high caliber. It need scarcely be added that the salaries paid by these states are well above the average.

*During the Second World War.* In December, 1941, when the United States entered the Second World War, the problem of producing adequate food supplies suddenly became vitally important. Enough food was needed to meet the demands of the United States and, at least in part, of its fighting allies. And, as conquered lands were gradually liberated, their starving populations required American food until they could repair their own depleted economies. American farmers were called upon to produce far more than they had ever produced before. "Food for victory" was the slogan, and the county agents directed the highly successful movement. They were assisted by more than a quarter of a million volunteer leaders. In war, as in peace, agricultural extension work proved its worth.

### AGRICULTURAL AND MINING EXPERIMENT STATIONS

Every state maintains an agricultural experiment station in connection with its agricultural college. These experiment stations were originally established as a direct result of a federal subsidy, but state appropriations now amount to three times the federal grant. Most of the customary conditions have been omitted from the federal offer, so that the states are free to conduct their stations without federal supervision or control. The experiments carried on at the stations cover a wide range—soils and fertilizers, field crops, horticulture, plant diseases, animal production, dairying, animal diseases, foods and human nutrition, rural home management, agricultural engineering and economics, and rural sociology. Numerous reports, bulletins, and miscellaneous publications of the experiment stations contain the results of experiments, and thus make this information available to the public.

A number of the states also maintain mining experiment stations, engineering experiment stations, or divisions of engineering research. This work is usually administered by the state university or the agricultural college. Studies are made of the origin and occurrence of minerals, methods of prospecting and mining, mineral analyses and tests, extraction and refining, properties and utilization of minerals, and preservation of safety and health in mining. Many experiments are conducted co-operatively with the federal Bureau of Mines. As in the case of agricultural experiments, results are published at frequent intervals.

## OIL AND GAS

**Conservation legislation.** The states have done very little to prevent wasteful exploitation of most of their mineral resources. Oil and gas, however, are exceptions to this general rule. Every state possessing substantial known deposits of oil and gas has enacted legislation to reduce waste. The first oil conservation measure was adopted by Pennsylvania more than half a century ago; a short time afterward New York and Ohio followed. These early laws were designed to protect oil- and gas-bearing sands from the infiltration of salt water. They provided merely that water should be cased off, that wells should be plugged in a specific manner when abandoned, and that the owners of adjacent land, in case of the failure of well owners to plug properly, might remedy the deficiency. A little later, as it became evident that generally accepted methods of oil production were causing the loss of immense quantities of natural gas, other laws were enacted for the specific purpose of preventing this waste. An Indiana statute of 1893, for example, provided that neither oil nor gas should be permitted to flow or escape into the open air for a period longer than two days after discovery. The constitutionality of this act was promptly attacked by one of the oil companies of the state, as contrary to the Fourteenth Amendment's due process clause. The company said, in effect, that it was interested only in the production of oil and that it could not produce oil without wasting gas. But the Supreme Court of the United States upheld the state's power of regulation, though upon rather narrow ground.[5]

PRODUCTION RESTRICTIONS. Somewhat later the oil-producing states enacted laws dealing with virtually every phase of oil and gas conservation, and establishing administrative agencies to make supplementary regulations and secure proper enforcement. It was found that unnecessary waste in the production of oil and gas could be prevented most readily by restricting production to the current market demand. Fair treatment of all the operators in a field was assured by prorating production among them. Voluntary proration agreements were encouraged in California for several years, but without substantial success. The other leading oil-producing states went still further and enforced production limits established by administrative decree. The validity of the Oklahoma law authorizing the corporation commission to restrict total production and to establish production limits for each operator was challenged by one of the affected companies as a violation of the due process and equal protection clauses of the Fourteenth Amendment to the federal Constitution. But the Supreme Court of the United States upheld the statute. "Every person has the right to drill wells on his own land and take from the pools below all the gas and oil that he may be able to reduce to possession including that coming from land belonging to others," declared Mr. Justice Butler, speaking for the Court, "but the right to take and thus to acquire ownership is subject to the reasonable exertion of the power of the state to prevent unnecessary loss, destruction, or waste."[6] Restrictions on the production of oil and gas were made effective by cooperative arrangements involving most of the important oil-producing states. Unfortunately, however, these restrictions were aimed more directly at the maintenance of prices than the conservation of oil supplies.

*During the Second World War.* The Second World War com-

---

[5] Ohio Oil Co. *v.* Indiana, 177 U.S. 190 (1900).

[6] Champlin Refining Company *v.* Corporation Commission of Oklahoma, 286 U.S. 210 (1932).

pletely transformed public oil policy. Laws to restrict output were no longer necessary; on the contrary, the problem was to stimulate production until it reached the highest possible level. Five million barrels of oil a day were needed, and this quantity could not be obtained without dipping into reserves. The task of regulating the oil industry under such circumstances was too big for the states, so the federal government promptly assumed control. It set up a Petroleum Administration and made it responsible for stimulating oil production and allocating supplies—first to the armed forces and then to industry. Another federal agency, the Office of Price Administration, was charged with the task of fixing the prices of petroleum products. So rapidly are the oil reserves of the United States being depleted by the requirements of total war that conservation will be absolutely necessary in the postwar period.

## WATER POWER

**Absolute federal control.** The federal government has taken the lead in the conservation of water power. Its control extends to water-power developments on navigable streams (through the right to regulate interstates commerce) and also to projects on the national domain. Since the justification for federal control in most instances is that streams are navigable, it becomes important to have a test of navigability. Such a test was established by the United States Supreme Court in 1871: "Those rivers must be regarded as public navigable rivers in law which are navigable in fact. And they are navigable in fact when they are used, or are susceptible of being used, in their ordinary condition, as highways for commerce. . . ." [7] This ruling stood for nearly three quarters of a century, but it was modified in 1940 by the Supreme Court, when it was called upon to determine the navigability of the New River. It held that the river was navigable, in spite of existing rapids, shallows, gorges, and other obstructions, because these barriers could be removed and the river made navigable in fact by the expenditure of a not unreasonable sum of money. "To appraise the evidence of navigability on the natural condition only of the waterway is erroneous," said the Court. "Its availability for navigation must also be considered." [8] This new criterion was attacked by Mr. Justice Roberts in a vigorous dissenting opinion. "If this test be adopted," he declared, "then every creek in every state in the Union which has

[7] Daniel Ball Case, 10 Wallace 557 (1871).
[8] United States *v.* Appalachian Electric Power Co., 311 U.S. 377 (1940).

enough water, when conserved by dams and locks or channelled by wing dams and sluices, to draw a boat drawing two feet of water, may be pronounced navigable because, by the expenditure of some enormous sum, such a project would be possible of execution. In other words, Congress can create navigability by determining to improve a non-navigable stream." And that is exactly what Congress can do, in the view of the Supreme Court, despite Mr. Justice Roberts' protest.[9] The effect of this decision has been to insure absolute federal control over all the water-power resources of the nation.

**State participation in conservation.** As early as 1920 a Federal Power Commission was established. In 1930 it was reorganized with additional powers, and five years later its authority was still further expanded. It now passes upon applications to construct power plants and grants licenses to responsible persons for periods not exceeding fifty years. It supervises the design, construction, and operation of each project, regulates the financial policy of each operating company, and controls such important matters as rates and services. The Federal Power Act does not, however, exclude the states from participation in the program of conserving water power. On the contrary, it recognizes the desirability of federal-state co-operation. No federal license is granted until the applicant has met all the requirements of state law. No federal regulation of rates, services, or financial policy is attempted if there is a state commission possessing adequate authority. The right of the state to acquire federally licensed projects upon payment of just compensation is expressly reserved. Until a state acts, however, the federal government continues to occupy the entire field of water-power regulation. In certain areas the federal government has undertaken direct construction and management of vast hydroelectric power projects, of which the best known is the Tennessee Valley development. The total cost of these undertakings will probably be more than three-quarters of a billion dollars.

Unfortunately, very few of the states have formulated any definite policies for conserving and developing their water-power resources. State public service commissions generally exercise a measure of control over companies that sell electricity developed from water-power, but this control is merely a phase of public utility regulation, not directly related to water-power development. There are, however, a few exceptions to the general rule of state inaction. Most notable is California, whose division of water resources in the department of

9 Mr. Justice McReynolds joined Mr. Justice Roberts in his dissent.

public works prepared a comprehensive state water plan as early as 1931.

## STATE PARKS

State parks serve the dual purpose of conserving natural resources and providing recreational areas for thousands of persons. The first state park was created in 1865, when the federal government gave the Yosemite Valley to California for recreational purposes. Yosemite has since been returned to the federal government and is now a national park, but numerous other tracts of land have been set aside by California as state parks, and a comprehensive park system has been developed. In 1885 the second state park was established, when Niagara Falls and a small strip of surrounding territory were set aside by the State of New York. Once again the primary object was the preservation of a great natural wonder. Other states followed slowly until about 1910, when the state park movement received fresh impetus from the increasing use of automobiles. State parks, created specifically for recreational purposes or for the preservation of places of natural beauty, were established in twenty-eight states by 1933. Then the federal government entered the picture, offering to aid the states in the development of their park areas by furnishing the labor of thousands of young men from the Civilian Conservation Corps. Financial assistance from the federal treasury was also provided. And as a result the total acreage of state parks doubled in five years. Every one of the states has now made some provision for the establishment of park areas. The parks are administered by a variety of agencies— the conservation commission, as in Iowa, the park commission, as in Arkansas, or the forestry and recreation commission, as in New Hampshire. In 1937 the states of New York and New Jersey created a joint commission to manage the Palisades Interstate Park, which parallels the Hudson River.

## STATE PLANNING

State planning was almost unknown before 1933, although city and regional planning were generally understood and accepted. But a few states had begun to prepare more or less systematic inventories of their resources. New York created a temporary commission on housing and regional planning in 1923, which made a number of important studies. In 1929 New Jersey and Wisconsin set up permanent state agencies to foster local planning. Then, in 1933, the fed-

eral government offered funds for the establishment of state planning boards. The response was enthusiastic and almost unanimous.
Every state except Delaware accepted the federal grant, and set up
some kind of planning agency. More recently, however, seven states [10]
have abolished their planning boards, and in many other commonwealths planning activities are narrowly restricted by inadequate
funds, lack of authority, or partisan politics.

**Activities.** The state planning boards perform a bewildering variety of activities. Some of them supervise and encourage local planning agencies. Some have made surveys of natural resources, population, transportation, education, health, housing—in fact, virtually
every phase of modern life. Nearly all the boards are concerned with
the utilization of land. They recognize that thousands of acres of
land are abandoned every year because the owners find it impossible
to wrest even a bare living from the soil and that these submarginal
areas must somehow be fitted into a planned public economy. To
date, however, state boards have prepared very few plans on any subject; instead they have devoted their time chiefly to the collection of
the factual information from which comprehensive plans may eventually be shaped. The planning boards of the several states range in
size from three members, as in Louisiana, to twenty-three, as in
Kansas. The governor and other state officers frequently serve ex
officio.

DURING THE SECOND WORLD WAR. After the United States entered
the Second World War, most of the State planning boards devoted a
considerable part of their time to the preparation of materials for war
agencies. They made maps and obtained data relating to camp sites,
emergency housing, army recreational facilities, and the like. They
studied the natural resources of their respective areas, and prepared
inventories of strategic war materials. Oddly enough, however, many
of the state planning boards were excluded from participation in postwar programs. The task of planning for postwar reconstruction and
development was frequently assigned to new agencies, specially created
for this purpose.

## SELECTED REFERENCES

Baker, G., *County Agent*, 1939.
Brinser, A., and Shepard, W., *Our Use of the Land*, 1939.

[10] Iowa, Kentucky, Maine, Nebraska, New York, Ohio, Texas. In New York, however,
there is a planning bureau in the Division of Commerce.

Bruner, H. B., and Smith, C. M., *Conserving Our Natural Resources*, 1938.

Comey, A. C., and Others, *State and National Planning*, Cambridge, Mass., 1937.

Connery, R. H., *Governmental Problems in Wild Life Conservation*, 1935.

Dahlberg, E. M., *Conservation of Renewable Resources*, Appleton, Wis., 1939.

Flynn, Harry E., and Perkins, Floyd E., *Conservation of the Nation's Resources*, 1941.

Folweiler, A. D., *Forest Fire Prevention and Control in the United States*, Baton Rouge, La., 1938.

———, *Theory and Practice of Forest Fire Protection in the United States*, St. Louis, Mo., 1937.

Gabrielson, Ira N., *Wild Life Refugees*, 1943.

Galloway, George B., *Postwar Planning in the United States*, 1942.

———, and Others, *Planning for America*, 1941.

Glover, K., *America Begins Again: The Conquest of Waste in Our Natural Resources*, 1939.

Hawley, R. C., *Forest Protection*, 1937.

Hynning, C. J., *State Conservation of Resources*, Washington, D.C., 1939.

National Resources Committee, *The Future of State Planning*, Washington, D.C., 1938.

———, *Regional Factors in National Planning and Development*, 1935.

National Resources Planning Board, *Human Conservation; The Story of Our Wasted Resources*, Washington, D.C., 1943.

———, *National Resources Development, Report for 1943, Part I: Postwar Plan and Program*, 1943.

———, *National Resources Development, Report for 1943, Part II: Wartime Planning for War and Postwar*, 1943.

———, *State Conservation of Resources*, 1942.

———, *The States and Planning*, 1942.

Pryor, W. C., and Pryor, H. S., *Water—Wealth or Waste*, 1939.

Renner, George T., *Conservation of National Resources; An Educational Approach to the Problem*, 1942.

Troup, R. S., *Forestry and State Control*, 1939.

# Chapter Twenty-Seven ❧ THE STATE AND BUSINESS

IT WAS long accepted as axiomatic by most Americans that business should be free from governmental supervision and control to the fullest possible extent. In recent years, however, this *laissez-faire* theory has been substantially modified—to some extent, even discarded. Twentieth century business has outgrown eighteenth century philosophy; depression and war have further emphasized the need for public control; and the result has been a rapid multiplication of governmental regulations, extending to every phase of business and professional activity. These regulations range from comparatively simple statutes or administrative decrees prohibiting the sale of adulterated foods and drugs to complex codes fixing the rates that may be charged by utility companies, prescribing the quantity and quality of service that must be rendered to the public, and establishing uniform accounting methods that must be adopted. Four main purposes underlie the control of business by the state: (1) production of revenue, (2) maintenance of free competition, (3) protection of public health and safety, and prevention of fraud, and (4) assurance of adequate service at reasonable rates in those businesses that are deemed essential to the public welfare.

## CORPORATION CHARTERS

**Abolition of legislative grants.** When several persons unite to form a business corporation, they must secure a charter from the state. At one time these charters were granted in every instance by special act of the legislature, with very unsatisfactory results. Valuable legislative time was wasted in discussion of matters that were essentially private—or at least of no great public importance; favoritism was shown in granting or withholding requested powers; and charges of bribery were common. So constitutional amendments were generally adopted to insure uniform and impartial treatment in granting charters. Ohio led the way in 1851, with the provision that "the general assembly shall pass no special act conferring corporate powers." Other states followed slowly; by the end of the century this clause or its equivalent had become a part of most state constitutions. Today, therefore, the legislature merely establishes a general policy for chartering corporations, and the details of the law are administered by the secretary of state or some other appropriate officer.

**Ineffectiveness of restrictions.** Numerous restrictive provisions, designed to protect the public interest, are found in the charter laws of the several states. These provisions are far from uniform, but they commonly deal with such matters as the purposes of incorporation, the minimum number of incorporators, the residence of incorporators, and the holding of corporation stock by other corporations. Approximately half of the states have requirements concerning paid-in capital and a few states prescribe the minimum amount of capital necessary to begin business. But evasion of these restrictions is comparatively easy in most jurisdictions. Thus, if a statute specifies that incorporators must be residents of the state, non-residents desiring to form a corporation need only secure the services of *bona fide* residents to act in their stead until the charter has been granted. The stock, once issued, can then be transferred to its real owners without violating the letter of the law. Or, to use another example, the requirement that every charter must state the purpose or purposes of incorporation can be nullified by including in the list of purposes almost every conceivable legitimate business activity. Most of the states view these evasions with equanimity, for they have discovered that lenient corporation laws attract would-be incorporators and thus swell the volume of state revenue from the granting of charters. A few commonwealths, following the early example of New Jersey, have deliberately adopted the policy of attracting incorporation business by lowering their standards almost to the vanishing point. Even mail-order incorporation is permitted in Delaware, Nevada, and a few other states. Thus the need for protection of the public interest is sometimes subordinated to the need for additional state income.

**Regulation of local versus interstate commerce.** Incorporation in one state does not confer the right to enter other states for the purpose of doing a local business. In this respect a corporation receives less protection than an individual, who may move freely across state boundaries without thought of interference. The federal Constitution declares that "The citizens of each State shall be entitled to all privileges and immunities of citizens in the several States," and the United States Supreme Court has ruled that these privileges and immunities include the right "to pass into any other State of the Union, for the purpose of engaging in lawful commerce, trade, or business, without molestation . . ." [1]     But this protection, enjoyed by every natural person who is a citizen, may not be shared by the corporation, an artificial person.     As previously pointed out,[2] a corporation is not a "citizen," as the term is used in the Fourteenth Amendment.     "The corporation, being the mere creation of local law, can have no legal existence beyond the limits of the sovereignty where created. . . . Having no absolute right of recognition in other states, but depending for such recognition and the enforcement of its contracts upon their assent, it follows, as a matter of course, that such assent may be granted upon such terms and conditions as those states may think proper to impose." [3]

It should be pointed out, however, that a corporation engaged solely in interstate commerce may enter any state of the Union at will and escape state interference with its affairs.     Regardless of its domicile, it may seek business through the mails.     Or it may send salesmen from state to state for the purpose of procuring orders, provided that such orders are subject to validation at the home office.     The matter of validation at the home office may seem unimportant, but it is sufficient to mark the difference between interstate and local commerce —and, therefore, between immunity from state control and complete subjection to state regulation.

It is becoming increasingly difficult for great corporations, with representatives in every state of the Union, to avoid "doing a local business" in the legalistic sense of the term.     Modern methods of distribution necessitate the concentration of goods at strategic points in many states, so as to facilitate prompt delivery.     Modern sales and service policies frequently involve the maintenance of local factory-controlled agencies.     To an increasing extent, therefore, business is assuming a "local" character as it expands to national proportions. This paradox is the source of complex legal problems, for problems inevitably arise when corporations doing business on a nation-wide scale are subjected to forty-eight different kinds of regulation.

And, in fact, forty-eight different kinds of regulation really exist. No two states have identical requirements for admitting foreign corporations to do business within their boundaries, and few states have

---

[1] Ward *v.* Maryland, 12 Wallace 418 (1871).
[2] See p. 47.
[3] Paul *v.* Virginia, 8 Wallace 168 (1868).

policies that even remotely resemble the policies of their neighbors. Some states admit foreign corporations on terms more favorable than those offered to corporations of their own creation; some permit foreign and domestic corporations to do business on equal terms; while others impose on foreign corporations heavy burdens from which domestic corporations are exempt. There is no general agreement as to whether foreign corporations should be encouraged or repressed, and this diversity of purpose naturally prevents unity of action. But every state is supreme in the regulation of business within its own boundaries, and those corporations that cannot remain beneath the sheltering cloak of interstate commerce must be prepared to accept the vagaries and uncertainties of state control.

## ANTI-TRUST LAWS

**National legislation.** The prevention of monopolies and combinations in restraint of trade has become chiefly a function of the federal government. In 1890 Congress enacted the Sherman Anti-Trust Act, which prohibits combinations in restraint of interstate trade. In 1914 it enacted two other important statutes: the Clayton Act, which defines certain abuses and restraints of trade more clearly than the Sherman Act; and the Trade Commission Act, which established an administrative agency—the Federal Trade Commission —to investigate alleged abuses and enforce the anti-trust laws. Since virtually all large business enterprises enter the field of interstate commerce, they come under federal jurisdiction. It is the Federal Trade Commission, therefore, that scrutinizes business practices most closely and displays greatest activity in combating monopolistic combinations.

**State legislation.** The prevention of unfair monopolies is not solely a federal responsibility, however. The states also have acted to insure free competition. Many of them had constitutional or statutory provisions directed against trusts and monopolies before the passage of the Sherman Act, and many others subsequently followed the example of the federal government by enacting anti-trust laws. To-day laws relating to monopolies and restraints of competition or trade are found in nearly all the states. These laws display wide variations. Some of them in sweeping terms prohibit trusts, monopolies, and all combinations that restrain trade or injuriously affect the public welfare. Others are directed against monopolies in special fields, such as the production and marketing of foodstuffs.   Certain business practices tending to restrain competition are sometimes specifically forbidden.

In recent years, however, the states have tended to look with favor upon business practices once regarded as highly undesirable.   Price maintenance, for example, which was formerly a punishable offense in many jurisdictions, is now almost universally permitted under certain conditions.   The California law of 1931, as amended in 1933, authorizes the producers of trade-marked goods to establish by contract the prices at which such goods may be resold and declares that resale at lower prices, even by non-contracting parties, is "unfair competition."   Nearly all the other states have since followed California's lead, and Congress has amended the federal anti-trust laws to exempt resale price contracts for trade-marked goods, when such contracts are permitted by state law.   In 1936 the Supreme Court of the United States unanimously upheld the California statute.[4]   Sales below cost are also prohibited in many states, except under certain specified conditions.   So, too, are price differentials between different communities, unless justified by the cost of transportation or service.[5]

## PURE FOOD AND DRUG ACTS

Laws to promote public health and safety are numerous and varied. In this category are the pure food and drug acts, now found on the statute books of every state, which prohibit the sale of diseased or adulterated food products, establish standards of purity for drugs, and specify that medicines containing dangerous ingredients shall be plainly marked.   In 1906 the federal government entered this field with the enactment of a law prohibiting the shipment in interstate commerce of adulterated or misbranded foods or drugs.   The federal statute was more comprehensive than most of the state laws adopted prior to that time, and within a year twenty-one states had modified their requirements to conform more nearly to federal standards. Most of the other states, in amending their food and drug laws from time to time, have been influenced to some extent by the federal act of 1906, and it is probable that they will be further influenced by the federal food, drug, and cosmetics statute of 1938.   But diversity in state legislation has never been eliminated.

[4] Old Dearborn Distributing Co. *v.* Seagram Distillers Corp., 229 U.S. 183 (1936).
[5] See Ewald T. Grether's excellent monograph, *Price Control under Fair Trade Legislation.*

Federal-state co-operation has been fostered by the establishment of an office of co-operation in the federal enforcement agency, and state-local co-operation is no longer merely the expression of a fond hope. The general plan of co-operative activity involves the inspection of factories and the control of intrastate trade by the states, the regulation of interstate and foreign shipments by the national government, and the examination of markets and local deliveries by the cities. The tendency in recent years has been to vest the state food and drug law administrators with considerable power to issue necessary regulations, and the result has been the steady growth of a body of administrative decrees supplementing and interpreting the provisions of the laws.

### PROTECTION FROM FRAUD

**Misrepresentation.** The states have enacted many laws designed to protect the public from fraud. Nearly every state has a statute directed at fraud in advertising; this statute commonly prohibits the circulation of any advertisement containing "an assertion, representation, or statement of fact that is untrue, deceptive, or misleading." Certain specific trade practices, such as the imitation of competitors' products or the sale of rebuilt machines as new products, are often declared to be misdemeanors. Sales contracts are generally regulated by state law, partly to prevent deception and partly to eliminate unnecessary misunderstandings.

**Securities regulation:** STATE BLUE-SKY LAWS. Among the most important statutory provisions aimed at fraud are the so-called "blue-sky" laws, now found in every state except Nevada. In 1911 a Kansas legislator, pointing out that the people of his state were losing millions of dollars each year through the purchase of worthless stocks and bonds, declared that some dishonest promoters would sell shares "in the bright blue sky itself." The statute that he sponsored, intended to protect the purchasers of securities, was speedily dubbed a blue-sky law, and the name is now applied to all similar legislation. At first the Kansas plan did not prove very popular. It was copied by a few states, but the others held aloof. The old common law principle of *caveat emptor*—let the buyer beware—was still the order of the day. Following the First World War, however, the rapid increase in national wealth and the boundless enthusiasm of the American people combined to make an especially fertile field for the operations of stock swindlers, and public opinion forced the general adoption of protective legislation. Not all the blue-sky laws are equally effective, however; some of them contain so many exemptions as to be practically worthless.

*Provisions.* The state blue-sky laws originally assumed several forms. Some of them applied only to the securities offered for sale, without attempting to regulate the dealers. Every security issue, or every issue of "speculative" securities, had to be approved by the state securities commission or other administrative agency before it might lawfully be sold within the state. Those states that limited the requirement of commission approval to speculative issues generally adopted complete though by no means uniform definitions of "speculative." Another type of blue-sky law was concerned only with dealers, on the assumption that honest men would not try to sell worthless stocks or bonds. Under the provisions of such a law dealers in securities had to be registered or licensed and were required to present evidence of good character and of an equitable plan of business. Nearly all the states now combine these two types of legislation by controlling both the securities and the dealers. Some states have established securities commissions or other separate agencies to administer the blue-sky laws, while others have relied on previously existing agencies, such as the railroad commission, the bank commissioner, the insurance commissioner, the secretary of state, or the attorney-general.

The blue-sky laws of four states—Delaware, Maryland, New Jersey, and New York—differ so radically from all other state legislation on the subject that they cannot be placed in any of the usual categories. Under these laws no attempt is made to register dealers or to examine securities in advance of sale, but appropriate court action is instituted by the attorney-general whenever it appears to him that fraud has been perpetrated. The protection thus afforded to purchasers of securities is sometimes known as "locking the stable door," because the administrative mechanism begins to operate after the damage has been done. In New York, however, where enforcement has been particularly rigorous, fairly satisfactory results have been obtained.

THE SECURITIES AND EXCHANGE COMMISSION. In 1933 and 1934 the federal government assumed a considerable part of the responsibility for regulating security issues. It established a Securities and Exchange Commission and prohibited the circulation in interstate commerce or through the mails of any prospectus advertising a security not listed with the commission. Every detail of new stock issues must be declared under oath; this information must include such matters as the company's financial condition, its purposes and business, its principal operators and owners, underwriting costs, commissions, and bonuses. Company directors are made civilly and criminally liable for any misrepresentation to investors. Moreover, the stock exchanges of the nation are brought directly under federal control.

FEDERAL-STATE CO-OPERATION. The federal regulation of securities through the Securities and Exchange Commission has no relation to purely local transactions, which remain within the jurisdiction of the states. In fact, the Commission has repeatedly made clear that it wishes to co-operate with the state commissions, instead of trying to put them out of business. Such co-operation has now been achieved to a considerable degree. Federal and state officials confer frequently concerning applications for registration, and they exchange information with regard to violations of the securities laws.

## REGULATION OF INTEREST RATES ON LOANS

**Usury laws.** Every one of the forty-eight states has established by statute a so-called legal rate of interest, which applies to certain contracts when the parties have failed to specify a particular rate. This rate ranges from five to eight per cent a year; usually it is six per cent. In addition to the "legal" rate, nearly every state [6] prescribes a maximum rate for interest on loans. This maximum rate may be the same as the legal rate; usually, however, it is somewhat higher, varying from six to twelve per cent. Interest charged in excess of the maximum lawful limit is declared to be usury, and usurious practices are punished by the forfeiture of all interest, as in Florida, the forfeiture of the principal, as in Oregon, or even by imprisonment under certain circumstances, as in California.

**Small-loan acts.** The theory that the borrower should be protected from excessive charges is by no means new; all the American colonies had usury laws, with heavier penalties than at present. In recent years, however, it has become evident that the usury laws frequently do more harm than good through their failure to recognize differences in risks, types of loans, costs, and security. Small loans to persons in dire need, often without security or with security of doubtful worth, cannot possibly be made by professional money-lenders at the legal maximum limit, even when the limit is twelve per cent. The cost of their business is too high, and the risk too great. A usury law that ignores this

---

[6] The only exceptions are Colorado, Maine, Massachusetts, and New Hampshire.

fundamental fact inevitably produces one of two results: either it drives professional money lenders from the small-loan field, thus multiplying the problems of the poor persons whose protection is sought, or else it draws into the field a group of unscrupulous Shylocks who willingly violate the law and charge exorbitant rates as compensation for the added risks they must assume. Nearly two thirds of the states, therefore, have supplemented their usury laws with small-loan acts, applying usually to loans of three hundred dollars or less. For such loans the lawful maximum rate is fixed sufficiently high to permit a reasonable return on invested capital even after the necessarily heavy losses have been deducted. Three and one half per cent a month is the most common limit. The small-loan laws are further strengthened by unusually heavy penalties for loans at rates in excess of the maximum and also by provisions concerning the periodic examination of money-lenders' records by state officials.

#### REGULATION OF BUSINESSES AFFECTED WITH A PUBLIC INTEREST

Certain businesses, such as banks, insurance companies, electric light and power companies, gas companies, and common carriers, are subject not only to ordinary governmental regulations designed to prevent unfair trade practices, promote the public health and safety, and prevent fraud, but also to special governmental control affecting every detail of their affairs—their accounting methods, the quality of their service, and, in most instances, their rate schedules. In wartime, of course, this distinction among different types of businesses may virtually disappear. Public control of prices, as well as quality and quantity of both goods and services, may be extended to all businesses that are even remotely connected with the war effort. Such a drastic plan for controlling business was in fact adopted by the federal government in 1942, only a few months after the United States entered the Second World War. Federal laws and regulations established maximum prices for thousands of articles, specified under what conditions they might be made and sold, and, with regard to some scarce commodities, even decreed who might buy them. These far-reaching regulations were generally considered a necessary part of the nation's total mobilization. In peacetime, however, they would not be accepted by the people or by the courts. Extensive public regulation has always been reserved for the banks, the common carriers, and the like.

**Distinguishing characteristics.** The question may well be asked, therefore, why these businesses may be so closely supervised. What characteristics do they possess that ordinary businesses lack? The generally accepted answer is that they are affected with a public interest. But that statement is not an explanation. As Justice Stone declared in his cogent dissent from the majority opinion in the case of Tyson *v.* Banton,[7] "the phrase 'business affected with a public interest' seems to me to be too vague and illusory to carry us very far on the way to a solution. It tends in use to become only a convenient expression for describing those businesses, regulation of which has been permitted in the past. To say that only businesses affected with a public interest may be regulated is but another way of stating that all those businesses which may be regulated are affected with a public interest." The Supreme Court of the United States has attempted a definition of public interest enterprises,[8] but its classification is so broad as to include every business that the courts have ever regarded as affected with a public interest, and so vague as to permit the inclusion of other enterprises from time to time, should changing conditions seem to warrant additions to the present list. It is, therefore, utterly worthless as a guide to underlying principles. The truth of the matter seems to be that no underlying principles exist.

SUPREME COURT DECISIONS. For many years the United States Supreme Court seemed willing to accept as binding practically every legislative declaration that a business was affected with a public interest. Legislative regulation, whenever attempted, was approved almost as a matter of course. Later, however, the Court refused to sanction a number of state laws extending the public interest principle. Thus it held in 1927, in the case of Tyson *v.* Banton,[9] that the fees charged by theater ticket agencies might not be fixed by statute. The next year it invalidated a New Jersey statute requiring private employment agencies to charge no higher fees than those deemed reasonable by the state commissioner of labor, on the ground that "an employment agency is essentially a private business." [10] Then, a few months later, came the decision that the business of selling gasoline was not affected with a public interest to the extent of permitting public regulation of rates.[11] In 1932 it was held that the business of manufacturing and selling ice was essentially private, and that the

[7] 273 U.S. 418 (1927).
[8] Wolff Packing Company *v.* Court of Industrial Relations, 262 U.S. 522 (1923).
[9] 273 U.S. 418 (1927).
[10] Ribnik *v.* McBride, 277 U.S. 350 (1928).
[11] Williams *v.* Standard Oil Co. of Louisiana, 278 U.S. 235 (1929).

number of those engaging in it might not be limited by legislative action.[12]

The Supreme Court adopted a liberal attitude in 1934 by upholding state regulation of milk prices. The New York legislature had created a milk control board and vested it with power to establish a retail price for milk, and this board had fixed nine cents a quart as the price to be charged by stores. A Rochester grocer, convicted of violating the board's order by selling two quarts of milk and a five-cent loaf of bread for eighteen cents, asked to have his conviction set aside on the ground that the price-fixing order of the milk control board was an unreasonable interference with a private business, but the Court refused to accept this point of view. "The milk industry in New York has been the subject of long-standing and drastic regulation in the public interest," declared Justice Roberts, speaking for the court in the case of Nebbia *v.* New York.[13] "In the light of the facts the order appears not to be unreasonable or arbitrary, or without relation to the purpose to prevent ruthless competition from destroying the wholesale price structure on which the farmer depends for his livelihood, and the community for an assured supply of milk." Although earlier decisions are not expressly overruled by the Nebbia case, there seems to be no escape from the conclusion that the Supreme Court has changed its attitude since it invalidated public regulation of the fees charged by employment agencies and theater ticket brokers.

*Variations in permissible regulation.* Even judicial determination of the fact that a business is affected with a public interest does not necessarily indicate the extent of public regulation that will be permitted. For businesses affected with a public interest may be affected in varying degrees, and therefore subject to varying types of supervision and control. Banks and telephone companies, for example, are both public interest enterprises, but the state's regulation of telephone companies is much more extensive than its regulation of banks. "To say that a business is clothed with a public interest," declared the United States Supreme Court in the case of Wolff Packing Co. *v.* Court of Industrial Relations,[14] "is not to determine what regulation may be permissible in view of the private rights of the owner. The extent to which an inn or a cab system may be regulated may differ

---

12 New State Ice Co. *v.* Liebmann, 285 U.S. 262 (1932).
13 291 U.S. 502 (1934).
14 262 U.S. 522 (1923).

widely from that allowable to a railroad or other common carrier. It is not a matter of legislative discretion solely. It depends on the nature of the business, on the feature which touches the public, and on the abuses reasonably to be feared. To say that a business is clothed with a public interest is not to import that the public may take over its entire management and run it at the expense of the owner. The extent to which regulation may reasonably go varies with different kinds of business. The regulation of rates to avoid monopoly is one thing. The regulation of wages is another. A business may be of such character that only the first is permissible, while another may involve such a possible danger of monopoly on the one hand, and such disaster from stoppage on the other, that both come within the public concern and power of regulation."

**Banking:** SUPERVISION FOR SECURITY. Every state exercises strict supervision over the banks that it has chartered to do business within its borders. This supervision does not extend to the charges made for bank services, but is aimed solely at greater security for depositors. Thus the state law commonly includes provisions concerning the minimum amount of capital stock for banks and the manner in which such stock must be subscribed; restrictions on the purposes for which bank loans may be made; requirements as to the amount and form of reserves; and definition of the obligations of bank stockholders. Half of the states permit branch banking, though branches are usually limited to the city or county in which the head office is located.

THE BANKING COMMISSIONER. The banking laws are enforced by a banking commissioner or other officer—sometimes known as the bank examiner, bank supervisor, or secretary of banking. This officer is commonly appointed by the governor, though he is chosen by the banking board in Oregon and by the corporation commission in Virginia. Two states—Mississippi and Tennessee—give the banks a voice in the selection of the chief banking officer. Florida and Illinois vest the duties of banking commissioner in the state auditor, who is chosen by the voters. Banking boards are found in but one third of the states; their functions are chiefly advisory.

*His powers.* Important powers are vested in the banking commissioner. He selected a staff of bank examiners who visit the banking institutions of the state and make such periodic investigations as are deemed necessary. In most states he is authorized to take charge of closed banks, liquidate their assets, and pay depositors. Usually he possesses a discretionary power to grant or refuse charters to new banks, though a number of states permit appeal from the banking commissioner to a board of review or to the courts.

A STATE-OWNED BANK. One state—North Dakota—has gone directly into the banking business in competition with private institutions. The state bank, established in 1919, is supervised by a three-member ex officio board which hires a full-time manager. Most of the deposits are from the state and its civil subdivisions, but many individual accounts are also maintained. The bank serves as fiscal agent for the state, frequently advancing the funds necessary to carry on various public activities and thus eliminating the need for short-term borrowing. It also supervises the management of several thousand farms acquired by the state as a result of foreclosures during the depth of the depression.

DEPOSIT GUARANTEES. During the decade prior to the First World War a number of states passed laws guaranteeing bank deposits. The customary procedure was to levy an assessment upon every bank operating under state law and to establish a depositors' guarantee fund with the money thus obtained. These laws were upheld by the courts, but they failed to meet the test of financial depression in 1929 and subsequent years. Guarantee funds were speedily exhausted, and several states were obliged to issue scrip in temporary payment of their obligations. The result was the repeal of every state law guaranteeing deposits. In 1933, however, the financial panic created widespread agitation for some form of insurance against loss of bank deposits, with the result that the federal government enacted a statute guaranteeing deposits, with maximum limits, in all member banks of the Federal Reserve System, as well as other banks accepting the provisions of the law. Whether the federal deposit guarantee system can withstand financial crisis more successfully than the guarantee systems of the states is not certain.

EXTENSION OF FEDERAL CONTROL. The federal government has long exercised a considerable measure of control over banking. In 1863, largely because of the difficulty of selling war bonds on reasonable terms, it established a national banking system and issued charters to approved banks applying for membership. These banks, therefore, came under national instead of state supervision. With the establishment of the Federal Reserve System in 1914, federal control became even more extensive. National banks were required to join the system, and state banks were permitted to do so if they conformed to federal standards. The nation's banking system was still further centralized by laws enacted in 1933 and 1935.

**Insurance:** THE INSURANCE COMMISSIONER. Insurance, also, is a business subject to strict public regulation. Every state except Arizona and Louisiana has an officer known as insurance commissioner, superintendent of insurance, or something of the sort; Arizona vests the duty of enforcing the insurance laws in the corporation commission, and Louisiana assigns this task to the secretary of state. The insurance commissioner is appointed by the governor in most states, though a few commonwealths specify other means of selection— popular election, as in Kansas, or election by the legislature, as in South Carolina. Technical qualifications are seldom prescribed.

*His powers.* The duties of the commissioner are numerous and far-reaching. Usually he exercises a measure of control over the incorporation of domestic insurance companies and the licensing of insurance companies from other states. Agents and brokers are subject to his supervision. From time to time he examines the records of all domestic companies for the purpose of determining the state of their finances. His powers in this respect are usually very broad. He may revoke a company's license to do business for unsound financing, violation of visitorial requirements, or a number of other reasons. The body of legislation that he is required to enforce generally includes statutes regulating the investment of insurance company funds, prescribing the procedure in the event that capital is impaired, specifying the forms of policies, prohibiting certain methods of getting business, requiring equitable treatment of policy holders, and assuring reasonable rates.

RATE REGULATION. Public regulation of the rates charged by insurance companies is an indication of the extent to which the insurance business is clothed with a public interest. Rates for fire, industrial compensation, and some other forms of insurance are commonly fixed by the companies through the rating bureaus of which they are members, but the rate schedules thus privately prepared must be submitted to the state insurance commissioner, who has the power to prevent discriminations and, in some jurisdictions, the power to order a general reduction if the level of rates seems too high. Life insurance rates are automatically controlled within narrow limits by statute prescribing the mortality table and rate of interest upon which reserves must be based. The Supreme Court of the United States has held that insurance is a business sufficiently affected with a public interest to justify public price fixing.[15]   It has also held, in a recent case, that an insurance company doing business across state lines is engaged in interstate commerce, and therefore subject to the authority of Congress.[16]   Whether this decision will lead eventually to comprehensive federal regulation of the insurance business is uncertain.

**Liquor industry.**   The need for strict public regulation of the liquor industry arises from the fact that liquor is a product inherently susceptible of abuse.   Many persons will use it immoderately, to their own detriment, if given the opportunity.   Therefore the state should restrict consumption within the narrowest possible limits—though bearing in mind, of course, that too great restriction tends to encourage law violation.   The liquor policies adopted by the several states since the repeal of the prohibition amendment in 1933 fall into three general categories: (1) sale by private persons, under a state licensing system; (2) sale by the state, through state-operated stores; and (3) prohibition of liquor sales throughout the state, or in those communities desiring such an arrangement.

Complete prohibition has become increasingly unpopular during recent years, even in the small group of states that originally elected to remain "dry" after the repeal of national prohibition; therefore it requires no more than passing mention.   The state store system has been adopted by sixteen states.[17]   Its essential feature is the establishment of a chain of retail stores for the package sale of liquor, under the management of a liquor control board or some similar agency.   The state thus holds a monopoly of package liquor sales. But sales by the drink require separate regulation.   Some of the so-called "monopoly" states permit licensed hotels and restaurants to sell intoxicants by the drink; others prohibit by-the-drink sales of all intoxicants, except light beer or beer and wine.   Under the license plan, which most states have adopted, the sale of intoxicants is a private matter, but is restricted to those persons who have been granted permits by the state liquor authority.   State laws regulate the hours of sale, the physical features of sales places, and the like.   Although one of the chief reasons for state control of intoxicants is supposed to be the restriction of consumption, this purpose is often forgotten by state legislators and administrators, who tend to encourage the ex-

[15] German Alliance Insurance Company *v.* Lewis, 233 U.S. 389 (1914).
[16] United States *v.* Southeastern Underwriters' Association, 322 U.S. 533 (1944).
[17] Alabama, Idaho, Iowa, Maine, Michigan, Montana, New Hampshire, Ohio, Oregon, Pennsylvania, Utah, Vermont, Virginia, Washington, West Virginia, Wyoming.

pansion of the liquor industry because it means additional tax revenue. This conflict of purposes is reflected in many state laws.[18]

**Public utilities.** Public control of business assumes its most complete form in the regulation of public utilities. These businesses, which are said to be essentially public in character, though owned and operated by private persons, differ from other enterprises affected with a public interest in that they enjoy special privileges such as the use of public property or the right of eminent domain. Not only may they be regulated, like banks, as to their financial structure; not only may they be supervised, like insurance companies, as to rates and quality of service; but in addition they may be compelled to serve all persons without discrimination. The list of utility enterprises is long and imposing. It includes wharves, docks, and bridges; telephone, telegraph, and power transmission lines; water, gas, and electric service; and transportation services such as car, bus, cab, and airplane lines, gas, oil, and express lines, and railroads. Nor does this enumeration make any pretense at completeness.

THE STATE REGULATORY AGENCY. The state agency created to supervise public utility affairs is variously known as public service commission, public utilities commission, or railroad commission. The early commissions were concerned solely with railroad control, and this fact explains the survival of the name "railroad commission" in a few states, despite the expansion of commission activity. In 1931 Oregon abolished its public service commission and substituted a single commission of public utilities. Shortly afterward its example was followed by Idaho, South Dakota and North Carolina. Elsewhere the commissions range in size from three members—the usual number—to seven members in Illinois, Pennsylvania, and South Carolina. Appointment by the governor is the most common method of selecting the commissioners, though popular election is still widely used in the South and Middle West. South Carolina vests the power of selection in the legislature. Terms of office are long, averaging about six years. But there are many contrasts, such as the ten-year term in New York and Pennsylvania and the two-year term in South Carolina. Technical qualifications for commissioners are seldom prescribed, either by law or custom. The inevitable result is that very few public service commissioners possess an adequate understanding of the complicated engineering

18 See *After Repeal*, by Leonard V. Harrison and Elizabeth Laine. See also *American Liquor Control*, by Marion Edward Stone.

and accounting problems they are called upon to solve. Therefore these problems are left to the technical staff, and commissioners busy themselves with "broad questions of public policy"—an euphemism for the repair of broken-down political fences.

*Extent of control.* Commission control usually extends to the approval of utility rates, the establishment of standards of service, the examination of financial practices for the purpose of preventing mismanagement, and the prescribing of uniform accounting methods. Rate control, of course, is most important. The fundamental purpose of utility regulation is to insure reasonable service at a reasonable price; therefore every public service commission possesses power to pass upon the charges made by the utility companies operating within its jurisdiction. Sometimes this power is limited to the fixing of maximum charges, but more commonly complete rate schedules are set up. Appeals from the commission's decisions may be taken to the courts, and such appeals are frequent. But every request for permission to charge a higher rate must first go to the public service commission, which makes a detailed study of all the facts involved.

Service standards, also, are important. A fair rate cannot be determined unless some agreement has been reached as to the quantity and quality of service to be given. Therefore the commissions are obliged to formulate and publish regulations covering these matters in great detail. Electric light and power companies, for example, are controlled by commission orders so numerous and so complete that their enforcement virtually necessitates a measure of commission participation in the management of the companies. These orders specify the conditions under which service may be secured, the aid that must be given to customers in selecting appliances best suited to their needs, the charges, if any, that may be made for extensions and service connections, the contents and form of bills, the deposits that may be required, the information that must be supplied to customers, and the manner in which complaints must be handled. Provision is made, also, for securing efficient service through the establishment of frequency requirements, together with statements of allowable voltage fluctuations. Other regulations deal with service interruptions, the location and testing of meters, and the prevention of accidents. Commission rules for other utilities are equally detailed, though necessarily covering other matters to some extent. Thus they deal with the installation of specified heating, ventilating, and safety devices on street cars, buses, and subway and elevated trains. Most commissions, though not all, possess the right to order service extensions. This power is important because it assures adequate service for newly developed areas, even though the amount of paying business may be comparatively small.

IMPORTANCE OF EFFECTIVE UTILITY REGULATION. The total investments in privately owned and operated public utilities amount to many billions of dollars. Some authorities believe that these investments represent one fifth of the entire productive wealth of the nation. When it is realized that the utility business is largely monopolistic, and therefore able to charge whatever the traffic will bear unless restrained from making exorbitant charges by the public service commission, the importance of effective utility regulation becomes apparent. An alert, honest commission, composed of competent technicians possessing adequate authority, can save huge sums that would otherwise swell the profits of the utilities. A commission that deviates from some of these specifications can transform regulation into a farce —or a tragedy. Unfortunately, most public service commissions have proved defective in one or more respects. And, in some states, it cannot be denied that public utility regulation has long hovered between tragedy and farce.

### HANDICAPS TO EFFECTIVE UTILITY REGULATION

**Poorly qualified commissioners.** Partisan politics often plays a part in the selection of commissioners, even in those states that vest the power of appointment in the governor. When the commissioners are popularly elected, of course, only an accident or a miracle can lead to the choice of properly qualified technicians. So the commissioners take office with political favors to be granted and political debts to be repaid. They cannot consider the public welfare until the welfare of their friends and followers has received due consideration. Even when commissioners are chosen solely on the basis of merit, it is usually well-nigh impossible to obtain outstanding men. For one thing, salaries are too low and tenure is too uncertain. Then, too, most of the leading technicians in the field are associated, quite naturally, with the utility companies. They can see no reason to jeopardize their future by accepting appointment to positions that will make them the guardians of the public interest against the interest of their former and probable future employers. Small appropriations, also, handicap most of the public service commissions. Technical staffs are undermanned, and equipment is inadequate.

**Incomplete jurisdiction of commission.** Public service commissions are seriously handicapped by inept and outworn legislation. In some states their authority does not extend to electric light and power lines. In others, although applying to all utilities, it does not include the right to prescribe uniform systems of accounting. One state—Delaware—has no state public service commission. The rules of commission procedure established by law are generally unsatisfactory and badly in need of revision. As recently as 1930 virtually all the public service commissions were without jurisdiction over holding companies. This denial of holding company control proved especially unfortunate, for it enabled the public utilities to escape effective regulation in a number of different ways. Within the last few years, however, this weakness has been recognized, and more than half of the state legislatures have enacted suitable statutes. Even more effective has been an act of Congress extending federal control over utility holding companies engaged in interstate commerce.

**The courts' theory of rate-making.** Fully as important as any other factor in destroying the effectiveness of utility regulation has been the attitude of the courts. For many years the federal and state courts. led by the Supreme Court of the United States, developed and applied a theory of rate-making that placed serious obstacles in the path of the commissions and virtually reduced valuation proceedings to a dignified and highly expensive game of blind man's buff.

Formula for utility valuation. In 1898, in the case of Smyth *v.* Ames,[19] the Supreme Court gave the first adequate statement of this theory. "We hold," it said, "that the basis of all calculations as to the reasonableness of rates to be charged . . . must be the fair value of the property being used by it for the convenience of the public." At first glance this statement seems entirely satisfactory. Certainly there must be some basis for determining the reasonableness of rates. When a public utility company applies for permission to increase its charges, the public service commission to which application is made must decide whether the present rates are unreasonably low. For if it does not permit the utility company to earn a reasonable return, it will deprive the company of its property without due process of law, in violation of the Fourteenth Amendment. A reasonable return must be allowed, therefore, and this return must be upon the "fair value of the property."

*Fair value of property.* But how is fair value to be determined?

[19] 169 U.S. 466 (1898).

The ordinary test of value, as applied to most goods and services, is selling price. An article or a service is worth exactly what it can be sold for. But this test is worthless in determining the value of public utilities, for utility properties are not daily bought and sold like clothing or foodstuffs. A few shares of utility stock or a few bonds may change hands, but these transactions cannot be accepted as an accurate index of the value of the entire property. Is it possible, then, to determine a public utility's value by capitalizing its earnings? This method of finding value, or selling price, is common in the field of competitive business. It cannot be used to ascertain the value of a public utility for rate-making purposes, however, because utility earnings are so closely related to the rates whose reasonableness is to be determined. The most obvious circular reasoning is involved in the statement that a public utility should be permitted to earn, say, six million dollars a year because this sum is a reasonable return upon its fair value of one hundred millions, and that the property is worth one hundred million dollars because it is capable of earning six million dollars annually. Such logic would make possible a complete justification of any rate, however large it might be.

*Difficulties of application.* If fair value is to be accepted as the basis for determining the reasonableness of utility rates, the usual tests of value cannot be applied. The "value" of a public utility must be something different from the value of a motor car or a pair of shoes. The Supreme Court realized this difficulty when it first enunciated the principle of a reasonable return upon the fair value of the property, and in the same case it established a formula of its own for finding value. This formula, as amended by subsequent court decisions, remained the basic principle of all valuation proceedings for nearly half a century. It was the starting point for every consideration of the reasonableness of rates by public service commissions. "In order to ascertain . . . value," said the Court, "the original cost of construction, the amount in permanent improvements, the amount and market value of bonds and stocks, the present as compared with the original cost of construction, the probable earning capacity of the property under particular rates prescribed by statute, and the sum required to meet operating expenses, are all matters for consideration."[20] Here, certainly, were enough factors to occupy the time and attention of the public service commissions. But how much weight should each factor receive? The Supreme Court answered that ques-

[20] Smyth *v.* Ames, 169 U.S. 466 (1898).

tion by stating that each of these elements of value should be given such consideration "as may be just and right in each case." Beyond that meaningless generalization it did not commit itself.

Over a period of years, however, and with the aid of subsequent court decisions, the public service commissions of the several states were able to gain some knowledge of the relative importance of the various elements of value as defined by the Supreme Court. They learned that certain factors, such as the amount and market value of bonds and stocks and the probable earning capacity of the property, might safely be accorded little more than lip worship. Other factors, such as the original cost of construction and the amount expended in permanent improvements, were deemed highly important.

*Prudent investment or reproduction cost?* Gradually two theories emerged as to the proper basis of utility valuation. One of these was the "prudent investment" theory; its advocates believed that the value on which a reasonable return should be allowed was the amount actually and prudently invested, including any additions to the original investment, with proper deductions for depreciation. The "reproduction cost" theory, on the other hand, was not concerned with the amount actually invested. Its proponents contended that the only true test of utility value was the cost of re-creating plant and equipment at present prices and with modern methods. Between these two theories yawned a wide gulf—as wide as the difference between the prices at the time of valuation and the prices at the time of original construction.

Let us suppose that a valuation for rate-making purposes was made in 1940. Most public utility companies were developed much earlier, during the days of relatively low price levels. It is easy to understand, therefore, why they heartily favored the reproduction cost theory. For under this theory a public utility's properties erected in 1910 at a cost of twelve million dollars might be worth seventeen millions in 1940, without regard to subsequent improvements, merely because of a change in the value of the dollar. If the theory of prudent investment were accepted instead, this company's properties would still be worth twelve million dollars in 1940—that is, omitting all consideration of depreciation and subsequent improvements in order to avoid unnecessary complications. In this instance, therefore, five million dollars would represent the difference between prudent investment and reproduction cost. Small wonder that the representatives of the utilities and of the public have seldom been agreed as to the proper basis of valuation!

The Supreme Court of the United States lent aid and comfort to both camps at different times. In Smyth *v.* Ames it mentioned both actual investment ("the original cost of construction, the amount expended in permanent improvements") and reproduction cost ("the present as compared with the original cost of construction") as factors to which just and proper weight should be given. Later it appeared to accept the theory of reproduction cost without qualification. Thus it said in 1909: "If the property . . . has increased in value since it was acquired, the company is entitled to the benefit of such increase." [21] But in 1923 it declared: "The refusal of the commission and of the lower court to hold that . . . the physical properties of a utility must be valued at the replacement cost less depreciation was clearly correct." [22] In 1937 it seemed to place considerable emphasis on prudent investment,[23] and five years later it even went so far as to hint its willingness to abandon the theory of reproduction cost.[24]

*Rejection of reproduction cost theory.* Not until 1944, however, was the traditional doctrine of Smyth *v.* Ames definitely thrown into the discard. The Federal Power Commission had ordered the Hope Natural Gas Company to reduce its rates, basing its order on a finding that the company was receiving an excessive return on the "actual legitimate cost" of its properties—in other words, the amount prudently invested. The company contended that its properties were worth nearly three times the actual investment because of changes in the price level, and it challenged the Federal Power Commission's right to ignore reproduction cost. But the Supreme Court upheld the Commission in a sweeping decision, making clear that rates based upon prudent investment would be upheld.[25]

Unfortunately, however, it did not accept the prudent investment theory in so many words, thus establishing a clear and workable theory of utility valuation. Instead, it declared itself willing to accept any theory that would produce reasonable results. "It is not theory but

21 Wilcox *v.* Consolidated Gas Co., 212 U.S. 19 (1909).

22 Georgia Railway and Power Co. *et al. v.* Railroad Commission of Georgia *et al.*, 262 U.S. 625 (1923).

23 Railroad Commission of California *et al. v.* Pacific Gas and Electric Co., 302 U.S. 388 (1937).

24 Federal Power Commission *v.* Natural Gas Pipeline Co., 315 U.S. 575 (1942).

25 Federal Power Commission *v.* Hope Natural Gas Co., 320 U.S. 591 (1944).

the impact of the rate order which counts," declared the Court, speaking through Mr. Justice Douglas. "If the total effect of the rate order cannot be said to be unjust and unreasonable, judicial inquiry under the act is at an end. The fact that the method employed to reach that result may contain infirmities is not then important." Such broad tolerance might be commendable, if it did not leave so many vital questions unanswered. Public service commissions are constantly engaged in the task of determining the value of utilities for rate-making purposes, and they must know what standards to use. For if they fail to use standards acceptable to the Supreme Court their findings will be declared invalid. But the Court itself refuses to give a direct answer. "Employ whatever methods you think best," it tells the commissioners. "We shall accept any standards that you may care to use, *provided the result is just and reasonable.*" And the members of regulatory commissions, both state and federal, can only shake their heads in bewilderment and ask: "How can we tell whether our findings are just and reasonable?" Surely the question of method is not unimportant, when different standards produce widely different results.

Mr. Justice Jackson, in a dissenting opinion, makes clear the dilemma in these words: "I must admit that I possess no instinct by which to know the 'reasonable' from the 'unreasonable' in prices and must seek some conscious design for decision. The Court sustains this order as reasonable, but what makes it so or what could possibly make it otherwise, I cannot learn." [26] Too much weight must not be given, however, to the confusion of thought evident in the majority opinion. One important fact stands out in this case: the willingness of the United States Supreme Court to accept utility valuations based solely on prudent investment. Apparently the long fight to eliminate reproduction cost from the rate base has been won, at least as far as the highest court of the land is concerned.

### STATE OWNERSHIP OF UTILITIES

Unless public regulation of the privately owned and operated utility companies can be made effective, the only practicable alternative seems to be public ownership. But public ownership of utilities has not proved very popular in the United States, except as applied to a few enterprises, such as roads, the post office, water supply, and garbage collection, which are now generally considered governmental func-

[26] Federal Power Commission *v.* Hope Natural Gas Co., 320 U.S. 645 (1944).

tions. State ownership, especially, as distinguished from federal or municipal ownership, has made but slight progress. There are, however, some examples of state ownership. A number of states own and operate grain elevators. State printing plants have been established in California and Kansas.[27] The State of Louisiana has expended large sums on the development of the port of New Orleans and now owns an extensive system of wharves and warehouses. In New York a state power authority has been established to control the development of hydro-electric power on the St. Lawrence River. Wisconsin is maturing comprehensive plans for state control of natural resources.

### REGULATION OF PROFESSIONS AND TRADES

The practice of certain professions and trades is restricted by state law to those persons who have satisfactorily demonstrated their proficiency. Examinations are held at stated intervals, and successful applicants are licensed to pursue their respective vocations. Restrictions of this sort, designed to protect the health or safety of the people, or protect them against fraud, are applied in different states and in varying degrees to physicians, dentists, osteopaths, chiropractors, optometrists, chiropodists, cosmetologists, pharmacists, veterinarians, nurses, embalmers, lawyers, accountants, engineers, architects, brokers, barbers, and plumbers.

The right of the state to fix the qualifications for persons engaged in some of these vocations has been established beyond doubt. The practice of medicine, for example, is subject to complete public control, and any regulations that the state may impose, short of mere arbitrary enactments, will be upheld by the courts.[28] Regulations concerning other professions and trades, also, are upheld under most circumstances and in most jurisdictions. Occasionally, however, a law providing for the examination and licensing of persons engaged in some vocation is set aside as bearing no reasonable relationship to the public welfare. Thus the Supreme Court of Maryland invalidated the state's 1935 barber act, because it imposed "requirements entirely out of proportion with the character and purposes of this trade. . . . In order to obtain a license, one must have had ten years of educational preparation." Such a standard indicated "an apparent design, although indefensible and unreasonable, to give to this simple and useful trade the characteristics and standards of a highly

---

[27] See p. 474.
[28] Dent *v.* West Virginia, 129 U.S. 114 (1889).

technical profession." [29]   Despite occasional adverse court decisions, however, the list of professions and trades subject to examination and license requirements is constantly growing, and state standards of technical proficiency are constantly being raised.

Separate boards of examiners for the several vocations conduct examinations and, in most states, issue licenses.   These boards may be united for administrative purposes under the control of a single department head, as in Illinois or Idaho.   Much more commonly, however, they are entirely independent of one another.   Their organization and powers vary widely, even within a single state.

## SELECTED REFERENCES

Barnes, Irston R., *Cases on Public Utility Regulation*, 1938.
———, *The Economics of Public Utility Regulation*, 1942.
Bauer, John, and Gold, Nathaniel, *The Electric Power Industry*, 1939.
Baum, Robert, *The Federal Power Commission and State Utility Regulation*, Washington, D.C., 1942.
Bonbright, James C., *Public Utilities and the National Power Policies*, 1940.
Bryant, John M., and Hermann, R. R., *Elements of Utility Rate Determination*, 1940.
Council of State Governments, *Securities Regulation in the Forty-Eight States*, 1942.
Fessler, James W., *Independence of State Regulatory Agencies*, 1942.
Grether, Ewald T., *Price Control under Fair Trade Legislation*, 1939.
Hall, Ford P., *The Concept of a Business Affected with a Public Interest*, Bloomington, Ind., 1942.
———, *Government and Business*, rev. ed., 1940.
Hunt, Edward E., ed., *The Power Industry and the Public Interest*, 1944.
Koontz, H. D., *Government Control of Business*, 1941.
Mosher, William E., and Crawford, Finla G., *Public Utility Regulation*, 1933.
New York Public Service Commission, *Regulation of Public Utilities during the War*, 1943.
Robinson, Louis N., and Nugent, Rolf, *Regulation of the Small-Loan Business*, Russell Sage Foundation, 1935.
Rohfing, C. C., and Others, *Business and Government*, 4th ed., 1941.
Scharff, M. R., and Others, *Depreciation of Public Utility Property*, 1941.
Stone, Harlan F., *Public Control of Business*, 1940.
Thompson, C. Woody, and Smith, Wendell R., *Public Utility Economics*, 1941.
Toulmin, Harry A., *Trade Agreements and the Anti-Trust Laws*, Cincinnati, 1937.
Weigel, Stanley A., *Fair-Trade Acts*, 1938.
Wilson, G. Lloyd, Herring, James M., and Eutsler, Roland B., *Public Utility Regulation*, 1938.
Wilson, Stephen, *Food and Drug Regulation*, Washington, D.C., 1942.

[29] Schneider *v.* Duer, 184 A. 914 (1936).

# Chapter Twenty-Eight THE STATE AND LABOR

"THE labor problem" is more than a phrase. Labor presents a most serious problem—or, more accurately, a large number of serious problems, including strikes, industrial accidents, and unemployment. The attempt to solve these problems has already produced a vast mass of legislation, and new labor laws are constantly swelling the total. Four main purposes underlie the labor legislation of the several states: the protection of the safety and health of the workers, the promotion of reasonable working periods and wage scales, the settlement of industrial disputes, and the reduction of unemployment.

## PROMOTION OF SAFETY IN INDUSTRY

**Prevention of industrial accidents.** The total number of persons injured in industry is appallingly high. In every state measures have been adopted to reduce industrial dangers, though these laws differ materially in scope and effect. Usually they prescribe minimum conditions of safety that must be maintained in every factory. Active parts of machines, such as saws, mangles, and emery wheels, must be screened or otherwise guarded. All mechanism for transmitting power must be equipped with adequate safety devices. Fire escapes must be installed, and safe exits must be provided. Safety requirements applicable to mines are common in the mining states. In some respects these requirements are even more important than the factory safety laws, for mining is an especially hazardous occupation. This fact is generally recognized, and the state mining codes are usually long and complex. Railroads, street car lines, and subway and elevated lines also come within the scope of governmental safety regulations. Such matters as track clearance, headlight power, and brakes are controlled by action of the state—or, in the case of interstate lines, the federal government. State laws frequently require railroad employees to pass tests of vision, including tests for color blindness. A number of states have enacted legislation designed to secure a greater measure of safety for workers engaged in the construction or repair of buildings. These laws relate to scaffolds, hoisting apparatus, signal systems, and inspection.

Despite the rapid spread of the movement for industrial safety during the last few years, state laws on the subject are still far from satisfactory. As a rule they apply only to certain specified occupations or processes, completely ignoring others that are equally dangerous but have escaped the legislature's attention. Lacking definite standards in many instances, they cannot readily be enforced. The more progressive states have obtained satisfactory results by passing outline laws [1] designed merely to express the legislative will in general terms, leaving the determination of specific rules to the industrial commission or similar agency. In this way the necessary element of flexibility is added to safety regulations. Desirable modifications need not await the next session of the legislature.

**Exclusion from certain industries:** CHILDREN. The prevention of industrial accidents is more than a matter of safety devices. It requires also the exclusion from certain industries of persons whose age, sex, or inexperience makes them especially susceptible to the hazards involved. Every state prohibits children from engaging in various kinds of labor before they reach a certain age, and some states extend this prohibition to include "any gainful occupation." Fourteen is usually the minimum age for general factory work, and eighteen is often fixed as the minimum for industries with a high accident rate. The contention has frequently been raised that child labor laws are an unreasonable and unconstitutional interference with individual liberty. Minors, it is said, share with adults the inalienable right to engage in any lawful occupation. But the courts have refused to admit the validity of this reasoning. In a long line of decisions they have established the principle that children are "wards of the state," and subject to special protective measures that might be unconstitutional if applied to the entire population.[2]

WOMEN. Women, also, are generally excluded from certain occupations, the list of occupations varying from state to state, but often including the cleaning of moving machinery and the operation of emery wheels. Manual labor by women in mines is forbidden in half of the states. Even more general are the prohibitions against the employment of women in occupations requiring constant standing. Some of these restrictions obviously aim to protect health quite as

[1] See pp. 211–213.
[2] See, for example, *In re* Spencer, 149 Cal. 396 (1906).

much as to prevent accidents. The courts uniformly uphold reasonable state laws prohibiting women's labor, for women, like children, are deemed in need of special protection.

MEN. Because the special protection of women and children cannot be extended to adult males without the risk of a judicial veto, laws excluding men from dangerous occupations are not of universal application. Instead they apply only to men whose inadequate physical or technical qualifications apparently unfit them for the proper performance of certain duties. State laws frequently prescribe rigid physical examinations for persons engaged in such dangerous occupations as mining, and forbid the employment of those who cannot meet the established standard of health. Even more important and far-reaching are the technical qualifications. Persons are not permitted to serve as railroad engineers, motion picture machine operators, elevator operators, or electricians—to mention but a few of the employments affected—unless they can demonstrate sufficient technical skill, and, in addition, present evidence of sobriety and good character. The elaborate qualifications prescribed for physicians, lawyers, architects, engineers, and others, sometimes in the interest of safety but more commonly for the protection of health or the prevention of fraud, have already been mentioned.[3]

### WORKMEN'S COMPENSATION

**Accident reports.** Virtually all the states require industrial accidents to be reported to some state authority. Massachusetts enacted such a law as early as 1886, and a number of other commonwealths followed its example before the end of the century, but these early statutes were poorly enforced. Injured employees had nothing to gain by supplying the necessary information; employers were reluctant to disclose facts that might indicate unsatisfactory working conditions; and state officials seldom bothered to prosecute. Thus the factual basis for a systematic plan of accident prevention was lacking. But conditions have materially improved since the adoption of workmen's compensation laws. The injured workman now has a definite pecuniary interest in reporting his case, and may reasonably be expected to do so promptly. Even today, however, thousands of industrial accidents are not reported—chiefly because they are not covered by the compensation laws.

**Accident compensation under common law.** The movement for

[3] See pp. 559–560.

workmen's compensation legislation arose from the unsatisfactory state of the common law concerning the liability of employers. Under common law this liability was narrowly restricted. It did not extend to injuries arising from the ordinary risks of the occupation, the extraordinary dangers of employment, the carelessness or negligence of the workman receiving the injury, or the carelessness or negligence of fellow workmen. Whenever an accident occurred, therefore, the injured employee had to institute a lawsuit in order to recover damages. At the outset he was handicapped by the law's delays. Lacking funds, he was seldom able to secure the best legal talent. At best he could hope for the payment of his claim only after a period of several years. At worst he would find his claim set aside because the employer had been able to establish some legal defense, such as the negligence of a fellow employee. Thousands of injured workmen learned from bitter experience the truth of the old maxim that delayed relief is no relief. Thousands of others accepted ludicrously small sums in full settlement of their claims rather than face the prospect of protracted litigation, with uncertainty as to the final outcome.

**Compensation laws.** Students of the problem of accident compensation became convinced that substantial justice could not be obtained under common law rules, or any mere modification of them. The remedy, they urged, was a system of compensation that would extend to all injured employees without regard to the relatively trivial matter of fixing the blame. Accidents were an inevitable accompaniment of modern industry; therefore industry should be made to bear the cost of providing proper medical treatment for disabled employees and caring for them and their families while disability continued. At first this reasoning was bitterly opposed, and some of the early compensation laws were declared unconstitutional. In 1911, however, four states [4] enacted workmen's compensation statutes that subsequently met the approval of the courts, and thus the movement was firmly established. It has since spread to every state except Mississippi.

PROVISIONS. The compensation laws provide for the payment of injured workers according to some established scale, the amount varying with the seriousness of the injury and the wage earned. The question of blame does not affect the payments, except that a certain percentage may be added if the employer violated the safety laws or

---

[4] California, New Jersey, Washington, Wisconsin.

deducted if the employee failed to make use of safety devices or received his injury while under the influence of liquor. Usually there is a short waiting period before payments begin. The compensation prescribed for various injuries varies widely from state to state. Some states require continuing benefits to dependents in the event of a workman's death, but such provisions are far from universal. Although the compensation laws of most states are optional, the option is more apparent than real, for employers who refuse to accept statutory liability are specifically deprived of their traditional common law defenses.

INSURANCE REQUIREMENTS. The additional liability imposed upon employers by the workmen's compensation laws necessitates some form of insurance. Recognizing that the cost of this insurance is high even under the most favorable circumstances, more than one third of the states have endeavored to keep it at a minimum by establishing state compensation insurance funds. In some of these states the employer is compelled to insure through the state fund; in others he is permitted to choose between state insurance and insurance with a private company. So-called "self-insurance" is permitted in some jurisdictions; in other words, the employer is permitted to assume his own risk under the compensation laws upon furnishing adequate proof of solvency.

DEFECTS. One of the most serious defects of workmen's compensation legislation, as found in most states, is its limited scope. Usually it covers the range of industrial employments rather thoroughly, but sometimes it applies only to occupations that have been designated as especially hazardous. Domestic service and agricultural work are almost always excluded, as are all casual employments. Liability under the compensation laws of twenty-two states does not extend to those employers who have only a few workmen, and in twenty-three states it does not relate to disability caused by occupational diseases. These restrictions have the effect of denying prompt and adequate relief to thousands of injured workers who happen to belong to the less favored groups.[5]

CONSTITUTIONALITY. The constitutionality of the principle of workmen's compensation legislation was determined beyond question

[5] See Walter F. Dodd's careful study, *The Administration of Workmen's Compensation.* See also Chap. VII of the 1943 edition of the U.S. Public Health Service's *Distribution of Health Services in the Structure of State Government.* This chapter is entitled "Industrial Health Activities by State Agencies."

in 1917, when the Supreme Court of the United States upheld the compensation laws of three states in a series of important decisions.[6] "It is evident," said the Court in the New York Central Railway case,[7] in answering the argument that the law was unreasonable because it imposed liability on the employer even if the employee were at fault, "that the consequences of a disabling or fatal injury are precisely the same to the parties immediately affected, and to the community, whether the proximate cause be culpable or innocent. Viewing the entire matter, it cannot be pronounced arbitrary and unreasonable for the state to impose upon the employer the absolute duty of making a moderate and definite compensation in money to every disabled employee, or, in case of his death, to those who were entitled to look to him for support, in lieu of the common law liability confined to cases of negligence."

## PROTECTION OF HEALTH

**Regulations to decrease occupational diseases.** Many state laws have been enacted for the purpose of protecting the health of workers. These laws are concerned in part with occupational diseases, which have become much more numerous and infinitely more serious in recent years. Some substances regularly used in industry are poisonous, and only the greatest care can protect the workmen who are required to handle them. Lead, for example, may cause lead colic or paralysis of the wrists. Sometimes long-continued contact with it is fatal. Radium, also, produces physical deterioration if not properly controlled. There are other occupational diseases produced, not by poisonous substances, but by unhealthful working conditions. Miners' hookworm, for example, is a constant menace in certain types of mining operations. Caisson disease, caused by breathing compressed air for long periods, often affects underwater workers. These are but a few of the many diseases traceable to specific occupations. Some poisonous substances once widely used in industry are now prohibited. More commonly, however, the states rely on regulation instead of prohibition to check the spread of occupational diseases. Factories are required to be properly ventilated, so as to reduce the hazard from dust and fumes. Wet cleaning methods, respirators, special work clothes, and wash and lunch rooms separate from the

---

[6] New York Central Railway Co. *v.* White, 243 U.S. 188 (1917); Hawkins *v.* Bleakly, 243 U.S. 210 (1917); Mountain Timber Co. *v.* Washington, 243 U.S. 219 (1917).

[7] 243 U.S. 188 (1917).

place of work are all important means of decreasing the danger from such diseases as lead poisoning, and are commonly required. One half of the states, led by California in 1911, have made provision for the reporting of occupational diseases, but as a rule these laws are poorly enforced.

**Exclusion from certain industries.** Reference has already been made to the exclusion of children from dangerous industries for the purpose of promoting industrial safety. On the ground of health, also, child labor is prohibited or narrowly restricted. Restrictions applying to women are found in most states. Men are excluded from certain occupations only if they cannot pass prescribed physical examinations. The object of these examinations is to weed out various groups of persons—those who are especially susceptible to particular trade maladies, those whose physical defects might interfere with the proper performance of their duties, and those suffering from contagious diseases that might be passed on to other workmen or to the purchasing public.

## RESTRICTION OF HOURS OF LABOR

Another matter that has attracted the attention of labor leaders, social workers, and statesmen is the length of the working day. Long hours destroy health, increase the likelihood of accidents, and leave insufficient time for recreation and mental improvement. There is a great deal of evidence to show that in certain occupations, at least, shorter hours actually result in increased output. In recent years, therefore, the trend has been definitely toward shorter hours of labor.

**Children.** Every state has enacted some laws concerning the length of the working day. Children, especially, are afforded a measure of protection against exploitation. Their working hours are generally limited to eight a day, and forty-eight a week, though six states still permit work for longer periods. The first state laws restricting the hours of children's labor were promptly challenged by employers as a violation of their rights under the Fourteenth Amendment to the federal Constitution, but the courts again declared what they had previously said in another connection—that children were poorly qualified to protect their own interests and therefore were entitled to receive the special protection of the state.[8]

**FEDERAL LEGISLATION.** Because many of the state child labor laws

8 Inland Steel Co. *v.* Yedinak, 172 Ind. 423 (1909).

were improperly drafted, poorly enforced, or unduly lenient as to hours of work, the federal government entered the field in 1916. Direct regulation of industrial conditions was beyond the scope of its authority, so it attempted to accomplish the desired result by indirection. Utilizing its power to regulate commerce, it prohibited the shipment in foreign and interstate commerce of goods produced in factories where children under fourteen were employed, or where children between the ages of fourteen and sixteen were employed more than eight hours a day. But this act was set aside by the courts as an unconstitutional invasion of the reserved sphere of state authority,[9] so Congress tried to accomplish its purpose in another way. This time it turned to the taxing power, and levied a tax of ten per cent on the net profits of factories employing child labor in violation of the conditions imposed. Once again, however, the Supreme Court interposed its judicial veto. "Grant the validity of this law," it said, "and all that Congress would need to do, hereafter, in seeking to take over to its control any one of the great number of subjects of public interest, jurisdiction of which the states have never parted with, and which are reserved to them by the Tenth Amendment, would be to enact a detailed measure of complete regulation of the subject and enforce it by a so-called tax upon departures from it. To give such magic to the word 'tax' would be to break down all constitutional limitation of the powers of Congress and completely wipe out the sovereignty of the states." [10] After this decision the federal government abandoned its attempt to regulate child labor until 1933, when it insisted upon the inclusion of anti-child labor clauses in most of the "codes of fair competition" established under the National Industrial Recovery Act. The subsequent collapse of the act, following another unfavorable court decision, marked the failure of this attempt at child labor control. A proposed amendment to the federal Constitution, authorizing Congress to limit, regulate, and prohibit the labor of persons under eighteen years of age, was placed before the states in 1924, but never received the approval of more than twenty-eight state legislatures—eight short of the necessary three fourths. Finally, in 1938, Congress once more attempted to regulate child labor through its control of interstate commerce. It prohibited industries engaged in interstate commerce from employing children under sixteen years of age. Certain exceptions were permitted, however, such as boys and

9 Hammer *v.* Dagenhart, 247 U.S. 251 (1918).
10 Bailey *v.* Drexel Furniture Company, 259 U.S. 20 (1922).

girls "employed in agriculture while not legally required to attend school." The Supreme Court upheld the law,[11] and thus an important victory was gained in the long fight against the evils of child labor. Much remains to be accomplished, however. Large numbers of children are engaged in agriculture—sometimes for long hours. Others work in a wide variety of businesses not affected by the federal law, such as retail stores, restaurants, hotels, repair shops, and bowling alleys. The trend of the war years has been toward increased employment of minors because of the labor shortage and the lure of high wages.

**Women.** Laws restricting the hours of labor of women in specified employments, or in general factory work, have been enacted by forty-four states.[12] Most of these states fix the maximum at eight or nine hours a day, but nine states still permit ten hours or even more. Weekly as well as daily limits, ranging from forty-four to sixty hours, are commonly established. When laws of this type first reached the courts they were declared unconstitutional,[13] but public opinion has long since compelled a reversal of this early judicial attitude. The Supreme Court of the United States has accepted the obvious fact that "women's physical structure and the performance of maternal functions place her at a disadvantage in the struggle for subsistence. . . . This is especially true when the burdens of motherhood are upon her. Even when they are not, by abundant testimony of the medical fraternity, continuance for a long time on her feet at work, repeating this from day to day, tends to injurious effects upon the body, and, as healthy mothers are essential to vigorous offspring, the physical well-being of woman becomes an object of public interest and care in order to preserve the strength and vigor of the race."[14] The constitutionality of legislation reasonably limiting the hours of labor of women is, therefore, no longer in doubt.

**Men.** Most state laws restricting the hours of labor of men apply only to public work, or to certain occupations that are considered especially dangerous or unhealthful, such as mining, smelting, or railroading. It has long been recognized that such laws are within the sphere of state power.[15] But what of maximum-hours legislation applying to all classes of workers in general manufacturing establish-

---

11 United States *v.* Darby Lumber Co., 312 U.S. 100 (1941).
12 The only exceptions are Alabama, Florida, Iowa and West Virginia.
13 See, for example, Ritchie *v.* Illinois, 155 Ill. 98 (1895).
14 Müller *v.* Oregon, 208 U.S. 412 (1908).
15 See, for example, Holden *v.* Hardy, 169 U.S. 366 (1898).

ments, or to workers in occupations that create no special hazard to life or health? The constitutionality of such legislation was long in doubt. In 1902 the State of New York enacted a law limiting the hours of labor of workmen in bakeries to ten a day, and three years later, when this statute was challenged before the Supreme Court of the United States in the important case of Lochner *v.* New York,[16] it was declared unconstitutional. The Court took the position that hours of labor were a matter of private bargaining between employer and employed and that the state might not interfere with his bargaining process except in the case of businesses particularly affecting the public health or safety. But this decision did not prevent further legislative attempts to fix maximum hours of labor for men in industry. Mississippi enacted a ten-hour day for all factory workers in 1912; Oregon followed with a somewhat similar statute the next year; and in 1915 North Carolina's general law fixed a limit of eleven hours. The Oregon law, which permitted three hours of overtime work in emergencies at one and one-half times the normal rate of pay, came before the United States Supreme Court in the case of Bunting *v.* Oregon,[17] and was declared valid. Without expressly reversing its opinion in Lochner *v.* New York, the Court quietly abandoned the doctrine of the Lochner case and accepted instead the proposition that hours of labor in all occupations were a matter of public concern, to be regulated by the legislature in such manner as it might see fit—subject, of course, to judicial review for the purpose of preventing mere arbitrary enactments.

Six years later, however, the United States Supreme Court created widespread consternation by casting doubt once more upon the validity of all comprehensive maximum-hours legislation. Referring to Lochner *v.* New York, the early case in which a ten-hour day for bakers was declared unconstitutional, Justice Sutherland said for the Court: "Subsequent cases in this Court have been distinguished from this decision, but the principles therein stated have never been disapproved."[18] This was news to most students of constitutional law. "I have always supposed," declared Chief Justice Taft in a noteworthy dissenting opinion, "that the Lochner case was . . . overruled *sub silentio.* . . . In Bunting *v.* Oregon . . . this Court sustained a law limiting the hours of labor of any person, whether man or woman,

16 198 U.S. 45 (1905).
17 243 U.S. 426 (1917).
18 Adkins *v.* Children's Hospital, 261 U.S. 525 (1923). For a consideration of the facts involved in this case, see p. 570.

working in any mill, factory, or manufacturing establishment to ten hours a day with a proviso as to further hours. . . . The law covered the whole field of industrial employment and certainly covered the case of persons employed in bakeries. Yet the opinion in the Bunting case does not mention the Lochner case. No one can suggest any constitutional distinction between employment in a bakery and one in any other kind of a manufacturing establishment which should make a limit of hours in the one invalid, and the same limit in the other permissible. It is impossible for me to reconcile the Bunting case and the Lochner case." For a time, therefore, two apparently inconsistent Supreme Court decisions delimited the power of the state to prescribe maximum hours of labor for all industrial workers.

Finally, in 1933, hours of labor in industry became a matter of federal concern when Congress enacted the National Industrial Recovery Act, designed in part to increase employment by narrowly restricting the hours of work of mercantile and clerical workers, artisans, mechanics, and laborers, and thus indirectly compelling the hiring of additional workmen. The "codes of fair competition" established under this act were declared unconstitutional by the Supreme Court of the United States, not only because they exceeded the scope of national authority but also because they represented an improper delegation of legislative power.[19]

But Congress was not discouraged. In 1938 it enacted a general law applying to all employees of firms whose products were shipped in interstate commerce. Maximum daily hours were fixed at eight, and maximum weekly hours at forty.[20] Longer hours were permitted, however, but only when compensated with overtime pay at one and one-half times the regular rate. Once again Congress was attempting to regulate labor conditions through its control of interstate commerce, as it had done when it enacted the first federal child labor law. That law had been declared unconstitutional in the case of Hammer *v.* Dagenhart,[21] but in the intervening years the Supreme Court's personnel had changed almost completely, and labor's need for protection had received increased public recognition. Astute observers were not surprised, therefore, when the Court upheld the law, and declared that Hammer *v.* Dagenhart "should be and now is overruled." [22] The

[19] Schechter *v.* United States, 295 U.S. 495 (1935).

[20] The act provided for a forty-four-hour maximum week during the first year, with gradual reductions to the ultimate maximum of forty hours.

[21] See p. 568.

[22] United States *v.* Darby Lumber Co., 312 U.S. 100 (1941).

Court went on to declare that reasonable hours of labor might be fixed by statute and that such legislation would not deprive employers of their property without due process of law.   Thus the right of Congress to safeguard the vast majority of American workmen against excessive working hours was established beyond the shadow of a doubt.

Very few states have followed the early lead of Mississippi, Oregon, and North Carolina in adopting a general policy of maximum hours of work in industry.   There have been a few exceptions, however. Montana has established an eight-hour day covering all occupations except farming and stock-raising, and this law has been approved by the state supreme court.[23]   In 1937 Pennsylvania prescribed an eight-hour day and forty-four-hour week as a maximum for all laborers, unless engaged in agriculture or domestic service.   Shortly afterward, however, the state supreme court declared the law unconstitutional, though not because of any objection to the principle of the eight-hour day.[24]

## WAGES

**Types of legislation:** PAYMENT OF WAGES.   Wages, like hours of labor, are a matter of utmost importance to the workers and have been made the subject of legislation in every state.   Some of these laws attempt to prevent unnecessary delays in payment of wages by specifying that payment must be made at regular intervals—usually two weeks. Others provide for payment in cash, rather than scrip or orders on the company store.   If a worker is discharged, he is permitted to collect his wages at once under the laws of many states.   Fines for breaches of shop discipline, bad work, or the like, which are widely used to reduce the real wage, are often subjected to state regulation or even prohibition.   These laws, unless purely arbitrary, receive the approval of the courts as a valid exercise of the police power.[25]

MECHANIC'S LIEN.   Another type of wage legislation, also accepted by the courts, is the so-called "mechanic's lien," which has long been recognized in every state.   Mechanics and other classes of workers

23 State *v.* Safeway Stores, 76 P. (2nd) 81 (1938).

24 The court's objection was based on a provision authorizing the Department of Labor and Industry to make exceptions to the general rules established by the legislature.   This provision, said the court, was a dangerous and unconstitutional delegation of legislative power to an administrative agency.   Holgate Bros. *v.* Bashore. 200 A. 672 (1938).

25 See, for example, McLean *v.* Arkansas, 211 U.S. 539 (1909); Knoxville Iron Co. *v.* Harbison, 183 U.S. 13 (1901); and Erie Railway Co. *v.* Williams, 233 U.S. 685 (1914).

engaged in the construction of buildings are permitted to bring suit for their wages against the value of the buildings or land on which they have been employed; thus they are protected against irresponsible contractors who cannot meet their payrolls. The types of property to which the lien applies vary from state to state. Public buildings and railroad properties are often exempted on the ground of public policy.

MINIMUM WAGES: *Women and children.* In 1896 the Australian state of Victoria took a bold step by fixing minimum wages for workers in certain industries where the wage scales were known to be particularly low. The movement spread to other occupations and to other states. Today minimum wage legislation, applicable to practically all workers except farm laborers, is in force in nearly every nation of Europe. The first American state to enact a minimum wage law was Massachusetts, in 1912. Other states followed, until the total had reached fifteen. Unlike the European laws, however, the American statutes applied only to women and children, on the theory that men could sufficiently protect their own interest in a living wage. In fact, the labor unions endorsed this attitude, for they believed that men could accomplish more by organization. In a few states the minimum wage for women and children was fixed by law. But this crude method of approximating a reasonable minimum proved unsatisfactory everywhere that it was tried, and most states adopted the more satisfactory plan of establishing wage boards to determine the proper minimum for each industry. These boards, composed of representatives of the employers, the employees, and the public, were usually voluntary bodies exercising only advisory functions, but their decisions as to minimum wages were generally accepted and enforced by the state commission or other administrative agency—subject, of course, to appeal to the courts.

It was inevitable that social legislation of this sort should be challenged as a violation of the freedom of contract guaranteed by federal and state constitutions. Both employee and employer, it was said, had an absolute right to obtain the best possible terms from each other as the result of private bargaining; and any legislation interfering with that right must be declared unreasonable and therefore void. At the outset this logic was lightly regarded by the courts. The Oregon minimum wage law was sustained by the state supreme court,[26]

[26] Stettler *v.* O'Hara, 69 Ore. 519 (1914).

and this decision was affirmed by the Supreme Court of the United States by an even vote of four to four, without opinion filed.[27]   But in 1923 came an authoritative statement of Supreme Court opinion, this time by a five-to-four vote, in the case of Adkins *v.* Children's Hospital.[28]   The law under consideration, enacted by Congress for the District of Columbia, authorized a commission to fix minimum wage standards for women in all occupations.   In sweeping language the Court declared this act unconstitutional and even branded it as potentially a great menace to employees.   "If, in the interest of the public welfare, the police power may be invoked to justify the fixing of a minimum wage, it may, when the public welfare is thought to require it, be invoked to justify a maximum wage. . . . The same argument which has been used here to strip the employer of his constitutional liberty of contract in one direction will be utilized to strip the employee of his constitutional liberty of contract in the opposite direction."

This decision was bitterly criticized by persons in all walks of life. Some characterized it as "a constitutional guarantee of the right to starve."   But the Supreme Court held resolutely to its position for more than a decade, voiding the minimum wage laws of Arizona, Arkansas, and New York.   In 1937, however, it specifically reversed its stand, overruling the Adkins case and upholding the minimum wage act of the State of Washington.   Chief Justice Hughes, speaking for the Court, declared that the protection of women and minors from the evils of starvation wages was an object closely related to the public welfare and that it might properly be promoted through the police power.[29]   Thus was won the long fight to legalize the minimum wage for women and children.   Minimum wage statutes, applying both to women and minors—or, in some instances, only to women—have now been adopted by twenty-seven states.

*All workers.*   But what of statutory minimum wages for all workers?   The argument used to justify such legislation for women and children—that they are "wards of the state" requiring special protection—can scarcely be applied to adult men.   Yet Congress has established minimum wage scales for men on several occasions.   In 1917 it temporarily regulated the wage schedules of interstate railroads in order to prevent a national calamity—a nation-wide strike of railroad

---

[27] 243 U.S. 629 (1917).
[28] 261 U.S. 525 (1923).
[29] West Coast Hotel Co. *v.* Parrish *et al.*, 300 U.S. 379 (1937).

labor; and the Supreme Court of the United States upheld the law as a proper emergency measure.[30]  The attempt to enforce minimum wage requirements in the so-called "codes of fair competition" prepared under the National Industrial Recovery Act of 1933 was necessarily abandoned when the Supreme Court invalidated the entire statute.  In 1935 the Guffey Coal Act attempted comprehensive regulation of the bituminous coal industry and, among other things, made provision for minimum wages.  It was declared unconstitutional on several grounds.[31]  There were two other congressional enactments, limited to agencies or groups more or less directly under federal control, and then came the most comprehensive of all national attempts at wage legislation—the Fair Labor Standards Act of 1938, fixing minimum wages [32] for all workers employed by firms engaged in, or shipping their products in, interstate commerce.  This statute went far beyond the traditional concept of minimum wage regulation, but it was upheld by the Supreme Court in United States *v.* Darby Lumber Co.,[33] the case that also established the right of Congress to enact comprehensive legislation concerning hours of labor.[34]  In 1944 New York took advantage of this new attitude of the highest court of the land and amended its minimum wage law to include men as well as women and children.

### COLLECTIVE BARGAINING

Virtually every student of labor problems emphasizes the important fact that the individual worker is at a serious disadvantage when bargaining with the individual employer.  The worker does not know the condition of the labor market; in many instances he must accept a proffered job on the employer's terms or face the alternative of starvation.  He cannot afford to wait, for he has no reserve of wealth.  Moreover, he lacks experience in making contracts and driving bargains.  At all times he faces the prospect of replacement by another worker or by a machine, and this danger tends to reduce him to a state of subservience.  By organizing with his fellows, however, the worker can overcome many of these handicaps and put himself more nearly on the level of the employer in bargaining power.  Quite

[30] Wilson *v.* New, 243 U.S. 332 (1917).

[31] Carter *v.* Carter Coal Co., 298 U.S. 238 (1936).

[32] Twenty-five cents an hour the first year, thirty cents an hour the next six years, and forty cents thereafter.

[33] 312 U.S. 100 (1941).

[34] See p. 569.

naturally, therefore, the movement for collective bargaining has made tremendous strides, especially among the more highly skilled laborers, and is manifested chiefly in formal workers' organizations known as labor unions.

For many years the labor unions had to overcome a series of legal handicaps. At first the courts took the view that they were combinations to restrain trade—and, therefore, unlawful organizations. Thus, in the early case of The People *v.* Fisher,[35] when the supreme court of the State of New York was called upon to consider an agreement among journeymen shoemakers not to make boots for less than one dollar per pair, it promptly branded the loosely knit shoemakers' organization as an unlawful conspiracy. A number of similar decisions in other states reflected the sentiment of the period. But in 1842 the supreme court of Massachusetts sustained the legality of labor organizations in an opinion so cogent that it had far-reaching influence upon the development of labor law in other states. "We think," said the court, "that associations may be entered into, the object of which is to adopt measures that may have a tendency to impoverish another, that is, to diminish his gains and profits, and yet so far from being criminal or unlawful, the object may be highly meritorious and public spirited. The legality of such an association will therefore depend upon the means to be used for its accomplishment. If it is to be carried into effect by fair or honorable and lawful means, it is, to say the least, innocent. . . ."[36] Today the right of labor to organize is no longer questioned.

### THE RIGHT TO STRIKE

**Approved reasons for striking.** The strike is labor's most powerful weapon, and any restriction of the right to strike necessarily weakens the bargaining power of the unions. Quite naturally, therefore, the representatives of organized labor contend that the right to strike is fundamental and may not be abridged by judicial action. Only the California courts accept this viewpoint, however; elsewhere the doctrine has been definitely established that a strike is lawful only if instituted for a proper purpose and conducted in a proper manner. There are, then, some objects that may lawfully be sought through the medium of a strike, and some that may not be sought in this man-

[35] 14 Wend. (N.Y.) 9 (1835).
[36] Commonwealth *v.* Hunt, 4 Met. 45 (Mass.) 111 (1842).

ner. Strikes for higher wages or shorter hours almost invariably
meet the approval of the courts—provided, of course, that unlawful
methods are not adopted. Dissatisfaction with sanitary or safety conditions, or with shop rules or apprentice regulations, is also considered
a proper reason for striking. On the other hand, strikes to compel
employers to hire more men than they require, or to continue certain
plant operations, are generally regarded with judicial disfavor.

THE CLOSED SHOP. For many years the courts were sharply divided
concerning the propriety of strikes to force employers to adopt the
"closed shop"—that is, a shop closed to all except union workmen.
Many state courts followed the leads of Massachusetts in holding such
strikes an unreasonable interference with the rights of employers and
non-union workmen; many other state tribunals accepted instead the
New York doctrine that workmen might legally strike for a closed
shop, even though acceptance of their demands involved the dismissal
of non-union laborers. The recent sharp swing of public opinion in
favor of the closed shop, as reflected in the National Labor Relations
Act of 1935 and in numerous state acts, has left little doubt that
closed-shop strikes are legal. Indeed, the National Labor Relations
Act goes so far as to authorize agreements requiring union membership as a condition of employment; and, during the war years, the
National War Labor Board has uniformly insisted that union members in good standing at the time of a collective bargaining agreement
must, as a condition of employment, remain members of the union
until the agreement has expired.[37]

SYMPATHY STRIKES. But even if we grant the legality of closed-
shop strikes, what shall we say of sympathetic strikes, carried on by
the workmen of one employer or the members of one union to aid
the workmen of another employer or the members of another union?
Until recently such strikes were commonly prohibited, on the ground
that the participants did not have a sufficiently direct interest. But
this rule was abandoned by the Supreme Court of the United States in
1941. A lower court had issued an injunction restraining peaceful
picketing, on the ground that no labor dispute existed, because the
pickets were not employees. When the matter was carried to the Supreme Court, however, it held that the lower court's injunction was
inconsistent with the right of free speech. "The right of free com-

[37] Unless they resign from the union within fifteen days after the National War Labor
Board has issued its order.

munication cannot be mutilated," declared the court, "by denying it to workers in a dispute with an employer, even though they are not in his employ." [38]

**Disapproved practices:** COERCION AND INTIMIDATION.    A strike may be outlawed, even though called for a legitimate purpose, if the workers engage in improper tactics.   It is obvious that a strike cannot succeed if the striking workmen are immediately replaced by other workmen of approximately equal skill; nor is it likely to succeed if customers continue to patronize the employer against whom it is directed.   The natural tendency of strikers, therefore, is to attempt to persuade other workmen from taking their places, and to induce customers to withdraw their patronage.   If persuasion fails, stronger arguments may follow.   Pleading may give way to intimidation.   It is at this point that the courts draw the line between proper and improper means of conducting a strike.   They hold that persuasion of employees, prospective employees, and customers is lawful, whereas threats, coercion, and intimidation are unlawful.

THE SIT-DOWN STRIKE.   One of the most effective means of preventing employers from continuing operations with non-striking employees is to remain on the job, but with folded arms.   This is the "sit-down" strike—a virtual seizure of the plant by striking employees who refuse to work and also refuse to vacate their posts.   Such strikes were widespread in the United States during the late 1930s, and were justified by some persons as a legitimate means of protecting the laborer's vested interest in his job.   But public opinion generally disapproved of the practice, and it received judicial condemnation from the Supreme Court of the United States in the important Fansteel case of 1939.[39]

WAR PLANT STOPPAGES.   During 1941, when the threat of war hung over the nation and most of its factories were busy with defense orders, the number of strikes increased rapidly.   Nearly four times as many men and women went on strike as in the preceding year.   Then came the actual declaration of war, and strikes lost much of their former popularity, though they did not completely disappear, despite labor's so-called "no-strike" pledge.   Finally Congress decided to take a hand. It passed, over the President's veto, a law forbidding strikes in government-held enterprises, and authorized government seizure of any plant, mine, or other enterprise in which a strike had been called.

[38] American Federation of Labor *v.* Swing, 312 U.S. 321 (1941).
[39] National Labor Relations Board *v.* Fansteel Metallurgical Corp., 306 U.S. 240 (1939).

When, therefore, the production of vitally needed war goods is delayed by labor disputes, the president as commander-in-chief may direct the army to take control, and order striking employees to return to their jobs. Continued refusal to work under such circumstances is a criminal offense. Wages and other conditions of employment in a plant seized by the government remain unaltered, unless a change is made by the National War Labor Board at the request of the operating government agency or a majority of the plant's workers. The president has seized a number of plants under the provisions of this act, restoring them to their private owners as soon as possible after eliminating the likelihood of further strikes. In peacetime such government interference would not be tolerated, but in time of war it is scarcely questioned.

**Remedies for unlawful strikes:** THE INJUNCTION. We have seen that the right to strike is not absolute; it must be exercised in a proper manner and for justifiable ends. So the question naturally arises: What remedies for unlawful strikes may be obtained by injured parties? Three distinct remedies are provided. One of these is the injunction, a court order forbidding the performance of certain specified acts. An employer who fears that the acts of his striking employees, or of their union, may result in "serious and irreparable" damage to his property has the right of appeal to the courts for protection; and the courts, if they agree that serious and irreparable damage may be done, will issue an injunction against the persons complained of, ordering them not to engage in one or more specified practices. If, despite this judicial warning, strikers do engage in prohibited practices, they are guilty of contempt of court and liable to summary punishment.

At one time the courts had virtually unlimited discretion as to the acts that might be forbidden, and they frequently used this power to restrict union activities. Not unnaturally, therefore, the unions brought pressure to bear on state legislatures to restrict the use of injunctions in labor disputes, and such laws were enacted in a number of states. The Arizona statute—the most drastic of the entire crop—went so far as to impose an absolute prohibition on the granting of injunctions "in any dispute concerning terms or conditions of employment," but it was voided by the Supreme Court of the United States as "a wrongful and highly injurious invasion of property rights" whereby "the owner is stripped of all real remedy." [40] In 1914 Con-

---

[40] Truax *v.* Corrigan, 257 U.S. 312 (1921).

gress withdrew the right of federal courts to grant injunctions in labor disputes "unless necessary to prevent irreparable injury to property or to a property right, . . . for which injury there is no adequate remedy at law." This statute was received with jubilation by the labor unions, but it was interpreted so narrowly by the courts as to add little to the rights which labor already possessed.[41] Thus the law stood, nonetheless, until 1932. But in that year Congress enacted the sweeping Norris–LaGuardia Act, which specified in great detail the conditions under which federal injunctions might or might not be granted and even listed eight specific acts, common to labor disputes, that might not be judicially restrained. The Supreme Court of the United States has upheld the provisions of this statute in a number of important cases.[42] More than half of the states have enacted anti-injunction laws of the Norris–LaGuardia type, and similar legislation has been considered in most of the other commonwealths. It seems, therefore, that employers can no longer rely on injunctions as a major source of protection.

THE CIVIL SUIT FOR DAMAGES. The second remedy provided by law for the employer whose business or property has been injured by an unlawful strike is a suit for damages against the persons responsible. In one case,[43] decided nearly forty years ago, a hat manufacturing company received a judgment of more than three hundred thousand dollars against the members of a union and succeeded in collecting most of the award. But the litigation required seven years, and at the end of the period the company was bankrupt. Most employers believe that the possibility of a civil suit against unions or their members provides little real protection because of the difficulty of establishing union responsibility for unlawful acts.

CRIMINAL PROSECUTION. Still another remedy exists: the arrest and prosecution of persons responsible for criminal acts arising out of strikes. Almost every long-continued strike involves many arrests—usually for such petty offenses as disorderly conduct, obstruction of traffic, disturbance of the peace, or trespass, but sometimes for serious crimes such as extortion, rioting, assault, or even kidnaping or murder. The public authorities are seldom neutral during a strike, and in many instances they permit their sympathies to influence their con-

41 Duplex Printing Press Co. *v.* Deering, 254 U.S. 443 (1921).

42 Lauf *v.* E. G. Skinner and Co., Inc., 303 U.S. 323 (1938); United States *v.* Hutcheson, 312 U.S. 219 (1941); Milk Wagon Drivers' Union *v.* Lake Valley Farm Products, Inc., 311 U.S. 91 (1940).

43 Loewe *v.* Lawlor, 208 U.S. 274 (1908).

duct. Sometimes striking workers are arrested on flimsy evidence and convinced without adequate proof; sometimes they are allowed to commit acts of violence with the tacit approval of the police. The effectiveness of criminal prosecution as a remedy for unlawful strikes varies widely, therefore, with the time, the place and the circumstances.

## OPEN *versus* CLOSED SHOP

**The "yellow-dog" contract.** One of the devices long used by union-smashing employers was the so-called "yellow-dog" contract, which bound the worker, as a condition of his employment, not to join a labor union. Such contracts were bitterly opposed, of course, by organized labor, and in a number of states they were prohibited by law. But the Kansas statute, which provided heavy penalties for employers who attempted to force non-union contracts upon their employees, was declared unconstitutional by the Supreme Court of the United States in 1915. "Conceding the full right of the individual to join the union," said the Court, "he has no inherent right to do this and still remain in the employ of one who is unwilling to employ a union man, any more than the same individual has a right to join the union without the consent of that organization." [44] This decision was a blow at organized labor, but at first employers found it of little value in fighting the unions, for it merely authorized employers to insist upon "yellow-dog" contracts, without providing any real remedy if the workers joined the union despite their non-union agreements. True, an employer could sue his employees for breach of contract if he could prove damages; but in practice he could never obtain such proof. His real grievance was against the labor unions, which often continued to proselyte among the workers despite their contracts of employment forbidding union membership.

**Prohibition of the non-union shop.** In one important case a coal company sought an injunction to restrain the United Mine Workers of America from attempting to unionize laborers who had signed "yellow-dog" contracts, and the injunction was approved by the Supreme Court of the United States on the ground that union organizers were committing an actionable wrong by inducing breach of contract.[45] That decision came in 1917, and its immediate result was the widespread adoption of non-union contracts by employers in all parts of

---

[44] Coppage *v.* Kansas, 236 U.S. 1 (1915).
[45] Hitchman Coal and Coke Co. *v.* Mitchell, 245 U.S. 229 (1917).

the United States.    Subsequent court rulings somewhat restricted the scope of the original decision,[46] but did not seriously injure the favorable position of employers.    So the unions set out to overcome their judicial defeats with legislative victories.    They brought strong pressure to bear on the state legislatures and Congress, and after 1930 they began to reap the reward of persistent, effective lobbying.    More than one third of the states enacted laws declaring non-union contracts to be contrary to public policy, and therefore unenforceable by injunction. The Norris–LaGuardia Act of 1932, to which reference has already been made,[47] contains a similar clause.    And the 1935 National Labor Relations Act goes still further by specifying that "it shall be an unlawful labor practice for an employer . . . by discrimination in regard to hire or tenure of employment or any term or condition of employment to encourage or discourage membership in any labor organization."    The United States Supreme Court has upheld this provision of the law; [48] in fact, it has even gone so far as to hold that an employer who refuses to hire workmen because of their union affiliations, even though he has never employed them before, is guilty of an unfair labor practice.[49]    Therefore it may fairly be said that in three decades the United States has swung from protection to virtual prohibition of the non-union shop.    A number of states have enacted statutes modeled after the National Labor Relations Act.

**Activities of the National Labor Relations Board.**    Not only does the National Labor Relations Act guarantee to workers the right of collective bargaining; it seeks to make this guarantee effective by establishing a board with extensive quasi-judicial and administrative powers.    The National Labor Relations Board assists employees in the designation of their representatives for bargaining purposes— a process that has been made infinitely more difficult by the division of organized labor into two opposing camps; it investigates alleged violations of workers' rights, as defined in the act; and it takes necessary steps to halt any violations that may be uncovered.    The powers of the board extend only to matters affecting interstate commerce, but the scope of interstate commerce is broadly defined.    When a board order directed the Jones and Laughlin Steel Corporation to re-

---

[46] See, for example, American Steel Foundries *v.* Tri-City Central Trades Council, 257 U.S. 184 (1921).

[47] See p. 580.

[48] National Labor Relations Board *v.* Jones and Laughlin Steel Corp., 301 U.S. 1 (1937).

[49] Phelps Dodge Corporation *v.* National Labor Relations Board, 313 U.S. 177 (1941).

instate some workers who had been dismissed for union activities, the company contended that it was engaged primarily in manufacturing—a local enterprise—and that its affairs were therefore beyond federal control. But the Supreme Court of the United States, in a five-to-four decision, thought otherwise. "In view of the respondent's far-flung activities, it is idle to say that the effect" of a plant shutdown on interstate commerce "would be indirect or remote. It is obvious that it would be immediate and might be catastrophic." [50] Thus manufacturing is brought within the sphere of federal authority, provided the raw materials are brought from other states or the finished product is sold across state boundaries.

### COMPULSORY SETTLEMENT OF INDUSTRIAL DISPUTES

It is obvious that strikes create serious industrial and social problems. Most of the states, therefore, have attempted to insure speedy and peaceful settlement of industrial disputes by establishing public boards of arbitration or conciliation. But the results have not been very satisfactory. In 1920 Kansas adopted the radical plan of prohibiting strikes, lockouts, picketing, and boycotting in certain essential industries, including not only the public utilities and other businesses generally said to be affected with a public interest, but also the coal, food, and clothing industries. A court of industrial relations was established, with full power to fix wages and prescribe working conditions in these businesses, and its decisions were made binding upon all parties concerned. Workers might quit their jobs as individuals, but they were forbidden to leave as a group for the purpose of bringing an employer to terms; and employers might close their plants. but they were restrained from locking out employees to gain some advantage in a trade dispute. From the outset this plan was bitterly opposed by organized labor, and many employers also regarded it with disfavor. In 1923, only three years after its adoption, it was greatly weakened by an adverse United States Supreme Court decision,[51] and two years later the entire scheme of compulsory arbitration, as applied to businesses not affected with a public interest, was declared unconstitutional by the Supreme Court.[52] Thereupon the

---

[50] National Labor Relations Board *v*. Jones and Laughlin Steel Corp., 301 U.S. 1 (1937).

[51] Wolff Packing Co. *v*. Court of Industrial Relations, 262 U.S. 522 (1923).

[52] *Ibid.*, 267 U.S. 552 (1925). It was in the first Wolff Packing Co. case that the Supreme Court attempted the classification of public interest enterprises to which reference was made in the preceding chapter. See p. 545.

Kansas legislature abolished the court of industrial relations, and an interesting chapter in the history of labor legislation came to an abrupt end.

### THE POSITION OF THE EMPLOYER

The labor laws enacted by the nation and the states in recent years have been designed primarily to overcome the serious handicaps formerly imposed upon workers by common law and statute. So successful have they been in this attempt that many employers now complain of the unfairness of public policy. They point out that the "unfair labor practices" forbidden by state and federal acts are, almost without exception, directed at employer activities; and they ask why certain union practices, such as the use of force or threats of force against non-strikers, should not also be labeled "unfair." [53] Another grievance arises from the inability of employers to enforce so-called "collective agreements." Employers agree with the union that they will maintain a specified scale of wages and hours, and they can be called promptly to account for failure to keep any part of their bargain. But the union does not contract to maintain a steady labor supply; therefore if union workers—as individuals—subsequently quit their jobs because of dissatisfaction with the agreements made in their behalf, the union cannot be held responsible. In many jurisdictions the law concerning the suability of unions still reflects the common law doctrine that union funds are the property of the members and therefore cannot be reached except by judicial action against the individuals involved. Whether these and similar matters reflect unreasonable discrimination against employers is, of course, a moot question. But no one can deny that labor has been highly successful in its recent efforts to affect the trend of governmental policy.

### PUBLIC AND PRIVATE EMPLOYMENT AGENCIES

Employment agencies have long been maintained by most of the state governments and also by the governments of many cities. These public agencies, which generally operate without charge, serve a useful purpose in bringing together those who desire work and those who desire workers. Until 1933, however, they were seriously handicapped by inadequate appropriations and untrained personnel; and they did not co-operate in any permanent nation-wide scheme of job-

---

[53] During the last five years a number of states have, in fact, passed laws defining certain unfair labor practices by labor groups.

finding. But in that year the federal government, which had successfully co-ordinated state and municipal employment agencies during the First World War, again entered the field, offering substantial grants to those states that would maintain employment offices in conformity with the standards prescribed by the United States Employment Service. The states were required to match federal funds dollar for dollar. Within a short time every state had accepted the federal offer, and a nation-wide system of employment offices—totaling about three thousand—had been established. The work of these offices was greatly increased, and the scope of their usefulness correspondingly extended, by the provision of the 1935 Social Security Act requiring all applicants for unemployment compensation to register at public employment offices. The federal government not only supervised state and local activities; it also found jobs for many persons. But its primary task in this regard was to refer laborers to federal and state emergency work projects. In late December, 1941—only a few weeks after the Japanese attack at Pearl Harbor—the President asked the governors of the several states to merge their state employment services with the United States Employment Service for the duration of the war. The governors agreed, and the step was taken promptly in order to achieve "complete responsiveness to the demands of national defense and speedy, uniform, effective action to meet rapidly changing needs."

The multiplication of public employment offices has by no means caused the elimination of private agencies. More than eight hundred private employment offices function in New York City in peacetime, and the number in other large metropolitan centers is very large. Some of these offices perform a useful service in supplementing public activities—particularly in specialized fields; but in the absence of public regulation they may engage in unethical practices. They may, for example, charge exorbitant fees, or give preference to applicants who pay extra fees; they may send applicants to distant points where no work exists or working conditions are unsatisfactory; or they may conspire with employers to split the fees obtained by hiring workers who are then discharged after a few days to make room for other workers. In some instances they may send women applicants to houses of ill fame. While such abuses may be confined to a comparatively small number of agencies, it has been found that they occur with sufficient frequency to necessitate strict public regulation of all private employment agencies. Most of the state regulatory laws follow the same general plan. They provide that private agencies must be licensed and bonded, and must use a specified form of register. The use of lodging and gambling houses as agency offices is forbidden.

## UNEMPLOYMENT INSURANCE

**The Social Security Act.** The most far-reaching plan for the solution of the unemployment problem is unemployment insurance. This device has been widely used in Europe during most of the present century, but it did not meet with popular favor in the United States until the crisis of post-1929 depression had forced millions of persons out of work. Then the President appointed a committee to study the entire problem of social security, and its recommendations became the basis for the Social Security Act of 1935, which establishes unemployment compensation on a nation-wide scale. The states actually impose the payroll taxes and administer the payment of benefits; but, as previously pointed out,[54] they have been forced into line by the action of Congress in imposing a tax of three per cent on the payrolls of employers and simultaneously offering to credit against the federal tax any amounts paid to the states for unemployment insurance, up to ninety per cent of the total. Some states might perhaps prefer to omit such taxes from their revenue systems in order to attract employers and build up their industries. But no employer, unless he belongs to one of the specifically exempted groups, can escape payment of the tax; he must make payment to the federal treasury if his own state has not seen fit to act. So state inaction benefits neither the employer nor the state; and as a result every one of the forty-eight commonwealths has enacted legislation acceptable to the federal government's Social Security Board.

STATE PLANS. The several state plans differ somewhat in minor details, but all conform to the same general set of specifications. Under their terms, any unemployed worker covered by the law may apply for compensation from public funds unless his unemployment is due to some improper cause, such as voluntary quitting or discharge for misconduct. Benefits may not be paid, however, during a preliminary period—usually two weeks; and after that their duration is strictly limited—most commonly to sixteen weeks in any fifty-two. The laws of the several states adjust benefits with reference to past earnings; usually they specify fifty per cent of full-time weekly wages, with a weekly maximum of fifteen dollars. Under the terms of the

[54] See pp. 373-374.

federal act employers of fewer than eight persons are exempt. More than half of the states have followed the federal lead in this respect, but ten commonwealths have applied their insurance schemes to every employer of one or more persons, and nine others have specified every employer of four or more. Other common exemptions include farm and domestic laborers, government employees, and workers in non-profit organizations. The states do not retain the money collected in payroll taxes; instead they deposit it in an unemployment trust fund administered by the federal government. Costs of administration are met by a grant to the states from the federal treasury.

CRITICISMS. The American version of unemployment insurance, as thus outlined, has been criticized by many persons, for a variety of reasons. Employers contend that it imposes too heavy a burden on industry. Workers complain that benefits are too low. Social workers declare that the number of exempted groups is too large, and students of government indicate that the supervisory powers of the federal government are too restricted. Most of these complaints have at least a partial basis in fact, and some of them will doubtless be corrected in the light of further experience. But at least a reasonable attempt has been made to protect the nation's workers against the more serious economic effects of unemployment. The restriction of benefit payments to a limited period in each year is, of course, a necessary feature of the insurance plan. Otherwise a serious depression might speedily deplete reserves and leave public authorities without funds for benefit payments. But government does not thereby limit its responsibility for the alleviation of human misery. It must still care for unemployed persons after benefit payments have ceased and their own funds have been exhausted. That is not an insurance matter, however; it is a problem of relief.

CONSTITUTIONALITY. The constitutionality of the unemployment compensation section of the Social Security Act was speedily challenged on a number of grounds: it involved federal coercion of the states; it made unreasonable discriminations, since it exempted some employers; it attempted to bring unemployment within the scope of congressional authority, contrary to the intent—and even the letter—of the federal Constitution. These contentions were considered by the Supreme Court of the United States and rejected in a sweeping decision which upheld the entire system of unemployment insurance.[55] The five majority members of the Court were unimpressed with Justice

[55] Steward Machine Co. *v.* Davis, 301 U.S. 548 (1937).

McReynolds' argument that the scheme interfered with the orderly processes of state government through "offers of seductive favors."

## SELECTED REFERENCES

Andrews, John B., *Administrative Labor Legislation; A Study of American Experience in the Delegation of Legislative Power*, 1936.

————, *Labor Laws in Action*, 1938.

Bowman, D. O., *Public Control of Labor Relations*, 1942.

Braun, Kurt, *The Settlement of Industrial Disputes*, 1944.

Commons, James R., and Andrew, James B., *Principles of Labor Legislation*, 1936.

Daugherty, C. R., *Labor Problems in American Industry*, 5th ed. rev., 1941.

Dawson, Marshall, *Problems of Workmen's Compensation Administration in the United States and Canada*, Washington, D.C., 1940.

Donaldson, McPherrin Hatfield, *Labor Problems in the United States*, 1939.

Duke University Law School, *Labor in Wartime*, Durham, N.C., 1942.

Epstein, A., *Insecurity: A Challenge to America*, 2nd ed. rev., 1938.

Kaltenborn, Howard S., *Governmental Adjustment of Labor Disputes*, 1943.

Leiserson, W. M., *Right and Wrong in Labor Relations*, Berkeley, Cal., 1942.

Lentz, Gilbert G., *Enforcement of the Orders of State Public Service Commissions*, Urbana, Ill., 1940.

Magnusson, Leifur, *Workmen's Compensation for Public Employees*, 1943.

Mariano, John H., *Wartime Labor Relations*, 1944.

Matscheck, W., and Atkinson, R. C., *Problems and Procedures of Unemployment Compensation in the States*, 1939.

Millis, H. A., *Labor's Risks and Social Insurance*, 2 vols., 1938.

Millis, H. A., and Others, *How Collective Bargaining Works*, 1942.

New York State Joint Legislative Committee on Industrial Relations, *The American Story of Industrial and Labor Relations*, Albany, 1943.

Pierson, Frank C., *Collective Bargaining Systems*, Washington, D.C., 1942.

Reed, George L., *Law of Labor Relations*, Newark, N.J., 1942.

Stewart, B. M., *Planning and Administration of Unemployment and Compensation in the United States*, 1938.

Taylor, A. G., *Labor Problems and Labor Law*, 1938.

Toner, Jerome L., *The Closed Shop*, Washington, D. C., 1942.

White, R. C., *Administering Unemployment Compensation*, 1939.

Wilson, A. T., and Levy, H., *Workmen's Compensation*, 2 vols., 1939.

APPENDIX

APPENDIX

# A MODEL STATE CONSTITUTION

## ARTICLE I

### BILL OF RIGHTS

**Section 100.** *Political Power.* All political power of this state is inherent in the people, and all government herein is founded on their authority.

**Section 101.** *Inherent Rights.* All men are by nature equally free and independent and have certain inherent rights; namely, the enjoyment of life and liberty, with the means of acquiring and possessing property, and pursuing and obtaining happiness and safety. These rights carry with them certain corresponding duties to the state.

**Section. 102.** *Legal Rights.* No citizen shall be disfranchised, or deprived of any of the rights or privileges secured to any other citizen, unless by the law of the land or the judgment of his peers; nor shall any person be deprived of due process of law, or be denied the equal protection of the laws. There shall be no imprisonment for debt and a reasonable amount of the property of individuals may be exempted from seizure or sale for payment of any debt or liabilities.

**Section 103.** *Right to Organize.* Citizens shall have the right to organize, except in military or semi-military organizations not under the supervision of the state, and except for purposes of resisting the duly constituted authority of this state or of the United States. Employees shall have the right to bargain collectively through representatives of their own choosing.

**Section 104.** *Searches and Seizures.* The right of the people to be secure in their persons, houses, papers and effects, against unreasonable searches and seizures, shall not be violated; and no warrants shall issue but upon probable cause supported by oath or affirmation, and particularly describing the place to be searched, and the persons or things to be seized. Evidence obtained in violation of this section shall not be admissible in any court against any person.

**Section 105.** *Writ of Habeas Corpus.* The privilege of the writ of habeas corpus shall not be suspended, unless, in case of rebellion or invasion, the public safety requires it, and then only in such manner as shall be prescribed by law.

**Section 106.** *Rights of Accused Persons.* In all criminal prosecutions, the accused shall have the right to demand a specific statement of the charges against him, and to appear and defend himself in person and by counsel; to meet the witnesses against him face to face; to have process to compel the attendance of witnesses in his behalf; and to have a speedy public trial in the county or district

---

1 Fourth Edition. Prepared by the Committee on State Government of the National Municipal League. Reprinted through the courtesy of the National Municipal League.

in which the offense is alleged to have been committed, unless he shall waive this right in order to secure a change of venue.

Section 107. *Double Jeopardy; Excessive Bail.* No person shall, after acquittal, be tried for the same offense. All persons shall, before conviction, be bailable by sufficient sureties, except for capital offenses when the proof is evident or the presumption great.

Section 108. *Right of Assembly.* The right of the people peaceably to assemble, and to petition the government, or any department thereof, shall never be abridged.

Section 109. *Freedom of Speech.* No law shall be passed abridging the freedom of speech or of the press.

Section 110. *Freedom of Religion.* No law shall be passed respecting the establishment of religion, or prohibiting the free exercise thereof.

Section 111. *Appropriations for Private Purposes.* No tax shall be levied or appropriation of public money or property be made, either directly or indirectly, except for a public purpose, and no public money or property shall ever be appropriated, applied, donated, or used directly or indirectly, for any sect, church, denomination, or sectarian institution. No public money or property shall be appropriated for a charitable, industrial, educational or benevolent purpose except to a department, office, agency or civil division of the state.

Section 112. *Freedom from Legislative Abuses.* The power of the state to act in the general welfare shall never be impaired by the making of any irrevocable grant of special privileges or immunities.

Section 113. *Eminent Domain.* Private property shall not be taken or damaged for public use without just compensation.

## Article II

### SUFFRAGE AND ELECTIONS

Section 200. *Qualifications for Voting.* Every duly registered citizen of the age of twenty-one years who shall have been a citizen for ninety days, and an inhabitant of this state for one year next preceding an election, and for the last ninety days a resident of the county and for the last thirty days a resident of the election district in which he or she may offer his or her vote, shall be entitled to vote at such election in the election district of which he or she shall at the time be a resident, and not elsewhere, except as hereinafter provided, in the election of all officers that are now or hereafter may be elective by the people, and upon all questions which may be submitted to the vote of the people, provided that no person shall become entitled to vote unless such person is also able, except for physical disability, to read and write English; and suitable laws shall be passed by the legislature to enforce this provision.

Section 201. *Absent Voting.* The legislature may, by general law, provide a manner in which qualified voters who may be absent from the state or county of their residence may register and vote, and for the return and canvass of their votes in the election district in which they reside.

Section 202. *Disqualifications from Voting.* No person who shall receive, accept, or offer to receive, or pay, offer or promise to pay, or withdraw or withhold or threaten to withdraw or withhold any money or other valuable consideration as a compensation or reward for the giving or withholding of a vote at an election shall vote at such election. No person under conviction of bribery or of any infamous crime shall exercise the privilege of the suffrage.

Section 203. *Residence.* For the purpose of voting, no person shall be deemed to have gained or lost a residence by reason of his presence or absence, while employed in the service of the United States; nor while engaged in the navigation of the waters of this state, or of the United States, or of the high seas; nor while a student at any institution of learning; nor while kept at any almshouse, or other asylum, or institution wholly or partly supported at public expense or by charity; nor while confined in any public prison.

Section 204. *Registration of Voters.* Laws shall be made for ascertaining, by proper proofs, the citizens who shall be entitled to the privilege of the suffrage and for the registration of all qualified voters. Registration shall be upon personal application in the case of the first registration of any voter and shall be completed at least ten days before each election. Such registration shall be effective so long as the voter shall remain qualified to vote from the same address or for such other period as the legislature may prescribe.

Section 205. *Methods of Voting.* Voting at all elections or on referenda shall be by voting machine or by such other method as may be prescribed by law, provided that secrecy of voting be preserved.

Section 206. *Election Officers.* All officers and employees charged with the direction or administration of the election system of the state and of its civil divisions shall be appointed in such manner as the legislature may by law direct, provided that appointment shall be made according to merit and fitness, to be determined, so far as practicable, by competitive examination.

## ARTICLE III

### THE LEGISLATURE

Section 300. *Legislative Power.* The legislative power shall be vested in a legislature, which may delegate to other public officers the power to supplement statutes by ordinances, general orders, rules, and regulations, provided a general standard or principle has been enacted to which such delegated legislation shall conform. All such delegated legislation, promulgated by state officers, departments, officers, or agencies, shall be reported to the legislative council, and shall be adopted and published in accordance with a fair procedure prescribed by law.

Section 301. *Composition of the Legislature.* The legislature shall be composed of a single chamber of such number of members as may be prescribed by law, but not to exceed ............ members. Except as otherwise provided in this constitution, any qualified voter shall be eligible to membership in the legislature.

Section 302. *Election of Members.* The members of the legislature shall be chosen by the qualified voters of the state for a term of two years by proportional representation, under a method to be prescribed by law. For the purpose of electing members of the legislature, the state shall be divided into districts, composed of contiguous and compact territory, from each of which there shall be elected from three to seven members, in accordance with the population of the respective districts. The term of members of the legislature shall begin on the first day of December next following their election.

Section 303. *Apportionment.* After each decennial census, the secretary of the legislature shall reallot the number of members assigned to each district, in accordance with the changes in the population of the several districts. The boundaries of the districts and the total number of members may be altered only by law and not more frequently than once in each census period.

Section 304. *Time of Election.* The election of members of the legislature shall be held on the Tuesday next following the first Monday in November in the odd numbered years, beginning in 19......

Section 305. *Vacancies.* Whenever a vacancy shall occur in the legislature, it shall be filled by a majority vote of the remaining members from the district in which said vacancy occurs. If, after thirty days following the occurrence of a vacancy, it remains unfilled, the governor shall appoint some eligible person for the unexpired term.

Section 306. *Compensation of Members.* The members of the legislature shall receive an annual salary, as may be prescribed by law, but the amount thereof shall neither be increased nor diminished during the term for which they are elected.

Section 307. *Sessions.* The legislature shall be deemed a continuous body during the biennium for which its members are elected. It shall meet in regular sessions quarterly or at such times as may be prescribed by law. Special sessions may be called by the governor or by a majority of the members of the legislative council.

Section 308. *Organization and Procedure.* The legislature shall be judge of the election, returns and qualifications of its members, and may by law vest in the courts the trial and determination of contested elections of members. It shall choose its presiding officer, and a secretary who shall serve for an indefinite term. It shall determine its rules of procedure; it may compel the attendance of absent members, punish its members for disorderly conduct and, with the concurrence of two-thirds of all the members, expel a member; and it shall have power to compel the attendance and testimony of witnesses and the production of books and papers either before the legislature as a whole or before any committee thereof.

Section 309. *Legislative Immunity.* For any speech or debate in the legislature, the members shall not be questioned in any other place.

Section 310. *Local and Special Legislation.* The legislature shall pass no
special act in any case where a general act can be made applicable, and whether
a general act can be made applicable shall be a matter for judicial determination.
No local act shall take effect until approved by a majority of the qualified voters
voting thereon in the district to be affected, except acts repealing local or special
acts in effect before the adoption of this constitution and receiving a two-thirds
vote of all members of the legislature on the question of their repeal.

Section 311. *Transaction of Business.* A majority of all the members of the
legislature shall constitute a quorum to do business but a smaller number may
adjourn from day to day and compel the attendance of absent members. The
legislature shall keep a journal of its proceedings which shall be published from
day to day. The legislature shall prescribe the methods of voting in legislative
matters, but a record vote, with the yeas and nays entered in the journal, shall be
taken on any question on the demand of one-fifth of the members present.
Mechanical devices may be employed to record the votes of members.

Section 312. *Committees.* The legislature may establish such committees as
may be necessary for the efficient conduct of its business. Each committee shall
keep a journal of its proceedings as a public record. One-third of the members of
the legislature shall have power to relieve a committee of further consideration of
a bill when the committee to which it was assigned has not reported on it. Notice
of all committee hearings and a clear statement of all subjects to be considered at
each hearing shall be published one week in advance in the journal.

Section 313. *Bills and Titles of Bills.* No law shall be passed except by bill.
Every bill, except bills for appropriations and bills for the codification, revision or
rearrangement of existing laws, shall be confined to one subject, which shall be
expressed in the title. Bills for appropriations shall be confined to appropriations.

Section 314. *Passage of Bills.* No bill shall become a law unless it has been
read on three different days, has been printed and upon the desks of the members
in final form at least three legislative days prior to final passage, and has received
the assent of a majority of all the members of the legislature. No act shall become effective until published, as provided by law.

Section 315. *Action by the Governor.* Every bill which shall have passed the
legislature shall be presented to the governor; if he approves he shall sign it, but
if not he shall return it with his objections to the legislature. Any bill so returned
by the governor shall be reconsidered by the legislature and if, upon reconsideration, two-thirds of the members present shall agree to pass the bill it shall become
a law. In all such cases the vote of the legislature shall be by roll call, and
entered on the journal.

If any bill shall not be signed or returned by the governor within fifteen days
after it shall have been presented to him it shall be a law in like manner as if he
had signed it, except that, if the legislature shall be in recess at the end of such

fifteen day period, the governor may return it with his objections upon the re-convening of the legislature, and if the legislature shall adjourn finally before the governor has acted on a bill that has been presented to him less than fifteen days before, it shall not become law unless the governor sign it within thirty days after such adjournment.

Section 316. *Referendum on Legislation.* Any bill failing of passage by the legislature may be submitted to referendum by order of the governor, either in its original form or with such amendments which were considered by the legislature as he may designate. Any bill which, having passed the legislature, is returned thereto by the governor with objections and, upon reconsideration, is not approved by a two-thirds vote of all the members but is approved by at least a majority thereof, may be submitted to referendum by a majority of all the members of the legislature. Bills thus submitted to referendum shall be voted on at the next succeeding general election occurring at least sixty days after action is taken to submit them, unless the legislature shall provide for their submission at an earlier date.

Section 317. *Legislative Council.* There shall be a legislative council consisting of not less than seven nor more than fifteen members, chosen by and from the legislature. Members of the legislative council shall be chosen by the legislature at its first session after the adoption of this constitution and at each subsequent session following a general election. Members of the legislative council shall be elected in such manner as the legislature shall direct, and when elected shall continue in office until their successors are chosen and have qualified. The legislature, by a majority vote of all its members, may dissolve the legislative council at any time and proceed to the election of a successor thereto.

Section 318. *Organization of Legislative Council.* The legislative council shall meet as often as may be necessary to perform its duties. It shall choose one of its members as chairman, and shall appoint a director of research; it shall adopt its own rules of procedure, except as such rules may be established by law. The secretary of the legislature shall serve ex officio as secretary of the council.

Section 319. *Duties of the Legislative Council.* It shall be the duty of the legislative council to collect information concerning the government and general welfare of the state and to report thereon to the legislature. Measures for proposed legislation may be submitted to it at any time, and shall be considered and reported to the legislature with its recommendations thereon. The legislative council may also recommend such legislation, in the form of bills or otherwise, as in its opinion the welfare of the state may require. Other powers and duties may be assigned to the legislative council by law. The legislature may delegate to the legislative council authority to supplement existing legislation by general orders. No such general orders shall be effective until published as provided by law.

Section 320. *Compensation of Members of the Legislative Council.* Members of the legislative council shall receive such compensation, additional to their compensation as members of the legislature, as may be provided by law.

## ARTICLE IV

### INITIATIVE AND REFERENDUM

Section 400. *The Initiative.* The people reserve to themselves power by petition to propose laws and amendments to this constitution, and directly to enact or reject such laws and amendments at the polls. This reserved power shall be known as the initiative.

Section 401. *Initiative Procedure.* An initiative petition shall contain either the full text of the measure proposed, or an adequate summary thereof, and, to be valid, shall be signed by qualified voters equal in number to at least ...... per cent of the total vote cast for governor in the last preceding general election at which a governor was chosen. An initiative petition proposing a constitutional amendment shall be signed by ...... [a greater] per cent of the qualified voters of the state than is required for a petition proposing a law. Not more than one-fourth of the signatures counted on any completed petition shall be those of the voters of any one county. Initiative petitions shall be filed with the secretary of the legislature, and the question of adopting any measure therein set forth shall be submitted by him to the qualified voters at the first regular state election held not less than sixty days after such filing, except that a constitutional amendment so proposed shall be submitted at the second regular state election after such filing.

Section 402. *The Referendum.* The people also reserve to themselves power to require, by petition, that measures enacted by the legislature be submitted to the qualified voters for their approval or rejection. This reserved power shall be known as the referendum.

Section 403. *Referendum Procedure.* A referendum petition against any measure passed by the legislature shall be filed with the secretary of the legislature within ninety days after the adjournment of the session at which such measure was enacted, and to be valid, shall be signed by qualified voters equal in number to not less than ...... per cent of the total vote cast for governor at the last preceding general election at which a governor was chosen. Not more than one-fourth of the signatures counted on any completed petition shall be those of the voters of any one county. The question of approving any measure against which a valid referendum petition is filed shall be submitted to the voters at the regular or special state election held not less than thirty days after such filing.

Section 404. *Effect of Referendum.* A referendum may be ordered upon any act or part of an act, except acts continuing existing taxes and acts making appropriations in amounts not in excess of those for the preceding fiscal year. When the referendum is ordered upon an act, or any part of an act, it shall suspend the operation thereof until such act, or part, is approved by the voters.

The filing of a referendum petition against one or more items, sections, or parts of an act shall not delay the remainder of the measure from becoming operative. No act shall take effect earlier than ninety days after the adjournment of the legislative session at which it was enacted, except acts declared to be emergency measures. If it be necessary for the immediate preservation of the public peace, health, or safety that a measure become effective without delay, the facts constituting such necessity shall be stated in a separate section, and if, upon a record vote entered in the journal, two-thirds of the members elected to the legislature shall declare the measure to be an emergency measure, it shall become effective at the time specified therein; but no act granting or amending a franchise or special privilege, or creating any vested right or interest, other than in the state, shall be declared an emergency measure. If a referendum petition be filed against an emergency measure, such measure shall be operative until voted upon, and if not approved by a majority of the qualified voters voting thereon, it shall be deemed repealed.

Section 405. *Special Elections.* Any referendum measure shall be submitted to the qualified voters at a special election if so ordered by the governor or if a separate petition requesting a special election be signed by ...... per cent of the qualified voters. Any such special election shall be held not less than one hundred and twenty nor more than one hundred and fifty days after the adjournment of the legislative session at which the act was passed.

Section 406. *Passage of Constitutional Amendments and Laws by the Initiative and Referendum.* Each measure shall be submitted by a ballot title, which shall be descriptive, but not argumentative or prejudicial. The ballot title of any initiated or referred measure shall be prepared by the legal department of the state, subject to review by the courts. The veto power of the governor shall not extend to measures initiated by, or referred to, the qualified voters. Any measure submitted to a vote of the qualified voters shall become law or a part of the constitution only when approved by a majority of the votes cast thereon, provided that, in addition, no initiative measure or constitutional amendment shall become effective unless the affirmative votes cast therefor shall equal 30 per cent of the total vote cast for governor at the last preceding general election at which a governor was chosen. Each measure so approved shall take effect thirty days after the date of the vote thereon, unless otherwise provided in the measure. If conflicting measures referred to the people at the same election shall be approved by a majority of the votes cast thereon, the one receiving the highest number of affirmative votes shall prevail to the extent of such conflict.

Section 407. *Restrictions on Direct Legislation Procedure.* The initiative shall not be used as a means of making appropriations of public funds, nor for the enactment of local or special legislation. No measure submitted by the initiative shall contain therein the name of any person to be designated as administrator of any department, office or agency to be established by the proposed law or constitutional amendment.

Section 408. *Provisions Self-Executing.* The initiative and referendum provisions of this constitution shall be self-executing, and shall be treated as mandatory. Laws may be enacted to facilitate their operation, including provision for verification of signatures on petitions, but no law shall be enacted to hamper, restrict or impair the exercise of the powers herein reserved to the people. No measure adopted by vote of the qualified voters under the initiative and referendum provisions of this constitution shall be repealed or amended by the legislature within a period of three years except by a two-thirds vote of all of the members of the legislature.

ARTICLE V

THE EXECUTIVE

Section 500. *Establishment of the Executive.* The executive power of the state shall be vested in a governor, who shall be chosen by the direct vote of the people for a term of four years beginning on the first day of December next following his election.

Section 501. *Election of the Governor.* The election for governor shall be held on the Tuesday next following the first Monday in November in each alternate odd numbered year, beginning in 19...... Any qualified voter of the state shall be eligible to the office of governor.

Section 502. *Legislative Powers.* The governor shall, at the beginning of each session, and may at other times, give to the legislature information as to the affairs of the state, and recommend such measures as he shall deem expedient. He shall have the power of veto over bills approved by the legislature, as in this constitution prescribed.

Section 503. *Executive and Administrative Powers.* The governor shall take care that the laws are faithfully executed. He shall commission all officers of the state. He may at any time require information, in writing or otherwise, from the officers of any administrative department, office or agency upon any subject relating to their respective offices. He shall be commander-in-chief of the armed forces of the state (except when they shall be called into the service of the United States), and may call out the same to execute the laws, to suppress insurrection or to repel invasion.

Section 504. *Judicial Powers.* The governor shall have power to grant reprieves, commutations and pardons, after conviction, for all offenses, subject to such regulations as may be prescribed by law relative to the manner of applying therefor.

Section 505. *Oath of Office.* The governor and all officers of the state, and of all civil divisions thereof, shall, before entering upon the duties of their respective offices, take and subscribe the following oath or affirmation: "I do solemnly swear (or affirm) that I will support and defend the constitution of the United States and the constitution of the State of ...................., and that I will faithfully discharge the duties of the office of ................ to the best of my ability."

Section 506. *Administrative Manager.* The governor shall appoint an administrative manager of state affairs, whose term shall be indefinite at the pleasure of the governor. The governor may delegate any or all of his administrative powers to the administrative manager. The administrative manager shall be assisted by such aides as may be provided by law, but all such aides shall be appointed and shall hold office under civil service regulations.

Section 507. *Administrative Departments.* There shall be such administrative departments, not to exceed twenty in number, as may be established by law, with such powers and duties as may be prescribed by law. Subject to the limitations contained in this constitution, the legislature may from time to time assign by law new powers and functions to departments, offices and agencies, and it may increase, modify, or diminish the powers and functions of such departments, offices, or agencies. All new powers or functions shall be assigned to departments, offices or agencies in such manner as will tend to maintain an orderly arrangement in the administrative pattern of the state government. The legislature may create temporary commissions for special purposes or reduce the number of departments by consolidation or otherwise.

The heads of all administrative departments shall be appointed by and may be removed by the governor. All other officers in the administrative service of the state shall be appointed by the governor or by the heads of administrative departments, as provided by article IX of this constitution and by supporting legislation. No executive order governing the work of the state or the administration of one or more departments, offices and agencies, shall become effective until published as provided by law.

Section 508. *Executive-Legislative Relations.* The governor, the administrative manager, and heads of administrative departments shall be entitled to seats in the legislature, may introduce bills therein, and take part in the discussion of measures, but shall have no vote.

Section 509. *Removal of the Governor.* The legislature shall have the power of impeachment by a two-thirds vote of the members elected thereto, and it shall provide by law a procedure for the trial and removal from office of all officers of this state. No officer shall be convicted on impeachment by a vote of less than two-thirds of the members of the court hearing the charges.

Section 510. *Succession to Governorship.* In case of the failure of the governor to qualify, or of his impeachment, or of his removal from office, death, resignation, inability to discharge the powers and duties of his office, or absence from the state, the powers and duties of the office shall devolve upon the presiding officer of the legislature for the remainder of the term, or until the disability be removed.

## ARTICLE VI

### THE JUDICIARY

Section 600. *Establishment of the Judiciary.* The judicial power of the state shall be vested in a General Court of Justice, which shall on and after January 1, .........., exercise the judicial power heretofore vested in any court in the state. The legislature shall provide by law for a supreme court department, and for such other departments, divisions, or special tribunals, and for such judges as may be required to handle the judicial business of the state properly.

**Section 601.** *Jurisdiction of the Courts.* The General Court of Justice shall have jurisdiction to hear claims against the state, and such other powers and jurisdiction as may be conferred upon it by law. The legislature may delegate to the judicial council the power to determine by general rules the jurisdiction of departments of the General Court of Justice other than the supreme court department.

**Section 602.** *Selection of Judges.* The chief justice shall be elected by the qualified voters of the state at a general election on the first Tuesday after the first Monday in November, in an odd numbered year, beginning two years after the first election of governor under this constitution. He shall hold office for a term of eight years, beginning on the first day of December next following his election.

The chief justice shall be a member of the supreme court department and shall appoint the judges of the various departments of the General Court of Justice from an eligible list containing three names for such vacancy, which shall be presented to him by the judicial council. The term of office of each judge so appointed shall be twelve years, subject to removal as hereafter provided. After any judge appointed by the chief justice shall have served for four years, the qualified voters of the state or of the judicial district which he is serving shall decide at the next regular election whether such judge shall be retained or removed from office. A separate ballot shall be used (unless voting machines are employed) in such election on which there shall appear no other question than that of the retention or removal of such judge. If a majority of the votes cast are against retaining such judge in office, the chief justice shall appoint his successor for a term of twelve years, subject to recall as provided in this section. If a majority of the votes cast are in favor of retaining such judge, he shall continue in office until the end of his term. All vacancies caused by death, resignation, or retirement shall be filled in like manner, for the full term.

**Section 603.** *Powers of the Chief Justice.* The chief justice shall be the presiding justice of the supreme court department and a member of any division thereof. He shall preside over meetings of the judicial council, and shall be the executive head of the General Court of Justice, exercising such powers as are herein conferred or may be hereafter conferred by law, or by rules, not in conflict herewith or with the statutes, made by the judicial council. It shall be the duty of the chief justice to organize and administer the General Court of Justice. He shall cause to be published an annual report covering the business done by each department of the General Court of Justice and stating the condition of the dockets at the close of the year. He may require periodic or special reports from the presiding justices of the several departments on the state of judicial business and operation of said departments. He shall appoint the clerk and such other ministerial agents of the supreme court department as may be authorized by law.

**Section 604.** *Judicial Districts.* The judicial council shall have power to alter the districts into which the state may be divided for the handling of judicial business, in so far as the legislature does not otherwise provide, but any such order of the council may be amended or revoked by the legislature.

Section 605. *Judges of Inferior Court Departments.* The chief justice shall assign the judges of the inferior court departments to the several districts. Any judge shall be eligible to sit under temporary assignment in any district.

There shall be a presiding justice in each district, who shall be appointed by the chief justice from among the judges of such district, and who shall serve until his retirement or his removal as presiding justice by the judicial council. The presiding justice in each district shall have control over the calendars in the courts in his district and over the assignment of judges within his district, subject to rules made by the judicial council, and shall appoint clerks, magistrates, and such other ministerial agents as are authorized by law for his district.

Section 606. *Establishment of Judicial Council.* There shall be a judicial council, to consist of the chief justice, and one justice of the supreme court department and two judges of the inferior court departments to be designated for four years by the chief justice; three practicing lawyers, to be appointed by the governor for overlapping terms of three years, from an eligible list containing three times as many names as there are appointments to be made and presented to him by the governing board of the state bar association; three laymen citizens of the state, to be appointed by the governor for overlapping terms of three years; and the chairman of the judiciary committee of the legislature. The judicial council shall meet at least once in each quarter, at a time and place to be designated by the chief justice.

Section 607. *Powers of the Judicial Council.* The judicial council, in addition to other powers herein conferred upon it or hereafter conferred by law, shall have power to make or alter the rules relating to pleading, practice, or procedure in the General Court of Justice, and to prescribe generally by rules the duties and jurisdiction of masters and magistrates; and also to make rules and regulations respecting the duties and the business of the clerk of the General Court of Justice and his subordinates and all ministerial officers of the General Court of Justice, its departments, divisions, or branches. The legislature may repeal, alter, or supplement any rule of pleading, practice, or procedure, by a law limited to that specific purpose. No such rule made by the judicial council shall be effective until published as provided by law.

Section 608. *Removal of Judges.* The legislature may, upon due notice given an opportunity for defense, remove from office any judge, upon the concurrence of two-thirds of all the members elected. Judges of the inferior departments of the General Court of Justice and all ministerial agents of the General Court of Justice may be removed, for cause, after due notice and opportunity for defense, by the judicial council.

Section 609. *Compensation of Judges.* All remuneration for the services of judges and court officials provided for under this constitution shall be paid from an appropriation by the legislature. The annual compensation paid to any judge shall be neither increased nor diminished during the term of office to which he shall be elected or appointed. The legislature may by law provide for the apportionment among the several counties of the state of the expense of the maintenance of the General Court of Justice.

Section 610. *Fees, Costs, and Fines.* All fees collected in any department of the General Court of Justice and all masters' fees shall be paid to the clerk of said court and shall be accounted for by him monthly and paid to the state treasury. The judicial council shall have power to establish or alter fees to be collected in the several court departments of this state, subject to such general regulations as the legislature may by law establish.

Section 611. *Ineligibility of Judges to Other Offices.* No judge shall hold any office or public employment, other than a judicial office, during the term for which he shall have been elected or appointed, and no judge shall engage in the practice of law or other private employment during his continuance in office. No judge shall be eligible for election to any non-judicial office until two years after the expiration of the full term for which he was appointed or elected.

Section 612. *Disqualifications in Certain Cases.* No judge shall sit in any case wherein he may be interested, or where either of the parties may be connected with him by affinity or consanguinity within such degrees as may be prescribed by law, or where he shall have been of counsel in the case, or in the trial of which he presided in any inferior court.

Section 613. *Writ of Habeas Corpus.* Each judge of any department of the General Court of Justice shall have power to issue writs of habeas corpus.

## ARTICLE VII

### FINANCE

Section 700. *Powers of Taxation.* The power of taxation shall never be surrendered, suspended, or contracted away.

Section 701. *Borrowing Power.* The credit of the state or any civil division thereof shall not in any manner, directly or indirectly, be given or lent to or used in aid of any individual, association, or private corporation.

Section 702. *Debt Limitations.* No debt shall be contracted by or in behalf of this state unless such debt shall be authorized by law for a single project or object distinctly specified therein; and no such law shall, except for the purpose of repelling invasion, suppressing insurrection, defending the state in war, meeting natural catastrophes, or redeeming the indebtedness of the state outstanding at the time this constitution is approved, take effect until it shall have been submitted to the qualified voters at a general election and have received a favorable majority of all votes cast upon such question at such election; except that the state may by law borrow money to meet appropriations for any fiscal year in anticipation of the collection of the revenues of such year, but all debts so contracted in anticipation of revenues shall be paid within one year.

Section 703. *The Budget.* Three months before the opening of the fiscal year, the governor shall submit to the legislature a budget setting forth a complete plan of proposed expenditures and anticipated income of all departments, offices and agencies of the state for the next ensuing fiscal year. For the preparation of the budget the various departments, offices and agencies shall furnish the governor such information, in such form, as he may require. At the time of submitting the budget to the legislature, the governor shall introduce therein a general appropriation bill to authorize all the proposed expenditures set forth in the budget. At the same time he shall introduce in the legislature a bill or bills covering all recommendations in the budget for new or additional revenues or for borrowing by which the proposed expenditures are to be met.

Section 704. *Legislative Budget Procedure.* No special appropriation bill shall be passed until the general appropriation bill, as introduced by the governor and amended by the legislature, shall have been enacted, unless the governor shall recommend the passage of an emergency appropriation or appropriations, which shall continue in force only until the general appropriation bill shall become effective. The legislature shall provide for one or more public hearings on the budget, either before a committee or before the entire legislature in committee of the whole. When requested by not less than one-fifth of the members of the legislature it shall be the duty of the governor to appear in person or by a designated representative before the legislature, or before a committee thereof, to answer any inquiries with respect to the budget.

The legislature shall make no appropriation for any fiscal period in excess of the income provided for that period. The governor may strike out or reduce items in appropriation bills passed by the legislature, and the procedure in such cases shall be the same as in case of the disapproval of an entire bill by the governor.

Section 705. *Expenditure of Money.* No money shall be withdrawn from the treasury except in accordance with appropriations made by law, nor shall any obligation for the payment of money be incurred except as authorized by law. No appropriation shall confer authority to incur an obligation after the termination of the fiscal period to which it relates. The governor shall have authority to reduce expenditures of state departments, offices and agencies under appropriations whenever actual revenues fall below the revenue estimates upon which the appropriations were based and, through allotments or otherwise, to control the rate at which such appropriations are expended during the fiscal year, provided that the legislature may exempt specific appropriations from the exercise of this power by the governor.

Section 706. *Purchasing Methods.* All public purchases made by the government of this state, or by any of its cities, counties, or other civil divisions, shall, so far as practicable, be made under a system of competitive bidding. Centralized purchasing shall be practiced, wherever practicable, within individual civil divisions, and the legislature may by law authorize co-operative purchasing by two or more civil divisions.

Section 707. *Post-auditing.* The legislature shall, by a majority vote of all its members, appoint an auditor who shall serve during its pleasure. It shall be the duty of the auditor to conduct post-audits of all transactions and of all accounts kept by or for all departments, offices and agencies of the state government, to certify to the accuracy of all financial statements issued by accounting officers of the state, and to report his findings and criticisms to the governor and to a special committee of the legislature quarterly, and to the legislature at the end of each fiscal year. He shall also make such additional reports to the legislature and the proper legislative committee, and conduct such investigation of the financial affairs of the state, or of any department, office or agency thereof, as either of such bodies may require.

Section 708. *Excess Condemnation.* The state, or any civil division thereof, appropriating or otherwise acquiring property for public use, may, in furtherance of such public use, appropriate or acquire an excess over that actually to be occupied by the improvement, and may sell such excess with such restrictions as shall be appropriate to preserve the improvement made. Bonds may be issued to supply the funds in whole or in part to pay for the excess property so appropriated or acquired; and such bonds, when made a lien only against the property so appropriated or acquired, shall not be subject to the restrictions or limitations on the amount of indebtedness of any civil divisions prescribed by law.

## ARTICLE VIII

### LOCAL GOVERNMENT

Section 800. *Organization of Local Government.* Provision shall be made by general law for the incorporation of counties, cities, and other civil divisions; and for the alteration of boundaries, the consolidation of neighboring civil divisions, and the dissolution of any such civil divisions.

Provision shall also be made by general law (which may provide optional plans of organization and government) for the organization and government of counties, cities, and other civil divisions which do not adopt locally framed and adopted charters in accordance with the provisions of section 801, but no such law hereafter enacted shall become operative in any county, city, or other civil division until submitted to the qualified voters thereof and approved by a majority of those voting thereon.

Section 801. *Home Rule for Local Units.* Any county or city may frame and adopt a charter for its own government in the following manner, subject to such further regulations as to the manner of framing and adopting a charter as may be provided by general law:

(a) The legislative authority of the county or city may, by a majority vote of its members, and upon petition of 10 per cent of the qualified voters thereof shall forthwith, provide by ordinance or resolution for submission to the qualified voters of the question, "Shall a commission be chosen to frame a charter for the county [or city] of ...........?" The ordinance or resolution shall require that the question be submitted to the qualified voters at the next regular election, if one shall occur not less than sixty nor more than one hundred and twenty days after its passage; otherwise, at a special election to be called and held within the time aforesaid. The ballot containing such question shall also contain the names of candidates for the proposed commission, but without party designation. Such candidates shall be nominated by petition signed by not less than 1 per cent of the qualified voters of such county or city and filed with the election authorities at least thirty days before such election, provided, however, that in any case the signatures of 1,000 qualified voters shall be sufficient for the nomination of any candidate. If a majority of the qualified voters voting on the question of choosing a commission shall vote in the affirmative, then the nine candidates receiving the highest number of votes (or if the legislative authority of the state provides by general law for the election of such commissioners by means of proportional representation, then the nine chosen in the manner required by such general law) shall constitute the charter commission and shall proceed to frame a charter for such county or city. The legislative authority of such county or city shall, if so requested by the charter commission, appropriate money to provide for the reasonable expenses of the commission and for the printing of any completed charter and any separate and alternative provisions thereof and their distribution to the qualified voters as required by subsection (b) of this section.

(b) Any charter framed as provided in subsection (a) of this section shall be submitted to the qualified voters of the county or city at an election to be held at a time to be determined by the charter commission, but at least thirty days subsequent to the completion of the charter and its distribution among the qualified voters and not more than one year after the election of the charter commission. Any part of such a charter, or any provision alternative to a part thereof, may be submitted to be voted upon separately. The commission shall make provision for the distribution, not less than fifteen days before any such election, of copies of the proposed charter, and of any separate parts and alternative provisions thereof, to the qualified voters of such county or city. Any charter so proposed which is approved by a majority of the qualified voters voting thereon, with the addition of such parts and as modified by such alternative provisions as may have been separately submitted and similarly approved by a majority of those voting on any such parts or provisions, shall become the organic law of the county or city at the time fixed in such charter, and shall supersede any existing charter and all laws affecting the organization and government of the county or city which are in conflict therewith. Within thirty days after its approval the election authorities shall certify a copy of the charter to the state officer charged by law with the supervision of civil divisions, who shall file it as a public record in his office and publish it as an appendix to the session laws enacted by the legislature.

(c) Amendments to any such charter may be framed and submitted by a charter commission in the same manner as provided in subsections (a) and (b) for framing and adopting a charter. Amendments may also be proposed by a majority vote of the legislative authority of the county or city, or by petition of 10 per cent of the qualified voters thereof; and any such amendment, after due public hearing before such legislative authority, shall be submitted to the qualified voters of such county or city at a regular or special election as in the case of the submission of the question of choosing a charter commission. Copies of all proposed amendments shall be sent to the qualified voters. Any such amendment approved by a majority of the qualified voters voting thereon shall become a part of the charter of the county or city at the time fixed in the amendment and shall be certified to and filed and published by the state officer charged by law with the supervision of civil divisions, as in the case of a charter.

Section 802. *Powers of Local Units.* Counties shall have such powers as shall be provided by general or optional law. Any city or other civil division may, by agreement, subject to a local referendum and the approval of a majority of the qualified voters voting on any such question, transfer to the county in which it is located any of its functions or powers and may revoke the transfer of any such function or power, under regulations provided by general law; and any county may, in like manner, transfer to another county or to a city within its boundaries or adjacent thereto any of its functions or powers, and may revoke the transfer of any such function or power.

Section 803. *County Government.* Any county charter shall provide the form of government of the county and shall determine which of its officers shall be elected and the manner of their election. It shall provide for the exercise of all powers vested in, and the performance of all duties imposed upon, counties and county officers by law. Such charter may provide for the concurrent or exclusive exercise by the county, in all or in part of its area, of all or of any designated powers vested by the constitution or laws of this state in cities and other civil divisions; it may provide for the succession by the county to the rights, properties, and obligations of cities and other civil divisions therein incident to the powers so vested in the county, and for the division of the county into districts for purposes of administration or of taxation or of both. No provision of any charter or amendment vesting in the county any powers of a city or other civil division shall become effective unless it shall have been approved by a majority of those voting thereon (1) in the county, (2) in any city containing more than 25 per cent of the total population of the county, and (3) in the county outside of such city or cities.

Section 804. *City Government.* Except as provided in sections 802 and 803, each city is hereby granted full power and authority to pass laws and ordinances relating to its local affairs, property and government; and no enumeration of powers in this constitution shall be deemed to limit or restrict the general grant of authority hereby conferred; but this grant of authority shall not be deemed to limit or restrict the power of the legislature to enact laws of statewide concern uniformly applicable to every city.

The following shall be deemed to be a part of the powers conferred upon cities by this section:

(a) To adopt and enforce within their limits local police, sanitary and other similar regulations, not in conflict with general laws uniformly applicable to all cities.

(b) To levy, assess and collect taxes, and to borrow money and issue bonds, within the limits prescribed by general laws uniformly applicable to all cities; and to levy and collect special assessments for benefits conferred.

(c) To furnish all local public services; and to acquire and maintain, either within or without its corporate limits, cemeteries, hospitals, infirmaries, parks and boulevards, water supplies, and all works which involve the public health and safety.

(d) To maintain art institutes, museums, theatres, operas, or orchestras, and to make any other provisions for the cultural needs of the residents.

(e) To establish and alter the location of streets, to make local public improvements, and to acquire by condemnation or otherwise property, within its corporate limits, necessary for such improvements, and also to acquire additional property in order to preserve and protect such improvements, and to lease or sell such additional property, with restrictions to preserve and protect the improvements.

(f) To acquire, construct, hire, maintain and operate or lease local public utilities; to acquire, by condemnation or otherwise, within or without the corporate limits, property necessary for any such purposes, subject to restrictions imposed by general law for the protection of other communities; and to grant local public utility franchises and regulate the exercise thereof.

(g) To issue and sell bonds, outside of any general debt limit imposed by law, on the security in whole or in part of any public utility or property owned by the city, or of the revenues thereof, or of both, including in the case of a public utility, if deemed desirable by the city, a franchise stating the terms upon which, in case of foreclosure, the purchaser may operate such utility.

(h) To organize and administer public schools and libraries, subject to the general laws establishing a standard of education for the state.

(i) To provide for slum clearance, the rehabilitation of blighted areas, and safe and sanitary housing for families of low income, and for recreational and other facilities incidental or appurtenant thereto; and gifts of money or property, or loans of money or credit for such purposes, shall be deemed to be for a city purpose.

Section 805. *Public Reporting.* Counties, cities and other civil divisions shall adopt an annual budget in such form as the legislature shall prescribe, and the legislature shall by general law provide for the examination by qualified auditors of the accounts of all such civil divisions and of public utilities owned or operated by such civil divisions, and providing for reports from such civil divisions as to their transactions and financial conditions.

Section 806. *Conduct of Elections.* All elections and submissions of questions provided for in this article or in any charter or law adopted in accordance herewith shall be conducted by the election authorities provided by general law.

## ARTICLE IX

### THE CIVIL SERVICE

Section 900. *General Provisions.* In the civil service of the state and all of its civil divisions, all offices and positions shall be classified according to duties and responsibilities, salary ranges shall be established for the various classes, and all appointments and promotions shall be made according to merit and fitness to be ascertained, so far as practicable, by examinations, which, so far as practicable, shall be competitive.

Section 901. *Administration and Enforcement.* There shall be a department of civil service which shall, in accordance with the provisions of this article and the laws enacted pursuant thereto, administer the personnel functions of the state and of such of its civil divisions as elect to come under the jurisdiction of the department. For the administration of the personnel functions of civil divisions that do not elect to come under the jurisdiction of the department, and which do not make provisions for the administration of their personnel functions in a home rule charter adopted pursuant to section 801 of this constitution, provision shall be made by law. No payment for any employment hereunder shall be made without the affirmative certification by the department, or of a designated local authority in the case of a civil division over which the department does not have jurisdiction, on each payroll or claim as to the legality of such employment. The legislature shall enact laws necessary to carry out the provisions of this article and the department shall make such rules as may be necessary to carry out the provisions and intent of such laws.

Section 902. *Legislative and Judicial Employees.* Employees of the legislature shall be selected in conformity with the provisions of this article and shall be appointed and supervised by the secretary of the legislature. Employees of the courts, including clerks of the courts, bailiffs, probation officers, parole officers and other technical employees likewise shall be selected in conformity with the provisions of this article, and shall be appointed and supervised as provided in this constitution or as may be prescribed by law.

## ARTICLE X

### PUBLIC WELFARE

Section 1000. *Public Education.* The legislature shall provide for the maintenance and support of a system of free common schools. wherein all the children of this state may be educated, and of such other educational institutions, including institutions of higher learning, as may be deemed desirable.

Section 1001. *Public Health.* The protection and promotion of the health of the inhabitants of the state are matters of public concern and provision therefor shall be made by the state and by such of its civil divisions and in such manner and by such means as the legislature shall from time to time determine.

Section 1002. *Public Relief.* The maintenance and distribution, at reasonable rates, or free of charge, of a sufficient supply of food, fuel, clothing, and other common necessities of life, and the providing of shelter, are public functions, and the state and its civil divisions may provide the same for their inhabitants in such manner and by such means as may be prescribed by law.

Section 1003. *Public Inspection of Private Charitable, Correctional, or Health Institutions and Agencies.* The state shall have the power to provide for the inspection by such state departments, offices or agencies, and in such manner as the legislature may determine, of all private institutions and agencies in the state, whether incorporated or not incorporated, which are engaged in charitable, correctional, or health activities.

Section 1004. *Public Housing.* The state may provide for low rent housing for persons of low income as defined by law, or for the clearance, replanning, reconstruction and rehabilitation of substandard and insanitary areas, or for both such purposes, and for recreational and other facilities incidental or appurtenant thereto, in such manner, by such means, and upon such terms and conditions as may be prescribed by law.

Section 1005. *Conservation.* The conservation, development and utilization of the agricultural, mineral, forest, water and other natural resources of the state are public uses, and the legislature shall have power to provide for the same and to enact legislation necessary or expedient therefor.

Section 1006. *Sightliness, Order and Historic Associations.* The natural beauty, historic associations, sightliness and physical good order of the state and its parts contribute to the general welfare and shall be conserved and developed as a part of the patrimony of the people, and to that end private property shall be subject to reasonable regulation and control.

Section 1007. *Powers of the State.* The enumeration in this article of specified functions shall not be construed as a limitation upon the powers of the state government. The state government shall have full power to act for the government and good order of the state and for the health, safety, and welfare of its citizens, by all necessary and convenient means, subject only to the limitations prescribed in this constitution and in the constitution of the United States.

## ARTICLE XI

### INTERGOVERNMENTAL RELATIONS

Section 1100. *Federal-State Relations.* Nothing in this constitution shall be construed in such manner as to impair the constitutionality of any act passed by the legislature for the purpose of making effective the co-operation of the state with the federal government under any legislation which Congress has the power to enact.

Section 1101. *Interstate Relations.* The legislature shall provide by law for the establishment of such agencies as may be necessary and desirable to promote co-operation on the part of this state with the other states of the Union. The legislature may appropriate such sums as may be necessary to finance its fair share of the cost of any interstate activities.

Section 1102. *Co-operation of Governmental Units.* Agreements may be made by any county, city, or other civil division with any other such civil division or with the state, or with the United States for a co-operative or joint administration of any of its functions or powers, and the legislature shall have power to facilitate such arrangements.

Section 1103. *Consolidation and Co-operation of Local Units.* The legislature may, by appropriate legislation, facilitate and encourage the consolidation of existing civil divisions, or the establishment of co-operative enterprises on the part of such civil divisions.

## ARTICLE XII

### CONSTITUTIONAL REVISION

Section 1200. *Amending Procedure.* Amendments to this constitution may be proposed by the legislature at any two regular sessions, a period of six months having intervened between each passage of such a proposal, or by the initiative as provided in Section 401. Any such amendment presented in the legislature and twice agreed to by a majority of all the members shall be entered each time on the journal, with a record of the roll call vote, and submitted after the second legislative action to a vote of the qualified voters by the legislature, at the first regular or special state election held not less than three months after date of adjournment.

Section 1201. *Constitutional Conventions.* The legislature, by vote of a majority of all the members entered by roll call vote on the journal, may at any regular session provide for the submission of the question, "Shall there be a convention to amend or revise the constitution?" to the qualified voters of the state at any regular election. If approved by a majority of the qualified voters voting on said question, the legislature shall at its next session provide by law for convening such a convention four months after the date of the election of the delegates thereof, and it shall provide for a preparatory commission to assemble information relating to constitutional questions for the assistance of the delegates. The secretary of the legislature shall submit the question, "Shall there be a convention to amend or revise the constitution?" to the qualified voters at the general election in 19........ and in every twentieth year thereafter.

Delegates to the convention shall be chosen at a special election to be held not less than three months nor more than six months after approval of the proposition to call a convention. Delegates shall be elected in the same manner as members of the legislature, by proportional representation. Except as otherwise provided herein, any qualified voter of the state shall be eligible to membership in the convention. As many delegates shall be elected to the convention from each existing legislative district as there are representatives in the legislature from that district; in addition, there shall be elected from the state at large, by the Hare system of proportional representation, a number of delegates equalling one-fifth of the membership of the legislature.

No proposal shall be submitted by the convention to the qualified voters as herein provided, unless it has been read on three different days, in the convention, has been printed and upon the desks of the delegates in final form at least three days on which the convention was in session, prior to final passage therein, and has received the assent of a majority of all the delegates. The yeas and nays on any question shall, upon request of one-tenth of the delegates present, be entered in the journal. The proposals of the convention shall be submitted to the qualified voters at the next regular election held not less than three months after the adjournment of the convention, either as a whole or in such parts and with such alternatives as the convention may determine. All such proposals approved by a majority of such qualified voters voting thereon shall become effective thirty days after the date of the vote thereon, unless a different time is provided therein, provided that the affirmative vote thereon shall equal 30 per cent of the total vote cast for governor in the last preceding general election at which a governor was chosen.

Section 1202. *Self-Executing Character of Provisions.* The provisions of this constitution affecting its amendment or revision shall be self-executing but legislation may be adopted to facilitate their operation. If conflicting measures submitted to the qualified voters at the same election shall be approved, the one receiving the highest number of affirmative votes shall become law as to all conflicting provisions.

## ARTICLE XIII

### SCHEDULE

Section 1300. *Former Laws to Remain in Force.* All laws in force in this state at the time of the adoption of this constitution, not inconsistent therewith, shall continue in force until specifically amended by the legislature, as if this constitution had not been adopted, and all rights, actions, prosecutions, and contracts shall continue except as modified thereby.

Section 1301. *Officers.* All officers now filling any office by election or appointment shall continue to exercise the duties thereof, according to their respective commissions or appointments, until their successors shall have been selected in accordance with this constitution or the laws enacted pursuant thereto and shall have qualified.

Section 1302. *Choice of Officers.* The first election of governor under this constitution shall be in 19....... The first election of chief justice under this constitution shall be in 19....... The first election of members of the legislature under this constitution shall be in 19.......

Section 1303. *Establishment of the Legislature.* Until otherwise provided by law, members of the legislature shall be elected from the following districts: The

first district shall consist of the counties of .............. and ...............,
and said district shall be entitled to ......... members in the legislature, etc.
[The description of all the districts from which the first legislature will be elected
should be inserted in similar language.]

A system of proportional representation for the election of the members of the
legislature shall be prescribed by law. In the event that no such system shall be
provided by law, the members of the first legislature under this constitution shall
be selected by the Hare system of proportional representation, each voter having a
single transferable vote, under regulations promulgated by the governor.

Section 1304. *Establishment of the Judiciary.* All courts in this state existing
at the time when this constitution becomes effective shall constitute departments
or divisions of the General Court of Justice until the legislature or the judicial
council, subject to legislative approval, shall otherwise provide. The justices of
the [here name the highest court of the state] and the judges of the [here name
all the courts of the state except justice of the peace courts] holding office on the
first day of January, 19......, shall constitute the first judges of the General Court
of Justice, and shall continue to serve as such for the remainder of their respective
terms and until their successors shall have qualified.

The justices of the [here name the highest court of the state] shall become
justices of the supreme court department of the General Court of Justice, and
the judges of the existing inferior courts shall be assigned by the chief justice to
the other departments of the General Court of Justice, due regard being had to
their position in the existing judicial structure. As nearly as may be, each judge
shall be assigned to a district containing all or part of the district in which he
served regularly as a judge prior to the adoption of this constitution.

Justices of the peace shall be attached as magistrates to that department of the
General Court of Justice exercising general jurisdiction in the county in which
they reside. The judicial council may reduce the number of such magistrates in
any county as vacancies occur.

Section 1305. *Judicial Districts.* Subject to alteration by the judicial council
or by law, the state shall be divided into the following judicial districts, namely:

First District: The first district shall comprise [and so forth].

Section 1306. *Judicial Rules.* The rules in force at the time the General Court
of Justice shall be established, regulating pleading, practice, and procedure in the
courts consolidated by this constitution, which are not inconsistent herewith,
shall constitute the first rules of court for the appropriate departments of the
General Court of Justice, but subject to the power of the judicial council to make
or alter such rules.

# TABLE OF CASES

# PROBLEMS

## Part One: STATE GOVERNMENT

### Chapter One. HISTORY OF AMERICAN STATE GOVERNMENT

1. Examine the constitution of your state, and list the clauses that bear evidence of having been influenced by the colonial period of American history.
2. Compare the federal Constitution, as adopted in 1789, with the first state constitutions. What fundamental differences do you observe?
3. Compare the states' rights philosophy of the pro-slavery statesmen prior to the Civil War with the states' rights philosophy of the present-day statesmen representing the wealthy industrial states.
4. Study the government of one of the Southern states during the period of reconstruction following the Civil War.
5. Make a list of the functions performed by your state government in 1900, and note the large number of functions added since that year. Is this trend likely to continue?

### Chapter Two: FEDERAL-STATE RELATIONS

1. Prepare a list of the factors that seem to indicate a further expansion of federal power at the expense of the states, and also a list of the factors that may check this trend. Do you believe that further federal expansion is inevitable?
2. In what respects are the present methods of apportioning federal aid among the states unsatisfactory? What bases of apportionment would you suggest?
3. Write a paper on the legal aspects of the removal from the Pacific Coast of persons of Japanese ancestry.
4. Prepare a brief history of the extradition of fugitives in the United States.
5. Should the federal government be permitted to tax the income from state and municipal bonds? Discuss this question in detail.
6. Select one of the states admitted into the Union since 1875, and trace the history of its transition from territory to state.

### Chapter Three: INTERSTATE RELATIONS

1. Prepare a brief report on the evils of diversity in state legislation and state administrative practices.
2. Describe the organization and activities of the National Conference of Commissioners on Uniform State Laws.

3. Summarize the reports and recommendations of the Interstate Commission on Conflicting Taxation.

4. What has been done by your state to promote the movement for interstate co-operation?

5. Write a brief history of the National Association of Secretaries of State or the National Association of Attorneys General.

## Chapter Four: STATE CONSTITUTIONS

1. Examine the constitution of your state, and make a list of the sections dealing with matters that might, in your judgment, be regulated more satisfactorily by the legislature.

2. If you were drafting a bill of rights for a present-day constitution, what rights would you include as essential to the welfare of the people of the state?

3. Compare the constitution of your state with the National Municipal League's model state constitution. Note the outstanding differences.

4. How many times has the present constitution of your state been amended since its adoption? Note the nature of the changes that have been made.

5. Contrast the policies of a number of states in gathering information for the use of constitutional conventions. Note especially the careful preparations of Massachusetts (1917), Illinois (1920), and Missouri (1943).

6. Examine the debates of a recent state constitutional convention. Can you discover economic motives for the attitudes of the various members?

## Chapter Five: NOMINATIONS AND ELECTIONS

1. Examine the election laws of your state. How do they differ from the model election administration system prepared for the National Municipal League by its Committee on Election Administration? The report of this committee was published as a supplement to the *National Municipal Review*, Vol. XIX, No. 9, September, 1930.

2. Observe the operation of the election system in your state on election day. What suggestions can you offer to—
   a. Reduce cost.
   b. Prevent fraud.
   c. Make voting easier for the average voter.
   d. Increase the speed of vote-counting?

3. Study the results of compulsory voting in Europe or Latin America. Do you believe that the United States would be justified in adopting such a plan?

4. The State of Iowa is considering the advisability of establishing a literacy test for voting. Prepare a paper presenting both sides of the matter, with emphasis on the experience of those states that have used literacy tests.

5. What percentage of the eligible voters in your community actually voted

at the last state election? Talk with a number of persons who did not vote, and try to learn their reasons for staying away from the polls.

## *Chapter Six:* PARTIES AND POLITICS

1. Study the organization of the major political parties in your community. To what extent do the rank and file of the party members participate in party affairs and influence party decisions?

2. Make the acquaintance of your precinct leader (or leaders, if both of the major parties are organized in your precinct). What methods do they employ to secure support for their candidates?

3. How many private organizations in your community are interested in influencing legislation? What methods do they employ to secure the adoption of laws that they have sponsored or indorsed?

4. Trace the newspaper accounts of some recent graft prosecution, and note the methods used by the political machine to enrich its members.

5. Who is the boss of your city or state? Study the history of his life, as far as you can obtain the facts from the newspapers or other sources, and try to learn the methods that he uses to remain in power.

## *Chapter Seven:* DIRECT LEGISLATION AND THE RECALL

1. Obtain a list of the initiative and referendum measures submitted during the last five years to the people of your state—or to the people of a neighboring state, if your state does not employ the initiative and referendum for ordinary legislation. What percentage of these measures dealt with non-technical matters on which sound popular judgments might well have been formed?

2. Describe briefly the procedure established for direct legislation in your state or some neighboring state.

3. Contrast the California and Oregon official publicity pamphlets. Which type do you prefer? Defend your choice.

4. Prepare a brief history of the recall in one of the eleven recall states.

5. Draft a model state constitutional amendment authorizing the use of the recall. Defend briefly the principal provisions of the amendment.

## *Chapter Eight:* STATE LEGISLATURES

1. Write a brief history of the legislature of your state.

2. Study the unicameral legislature of one of the Canadian provinces. Describe its organization and work.

3. Conduct a proportional representation election with some group of which you are a member. For an excellent concise description of the method of count-

ing ballots, see *Leaflet No. 5* of the Proportional Representation League. Hoag and Hallett's *Proportional Representation* treats the subject in great detail.

4. Make a list of important measures enacted by the legislature of your state during the last ten years, and note how the members voted on these measures, if their votes are recorded. Do you observe a sharp dividing line between urban and rural interests?

5. Write the story of a recent impeachment trial in your state or some neighboring state.

6. What limitations are imposed upon legislative action by the constitution of your state? Examine the records of the convention that prepared the present constitution, and try to determine why these limitations were imposed. How many of them should be retained?

## *Chapter Nine:* THE LEGISLATIVE PROCESS

1. What are the powers and duties of the lieutenant governor of your state or of a neighboring state? Of what commissions and boards is he an *ex officio* member?

2. How many stenographic and clerical workers are employed by the two houses of your state legislature? How are they chosen? Do you observe any evidences of nepotism?

3. How many bills were introduced at the last session of your state legislature? Trace briefly the history of these bills—how many were reported from committee, how many actually received consideration on the floor of either house, how many were passed during the last forty-eight hours of the legislative session.

4. Note the number and duties of the committees of the two houses of your state legislature. How many of these committees could be eliminated without a reduction of legislative efficiency?

5. Examine the records of the last session of your state legislature. To what extent did each house follow the recommendations of its committees?

6. Study the work of the legislative reference bureau of your state or a neighboring state.

## *Chapter Ten:* STATE EXECUTIVES

1. How many bills have been vetoed by the governors of your state during the last twenty years? In how many instances have these vetoes been overridden by the legislature?

2. Study the operation of the governor's power of item veto, as found in your state or a neighboring state.

3. What is the extent of the governor's removal power in your state? How freely does he exercise that power?

4. Does the governor of your state regularly act on the recommendations of

members of the legislature in making appointments? To what extent does the senate refuse to approve nominations made by the governor?

**5.** How many times has the National Guard of your state been called into active service during the last twenty years? For what purposes has it been called?

**6.** Study the organization of the state auditor's office in your state. Does the present auditing procedure seem reasonably satisfactory?

## *Chapter Eleven:* STATE COURTS

**1.** Study the operation of the magistrates' courts in your city. What qualifications do the magistrates possess for their work? Is a real effort made to do substantial justice?

**2.** Prepare a chart showing the organization of the judicial system of your state.

**3.** Examine the organization and work of the judicial council in some state that has created such a body. What results has it accomplished?

**4.** How are members of the petit jury chosen in your community? Can you suggest ways to improve the present method of selection?

**5.** Select a state that has enacted a declaratory judgment statute, and find what results that statute has given. Compare the statute with the model declaratory judgment law prepared by the Conference of Commissioners on Uniform State Laws.

## *Chapter Twelve:* STATE CONTROL OVER LOCAL GOVERNMENTS

**1.** Trace the movement for local self-government in some state that has not yet adopted municipal home rule. What measure of control do the cities of the state exercise over their own affairs?

**2.** Give five instances of legislative control of cities and five instances of administrative control of cities in your state.

**3.** What has been the attitude of the courts of your state or of a neighboring state toward classification of cities by the legislature? Examine the decisions of the state supreme court.

**4.** What evidences of increasing state centralization can you find in your state? Do you think that this movement is likely to prove stronger than the movement for local self-government?

**5.** Study the relations of some nearby large city with the county in which it is situated. Do you find instances of unnecessary duplication or conflicts of authority?

## *Chapter Thirteen:* CITY GOVERNMENT

**1.** Examine the organization and work of the bureau of municipal research in your city or some nearby city where a research bureau has been established.

2. Prepare charts showing the governmental organization of several large cities operating under the mayor-council form of government.

3. Describe the organization of your city council—how the presiding officer is selected; how clerical and stenographic employees are chosen; how many standing committees have been created; the size of these committees; how committee memberships are determined.

4. Note the relations of the city manager and the council in your city or some nearby city that has adopted the council-manager form of government. Does the manager ever interfere with the council's task of policy determination? Does the council ever interfere with the manager's task of administration?

5. Is the trend in American city government toward the selection of local men as managers or the selection of out-of-town men? See the issues of Public Management and the Municipal Year Book.

6. How are employees selected for the municipal service in your community? Is a serious effort made to secure the best men and women available? If no formal merit system exists, what procedure is followed?

## *Chapter Fourteen:* COUNTY GOVERNMENT

1. Prepare a chart showing the governmental organization of your county. What changes in the present organization would you advocate?

2. Describe the organization and work of the treasurer's office in your county. What qualifications does the present treasurer possess? Note his training and previous experience.

3. What are the duties of your county clerk? How well does he perform these duties?

4. Examine the budget system of your county, or of some county in a neighboring state that requires county budgets. Does the existing budgetary procedure seem reasonably satisfactory? Are all items of county expenditure and revenue included in the budget?

5. How are your county's employees selected? Is an attempt made to secure properly trained persons? Are dismissals ever made for political reasons?

## *Part Two:* STATE ADMINISTRATION

## *Chapter Fifteen:* STATE ADMINISTRATIVE ORGANIZATION

1. How many administrative officers are popularly chosen in your state? Which of them possess important policy-determining powers? Analyze the powers assigned by the constitution and the laws.

2. Select some state whose government has been carefully surveyed in recent years, and compare the recommendations of the surveying agency with the changes actually made.

3. Make a list of the administrative agencies in your state government that are headed by boards or commissions, and a separate list of the agencies that are headed by individuals. Examine the functions of all these agencies. Would you replace some boards or commissions with individuals, or some individuals with boards or commissions?

4. Examine the statutes enacted at the last session of your state legislature. How many of them are "outline" laws, vesting considerable discretion in administrative agencies?

5. Prepare a chart showing the organization of the administrative branch of your state government as it existed fifty years ago, and another chart showing the present-day organization. What differences do you note?

## *Chapter Sixteen:* PERSONNEL

1. Study the operation of the merit system in some state that has adopted it.
   a. To what extent are appointments actually made on a merit basis?
   b. Are formal examinations used for the selection of high-salaried technicians in the administrative service?
   c. What has been the practical effect of legislation giving preference to veterans?
   d. What procedure is followed in dismissing employees?
   e. Is a system of efficiency records maintained?

2. Study the operation of the pension system in one of the states that has adopted a comprehensive system applying to all employees.

## *Chapter Seventeen:* STATE EXPENDITURES

1. Trace the growth of expenditures by your state government from 1915 to the present, and note the changes in the relative importance of the several items. The necessary data can readily be found in the annual reports published by the United States Census Bureau.

2. For what purposes are payments made from the state treasury of your state to local units of government? What conditions, if any, are attached to these grants? Is a serious effort made to enforce the conditions imposed?

3. What items of state expenditure are likely to increase most rapidly during the next decade? Why?

4. Study the budget procedure of your state. Can you offer any suggestions for improvement?

5. How are supplies and equipment purchased in your state? Is the present arrangement satisfactory?

## *Chapter Eighteen:* STATE REVENUES

1. Trace the growth of the revenues of your state government from 1915 to the present, and note the changes in the relative importance of the several sources of revenue.

2. What classes of property are exempt from payment of the general property tax in your state? What changes, if any, would you advocate in the present policy of exemptions?

3. Make a study of the methods of assessing real estate in your community. Note the assessment procedure, and compare the assessed value of a number of properties (if the assessment records are public) with the selling price of those properties, as obtained from the records of a title insurance company or a real estate agency.

4. What is the method of taxing personal property in your community? What classes of personal property are taxed?

5. What have been the effects of the industrial depression of the 1930s and the war of the 1940s upon the state tax systems? See the annual reports of the United States Census Bureau, *Financial Statistics of States,* and more recently, *State Finances.*

6. What taxes are imposed upon corporations, foreign and domestic, by your state government?

## *Chapter Nineteen:* STATE INDEBTEDNESS

1. Trace the growth of the debt of your state government. What are the principal purposes for which bonds have been issued since 1900?

2. Prepare a brief history of the state debts incurred during the Revolution, and immediately afterward.

3. Compare the provisions of your state constitution concerning indebtedness with the corresponding provisions of the Model State Constitution. Can you account for their differences on the ground that the clauses of your state constitution are made necessary by local conditions?

4. Trace the fluctuations in the interest rates of state bonds during the last half-century. Do you observe a long-range trend? If so, how do you account for it?

5. Obtain copies of the capital budgets of a number of states. What similarities and differences do you observe?

## *Chapter Twenty:* ENFORCEMENT OF LAW

1. Study the organization and work of the state police in your state or a neighboring state. What suggestions can you offer for improvement?

2. How is the police force organized in your local community? What training is given to members of the force?

3. Examine the relations of the sheriff and the municipal police in your community. Do conflicts of authority sometimes occur?

4. Make a careful comparison of the relative importance of indictment and information as methods of initiating prosecution in some state where both methods are used. What merits and defects have these methods revealed in practice?

5. Study the system of assigned counsel for poor persons accused of crime in some state that has not adopted the public defender system.

6. Observe the organization and work of the coroner's office in your community. To what extent are modern scientific methods employed in the determination of causes of death?

## *Chapter Twenty-One:* CORRECTION

1. Write the story of the shipment of English criminals to the American colonies during the seventeenth and eighteenth centuries.

2. Visit the county or city jail in your community, and observe the manner in which it is conducted. Is any attempt made to segregate convicted criminals from those persons awaiting trial?

3. Visit the nearest state penitentiary, and note the living and working conditions. What provision is made for the recreation of prisoners?

4. How are the prison officials and guards chosen in your state? Is any attempt made to secure efficient men, or is selection made on the basis of political influence? What training, if any, do new guards receive before they are assigned to duty?

5. Study the operation of probation and parole in your state. Is any serious effort made to supervise the persons who have been placed on probation and parole?

6. What agency is responsible for granting pardons in your state? How does it obtain the information necessary for its decisions?

## *Chapter Twenty-Two:* WELFARE

1. Describe briefly the organization and administration of the Community Chest in your city.

2. Visit your county almshouse, and observe how it is managed. Is work provided for those inmates who are capable of working? What recreational facilities are furnished?

3. Study the operation of your state's old age pension law. What agency is responsible for its administration? Are pension allowances adequate? What methods are used to detect impostors?

4. Describe the system of placing homeless children in private homes, as it

operates in your community. How many families eventually return the children instead of adopting them? How thoroughly are families examined before children are entrusted to their care? How carefully are families and children supervised after placement?

**5.** Examine the mothers' aid law of your state, and note the manner in which it is administered. What defects do you observe in the law or its administration?

**6.** Describe the organization and activities of the state agency or agencies administering charity in your state.

## *Chapter Twenty-Three:* EDUCATION

**1.** Study the relations of state and local school authorities in your state. Do you favor a further extension of state control, or do you believe that the local school officials should be protected from additional encroachments on their authority?

**2.** What are the relations of the county school superintendent and the county school board in your state? Do you think that the present arrangement is satisfactory? If not, what changes would you suggest?

**3.** Enumerate the powers and duties of your state superintendent of public instruction. How is his office organized to carry on its various activities?

**4.** What provisions for teacher training have been made by your state government? Has a minimum salary law applying to teachers been enacted? Is it enforced in all sections of the state?

**5.** What public supervision over private schools is exercised in your state? Is a serious attempt made to insure the proper training of private school teachers?

**6.** Visit a state school for handicapped children. What methods are employed in training these children? What are the subjects of instruction?

## *Chapter Twenty-Four:* HEALTH

**1.** Study the organization of your state health department. Enumerate the services that it performs, and note the date that each of these services was added to the list.

**2.** Trace the relations of state and local health authorities in your state. Has state supervision resulted in higher standards of local health work?

**3.** Should smallpox vaccination be made compulsory? What proposals for compulsory vaccination have been made in your community? What groups have opposed the movement?

**4.** Study the relations of public and private agencies in the control of tuberculosis. Have these relations proved entirely satisfactory?

**5.** Visit your state public health laboratory, and write a brief description of its organization and work.

**6.** Prepare a summary of the proposals for socialized medicine that have been made in Congress and in various state legislatures.

## Chapter Twenty-Five: HIGHWAYS

1. Write a brief history of the good highway movement in your state.

2. Study the relations of the federal government, your state and its local sub-divisions in highway construction and maintenance.

3. Prepare a report on the proposals that have been made in Congress and elsewhere for expanded programs of highway construction in the postwar era.

4. Trace the history of the movement to transfer a portion of gasoline tax receipts from highways to other activities. What groups favor this change and what groups oppose it? In your judgment, would such a change be desirable?

5. What steps have been taken by your state highway department to reduce automobile accidents?

## Chapter Twenty-Six: NATURAL RESOURCES

1. Describe the forest fire prevention work of your state or a neighboring state. What part is played by the federal government and by private agencies in forest fire protection?

2. Summarize the fish and game laws of your state. By whom are these laws administered?

3. Observe the work of the county agent in your county or a neighboring county. Write a brief description of his principal duties and the manner in which he performs them.

4. Visit your state agricultural experiment station. What are its principal activities?

5. Write the recent history of public control of the petroleum industry.

6. Study federal-state relations in the development of water-power. What has been done by your state to conserve its water-power resources?

## Chapter Twenty-Seven: THE STATE AND BUSINESS

1. Summarize the laws of your state concerning the incorporation of business enterprises.

2. Study the operation of the small-loan act of your state or a neighboring state. What defects has it revealed in practice? What agency administers it?

3. What effect did the financial panic of 1933 have upon the banking laws of the several states? Describe the work of the banking commissioner of your state.

4. What service standards have been established by the public service commission of your state for electric light and power companies? For street railway companies? What penalties are provided for failure to comply with these standards?

**5.** Make a list of all the publicly owned and operated utilities in your community. Are they self-supporting?

**6.** How many agencies in your state government are responsible for examining and licensing persons who desire to practice professions and trades? Describe the organization and work of these agencies.

## *Chapter Twenty-Eight:* THE STATE AND LABOR

**1.** Examine the system of workmen's compensation in your state. Are the rates of compensation adequate? What provision, if any, is made in the law for the compensation of persons affected by industrial diseases?

**2.** Write a brief history of the growth of the labor union movement in your state.

**3.** Prepare a comprehensive account of a strike in your state or a neighboring state—the issues involved; the steps taken by the strikers and by the employers to gain their respective ends; the attitude of the public authorities; the final settlement.

**4.** Describe the organization and work of public employment offices in your state.

**5.** Talk with a number of employers in your community, and learn their criticisms of existing labor laws. Do you think that these criticisms are justified?

INDEX

# INDEX